South African

Human Resource Management

for the Public Sector

Editors:

Ernst van der Westhuizen
Jacobus Wessels

South African Human Resource Management for the Public Sector
First published 2005
Reprinted 2009
Second edition 2011

Juta & Co Ltd
First Floor, Sunclare Building, 21 Dreyer Street, Claremont, 7708
PO Box 14373, Lansdowne, 7779, Cape Town, South Africa

© 2011 Juta & Company Ltd

ISBN 978-0-70218-863-3

Project Manager: Debbie Henry
Editor/ Proofreader: Christine de Nobrega
Typesetter: Ashley Richardson
Cover designer: Marius Roux
Printed in South Africa by Impressum Print Solutions

Contents

Preface

Any author who intends to write a textbook does so for a variety of reasons. The editors of this textbook have decided to get involved in this project for two reasons. First, we believe that we have a unique contribution to make to the field of study and second, we are of the opinion that existing texts have shortcomings that we would like to address. Although it may sound egotistic, these two reasons describe our motivation for writing this text on public sector human resource management.

South African Human Resource Management for the Public Sector is an adaptation for the public sector of the well-known book *South African Human Resource Management: Theory and Practice*, by Ben Swanepoel, Barney Erasmus, Marius van Wyk and Heinz Schenk.

Few of you who read this textbook will disagree that the last few years have brought fundamental challenges to the South African public sector. The complete transformation of the South African society, coupled with the fact that one can nowadays almost refer to 'borderless public service delivery', means that South African public sector institutions are faced with external environmental forces requiring change and transformation within the institution in order to be able to survive and develop. It is well known that the way in which we manage the people within our institutions in the public sector – the employees, the human resources – holds the key to managing these forces of change and transformation in today's highly competitive environment.

The foundation of this book is the belief that successful public-sector human resource management is a prerequisite for overall institutional success, and that human resource management is therefore a tripartite management responsibility at all levels (political executives, line function employees and human resource specialists), which requires a strategic and general management approach. In addition, because a strategic approach implies a good 'fit' between internal and external environments, the heart of this text consists of the unique South African public-sector human resource management challenges.

These challenges relate to such aspects as dealing with changing worker expectations, strategically implementing affirmative action, coping with fast-changing labour legislation, enhancing service delivery, dealing with unions, contracting out services, increasing emphasis on quality, performance, efficiency and cost-effectiveness, devolving of managerial responsibility and accountability, introduction of more participative organisational structures, introduction of less rule-bound cultures, development of more effective computerised management information systems and the introduction of more flexible staffing and recruitment practices.

This textbook recognises that the human resource function should not be relegated to some separate personnel 'back room'. All public-sector managers should explore and adapt human resource management strategies and practices that add value within the South African public sector environment – an environment which, although showing many similarities, is quite distinct from that of the private sector.

The structure of this book

In order to assist practising South African public sector managers and students (who have no human resource management experience), this text is divided into six parts, covering 17 chapters.

- **Part 1:** Orientation and theoretical overview contains three chapters and has the overall aim of introducing public-sector human resource management as a field of study from a general international, national and specific public administration perspective. It specifically covers the broad South African public administration environment, which has an ongoing influence on the public-sector human resource function. Certain theoretical perspectives on public-sector human resource management are comprehensively dealt with in Chapter 3.
- **Part 2:** Strategising and planning for public-sector human resources consists of two chapters covering the longer term preparatory decisions that every senior management team in the South African public sector has to consider. It deals with the strategic human resource management process in relation to the overall approaches we have to follow in managing human resources. In addition, with respect to planning, it shows us how to balance workforce supply and demand.
- **Part 3:** Obtaining suitable public human resources consists of three chapters dealing with strategies, processes and practices involved in staffing our public sector organisations with the right quality and quantity of people. It specifically covers affirmative action because of its prominence in the South African public sector context.
- **Part 4:** Utilising and developing public sector employees are made up of three chapters. The spectrum of topics covered includes appraising and managing work performance, career management in the public sector and structuring learning programmes for public officials.
- **Part 5:** Compensating and caring for public sector employees focuses in three chapters on basic wage and salary structures, incentives and other benefits, and the non-material ways of caring, namely the health and safety of officials, and counselling.
- **Part 6:** Managing public sector employee relations consists of three chapters dealing comprehensively with the challenges posed to public sector managers in terms of labour relations. Special attention is devoted to historical developments and the legal context of public-sector labour relations. The focus is specifically directed upon the establishment of climates of trust, co-operation and strike handling. The individual dimension of employment relations is also addressed, and communication, grievance handling and discipline are well covered.

This book has several distinguishing features. It covers fundamental human resource material such as recruitment, selection, labour relations and dismissal. The milieu of the public sector human resource function and strategic public human resource management are used as integrating themes. Practical applications, such as how to recruit staff, appraise performance, establish pay plans and manage labour relations, are also presented in order to provide the reader with human resource management skills that are essential for the public sector.

By covering a broad spectrum of topics, integrating all of them into the whole and blending them with a unique South African public sector flavour, we believe that this textbook on Public Sector Human Resource Management will enhance the appreciation and understanding of this all-important public management challenge facing all South African public sector institutions. The ideas introduced in this book do not aim to be comprehensive and definitive. Therefore, certain topics which are covered in Swanepoel's book, such as 'Motivating employees', 'Leading employees' and 'Managing change and transformation' have not been included in this book. This is due to a lack of space and, because we presuppose that those reading the book may be better served by focusing on the real context of the human resource function, rather than by underlining the significance of such peripheral issues. Consequently, the discussion is deliberately selective, emphasising certain major ideas around the human resource function to stress their importance to the responsibilities of both the line function employees and the human resources specialists.

Michael Stahl, who worked in the Environmental Protection Agency of the federal government in the United States of America, once said during an interview:

> If you are considering a career in the public service, take the time to reflect on your motivation for entering the public service, because there are 'right' and 'wrong' reasons. You are entering for the right reasons if you want to make a contribution to the solution of social problems, promote democratic values and ethical standards on using the powers of government, and if the concept of serving the public good is a passion. You are entering for the wrong reasons if you are looking for public adulation and recognition for your accomplishments, seeking material or financial rewards as compensation for your hard work, or expecting to acquire levels of power and change the world according to your own plan (Denhardt 1995: 28; White 1945: 313).

Reviewers of the first edition suggested a more integrative style of presentation. The authors, therefore, have included the following additions to the second edition:
- **Did you know** questions: These are included to stimulate interest and to highlight current issues in the field.
- **Focus on research** activities: These are intended to encourage the reader to read up on the latest research reports (national and international) in the field.

- **Spotlight on the law** activities: In recent years, the traditional boundaries between the public and private sectors have become increasingly blurred as all labour legislation currently apply to both sectors. In addition, the public sector has adopted business-orientated management policies and practices. Currently, there is a significant degree of court decisions within the ambit of HRM-related legislation, which impact on the day-to-day management of human resource affairs in the public sector. Hence, this edition does try to accommodate relevant court cases in both the public *and* private sectors. These court cases are linked to specific chapters, which will help to demonstrate some of the activities one may experience if you choose a career in public human resource management. A brief summary of the court cases are presented in the text. However, full reports of court decisions can be found at http://www.saflii.org/content/south-africa-index.

Acknowledgements

Many people, some directly and others indirectly, have contributed to this book. From our work with members of the Department of Public Service and Administration, we gained a special appreciation of the complexities of the locus of public sector human resource management. Colleagues in the Public Service Commission were also a great source of help. These colleagues provided us with lengthy reports on contemporary human resource issues.

We would also like to express our thanks and appreciation to colleagues and friends at the Department of Public Administration and Management at UNISA, who were continually of great help during the project. We sincerely trust that we have correctly reflected the content of the human resource function as it was clarified during the many conversations that we had.

This book is an adaptation for the public sector of the original book entitled *South African Human Resource Management: Theory and Practice* by Ben Swanepoel, Barney Erasmus, Marius van Wyk and Heinz Schenk.

While completing the book, we realised that others have contributed in a unique way and provided the balance along the road. We especially want to offer thanks to our Heavenly Father, who supported us on a spiritual level. Finally, we would like to extend a special word of thanks to our families who kept it all together for us.

About the editors and authors

Editors

Prof Ernst J van der Westhuizen is Professor of Public Administration in the Department of Public Administration and Management at the University of South Africa (UNISA). He received his DAdmin in Public Administration (an empirical study on quality circles in the South African public service) from UNISA in1993. He joined the teaching profession in 1988 following a career in human resources in the public service. He has authored numerous articles for local as well as international accredited journals. He has addressed many international and local conferences on public management, human resource management, public sector reform and ethics. He has also completed different study tours in Europe, including countries such as England, the Netherlands, Bulgaria, Slovenia and Hungary. Prof. van der Westhuizen is registered as Master HR Practitioner with the South African Board for People Practices. He also received the Researcher of the Year Award in the School of Management Sciences at the University of South Africa.

Prof Jacobus S Wessels is Professor of Public Administration and currently a Research Manager and head of the Academic Research Support Unit (ARSU) in the College of Economic and Management Sciences at the University of South Africa. The National Research Foundation has rated him as an 'Established Researcher' (C3) during 2006. During 2009 he received the Researcher of the Year Award from the School of Management Sciences at Unisa. His fields of interests are: Research Methodology, ethics in public administration, curriculum development and lifelong learning. Before he joined Unisa in January 1995, he gained six years of extensive multi-disciplinary research experience at the Human Sciences Research Council (HSRC) and before that, eight years of experience in the South African public service. He holds a DPhil degree from the University of Pretoria. He is co-editor of, and contributor to a scholarly book *Reflective Public Administration: views from the South*. He is also author and co-author of many publications in scientific journals, as well as other reports and contributions. He has read numerous papers at local and international conferences. He was a member of the editorial committee of an accredited journal for eleven years and for some years, he was also a member of the national executive of a professional association. He has received various grants enabling him to travel abroad and to participate in international conferences. He is a member of the Association of Southern African Schools and the Departments of Public Administration and Management (ASSADPAM), the South African Association of Public Administration and Management (SAAPAM), and the *Suid-Afrikaanse Akademie vir Wetenskap en Kuns* (South African Academy of Science and Arts).

Authors

Prof Ben Swanepoel, the original editor of *South African Human Resource Management: Theory and Practice,* is a former member of the University of Southern Queensland (USQ) in the Faculty Business (and a former Head of Department and acting Head of School). He is a former president of IRasa (Industrial Relations Association of South Africa) and also used to be a part-time commissioner of the CCMA. Ben has authored and co-authored numerous books in South Africa and articles internationally. For a number of years now, he has also been privileged to gain international academic leadership and managerial experience.

Prof Barney Erasmus is the Vice-Principal: Operations of the University of South Africa. Having formerly achieved success in roles such as Head of the Centre for Business Management, Head of the Department of Business Management, and later also Director of the School of Management Sciences, Barney was seconded to his current role during 2006. He is registered with the South African Board for Personnel Practice, has authored and co-authored numerous books and articles in the fields of human resource development, labour relations and human resource management, and acts as consultant in these fields as well as in general management.

Prof Heinz Schenk is the Head: Department of Human Resource Management of the University of South Africa. Heinz has proven his managerial capabilities having successfully occupied positions such as Executive Director: Human Resource Management at the former Technikon Southern Africa and his current position. He is registered as an industrial psychologist and also as a (generalist) Master Practitioner of the South African Board for Personnel Practice, where he serves on the education committee and also as a registered mentor. He has co-authored and contributed to various textbooks in the broad field of HRM.

The late **Marius van Wyk**, former Professor of Labour Law and Business Ethics at the Graduate School of Business Leadership of the University of South Africa.

A typical working day in the life of a human resource manager working in the public sector

Thabo Matsimela is the Chief Director, Human Resources (head of the human resource office), of the Department of Health in Pretoria. He heads a human resource office organised into six divisions – Strategising and Planning, Recruiting, Selecting and Appointing, Utilising and Developing, Remunerating and Caring, and Employee Relations. Thabo is caught up in the middle of a public sector human resource function that is confronted with some of its biggest challenges since it started taking shape as a separate staff function some 90 years ago. This renewed onslaught is brought about by a series of complex influences transforming the function from a narrowly defined bureaucratic approach into a more people oriented one. Since 1994, there has also been an increased realisation of the critical importance of approaching public sector human resource management from a strategic perspective in order to realise institutional success. All of these pose numerous challenges, threats and opportunities to Thabo and the human resource office. Thabo's life is further complicated by a rapidly changing and diversifying workforce, increasingly legal and regulatory changes, declining budgets, declining confidence in public service delivery, demands for productivity improvement, virtual government, decentralisation of the human resource function and epidemic health threats such as HIV/AIDS.

- **06:00** – It is the year 2010, and another Monday morning has dawned for Thabo and his family. He reads the newspaper, which reports an increase in the country's unemployment rate. A higher unemployment rate will increase the number of people seeking work. He pauses for a while and immediately thinks how the pending layoffs in the Department will add to the unemployment crisis. These forthcoming layoffs are related to the Department's decision to contract with the private sector for services in the area of health clinics and transportation (ambulances). Many of the line function employees in the Department have consulted with him about the best way to deal with the human resource issues that arise from contracting out services. Since all public service institutions are affected by the White Paper on Public Service Delivery (Batho Pele), its contents will also have to be taken into consideration in this regard. Thabo also reads in the newspaper that the Director-General (head of the Department of Health) has rejected demands from health workers for salary increases. The trade unions, in turn, are reluctant to endorse the Director-General's proposals for reinventing and reengineering plans. Further, the newspaper reports that labour unrest among five provincial hospitals could result in a situation in which other unionised employees, who have already reached a settlement with management, could be negatively affected. Thabo already has a scheduled meeting later today with the Department's negotiation team to formulate a strategy around the hopes of preventing a strike. The newspaper also contains a story explaining some of the details in a lawsuit filed against a male manager in the Department who is sexually harassing one of his female employees. The training section has been involved in undertaking sexual harassment training sessions throughout the 2004 financial year, in order to provide guidelines in such cases. This has definitely helped to reduce the Department's legal exposure.

- **07:00** – Thabo arrives at his work premises after having dropped off his two daughters at school (his son is in hospital – he has broken his leg in a soccer match). His wife, who works at the City of Tshwane as a financial consultant, is on a three-day strategic planning session, and was not able to transport the kids this morning. Since they are also a dual-career couple, he finds the conversation in the parking area very interesting. There are other staff members who are in the same situation, and who feel there is a need for on-site child-care facilities, as well as more flexible working conditions. A staff member once revealed that, if the Department had these facilities available, it would be more competitive in its recruitment efforts.

  Arriving in his office, Thabo switches on the computer to see what the weather is like in Cape Town. He will be flying down to Cape Town tonight, where he has to appear tomorrow before the Parliamentary Portfolio Committee of Public Service and Administration in the National Assembly to answer certain questions about human resource matters in the Department of Health. After getting settled in his office, he requests his administrative assistant, Miriam Campbell, to do the following instructions:
  - Pick up the air tickets, hotel accommodation reservations and vehicle reservations at Jabulani Travel Agency, the on-site travel agency for the Department.
  - Make an appointment with Supa Quick so that his car can be fitted with new tyres while he is in Cape Town.
  - Forward last Thursday's minutes of the meeting with the Director-General to all four of the directors in the human resource office by e-mail with a request to comment on the proposals regarding the new promotion policy for senior nurses.
  - Make a copy of the paper on affirmative action delivered at a workshop organised by the Department of Public Service and Administration. The content of this paper needs to be discussed at next Wednesday's meeting with the four human resource directors.
  - Make sure that a copy of the White Paper on Affirmative Action in the Public Service is made. Make the copy available to Mary Mahola, head of the Affirmative Section, and arrange a meeting between himself and Miriam for next Thursday. Strategies need to be discussed for the gathering of data for the next affirmative action report that must be provided to the Department of Labour.

Thabo's Monday schedule continues:
- **08h00** – Staff meeting with Miriam; they discuss the new office rules that have to be compiled, a delegation of powers manual that has to be finalised and Miriam's merit report. Thabo asks Miriam to go through all the e-mail messages and make

copies of those relating to the week's activities. He will work through the e-mails on the plane to Cape Town.

- **08:45** – Staff meeting with Marie Gildenhuys, Director of Finance. The meeting focuses on the making operational the new computer package for the payment of salaries.
- **10:30** – Conduct employee orientation programme for new staff of the Department.
- **11:00** – Staff meeting with department heads concerning the implementation of a new performance measurement programme.
- **12:00** – Staff meeting with Director-General, chief directors and directors on the recruitment plan for 2005.
- **13:00** – Lunch in the staff canteen with legal counsel on the status of the pending lawsuits and sexual harassment charge. On his way out of the canteen, he meets Patrick Mabete, chairperson of the Social Club, who reminds him that they have to sort out the matter of members' contributions.
- **14:00** – Meeting with the labour negotiating team regarding bargaining issues.
- **14:30** – Meeting with university contractors on the content of management development programmes.
- **15:00** – Staff meeting with Miriam on review plans for updating all job descriptions.
- **15:30** – Proofread the Cabinet memorandum about a new appointment policy for the Department. Replies to urgent e-mail messages.
- **16:00** – Attends the welcoming ceremony for the Deputy Director-General (second in charge of the Department).
- **17:00** – Collects the car at the Avis carport and departs for Johannesburg International Airport (flight SA317) from Johannesburg to Cape Town. Reminds Miriam to call the hospital to enquire about his son's health. Confirms with Miriam to pick up his two daughters at the day-care centre and take them to his parents, who will look after them until he has arrived back from Cape Town.

Although Thabo has a busy day structured around different meetings, he also tries to arrange for time each day to consider the longer range strategies. These include such issues as the implementation of performance measurement in key units in the Department, incentive pay schemes for selected employees, online access to human resource (and other relevant fields), Acts, regulations, white papers, collective agreements and management guides, and a cafeteria-style employee benefit plan.

Thabo's typical working day shows the broad range of activities that might be faced by today's public sector human resource manager. It illustrates the complex environment within which the human resource function takes place. These challenges require unique skills of those involved in the human resource function. In this regard, we must note that 21st-century public sector human resource management embraces a broader and more strategic approach – a so-called people-focused style of managing people. It also means that the human resource function can no longer operate in isolation. An analysis of the various meetings above shows that the human resource function cannot take place without other strategic partners in the institution. Almost every operational decision has human resource implications and there has to be a partnership between line function employees and the human resource specialists.

As Thabo settles into his seat on flight SA317, he closes his eyes and can't help but think about his challenging and exciting job and career. He thinks of the importance of human rights (Constitutional rights) in the public sector workplace and realises that this requires completely new ways of working. For example, public sector employees have considerable rights to privacy. These rights apply, for instance, to such issues as alcohol and drug testing, pre-employment background checks and religious freedom. Furthermore, the emerging virtual public sector workplace (or 'virtual government' as it is better known) is in our midst. This implies that some traditional nine-to-five workplaces with fixed central office locations are replaced with more flexible working arrangements, such as telecommuting and contract labour. In addition, we recognise cultural diversity, which is a worldwide phenomenon requiring a unique sensitivity towards one another in the workplace. The composition of the South African public sector workforce is more diverse – more representative of the nation's demographics – than ever before. (Adapted from Berman, Bowman, West, & Van Wart 2001: 4–7; Starling 1993: 3–7; Van der Westhuizen 2000: iii–iv)

Orientation and theoretical overview

WORK occupies a central part in life. In general, adult people have to engage in some form of work activity to earn a living. Most do so within the context of an institution in which they are employed. Such people can be classified as the personnel, staff, workers, employees or 'human resources' of an institution. A public sector institution is one type of institution to which human resources can offer their labour (knowledge, skills and energy). Because the government provides multiple public services, enforces numerous laws and regulations and is involved in many court decisions, it could be classified as a labour-intensive sector. Obviously, all these activities require human resources. How well the public sector operates depends principally on the quality of the human resources and the way in which the knowledge, skills, attitudes and talents of these people are managed in the various institutions. Research has proven that the successful management of human resources has a definite positive relationship to the performance of institutions (Sherman, Bohlander & Snell 1998: 29). This is why it is so beneficial to study public sector human resource management – an interesting, dynamic and challenging field of study. The overall aim of this book is to provide information on state-of-the-art theory and practice of human resource management from a South African public administration perspective. It is aimed at facilitating learning about the management of people in relation to their work and to the institutions for which they work in the South African public sector.

In Part 1, we will seek a clear understanding of the political, institutional, ethical, historical and theoretical context of Public Sector Human Resource Management. These are the pillars on which the discipline rests. Therefore, it is necessary to provide a brief overview and orientation to the subject field. In more specific terms, we will examine the milieu or environment within which Public Sector Human Resource Management takes place – in other words, those factors that make the discipline unique and which distinguish it from other disciplines. We will also examine the theoretical perspectives underpinning the discipline by paying attention to the international and national contributions made. Part 1 ends with a brief note on contemporary perspectives of Public Sector Human Resource Management.

Although we will introduce you to many different areas of Public Sector Human Resource Management in Part 1, we will do so from a particular point of view. In adopting this view, we have been able to develop a unifying theme in the analysis of human resource management work in the public sector. Most importantly, we will emphasise the management context of human resource management. In this regard, we will familiarise you with the management tasks and skills and the way in which the practices are related to these. In addition, we will consider the uniqueness of

Public Sector Human Resource Management. What this means is that the human resource function is distinguished by its pursuit of democratic values and principles (or outcomes) as spelt out in the Constitution of the Republic of South Africa, 1996 (Section 195(1)) and in the White Paper on Human Resource Management in the Public Service of 1997 (Chapter 2). The important thing about this is that almost every activity of a public sector manager is influenced by these values and principles. In executing your daily work at public offices, you are obligated not only to synchronise all these tasks, skills, practices, values and principles, but you have to be responsive to the public interest. This may sound rather abstract and may appear to be a particularly complex approach, since the human resource function renders a service to other employees in the institution and not directly to the public. Nevertheless, as will be seen in Part 1, in delivering professional services to other employees, these employees are motivated, and, in being motivated, they are in a position to deliver better services to the public.

1   General introduction

Purpose

The purpose of this chapter is to provide a broad overview of public sector human resource management so that the reader may have better insight into the nature and content of the study field.

Learning outcomes

After you have read this chapter, you should be able to:
- Describe and discuss the concept of 'public sector human resource management' (PSHRM in short).
- Demonstrate the fact that PSHRM has a management perspective.
- Explain that HRM also takes place in the public sector and therefore has a 'public' dimension requiring specific unique skills and competencies.
- Describe the key role that resources play in a public sector organisation to guide the HR function optimally.
- Demonstrate the fact that PSHRM is a strategic tripartite division of responsibilities between the executive political managers, line function employees and human resource specialists.
- Demonstrate sensitivity to the most important ethical guidelines designed to ensure professional behaviour among public sector employees.
- Outline the scope of the integrated PSHRM process that mainly comprises four activities, namely key functions and practices, management tasks, additional management skills and specific outcomes.

1.1   Introduction

There are more than one million people employed by the different public sector institutions in South Africa. If one is in charge of managing these huge numbers of employees, the question immediately arises according to what criteria would you recruit, select, train, discipline, promote and pay them. All these activities require the skills and competencies of human resources. Today, the underlying assumption is that 'managing people' is the most complex dimension of management. To a very large extent, the South African nation's ability to achieve success through effective public service delivery depends on the performance, honesty and motivation of public employees. This emphasises the fact that public sector human resource management is important. In this chapter, we are going to take an overview of the essentials one should know about public sector human resource management and provide information on state-of-the-art theory and practice from a South African public sector perspective.

1.2 The meaning of public sector human resource management (PSHRM)

There are different opinions and viewpoints regarding the meaning of the concept of 'public sector human resource management'. Some adopt a 'generalist' perspective, while others (the 'absolutists') view the concept of PSHRM as denoting a very specific style or way of managing people at work. Although the absolutist approach is not presented in this book, the authors also do not subscribe to the approach of 'old wine in new bottles'.

In this book, public sector human resource management as a field of study, theory and practice is taken to be that part of management concerned with all the factors, decisions, principles, strategies, operations, practices, functions, activities, methods, processes and procedures related to employees in public sector institutions, all the dimensions related to people in their employment relationships, and all the dynamics that flow from it. These are all aimed at helping to ensure continuous success of public sector institutions through 'good fit' employment relationships in turbulent and ever-changing environmental conditions.

The perspective taken is thus broad rather than narrow, in that PSHRM is viewed as referring to all practices and decisions aimed at continuously achieving an optimal match or fit between work, the human resources required to execute the work of public sector institutions, and the environment in which these institutions operate.

A variety of job titles and names have been used in the field of human resource management (HRM), for example, personnel management, personnel administration, manpower management, people-power management and human resource management. Different names have also been given to the structures and persons concerned with the HR function. In this regard, it has been common practice to refer to the section/unit dealing with HR matters as the personnel department, personnel section, human resource department, human resource division, personnel office or human resource section. People who specialised in and who have been specifically tasked with the HR function have been referred to as personnel officers, personnel managers, personnel directors, heads of personnel, human-resource managers or human-resource executives.

Given all these titles and names, we can see that it is already difficult to start explaining the meaning of the concept of PSHRM. However, the authors are of the opinion that a good starting point would be to concentrate on certain characteristics inherent to the concept. Some of the more important characteristics of PSHRM (which may or may not form part of the approaches or perspectives taken by others) are outlined below:

- It has a management perspective.
- It focuses on the public sector and therefore has a unique 'public' sector dimension.

- It utilises certain resources to guide the HR function optimally. It is a tripartite division of responsibilities assigned to executive political managers, line function employees and human resource specialists to achieve certain institutional objectives.
- It is guided by certain professional ethical guidelines designed to ensure professional behaviour.
- It is an integrated process that mainly comprises four activities that are connected with each other, namely key functions and practices, management tasks, additional management skills and specific outcomes which have long-term consequences. All these activities are directed towards the purpose of enhanced performance (better service delivery) of public sector institutions.

All these characteristics and other aspects that form the basis of good PSHRM will be discussed in this introductory chapter.

1.3   The management perspective of PSHRM

Public sector institutions are non profit-seeking institutions. But this does not mean that public sector institutions do not fulfil a particular role in life and therefore have no purpose for their existence. All public sector institutions consist of people who are supposed to interact consciously in an endeavour to achieve certain institutional goals by serving a particular need in society. Therefore, all public sector institutions strive towards being successful. Success, in this context, means doing the right things (being effective) in the right way (being efficient). The 'right things' refer to the specific services which a particular public sector institution serves to provide. Providing such services constitutes the basic *raison d'être* of any institution that is established to satisfy society's needs. Furthermore, all public sector institutions also have to do things the right way. This means that, in providing these 'right services', public sector institutions must also function in such a way that all the stakeholders – in particular the citizens/ customers or end users of these services – are satisfied. The nature and quality of the services must be right, and they must be provided at the right price, at the right time and at the right place. If the citizens/customers are satisfied and they use the services, the institution's chances of being successful are better.

Students of management (including public sector human resource management) therefore study all the activities and decisions of public sector managers (including public human resource managers), which aim to ensure the success of their institutions and the gradual improvement of the quality of life of all their stakeholders (such as the citizens/customers, the employees and the community at large). In this sense, the institution is goal driven and public sector managers are responsible for ensuring goal achievement. Management, as a field of study, is complex and vast. It is concerned with the utilisation and mobilisation of all of a public sector institution's resources so that it can be successful and survive in the changing environment within which any institution exists and operates. These resources can be tangible or intangible. They include natural resources such as water and land, financial resources such as cash, technological resources such as machinery, equipment and computer technology, information and knowledge-based resources, energy-related resources, and human resources. All of these resources have to be utilised, combined and transformed into need-satisfying services by a wide range of public sector institutions. It is the responsibility of management (which is also represented in the human resources field) to manage all of these resources.

But why is HRM important to all public sector managers? In answering this complex question, one may wish to list some of the HRM mistakes a manager typically wants to avoid, such as the following (Dessler 1981: 3):

- Hiring the wrong person for a specific post;
- High staff turnover;
- Employees not performing well;
- Inefficient job interviews;
- Court cases because of discriminatory actions;
- Unsafe working conditions;
- Pay inequities;
- Incompetent staff; and
- Unfair labour practices.

Remember that being successful is the bottom line of managing and as a manager you will have to achieve results through people. A public sector manager could do everything else right – have brilliant policies and plans, set up proper organisational structures and use modern technology – and yet still fail as a manager in the HR arena. This is possible through hiring the wrong people, not motivating employees properly and not providing enough training opportunities.

Normally, the management function materialises on three levels of management in the public sector, namely the junior, middle and senior management level.

How human resource managers in the public sector are employed may vary from level to level. In this book, we will mainly consider the human resource knowledge and skills associated with senior public sector managers.

DID YOU KNOW?

The White Paper on Human Resource Management in the Public Service of 1997 defines a manager in the public service as anyone who takes responsibility for other people's work. According to this definition it also includes first-level supervisors or junior managers.

1.4   The 'public' dimension of PSHRM

Now that we have clarity on the management part of PSHRM, it is necessary to determine what the 'public' dimension entails in the larger context of public administration. The word 'public' in the term PSHRM tends to be rather complex and difficult to explain because the public sector covers such a wide terrain (Bovaird & Löffler 2003: 4–5). One way to map out the boundaries of the public sector would be to identify the wide array of public sector institutions within which HRM takes place (Van der Westhuizen 2000: 8). In general terms, the concept 'public sector' constitutes the public service (which includes employees in government departments at national and provincial level) and local government, as well as a host of statutory bodies, parastatals and quasi-government institutions. In more specific terms, it implies that HRM takes place within institutions such as the Department of Health on the national level, the Gauteng Provincial Administration on the provincial level, and the Department of Recreation and Culture in the City of Tshwane on the local level. It also takes place in parastatals (such as the South African Reserve Bank), state-owned enterprises (such as the South African Post Office) and other institutions including universities and technicons. If one further subdivides the public service, one will find that PSHRM takes place in the following institutions:

- Service delivery agencies (such as the Departments of Health and Education);
- Security agencies (such as the South African Police Service and the South African National Defence Force);
- Administrative agencies (normally referred to as the 'civil service' – these agencies were established to ensure the effective administration of governmental functions); and
- Statutory agencies (for example, the Public Service Commission and the Auditor-General) (Adler 2000: 5–6).

It is clear from the above arguments that the activities of PSHRM basically unfold in institutions that make up the public sector (the broader framework) or the public service. This book will focus on managing people within these two broad institutional settings. This is why it is necessary for the author to continually refer to the 'public sector' in certain cases and to the 'public service' in other cases.

1.5 Resources for PSHRM

In any given situation, a public sector manager has four basic resources at his or her disposal in order to execute the HR function successfully. These resources are roughly classifiable as financial, physical, informational and human resources. An important responsibility that faces the public sector manager is to ensure that these resources are utilised optimally. Some of the key items provided for under each category of resources are the following:

- Financial resources (salaries, wages, and petty cash funds);
- Physical resources (buildings, lecture rooms, computers, cell phones, tables and chairs);
- Informational resources (annual reports, research reports, data on survey questionnaires, post records, leave records, remuneration systems, human

resource planning systems, service records, training records, statutes, regulations and instruction codes); and
- Human resources (human resource managers, line function personnel, technical and administrative personnel and other human resource specialists).

It can be stated categorically that human resources probably play a larger and more strategic role than the other resources because public sector managers in any public sector institution have the responsibility to take decisions on how to utilise the other resources. In this regard, Likert (in Marx 1986: 18–19), one of the well-known management authors, long ago wrote:

All the activities of any enterprise are initiated and determined by the people who make up the institution. Plants, offices, computers, automated equipment and all else that a modern firm uses are unproductive except for human effort and direction [...] Of all the tasks of management, managing the human component is the central and most important task, because all else depends on how well it is done.

DID YOU KNOW?

About 1.2 million employees operate in national state departments and provincial administrations, accounting for over 50% of public expenditure. This means that human resources should actually be regarded as the most valuable resource and that its strategic and efficient management should form the cornerstone of all public service activities.

This brings us to reasons why human resources should be regarded as the most important resource in the public sector. First, the increase in numbers of professional occupations, such as lawyers, medical practitioners and engineers, is expecting more advanced HRM practices and systems. Second, because human behaviour cannot be monitored and controlled mechanically, special attention should be paid from a HR perspective to gain positive results. Third, it can be assumed that, if an employee has been placed correctly, undergone the correct training, and receives an acceptable remuneration package, such a person can probably make a positive contribution towards the enhanced performance of a public sector institution (Van der Westhuizen 2000: 11).

1.6   PSHRM as a specific responsibility

In accordance with Section 7(3)(b) of the Public Service Act 103 of 1994, public managers (including human resource managers) are responsible for the efficient management and administration of public sector institutions, including the effective utilisation and training of staff, the maintenance of discipline and the promotion of sound labour relations. The focus falls squarely on the term 'responsibility'. Undoubtedly, responsibility in terms of PSHRM has wide and varied implications. In this regard, the White Paper on Human Resource Management in the Public Service of 1997 clearly states that HRM will no longer be the sole responsibility of

HR specialists, but rather a dual responsibility between HR specialists and all other public sector managers. Because PSHRM takes place in the public domain, one can add another role player here, namely 'political managers'. In brief, this involves a tripartite division of responsibilities between the executive political heads (political managers), the line function employees (mostly managers), and human resource specialists (including HR managers). Basically, political responsibility involves the establishment of 'political' and 'executive' HRM policy with the human resource office – which in the South African case is the responsibility of the Department of Public Service and Administration (DPSA) – and co-ordination of this policy between the different institutions and sections/units. It also involves ensuring that this policy is implemented successfully. Additional political responsibilities are vested in the powers and functions of the Public Service Commission (PSC). These responsibilities are presented in Section 196 of the Constitution of the Republic of South Africa, 1996 (the 1996 Constitution). According to the 1996 Constitution, the PSC is responsible for investigating, monitoring and evaluating the human resource practices of the public service. Basically, this responsibility involves a so-called 'watchdog role'.

The other two role players, namely the line function employees and the human resource specialists (sometimes referred to as the 'staff' component), have a unique responsibility or relationship, and in a sense one could refer to this as a line-staff partnership. In order to understand the meaning of this line-staff partnership, it is best to begin with a distinction between line function employees and human resource specialists (staff employees).

Line function employees are directly involved in accomplishing institutional goals and delivering services to the public. Doctors and nurses in state hospitals are examples of line function employees. HR specialists (staff employees), on the other hand, assist, support and advise line-function employees in accomplishing the set goals. For this line-staff partnership to be effective, line-function employees and HR specialists will have to work together strategically and proactively so that the central purposes of government are realised.

Today there is also a strong view that this partnership involves the establishment of strategic linkages between HR policies and practices and the attainment of institutional objectives (Tompkins 1995: 4). This brings us to HR-related responsibilities between line-function employees and human resource specialists. The responsibilities of line function employees may include, among others, the following:

- Establishing job qualifications;
- Selecting and orienting new employees;
- Interpreting and executing HR policies and regulations;
- Training and developing employees;
- Improving the job performance of each employee;
- Controlling labour costs;
- Protecting health and physical conditions of employees; and
- Initiating disciplinary actions.

The HR specialist, by contrast, may be responsible for, among others, the following:

- Drafting HR policies for consideration by upper management (in our case, the Department of Public Service and Administration);
- Consulting with line function employees about the compliance with HR laws, regulations and other instructions;
- Providing of routine HR services (for example, screening of job applicants, negotiating collective agreements, and administering pay and benefit programmes);
- Evaluating the successfulness of current HR policies and procedures (this role is exercised by the Public Service Commission);
- Monitoring the activities of line function sections/units to ensure that the law and regulations are complied with (another role that is executed by the Public Service Commission); and
- Notifying the Treasury of HR budget proposals.

Table 1.1 summarises a more selective and detailed list of the way in which HR-related responsibilities may be shared between the HR specialists and line-function employees. Two HR functions and practices, namely recruitment and selection and labour relations, provide the illustration here.

Table 1.1   Division of responsibilities shared between HR specialists and line-function employees

Main areas of activity	Involvement of HR specialist	Involvement of line-function employee
Recruitment and selection	• Design policies and procedures for fair and equitable recruitment and selection in order to contribute to the institution's corporate strategy and the relevant unit's business plan. • Develop sources of qualified applicants from the international and external labour market. This action requires carefully planned community relations, speeches, advertisements, and active university, technikon, college, and high school recruiting. • Conduct skilled interviews, give scientific employment tests, make thorough reference checks, and screen applications in line with employment laws. • Refer best candidates to the relevant line function employee, after physical examinations and qualifications for the posts have been carefully evaluated.	• Prepare requisition outlining specific qualifications of employees required to fill specific posts. • Assist the HR office to create a positive image that will attract the 'best' candidates. Interview and select from candidates screened by HR. • Make specific job assignments to individual employees and teams. Brief new employees on details such as safety rules, pay and hours of work.

Main areas of activity	Involvement of HR specialist	Involvement of line-function employee
Recruitment and selection	• Give new employees preliminary briefing about the institution, benefit plans, general safety, and first aid, etc.	
Labour relations	• Diagnose underlying causes of labour difficulties, anticipate disruptions, work with line function employees on preventive measures to stabilise and build trust in relationships. • Do research in preparing professional labour contracts. • Act as management spokesperson or adviser to institution negotiators in bargaining with unions or liaison with institution lawyers on technical matters. • Train all levels of management in contract interpretation and administration; handle legal and nonlegal interpretation questions. • Design disciplinary policy and procedure manuals. • Monitor the effectiveness of the policies and procedures. • Give advice to line function employees on disciplinary problems. • Organise training for line function employees about disciplinary issues. • Issue warnings in later stages of the disciplinary procedure. • Maintain central records of disciplinary action taken. • Participate in the design of the grievance policy and procedure manual. • Inform and train employees in grievance handling.	• Establish day-to-day relationship of mutual respect and trust with union representatives; apply labour laws and contracts consistently. • Advise institution negotiators of contract changes. • Assist in bargaining sessions where department/unit issues are at stake, and give technical advice. • Apply seniority principles in promotions, transfers, layoffs, etc. • Conduct informal disciplinary interviews. • Issue formal warnings outlined in the disciplinary policy and procedures manual. • Maintain records of warnings issued. • Deal initially with grievances raised by employees as part of the formal grievance policy and procedure. • Is likely to be involved in negotiation on a wide range of issues.

Source: Adapted from Foot & Hook (1996: 21–25) and Dessler (1981: 8–9)

1.7 Public sector human resource management as an integrated process

The matter of how best to promote better service delivery in the public sector involves ensuring that all institutions, teams, and individuals perform well. However, there are no easy solutions to the issue of improved institutional performance if it is to be done properly. If public sector employees are to think and act in such a way that leads towards improved institutional performance, they must have a clear understanding of the way in which their efforts contribute in an integrated manner towards the desired service-delivery levels. The model in Figure 1.1 is designed to show the diverse and integrated activities associated with PSHRM. It should be clear from the model that PSHRM is presented as an integrated process comprising a number of different activities that have numerous connections between them. Public sector managers are expected to make key strategic connections between the key HR functions and practices, the HR management tasks, additional HR management skills and the outcomes that are at stake. The model also reflects the structure of this book.

1.7.1 Key PSHRM functions and practices

The term HR function refers to the activities for which line function employees and HR specialists are jointly responsible. In short, a function is a specialised professional activity to realise effective institutional performance and service delivery. In contrast to the HR management tasks – policy determination, organising, financing and controlling – the HR function deals primarily with the people-related aspects of management. These specialised professional HR functions and practices are delivered to line-function employees in order to achieve the objectives of the relevant institution. The primary HR functions and practices include the following:

- **Strategising and planning for public sector human resources:** This task involves establishing institutional objectives and formulating, integrating and implementing strategies for achieving them. It also includes strategic HR planning, which allows public sector institutions to anticipate future HR needs and to adjust to the internal and external environment in the process of reaching institutional objectives.
- **Obtaining (provision of) suitable human resources:** This task embraces the formulation and implementation of equal employment opportunity requirements and affirmative action policies, the recruiting of qualified job applicants, and the selection and appointment of those applicants who best comply with the requirements of open job positions.
- **Utilising and developing public sector employees:** The content of this task centres on appraising, career management and learning, and training and development.
- **Remunerating and caring for public sector employees:** The premise is that the employer is consciously involved in remunerating, providing incentives and counselling.

- **Public sector employee relations:** Public sector employee relations involve undertaking such activities as labour relations, dismissal, redundancy and outplacement.

Source: Hosking (2010: Online)

Figure 1.1   PSHRM as an integrated activity

?

DID YOU KNOW?

Public sector institutions should have wellness strategies in place. Key initiatives in your wellness strategy should be an HIV management programme, a flu vaccination programme before winter, an anti-TB programme, blood pressure and cholesterol checks and a diabetes awareness programme. But these largely address physical conditions. What about the emotional and mental wellness of your people? That's why stress reduction workshops, parenting workshops and relationship workshops are also important, as well as help line facilities to support staff in a multitude of creative ways.

Source: Hosking (2010: Online)

1.7.2 HR management tasks

Apart from the functions and practices, PSHRM also covers the field of management tasks. Whatever one's philosophy is towards work, it is through management that all the efforts of a public sector institution are directed towards goal achievement through such tasks as policymaking, organising, financing and controlling. There are various management models that one can utilise as an analytical framework for reference, but for the purposes of this book we have decided on the above set of management tasks as the basic model. These management tasks are enabling activities that typify the work of all public sector managers, including HR managers.

The first management task, namely policy making, is certainly one of the most important tasks of the public sector manager. HR policy is the cornerstone of all HRM activities because it gives direction and serves as an instrument that enables the public sector manager to lead the institution concerned to the achievement of its objectives (Van der Westhuizen 2000: 16). HR policy guidelines in the public sector are embodied in such documents as statutes, bills, draft bills, regulations, codes of instruction, white papers, green papers, collective agreements and management guides. The Public Service Act 103 of 1994 is an example of an official statute governing PSHRM. A number of key HRM responsibilities can be identified under the management task of policymaking, but only one will be highlighted here. First, it is of the utmost importance that the public sector manager remains abreast of all policy measures embodied in documents just mentioned. (See Appendix 1 to this chapter for the steps required to establish public sector human resource policy.) During 2006, the Public Service Commission conducted a study on the management of HIV and AIDS in the public service. The results are shown in the Focus on Research 1.1 feature on page 15.

The second management task, namely organising, is an enabling process that comprises of the following (Van der Westhuizen 2000: 21):
- The creation of an organisational hierarchy;
- Allocation of duties and responsibilities, and also of delegation of authority to subordinate institutions and individual workers; and
- Determination of the relationship between individual workers and groups in order to promote co-ordination.

FOCUS ON RESEARCH 1.1
Report on the evaluation of the policy framework on managing HIV and AIDS in the public service

During 2006, the Public Service Commission carried out a research project, its primary aim to determine the extent at which the public service was implementing the policy framework, and to monitor the progress made on the establishment of employee assistance programmes and their impact on providing services to people living with HIV and AIDS. It also sought to identify opportunities and threats regarding HIV and AIDS in the workplace, and best practices to minimise such threats and to optimise opportunities to sustain a stable public service.

One of the main findings of this research project indicated that, although general health promotion programmes have been introduced in a large number of state departments, there was still a lack of programmes specifically targeting aspects of HIV and AIDS in the workplace, such as programmes aimed at promoting openness, acceptance, care and support for those living with HIV and AIDS, programmes aimed at reducing HIV and AIDS-related diseases, as well as awareness and training programmes regarding HIV and AIDS.

Source: Republic of South Africa (2006: 46)

The following HRM responsibilities may be included (Van der Westhuizen 2000: 27):
- Orientation of HR employees regarding their place in the greater order of the organisational hierarchy;
- Assignment of work to HR employees;
- Drawing up and regularly revising duty rosters;
- Advice about which employees are ready for promotion; and
- Ensuring that prescribed forms are used correctly such as forms for resignations, dismissals, and appointments.

Thus far we have focused on two management tasks, namely policymaking and organising. The third one we have to concentrate on is financing. The financing task is an enabling activity that has to be executed to make funds available so that the HR functions and practices can be implemented. In general terms, HRM responsibilities in the financing task involve the following (Van der Westhuizen 2000: 28–30):
- Preparing draft budgets for submission to higher institutions, such as Parliament;
- Determining measures for the spending of money that has been allocated; and
- Bookkeeping, including exercising control over all HR-related financial transactions.

This brings us to the fourth and last management task of the public sector manager, namely controlling. Controlling of the HR functions and practices involves a wide-ranging group of activities that have to be undertaken to ensure that human resources are utilised effectively and efficiently. The controlling task involves the setting of standards, checking to see how actual performance compares with these standards, and taking corrective action as required. The following are some of the HRM responsibilities which involve the exercise of control (Cloete 1997: 41):

- Submission of annual and special reports to Parliament;
- Investigation, monitoring and evaluation of personnel practices by an independent and impartial central personnel agency, such as the Public Service Commission; and
- Appointment of committees or commissions to conduct enquiries into the performance of HR functions and practices.

1.7.3   Additional PSHRM skills

Thus far, we have covered the HR functions and practices and HR management tasks. These functions and practices and management tasks are indispensable to PSHRM. However, the HR functions and practices and HR management tasks must not be seen in isolation. This is why we have referred in section 1.7 to HRM as an 'integrated process'. In addition to these functions, practices and tasks, the public manager is also responsible for additional HRM skills. These additional skills are usually implemented in conjunction with the HR functions, practices, and management tasks. Cheminais *et al* (1998: 15) refer to these additional skills as conceptual, human (interpersonal) and technical.

First, conceptual skills refer to the mental ability to see the relevant HR office as a whole and complex system and to co-ordinate and integrate all the interests and activities. When approaching HRM conceptually, one will have to display the following skills: (1) working out well-conceived plans in collaboration with subordinate employees, and (2) taking rational and informed decisions about HR issues.

Second, people skills refer to the ability to work with, understand, and motivate people. In essence, one's people skills can be judged by (1) how successfully one communicates with others, and (2) the extent to which one is involved in motivating employees.

Third, technical skills refer to the ability to apply professional, functional, and specialised knowledge and expertise to ensure that HRM takes place smoothly. In practice, this involves the ability to apply techniques and procedures in a specialised field of HRM (as in the selection of employees when specialised personality tests need to be analysed).

1.7.4   PSHRM outcomes

In general, citizens expect public sector institutions to perform well. In this notion of 'performing well', we can detect what people look for in terms of 'good government services'. Although there will always be considerable disagreement about what it means to 'perform well', citizens expect public sector institutions to reach their mandated purposes efficiently and effectively. However, there are different yardsticks by which to measure government performance and, in this case, the outcomes of public sector human resource management provide the measurement. Therefore, public sector managers must have a clear understanding of the way in which their inputs contribute to the final HR outcomes or results. While executing the HR functions and practices, HRM tasks and additional management skills, public sector managers must bear in mind that all these activities need to be performed so that specific outcomes are achieved. These outcomes have to be representative of the products of the HR functions and practices, management tasks and additional management skills. The outcomes can also be viewed as markers of measurement. They are derived from the 1996 Constitution and are summarised in the White Paper on Human Resource Management in the Public Service (Republic of South Africa 1997: 20-21) as follows:

- **Promoting fairness:** All actions and decisions of public service employees within the context of PSHRM must be objective, consistent, equitable and without prejudice.
- **Applying equity principles:** It is undoubtedly true that the present government inherited a public service that is deeply marked by inequalities and unfairness on almost every level of public administration. Every effort should be made to apply corrective measures to ensure that human resource practices are free from discrimination. Further issues to be included refer to the removal of invisible barriers and unjustness that will impede equal employment opportunities.
- **Encouraging accessibility:** In line with overall government policy, considerable emphasis should be placed on accessibility in relation to employment, management and information. Since HRM is subject to the application of the 1996 Constitution it is essential that all human resource activities must contribute to this outcome.
- **Fostering transparency:** In keeping in line with the principles of democratic public administration, all HRM activities must be open and subject to public scrutiny within reasonable limits. However, public scrutiny also implies that HRM activities must be allowed to operate unrestrained, subject to the application of the values and principles highlighted in the 1996 Constitution and other relevant legislation.
- **Demonstrating accountability:** According to the Senior Management Service: Public Service Handbook (Republic of South Africa 2003: Annexure A), responsibilities for senior managers (including their human resource management responsibilities) are clearly defined. This handbook specifically states that the appointment of senior managers will be subject to the signing of an employment contract and a performance agreement. This signifies that individual employees will be held accountable for discharging their responsibilities conscientiously and with probity and integrity.
- **Increasing professionalism:** A code of conduct has been developed, published and implemented for the South African public service. This means that PSHRM will be conducted competently and reflect the highest moral and ethical standards. What are ethical standards? Generally, ethics is concerned with what is good or bad and right or wrong. More precisely, it deals with standards of morality and integrity

and of honourable and acceptable behaviour, which are developed by an individual or by institutions (such as churches), groups of people (such as classmates) or the community (such as parents). These ethical standards (or 'professional ethical guidelines' as they are better known in general public administration language) are influenced by factors in the political and social spheres. First, in any democratic state, certain political doctrines serve as guidelines for the behaviour of public servants. For example, Section 2 of the 1996 Constitution provides that the Constitution will be the supreme law for all South African public sector institutions and their activities, including PSHRM. In addition, another factor in the political sphere, namely that of 'political supremacy', implies that public sector managers have to accept Parliament as the policymaking authority. In other words, Parliament has to provide guidelines on how PSHRM should function. Second, PSHRM is also inseparable from the social sphere within which it operates. In this sense, the cultural and historical backgrounds of the various communities prescribe ethical norms and standards such as sincerity, honesty, and integrity.

An example of the application of the HRM outcome 'equity' in the workplace is shown in Spotlight on the Law 1.1 below.

SPOTLIGHT ON THE LAW 1.1
Unfair dismissal

The Labour Relations Act 66 of 1995 automatically regards a dismissal based on the basis of an employee's age as unfair. However, the Act provides that dismissals based on age are not unfair if the particular employee had reached the agreed retirement age as prescribed in the employment contract. Although this is a general principle it does not apply in certain circumstances.

In *Datt v Gunnebo Industries* [2005] 5BLLR 449 (LC), Mr Datt had worked for the company for many years. Mr Datt's original employment contract did not specify a retirement age. However, two months before his retirement age he signed a revised employment contract specifying the retirement age as 65 years (rules of the provident fund). On Datt's 65th birthday the chief executive officer (CEO) requested him to proceed with his duties at work 'until such time as we mutually agree that you should take retirement'. The CEO's successor was of the opinion that Datt was a risk and indicated to him to retire. This was done, but Datt claimed that his forced retirement constituted an automatically unfair dismissal. The court ruled that Datt's dismissal was automatically unfair and he received compensation equivalent to two years' salary.

Source: Grogan, Jordaan, Maserumule & Stelzner (2009: 22–23)

In dealing with PSHRM outcomes, one is indeed required to balance competing pressures with one another. The clarifying of outcomes raises the awareness of different aspects of PSHRM. Here, too, public sector managers have a difficult task at hand since their actions (if applied correctly) will be continually under the spotlight to see whether they have realised the outcomes. PSHRM actions will always be measured against such complex issues as the following:

- Querying, in particular instances, the high pay levels of line function employees when staff members in staff sections are paid low wages (fairness);
- Complying with instructions to include job applicants for consideration who are HIV-positive (equity);
- Allowing, within the rules, outside researchers to do study projects on HR matters in a public sector institution (accessibility);
- Reporting to fellow workers in a transparent and honest way about impending layoffs (transparency);
- Accepting the decision of a disciplinary enquiry when accused of certain transgressions and being prepared to resign in such a case (accountability); and
- Reporting to higher authority observations of employees loafing and loitering (professionalism).

Central to the understanding of the outcomes concept is the principle that public sector institutions that succeed in achieving the outcomes will deliver better services that those that do not strive towards it. The outcomes identified here are by no means exhaustive. However, we have examined those which are generic to everyday PSHRM and with which public sector managers are mostly concerned.

1.8 Enhanced institutional performance (better service delivery)

A question most frequently asked nowadays is: 'Can human resource management really have a positive impact on a public sector institution's performance or service delivery levels?' Many stakeholders in the public administration field would contend that the answer is 'no'. The most commonly quoted illustration in this regard is the stereotyped view of line-function employees that sees HRM as a clerical job which lacks a focus on performance. In essence, this view holds that, as a staff or advisory function, PSHRM does not have a direct link to enhanced performance or better service delivery. As a result of this view it is wrongly believed that HRM is not associated with performance enhancement. Fortunately, this view has been proved wrong and has been largely rejected. It has already been found that HRM techniques, procedures and systems, as applied by line function employees and HR specialists in their 'human resource role', have a real impact on performance and service-delivery levels of public sector institutions.

Researchers have found, for example, that the use of screening tests has resulted in the identification of high-potential candidates and has saved employers millions of rand per year. Another example refers to the implementation of occupational health and safety programmes. These programmes, which are also HRM related, can reduce costs incurred by lost-time accidents and illnesses. The fact is that almost every aspect that will be discussed in this book – human resource planning, recruiting, selecting, appointing, appraising, remunerating and labour relations – will have a measurable effect on the performance of public sector institutions. Every human resource activity has an influence on all the others. All the HR activities – the appointment of people, the provision of training, the measurement of performance, and the exercise of discipline – affect performance, not only of individuals but of the institution as a whole.

1.9 The integrated relationship of PSHRM functions and practices, HRM tasks, additional HRM skills and HR outcomes

None of the four main areas of PSHRM is executed independently and is an end in itself. Figure 1.2 illustrates the integration of the HR functions and practices, HRM tasks, additional HRM skills and HR outcomes. Disciplining, as one of the most complex HR functions and practices, is used here as the example.

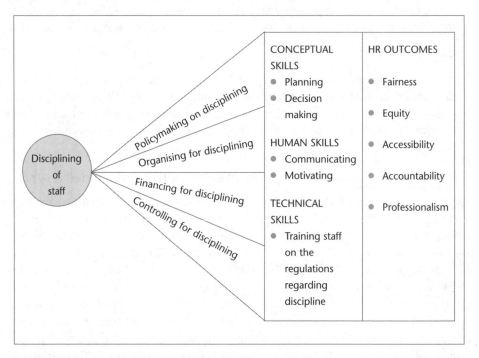

Source: Adapted from Van der Westhuizen (2000: 48)

Figure 1.2   Integration of HR functions and practices, HRM tasks, additional HRM skills and HR outcomes

The simplified model in Figure 1.2 signifies that all the above activities must be carried out simultaneously to make PSHRM operative. It also explains the integrated nature of PSHRM in the application of disciplinary measures in any given public sector institution. Further, by studying the chain relationship in the above model, one will soon come to the conclusion that almost every disciplinary action is interrelated with and influences the other human resource functions and practices, tasks, skills and outcomes. The basic process can be summarised in the following way: During the application of disciplinary measures, it is important that the public sector manager understands the policy guidelines on discipline and how to apply them in practice. It is also necessary to ensure that these policy guidelines should be communicated to all employees so that they know what is expected of them. In this way, the disciplinary process is structured and executed in an orderly manner. However, this is only the beginning of the disciplinary process. Management must also plan which people will be responsible for administering the disciplinary function. Furthermore, it must also be decided how much money will be allocated to the budget for the disciplining of staff. At the same time, management must decide how the transgressors will be dealt with so that they do not feel worthless after disciplinary action has been taken. During the execution of the disciplinary process, it is important that actions must be objective, consistent, and equitable.

1.10   Review

This chapter has introduced you to the nature and content of human resource management and the way in which it fits into the South African public sector. Specific attention has been devoted to the meaning of public sector human resource management, the management part of the human resource function, the 'public' dimension of PSHRM, the key responsibilities of a public sector resource manager and the integrated nature of the field.

1.11   Self-evaluation questions

1. Briefly explain what 'public sector human resource management' is all about.
2. 'Public sector human resource management has a management perspective.' Discuss this statement.
3. What does the term 'public' entail in PSHRM?
4. What resources can a public sector human resource manager utilise to guide the HR function optimally?
5. Can you mention the tripartite responsibilities of PSHRM? Briefly elaborate on the line-staff partnership in this regard.
6. Identify the four integrated activities associated with PSHRM and indicate how all these activities are connected to each other ensuring enhanced institutional performance.

Bibliography

Adler, G. 2000. *Public service labour relations in a democratic South Africa.* Johannesburg: Witwatersrand University Press.

Andrews, Y. 1985. *Die personeelfunksie.* Pretoria: HAUM.

Berman, EM, Bowman, JS, West, JP, & Van Wart, M. 2001. *Human resource management in public service: Paradoxes, processes, and problems.* London: Sage.

Botes, P. 1994. *Aspects of supervision: A guide for the contemporary public manager.* Halfway House: Southern.

Bovaird, T, & Röffler, E. 2003. *Public management and governance.* London: Routledge.

Cheminais, J, Bayat, S, & Van der Waldt, G. 1998. *The fundamentals of public personnel management.* Cape Town: Juta.

Cloete, JJN. 1997. *Personnel administration and management.* 4th edn. Pretoria: Van Schaik.

Dessler, G. 1981. *Personnel management: Modern concepts and techniques.* Reston, VA: Reston Publishing.

Dresang, DL. 2002. *Public personnel management and public policy.* 4th edn. New York: Longman.

Du Toit, DFP, & Van der Waldt, G. 1997. *Public management: The grassroots.* Cape Town: Juta.

Foot, M, & Hook, C. 1996. *Introducing human resource management.* London: Longman.

Grogan, J, Jordaan, B, Maserumule, P & Stelzner, S. 2009. *Juta's labour law update 2009.* Cape Town: Juta.

Hays, SW, & Kearney, RC. 1995. *Public personnel administration: Problems and prospects.* Englewood Cliffs, NJ: Prentice-Hall.

Hays, SW, & Reeves, TZ. 1989. *Personnel management in the public sector.* Dubuque, Iowa: Brown.

Hosking, A. 2010. Get well soon (Editorial). *HR Future,* No 2, 4. [http://www.hrfuture.net].

Klingner, DE, & Nalbandian, J. 1985. *Public personnel management.* Englewood Cliffs, NJ: Prentice-Hall.

Levine, CH, Peters, BG, & Thompson, FJ. 1990. *Public administration: Challenges, choices and consequences.* London: Scott Foresman/Little.

Marx, FW. 1986. *The personnel and public relations functions in the business enterprise.* Pretoria: HAUM.

Moore, P. 1985. *Public personnel management: A contingency approach.* Lexington, MA: Lexington Books.

Nigro, FA, & Nigro, LG. 1986. *The new public personnel administration.* Itasca, Minnesota: Peacock.

Sherman, A, Bohlander, G, & Snell, S. 1998. *Managing human resources.* 11th edn. Cincinnati, OH: South Western/Thompson.

Starling, G. 1993. *Managing the public sector.* Ontario: Dorsey.

Swanepoel, B, Erasmus, B, Van Wyk, M, & Schenk, H. 2003. *South African human resource management: Theory and practice.* 3rd edn. Cape Town: Juta.

Tompkins, J. 1995. *Human resource management in government: Hitting the ground running.* New York: Harper Collins.

Uys, F, Van der Westhuizen, EJ, Smith, FH, & Rowland, RW. 1998. *Organisasieleer en Personeel-administrasie:* Enigste studiegids vir PBL201-E/PBA201-U (Publieke Administrasie). Pretoria: University of South Africa.

Van der Westhuizen, EJ. 2000. *Public Human Resource Management:* Study guide 1 for PUB302- F (Public Administration). Pretoria: University of South Africa.

Acts of legislation

Republic of South Africa. 1994. The Public Service Act (Proclamation 103 of 1994). Government Printer. [http://www.polity.org.za/html/govdocs/legislation/1994]

Republic of South Africa. 1996. The Constitution of the Republic of South Africa (1996). Government Printer. [http://www.polity.org.za/html/ govdocs/legislation/1996]

Government white papers

Republic of South Africa. 1997. White Paper on Human Resource Management in the Public Service. Government Gazette 390 (18594). [http://www.dpsa.gov.za/ docs/policy/white-papers/pservice]

Government reports

Republic of South Africa. 2006. Report on the evaluation of the policy framework on managing HIV and AIDS in the public service. Public Service Commission. [http://www.psc.gov.za/docs/reports/2006/report_eva_policy_framework_hiv_aids_policy.pdf]

Management guides

Republic of South Africa. 2003. Senior Management Service: Public Service Handbook. Department of Public Service and Administration. [http://www.dpsa.gov.za/ documents/sms/publications]

APPENDIX A

Policy making for public sector human resource management

Before any human resource legislation can be taken to Parliament for approval, it is usually embodied in a 'green paper' by the relevant political manager/head (minister), after which it is published in the Government Gazette for comment by all the relevant role players. The green paper is the document on which the subsequently published 'white paper' is based. After all the information contained in the various commentaries is incorporated, a white paper is published in the Government Gazette for further comment. The White Paper on Human Resource Management in the Public Service of 1997 is an example of a white paper published by the Minister of the Public Service and Administration (the responsible minister of public sector human resource management) in the Government Gazette. Once all the commentary has been dealt with, the white paper is embodied in legislative proposals by the Department of Public Service and Administration, whereupon it is submitted to the Cabinet for approval. If the Executive Authority – the Cabinet or government – is of the opinion that its new policy has legislative implications, it formulates a draft bill to be published for further comment. After this, the white paper becomes official policy of the Executive Authority – or government. It may also be given to important role players in the human resource environment for specific comment.

Once all the commentary has been dealt with again, the draft bill is passed on to legal advisers in the government so that its legal implications can be determined. It is then taken to Parliament and placed on the 'Order Paper'. When the draft bill has reached the parliamentary phase, it is referred to as 'the first reading stage'. At the same time, it is also referred to the relevant portfolio committee, namely the Committee for Public Service and Administration, for further consideration. The portfolio committee comprises members of all the political parties represented in Parliament. This committee is responsible for refining the draft bill further and is authorised, for example, to approach human resource specialists to assist it in this regard. Once the committee has gained consensus about the draft bill, it goes back to Parliament for further debate. After both houses in Parliament (the National Assembly and the National Council of Provinces) have approved the draft bill, it goes back to the President for his signature, and it is then published in the Government Gazette and accepted as official legislation from a specified date.

At this stage, the policy is referred to as 'political policy' because it is approved by political representatives in Parliament. Cases in point are the Public Service Act of 1994 and the Public Service Commission Act of 1997, which are referred to as official statutes governing public sector human resource management in the South African public service. Since it is impossible in practice for legislators to write details into law, executive political heads or ministers (who are in charge of public institutions and are therefore responsible for ensuring that legislation is properly administered) are allowed to formulate 'executive policy'. This arrangement enables executive political heads to embody their views in regulations published as a supplement to the statutory provisions. In practice, this means that the Minister of Public Service and Administration is authorised to issue regulations about certain human resource matters, such as appointments and promotions. Accordingly, Public Service Regulations may be issued in terms of Section 42 of the Public Service Act of 1994.

The process of policymaking does not end there, however. In addition, 'administrative policy' and 'operational policy' also have to be determined. Administrative policy is usually determined by the central personnel agencies (the Department of Public Service and Administration and the Public Service Commission) and the chief executive officers or heads of public sector institutions such as state departments (usually referred to as 'directors-general'). When policy is determined, decisions have to be made about such matters as qualifications required at appointment, and the decisions have to be within the legal framework of parliamentary legislation, ministerial regulations, and codes of instruction.

Administrative policy usually culminates in specific codes of instruction (such as collective agreements and management guides) and is put in place to support laws and regulations. Operational policy for human resource management is determined by human resource specialists in conjunction with the various line function managers and their personnel who are employed in public sector institutions. However, these persons do not have extensive discretionary powers to refine policy which is already specified in elaborate detail in legislation, regulations, and other codes of instruction. Practical arrangements concerning place and time still have to be cleared up, however, and these arrangements can be called operational policy (Van der Westhuizen 2000: 17–18).

2 The milieu of the public sector human resource function

Purpose

The purpose of this chapter is to contextualise the South African public sector human resource function.

Learning outcomes

After you have read this chapter, you should be able to:
- Explain the influence of the variables and changes at a global level on human resource management in the South African public sector.
- Provide a statistical overview of the composition of the South African public service.
- Describe the implications of the constitutional values for public sector human resource management.
- Give examples of legislation and policies applicable to public sector human resource management in South Africa.
- Explain the functions of the major role players in the public sector human resource system in South Africa.
- Describe the contemporary trends in and challenges for public sector human resource management.

2.1 Introduction

People are central to government's effort to execute its functions and to render services to the public; they are the targets of government's actions, and they are also the means through which government has to execute and fulfil its responsibilities to the country's citizens. People form one of the various categories of resources necessary to deliver services to the public. These human resources are thus indispensable for government to execute its functions and render services. The government of the day may have brilliant political agenda, excellent public policies and legislation, physical resources such as land and buildings, and access to vast amounts of financial resources. However, without human resources, no government will be able to deliver.

Human resources, also known as staff or personnel, do their various jobs as employees of the manifold public institutions. As these public institutions do not exist in isolation, the human resource management within them must thus be contextualised in terms of the milieu external to these institutions. Although this macro external milieu constantly changes, it is important to establish some framework of factors that may have an impact on the way people are managed.

This chapter focuses on the wider context of human resource management in the South African public sector, namely the variables and changes at a global level, the composition of public officials in South Africa, constitutional values and principles, the legislative framework, human resource systems in the public service and contemporary trends.

The point of departure, however, is that South Africa is part of an even wider system, namely the international global system.

2.2 Variables and change at a global level

As we are moving further into the third millennium, we can safely say that the world is in the midst of multifaceted and revolutionary change. From the perspective of world politics and international power relations, an era has dawned in which there is growing appreciation for and acceptance of more democratic systems worldwide. The oppressive, authoritarian and communistic systems that were common for a long period in the world's history have been making way for democracies. A shift has been taking place from a largely bipolar world order towards a multi-polar order. For many years, the United States of America (USA) and the Soviet Union, as the two world 'superpowers' with their distinctive systems of free enterprise and state socialism respectively, had taken centre stage in debates over world politics and economics. Instead of this bipolar order, we now have a situation in which different power blocs are developing. Not only did the Soviet Union collapse soon after the fall of the Berlin Wall and the reunification of East and West Germany, but a confederation of major European countries, the European Economic Community (EEC), was formed, and a gradual shift of economic power towards the East Asian bloc has also taken place. It has been estimated, for instance, that over the period from 1992 to 2000, 40% of new purchasing power in the world would have come from East Asia (De Villiers & Slabbert 1996). Also, with the relative declining prominence of the USA, the conclusion of the North American Free Trade Agreement (NAFTA) has resulted in the formation of a North American trade bloc consisting of the USA, Mexico and Canada.

Simultaneously with these trends in international relations and the world politico-economic order, a revolution has been taking place in the field of technology. This is true especially in the field of information and communication technology. The move from the industrial age into the information age is resulting in an almost boundary-less world with individuals, businesses, governments, etc. becoming more and more interconnected through computers and online systems such as the Internet. Information flow and distance have become crucial variables in transactions between countries and organisations. Revolutionary technological developments have thus created the foundation for more free trade and for faster moving economic transactions and systems across the globe.

A more open and global world order has thus come into existence. Due to these advances in communication technology, the abilities of governments to control information (and thus their sovereignty) have been severely curtailed. These and other developments – such as the establishment of economic blocs and more free trade between nations, which has been further facilitated by developments such as the establishment of the World Trade Organisation (WTO) – has made it more difficult for governments to retain control over information and money flows, thus impacting negatively on their ability to maintain systems of nation-state sovereignty.

All these complex and multifaceted developments are making for a whole new 'global village' in which the internationalisation of markets is commonplace. New markets arise with the concomitant potential to compete across boundaries. Companies are setting up operations in other countries and entering into business alliances outside their home countries. Thus, South African institutions now have to compete not only with the providers of products and services from other countries on our local markets, but they can also compete with others in markets within other countries. Similarly, our business leaders have to decide whether or not they are interested in setting up operations beyond the boundaries of South Africa. These ventures pose additional challenges to the Departments of Trade and Industry and Foreign Affairs and their officials.

In this competitive world economy, the management of organisations thus have constantly to seek ways of improving their performance in order to survive. So-called total quality and high performance systems have thus come to the forefront, placing new demands on the management of human resources. Within this context of global competition and free trade, countries are tied via their business economic structures into a game of vigorous competition for foreign investment to stimulate growth. At the same time (or rather as a result of this), labour has become a more fluid 'production factor' in what can almost be termed a global labour market. In a nutshell, due to variables and forces that are experienced internationally – such as increased competition, the accelerated pace at which economies (and thus private and public institutions) have to operate, the free flow of money, information, products, and people, the wave of high-tech developments and the general trend towards more democratic value systems – the world of work and human resource management in South Africa, as elsewhere in the world, is faced with a multitude of complex challenges and forces. Apart from these rather generic factors that are experienced worldwide, other variables and forces are unique to the peculiar South African situation.

2.3   Public officials in South Africa: Statistical variables

When we think of officials in the public service, we invariably imagine people in government institutions all over the country busy executing government functions or providing services. In order to construct a representative picture of all public officials, it is therefore necessary to classify them according to the particular characteristics that they have in common within the context of various social and demographic dynamics. A statistical overview of the South African public service will enable the reader to assess the impact of the societal milieu (specifically with regard to inequalities in the income status in South Africa) on the composition of the public service.

2.3.1 General

As indicated above, the challenges and complexities facing South Africa cannot be separated from broader international developments. For South Africa to survive in this international arena of competition, tremendous efforts will be required from all its citizens, especially the stakeholders of the organisations that deliver the goods. A major challenge in this regard is the need to balance the inherent intricacies and tensions which have resulted from our history of gross unfair discrimination and inequality with the need to stimulate and develop the economy.

Fundamental to the success of any country is, apart from its natural resources, its people. The people of any country make the difference between success and failure. Demographic statistics cannot, however, be detached from the circumstances within which the people of the country live and make a living.

South Africa's complex socio-political-economic setup is founded today to a large extent on the history of the country. Reference to our history shows clearly that the legacies of the apartheid system have permeated all aspects of our lives. The pressures and demands facing South Africa in a global economy – where competitiveness is the watchword – must be seen against the background of the major threat (or challenge) to our country: the problem of inequality.

Although South Africa's single major objective may be to stimulate the economy in order to create the means to improve the quality of life of all the country's inhabitants, the real problem that we face is that of the gross socio-economic inequality in our society. Reconciling these two dynamic realities (inequality and growth) embodies one of the greatest challenges facing the country. Whereas some parties (such as organised labour) are fighting to eradicate the socioeconomic inequalities through strategies aimed at wealth redistribution, captains of business and industry are adamant that, in order to enrich the historically deprived, wealth has first to be created. To them, creating wealth means but one thing: business organisations and public institutions have to become competitive and efficient in international terms. This may mean adopting measures to cut costs, to become 'lean and mean', which may include cutting labour costs and improving labour productivity. To the deprived, the immediate objective is to get that which was historically denied them or taken away from them. The essence of the debate thus concerns what comes first: wealth creation or wealth redistribution. This dynamic tension boils over directly into the relations between the parties in the workplace, which means, in the simplest terms, relations between the employer and the employee.

2.3.2 Social and demographic dynamics

In a book such as this one, the departure point of contextual analyses ought to be the situation of human resources in the country. We shall therefore focus briefly on some important demographic and social variables.

2.3.2.1 Notes on the South African population

The mid-year estimates of Statistics South Africa (Republic of South Africa 2010a) shows that the South African population has doubled over the past three decades, with the country's population estimated at 49.99 million people. Of these, 79.4% classified themselves as African, 9.1% as white, 8.8% as coloured, and 2.6% as Indian/Asian (see Figure 2.1) (South Africa 2010a). The age distribution is typical of a developing country as nearly one-third (31%) of the population is aged younger than 15 years while approximately 7.6% is 60 years or older. A total of 48.67% of South Africans are male, while 51.33% of the population are female (Republic of South Africa 2010a). Although most of the statistics in this book will be already obsolete by the time you read it, you can obtain the most recent statistics on the South African population from the StatsOnline (see Focus on Research 2.1 below).

FOCUS ON RESEARCH 2.1
Most recent mid-year population estimates for South Africa

RESEARCH

Researchers on public human resource management need the most recent statistics on their specific country's population composition in order to contextualise their research. Statistics South Africa (Republic of South Africa 2010a) provides this statistics online on their web site at http://www.statssa.gov.za/publications/. The mid-year estimates for 2010 are summarised as follows:

- This release uses the cohort-component methodology to estimate the 2010 mid-year population of South Africa.
- The estimates cover all the residents of South Africa at the 2010 mid-year, and are based on the latest available information. Estimates may change as new data become available.
- For 2010, Statistics South Africa (Stats SA) estimates the mid-year population as 49.99 million.
- Fifty-one per cent (approximately 25.66 million) of the population is female.
- Gauteng comprises the largest share of the South African population. Approximately 11.19 million people (22.4%) live in this province. KwaZulu-Natal is the province with the second largest population, with 10.65 million people (21.3%) living in this province. With a population of approximately 1.10 million people (2.2%), Northern Cape remains the province with the smallest share of the South African population.
- Nearly one-third (31.0%) of the population is aged younger than 15 years and approximately 7.6% (3.8 million) is 60 years or older. Of those younger than 15 years, approximately 23% (3.52 million) live in KwaZulu-Natal and 19.3% (2.99 million) live in Gauteng.
- Migration is an important demographic process in shaping the age structure and distribution of the provincial population. For the period 2006–2011 it is estimated that approximately 211 600 people will migrate from the Eastern Cape; Limpopo is estimated to experience a net out-migration of just over 140 000 people. During the same period, Gauteng and Western Cape are estimated to experience a net inflow of migrants of approximately 364 400 and 94 600 respectively.
- Life expectancy at birth is estimated at 53.3 years for males and 55.2 years for females.
- The infant mortality rate is estimated at 46.9 per 1 000 live births. ▷

- The estimated overall HIV prevalence rate is approximately 10.5%. The total number of people living with HIV is estimated at approximately 5.24 million. For adults aged 15–49 years, an estimated 17% of the population is HIV positive.
- For 2010, this release estimates that approximately 1.6 million people aged 15 and older; and approximately 183 000 children, would be in need of ART (anti-retroviral therapy).
- The total number of new HIV infections for 2010 is estimated at
- 410 000. Of these, an estimated 40 000 will be among children.

The South African population consists of the following groups: the Nguni people (consisting of the Zulu, Xhosa, Ndebele and Swazi); the Sotho-Tswana people, who include the Southern, Northern, and Western Sotho (Tswana); the Tsonga; the Venda; Afrikaners; English speakers; coloureds; Indians, and those who have immigrated to South Africa from the rest of Africa, Europe and Asia and who maintain a strong cultural identity. Groups of the Khoekhoen and the San people also live in South Africa.

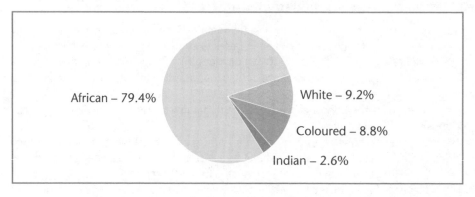

Figure 2.1   Percentage of the population of South Africa by population group

The language of most South Africans is Zulu (23.8%), with Xhosa second (17.6%), and Afrikaans third (13.3%) (Republic of South Africa 2010b). The male to female ratio is approximately 48:52 and the urban to non-urban distribution ratio is approximately 64:46. More than half of the country's population is concentrated in three regions: KwaZulu-Natal (21%), Gauteng (18%), and the Eastern Cape (16%).

By international standards, South Africa's population is growing rather rapidly. It grew at an annual rate of approximately 2.3% over the past two decades of this century. The growth of the African population is particularly high at about 2.6%. Some project that our population will have reached between 50 and 57 million by 2010. The impact of the influx of foreigners from our neighbouring countries should, however, not be underestimated in these population growth statistics. According to Barker (1999: 56), 'reducing the high population growth rate should be an important priority for the country, to relieve pressures on social services, the environment and finding employment'. The Institute for Future Research (IFR) at the University of

Stellenbosch singles out food production, water resources, education, housing and health services as those areas most threatened by the population explosion (Cloete, 1996). As far as food production is concerned, too large a population creates the problem of having to produce more food on existing agricultural land. It is estimated that only 10.7% of the total surface of the country is devoted to agriculture.

With regard to water resources, the IFR points out that there has always been a shortage in South Africa. It is estimated that South Africa will be without sufficient water between 2020 and 2030 unless drastic steps are taken. Approximately 88% of all fresh water is used by the agricultural and industrial sectors, which leaves only 12% for domestic use. Domestic consumption is expected to increase sharply in future.

Together with this, the agricultural sector will have to increase food production by 50% between now and 2026 in order to feed an additional 23 million people. This will put further pressure on water resources. As for the education levels of the South African population, African black females have the lowest educational attainment in the country, followed by African males.

Figure 2.2 shows that 43.5% of the population has either no education or some primary education. It is a disturbing fact that 93.8% of the population has no educational qualifications beyond school.

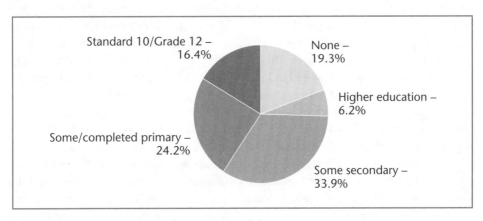

Figure 2.2   Percentage of the population aged 20 years or over, by highest level of education completed

Among all people aged 20 years or over, more than 20% have received no education and only 6% have post-school qualifications. Among Africans, 12.1% have passed Matric and only 3% have post-matriculation qualifications. At the upper end of the educational scale, 40.7% of whites have passed grade 12, and 30% of white males and 24% of white females have post-Matric qualifications.

The South African provinces' respective proportions of people aged 20 years or over with no education are shown in Figure 2.3 on page 32.

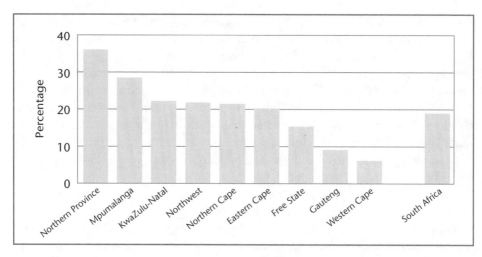

Figure 2.3   Percentage of the population aged 20 years or over with no education, per each province and in South Africa overall

The IFR estimates that the total school-going population will grow to more than 13 million by the year 2006. An average annual increase of more than 160 000 pupils is thus expected. This will mean that about 330 schools with an average of 500 pupils will have to be built annually. With regard to housing, the IFR says that it is almost impossible to meet the demand. The backlog is already about three million units, while the population is expected to increase at a rate of more than 2% over the first decade of the new millennium.

In respect of health services, it is estimated that, up to the year 2006, 710 doctors and 2 969 nurses will have to be trained annually. That does not take retirement, deaths and emigration into account. In respect of HIV and AIDS, there is still a great deal of debate regarding facts and figures. Some estimates are that the epidemic is growing at a faster rate in South Africa than in most other African countries, and that between three million and eight million South Africans were carrying the HI-virus by the end of the twentieth century. Over the next decade, millions more of South Africa's people could be infected (see Chapter 14).

Other important characteristics of the South African society include high rates of crime and violence, high expectations and growing impatience for drastic improvements in quality of life by most, and a fear of losing everything by others. There are feelings of mistrust and uncertainty, and racist attitudes continue to thrive as the country transforms itself towards a more open and democratic society. Tensions between reconciliation and nation building on the one hand and retribution and dissent on the other have to be balanced and managed.

So while the rest of the world continues to progress and develop at a dramatic pace, South Africans are now urged to stop spending energy, time and resources in focusing on the past. The current situation in our country has created a very complex external environment, which impacts on the management of human resources within our organisations. There are, however, numerous other socio-economic dynamics that play an equally important role, and these also have to be understood.

2.3.2.2   The South African public service: Statistical overview

By the end of March 2008, the South African public service had almost 1 204 525 people (including members of the South African National Defence Force) in its employ. The priority of the government of the day, with regard to types of services rendered to society, is shown by the following statistics: 63% of the staff are attached to the social services sector (health, social development and education), followed by 20% in the criminal justice cluster (Republic of South Africa 2010c).

With the composition of the South African population in mind (refer Figure 2.1), the South African government does have a sound affirmative action policy (see Chapter 6). The overall profile of the public service seems to be close to achieving perfect representative status, matching the population profile in terms of both race and gender. Of the nearly 1 204 525 public servants, approximately 56% are women and 44% are men – 6 percentage points more women than December 1998 (Republic of South Africa 2010). Almost 85% of the public servants are black (African, coloured and Indian), compared to the national profile of about 90%. This is also an increase of nearly 3 percentage points since December 1998. By April 2002, the senior management levels included 68% black people (including coloureds and Indians), compared to 41% in 1999 (Republic of South Africa (2006: 25)).

2.4   Constitutional values and principles

We are convinced that the public sector is different from both the private and non-profit sectors. This view is shared by Ban and Riccucci (2002: 2), who attribute this difference to 'law' and 'politics'. It is evident from the previous paragraphs that the South African public service is diverse in all respects. Considering the diversity evident in the backgrounds and upbringing of people, it would be reasonable to deduce that the values held by an individual could and probably would differ from those held by others. For the conduct of public administration, differences in the value make-up of public servants could present a problem. Obviously, some uniformity in approach and conduct is required of those providing public services. This implies that there should be substantial agreement as to the norms and standards of behaviour and conduct that are to be applied by public officials in the performance of their duties (Robson 1999: 158).

The Constitution of the Republic of South Africa, 1996 (henceforth referred to as 'the Constitution') and other laws constitute the immediate sources of ethical direction to public officials in general and public human resource practitioners in particular. The Constitution is '[...] the supreme law of the Republic; law or conduct inconsistent with it is invalid, and the obligations imposed by it, must be fulfilled' (Republic of South Africa 1996: Section 2). It is the final arbiter and enforcer of what is good and right and correct. To fulfil its primary ethical function effectively, the Constitution must be accepted by general consensus of the people (Robson 1999: 158). Some key parts of the Constitution need to be highlighted for the purpose of this discussion.

The Constitution declares the Republic to be a democratic state, founded on a number of values. These include principally human dignity, the achievement of equality, the advancement of human rights and freedoms, non-racialism, non-sexism, the rule of law, universal adult suffrage, and accountability, responsiveness and openness. In committing himself or herself to a career in the public service, the public servant – as a key role player in the national effort aimed at making society and the state 'work' – is bound by the democratic nature of the state and the values which support it. He or she is under an unqualified obligation to understand and appreciate those values and to strive consciously to ensure that his or her day-to-day activities are guided by them. For the thinking public servant, the lead statement of the Constitution thus serves as an authoritative cue to the ethical performance of his or her duties (Robson 1999: 159).

Public sector human resource managers and practitioners are confronted on a daily basis with such concepts as human dignity, equality and other rights and freedoms. The meanings of these concepts are comprehensively spelt out in the second chapter of the Constitution, which contains the Bill of Rights. Here is a repository of the best of human thought concerning the individual and the state. It is to be studied and reflected on by each and every human resource manager and practitioner. It is to be noted that the Bill of Rights goes considerably beyond the 'classical' rights of equality, freedom of movement, freedom of association, freedom of expression, and others, to encompass also so-called second- and third-generation rights pertaining to the environment, housing, health care, food and water, social security and education. Public servants are legally bound by the Bill of Rights in the performance of their duties (Robson 1999: 159).

In its chapter dealing with public administration, the Constitution requires public administrators to be governed by '[...] the democratic values and principles enshrined in the Constitution' (Republic of South Africa 1996: Section 195(a)). A number of principles are listed, such as the following:

- The promotion and maintenance of a high standard of professional ethics;
- Efficient, economic and effective use of resources;
- A developmental orientation;
- Impartial, fair and equitable provision of services;
- Responsiveness to people's needs and encouragement of the public to participate in public policymaking;
- Public accountability;
- Transparency;
- Good human resource management; and
- Broad representativeness.

There is a wealth of virtuous capital here for the public administrator to draw on (Robson 1999: 159).

The Constitution states the democratic ideal, indicates the core values underlying that ideal, enshrines the rights of people and sets certain key requirements for the conduct of public administration. By doing that, it has provided public human resource managers and practitioners with a rich store of ethical substance to inform and guide their day-to-day activities. As we have seen in Chapter 1, the White Paper on Human Resource Management in the Public Service (Republic of South Africa 1997: Chapter 2) derives the values for public human resource management from the Constitution.

2.5   Legislative and policy framework

Human resource management in the South African public service occurs within a definite legislative and policy framework. The following are examples of such Acts of legislation and white papers, the relevance of which is discussed in various chapters of this book:

- The Public Service Act, 1994;
- The White Paper on the Transformation of the Public Service, 1995;
- The Public Service Laws Amendment Act, 1997;
- The White Paper on Public Service Training and Education, 1997;
- The White Paper on Human Resource Management in the Public Service, 1997;
- The Green Paper on a Conceptual Framework for Affirmative Action and the Management of Diversity in the Public Service, 1997;
- The Employment Equity Act, 1998;
- The White Paper on Affirmative Action in the Public Service, 1998; and
- The Public Service Regulations, 2001.

Each of the above documents directs the activities of human resource managers in the South African public service in one way or another. These documents also form the foundation for the human resource management system for the public service.

2.6   Human resource system for the South African public service

The human resource system for the South African public service is characterised by the presence of four major role players, namely the Department of Labour, the Department of Public Service and Administration, the Public Service Commission and national departments and provincial administrations.

2.6.1   Department of Labour

The Department of Labour, similarly to human resource management in the private sector, is responsible for the maintenance of the generic policy and legal framework for human resource management in the country. For more information, visit the departmental web site at http://www.labour.gov.za/

2.6.2 Department of Public Service and Administration

The Department of Public Service and Administration focuses, in terms of human resources, solely on the public service. (For more information visit the departmental web site at http://www.dpsa.gov.za/) Its tasks include the following (Republic of South Africa 1997: 7.1.4):

- To ensure that human resource policies are supported by key stakeholders;
- To get support for human resource policies from organised labour at national level;
- To ensure that the statutory framework supports the practical application of new human resource management policies;
- To ensure that human resource management policies are aligned with other transformation initiatives;
- To ensure that centrally controlled systems, such as PERSAL, are developed to support national departments' and provincial administrations' implementation of the new human resource management policies; and
- To assist national departments and provincial administrations in implementing the new human resource management policies by providing guidance and, in conjunction with training suppliers, help to develop capacity.

2.6.3 Public Service Commission

The Public Service Commission (PSC) is one of the institutions created by the Constitution to promote democratic values and principles in South Africa. In terms of Section 196 of the Constitution, the PSC is responsible for the monitoring and evaluation of the implementation of human resource policies. In the process of monitoring and evaluation, the Public Service Commission publishes its findings as public reports. The following are examples of reports (available at http://www.psc.gov.za/) on aspects of human resource management that have been published recently:

- An Evaluation of Integration and Co-ordination in the Integrated Sustainable Rural Development Programme;
- Assessment of the State of Human Resource Management in the Public Service;
- Consolidated Report on Inspections of Service Delivery Sites: South African Police Service;
- Fact Sheet: Grievance Resolution for the 2008/09 Financial Year; and
- Report on the Assessment of the Public Sector Education and Training Authority's [PSETA's] Contribution Towards the Development of Skills and Career Progression Prospects in the Public Service (see 'Did you know?' on page 37).

2.6.4 National departments and provincial administrations

National departments and provincial administrations are the actual service-delivery agencies utilising the human resources that make up the public service. (For an updated list, visit the web site http://www.info.gov.za/aboutgovt/dept.htm). These departments and administrations are responsible for the following tasks, among others, in this human resource system (Republic of South Africa 1997: 7.1.3):

- Adopting new approaches to human resource management;
- Creating or developing infrastructure and systems to support new human resource management practices;
- Ensuring that line managers have the requisite human resource management skills; and
- Acquiring and utilising human resources within national legal and policy frameworks in order to render public services to the public.

DID YOU KNOW?

The Public Service Commission (PSC) takes its powers and functions from Sub-section 196(1) of the Constitution of the Republic of South Africa, 1996. This sub-section reads as follows:

1. The powers and functions of the Commission are:
   a. To promote the values and principles set out in section 195, throughout the public service;
   b. To investigate, monitor and evaluate the organisation and administration, and the personnel practices, of the public service;
   c. To propose measures to ensure effective and efficient performance within the public service;
   d. To give directions aimed at ensuring that personnel procedures relating to recruitment, transfers, promotions and dismissals comply with the values and principles set out in section 195;
   e. To report in respect of its activities and the performance of its functions, including any finding it may make and directions and advice it may give, and to provide an evaluation of the extent to which the values and principles set out in section 195 are complied with; and
   f. Either of its own accord or on receipt of any complaint:
      i. To investigate and evaluate the application of personnel and public administration practices, and to report to the relevant executive authority and legislature;
      ii. To investigate grievances of employees in the public service concerning official acts or omissions, and recommend appropriate remedies;
      iii. To monitor and investigate adherence to applicable procedures in the public service; and
      iv. To advise national and provincial organs of state regarding personnel practices in the public service, including those relating to the recruitment, appointment, transfer, discharge and other aspects of the careers of employees in the public service; and
   g. To exercise or perform the additional powers or functions prescribed by and Act of Parliament.

2.7 Contemporary trends and challenges for public sector HR management

Reflecting on contemporary trends and challenges for human resource management in the public sector is essentially a contextualised issue. The White Paper on the

Transformation of the Public Service (Republic of South Africa 1995: Chapter 4) refers to an international movement in re-evaluating the role of the state and the public service in society. According to this white paper, this trend has been in response to such factors as the following:

- The growing impact of global markets, competition, and financial mobility;
- The increasing trend toward economic liberalisation and political democratisation;
- The increasing international spread of communications and information technology; and
- The worsening economic crisis in the developing world and the impact of IMF/World Bank structural adjustment programmes.

Within the context of re-evaluating the role of the state and the above-mentioned factors, the major trends characterising human resource management in the South African public service during the first ten years since 1994, when the ANC took over the government, can be summarised as follows (Republic of South Africa 1995: Chapter 8):

- Creating a unified and integrated service;
- Restructuring the senior management echelon into a Senior Management Service (SMS); and
- Creating a leaner and a more cost-effective public service.

After the first ten years, the Public Service Commission (Republic of South Africa 2004: 39) has identified the following challenges or priorities for the South African public service:

- Better assessments of the State capacity and performance;
- The improvement and strengthening of public management;
- Better fostering and nurturing of public service leadership;
- A general focus on implementation and service delivery; and
- The acceleration of social development and the effective address of poverty.

These challenges will impact directly or indirectly on the planning for and strategies of human resource management in the South African public service. They will also influence such aspects as the utilisation and development of public sector employees, remuneration and labour relations.

2.8   Review

This chapter has outlined briefly the milieu of human resource management in the South African public service. It is clear that the macro context – characterised, among other factors, by increased competition, the accelerated pace at which private and public institutions have to operate, and the general trend towards more democratic value systems – cannot be ignored by human resource managers in the South African public service. It is this context that makes it necessary to consider the overall profile of the public service in terms of its representativeness.

The general trend towards a democratic value system is also reflected by the Constitution of the Republic of South Africa, which provides public human resource managers and practitioners with a rich store of ethical substance to inform and guide their day-to-day activities. Some of the values enshrined in the Constitution are fairness, equity, accessibility, transparency, accountability, participation, and professionalism. These values are also reflected by the various legislation and policies applicable to human resource management in the South African public service.

This chapter has also given a brief overview of the four major role players in the human resource system of the South African public service, namely the Department of Labour, the Department of Public Service and Administration, the Public Service Commission, and national departments and provincial administrations. In conclusion, we have reflected on contemporary trends and challenges for human resource management. Some of the trends relevant to human resource management in the South African public service seem to be political change (worldwide, but specifically in South Africa), economic changes, social and demographic changes, technology changes, the integration, unification, and restructuring of the South African public service and senior management, as well as a leaner and more cost-effective public service. Various challenges in terms of performance assessment and the improvement of leadership and service delivery have also been identified.

2.9 Self-evaluation questions

1. Name the most prominent global variables and changes and discuss their real or possible effect on HR management in the South African public service.
2. Compare the composition of the South African population with the composition of the South African public service in terms of race and gender. Give your own assessment of the comparison.
3. Name the most prominent values one can derive from the Constitution of the Republic of South Africa.
4. Discuss the implications of the constitutional values for public human resource management in South Africa.
5. Give examples of legislation and policies applicable to public human resource management in South Africa.
6. Explain the possible effect of the various legislation and policy documents on human resource management in the South African public service.
7. Name the major role players in human resource management in the South African public service.
8. Discuss the respective functions of the major role players in human resource management in the South African public service.
9. Discuss the contemporary trends in public human resource management.
10. Discuss the challenges for human resource management in the South African public service.

Bibliography

Ban, C, & Riccucci, NM. 2002. *Public personnel management: Current concerns, future challenges.* 3rd edn. New York: Longman.

Barker, FS. 1999. *The South African labour market: Critical issues for renaissance.* Pretoria: Van Schaik.

Burger, D. (Ed.) 2002. *South Africa yearbook 2002/03.* Government Communication and Information System. [http://www.gov.za/structure/pubserv]

Cloete, G. 1996. Oorbevolking kan HOP verongeluk, *Finansies en Tegniek,* 26 January.

De Villiers, AS, & Slabbert, JA. 1996. *The South African organisational environment.* Johannesburg: Rand Afrikaans University.

Powell, TA, & Buchmann, C. 2003. *Effects of spatial segregation and local labour markets on the occupational status and income of black and white South Africans.* [http://www.soc.duke.edu/~cbuch/web/Powell_Buchmann]

Robson, IH. 1999. Professional ethics from day to day: A practitioner's reflection. In JS Wessels & JC Pauw, *Reflective public administration: Views from the South.* Cape Town: Oxford University Press.

Acts of legislation

Republic of South Africa. 1996. *The Constitution of the Republic of South Africa,* 1996. Government Printer. [http://www.polity.org.za/html/govdocs/legislation/1996]

Government white and green papers

Republic of South Africa. 1995. *White paper on the transformation of the public service.* Department of the Public Service and Administration. [http://www.dpsa.gov.za/docs/policy/white-papers/transform95]

Republic of South Africa. 1997. *White paper on human resource management in the public service.* Department of the Public Service and Administration. [http://www.dpsa.gov.za/docs/policy/white-papers/pservice]

Government reports

Republic of South Africa. 2004. *Report on the State of the Public Service.* Public Service Commission.

Republic of South Africa. 2006. *An Audit of Affirmative Action in the Public Service.* Pretoria: Public Service Commission. Accessed online on 9 August 2010. http://www.psc.gov.za/home_docs/Low-rez%20Document.pdf.

Republic of South Africa. 2010a. *Mid-year population estimates 2010.* P0302. Available online at: http://www.statssa.gov.za/PublicationsHTML/P03022010/html/P03022010.html. Accessed on 9 August 2010.

Republic of South Africa. 2010a. *South Africa's population.* [http://www.southafrica.info/about/people/population.htm; accessed on 9 August 2010]

Republic of South Africa. 2010b. *The languages of South Africa.* [http://www.southafrica.info/about/people/language.htm: accessed on 9 August 2010] Republic of South Africa. 2010c. *The public service.* [http://www.info.gov.za/aboutgovt/publicadmin/ps.htm: accessed at 9 August 2010]

3 Theoretical perspectives on public sector human resource management

Purpose

The purpose of this chapter is to provide the reader with a clear and broad overview of the theoretical developments in public sector human resource management (PSHRM) in order to comprehend the contemporary South African perspectives.

Learning outcomes

After you have read this chapter, you should be able to:
- Demonstrate an awareness of the developments of HRM in an international historical context.
- Describe the historical development of HRM in South Africa.
- Describe the evolutionary nature of employment practices in the PSHRM field in a historical context.
- Provide a contemporary South African perspective of PSHRM.
- Explain how one can pursue a career in the HR field in South Africa.
- Identify the role of the South African Board for Personnel Practice (SABPP) in HRM in South Africa by explaining its philosophy, strategy and objectives.
- Outline the process of registration with the SABPP.
- Explain how one can remain a valued HR specialist in South Africa by doing extensive networking and reading in the subject field.

3.1 Introduction

In Chapter 2, you were introduced to the milieu of public sector human resource management (PSHRM). Milieu was used as a key concept to explain the surroundings and setting of the public domain in which the human resource function takes place; in other words, we discussed the context of the public sector human resource management sphere. In Chapter 3, we will introduce some theoretical perspectives that underpin the discipline. Without some degree of reflection on the themes that have traditionally characterised human resource management work in the past, actions and thoughts for the future are sterile and will not be clearly guided. Various individuals, groups and disciplines have contributed to the development of public sector human resource management. The relevant literature makes it clear that contributions were made from the earliest times. What is important to note, however, is that these contributions offer distinct and varied ideas about the way in which the human resource function should be managed, according to their historical and topical context. Nevertheless, a closer analysis of the content reveals that, together, they have had a cumulative effect, continuously influencing the body of knowledge (theory) and practice (pool of practical skills) of human resource management. For this reason, it is necessary to consider the evolution of human resource management (HRM) as it has unfolded through the centuries. A brief review of the international, national and public sector perspectives will be provided in order to learn as much as possible about what constitutes 'good' public sector human resource management. In the following sections, an overview will be given as to where public sector human resource management comes from and where it stands today.

3.2   The international historical context of HRM

Few areas of management research, teaching or writing have evoked as much debate as that which abounds in the literature concerning the field of human resource management. It seems that this proliferation and variety of ideas stems partly from international and historical differences that have developed in theories relating to this field of knowledge and practice. It is therefore necessary to focus briefly on this concept in a historical and international context.

3.2.1   Brief evolutionary overview

As we enter the twenty-first century and look back in time, it seems that not only life in general but working life in particular is significantly different today from what it used to be; it can, however, be concluded with reasonable certainty that it will be even more significantly different another fifty years from now.

Before the Industrial Revolution, most people were engaged in home crafts or in agriculture. There was virtually no such thing as modern-day employment or employment relationships. With the coming of the Industrial Revolution, however, daily life and the world of work changed dramatically as technological developments led to the establishment of factories where people went to work. Working life came to be removed from the family or household context. Specific employer-employee relationships were established, which had to be managed by those in charge of and responsible for these factories and related institutions. The real origins of human resource management practice can hence be traced back to all those efforts by employers who, over the years, tried to devise ways to maintain and utilise their workers better. For example, Robert Owen (1771–1858), a Scottish textile manufacturer, spent company profits on efforts to improve the living and working conditions of his labour force. These efforts included the provision of villages for workers near their places of work, schooling facilities and decent health and sanitation facilities in his cotton mill factories (Beach 1980; Cuming 1989). On the other hand, in the United States of America, the earliest strike ever to be documented was organised by Philadelphia printers who claimed minimum weekly wages as long ago as 1786. In addition, as early as 1794, Albert Gallatin had already established the first profit-sharing scheme in the USA at his glass works in Pennsylvania (Cherrington 1983: 15).

During the period from 1880 to 1920, three important changes came about: a massive growth in factory-type work, serious efforts to improve the general welfare of factory workers, and scientific management to improve production levels. Due to a growth in larger factories, an American, Frederick W. Taylor (the so-called father of scientific management) began his research. He propagated the use of 'scientific techniques' to elicit higher output, accompanied by higher wages, through a differential piece-rate wage incentive system. He believed in using scientific methods to study working conditions and jobs to identify the 'best working methods' (tools, equipment, machinery and process) and to recruit and appoint the 'right' people for the 'right' jobs. Scientific protagonists, such as Taylor, the Gilbreths and Henry Grant, also advocated clearly defined jobs with concomitant organisational structures.

Hugo Munsterburg's famous book, *Psychology and Industrial Efficiency*, was published in 1913 – a work regarded by many as the authoritative source in the field of applying psychological knowledge to the management of work and human resources. These developments made important contributions to existing knowledge on such aspects as training techniques, the relationship between working conditions and work performance, work motivation and morale, and performance evaluation.

During the period from 1924 to 1933, Elton Mayo and some of his colleagues at Harvard University also conducted a series of research studies at the Hawthorne Works of the Western Electric Company in Chicago, USA. Their work related to the role of aspects such as lighting, rest pauses and group norms on work performance levels, and laid the foundation for the so-called human relations movement that highlighted the social drives of humankind within the context of the workplace. This movement, which marked the beginning of the era of applying behavioural sciences in the workplace, put forward the view that employees could not be seen merely as 'factors of production' just like materials, money and natural resources. Human resource management (or 'personnel management' as it was known in those days) thus became appreciated and recognised as a distinct field of theory and practice.

During the 1950s and 1960s, various behavioural scientists influenced the human relations school of thought. Humanistic psychologists such as Abraham Maslow (1954), Chris Argyris (1957), Douglas McGregor (1960), and Frederick Herzberg (1966) were prominent figures in this regard. In 1965, Miles published an article in the *Harvard Business Review* in which he explicitly made the distinction between human relations and human resources. Whereas, in the former, the emphasis was said to be on the human aspect, on the 'softer' issues of supportive, friendly people management styles in which employees' feelings and needs were emphasised, the latter was said to emphasise the potential value of the resource aspect in terms of which each employee's potential talents, qualities and abilities would contribute. In a broader sense, Becker's work, *Human Capital* (1964), in many respects laid the foundation for the idea of human resource management. Frederick Herzberg's *Work and the Nature of Man* (1966) also made major contributions to developments in this field. He emphasised the necessity of incorporating certain 'motivational' principles (such as challenging work and responsibility), as well as 'hygiene' principles (such as good pay and good interpersonal relations between superiors and subordinates), in the design of work, processes and systems to manage people who execute the work in organisations. Rensis Likert's work (1967) emphasised the quantification of all these aspects through the development of the first human resource accounting systems. This again emphasised the 'harder', economic, or 'business value' aspects of human resource management. Employees were considered as highly valued assets rather than as cost factors of production.

? DID YOU KNOW?

HRM in developing countries were/are influenced by the following main factors:
- Religious influences, such as Islam, Hinduism, Buddhism, traditional beliefs in spirits, fetishes and gods;
- Traditional cultural beliefs, such as Confucianism, African traditional practices and caste in India; and
- Western colonial influences, such as predominance of a particular language, and modern influences, such as organisational development techniques.

Source: Wilkinson, Bacon, Redman & Snell (2010: 396)

3.3 Historical perspectives on HRM developments in South Africa

In Section 3.2, we looked at human resource management from a general international and historical perspective. In sum, we have seen that there have been various traditions in human resource management and that each phase of development has its own historical pedigree. Each evolutionary step forward in the development of the discipline internationally can be seen as an investment to enhance the value of the worker for the institution. Perhaps most notable among these developments have been the introduction of the concept of 'management' and the role managers can play in the day-to-day handling of human resource affairs.

An analysis of the developments that have occurred in the South African labour environment over the past several decades reflects this nation's history and shows us that management is an important role player in the process. In South Africa, management has evolved through various sophisticated human-resource management systems from early times for developing, maintaining and motivating its employees. Although by now you should already have a fair idea of our approach to HRM in this book, this section is intended to introduce some additional important issues that underpin HRM theory and practice in South Africa.

3.3.1 The world of work in pre-industrial South Africa

Because South Africa was chiefly an agrarian society prior to the discovery of diamonds in 1867 and gold in 1872, most of the country's inhabitants were engaged in subsistence and agrarian activities. The San people, probably the first inhabitants of South Africa, were highly competent hunters. The Khoekhoen, who lived at the Cape when the first Europeans came ashore in 1488, were nomadic herdsmen and also proficient hunters. These indigenous peoples bartered their cattle in exchange for the copper, beads, iron and tobacco offered by the early European visitors. Later, some of the Khoekhoen became the servants and slaves of the Dutch settlers.

As more and more immigrants settled at the Cape after Jan van Riebeeck arrived in 1652 to set up a refreshment post, trade between these groups increased. The Khoekhoen provided fresh vegetables and fruit. More people were required to help build the growing settlement. Many of the passing crewmen stayed on, and the first Cape community thus came to include skilful people such as millers, bakers and blacksmiths.

Because the settlers needed more and more help, and the Khoekhoen people were reluctant to work for them, Van Riebeeck, who was well acquainted with the slave trade in the East, arranged for the first shipment of slaves from Angola in 1658.

DID YOU KNOW?

The Dutch Indian Company (VOC) 'imported' more slaves to Cape Town in response to the colonists' (European settlers') demands for more labour. The VOC imported these slaves from East Africa, Madagascar and its possessions from the East Indies. The slaves had to work hard maintaining gardens and buildings, chopping trees and working on farms for six days a week – all without pay. Their working conditions were poor and they were often punished, for example, by taking away their tobacco rations if they did not perform or behave as required.

Source: Republic of South Africa (2006: 30)

Finnemore and Van der Merwe (1992: 17) state that 'by the end of the 18th century slavery had become an integral part of the Cape Colony. The nomadic Boer farmers carried these ideas into the interior, where manual labour was expected to be done by blacks who rendered their services to the farmer in return for squatting rights.'

The basic relationship was thus mainly one of slavery – of master and unpaid captive servant. Slaves, as the property of the owners who bought them at auctions, had to obey their masters and work hard without obtaining anything in return. In these early days, there was no other form of 'personnel management' (if we can call it that at all). Slavery was eventually officially abolished in 1834 (Nel & Van Rooyen 1993: 54), and the first formal regulation of some form of individual employment relationship came into being with the Masters and Servants Act of 1841. Later, the Masters and Servants Act 15 of 1856 repealed the Act of 1841 and increased the strict legalistic and paternalistic nature of 'people management' in South Africa. Servants were subjected to a host of rules and Acts, dealing with such matters as failure to commence work on an agreed date, intoxication, disobedience to the master, unauthorised absence from work, substandard work performance, negligence and the use of abusive language. These were all viewed in terms of this Act (15 of 1856) as offences punishable by imprisonment with or without hard labour for a period of not more than one month (Nel & Van Rooyen 1993: 54). The personnel, or rather servants, were thus managed in a very strict, almost subhuman manner. They were motivated in a negative way (with threats of punishment), and did not enjoy any real form of security or any guarantees of the protection of their well-being.

3.3.2 People and work after the South African industrial revolution

With the discovery of diamonds and gold and the accompanying advent of the South African industrial revolution in the late 1860s and 1870s, life and the world of work in this country changed dramatically.

The need arose for mining and engineering-related skills to mine the diamonds and gold. Other industries, such as building, engineering and the railways, developed around the mining industry. In order to satisfy the need for skilled people in these areas, European immigrants (mostly from the United Kingdom due to the colonial relationship) were recruited. These skilled people were paid high wages because of the increasing demand for their services and knowledge. In the meantime, local inhabitants were utilised to perform some of the less skilled tasks in these industries. There was thus an increased movement away from traditional, mainly agrarian, subsistence and household activities as people entered into formal employment relationships with the growing number of industrial types of organisation.

While the need increased for cheap labour to support the skilled workers, the latter kept their labour scarce by establishing trade unions (the first one was the Amalgamated Society of Carpenters and Joiners of Great Britain, established during December of 1881), by limiting membership exclusively to the British skilled worker (excluding blacks as well as Afrikaans-speaking whites), by preventing the entry of others into these jobs, and by resisting job fragmentation.

The ideas of scientific management (Taylorism) were also 'imported' in the sense that, as mechanisation increased, mining employers turned their attention to breaking down the many skilled jobs into smaller, simpler units in order to be able to employ cheaper, unskilled or semi-skilled labour to perform these tasks. This was resisted by the unions. Strict control was thus very much the watchword of people management during these times. Not only was labour mobility and entry into certain job categories strictly controlled, but mine owners also tried to control the supply of cheap labour by extending unskilled workers' employment contracts, for example (Finnemore & Van der Merwe 1992: 18). Rules and regulations on the mines were extensive. A regulation which required miners who came off duty to be stripped and searched led to the first official strike in South Africa, which took place on the Kimberley diamond fields in 1884.

In 1886, the Witwatersrand Chamber of Mines was formed, and, after brainstorming the labour problems faced by mine owners, it was decided to attempt to lower the wages of black workers (which had by now started to rise due to shortages of cheap labour). In 1897, white miners went on strike when attempts were also made to lower their wages in line with the wages of black mine workers. The late 1800s and early 1900s were thus characterised by the legalistic management of people, strict control and a lack of flexibility, with little room for individualism in employment relations. There was also an underlying lack of concern for the workers' needs, which resulted in increased conflict in the field of people management in South Africa. This is clearly demonstrated by the relatively high number of strikes which occurred during these years (for example, seven strikes between 1904 and 1908) (Nel & Van Rooyen 1993: 57). Workers were required to work very hard and for very long hours. In 1907, for example, white miners went on strike due to dissatisfaction with their heavy workloads (according to them, they had to supervise too great a number of drill bits). The widespread strike of 1913 (involving some 20 000 strikers) was initially the result of dissatisfaction with the decision of the management of Kleinfontein Gold Mine to compel underground mechanics to work longer hours on Saturdays (from 07:00 to 15:30 and not to 12:30) (Cunningham, Slabbert, & De Villiers, in Slabbert, Prinsloo, and Bakker 1990: 2.5).

The result of this widespread dissatisfaction was that the majority of workers joined trade unions; while management practices relating to the individual were still sadly deficient, collective aspects were becoming increasingly important during this period of personnel management in South Africa. Nel and Van Rooyen (1993: 59), for example, report that 'during the period of 1915 to 1917, there was a fourfold increase in worker representation through trade unions'. By 1921/22, white-led trade union membership figures had grown to approximately 118 000 and, between 1918 and 1922, organised collective industrial action (strikes) involved, on the average, 42 000 black workers striking for 16.8 days each (Cunningham et al, in Slabbert et al 1990: 2.4–2.6; Coetzee 1976: 6, 12). Trade unions thus played a prominent role in sensitising management in South Africa to the needs of workers. Most of the dissatisfaction on the mines can also be traced back to the strong racial undertones characterising people management practices at this time.

As secondary industries (mainly manufacturing) grew along with the expanding mining industry, and in line with 'scientific management' thinking, mass production increased and the need arose for predominantly semi-skilled workers in industries such as furniture, clothing and shoe manufacturing. Many white females and black males were prepared to do this type of work for lower wages than those paid to skilled labourers. Whereas whites in the mining industry were largely to be found in supervisory positions, there was a greater mix of race groups on the shop floors of these manufacturing institutions (Finnemore & Van der Merwe 1992: 22). The spectrum of people who had to be managed throughout industrialised South Africa was thus basically multiracial and multicultural (due to the presence, for example, of former slaves and indentured labourers of Asiatic or Chinese origin) and not limited only to the male sex. Although there were efforts during the late 1920s and in 1930 to establish a culture of non-racialism in South African industrial relations (for example, the multiracial conference of 1930, which resulted in the establishment of the South

African Trades and Labour Council, which called unsuccessfully for the inclusion of blacks under the Industrial Conciliation Act) (Finnemore & Van der Merwe 1992: 22), race continued to play a dominant role in all people management issues in South Africa. Various labour-related Acts made sure of this. For example, in terms of the Industrial Conciliation Act 11 of 1924, later repealed by Act 36 of 1937, blacks were excluded from the definition of 'employee'.

Partly due to the high cost of industrial action and the rise in collectivism (trade unionism) in South Africa, awareness of the necessity for greater sensitivity towards the needs, welfare and rights of employees gradually increased during the first three to four decades of the 20th century.

? DID YOU KNOW?

The Industrial Conciliation Act 36 of 1937 and the new Wage Act 44 of 1937 can, for example, be viewed as the first attempts (although partly) by government to provide, among others, for the welfare and rights of certain groups of workers and to remove the need to belong to trade unions.

Source: Nel & Van Rooyen (1993: 62)

Although union membership figures generally kept on growing (black workers, for example, organised and went on to form the Council for Non-European Trade Unions in 1941, claiming 158 000 individual members and 119 union members in 1945), managers gradually began to realise that people are not the same as other production factors and cannot simply be treated and controlled like extensions of the machine. In South Africa, as in other parts of the world, it became clear that people as employees needed some form of special treatment.

3.3.3   Isobel White and the advent of personnel management in SA[1]

South Africa was indeed fortunate that Isobel H.B. White, the wife of a professor who was appointed to the chair of Classics at Rhodes University College, Grahamstown, in 1938, accompanied her husband to South Africa. Isobel White can truly be regarded as the mother of South African personnel management. It was, for instance, her pioneering work that eventually led to the establishment of the Institute of Personnel Management of South Africa.

Towards the end of 1940, Mrs White gave her first six lectures on industrial psychology at Rhodes University College, at that time a residential college of the University of South Africa. She began to conduct research in the personnel field during the 1940s, published extensively and addressed various meetings in order to propagate and publicise the need for personnel managers and welfare officers in larger factories in South Africa. The need for a new attitude towards labour was researched by White during 1941. The research results have shown that a matter such as training needed attention, as is shown in Focus on Research 3.1 on page 49.

FOCUS ON RESEARCH 3.1
Investigation on personnel related problems

In September 1941, Isobel White was requested to conduct pilot research at seven footwear factories in the Port Elizabeth area, with the aim of investigating possible personnel-related problems. A report with a series of recommendations for future work subsequently followed. In October 1941, she addressed a special joint meeting in Port Elizabeth of the South African Institute of the Boot and Shoe Industry, and the Port Elizabeth (Shoe Trade and Training Industry) Managers' and Foremen's Association, on 'Human Problems of Management'.

In this paper she emphasised, for example, the need for a new attitude towards labour, including the training and follow-up of new employees, and the necessity of fostering a spirit of co-operation between management and non-management employees. She also emphasised the need for paternalistic practices related to the maintenance of employee health, proper nutrition, and the importance of 'good working conditions for workers'.[2]

She also published two articles in the *South African Industry & Trade Journal*, under the heading 'Selecting employees for maximum efficiency'. Mrs White was subsequently requested to carry on with her personnel research work as an Assistant Research Officer with the Leather Industries Research Institute, Rhodes University College, from January 1942. In recognition of her pioneering work in South Africa, Isobel White was elected to the Fellowship of the Institute of Personnel Management of Great Britain (then called the Institute of Labour Management) in 1943.

She also worked on aptitude tests and recruitment methods. In addition, because of her intense interest in the general welfare of workers, she established a Factory Welfare Board in Port Elizabeth in 1944, to work towards the improvement of the general environment of factory workers. This Board consisted of representatives of footwear manufacturers, the Red Cross, factory inspectors and Child Welfare.

Her research work also emphasised welfare aspects and related these to analyses of factors such as employee absenteeism and labour turnover. Various articles in this regard subsequently appeared in *The Manufacturer*, *The Engineer* and *Industry and Trade*, and awareness of the need for welfare supervisors and personnel managers was thus spread.

Having attempted to sensitise managers to the need for these specialists, Mrs White felt that the time was right to work more formally towards the establishment of an official personnel management training course at tertiary level. In this regard, she realised that South Africa had its own unique situation and that a course in personnel management in South Africa had to have its own character.

The need to introduce an obligatory scheme of welfare supervision was also advocated by Isobel White. In 1945, she advanced her reasons for this as follows (White 1945: 313):

1. The Factories Act will remain a dead letter unless someone is appointed to see that the spirit of the Act is carried out, for example, supervision of cloakrooms, washing accommodation, rest rooms, etc.

2. First Aid
3. Extra supervision is necessary because of the influx of women and young people. Married women also raise a special problem, unless there is someone outside of the production side to whom these employees can take their personal problems. Employees who are worried are not efficient and production will always be hampered.
4. Utilisation of manpower: The welfare supervisor can ensure that each one is doing the job for which he is mentally and physically capable. This induces contentment.
5. Canteens: Much more attention must be paid to the nutrition of our industrial workers. The importance of a sound midday meal in preventing fatigue and ill-health cannot be overrated.
6. Working conditions: Supervision of lighting, seating, ventilation, etc.
7. Resolving problems, mental and physical, in so far as they affect the relations between the individual and the organisation by personal influence and by calling in all the resources which the organisation provides.

In January 1944, White instituted a special postgraduate Diploma in Personnel Welfare and Management at Rhodes University College. Recognition for this diploma was obtained from the Institute of Labour Management (Great Britain).

As more and more personnel managers and 'welfare supervisors' went to work in factories throughout South Africa, it was realised that these specialists felt somewhat isolated. South Africa's mother of personnel management thus felt it necessary to establish some forum for interaction among these specialists. A local branch of the Institute of Personnel Management (UK) was thus formed in Port Elizabeth in 1945.

In the light of the developments described above, it is clear that, in the beginning, personnel management in South Africa had very much a welfare-oriented and paternalistic character. It was also sometime during 1945/46 that the South African mining industry's first personnel department was set up, also presumably very much along the lines of welfarism and personnel administration.

By 1955, however, there were signs of a gradual shift from welfarism to human relations. Isobel White's address delivered to a one-day conference of the Port Elizabeth branch of the SA Institute of Personnel Management on Tuesday, 9 August 1955 (the first conference of this kind in South Africa) illustrated this shift in thinking (White 1955: 1–2).

From the extract quoted below (White 1955: 4–6), it can be seen that, as early as 1955, personnel management in South Africa had started to focus on a much broader range of issues. In the same address, White referred to the importance of training all supervisors of people in 'the understanding of human beings and on leadership'. Other aspects which featured strongly included wage incentives, merit rating schemes, selection and training of supervisors, motivation of people, attending to morale problems, and grievance handling. The human relations movement was thus also propagated in South Africa at that stage.

Isobel White's address to the IPM in 1955

In the past the emphasis has been placed on the welfare aspects, on the housing of the worker, on establishing standards of good cloakrooms and their equipment, washing facilities and good general working conditions. Attention was given to the provision of adequate lighting, protective clothing, rest pauses and canteen facilities. The personnel manager in earlier days was very much concerned with recreation, social clubs, arranging holiday camps and other activities concerned with the maintenance of health. Students in training were taught the importance of these welfare aspects, were encouraged to undertake research in them. They were taught how to educate and convince employers on the need for expenditure on these activities in order to get a more efficient and contented staff.

Now, it is true that many of these 'welfare activities' are admirable in themselves, but they dealt exclusively with the individual worker in relation to his environment, not with the individual in relation to the group whether co-workers, supervisors or management. Much of the work included in this category has now been covered in our factory legislation and we take these standards for granted [...] Nothing will illustrate the great change in emphasis of which I have spoken more than the successive changes of name which have occurred since the foundation of the Institute in 1909 from Institute of Welfare Workers to Institute of Labour Management and finally to its present title. Today we have moved away from the conception of the factory as a kind of hygienic cowshed where the cows, if given every physical condition that is conducive to content will produce an ever-increasing volume of milk, to one where we realise that we are employing human beings who react in different ways not only to each other but to those who are leading them. The Personnel Manager has, therefore, become much more concerned not so much with the battle for staff comfort [...] but with the human relations side of this job. The function of the Personnel Manager thus becomes:

- Recruitment
- Employment
- Incentives
- Morale

The worker is a human being who is also a member of a team [...] It is now clear that the most important single factor in determining output is the emotional attitude of the worker towards his work and his workmates [...] The main problem is how to apply the carrot and stick theory when jobs are open to choice [...] The modern manager, therefore, is not so concerned with machines and materials but with handling people. The need for social skills is a further reason for the interest shown in problems of motivation and morale today [...] One of our crying needs is to find leaders and it is one of the concerns of the Personnel Manager to select leaders and, having found them, to develop them.

Source: White (1945: 313)

In the meantime, the National Party came to power in 1948. The rigid policy of racial segregation that was subsequently institutionalised had direct implications for South African workplaces and workers.

A variety of legislation was enacted during this period to ensure an 'apartheid system of people management' in South African institutions, a system which represented an embodiment of current thinking, and which was expressed as follows in the senate by Dr HF Verwoerd in 1954 (Cunningham *et al.*, in Slabbert *et al.* 1990: 2.11):

> [...] Natives will be taught from childhood to realise that equality with Europeans is not for them [...] What is the use of teaching a Bantu child mathematics when it cannot use it in practice? [...] That is absurd [...] Education must train people in accordance with their opportunities in life [...] the opportunities are [...] manual labour.

Separate labour-related legislation was thus enacted for blacks in South Africa. The Black Labour (Settlement of Disputes) Act 48 of 1953 was, for example, a result of the Botha Commission's (appointed in 1948) recommendations, and later had to complement the Industrial Conciliation Act 28 of 1956 (which repealed Act 36 of 1937). In terms of the former Act, black workers who had problems or disputes with their white employer-managers had to deal with them through a committee system. Clearly, already in the fifties, there were signs of a very particular South African approach to human resource management, the emphasis being on racial discrimination and a partnership between HR specialists and line function employees.

Interest in the personnel field grew quite rapidly in South Africa during the 1940s and 1950s. The Johannesburg branch of the Institute of Personnel Management, for example, grew so rapidly that it was registered as the South African Institute of Personnel Management in 1959.

3.3.4   The period following Republic status

Personnel management as a field of study, research and practice in South Africa had already become relatively well established at the time when South Africa attained Republic status. On 20 October 1964, all provincial units of the Institute of Personnel Management joined forces to form a single national body, retaining the name South African Institute of Personnel Management.

Estimates from early research (Langenhoven & Verster 1969) indicate that, by 1964, South African institutions probably had a ratio of personnel staff to a total number of employees of 0.97:100. Although the black to white ratio of total staff complements was in the region of 1.67:1, the ratio of black to white personnel staff was only approximately 0.93:1.

By 1969, there were also signs of a qualitative shift in personnel people in terms of their qualifications. Approximately 8.8% of staff performing personnel work were graduates. Of these, 3.36% had majored in Psychology, and 1.31% held degrees with Industrial Psychology as a major subject. An example of a South African study focusing on the characteristics of personnel management during the late 1960s is described in Focus on Research 3.2 on page 53.

FOCUS ON RESEARCH 3.2
Characteristics of personnel management in South Africa (1969)

RE EA CH

Research indicated that, by 1969, personnel management in South Africa had the following characteristics:

- The majority of institutions did not have a separate personnel department.
- Personnel departments were relatively small and consisted mainly of personnel without formal post-matriculation qualifications.
- Use was made of personnel specialists, particularly in areas such as employment, salary and wage administration, and training and development.
- The most general subsections into which personnel departments were organised included (in order of priority): general personnel administration; employment (including recruitment and selection); training and development; welfare, sport, pension, and related personnel services; salary and wage administration, and medical schemes and medical services.
- The emphasis in personnel work fell on administrative/clerical, routine work and also, to some extent, on paternalistic, welfare-related activities.
- Most of the people in the personnel field who actually did have formal qualifications were graduates in the social sciences (and there weren't many.)

Source: Langenhoven & Verster (1969); Marx (1969)

As can be seen, the emphasis was on individualism rather than on collectivism, and there had been a gradual movement towards the human relations approach, especially as far as white employees were concerned. Racialism was a dominant force and was rigorously controlled in the South African workplace. Two other trends did, however, start to emerge:

- A realisation of the need for more of a 'human resources approach', and
- A gut feeling that collectivism (trade unions) would become more prominent.

3.3.5   The decade that shaped the future

The decade 1969–1979 brought with it all the signs of what was to follow later during the eighties, particularly with regard to the collectivism of black employees. Durban dock workers went on strike in 1969, African workers launched isolated efforts to organise themselves from early 1970, huge numbers of contract workers went on strike on the diamond mines of Namibia (then still South West Africa and controlled by Pretoria), and, in 1972, the approximately 9 000 black workers who had embarked on strike action cost management 74 000 shifts (including the Putco strike in June 1972, which stranded 120 000 commuters) (Friedman 1987: 44–45).

Yet the real rebirth of African collectivism only started in 1973, with the outbreak of the biggest wave of strikes in the country since World War II. Friedman (1987: 40) states that 'between 1965 and 1971, less than 23 000 African workers had struck. In the first three months of 1973, 61 000 stopped work. By the end of the year, the figure had grown to 90 000 and employers had lost 229 000 shifts.'

The Natal strikes highlighted the fact that the system of black worker representation – and, in fact, the total approach to the management of black workers in South African institutions – was deficient and that too little proper interaction was taking place between management and black workers (Nel & Van Rooyen 1993: 68). This wave of strikes also emphasised the need to review labour legislation, and the Black Labour Relations Regulation Amendment Act 70 of 1973 followed as a result. Committees (liaison committees in particular) were increasingly being established to communicate with black workers (Friedman 1987: 56).

However, in addition to the collectivism aspect, more and more people had begun to realise the importance of the role of the black worker. A number of examples can serve to illustrate this. In 1973, for example, training centres were set up and tax benefits offered for the training of African workers (Friedman 1987: 52). In July 1973, the Institute of Personnel Management (Southern Africa) – having changed its name from the South African Institute of Personnel Management on 2 February the same year – published the first edition of *People & Profits* and, in this very first edition, an article appeared about black advancement efforts by the Anglo American Corporation (Nattrass 1973: 9–12). In the same edition, and following from the 1973 strikes, a checklist for action in case of strikes was published, as well as an article on the representation of black workers. In the November 1973 edition of this journal, the need to train blacks for higher level jobs and to channel their potential into the field of technology was emphasised by two different experts (Natrass 1973: 5; Jacobsz 1973: 22). In the December 1973 edition, W. Bagwa (1973: 12–16) pleaded for the improvement of welfare facilities for black employees. In the very next edition, the need to educate African workers in order to help them to participate meaningfully in committees was emphasised, as was the importance of utilising the black personnel officer as 'the linkman' (Douwes Dekker 1974: 5–7; Dickenson 1974: 8–19).

After the 1976 strikes on the Witwatersrand, it again became apparent that labour legislation in South Africa, as far as it concerned the collective bargaining rights of black workers, was totally inadequate and needed to be completely updated. Eventually, Professor Nic Wiehahn, previously of the University of South Africa, was appointed as chairman of a commission of inquiry into South African labour legislation – an investigation which was to lead to a break with statutory racialism in the workplace and which, therefore, significantly altered South Africa's system of industrial relations.

Another important development which took place in the late seventies was the drive to professionalise personnel work in South Africa. By mid-1978, the initiative had already been taken and the professionalisation of personnel management practice in South Africa was well under way. Gary Whyte, the 1977 president of the Institute of Personnel Management (SA), presented a paper on this topic at the IPM's Twenty-first Convention in September 1977. Professor H.P Langenhoven published an article in this regard in the June 1978 edition of *People & Profits*, and, after this, the debate gained momentum (Langenhoven 1978: 14–15; Whyte 1978: 9–10).

The concept of human resources had, by this time, also come to be used more often. In 1978, BU Lombard (after returning from the USA) published an article in the *South African Journal of Labour Relations*, entitled 'Human Resources Management: A New Approach for South Africa' (Lombard 1978: 12--24). The IPM's journal, *People & Profits*, furthermore, started to feature regular articles on industrial relations issues by 1978/79, reflecting the then growing importance of the collective dimension of personnel management in South Africa. Another South African study focusing on the characteristics of personnel management during the late 1970s is described in Focus on Research 3.3.

FOCUS ON RESEARCH 3.3
Characteristics of personnel management in South Africa (1979)

The year 1979 saw the publication of some very interesting research results stemming from a survey on developments in personnel management in South Africa conducted by the University of the Orange Free State (Verster 1979). The findings revealed that, by 1979, personnel management in South Africa had acquired the following characteristics.

- Many institutions had independent personnel departments.
- In most cases, the top personnel official was called a personnel manager – often a group personnel manager or personnel director.
- As a rule, this top-level personnel official reported to the general manager or to a member of the board.
- People performing personnel work exclusively held more clerical positions than managerial or professional positions, especially in the case of black personnel staff.
- The ratio of people performing personnel work to total staff establishment was in the region of 1.26:100.
- Approximately 21% of those performing personnel work had post-matriculation qualifications.
- Approximately 3.4% of the personnel staff had degrees with Industrial Psychology as a major subject.
- Another approximately 3.6% had postgraduate qualifications in a behavioural science.
- Changes in emphasis in personnel management practice from 1976 to 1979 resulted in the emergence of the following top three priority areas: (1) the upgrading of black workers, (2) employee training, and (3) industrial relations.
- More money, time and manpower were spent on administrative personnel work than on professional aspects of personnel management.
- Personnel research work was neglected and viewed as the black sheep of personnel work.

3.3.6 HRM developments in a post labour-apartheid decade

The South African government's acceptance in principle of the Wiehahn Commission's recommendation that racialism no longer be a consideration in the South African labour dispensation gave rise to a new era of personnel management in South Africa – an era in which black employees were no longer to be excluded from the statutory labour machinery of the country.

The realisation of the increasing importance of trade unions led institutions in South Africa to pay increasing attention to the human resource aspects of management. In 1980 – in one of the first articles in the IPM's journal with a title referring to 'human resources management' (rather than personnel management) – CH Diessnack (1980: 5) specifically stated that 'a new union will increase payroll costs by 20% with no increase in production'. The 'hard' aspects of human resource management – the impact of people management practices on the bottom line of institutions, thus also came to the fore by the time collectivism gained more official prominence.

Trade union membership figures increased throughout the eighties, and along with these huge organising efforts came the signs of increasing adversarialism in the relationships between (especially black) employees and their trade unions on the one side and employers (and managers, mostly white, as their representatives in the workplace) on the other side. The unions displayed a great deal of militancy, and industrial action became a frequent challenge in the area of human resource management in South Africa. Whereas the number of reported strikes stood at 179 for the ten-year period from 1970 to 1979, the corresponding number for the five-year period from 1983 to 1987 was 3 135.

However, the individual dimension of personnel management in South Africa also matured to some extent during the eighties, in particular as far as certain traditional functional areas of personnel management were concerned. Attention was being paid to a whole range of aspects. During the first five years of the eighties, aspects which were emphasised in journal articles included manpower planning, selection, training and development, organisation development, job evaluation and remuneration, career planning, performance appraisal, manpower information systems, and especially black advancement and labour productivity (apart from the large number of industrial relations-related articles and books which were published).

In October 1983, the professionalisation of the personnel field in South Africa became a reality with the inauguration of the first South African Board for Personnel Practice (SABPP). The following was reported in June 1983 (IPM News Update 1983: 4–5):

> In the first two weeks of registration, over 300 applications were received! [...]
> The Registrar for the Board, Mr Wilhelm Crous, said that he was 'overwhelmed' by the response [...] the Board was now 'truly launched', and will play a 'meaningful role' in South Africa's fields of personnel, training and industrial relations.

Meanwhile, on 30 November 1985, COSATU (Congress of South African Trade Unions), the giant trade union federation, was born, with an initial membership of 33 trade unions. In 1987, strike action in South Africa reached a peak, with 1 148 recorded strikes and 5 825 231 person days lost. During the eighties, much of the industrial unrest was motivated by political factors because the majority of South Africa's people were disenfranchised, the trade unions being their only legitimate public forum. Human resource management in South Africa thus became politicised to a great extent during the eighties, and trade unions were very instrumental in the political transformation of the country.

In the meantime, in 1985, another dimension was added to the concept of personnel management in South Africa with Pansegrouw's definition of 'strategic HRM' (Pansegrouw 1985). In 1987, Hill (1987: 6–9) also proposed the adoption of a 'strategic approach to human resources management' by South African institutions. In Focus on Research 3.4, the findings of the 1985 research done on the responsibilities of the HR function are explained.

FOCUS ON RESEARCH 3.4
Responsibility of the human resource function

RESEARCH

Research findings published in 1985 showed that the responsibility for decision making with regard to people-related issues had been transferred to the personnel and/or industrial relations departments of South African institutions. According to Horwitz (1988: 6–7), however, this was contrary to a typical international shift from 'functionally oriented personnel management' to a more line driven, general management conception of HRM. In the same article, in which Horwitz speculated about the differences between 'functional, specialist and professional personnel management' on the one hand and 'a generalist, organisational conception of HRM' on the other, it was proposed that the differences should be viewed as orientational rather than as substantive, and that the two approaches linked to the terms should not be regarded as being mutually exclusive.

Source: Hall (1985: 6)

Meanwhile, also in 1987, the first local comprehensive academic textbook on the personnel field was published. In this publication, the authors held that, due to the rapid developments in industrial relations in South Africa over the preceding decade, employers had been compelled to 'resort to the employment of industrial relations specialists to cope with the new demands [...]', and that '[...] the task of the industrial relations manager may come to be as important as that of the human resource manager' (Gerber, Nel & Van Dyk 1987: 315–316). Industrial relations thus became a distinct and extremely important area of people management during the eighties, and such aspects as collective bargaining (negotiating recognition and other agreements with trade unions), dispute handling, strike management, and fair discipline and labour practices took centre stage in the management of most South African enterprises (see, for example, Horwitz 1988).

Towards the latter part of 1988, other important aspects which began to feature prominently in the literature on personnel management included worker participation, violence and HIV/AIDS.

3.3.7 HRM during a period of transitional politics in the 1990s

By the end of the eighties, the South African economy was in recession due to political instability, disinvestment and sanctions imposed by overseas countries, and rising labour unit costs (lower labour productivity and higher wages), among other factors. Poor economic growth had resulted in large-scale unemployment and job creation had become one of the major challenges (Finnemore & Van der Merwe 1992: 37). Against the background of the gloomy economic situation, the socio-economic backlogs suffered by the majority of black South Africans became increasingly more apparent. South Africa was in the midst of political and socioeconomic turmoil – a situation felt by virtually every employer and employee.

On 2 February 1990, South Africa's newly elected State President, FW de Klerk, announced the government's intention of trying to resolve South Africa's socio-political problems through negotiations with all stakeholders, thus effectively turning around the world of each and every South African. The stage was set for major transformations in the country and the idea of a 'new South Africa' and a 'post-apartheid era' echoed throughout the land. This situation, however, also brought along with it certain dynamics and challenges which spilled over into the world of work and people management.

Employers became increasingly aware that not only did they have a welfare role to fulfil in respect of their employees, but they also had to exhibit a broader social responsibility. For example, Wilhelm Crous, the then Executive Director of IPM (SA), stated in March 1990 that, as political problems were solved, other areas of pressing concern, such as unemployment, housing, education and training, and health, had to be addressed (Crous 1990: 3). Consequently, during the early 1990s, many of the personnel-related publications dealt with these types of issue.

In 1990, the SABPP made available a Board Paper which spelled out a 'Generic Competency Model for Human Resource Practitioners', as developed by the human resources group of Eskom, the national electricity utility. This broad framework identified the knowledge, the skills, and the experiential and behavioural base required to perform competently at the various levels in the HR profession in South Africa. By this time, the role of HR practitioners in South Africa had broadened, and many managers were turning to them to act as change agents and to help with demands and problems which had no clear-cut, ready-made answers.

The SABPP (1990: 4–5) published this framework or model which was to serve as a guideline for the development of HR practitioners in South Africa. It basically became a guide to the identification, development and evaluation of the competencies (knowledge, skills, and experiential and behavioural base) required of professional specialists at various levels in the HR field in South Africa. The framework is presented in Figure 3.1 on page 59.

COMPETENCE	=	EDUCATION	+	TRAINING	+	APPLICATION	+	VALUES

Level	Knowledge base	Skills base	Experiential base		Behavioural base
Managerial	**Social sciences** 1 Industrial psychology 2 Industrial sociology 3 Industrial law/labour law **Business sciences** 4 Business management 5 Economics 6 Accounting 7 Statistics 8 Computer systems	**Functional** 1 Research methodology 2 Measurement 3 Assessment 4 System design 5 Group process 6 Mentoring 7 Consulting **Managerial** 8 Leadership 9 Planning 10 Budgeting 11 Communication 12 Marketing and promotion 13 Negotiating 14 Change management 15 Monitoring 16 Reporting	**Employee level** *Deployment* 1 Recruitment 2 Selection 3 Career management 4 Termination 5 Retirement planning *Administration* 6 HR policies 7 HR procedures 8 Job evaluation 9 Compensation management 10 Employee assistance programmes 11 Occupational health 12 Industrial relations agreements 13 Disciplinary procedure 14 Grievance procedure 15 Accommodation and feeding 16 Recreation *Performance development* 17 Course design 18 Induction/orientation 19 On-job training 20 Off-job training 21 Performance assessment 22 Development counselling 23 Job advancement 24 Educational assistance	**Group level** *Intragroup functioning* 25 Team development 26 Conflict management 27 Participation *Intergroup functioning* 28 Matrix management 29 Cross-cultural environments 30 Industrial relations structures 31 Trade union relationships 32 Collective bargaining **Organisational level** *Corporate strategy* 33 Business planning 34 Manpower planning 35 Succession planning *Corporate structure* 36 Organisation design 37 Job design 38 Resource utilisation *Corporate functioning* 39 Corporate values 40 Employee motivation 41 Opportunity equilisation 42 Human resource surveys	**Professional** 1 Systemic thinking 2 Measurement orientation 3 Objectivity 4 Judgement 5 Innovation 6 Assertiveness 7 Accountability 8 Integrity 9 Confidentiality 10 Flexibility **Interpersonal** 11 Respectfulness 12 Recognition 13 Responsiveness 14 Empowerment 15 Consultation **Managerial** 16 Customer focus 17 Quality focus 18 Cost focus 19 Results focus

Figure 3.1   The generic competency model for HR practitioners

Gradually, the nature of industrial relations also began to show signs of a need for change. Unions and management seemed to become aware that there were areas of common ground. The parties involved had to follow the dictates of the socioeconomic reality and began to realise that outright hostility and severe adversarialism could lead to their mutual demise, especially at a time when economic conditions and business confidence had reached dangerously low levels. Business not only had to become more competitive (especially internationally) so that jobs could be preserved, but also had to grow so that new job opportunities could be created. All of this called for the development and better utilisation of all of the country's human resources, as well as participation and better co-operation by all the stakeholders in the South African industrial relations community. A culture of greater co-operation was necessary, and aspects such as 'social contracts' at national level and joint decision making at the institutional level were increasingly emphasised in the publications of the day.

From early 1992, representatives of business and labour engaged in bilateral negotiations with the aim of setting up a national, tripartite economic forum which would include representatives of the government. Eventually, the National Economic Forum was formally launched on 29 October 1992.

The findings of a survey conducted among a number of prominent South African institutions, and covering more than 1.2 million employees, were released in a report published by SPA Consultants in 1992. In this report certain human resource priorities in the medium to short term were identified. These priority areas included such aspects as education/training; affirmative action, discrimination and white resistance; industrial relations (with particular reference to shop-floor relationships and bargaining levels); business literacy; social responsibility and violence (SPA Consultants 1992: 6–24).

In 1994, the South African Board for Personnel Practice (SABPP) (now known as the South African Board for People Practices) requested the Human Sciences Research Council (HSRC) to launch an investigation to determine the supply and demand of personnel practitioners in South Africa.[3] The results of this study are presented in Focus on Research 3.5 on page 61.

Soon after the 1994 'political miracle', the development of a whole new labour legislative environment was kick-started by a 'five-year plan' of the Department of Labour. A stream of new labour-related laws provided the impetus for a renewed awareness of what the 'people-centred philosophy' of the government meant. On 5 May 1995, the National Economic, Development and Labour Council (NEDLAC) came into existence through Act 35 of 1994. In broad terms, this body was created to facilitate the social dialogue between the representatives of the major stakeholders and role players, namely labour, business, government and the 'socially excluded' (such as the unemployed) on all socio-economic and labour matters. In particular, one of NEDLAC's functions in terms of the statute was to seek to reach consensus on proposals regarding labour market policy and labour legislation before any of these were to be introduced through Parliament.

One of the first pieces of labour legislation that went this route was the Labour Relations Act 66 of 1995, which eventually came into operation during November 1996.

FOCUS ON RESEARCH 3.5
Study by the Human Sciences Research Council (HSRC)

RESEARCH

The 1994 study by the HSRC to investigate the supply and demand of personnel practitioners in South Africa revealed the following research results:

- The role of human resource specialists was changing from the provision of primarily support services to involvement in the core business of organisations. Human resource practitioners in South Africa were increasingly being expected to participate in the general strategic management of institutions.
- Devolution of the HR function, a shift of the responsibilities for HRM from human resource specialists to line-function employees
- Institutions were also apparently tending to 'downsize' their in-house human resource departments or functions, increasingly making use of independent consultants.
- Institutions were apparently becoming more democratised, making greater use of worker participation and shifting from authoritarian to more participative management styles.
- The importance and high priority of affirmative action had also been identified, and all the institutions that took part in the investigation were at that stage involved to some extent in affirmative action.
- An increasingly strong focus on human resource development, which was becoming competency based and modular, with the trend towards matching it with a 'national qualifications framework'. There was also an increased emphasis on the development of basic skills, such as literacy and numeracy, as well as on accelerated management development.
- Implementation of the Reconstruction and Development Programme (RDP). These efforts included participation in the upliftment of local communities through such initiatives as the provision of housing, water, health facilities and educational opportunities.
- Revolutionary developments in the field of information technology were affecting the work of South African HR specialists.

Other new labour-related statutes that followed this route included the South African Qualifications Authority Act 58 of 1995, the Basic Conditions of Employment Act 75 of 1997, the Employment Equity Act 55 of 1998, the Skills Development Act 97 of 1998 and the Skills Development Levies Act 9 of 1999. (Relevant aspects of these Acts are discussed elsewhere in the book in Chapters 6, 11 and 15.)

The overall purpose of the South African Qualifications Authority Act 58 of 1995 is spelt out in the statute as being to provide for the development and implementation of a National Qualifications Framework (NQF) and to establish the South African Qualifications Authority (SAQA) for this purpose. This was meant to facilitate the establishment of an integrated system that would enhance access to and mobility and progression within an integrated national framework for learning (integrating all forms of learning, such as education, training, formal, informal, on-job and off-job). This new system would facilitate an improvement in the general quality of education and training in the country – especially as these relate to redressing the effects of past unfair discrimination – and that it would enhance the personal development and employment opportunities of the people of the country. This, as is widely accepted today, is a prerequisite for South African institutions to become more competitive, for the country's economy to grow, for growing job and work opportunities and for the general socioeconomic development of the nation as a whole.

In line with this need to transform the ways in which human resources are managed and developed in South Africa, an initiative was launched by the SABPP (South African Board for Personnel Practice) during the first half of 1998 to establish a Standards Generating Body for the human resources field, in terms of the National Qualifications Framework (NQF). For this purpose, the SABPP arranged a workshop for 29 April 1998 in Midrand. A wide range of stakeholders attended and participated in the process of crafting a Standards Generating Body for human resource management in terms of statutory guidelines. A Steering Committee to this effect was established in August 1998, with the task of establishing such a Standards Generating Body. By mid-1999, an application was made to SAQA for the formal recognition of an establishment of a Standards Generating Body for human resource management and practices under the Business, Commerce and Management Studies National Standards Body (NSB 03).

3.4   A history of employment practices in PSHRM

Public sector human resource management in its fullest variety has always been influenced by the political, social and cultural environment within which it operates. Therefore, one will find that public sector human resource management systems in South Africa may differ from those of corresponding institutions in other countries. At the heart of contemporary public sector human resource management in South Africa is the assurance that public sector employees will be treated according to the principles of a constitutional democracy. In practice, it is expected that the human resource systems are likely to be influenced by the democratic concerns as reflected in the Constitution of the Republic of South Africa, 1996. But, until 1996 and the inception of the new Constitution, different traditions, legacies and approaches helped shape the way in which public sector managers (line-function employees and HR specialists) hire and manage their employees. An adequate way of categorising these traditions, legacies and approaches is to refer to them as human resource systems. In the following sections, we shall see how the evolution of human resource management systems took place by providing an overview of where the systems came from (early developments) and where they stand today.

3.4.1   Early developments

Generally speaking, public services periodically undergo reforms that automatically transform their structures, processes, systems and operations. Many of the reforms occur as a result of changing forces in society. Normally, the dominant values in these forces become the focus point of the political system in the form of legislation, executive instructions, and judicial decisions. Needless to say, these resulting reforms often hold important changes for human resource management practices. Many different values have shaped the nature and content of public sector human resource management in the past. Values that have been particularly influential are merit, political neutrality, representativeness and efficiency (Tompkins 1995: 54–55). The meanings of these values and the way in which they have been realised in the various public sector human resource management systems will be clarified in the following paragraphs.

DID YOU KNOW?   ?

The history of employment practices or systems can be traced back to ancient and medieval times. It was King Hammurabi of Babylon (BC 2000) who first employed a system of accountable reporting on the remuneration of personnel. Though Confucius, the well-known Chinese philosopher, was not the first to propagate human resource management practices, he was of the opinion that public service delivery could be improved by appointing honest and able personnel.

For the sake of chronological order, the developments of human resource management systems can be classified under the following headings: the personal service system, the spoils system and the commodity system.

3.4.1.1 The personal service system

The personal service system was developed during the time of the medieval feudal lords. In these early times of public administration, all officials were appointed by and were responsible to a king or any other kind of ruler. This system of administration resulted in a situation in which employees served a king or another kind of single ruler (an individual person) and not an institution or the public at large. In other words, all government functions were centralised at one point (Megginson 1967, in Uys *et al.* 1997: 168). Even the proponents of the personal service system could not have foreseen the evolutionary democratic developments that would soon become associated with the politics of these times. These political developments began to set the stage for the expansion of government activities that made it practically impossible for a king or any type of ruler to adhere to all public sector activities. As a result, the king's or ruler's functions were delegated to councils. In addition, some court officials were assigned to these councils to perform certain public sector tasks. However, the king or ruler could still manipulate the hiring and firing process.

3.4.1.2 The spoils system

The incapacity of the personal service system soon led to a strong and active reform movement for something new. Changes were made, and royal sovereignty (where the king was the absolute ruler) was replaced by parliamentary government.

Basically, this implies that the right to hire (appoint) and fire (dismiss) people gradually shifted from the authority of the king to that of political representatives, more specifically ministers (Rosenbloom & Goldman 1989: 187; Uys *et al.* 1997: 169). Political representatives began to realise the importance of public servants' loyalty to the government of the day in order to execute policies successfully. In other words, public servants needed to be in support of the policies of the political party in power. Therefore, the emphasis was placed on political appointments, especially in the senior management echelons, and the focus was on hiring for temporary periods for as long as the dominant political party was in power (Denhardt & Hammond 1992: 261).

Simultaneously, the notion developed that 'to the victor belong the spoils'. This means the ability to give public service jobs to those people supporting the political party in power.

? DID YOU KNOW?

Through the spoils system, public employment was used as a resource to be distributed to followers and winners of the electoral game. As a consequence, civil systems became heavily politicised. The spoils system soon became associated with negative effects, such as a serious decline in administrative ethics and efficiency. It boosted corruption and abuse, and it could not survive the growth of government functions and the expansion of public service institutions.

3.4.1.3 The commodity system

Another employment practice that developed during the early times was the commodity system. The Industrial Revolution, which was a period characterised by early capitalism, played a major role in establishing some of the principles of the commodity system (Uys *et al.* 1997: 171-172). The main idea of the commodity system rested on the principle that a worker was considered to be a commodity of varying quantity, quality and type that was contractually purchased and sold at a certain negotiable price. In this fashion, the worker pursued a career. To a limited extent, the principles of this system were gradually applied to the public sector over the years, and the use of consultants and contractors is a modern manifestation of the system.

3.4.2 Modern approaches

It was during the time of the above developments that abuse was the order of the day, and corruption was becoming a normal way of executing public sector work. It soon became evident that these factors set the stage for reform and that the existing human resource management systems, developed during these early times, had flaws in their practical application. Even more important, however, was that the quality of public services in general declined in these periods. Many questions have also been put forward about the politicisation of the public sector and the negative impact of this on the efficient delivery of services. It was an acknowledged fact that changes were required for reforming human resource management systems and practices in the public sector. This acknowledgment provided the basis for modern developments.

3.4.2.1 The merit system

The foundation of the merit system was laid in the USA with two landmark pieces of legislation, namely the Pendleton Act and the Civil Service Reform Act. The cornerstone of the merit system rested on the following principles: (1) that the selection and appointment of public officials should be based on merit – the ability to perform competently rather than any form of political favouritism; (2) that those public officials who were hired should have tenure in office regardless of political changes; and (3) that the establishment of an independent central service commission could protect the public service against incursions by patronage-oriented politicians (Denhardt 1995: 200; Rosenbloom & Goldman 1989: 191–192).

DID YOU KNOW?

The merit system has also become firmly established in the South African public service, especially with the proposal of the White Paper on Human Resource Management in the Public Service of 1997. This White Paper was proposed in order to restore the merit principle to its fullest consequences because of some backlogs created by the previous political dispensation of apartheid (before 1994), which was ineffective, discriminatory and inefficient. Through the White Paper, the government has embarked upon a comprehensive and changing human resource management culture with new guidelines for policies, which include increased competition for positions, a career service, selection on merit (with the reservation of employment equity and affirmative action), recruitment from all sections of the population, multi-skilling, improved performance management and redeployment.

3.4.2.2 New public personnel administration and management system

The new public personnel administration and management system emphasises radically different values from those of the merit system. During this phase, emphasis was placed on different considerations in the public sector human resource management field. Perhaps its key underlying value is that constitutional and other rights for public officials were created in the process. Other factors contributing to the changes of new human resource management policies during this era have been: (1) its expansive views on collective bargaining; and (2) legislative, judicial and administrative policy requirements for equal job opportunities and affirmative action programmes (Hays & Kearney 1995: 297–300; Uys *et al.* 1997: 177).

More specifically, different types of human resource management sub-systems and practices have evolved from the new public personnel administration and management phase.

The collective bargaining sub-system

The first is the collective bargaining sub-system. Generally, collective bargaining means negotiation between representatives of the employer and representatives of the union on issues of employment. In reality, the main purpose of the bargaining process is to reach decisions bilaterally rather than unilaterally, and to have a win-win situation for both the employer and the union. In addition, it is supposed to create a partnership between management and the unions for the sake of improved public human resource management.

In the past, unions did not play a significant role in the day-to-day managing of human resource matters in the South African public sector. It was only during the 1990s, with the advent of a constitutional democracy in this country, that the public sector was really brought under the ambit of the Labour Relations Act 66 of 1995. Since the 1990s, there has been a rapid rise in the number of unions and union members (Adler 2000: 95). Today there are nearly 20 unions, representing 980 000 public officials. Over the years, the collective bargaining system has been streamlined and today there is an incredible variety in the kinds of labour-management relationship.

The equal employment opportunity and affirmative action sub-system

Nevertheless, public sector human resource management systems in the new public personnel administration and management era were certainly not limited to the collective bargaining system. A second sub-system, the equal employment opportunity and affirmative action system, is probably one of the most prominent modern developments that has been put into operation in the public sector. Basically, equal employment opportunity implies a ban on discrimination in employment on the basis of race, gender, colour, religion and disability, among other factors (Uys *et al.* 1997: 179). Affirmative action is a more active approach and involves '[...] additional corrective steps that must be taken so that those who have been historically disadvantaged by unfair discrimination are able to derive full benefit from an equitable employment environment' (Republic of South Africa 1998). The equal employment opportunity and affirmative action system tend to have a definite effect on public sector human resource management in the sense that it raises an ethical dilemma. This dilemma is derived primarily from two interrelated viewpoints. First, there is a group that argues that it is necessary and desirable to 'bend the rules' in order to make up for discriminatory behaviour in the past. A second group is of the opinion that equal employment opportunity and affirmative action will result in the lowering of employment standards. According to this group, it will ultimately cause poor service delivery.

In moving towards a representative public sector, the government has developed a comprehensive policy framework. It is important to emphasise that this policy framework should be understood and applied within the supreme guidelines of the Constitution of the Republic of South Africa, 1996. In this regard, the concept of representativeness is firmly established in Chapter 10 of the 1996 Constitution. Similarly, a number of other equal employment opportunity and affirmative action policy mechanisms were put on the table, including the following:

- The Employment Equity Act 55 of 1998;
- The White Paper on the Transformation of the Public Service of 1995, which extensively deals with representativeness and affirmative action (where targets and time frames are set);
- The White Paper on Affirmative Action in the Public Service of 1998; and
- The White Paper on Human Resource Management in the Public Service of 1997, which values diversity management as highly important.

Since the introduction of the new policy framework, many court cases have seen the light. For example, in *Hoffman v South African Airways (SAA)* (2000) 21 ILJ 891 (W), the SAA contended that Hoffman was incapable of performing the work of a flight attendant because of his positive HIV status. The High Court agreed. However, the Constitutional Court held that SAA had failed to prove that the appointment of Hoffman as a cabin attendant would pose any significant threat to passengers using the airline. Although it was argued that that the business (economic) needs of the airline were important, the Constitutional Court found that the constitutional right of HIV-positive people needs to be protected against 'stigmatisation and prejudice' and that the latter was of greater social value (Grogan 2008: 298). A further example of discrimination in the workplace is provided in Spotlight on the Law 3.1.

SPOTLIGHT ON THE LAW 3.1
Race discrimination

Mutale v Lorcom Twenty-Two CC (2009) 30 ILJ 634 (LC) provides an example of discrimination based on unfair compensation. First, Mutale alleged that the employer committed an unfair labour practice by racially discriminating against her in the computation of her salary. Second, she alleged that she was subjected to an automatically unfair dismissal after she had indicated to the employer that she wanted to take an action against it by exercising a right conferred by the Labour Relations Act 66 of 1995.

Any discrimination of an employee on the grounds of race has no place in employment practices. The court found that there was no other ground on which the disparity of the computation of her salary was founded other than race. The employer's decision was clearly based on arbitrary grounds when its progression in about 30 months of her employment with the respondent is considered. The employer chose to deny its racist practice instead of leading evidence to prove the fairness thereof.

The employer was ordered to pay Mutale compensation equal to 20 months' salary for her unfair dismissal and a further amount equal to 24 months' compensation for discriminating against her.

Source: Grogan, Jordaan, Maserumule & Stelzner (2009: 22); Legal Information (2010: Online)

The client-oriented sub-system

Another new public personnel administration and management system is the client-oriented sub-system. In the past, many public sector institutions had an inward approach, focusing their attention on the activities executed within the institution rather than on its external clients. This pattern of doing things placed emphasis on bureaucratic conformity and improved service delivery was not targeted. During the last few years, however, the emphasis has shifted to quality service delivery. In essence, the following fundamental reasons were identified for this approach:

- The community had more complex expectations of public services.
- Improved service delivery attracted public attention.
- Devolved management authority allowed more decision-making discretion in meeting the needs of the community.

The client-oriented system forced governments to become immediately involved in service-delivery issues that put the client first. The South African government was no exception and soon a new strategy on public service delivery saw the light. The guiding principle of this new strategy was that the public service must be of 'service' to the citizens. Eight principles for transforming public service delivery – the Batho Pele principles – have been identified and formalised in the White Paper on Transforming Public Service Delivery of 1997. The Batho Pele principles are, in every sense, part and parcel of public sector human resource management and include:

- Consulting users of services about the level and quality of services;
- Setting the level and quality of service standards;
- Increasing equal access to services;
- Ensuring courtesy and consideration to all citizens with regard to service delivery;
- Providing full and accurate information on services;
- Increasing openness and transparency on the costs of service delivery;
- Remedying mistakes and failures in service delivery by means of apologies and explanations; and
- Providing the best possible value for money in service delivery.

The management sub-system

In contrast to the client-oriented system, another interpretation of the new public personnel administration and management system was found, namely the management sub-system. The management sub-system has been referred to, among other things, as 'managerialism', 'new public management', 'market-based public administration', 'the post-bureaucratic paradigm' and 'entrepreneurial government' (Hughes 1998: 52). Hood (1991, in Hughes 1998: 61–62) considers the managerialist sub-system as comprising the following features:

- Hands-on professional management in the public service;
- Specific standards and measures of performance;

- Greater emphasis on output controls;
- More emphasis on private sector styles of management practice; and
- Greater discipline in resource use.

In this spirit, the concept of managerialism soon developed firmly as an employment practice in the USA under the name of the 'Senior Executive Service'.

DID YOU KNOW?

?

A similar dispensation (other than in the USA) of 'managerialism' started in the South African public service under the name of the 'Senior Management Service'. One of the key features of the Senior Management Service was to 'professionalise' the senior management echelon. In addition, there would be a strengthening of management capacity so that government departments might convert policy directives effectively into practice and utilise the resources allocated to them efficiently. So, the Public Service Act 103 of 1994, the Public Service Regulations of 2001 (promulgated under Section 41 of the Public Service Act), the Handbook for the Senior Management Service, other directives issued by the Minister of Public Service and Administration, and the resolutions of collective agreements constitute the overall policy framework within which the Senior Management Service is to be administered.

Source: Republic of South Africa (2000c: 1)

The management flexibility sub-system

Perhaps the most recent approach that developed during the new public personnel administration and management phase is the management flexibility sub-system. In part, the rationale behind this sub-system is that political executives (heads of government departments) and senior managers are responsible for controlling the human resource management functions. It is argued that central personnel agencies (such as the Department of Public Service and Administration) and the human resource offices in line departments have built up too many control measures over the years. One way of overcoming this obstacle is to eliminate the multiplicity of unnecessary control measures in human resource management affairs (Uys *et al.* 1997: 183). In this regard, the government has initiated one of the most heralded developments in public sector human resource management, which is related to the principles of the management flexibility sub-system, namely the 'Public Service Management Framework'. This framework assists the government in becoming more client-centred. Moreover, it devolves and decentralises powers to lower levels of management. The framework is embodied in the Public Service Regulations of 2001 and serves as a management tool by setting minimum requirements for public sector managers in realising set objectives.

The integrated human resource management sub-system

A final new public personnel administration and management development is the integrated human resource management sub-system, the principles of which form the basis of this book. In the previous political dispensation before 1994, public service acts, regulations, codes and management guidelines demanded obedience to rules. Needless to say, the comprehensive nature of this rule-bound style of managing public sector affairs had a substantial negative impact on service delivery because there was less emphasis on results. The focus that was placed on rules resulted in a public sector that was not always capable of serving the needs and expectations of the majority of the people (Adler 2000: 12; Republic of South Africa 1999: 9). Since 1994, the priority has been on managing for better results. This perspective entails an integrative approach to all aspects of public administration in the public sector human resource management arena. In practice, it means a 'tying it all together' approach to all main human resource activities and operational work. It implies a commitment to aligning the operational vision, mission and objectives with human resource management strategies, information programmes, financial plans and organisation structures.

A strong case could be made for a so-called integrative approach to public sector human resource management. This approach views public sector human resource management in an integrated manner, which gives it a strategic element that allows for co-operation from all the different role players in order to enhance performance and service delivery capacity. Each action in the public sector has an influence on human resource activities. For example, if it is decided to build a new hospital, human resource policies must be put into place, new structures must be designed, and people must be hired, trained and appraised. All these have an effect on service delivery. It is this interrelatedness among all public sector human resource management activities that forms the basis of the integrated human resource management sub-system (also see Chapter 1). The Public Service Regulations of 2001 entail an integrated framework designed to promote effective performance of all public sector human resource management activities. This integrated framework allows for (1) strategic interventions, decisions, and activities across and within public service institutions that link day-to-day work and strategic goals; and (2) the design of all human resource management systems to recruit, support, develop, and pay staff members and set them up to perform well.

3.5 Contemporary South African perspectives of PSHRM

In Section 3.2, we discussed the international variations in the debate regarding definitions of the concept of HRM. We have also considered the variety of opinions and viewpoints regarding the meaning of the concept 'public sector human resource management'. Some adopt a generalist perspective, while others (the 'absolutists') view the concept of HRM as denoting a very specific style or way of managing people at work. The following points summarise the approach taken in this book:

- In this book, public sector human resource management as a field of study, theory and practice is taken to be that part of management concerned with all the factors, decisions, principles, strategies, operations, practices, functions, activities and methods related to employees in public sector institutions; all the dimensions related to people in their employment relationships, and all the dynamics that flow from it, all of which are aimed at helping to ensure continuous institutional success of public sector institutions through 'good fit' employment relationships in turbulent and ever-changing environmental conditions.

■ The perspective taken is thus broad rather than narrow, in that PSHRM is viewed as referring to all practices and decisions aimed at continuously achieving an optimal match or fit between work; the human resources required to execute the work within an institutional context; and the environment. The days of seeing human resource management as only a specialised and technical staff (supportive) activity are over. What is important today is that the human resource function must be involved in all aspects of an institution's activities. Public sector employers will increasingly have to make sure that employees perform at an optimal level so that the overall strategy and goals can be achieved. This implies that human resource management policies and practices must mesh with all other institutional policies and practices to ensure the efficient and cost-effective use of human resources (Tompkins 1995: 15). This requires an integrative perspective of managing human resources that is a fundamental managerial shift away from personnel administration to human resource management.

Some of the more important characteristics of the above perspectives (which may or may not form part of the approaches or perspectives taken by others) are outlined below:

■ Human resources are viewed as an institution's most important and valued asset. The workforce of any institution determines what value will be added to all the other resources utilised by an institution in its striving towards success. The institution's value system and culture, and the quality and commitment levels of its human resources ultimately exert the greatest influence on the institution's ability to change continuously in line with the demands of its environments.

■ Public sector human resource management is viewed from a visionary perspective. This implies that human resource management systems and processes should be put into place that will result in a diverse and competent workforce that is capable of, and committed to, delivering high-quality public services.

■ All public sector managers are involved in human resource management to a greater or lesser extent, depending on the particular management level (junior, middle or senior) on which the person is operating. Human resource management is a general management function shared, on the one hand, by all HRM managers, functionaries or specialists and, on the other hand, by all those involved in the management of people (line managers) within the context of getting the work of an institution done. An interesting issue that cuts across the field of PSHRM is the growing awareness of the importance of re-establishing the strategic linkages between HRM specialists and line function employees. This is a very complex issue in its own right. There is, of course, a notable prerequisite in this regard. Success will require a line-staff partnership in which line function employees and human resource specialists work closely together in a strategic manner in order to accomplish the central objectives of the public sector (Tompkins 1995: 3–4). For various reasons, things occasionally do not work out in this line-staff partnership as would normally be expected. Where line function employees and HR specialists work together, there is frequent difference and conflict. Because they differ on who has the authority to make decisions, and because they have different objectives, conflict cannot be avoided at all times. This conflict potential is most dominant when decisions are taken jointly on such human resource issues as discipline, physical working conditions, termination of services, transfers and promotions.

- Public sector human resource management is viewed from a contingency perspective. There is no single 'best' model of PSHRM in an absolutist sense, and the management of human resources is not only contingent upon institutional strategies (corporate and/or business) but is also influenced by a magnitude of other, ever-changing factors and circumstances, both internal and external to the institution. Flexible people management, which will vary according to situational factors, is thus supported.

- An open systems and integrated public sector human resource management perspective is adopted. The human resource system of any institution is taken to be one of the many sub-systems in the institution, with the institution also being viewed as an open system existing and functioning in an ever-changing external environment of which it is itself a sub-system. The aim of integrated public sector human resource management is to ensure that services are shaped to meet clients' needs. In practice, it means public sector human resource managers will have to integrate their human resource planning activities with strategic and operational objectives, service delivery needs, and mandates.

- Human resource management, as viewed from a holistic perspective, is taken to be a comprehensive field of theory and practice, which includes topics that were traditionally studied by personnel management scholars, as well as any contemporary topics covering more proactive, innovative and alternative approaches to the management of the human factor at work. There are several contemporary initiatives throughout the public sector aimed at realising this holistic perspective. These can be summarised as multi-skilling, decentralised human resource management, developmental performance management, needs-driven training and education, accountability for results, employment equity, continuous employment contracts, flexible working patterns, a career public service, increased competition, lateral transfers, secondments, re-employment, succession planning, strengthening of management capacity, improved service delivery, electronic human resource management, and the learning organisation.

- Public sector human resource management has both 'hard' and 'soft' characteristics. The former refers to the rational (quantitative and calculative) and economic/financial aspects of people management (such as psychometric evaluation and measurement of work performance and the audit and/or evaluation of PSHRM – including human asset accounting – as well as the formal, rational functions or activities involved in workforce forecasting and planning). The soft aspect emphasises the incorporation of the human dimension (as advocated by human relationists and the work of Herzberg, for example) in the decisions and practices concerning PSHRM, and it emphasises the idea that human resources cannot be dealt with in the same way as other production factors or resources because much more complex and intangible issues (such as feelings, attitudes, perceptions, and human needs) are involved.
- The promotion of a professional service ethos is generally considered to be essential for effective public sector human resource management. The professional ethical behaviour of all public sector employees is thus supported. In this regard, the following values and principles are supported, as summarised in the Constitution of the Republic of South Africa, 1996:
  - A high standard of professional ethics;
  - Efficient, economic, and effective use of human resources;
  - Developmental orientation to human resource management;
  - Provision of human resource services that are fair, equitable, and without bias;
  - Public participation in human resource policymaking;
  - Accountable human resource management;
  - Transparency in providing clients with timely, accessible, and accurate information on human resource matters; and
  - Good human resource management practices to maximise human potential.

Institutional success is not only influenced by the extent to which public sector human resource strategies and practices are closely linked with, and make important contributions to, the institution's strategic objectives and plans. It is also influenced by the degree to which the various aspects of HRM are synchronised with each other and managed in an integrated, coherent way, with the aim of fostering a culture conducive to institutional success.

In concluding this section, it is appropriate to refer to some of the most recent attempts to define and demarcate the field of human resource management in South Africa. In Section 3.3.7, it was indicated that, by the end of 1999, an initiative to establish a Standards Generating Body for human resource management and practices under NSB 03 (The National Standards Body for Business, Commerce and Management Studies) was under way as part of the implementation of the NQF (National Qualifications Framework). In the application submitted to the South African Qualifications Authority to this effect during mid-1999, the human resource management and practices sub-field was described as being concerned with the following:

- All the decisions, strategies, factors, principles, operations, practices, functions, activities, and methods related to the management of people as employees in any type of institution, including SMMEs and virtual institutions;
- All the dimensions related to people in their employment relationships, and all the dynamics that flow from them (including the realisation of the potential of individual employees in terms of their aspirations); and
- All activity aimed at adding value to the delivery of goods and services, as well as to the quality of work life of employees, and hence helping to ensure continuous institutional success in transformative environments.

It should, however, be borne in mind that this description is by no means final, as part of the process of developing standards is the challenge to refine the definition and to determine the scope of HRM in the South African context. As the broader context of HRM changes and unfolds into the twenty-first century, it can be expected that the nature of the HRM field and the way in which it is defined will also change.

3.6   Pursuing a career in the HR field in South Africa

The question arises: How does one embark on a professional career in this field in South Africa?

Although, traditionally, HR specialists did not require formal qualifications and could become top-level managers through experience in administrative personnel departments, over the past two decades or so, HRM has become such a complex and demanding field of theory and practice that true professionalism has come to be regarded as a major requirement for HR specialists.

As mentioned earlier, HR departments have traditionally been the administrative sections in many institutions. Consequently, the typical HR department is involved in data gathering, record keeping and other clerical work. Personnel clerks or officers who have no tertiary qualifications thus still carry out important supportive work which has to be executed in any institution (such as record keeping on leave and absenteeism, preparing the payroll inputs, and processing medical aid and insurance claims). However, in order to gain access to a professional career in HRM, one has to undertake additional education, training and development in the field of HRM. External factors, such as changes in workforce demographics, changing values in society, economic pressures, globalising competition, and corporate reorganisation, require the inputs of a new breed of HR specialists – HR professionals who can add value to institutional success, employee well-being and a better society in general. These realities pose peculiar challenges to those interested and involved in the HR field in South Africa – challenges which call for HR professionalism.

A definite course of action must be determined and followed in order to become a highly valued HR specialist. Apart from studying for the recognised qualifications, it is often desirable to gain general public sector management experience in order to understand the type of work in which an institution's human resources are really involved. This is where integrative HRM thinking begins. However, a crucial aspect is gaining the necessary relevant knowledge base regarding the human factor within the institutional context.

Most tertiary educational institutions in South Africa offer courses in fields relevant to HRM. General social science studies in the fields of psychology or sociology help to provide knowledge of human and behavioural processes in institutional contexts. Similarly, legal studies can provide knowledge of relevant legal requirements which have a bearing on the acquisition, utilisation and separation of the institution's human resources.

On the other hand, disciplines such as industrial psychology, business economics, or business management, as well as public administration, can provide an important foundation in the HRM field. Many tertiary educational institutions in South Africa offer specialised post-matriculation courses in HRM or personnel management. These include universities, technicons, technical colleges and other business/management educational schools or centres where one can obtain qualifications in this interesting and dynamic field. Furthermore, most of the South African universities' postgraduate business schools offer modules specialising in human resource-related topics.

In addition to obtaining the necessary qualifications, one must also seek employment in the HR field in order to gain the relevant experience and to apply the theoretical knowledge gained through studies.

Because of the complex and dynamic challenges currently facing the HRM field, more stringent requirements are being applied to those wishing to become true HR specialists. Cuming (1989: 45), for example, says in this regard that 'the status of any profession depends in large measure on its requirements and methods for entry into membership and on the existence of a code of professional conduct'. This means that, in order to be called an HR professional, one really has to be a professional person, involved in a particular profession.

> In this regard, a profession can be said to be characterised by the existence of a common body of knowledge, a procedure for certifying members of that profession, a set of standards of ethical conduct, and a communication system that can facilitate the exchange of ideas and self-regulation (Cherrington 1983: 26).

Thus, to be an HR professional not only requires a professional approach to HR practice but also some form of official professional recognition. In South Africa, one can become an official HR professional through registration with the South African Board for People Practice (SABPP).

3.7   Professionalism in HRM and the SABPP

In 1990, the Chairman of the SABPP, Gary Whyte, explained the reason for the decision to set up the SABPP in 1982 (Whyte 1990: 33):

Just like chartered accountants and professional engineers have to be 'registered', and every profession needs to have set standards (related to education and training of new entrants, registration and professional conduct), which are fully credible and are hence set by an impartial body, the need arose for a similar body and registration process in the personnel field.

Whyte (1990: 33) then went on to say: 'There was a groundswell of opinion and feeling, expressed by the members of the personnel fraternity that they wanted to pursue the goal of professionalism.' Consequently, in 1976, an Ad Hoc Committee on Professional Recognition for Personnel Practitioners was established, paving the way for the eventual establishment of the SABPP on 15 October 1982.

The South African Board for People Practices' mission is to establish, direct and sustain a high level of professionalism and ethical conduct in personnel practice in South Africa.

If a person is registered with the SABPP, this serves as an indication to employers, fellow employees, and all other interested parties that this person meets the very high standards of professional performance and ethical conduct set by the Board; it is also a form of recognition of the individual's professional status and of the contributions which he or she has made to the HR field. Employers often demand registration with the Board as one of the criteria necessary for appointment to HR positions. By setting and protecting these standards of professionalism, the SABPP, as an impartial and independent body, protects the public, the Board's registered practitioners, and their employers. The SABPP monitors the application of (and thus ensures the protection of) professional standards and conduct in the HR field.

3.7.1   Philosophy, strategy and objectives of the SABPP

The philosophy of the SABPP is to enable those engaged in the HR profession to make a significant contribution as follows:
- To the institution, in terms of its management and utilisation of HR;
- To the individual, in terms of his or her needs and aspirations; and
- To the community at large, in terms of an enhanced quality of life.

The Board's strategy is to promote, direct and influence the development of the human resources profession; to review competency standards for the education, training and conduct of those engaged in the profession; to advise involved parties on the development and attaining of those competencies; and to evaluate such attainment.

The SABPP is committed to (values) objectivity, fairness, consistency and integrity in all its functions. The quality assurance system of the SABPP ETQA strives to contribute to the economy of South Africa. The SABPP links the achievement of quality to equity and the fostering of innovation and diversity. With a customer-centred focus the SABPP will work in a consultative and co-operative mode with partners and stakeholders, offering service excellence being professional in all our dealings building and maintaining trust and confidentiality. The SABPP strives to facilitate the delivery of high quality HR practice (South African Board for Personnel Practice, 2010). The SABPP's objectives rest on the following four pillars of professionalism (South African Board for People Practices, 2010):

- Mastery of a particular intellectual skill, acquired by training and education;
- The adherence by members to a common code of values and conduct;
- A regulating or administrating body; and
- Acceptance of a duty to society as a whole.

3.7.2 Registering with the SABPP: Levels, categories, processes and procedures

Individuals who are interested in registering with the SABPP can apply for registration at various levels. It is also possible to register in more than one category; in other words, one can register both as a Specialist and Generalist.

DID YOU KNOW?   **?**

The Board's charter provides for registration in the following specialist categories:

1. Planning, recruitment and selection
   - Workforce planning and personnel cost
   - Recruitment and selection
   - Induction
2. Learning and development
   - Development of trainers/facilitators/ educators, including management development/ leadership development
   - Career development/ Developing workplace skills plan
   - Coaching and mentoring
3. Rewards management
   - Job evaluation and person-based systems
   - Incentives
   - Benefit
   - Salary and wage structuring
4. Employment relations
   - Risk and conflict management
   - Dispute settlement
   - Collective bargaining and negotiations

- Labour law specialist and diversity dynamics
- Employee/stakeholder relationships
5. Safety, health and environment
   - Safety and health
   - Wellness
   - Environment
   - EAP
   - Research
6. Organisation development
   - Change management
   - Re-engineering, performance and research
7. HR information systems
   - HR data management
   - Business process improvement
   - Information systems design, maintenance and management
8. HR administration
   - HR reporting
   - Record keeping
   - Organising, scheduling and HR compliance

Source: South African Board for People Practices (2010: Online)

Registered practitioners who meet certain additional criteria set by the Board may act as mentors, upon invitation by the Board. Such individuals will gain enhanced status and will have the opportunity to make additional contributions to the field by helping new entrants to the profession to qualify for higher levels of registration.

The requirements set for registration at the various levels differ, but usually consist of a combination of relevant experience and qualifications. The professional registration levels and post-nominal titles are as follows (South African Board for Personnel Practice 2004b):

- **Master HR Practitioner (MHRP)**
  NQF level 8 postgraduate 3 and 4/Master's or Doctorate
- **Chartered HR Practitioner (CHRP)**
  NQF level 8 postgraduate 1 and 2/Honours, BTech or Master's Diploma
- **HR Practitioner (HRP)**
  NQF level 7/three years' post-matriculation study/National Diploma or Degree
- **HR Associate (HRA)**
  NQF level 6/two years' post-matriculation study/SGB diploma
- **HR Technician (HRT)**
  NQF level 5/one year post-matriculation study/certificate

New non-professional registration levels:
- Affiliate;
- Full-time student; and
- Candidate.

Apart from the qualification requirement mentioned at each level, appropriate experience, proven competence and continued professional development are always requirements at each level. In addition to these requirements, the Board provides certain other guidelines regarding the qualifications and relevant experience required in order to qualify for registration. These guidelines are usually provided quantitatively by means of credits which are calculated according to predetermined values (such as one credit for one year's appropriate experience if one wants to register as an HR practitioner). They are also provided qualitatively, which normally relates to the type of experience required (such as in training and development or industrial relations) and the depth of involvement in the particular HR field.

Guidelines are also provided regarding the relevance of different study courses. The Board may furthermore request an applicant to attend a professional interview in a case where there is any doubt as to the applicability of an applicant's experience and/or qualifications.

3.7.3 Process and procedure for registering

Any person who is interested in registering can request the Registrar: SABPP to provide him or her with the necessary documentation.

After the relevant documentation has been studied, and if the person thinks that he or she qualifies for registration, the necessary application forms are to be completed and returned to the SABPP, together with a nominal registration fee, certified copies of all relevant certificates, a detailed curriculum vitae (CV), a job description of the person's current post, and recommendations from at least two persons (preferably registered with the SABPP) (South African Board for People Practices (2010: Online)).

3.8 Remaining a valued HR practitioner: Networking and reading

Individuals who choose a career in the public sector human resource field specifically, and who want to become successful professionals, must continuously keep abreast of the latest developments in the relevant fields in order to ensure that they remain knowledgeable, valued, state-of-the-art HR practitioners. They must constantly add to their knowledge of the relevant fields and keep in contact with other professionals. It may not be too difficult to obtain the necessary qualifications, to gain the required experience, or even to register with the SABPP, but to remain a highly valued and well-respected HR practitioner means that one must be prepared to go the extra mile. In this regard, it is necessary at least to read extensively and to become a member of other associations where interaction with others with similar interests can take place.

The Institute of People Management (Southern Africa) (IPM) is a very prominent body or association in the HR field in South Africa. Other relevant associations include the Industrial Relations Association of South Africa (IRASA), which is affiliated to the IIRA (International Industrial Relations Association), the Society for Industrial Psychology (SIP), the Employee Assistance Professionals Association (EAPA South Africa), the Association of Southern African Schools and Departments of Public Administration and Management (ASSADPAM) and the South African Association for Public Administration and Management (SAAPAM). By joining associations such as these, individuals can come into contact with other professionals who also want to stay on top of their professions. Knowledge and experience can be shared and ideas exchanged and, in this way, not only will the individual enhance his or her own level of professionalism and competence, but the community as a whole will also benefit.

Because of the importance of the IPM, it is necessary to highlight its role in South Africa and to distinguish it from the SABPP.

The IPM (SA) was established in 1946, and, although (like the SABPP) it is also concerned with the question of professional competence in the HR field, there is a difference in emphasis. In this regard, Whyte (1990: 33) commented:

The IPM is concerned with promotion and development, which it achieves through activities such as its diploma programmes, its Convention, its Journal, and its seminars. The Board focuses on enablement, which it does through standard setting in areas like registration, education, candidate training, and norms of professional conduct. The Board confines itself to 'Personnel Practice', which is concerned with the unique role of the functional specialist. The remit of the IPM is much wider. It concerns itself with 'Personnel Management' (or 'Human Resource Management', if you prefer), which refers to the generic role of managing people at work.

Apart from the networking that can be undertaken by joining associations such as the IPM or IRASA, and by actively taking part in the activities of these organisations, it is also of extreme importance to read extensively in the relevant field. Reading relevant journals is thus an important part of trying to remain a valued HR practitioner in South Africa. Some of the more prominent South African and international publications are listed below:

Some HRM-related journals

South African
- Administratio Publica
- Contemporary Labour Law
- Employment Law
- HR Future
- Journal of Public Administration
- Management Today
- People Dynamics (Official publication of the IPM)
- Politeia (Journal of the Departments of Political Sciences and Public Administration, University of South Africa)
- South African Journal of Labour Relations
- South African Journal of Human Resource Management

International
- The American Review of Public Administration
- Harvard Business Review

- Human Resource Management
- International Journal of Human Resource Management
- The Journal of Human Resources
- The Journal of Industrial Relations
- Journal of Organizational Behavior
- Human Resource Management Journal
- British Journal of Industrial Relations
- European Industrial Relations Review
- Personnel Journal
- The Personnel Administrator
- The Public Manager
- Industrial Relations Journal
- Industrial and Labor Relations Review
- Personnel Management
- Public Management Review
- Public Money and Management
- Review of Public Personnel Administration
- Public Personnel Management
- The International Journal of Public Sector Management

In addition, several publications of the Department of Labour can keep one abreast of general developments in the field of human resources in South Africa.

3.9 Review

In this chapter, we have discussed the theoretical aspects of public sector human resource management from a South African perspective. Although we have devoted attention to the role that history has played in the field, we have also looked at more recent developments. We have accordingly examined the contributions made by well-known international experts in the field. In analysing HRM in South Africa, we have paid special attention to the pioneering work of Isobel White and to her influence on HRM in this country.

We have also considered some contemporary perspectives of PSHRM. The South African public sector human resource specialist is confronted with a variety of challenges in the external environment, which call for a professional approach to the managing of people in the public sector. In order to equip oneself for these challenges, one can study for professional HR qualifications and also register with the SABPP. As PSHRM specialists seek to professionalise themselves, they must constantly add knowledge to their relevant fields of expertise by becoming involved in reading extensively in the subject field and by joining professional associations and subscribing to professional journals.

3.10   Self-evaluation questions

1. Are you of the opinion that HRM in South Africa has been influenced by international developments in the field?
2. One often hears that the HRM ideas created during the Industrial Revolution are still widely used in South African HRM. Do you agree with this statement?
3. Explain the pioneering role played by Isobel White in establishing the principles of HRM in South Africa.
4. Would you agree that HRM was extensively influenced by the political conditions in the country, especially during the apartheid years? Give reasons for your answer.
5. Much has been said about HRM developments during the 1990s. Describe some trends that you believe had an impact on HRM during those years.
6. How did the evolution of PSHRM systems take place?
7. As a human resource management specialist, how would you go about describing a contemporary South African perspective of PSHRM?
8. Suppose that you are approached by a friend who would like to pursue a career in the public sector human resource management field in South Africa. What advice would you give him or her regarding the nature of such a career, how to enter the field, what to study and read, and which institutions and associations to approach?
9. What are the options available to professionalise oneself in PSHRM? Consider, in this regard, the role of the SABPP and ways in which one can go about networking and reading.

3.11   End notes

1. This section is based largely on personal notes of I.H.B. White (kindly supplied by the IPM (SA)), on publications by I.H.B. White, and on a personal interview with I.H.B. White conducted by Professor Ben Swanepoel.
2. Eastern Province Herald, Friday, 31 October 1941.
3. This section is based on and adapted from The Supply and Demand of Personnel Practitioners in South Africa, published by the Human Sciences Research Council.

Bibliography

Adler, G. 2000. *Public service labour relations in a democratic South Africa.* Johannesburg: Witwatersrand University Press.

Anglo sticks its neck out: Dr Alex Boraine plans for black advancement. 1973. *People & Profits,* 1(1), July, 3-28.

Bagwa, W. 1973. Welfare facilities for black employees. *People & Profits,* 1(6), 12-16.

Beach, DS. 1980. *Personnel: The management of people at work.* 4th edn. New York: Macmillan.

Botha, B. 1992. Window for opportunity. *People Dynamics,* 10(12), 7.

Cherrington, DJ. 1983. *Personnel management: The management of human resources.* Dubuque, Iowa: Brown.

Coetzee, JAG. 1976. *Industrial relations in South Africa.* Cape Town: Juta.

Crous, W. 1990. 'n Nuwe Suid-Afrika op die horizon: Implikasies vir die menslike hulpbronbestuurder. *IPM Journal,* 8(8), 3.

Cuming, MW. 1989. *The theory and practice of personnel management.* Oxford: Heinemann.

Cunningham, PW, Slabbert, JA, & De Villiers, AS. 1990. The historic development of industrial relations. In JA Slabbert, JJ Prinsloo & W Backer (eds.), *Managing industrial relations in South Africa.* Pretoria: Sigma.

Denhardt, RB. 1995. *Public administration: An action orientation.* Bonn: Wadsworth.

Denhardt, RB, & Hammond, BR. 1992. *Public administration in action: Readings, profiles, and cases.* Pacific Grove, CA: Brooks/Cole.

De Witt, D. 1998. HR challenges for organisational transformation. *Management Today.* 13(10), 33-35.

Dickenson, J. 1974. The linkman: Selection and training of the black personnel officer. *People & Profits,* 1(7), 8-19.

Diessnack, CH. 1980. Financial impact of effective human resources management. *People & Profits,* 7(10), 5.

Douwes Dekker, L. 1974. Workers' education: A prerequisite for effective works committees. *People & Profits,* 1(7), 5-7.

Finnemore, M, & Van der Merwe, R. 1992. *Introduction to industrial relations in South Africa.* Johannesburg: Lexicon.

Friedman, S. 1987. *Building tomorrow today: African workers in trade unions 1970-1984.* Johannesburg: Ravan Press.

Gerber, PD, Nel, PS, & Van Dyk, PS. 1987. *Human resources management.* Johannesburg: Southern.

Grobler, PA. 1993. Strategic human resource management models: A review and a proposal for South African companies. *Management Dynamics: Contemporary Research,* 2(3), 17.

Grogan, J. 2008. *Workplace Law.* Cape Town: Juta.

Grogan, J, Jordaan, B, Maserumule, P, & Stelzner, S. 2009. *Juta's Labour Law Update 2009.* Cape Town: Juta.

Hall, R. 1985. Some changes in management practice in the Transvaal. *Industrial Relations Journal of South Africa,* 2nd quarter, 6.

Hays, SW, & Kearney, RC. 1995. *Public personnel administration: Problems and prospects.* Englewood Cliffs, NJ: Prentice-Hall.

Henry, N. *Public administration and public affairs.* Englewood Cliffs, NJ: Prentice-Hall.

Hill, A. 1987. The strategic approach to human resources management. *IPM Journal,* 5(9), 6-9.

Horwitz, FW. 1988. Personnel management or human resource management: Euphemism or new paradigm? *IPM Journal,* 6(12), 6-7.

Hughes, OE. 1998. *Public management and administration: An introduction.* New York: Palgrave.

IPM News update: South African Board for Personnel Practice. 1983. *IPM Manpower Journal,* 2(2), 4.

Jacobsz, FP. 1973. Herstrukturering van arbeid: 'n Voorvereiste vir ekonomiese groei. *People & Profits,* 1(5), 22.

Langenhoven, HP, & Verster, R. 1969. *Survey of personnel management in South Africa.* Bloemfontein: Personnel Research Division, University of the Orange Free State.

Langenhoven, HP. 1975. *The present state of black personnel management in South Africa.* Bloemfontein: Personnel Research Division, University of the Orange Free State.

Langenhoven, HP. 1978. Industrial psychology and personnel management do not mean the same thing. *People & Profits,* 5(12), 14-15.

Lee, YS. 1992. *Public personnel administration and constitutional values.* London: Quorum.

Lombard, BU. 1978. Human resources management: A new approach for South Africa. *SA Journal of Labour Relations,* December, 12-24.

Makoane, S. July 2001. Challenges of the new HR world. *HR Future,* 1(5).

Marx, FW. 1969. *Aspects of personnel management.* Pretoria: University of Pretoria.

Natrass, N. 1973. Effective supervision of black employees: Techniques that get results. *People & Profits,* 1(5), 5.

Nel, PS, & Van Rooyen, PH. 1993. *South African industrial relations theory and practice.* Pretoria: Van Schaik.

Norman, P. 1998. Critical challenges ahead for HR in business transformation. *Management Today,* 14(2), 14-16.

Pansegrouw, G. 1985. Strategic human resource management: An emerging dimension. Parts 1 & 2. *IPM Journal,* 4(5), 22-30; 4 (6), 8-15.

Rosenbloom, DH, and Goldman, DD. 1989. *Public administration: Understanding management, politics, and law in the public sector.* New York: Random House.

Slabbert, JA, Prinsloo JJ, & Backer W. 1990. (Eds.) *Managing industrial relations in South Africa.* Pretoria: Sigma.

South African Board for Personnel Practice (SABPP). 1990. *Generic competency model for human resource practitioners.* (Board paper of the South African Board for Personnel Practice. Johannesburg): Eskom, Human Resources Performance Management.

South African Board for Personnel Practice. 2004a. *Introduction: History and composition: Objectives and activities* [http://www.sabpp.co.za/intro].

South African Board for Personnel Practice. 2004b. Professional registration with the SABPP [http://www.sabpp.co.za/registration/intro].

South African Board for People Practices. 2010. *Commitment to Standards: Mission, Strategy and Value Statements* [http://www.sabpp.co.za/sabpp/commitment-to-standards.html].

Southern African Legal Information Institute. 2010. *South Africa: Labour Court.* [http://www.saflii.org/za/cases/ZALC/].

SPA Consultants. 1992. Human resources survey in 23 well-known South African organisations, 6-24.

Tompkins, J. 1995. *Human resource management in government: Hitting the ground running.* University of Montana-Harper Collins.

Stillman, RJ. 1992. *Public administration: Concepts and cases.* Boston, MA: Houghton Mifflin.

Uys, F, Van der Westhuizen, EJ, Nealer, EJ, Smith, FH, Clapper, VA, Rowland, RW, & Van Wyk, WJ. 1997. *Organisational theory & personnel administration.* Pretoria: University of South Africa.

Van Wyk, C. 1989. The human resource practitioner's changing role. *IPM Journal,* 7(9), 13-14.

Veldsman, T. 1998. The making of a people miracle. *Management Today,* 14(2), 35.

Verster, R. 1979. Personnel management in South Africa. Bloemfontein: Personnel Research Division, University of the Orange Free State.

Visser, P, Douwes Dekker, L, Majola, A, & Brenner, D. 1991. Community conflict and violence: A human needs perspective. *IPM Journal,* 10(2), 22.

White, IHB. 1944/45. Personnel management in South Africa: Labour management. *Journal of the UK Institute of Personnel Management,* 144.

White, IHB. 1945. Personnel management in industry. In *Personnel research in South Africa.* Grahamstown: Personnel Research Section, Leather Industries Research Institute.

White, IHB. 1955. *The effect of the changing social and economic situation on the training and experience demanded of the personnel manager.* Address delivered at a one-day conference of the Port Elizabeth branch of the SA Institute of Personnel Management on 9 August, 1955.

Whyte, GS. 1978. The professionalism of personnel management. *People & Profits*, 5(12), 9–10.

Whyte, GS. 1990. IPM and SABPP: How do they differ? (IPM in interview with Gary Whyte). *IPM Journal*, 8(7), 33–34.

Wilkinson, A, Bacon, N, Redman, T, & Snell, S. 2010. *The SAGE Handbook of Human Resource Management.* Los Angeles: Sage.

Acts of legislation

Republic of South Africa. 1996. The Constitution of the Republic of South Africa (1996). Government Printer.

Republic of South Africa. 1995a. The Labour Relations Act (Act 66 of 1995). Government Printer. [http://www.polity.org.za/html/govdocs/legislation/1995/act95]

Government regulations

Republic of South Africa. 2001a. Public Service Regulations of 2001 (promulgated under Section 41 of the Public Service Act, Proclamation 103 of 1994). Government Gazette, 427 (21951). Government Printer.

Government white and green papers

Republic of South Africa. 1995b. White paper on the Transformation of the Public Service. 24 November 1995. Government Gazette, 365 (16838).

Republic of South Africa. 1997a. White paper on Transforming Public Service Delivery (Batho Pele). 1 October 1997. Government Gazette, 388 (18340).

Republic of South Africa. 1997b. White paper on Human Resource Management in the Public Service. 31 December 1997. Government Gazette, 390 (18595).

Republic of South Africa. 1998. White paper on Affirmative Action in the Public Service. 23 April 1998. Government Gazette, 564 (18800).

Government reports

Republic of South Africa. 2000a. Annual Report of the Department of Public Service and Administration for the Year 1999/2000. Department of Public Service and Administration. [http://www.dpsa.gov.za/docs/reports/annual99-00]

Republic of South Africa. 2000b. Report on the State of Representativeness in the Public Service. Public Service Commission.

Management guides

Republic of South Africa. 1999. *Baseline Implementation Guide.* Department of Public Service and Administration. [http://www.dpsa.gov.za/documents/baseline/part1]

Republic of South Africa. 2001b. Policy Statement on the Establishment of a Senior Management Service in the Public Service. Department of the Public Service and Administration. [http://www.polity.org.za/govdocs/policy/sms-aug00]

Republic of South Africa. 2001c. *Public Service Handbook: Senior Management Service.* Department of Public Service and Administration.

Other government documents

Republic of South Africa. 2007. 2006/2007 *South African Yearbook.* Government Communication & Information System.

Part 2

Strategising and planning for public sector human resources

IN PART 1, we explained that, in our view, human resource management (HRM) ought to be managed in accordance with a strategic approach. The need for such an approach in South Africa was already being mooted in the early eighties. However, in the public sector, it tends to be regarded as an activity of more recent concern. Although the strategic approach to PSHRM is a recurrent theme throughout this book, the aim of Part 2 is to clarify specific aspects of this approach in greater detail.

We have already noted that public service delivery is a strongly labour-intensive activity. In Chapter 1, we saw that the total South African public service comprises more than one million people. This figure is likely to stay the same well into the foreseeable future. Because so many people are employed in the public sector, it is essential that public sector managers have to think many years ahead about the number and type of human resources they will need and about how to get, keep and optimally utilise these human resources. Strategies will therefore have to be developed within the parameters set by the budgetary process. Strategy, in this regard, will include the adopting of wide-ranging techniques, such as organisational redesign, process re-engineering and outsourcing. Applied in a narrow sense, strategising and planning for human resources refers to staffing. This means, of course, those employment practices that are directed at obtaining suitable human resources for public sector institutions – the recruiting, selecting, appointing and orientating of employees – the topics of Part 3.

We could extend the applicability of the strategising and planning function even further. It is applicable to other human resource tasks, such as promotion, redeployment, training and development, career management, reduction and retention. Depending on the results of a strategic planning exercise, strategies need to be developed and implemented in terms of the specific human resource needs. In the process of developing strategies and working out human resource plans, it is important to bear in mind that human resource management does not take place in a vacuum. There are, of course, many variables that individually or collectively influence the human resource function in the public sector. These variables provide guidelines for all PSHRM activities. Therefore, it is important for the public sector manager to take note of these variables and to realise that PSHRM is shaped by the nature, purpose, and context of government (the political field), the existing public sector management framework (organisational structures and policies), the prevailing social values (for example, religious influences), and public interests and changes (for example, economic changes) that are taking place on a continuous basis. These contextual public sector variables need to be strategically scrutinised and planned against in order to arrive at effective human resource management decisions. This is the subject of Part 2.

Strategic public sector human resource management

Purpose

The purpose of this chapter is to give an overview of the principles of strategic public sector human resource management to enable public officials to make strategic decisions about the human resource function.

Learning outcomes

After you have read this chapter, you should be able to:

- Explain the emergence of strategic public sector human resource management.
- Explain the meaning of public sector human resource management.
- Describe what a 'strategic approach to public sector human resource management' entails.
- Devise and implement the following six-step process for strategic public sector human resource management: (1) considering the corporate plan, (2) scanning environmental conditions, (3) establishing specific objectives, (4) deciding on an integrated human resource management strategy, (5) drafting and implementing of public sector human resource management business plans, and (6) monitoring, evaluating and reporting.
- Apply environmental scanning to determine which factors have an immediate impact on public sector human resource matters.
- Distinguish between two different public sector human resource management strategy options, namely the corporate strategy and the business strategy.
- Draw up a public sector human resource management business plan.
- Monitor, evaluate, and report on the results of the public sector human resource management process.

4.1 Introduction

As we have already indicated, one of the posing challenges at present for public sector managers is that they are becoming more involved in formulating, integrating and implementing strategies in public sector institutions. The efforts to formulate, integrate and implement sound HRM strategies are designed to achieve efficient public service delivery. Compared with the past, human resource management is regarded nowadays in a new light in the public sector. It is no longer viewed as a highly specialised and technical staff activity. There is a growing tendency to acknowledge human resources as a vitally important factor for the public sector's success and to recognise that the human resource function must be involved in all aspects of a public sector institution's activities. Hence, it is essential that all public sector employees must perform at an optimal level so that the overall strategy, purpose and objectives of government can be achieved. To this end, key concepts will be clarified, and the link between the general strategic management of public sector institutions and strategic human resource management will be explained. The focus will then fall on management decision making in the formulation of human resource strategies. This will be followed by a discussion of other long-term decisions relating to HRM.

4.2 The emergence of strategic public sector human resource management (PSHRM)

In the previous political dispensation, HRM was managed, to a great extent, according to a rigid pattern, leaving little scope for individual public sector managers to take decisions or make plans on their own. However, the post-1994 public sector faces enormous challenges for HRM. These challenges have found practical expression through a comprehensive programme of new policy initiatives. What is evident in these changes is that the primary locus (the functional locality) of HRM has evolved from performing routine personnel work (personnel administration), to enhancing service delivery through a line-staff partnership, to managing human resources in ways that are strategically linked to government objectives (strategic public sector human resource management) (Republic of South Africa 1997: 9). This approach strongly propagates the notion of assigning managerial results closest to the point of service delivery.

No one today disputes the fact that the theory and practice of HRM has been enormously influenced since the late 1980s. These influences are largely attributable to the political changes that had started taking place during these times: the impacts of technology, demographic changes, a changing workforce (more women and black people working in the public sector), changing legal climate, globalisation and restructuring (downsizing, rightsizing and outsourcing), and increased decentralisation of management authority. PSHRM is therefore no longer reduced to an administrative task undertaken by a specialist group of human resource specialists applying centrally devised regulations, but is concerned much more with the development of human resource strategies that are integrated with the strategic and operational plans. In doing so, public sector managers will, for example, have to make sure that these human resource strategies will include specific employment equity objectives and targets for achieving a representative public sector workforce (Republic of South Africa 1995: 20–22). Strategic public sector human resource management is even more evident if one looks at the management principles set by government for the public sector.

DID YOU KNOW?

The strategic HRM principles in the public service are the following:
- Increased delegation of managerial responsibility and authority;
- Development of a service delivery-oriented, multi-skilled and multi-cultural workforce; and
- Continuing drive for efficiency and effectiveness.

Read more about the strategic plan of the Department of Public Service and Administration for the period 2010–2014. This plan is available at: http://www.dpsa.gov.za/documents

Source: Republic of South Africa (1997: 10)

Each of the management principles outlined above is likely to create its own particular human resource management opportunities. To take only one example, delegated responsibility will require public sector managers at every level to develop skills that have hitherto been required of only a few. In more practical terms, it means that all public sector managers will need to get involved in strategic human resource activities as well. The implication of this, when applied to SHRM, is far-reaching. The mere fact that human resources form the major component of resources in the public sector implies that their management should be considered as a strategic activity. Undoubtedly, it cannot continue to be the sole responsibility of human resource specialists. All public sector managers, irrespective of the management level on which they operate, will have to be skilled in managing people. Therefore, HRM will no longer be assigned to human resource specialists, but will become a core competency for all (Republic of South Africa 1997: 23). The idea of incorporating SHRM activities and plans into the institution's corporate plan entails numerous activities. Above all, it involves establishing a strategic planning process, strategic decision making at all levels, consideration of the vision, mission, objectives, plans, strategies and values, and the deploying of financial, informational and human resources. In addition, the outcome of the strategic planning process ends in the writing of a business plan.

4.3 The meaning of strategic public sector human resource management

In the spirit of what has been written so far, we now need to elaborate on some relevant terms for the analysis of the concept PSHRM. We shall begin by taking a closer look at the term 'strategic management'.

4.3.1 Strategic management

Chapter 1 emphasises the fact that management is based on a process of policymaking, organising, financing and controlling. Strategic management is thus the application of this management process at the top level of the institution. At this level, the focus is on the success of the institution as a whole over the long term, within the context of a changing and competitive environment. Smith, Arnold, and Bizell (1988: 5) provide the following definition:

'Strategic management is the process of examining both present and future environments, formulating the institution's objectives and making, implementing and controlling decisions focused on achieving these objectives in the present and future environments.'

In the same vein, Pearce and Robinson (1991: 18) describe strategic management as 'the set of decisions and actions that result in the formulation and implementation of plans designed to achieve a company's objectives. Because it involves long-term, future-orientated, complex decision making and requires considerable resources, top management participation is essential.'

The process of strategic management is described by most authors as consisting of strategy formulation and strategy implementation. Although it is self-evident that the distinction between the two is not watertight and that they are interdependent, Schendel (1992) points out that there '[...] are two different types of activities here: shaping has to do with finding strategy, implementing has to do with using strategy'.

In defining these two broad activities, different components or tasks in the strategic management process can be identified. It must, however, be emphasised that, although for conceptual and analytical purposes these tasks/components of the process are separated (and even treated by some as a series of discrete steps in the process), in practical reality they are often performed simultaneously or in a different order, making the whole process interactive and dynamic by nature. Nevertheless, in order to facilitate learning, most authors describe the strategic management process in terms of these different tasks, steps, components, or sub-processes. The same approach is followed here.

Environmental scanning and analysis entails a thorough study of all the factors or variables, both external and internal to the institution. The ultimate aim is to create the necessary match or fit between the two. This is often referred to as 'SWOT analysis', and involves the process of analysing and synchronising the institution's internal strengths and weaknesses, and the opportunities and threats coming from the external environment.

Developing a vision and/or mission is another facet of strategic management. This direction-setting task concerns determining exactly what service delivery field you are in and what service you want to be in. Other components of strategy formulation include the formulation of different types of strategy, such as generic business strategies, corporate and grand strategies, functional strategies, drafting policies, and identifying and defining so-called critical success factors (CSFs) or key strategic issues (KSIs) within the context of the business plans that are drafted.

The implementation of a strategy entails creating the necessary structures and also establishing a culture whereby all the role players actually work towards overall mission accomplishment. It is all about mobilising resources towards mission accomplishment.

Throughout the process, it is important continuously to monitor and evaluate the extent to which strategic decisions match or fit the changing circumstances, as well as the extent to which they are actually being implemented.

Finally, it must be emphasised that strategic management cannot be regarded simply as a neatly packaged set of rational decisions and related behaviour. The role of the socio-organisational side (the 'political' or 'softer' side of management) has become increasingly important. Factors such as the ideologies of managers, the motivations and frames of reference that they have, their perceptions, and the role of so-called cognitive maps and cognitive processes all play a very significant part in the process of strategic management. Wood (1996: 4) says the following in this regard: 'Ideological differences saturate the presumably rational institutional process of decision making [...] We need to understand how we in business organisations are guided by ideology.'

Strategic management, then, is best seen as a process. This means it can be seen as a process in which all workers – who often have special knowledge and skills (in other words, competencies) in a specific area (such as human resource management) – contribute to the overall performance of the public sector institution. One must remember that a public sector manager is a person who is firstly a manager who is responsible to realise strategically the overall objectives of the institution where he or she is employed. This same manager is secondly a manager charged with HRM responsibilities such as recruitment, selection, training, and labour relations. To summarise this point, public sector managers should not manage their own section's work for the benefit of that section only. They should rather manage it in such a way as to contribute to the benefit of the whole public sector institution. This goes for public human resource managers as well.

4.3.2   Strategic public sector human resource management

From the foregoing, it can be concluded that, by strategic public sector human resource management, we mean those long-term, senior-level management decisions and actions regarding employment relationships that are made and performed in a way that is fully integrated with the overall general strategic management of public sector institutions.

Strategic human resource management thus chiefly concerns synchronising and integrating the institution's strategic needs and plans with all those aspects stemming from and relating to the management of employees. A strategic approach to HRM also requires that we focus on the contributions human resource specialists make to the overall success of the institution. In other words, the way in which they contribute to the directing of the broader activities of the institution (Leopold *et al.* 1999: 22). From the strategic management perspective, this has a major implication for human resource management in particular. All public sector managers (including human resource managers) are part of the management cadre, and all of them are responsible for reaching the objectives of government in the most efficient and effective way. Therefore, every one of them has a role in strategy making, namely shaping and directing the institution in the face of all opportunities and threats that arise in the environment. Every public sector manager, thus, is a key role player, however humble, in contributing to the strategic processes of the public sector. This brings another aspect to the fore: adopting this strategic perspective to HRM implies that the term 'public sector human resource manager' can almost be viewed as a misnomer. This is to say that human resource managers are not there to manage 'human resources'. They are actually there to help manage the public sector in its totality, ensuring that it is resourced with the right human resource knowledge, skills, and competencies to help it to survive in the long term.

Strategic human resource management is not to be viewed as something separate from or subordinate to the formulation and/or implementation of corporate or business strategies of public sector institutions. It is also not to be seen as something which has only to do with either general strategy formulation or with strategy implementation. On the contrary, it is viewed as an integral part of general strategic management. Aspects related to or connected with the management of employment relationships permeate all facets of general management strategy formulation and implementation. Public sector strategy cannot be formulated without incorporating the relevant human resource-related issues. If, for instance, the senior management of a public sector institution decides to diversify (diversification strategy) into different segments or lines of service delivery, the human resource-related implications that will have to be considered include peculiar labour market conditions in those segments or lines of service delivery (for example, supply/demand of labour, skills needed, wage levels/ labour costs, and trade union activity/strategies).

Similarly, the human resource-related requirements will be quite different in a public sector institution that is following a strategy of innovation from one in which a strategy of retrenchment/turnaround is followed. In the case of the latter, the emphasis will be on cost reduction and/or asset reduction. If, for example, a public sector institution experiences a phase of decline (because of an economic recession, for instance), it may decide to embark on such a strategy with the hope of recovering later. In such a case, emphasis will be on strategies to reduce the size of the workforce by natural attrition and/or by means of retrenchment/redundancy packages. Should people still be required in certain critical areas because of voluntary separations in those areas, the emphasis will only be on short-term employment relationships.

On the other hand, if the strategy is one of innovation, the public sector institution's aim will be to deliver the best service by concentrating on bringing out new or improved services. This strategy can, however, only be considered if there is the will to employ, train for, and facilitate worker creativity and flexibility.

Thus, although many textbooks on general strategic management deal with the human side of things only when strategy implementation is discussed (focusing on aspects like leadership, culture and reward), it is clear that human resource issues should also be viewed and dealt with as an integral part of the strategy formulation phase. When the senior management of a public sector institution defines the vision/ mission statement of the institution, it should be borne in mind that such a statement is important also for the employees. This type of statement can go a long way in getting employees to identify with the institution and to support it or to be committed. Such a mission statement should not only outline the typical service orientation of the institution, but it should also be 'employee friendly' and explicitly state what the institution's stance towards the management of employee-related affairs is. Furthermore, when SWOT analyses are executed as part of strategy formulation, it is often realised that many of the external threats/opportunities and/or the internal strengths/weaknesses are actually related to human resources.

Similarly, the design of organisational structures (the notion of 'structure follows strategy') relates to the way in which the work of the institution is organised – and this is clearly a people-related issue. The same holds true for a strategy implementation issue such as trying to elicit and maintain employee behaviour that will be in line with what is required. Rewarding employees for behaving/performing in such a way that strategy is implemented is clearly a human resource management issue.

Not so long ago, public sector human resource management followed the incremental pattern of planning for human resource activities. These planning options mainly related to the tradition that all public sector work (including the human resource function) was associated with budgeting, and that all decisions needed to centre on budget allocations. This led to the incremental approach of managing public affairs, in which the search for alternative solutions to a problem was ceased when a satisfactory, but not necessarily optimal solution was found. It goes without saying that the result of this pattern of public sector human resource management normally resulted in minor adjustments to the status quo (Dresang 2002: 125–125).

Consequently, we were faced with a situation where matters were not looked at strategically. This meant that comprehensive solutions could not be found. In part, incrementalism, in terms of managing people strategically, means accepting current human resource positions and structures as the basic framework within which one has to operate. For example, when increases or decreases in the number of positions are foreseen human resource decisions are based on budgetary exercises. In the past, mainstream public administration has always coped with fewer people during times of budgetary constraints by not filling vacancies, rather than by analysing how they might creatively redeploy existing employees. Although routine work is essential in the human resource field to ensure that work is done consistently, it is essential that comprehensive and rational decisions are taken for long-term planning purposes.

Thus, the adoption of a more modern strategic public sector human resource management approach, excluding incrementalism, is more acceptable. Recently social psychologists told us that, despite the limits we have in terms of available information and analytical abilities, we are still in a position to identify and weigh objectives and do calculations on the best way to achieve institutional success.

> **DID YOU KNOW?**
>
> The vision, mission and values for HRM in the South African public service are as follows:
> - **Vision:** Human resource management in the public service will result in a diverse, competent and well-managed workforce, capable of and committed to delivering high-quality services to the people of South Africa.
> - **Mission:** Human resource management in the public service should become a model of excellence, in which service to society stems from individual commitment instead of compulsion. The management of people should be regarded as a significant task for those who have been charged with that responsibility and should be conducted in a professional manner.
> - **Values:** The following values, which are derived from the 1996 Constitution, will underpin human resource management in the public service: professional ethics, efficiency, effectiveness, fairness, equity, accessibility, transparency and accountability.

However, at the centre of this new strategic public sector human resource management approach lies the adoption of a set of procedures to guide those participating in the process. This is the viewpoint that we apply to strategic PSHRM in this book. The procedures are designed to direct public sector managers to act systematically and to break out of the natural mould of making human resource decisions incrementally. This is a great advantage, since it tends to lead to greater strategic success. It is important to note, however, that, although human resource-related issues and decisions are dispersed throughout the process of general strategic management, the actual process of strategic public sector human resource management can also, for the purposes of analysis and conceptualisation, be subdivided into strategy formulation, structure that follows strategy, and strategy implementation.

4.4 Towards a model for strategic public sector human resource management

McGregor (in Tompkins 1995: 32) places the strategic management of human resources on the shoulders of people at all levels of management. He is of the opinion that the application of strategic management principles requires all public sector managers to '[...] learn to think systematically about the many connections between strategy and people'. With a systematic view of strategic public sector human resource management, formal human resource plans are processed and can be seen as preceding actions. The term 'processed' has been used to embrace the fact that strategic PSHRM consists of different phases (steps), requiring public sector managers to execute the process in a logical order. However, given the complexity of human resource work, we often anticipate the results of one phase influencing the other. Therefore, the actual sequence of the phases is rarely neat and orderly (Dresang 2002: 128). But practising strategic PSHRM in the public sector may not be such an easy task. In its broadest sense of application, this depends on the size, complexity and resources of the particular public sector institution. Figure 4.1 illustrates a strategic approach to PSHRM.

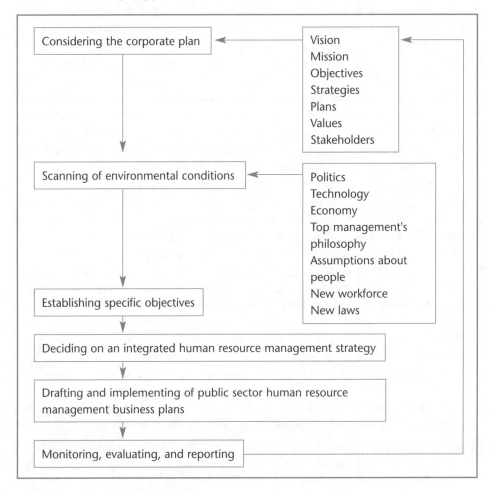

Figure 4.1   Strategic approaches to public sector human resource management

The six sections that follow will present a detailed discussion of the six phases in the strategic approach to PSHRM, as set out in Figure 4.1.

4.5   Considering the corporate plan

The importance of strategic PSHRM is that it has to start with the existing corporate plan of the relevant public sector institution. Typically, a public sector institution's corporate plan will present the scope of its operations in service delivery terms. It will spell out the 'who, why, what and whereto' of the institution. In essence, it refers to the domain that the institution stakes out for itself, and to its *raison d' être*. In this regard, all the different stakeholders of the institution have to be taken into account. In sum, the determining of the corporate plan includes the formulation of a vision, mission, objectives, strategies, and plans, the consultation of the different stakeholders, and the consideration of the relevant values that are at stake.

The fundamental purpose of a vision and mission of any public sector institution can be found in the needs of a society. If there were no need for certain services, there would be no opportunity for a public sector institution to be set up and maintained successfully. Another important aspect that has to be specifically catered for in the corporate plan is the impact of the various stakeholders on the human resource function. For example, the Department of Public Service and Administration plays an essential role in making policies with regard to the functions and organisational arrangements of the public service and with regard to employment and other practices, such as the promotion of broad representativeness, training, salaries, service conditions and labour relations (Republic of South Africa 2000a: 7). There are also other important stakeholder groups, such as political office bearers, the Public Service Commission, trade unions, employment agencies, professional bodies, the Treasury, the media and the broader community (Cheminais, Bayat, Van der Waldt, & Fox 1998: 37–40).

Another important aspect that impacts on the corporate plan is the values underlying PSHRM at a particular point in time. Nowhere in the field of public administration is the contest between the competing values played out more clearly than in the arena of human resource management (Denhardt 1995: 197). Public human resource systems continuously undergo transformation as a result of conflicting value orientations in the broader society. These value orientations are then shaped into political priorities in the form of legislation, executive orders, or judicial decisions (Tompkins 1995: 53). After some time, these values are clearly

SPOTLIGHT ON THE LAW 4.1
Unfair discrimination against an insulin-dependent diabetic

Section (6)(2)(b) of the Employment Equity Act 55 of 1998 provides that it is not unfair to 'distinguish, exclude or prefer any person on the basis of an inherent requirement of a job'. The complexity of the plea that discrimination is related to the 'inherent requirements of a particular job' is illustrated in *Independent Municipal & Allied Workers Union v City of Cape Town* (2005) 26 ILJ 1404 (LC). In this case, the City of Cape Town had imposed a blanket ban on the employment of insulin-dependent diabetics as fire-fighters. One of the employees, employed in the security services division of the City of Cape Town, applied for a post as fire-fighter. The municipality's occupational therapists indicated that it would be unsafe to the applicant, his colleagues and the public to employ him as a fire-fighter. The argument in this case was whether the municipality could fairly impose a blanket ban on the employment of insulin-dependent diabetics as fire-fighters. The Labour Court found that the blanket ban of the municipality was 'paternalistic' and offended the dignity of diabetics and their right to follow their chosen calling. The court ordered the municipality to employ the applicant as a fire-fighter if he passed the relevant employment tests.

Source: Grogan (2008: 298)

reflected in human resource management practices, processes and systems, and generally come to the surface in themes such as efficiency, effectiveness, equity and responsiveness. Managerial concern for applying these values may, during particular periods, differ from time to time, depending on the policies of the political party in power. Some values may be more influential than others. Currently, employment equity is regarded as one of the strategic values in the field. Spotlight on the Law 4.1 on page 96 has a look at one such case study.

4.6   Scanning of environmental conditions

As stressed before, PSHRM takes place in a political environment. In practice, this means that human resource decisions are affected by the interplay of politics and the issues surrounding the political arena. These political considerations become even more evident in the application of the different human resource management rules and regulations. For young appointees, things occasionally do not work out on the job as they originally expected because of the politics involved in the human resource environment. It has often happened in the past that students entering the public sector, who viewed their jobs in terms of the rational application of professional human resource expertise, soon became frustrated and left the service because of the involvement of political role players in the field. Thompson (in Tompkins 1995: 22) distinguishes, in this regard, between elective and generic personnel politics, as two categories of role players affecting the managing of human resource-related issues in the public sector.

On the one hand, elective personnel politics refers to the involvement of elected officials in the employment decisions of senior officials to ensure the public sector's responsiveness to political agendas. Generic personnel politics, on the other hand, refers to the attempts of various role players, such as political appointees, career public servants, legislators and interest group representatives, to change the nature and content of human resource policies. For example, human resource policies, such as employee rights, affirmative action and sexual harassment have often been used by these people as vehicles to mobilise change in the public sector. What is required, though, by those involved in the strategic PSHRM process, is a full understanding of the political issues involved in the environment and an ability to distinguish legitimate political demands from potentially illegitimate ones.

The human resource sub-system is seen as being influenced not only by politics but also by other factors in the external environment.

Human resource strategies do not exist in isolation, and they are essentially formulated to be used offensively or defensively to mediate between the preferences and frames of reference of management and the perceived environmental threats, opportunities, and constraints. Environmental influences need not, however, be accepted passively. Really proactive public sector managers will attempt to influence or shape their environments, even though such an approach will not necessarily make them immune to forces in the external environment.

It should be noted, however, that the 'external' environment does not only refer to factors or forces external to the institution, but also to those internal to the institution's human resource system. This means that, when environmental scanning is done from the perspective of human resource strategy formulation, not only are the relevant factors in the political, economic, social and technological (PEST) environments explored, but also those related to institutionally internal variables. This requires, first of all, the alignment of the institution's general business strategies with the human resource strategies. As the business strategies are being formulated and other PEST factors are scanned, particular attention should be paid to the relevant human resource-related implications. Similarly, as decisions related to the purely financial side of a public sector institution are made within the context of certain environmental trends that are analysed, the relevant human resource implications have to be actively searched for.

The reverse is also true, however. The potential financial and business strategy implications of particular human resource strategy-related factors have to be seriously considered when senior management does environmental analyses for the purpose of business strategy formulation. In order for the whole institutional system to be successful, all of the parts or sub-systems must work together. This is why it is so important to execute an integrated environmental scanning process.

? DID YOU KNOW?

The public service is currently experiencing several changes that impact their HR functions, including having greater exposure to the financial year (business cycle) fluctuations due to the weak economic conditions, the unwillingness of legislators to raise taxes, being under greater pressure from constituents to operate according to private sector efficiency principles, and facing greater competition from private-sector employers looking for workers with unique skill sets. In addition, the public service, along with many other public employers throughout the economy, also have to respond to growing demands from public officials to promote better work-life balance. For all of these reasons and more, public HRM scholars and practitioners need to take a much closer look at creative HRM strategies.

Source: Mastracci (2009: 20)

At this stage, you may wonder which particular factors need to be analysed. To draw up a complete list in this regard is neither possible nor feasible. Each public sector institution is different, and each institution's environmental make-up differs. However, there are two key characteristics of the public service environment that impact on the human resource function at present. These are a changing corps of workers and restructuring. A demographic survey unveiled in December 2002 showed that the public service in South Africa was acquiring a new, dynamic and changing corps of workers. The survey indicated that representative figures had already reached a stage where the race and gender composition of the public service was approaching a situation in which the make-up of the public service mirrored the make-up of the South African population. Table 4.1 gives an indication of the composition of the public service numbers by race and gender.

Table 4.1   Public servants distribution by race and gender as at October 2009

Race	Male	Female	Total	%
African	142 890	78 961	221 851	73.6
Asian	5 051	2 738	7 789	2.6
Coloured	20 150	11 105	31 255	10.4
White	23 337	16 895	40 232	13.4
Total	191 429	109 699	301 127	100
Percentage	63.6	36.4	100	

Source: Republic of South Africa (2010: 13)

In 1998, white males numbered 91 701, while in 2002 they were at 70 991. This clearly shows that the presence of white males is decreasing in the public service and that women are becoming the dominant group of workers. This has serious implications for PSHRM from a strategic perspective. Dual-career couples and single parents are some of the issues to address in this regard. This social trend calls for family involvement on the part of the government. An integral step in the development of strategic human resource interventions is the putting in operation of flexitime systems, nursery schools and maternity leave arrangements (including paternity leave benefits for the male worker) (Van der Westhuizen 2000: 60–61).

Another key characteristic of the public service environment that influences the human resource function strategically is the restructuring processes of the government that take place on a continuous basis. An essential element of the public service's transformation programme concerns the restructuring and rationalisation of the public service (Republic of South Africa 1995: 43). As a result of the apartheid system from 1948 to 1994, the public service was significantly fragmented structurally when the new constitutional dispensation came into force in 1994. Owing to these structural backlogs, efficient and effective service delivery was seriously affected. Thus, the situation was changed extensively, and the government embarked upon a comprehensive programme of administrative restructuring and rationalisation in creating a unified public service. One consequence of this was the welding together of the former four TBVC countries (Transkei, Bophuthatswana, Venda and Ciskei) and the nine self-governing areas (for example Lebowa and Kangwane) into a single integrated South African public service. This programme had, and still has, a dramatic impact on HRM, in which strategic processes such as downsizing, rightsizing, outsourcing and re-engineering were used to achieve the required results.

Now that we have discussed the contemporary environment within which public sector managers operate, let us elaborate on certain other environmental factors that affect the human resource function and for which one has to plan strategically. A further scan of the public service's environment might, for example, include the factors illustrated in Table 4.2.

Table 4.2   An environmental scan for the public service

Sector	Environmental scan
Technological developments	Hardware changes, satellites for videoconferencing, computers for word processing, CD Rom, e-mail and Internet communications, barcode scanners for registrations and office machines to send faxes and for photocopying. Non-hardware changes – management by objectives, quality circles and flexitime
Economic conditions	Interest rates, employment rates, inflations rate, strength of rand, tax revenues, budgets and recessions
Political influences	Role of elected officials, political appointees, legislators, and interest group representatives
Legal measures	Acts of Parliament, draft bills, regulations, and white papers
Resource providers	Parliament, Department of Public Service and Administration, Treasury, and Public Service Commission
Other factors	Top management's philosophy, your own basic assumptions about managing people, ethics and productivity

Source: Moore (1987: 7–12) and Van der Westhuizen (2000: 62–68)

Each of these factors will affect the human resource function's ability to attain its vision, mission, and objectives. Therefore, it requires a systematic process of strategic thinking that must be procedurally analysed. Strategic human resource decisions are required as a result of the scanning of the environment. Considering all these different factors in Table 4.2, the immediate question that arises is where to start with the scanning process. Basically, the environment can be scanned in terms of four major dimensions (Gòmez-Mejía, Balkin, & Cardy 1998: 31):

- Degree of uncertainty (how much information is available to make relevant and appropriate decisions);
- Volatility (how often the different environmental factors change);
- Magnitude of change (how drastic the changes are); and
- Complexity (how many different factors in the environment affect the organisation).

Table 4.3   Selected HR strategies for public sector institutions low and high on different environmental dimensions

Environmental dimension	Low	High
Degree of uncertainty	Detailed work planning Job-specific training Fixed pay High dependence on manager	Loose work planning Generic training Variable pay Multiple inputs for appraisals
Volatility	Control emphasis Efficient outputs Job-specific training Fixed pay	Flexibility Innovation Generic training Variable pay
Magnitude of change	Explicit job descriptions Formal hiring 'Make skills' Uniform appraisal procedures	Broad job classes Informal hiring 'Buy skills' Customised appraisals
Complexity	Control emphasis Internal recruitment Centralised pay decisions High dependence on manager	Flexibility External recruitment Decentralised pay decisions Multiple inputs for appraisal

Source: Gòmez-Mejia et al. (1998: 31)

It is clear from Table 4.3 that public sector institutions that are high on all four of these dimensions are more likely to benefit from human resource strategies that promote flexibility, diversity innovation, adaptability, decentralisation, integration, competition and responsiveness. As can also be seen from the above list, public sector institutions facing environmental factors that are low on uncertainty, volatility, magnitude of change and complexity will benefit from human resource strategies that allow for rationality, centralisation and orderliness, with a relatively predictable and stable environment. Normally, public service institutions tend to fall at the low end of the scale on all four of these dimensions. Therefore, public service type human resource strategies may tend to be more mechanistic in nature with an emphasis on activities such as performance appraisal as a developmental tool, individual-based pay, and a continuing concern for the terminated employee (Gòmez-Mejia *et al.* 1998: 32). (Also see Chapter 6 on affirmative action, a particular environmental factor that has to be constantly monitored in South Africa nowadays.)

In the process of analysing all such environmental factors, different methodologies can be used, including interviews with experts, scenario planning and document reviews. Typically, the aim would thus be not only to identify the variables but also to analyse how these factors may impact on the public service institution, the work that is to be done, the employees who have to do the work, and especially the managerial employees who have to manage the people -including the institution's HR department/section.

4.7 Establishing specific objectives

As emphasised in Section 4.5, strategic PSHRM must be based on the corporate plan of the public service institution. After the corporate plan has been consulted and the environment has been scanned, specific objectives can be established that will support the corporate plan (Fisher, Schoenfeldt, & Shaw 1990: 694). Formulating the institution's objectives with regard to its human resource systems thus requires an explicit statement outlining the means by which management intends to manage the relationship between the institution and its employees as important stakeholders. In the process of shaping this part of the institution's corporate plan, the crucial linkup and integration between human resource management and general management of operational affairs is thus to be facilitated (Byars & Rue 1997: 118). In the process of establishing objectives, management gives the public-sector institution and its members direction and purpose that could have the following important benefits (Fisher *et al.* 1990: 694):

- Objectives are a source of motivation in the sense that they describe the purpose of the institution to all members involved.
- Objectives serve as guidelines for all of the actions in the institution.
- Objectives provide the foundation for all decisions that need to be taken by different individuals and groups.
- Objectives also become the basis for the managing of work performance.

Basically, one can use two approaches in establishing human resource objectives strategically. One approach to objective setting begins at the top of the public sector institution where senior management formulates a statement of vision and mission that defines the institution's current and future service-delivery levels over the long term (Byars & Rue 1997: 118–119). This is referred to as the 'top-down' approach. Sometimes this type of objective-setting is vague and contradictory and could end in political compromise or very generally stated objectives (Dresang 2002: 127). These long-range objectives are formulated according to the institution's corporate plan. For example, it is stated in Section 195(1)(i) of the 1996 Constitution that public administration must be broadly representative of the South African people. This is a very general objective and it is not always easy to translate it into specific and exact human resource objectives. Another approach to objective-setting might be referred to as 'bottom-up'. Here, the objectives should be stated in terms of expected results and be short-term related, based on the content of long-term objectives. This approach to objective setting in strategic PSHRM emphasises that short-term objectives should have a time schedule, be expressed quantitatively, and involve all levels of management in the process. This has been referred to as the cascade approach. If properly used, the bottom-up approach involves both line function employees and HR specialists in the overall strategic PSHRM process. Especially during the early stages of the strategic PSHRM process, human resource specialists can play a vital role in influencing objective setting by providing correct and timely information about the organisation's human resources. To explain short-term objective setting in a less dry and abstract manner, we may consider an example of representativeness and affirmative action. In the White Paper on the Transformation of the Public Service (Republic of South Africa 1995) objectives are proposed that have specific time frames and are measurable. It is proposed that, within four years, all public service institutions must endeavour to be at least 50% black at management level. During the same period, at least 30% of new recruits to the middle and senior management echelons should be women.

4.8 Deciding on an integrated human resource strategy

In the process of determining a specific strategy, senior management has to make certain important decisions. Before we discuss in some detail the nature of particular strategic options, it is important first to reflect briefly on what decision making entails in this context.

The implementation of human resource strategies involves strategic choices (decisions) among specific human resource practices. These strategic human resource choices (decisions) are the different options that public sector management has available in designing its human resource systems. These institutions' choices (decisions) are strategic because they affect the institution's overall performance levels (in terms of service delivery) and therefore can be favourable or unfavourable in the long run. There are of course many different programmes that can be used separately

Performance appraisal	
Customised appraisals	Uniform appraisal procedures
Developmental appraisals	Control-oriented appraisals
Multi-purpose appraisals	Narrow focused appraisals
Training and development	
Individual training	Team-based training
On-the-job-training	External training
Job-specific training	Generic training
Remuneration	
Fixed pay	Variable pay
Job-based pay	Individual-based pay
Seniority-based pay	Performance-based pay

Source: Adapted from Fisher, Schoenfeldt and Shaw (1990: 696) and Gòmez-Mejia et al. (1998: 23)

Figure 4.2 Selective strategic HR choices

or together to implement a specific choice that has been opted for. Consideration of a public sector human resource programme, such as pay for performance, can lead to several alternatives or to the specific choice (decision) of a particular direction in which the public sector institution should move. Pay for performance, for example, may incorporate strategic human resource choices (decisions) or alternatives such as cash awards, lump-sum annual bonuses, raises based on performance appraisals, and an employee-of-the-month award (Gòmez-Mejia *et al.* 1998: 22). In Figure 4.2 on page 103, selective strategic human resource choices are compared with each other on two opposite poles of a continuum.

It is important to bear in mind that this list of strategic human resource choices is not exhaustive. Also bear in mind that very few public sector institutions fall at these extremes of the continuum. It is likely that some institutions will be closer to the right, some closer to the left, and some closer to the middle. Let's consider the three areas of choice more closely:

- **Performance appraisal:** In many ways, performance appraisal is the linchpin in strategic PSHRM. It involves the assessment of the work performance of all employees at all levels. There is a wide range of strategic human resource choices that public sector managers have at their disposal for performance appraisal. Some strategic human resource choices available are: (1) developing an appraisal system that is customised for specific employee groups (for example, by designing a different performance appraisal system for each group of posts versus using a uniform performance appraisal system throughout the public sector institution; (2) utilising the results of the appraisal data as a developmental tool to assist public sector employees improving their performance levels versus using performance appraisals as a control mechanism to iron out weak performers; and (3) designing the performance appraisal system with more than one objective in mind (for example, training, promotion, and selection decisions) versus designing it for a single objective (such as pay decisions).
- **Training and development:** Broadly speaking, training and development activities are implemented to help a public sector institution meet its knowledge and skill requirements. In addition, training and development efforts also help its employees to realise their maximum potential. Two aspects of training and development are receiving attention in the public sector. First, public sector institutions that are not committed to improving the work performance levels of their own employees will seek to employ skilled workers from external sources. There is nothing wrong with this type of human resource choice, because, during times of rapid change, this is sometimes the only way to acquire the needed expertise. The second human resource choice is made by public sector institutions that prefer to develop expertise in-house. In addition, public sector institutions face several strategic human resource choices in training and developing their employees. These may include: (1) deciding whether to provide training opportunities to individual employees or to teams; (2) deciding whether to opt for on-the-job-training or to

make use of external training opportunities; and (3) deciding whether to focus on job-specific training or generic training.

- **Remuneration:** Remuneration is any form of payment that public sector employees receive in exchange for their labour that is provided to a public sector institution. All remuneration levels and allowances are determined centrally by the Minister of Public Service and Administration for those employees who fall within the ambit of the Labour Relations Act 66 of 1995 and work in the public service. The strategic human resource choices (decisions) made with respect to remuneration are particularly important in implementing a specific human resource strategy, since public service institutions, generally, spend more than 70% of their budgets on personnel expenditure. This figure is an indication that, perhaps more than in any other area of PSHRM, remuneration practices should present the most important human resource choices. Some strategic human resource choices pertaining to remuneration are: (1) providing public sector employees with fixed salary scales, allowances, and benefit packages that change incrementally from year to year versus providing them with a variable range of salaries, allowances and benefit packages according to work performance; (2) remunerating public sector employees on the grading particulars of the job versus remunerating them for their individual contributions made to the institution; and (3) remunerating employees according to the exact time they have worked for the institution public sector versus remunerating them for the work performance delivered.

4.8.1 Strategy options

The success of strategic PSHRM is dependent on how well it matches all the other factors involved. Throughout all the attempts, one should always strive towards that one powerful prediction for human resource strategies, which is that particular match or 'fit' which will lead to better performance (service delivery) by the public sector institution as a whole. Basically, the concept of 'fit' refers to compatibility between human resource strategies and other key managerial and operational factors of the institution. There are obviously many of these factors facing public sector institutions, and, correspondingly, many fit options to consider in determining which human resource strategies will have a positive impact on the performance levels of the institution. The following institutional law is relevant in this regard: the relative contribution of a human resource strategy to the performance levels of a public sector institution increases in terms of: (1) the greater the fit between human resource strategies and the institution's overall corporate strategy; (2) the greater the extent to which the human resource strategy is in line with the environment in which the institution delivers its services; (3) the more the human resource strategy is correlated to the unique institutional features (features such as history, culture, leadership style, technology, senior management's philosophy and productivity concerns); and (4) the more human resource strategies enable the institution to benefit from its distinctive competencies (Gòmez-Mejia *et al.* 1998: 26–27).

It is clear that it is useful to conceptualise the different strategic options in the field of PSHRM. Decide what approach will be followed in managing the individual and collective dimensions within the relevant public sector institution. The individual and collective dimensions must be integrated at the stage at which the appropriate core idea and approach are evaluated. Obviously, the size of the relevant public sector institution and the complexity of service delivery options that are involved will play an important role in determining the individual and collective dimensions of strategy selection. Generally, strategy options take one of two generic forms: corporate strategy and business strategy. These options are summarised below.

4.8.1.1 Corporate strategy

The corporate strategy refers to the mix of activities, tasks, processes, practices and services the public service as a whole (single entity) decides to hold and the flow of resources (financial, physical, information and human resources) among those activities. This predominant overall corporate strategy is also referred to as a 'grand' strategy. In fact, the corporate strategy is a major plan of action for achieving the objectives of the public sector as a whole rather than those of a single public sector institution. A decision has to be made at senior management level (normally in the Department of Public Service and Administration) regarding the type of corporate strategy in which to get involved. The new 'Public Service Management Framework' (which is a management policy guideline compiled by the Department of Public Service and Administration) is an example of a corporate strategy followed at present in the public service as a whole. The new framework entails changing the way the public service operates in order to provide better services to the citizens.

It is a radical change from the past – the focus is now on the delivery of efficient and effective services as opposed to the past where the focus was on the preoccupation with rules and regulations for which the public service is so well known. It is an integrated approach to PSHRM to ensure that services are shaped to the needs of the citizens. In terms of the new Public Service Management Framework, it is expected of public sector institutions to: (1) establish and sustain a service delivery improvement programme and publish an annual statement of public service commitment; (2) develop policies or guidelines on internal work institution; (3) develop employment equity plans; and (4) develop manuals about how to implement and manage delegations (Republic of South Africa 1999: 15–36).

It is possible to see opportunities that might arise in seeking to link the above corporate strategy of the public service to strategic PSHRM options. Particularly, the establishment of a service delivery improvement programme may raise a strategic human resource issue of training and development, especially for front-line service personnel. This corporate strategy of service delivery improvement has brought renewed attention to a culture and ethos of service delivery (Republic of South Africa 1995: 17). Obviously, front-line service personnel are not properly trained in the principle of quality service delivery where the citizen comes first, and this human resource option needs to be redressed.

There are two major types of corporate strategy and matching human resource strategies, namely the stability strategy and the evolutionary strategy.

The stability strategy

This is a strategy in which citizens are served on the same service delivery level, which focuses on the same objectives, and which only seeks gradual improvement in performance levels. By following this strategy, a public sector institution sees the environment as not having such a significant influence on the daily activities and offering rather limited opportunities for expansion. Although, in this day, strategies based on stability will in practice be unlikely, especially in the light of the continuous changing environmental challenges we are faced with, such possibilities still cannot be completely excluded.

There are several human resource options available when one is opting for a strategy of stability. For public sector institutions pursuing this strategy, the most prominent human resource issues relate to utilising and developing employees. In this case, public sector managers know that there is little opportunity for upward mobility and there are no substantial opportunities for advancement. Human resource strategy options most appropriate under these stable environmental conditions are as follows: emphasising of efficiency detailed work planning, long-term career development, centralisation, a paternalistic attitude (reflected, for example, in a preferential approach towards laid-off employees when economic conditions improve, and retention of talented workers), focus on the motivation of employees, employment security, formal human resource planning, staffing from within, broad career paths, job enrichment, and employee involvement (Gòmez-Mejia *et al.* 1998: 27).

The evolutionary strategy

The evolutionary strategy involves   to its fullest capacity. To understand fully what is meant by change management, one has to look at the broader role of the state in society and the impact it has on public service delivery. In more recent years, many countries, including South Africa, have embarked on a thorough re-evaluation of the role of the state and the public sector. This could be attributed to a number of factors operating in the broader public sector environment. For example, the growing impact of international public administration, the increasing trend towards political democratisation, and the increasing international spread of communication and information technology.

DID YOU KNOW?

The relevant themes for change management in the public service are:
- A move away from centralised and corporate planning;
- A new role of the state to that of guiding and facilitating development;
- Trimming state expenditure and the size of the public service;
- Sub-contracting of public services to private sector and non-governmental agencies;
- Ensuring greater accountability and devolution of managerial authority and resource control;
- Increasing emphasis on quality, efficiency and cost-effectiveness;
- Developing a more effective citizen/customer orientation and a stronger service ethos;
- Increasing emphasis on human resource development and participative management;
- Improving financial planning and control systems; and
- Greater reliance on information technology and computerised management information systems.

Source: Adapted from the White Paper on the Transformation of the Public Service (Republic of South Africa 1995: 23–24)

Almost every theme presented above has serious human resource implications. Since 1995 till today, the government has developed many sophisticated devices to design the operations of public sector institutions. Many of these devices are based on change management theory principles with their origin mainly vested in the concept of managerialism. At the most general level, managerialism is a set of beliefs and practices that assume that social progress now lies through the achievement of continuing increases in economically defined productivity. It is further believed that increased productivity can only be realised by applying more sophisticated technologies. This can only be achieved through responsible public sector managers with a labour force that is disciplined in accordance with the productivity ideal.

Human resource options to best fit the above evolutionary corporate strategies include strategies, such as flexibility, diversity, decentralisation and entrepreneurship (Republic of South Africa 1997: 22–23). The implication of adopting these options, when applied to the management of human resources, is significant. It will mean that public service institutions will have to introduce early retirement opportunities, carry out comprehensive auditing of skills and competencies, appoint people from outside the public service, introduce redeployment, the development of new organisational cultures, total quality management, and training programmes to promote affirmative action, redirect human resources from administrative tasks to service provision, and implement a code of conduct (Republic of South Africa 1995: 43–72).

Perhaps one of the most complex human resource challenges, when opting for the evolutionary corporate strategy, is restructuring and rationalisation. Numerous programmes of restructuring and rationalisation have been reported in the South African public service since 1994. These moves were mainly undertaken to create

DID YOU KNOW?

In moving towards the principles of change management (in other words, transformation) the government has identified the following strategic evolutionary priority areas for transformation:

- Rationalising and restructuring to ensure a unified, integrated and leaner public service;
- Institution building and management to promote greater accountability and organisational and managerial effectiveness;
- Representativeness and affirmative action;
- Transforming service delivery to meet basic needs and redress past imbalances;
- Democratisation of the state;
- Human resource development;
- Employment conditions and labour relations; and
- Promotion of a professional service ethos.

Source: Republic of South Africa (1995: 25)

a unified and integrated public service. This could basically be seen as a 'merger' between the former administrations in South Africa, the TBVC states (Transkei, Bophuthatswana, Venda and Ciskei) and the self-governing territories (for example, Lebowa). In practice, the creation of a unified public service has involved three related processes, namely: (1) transferring of functions and organisational components from the above-mentioned units to the new national departments and provincial administrations; (2) rationalising of conditions of service; and (3) staffing of the new rationalised structures (Republic of South Africa 1995: 43).

There is evidence that the success rate of these unification and integration processes (in other words, mergers) is not very high. Some, if not all of these programmes, have experienced human resource management constraints. In the past, it proved to be a time-consuming process, which of course is not surprising, given the magnitude and complexity of the task. It has also resulted in uncertainty among staff and disrupted continuity, which has ultimately affected productivity levels negatively. However, human resource specialists can play an important role in both the pre- and post-unification and integration processes. Some guidelines for human resource specialists involved in a unification and integration process are presented on page 110.

4.8.1.2 Business strategy

Whereas corporate strategies apply to the entire public service, business strategies refer to the formulation and implementation of strategies for separate organisational components (for example, national government departments and provincial administrations) even if they are part of the larger public sector. This implies that public service institutions must develop their own human resource and work organisation policies, procedures, practices, manuals, guides, employment equity

Guidelines for human resource specialists for dealing with a unification and integration process (merger)

- Insist on early involvement, even as the combination is being considered. This allows a preventative stance.
- Document everything – record as much as possible in writing.
- Learn the other organisation's culture and plan for any possible cultural mismatch.
- As planning progresses, adopt a plan, announce, act – always announce beforehand so that those who are involved know what is going on.
- Inform those employees who are affected as soon as possible so that they can plan accordingly.
- Eliminate the 'we/they' attitude by mixing employees as much as possible at all levels in the newly established organisation.
- Communicate the process in all directions, through all the media and formal and informal leaders and to work groups.

Source: Adapted from Fisher et al. *(1990: 706)*

plans, delegations and authorisations according to their service-delivery objectives. This is very different from the past, when all these business strategies were determined centrally (Republic of South Africa 1999: 5). A business strategy can be regarded as an attempt to establish harmony between the broader public service's corporate strategy and the separate public service institution's business strategy. In addition, all efforts need to be in congruence with the external and internal factors in the environment. Two broad strategy options within the business strategy have been defined: the prospector and defender options.

The prospector strategy

Very generally the prospector strategy is associated with flexible, decentralised organisational structures and unstable environments that change rapidly to facilitate innovation and creativity among staff (Gòmez-Mejia *et al.* 1998: 30). The public service's present corporate strategy of decentralised management, where the aim is to minimise waste and maximise value, allows for flexible and creative prospector strategies. In this case, service standards are high on the priority list. Human resource strategies that match the orientation of a prospector strategy involve a wide range of options. Public service institutions pursuing a prospector strategy, for example, tend to go for external recruitment. Normally, prospectors try to recruit experienced, well-skilled employees from the outside.

In general, practitioners in the field increasingly focus on creative HRM strategies for attracting and retaining employees with special skills and institutional knowledge. An example of how the public service can effectively strategise for recruitment is set out in Focus on Research 4.1 on page 111.

FOCUS ON RESEARCH 4.1
Management strategies for recruiting

RESEARCH

This study sets out to examine the estimated effects of various job characteristics of IT professionals' (in the public sector) motivations to find different jobs. The researcher looked at several factors to predict employees' turnover intentions, including competitive compensation, opportunities for job security and professional advance, and control over work schedules.

The following hypotheses were used for the study:
- **H1:** Rates of compensation comparable to the private sector will increase the probability of an IT professional to work in federal government.
- **H2:** Greater opportunities for job security and professional advance will increase the probability of an IT professional to choose to work for the public sector rather than a private sector organisation.
- **H3:** Higher degrees of control over work schedules and worker self-determination related to work schedules will increase the probability of an IT professional to choose to work for the public sector rather than a private sector employer.

The research study revealed the following results:
- H1 is supported because it was determined through the study that higher compensation did increase the probability of an IT professional to work in the public sector.
- H2 is not supported by the evidence. It was found that greater opportunities for employment in the public sector than in the private sector may or may not increase the probability of an IT professional to work in the public sector. Greater employment opportunities in the public sector could spur flight to that sector.
- H3 is fully contradicted. Higher degrees of control over work schedules and worker self-determination related to work schedules actually decreased the probability of an IT professional to work in the public sector.

Source: Mastracci (2009: 30–32)

Another popular human resource strategy option for prospectors is to use results-oriented performance appraisal methods. In other words, prospectors appraise on the basis of final results – the need is for divergent, creative and unprogrammed behaviour to cope with changing environmental factors.

The defender strategy

Unlike prospectors, whose success primarily comes from efficiently serving a changing environment, the defender's key objective is to focus on improving the efficiency and effectiveness of existing work activities. Defenders prefer to maintain a secure position in a stable environment instead of expanding into new territory (Gòmez-Mejia *et al.* 1998: 29). In addition, defenders follow highly formal management patterns, they make use of organisational structures that are heavily centralised, and they seldom make major adjustments in their operations and technologies. The public service under the previous political dispensation (before 1994), in which public service delivery was to a great extent heavily centralised, provides an example of a defender strategy. The public service inherited by the current government promoted in many ways the social, economic, and political system of apartheid. Many human resource problems arose from the apartheid system because of the defender principles applied. Consider the following examples.

Because public sector employees were hired according to rigid apartheid rules and regulations, certain race groups (mainly blacks) were excluded from the staffing processes. This led to a lack of representativeness of all the people of South Africa in terms of race, gender and disability. Another aspect that needs special attention, which is an indication that a strong defender strategy was followed under the previous system, is the application of centralised control measures and top-down management principles (Republic of South Africa 1995: 17–18). Even more important to observe is the fact that the public service system was strongly oriented towards control of the majority of people's social lives. This resulted in a system in which public service institutions were highly authoritarian, centralised and rule bound in their service-delivery activities. Human resource defender strategy options that best correlate defenders' needs do not take risks. They tend to implement their defender strategy by appointing at the entry level and then developing their own high-level employees. Defenders focus on promoting their own employees. Therefore, they often get involved in extensive in-house training and development (Fisher *et al.* 1990: 711).

4.9 Drafting and implementing of PSHRM business plans

In essence, business plans are documents detailing the more medium-term plans and objectives of the organisation. Typically, such business plans cover five-year periods and are redrafted annually within the context of corporate planning, which is carried out in order to ensure the necessary fit between internal and external environments on a continuous basis. Taking into account the environmental scanning information, the SWOT analysis, the strategy decided upon, and the public sector institution's current and future strategic postures, medium-term moves are formulated to facilitate vision and mission accomplishment. Business plans will thus focus in more detail on various functional areas and on what ought to be done in these areas, by whom and how, in order to get strategy (corporate/business) implemented and to thus facilitate goal achievement. These business plans then typically form the basis for short-term, annual action plans. On the basis of such action plans, annual budgets are integrated to allow for appropriate resource allocation. In other words, resources (such as money, people, time, and information) are allocated so that action plans can be carried out, which in turn facilitates execution of the business plan, finally leading to strategy implementation, and vision and mission accomplishment.

When drafting the HRM business plan, the concept of fit is of crucial importance. Not only must the HR business plan fit the HRM strategy, but it must also fit the internal and external environmental factors – most notably the public sector institution's general corporate strategy.

In the process of drafting a business plan for human resource management, it is thus necessary not only to ensure that the business plan fits the HRM corporate strategy but also that the HRM corporate strategy's fit with the business strategy will be facilitated by the execution of the HRM business plan. In other words, the HRM business plan's purpose should basically be to put into operation or bring about the concept of fit between general corporate strategy and HRM business strategy. Although the selection/choice of an appropriate HRM corporate strategy must itself ensure that there is an alignment between corporate and HRM strategy, the various elements of the business plan must now clarify how the necessary fit will be achieved.

The above should serve to clarify some links between corporate strategy and HRM strategy. When drafting and implementing HRM business plans, the challenge lies in identifying the key areas or strategic priorities that require attention over the medium term in order to facilitate corporate strategy implementation. It may, for instance, be necessary to redesign the work, to rewrite job descriptions, to recruit new employees with different characteristics, to design a new performance management system and/or to redesign the institution's remuneration system. The emphasis thus shifts to different functional aspects of HRM, selecting the required strategic change interventions in each area and assigning responsibilities and allocating time limits in respect of each functional intervention. In this way, appropriate objectives can be formulated in order to monitor progress over time.

4.10 Monitoring, evaluating and reporting

The final step in the strategic PSHRM process is the monitoring, evaluating and reporting of results. An aspect of monitoring and evaluating that needs special attention is that it requires standards against which results can be measured. The message to convey is that, without these set standards, it is almost impossible to determine success or failure. Normally, monitoring and evaluating begins by comparing the vision, mission, and objectives that have been originally established with the final accomplishment (Dresang 2002: 141).

However, a monitoring and evaluating effort that ends with matching objectives and looking at accomplishments is incomplete. It is important that monitoring and evaluating be incorporated with reporting, and the government has realised the importance of this aspect. The particular format used to do reporting on human resource issues in the public service is addressed in the Public Service Regulations of 2001, Part III, J. The human resource report shall be compiled annually and submitted to Parliament, and shall include such information on planning, service delivery, organisation matters, job evaluation, remuneration, benefits, personnel expenditure, affirmative action, recruitment, promotions, termination of services, performance management, skills development, injury on duty, labour relations, leave and discharge due to ill health.

In general, strategic PSHRM rarely delivers in practice what it promises in theory. Unfortunately, it is not possible to know beforehand whether a public sector human resource programme will meet its vision, mission and objectives, and therefore a periodic monitoring and evaluation of human resource programmes is also necessary. Below is a series of important questions that should serve as a guideline in evaluating the appropriateness of human resource programmes.

Questions for testing the appropriateness of public sector human resource programmes

- Are the HR programmes effective tools for implementing HR strategies?
  - Are the proposed HR programmes the most appropriate ones for implementing the institution's HR strategies?
  - Has an analysis been done of how each of the past, current or planned HR programmes contributes to or hinders the successful implementation of the institution's HR strategies?
  - Can the proposed HR programmes be easily changed or modified to meet new strategic considerations without violating either a 'psychological' or a legal contract with public sector employees?
- Do the HR programmes meet resource constraints?
  - Does the public sector institution have the capacity (is it realistic) to implement the proposed HR programmes?
  - Are the proposed programmes leading to widespread confusion and will they create resistance among employees?
- How will the HR programmes be communicated?
  - Are the proposed HR programmes well understood by those who will implement them?
  - Does senior management understand how the proposed programmes are intended to affect the public sector institution's strategic objectives?
- Who will put the HR programmes in motion?
  - Is the HR department responsible for carrying out the proposed HR programmes?
  - Is senior management visibly and emphatically committed to the proposed programmes?

Source: Adapted from Gómez-Mejía et al. (1998: 34)

To be judged successful from the human resource side, you will have to evaluate how effectively you have used your human resources. HR audits are an effective tool that HR departments can use in monitoring and evaluating HR programmes. The following is a broad set of questions that can be asked during the HR audit (Gómez-Mejía *et al.* 1998: 36–37):

- Is the turnover rate exceptionally low or high?
- Are the people who are quitting good public sector employees who are frustrated in their present job, or are they marginal performers?
- Is the public sector institution achieving results from the funds it spends on recruitment and training, for example?
- Is the public sector institution complying with all regulatory guidelines?

- How well is the public sector institution managing employee diversity?
- Is the HR department providing the services that line staff need?
- Are HRM policies and procedures assisting the public sector institution in accomplishing its objectives?

4.11 Review

The focus of this chapter has been on the nature of strategy and strategic management and on the way in which public sector human resource management can be linked with the general strategic management of public sector institutions. The emphasis has been on options, choices and decision making in the formulation of human resource management strategies that have to match or fit the internal and external environmental conditions of the public sector institution. We have devoted special attention to the necessity of aligning the public sector institution's human resource strategies with its general corporate strategies.

Furthermore, we have explored a model for strategic PSHRM, including the steps you will need to know in managing public sector human resources effectively. The material in this chapter contributes a knowledge base on which to build your strategic PSHRM skills. We have emphasised that the application of strategic management principles requires a systematic view of human resource matters. Therefore, it is important that one executes the strategic PSHRM process in an orderly manner as explained in the model presented in this chapter.

4.12 Self-evaluation questions

1. The strategic approach to managing human resources in the public sector has emerged as one of the most important topical issues. Do you agree or disagree with this statement? Give reasons for your answer.
2. Describe what is meant by the concept of 'strategic public sector human resource management'. Explain in your answer why it is more acceptable nowadays to exclude incrementalism from the process.
3. The strategic public sector human resource management process consists of various steps that require those involved to execute the process in a logical order. Explain this process.
4. The second step in the strategic public sector human resource management process involves the scanning of the environment. Identify some of the contemporary environmental factors impacting on the human resource function.
5. What are the various strategy options for public sector human resource management?
6. When drafting a business plan for the human resource function in the public sector, the concept of 'fit' is of crucial importance. Elaborate on this concept.
7. Are you of the opinion that monitoring, evaluating, and reporting on the results of the public sector human resource management process is essential? Provide reasons for your answer.

Bibliography

Anstey, M. 1995. Can South African industrial relations move beyond adversarialism? Some comparative perspectives on the prospects of workplace forums in South Africa. *South African Journal of Labour Relations,* 19(4), 13.

Anthony, WP, Perrewe, PL, & Kacmar, KM. 1996. *Strategic human resource management.* Orlando, FL: Dryden.

Brewster, C, & Holt Larsen, H. 1992. Human resource management in Europe: Evidence from ten countries. *The International Journal of Human Resource Management,* 3(3), 409-434.

Byars, LL, & Rue, LW. 1997. *Human resource management.* Chicago: Irwin.

Campion, M, & Thayer, P. 1985. Development and field evaluation of an interdisciplinary measure of job design. *Journal of Applied Psychology,* 70, 29-34.

Cappelli, P, & Rogovsky, N. 1996. What do new systems demand of employees? *Business Day Supplement: Mastering Management Series,* Part 5, 1 April, 2.

Cheminais, I, Bayat, S, Van der Waldt, G, & Fox, W. 1998. *The fundamentals of public personnel management.* Cape Town: Juta.

Corporate Research Foundation. 1998. *The 49 best companies to work for in South Africa.* Halfway House: Zebra.

Crous, W. 1990. 'n Nuwe Suid-Afrika op die horizon: Implikasies vir die menslike hulpbronbestuurder. *IPM Journal,* 8(8), 3.

Dale, E. 1965. *Management: Theory and practice.* New York: McGraw Hill.

Denhardt, RB. 1995. *Public administration: An action orientation.* Bonn: Wadsworth.

Dessler, G. 1981. *Personnel management: Modern concepts and techniques.* Reston, VA: Reston Publishing.

De Witt, D. 1998. HR challenges for organisational transformation. *Management Today,* 14(1), 28-31.

Dresang, DL. 2002. *Public personnel management and policy.* 4th edn. New York: Longman.

Financial Mail Corporate Report. 1998. Unilever SA: Leader of the pack? *Financial Mail,* October 23, 1-56.

Fisher, CD, Schoenfeldt, LF, & Shaw, JB. 1990. *Human resource management.* Dallas, TX: Houghton Mifflin.

Gibson, JL, Ivancevich, JM, & Donnelly, JH. 1994. *Organizations: Behavior, structure, processes.* 8th edn. Burr Ridge, IL: Irwin.

Gómez-Mejía, LR, Balkin, DB, & Cardy, RL. 1998. *Managing human resources.* Englewood Cliffs, NJ: Prentice-Hall.

Grogan, J. 2008. *Workplace Law.* Cape Town: Juta.

Hackman, JR, & Oldham, GR. 1975. Development of the job diagnostic survey. *Journal of Applied Psychology,* 60, 159-170.

Harder, JW. 1996. Search for the virtual water cooler. *Business Day Supplement: Mastering Management Series,* Part 4, 25 March, 5.

Harris, P. 1986. Building a high performance team. *Training and Development Journal,* 40 (April), 229.

Hendry, C. 1997. *Human resource management: A strategic approach to employment.* Johannesburg: Butterworth Heinemann.

Hirschohn, PA. 1988. Management ideology and environmental turbulence: Understanding labour policies in the South African gold mining industry. MSc dissertation, Oxford University.

Horwitz, FM, & Franklin, E. 1996. Flexibility is the name of the game. *Business Day Supplement: Mastering Management Series,* Part 7, 15 April, 15.

Hughes, OE. 1998. *Public management and administration: An Introduction.* New York: Palgrave.

Ivancevich, JM. 1998. *Human resource management.* Boston, MA: Irwin.

Jarvis, D. 1998. The organiser's dilemma: Union responses to industrial restructuring. *South African Labour Bulletin,* 22(5), 27-33.

Johnson, C. 1986. An outline for team building: Cooperation, collaboration and communication are the key ingredients of an effective team. Training: *The Magazine of Human Resource Development,* 23 (January), 48.

Leopold, J, Harris, L, & Watson, T. 1999. *Instructor's manual: Principles, perspectives and practice.* London: Financial Times/Pitman.

Lewis, G. 1988. *Corporate strategy in action.* London: Routledge.

Lloyd, C. 1994. *Work organisation and world class management: A critical guide.* Senderwood, Johannesburg: Red Earth.

Mastracci, SH. 2009. Evaluating HR management strategies for recruiting and retaining IT professionals in the U.S. Federal Government. *Public Personnel Management,* 38 (2), 19-34.

Moore, P. 1987. *Public personnel management: A contingency approach.* Lexington, MA: Lexington Books.

Noe, RA, Hollenbeck, JR, Gerhart, B, & Wright, PM. 1994. *Human resource management: Gaining a competitive advantage.* Boston, MA: Irwin.

Pearce, JA, & Robinson, RB. 1991. *Strategic management: Formulation, implementation and control.* Homewood, IL: Irwin.

Ray, M. 1997. Weza Sawmill. *South African Labour Bulletin,* 21(2), 51–54.

Schendel, D. 1992. Introduction to the summer 1992 special issue on 'strategy process research'. *Strategic Management Journal,* 13, 1–4.

Shani, AB, & Lau, JB. 1995. *Behavior in organizations: An experiential approach.* 6th edn. Chicago: Irwin.

Sisson, K. 1989. (Ed.). *Personnel management in Britain.* Oxford: Basil Blackwell.

Smit, PJ, & Cronje, GJ de J. 1992. *Management principles.* Cape Town: Juta.

Smith, GD, Arnold, DR, & Bizell, BG. 1988. *Business strategy and policy.* 2nd edn. Boston, MA: Houghton Mifflin.

Storey, J. 1992. *Developments in the management of human resources.* London: Blackwell.

Stott, K, & Walker, A. 1995. *Team, teamwork and teambuilding.* New York: Prentice-Hall.

Swanepoel, BJ. 1995. 'n Strategiese benadering tot die bestuur van die diensverhouding. Unpublished doctoral dissertation, University of South Africa, Pretoria.

Tapscott, D, & Caston, A. 1993. *Paradigm shift.* New York: McGraw Hill.

Tompkins, J. 1995. *Human resource management in government: Hitting the ground running.* New York: Harper Collins.

Tompkins, J. 2002. Strategic human resource management in government: Unresolved issues. *Public Personnel Management,* 31(1) 95–110.

Tyson, S. 1987. The management of the personnel function. *Journal of Management Studies,* 24(5), 523–532.

Tyson, S, & Fell, A. 1986. *Evaluating the personnel function.* London: Hutchinson.

Van der Westhuizen, EJ. 2000. Public Human Resource Management: Study guide 1 for PUB302- F. Pretoria: University of South Africa.

Vecchio, RP. 1996. *Organizational behavior.* 3rd edn. Orlando, FL: Dryden.

Wood, JD. 1996. The nature of ideology. *Business Day Supplement: Mastering Management Series,* Part 16, 10 June, 2–4.

Government regulations

Republic of South Africa. 2001. Public Service Regulations of 2001. Government Gazette, 427 (21951).

Government white papers

Republic of South Africa. 1995. White Paper on the Transformation of the Public Service. 24 November 1995. Government Gazette, 365 (16838).

Republic of South Africa. 1997. White Paper on Human Resource Management in the Public Service. 31 December 1997. Government Gazette, 390 (18595).

Government reports

Republic of South Africa. 2000a. Public Service Review Report for the Year 1999/2000. Department of Public Service and Administration.

Republic of South Africa. 2000b. Annual Report of the Department of Public Service and Administration for the Year 1999/2000. Department of Public Service and Administration. [http://www.dpsa.gov.za/docs/reports/annual99-00]

Republic of South Africa. 2010. Assessment of the state of human resource management in the public service. Pretoria; Public Service Commission.

Management guides

Republic of South Africa. 1999. Baseline Implementation Guide. Department of Public Service and Administration. [http://www.dpsa.gov.za/documents/baseline/part1]

5 Strategic public sector human resource planning

Purpose

The purpose of this chapter is to provide insight into current practice in strategic public sector human resource planning.

Learning outcomes

After you have read this chapter, you should be able to:
- Explain the nature of HR planning.
- Describe the purpose and importance of HR planning.
- Identify the role players responsible for HR planning.
- List the five steps in the HR planning process.
- Explain the importance of consulting the corporate plan.
- Define the concept of job analysis.
- List the stages of the job analysis process.
- List the different uses of job analysis.
- Apply the different job analysis methods.
- Write a job description.
- Put together a job specification.
- Draw up an HR plan.
- Explain the importance of monitoring, evaluating and reporting on HR planning.

5.1 Introduction

So far we have focused on the broader context of strategic PSHRM. Now we begin a transition to a more technical approach, namely human resource planning. Surely one of the most difficult responsibilities facing the HR function is to decide the size of the staff complement required to render an efficient and effective public service that will satisfy the needs of the citizens/customers without wasting public funds. The task of HR planning becomes even more difficult when one analyses the nature and content of public service delivery. The public sector is a large employer with issues peculiar to itself. Consider, for example, the numerical strength of its workforce, the heterogeneity of its employees, and the large variety of occupations it encompasses (doctors, teachers, lawyers, engineers, correctional officers, police officers, etc.). HR planning is therefore an important facet of the public sector's strategic HRM efforts. Without a thoughtful HR plan, public sector managers will not be able to allocate resources effectively (including human resources), prioritise activities and reach objectives. But what does the concept of HR planning comprise in practice?

The outcome of work design is an organisation structure made up of various work units such as individual positions, sections, teams, etc. When a public sector institution has been operating for some time, the work to be performed by these units will already have been structured. However, even if work is not redesigned, it is still important to plan who will do the work, when and how. It is necessary to know what kinds of position, what types of work and what numbers of people with what kinds of competencies will be needed to ensure the successful operation of the public sector institution over the long term. When one starts to do a detailed analysis of such issues, the management process that has been put into motion can be termed human resource planning (traditionally also known as 'manpower planning'). The basis of such HR planning is information about what work is being done or may need to be done, and this information comes from job analysis.

In order to staff a public sector institution with suitable employees, jobs will have to be analysed, potential employees will have to be identified and encouraged to apply for positions, and the selection and appointment of employees will have to take place. To do this, it is important to plan in advance what work needs to be done and what positions may become vacant. One must also project and profile the need to fill these positions. Effective human resource management in an organisation cannot take place without proper HR planning, of which job analysis is an important part.

5.2   The nature of HR planning

HR planning can be viewed as the process of developing and implementing plans and programmes to ensure that the right number and types of individuals are available at the right time and place to perform the work necessary to achieve a public sector institution's objectives (Dolan & Schuler 1987: 41). HR planning must be directly linked to corporate and business planning – it addresses the major objectives of the institution in that it spells out what types of people will in future be needed to execute the work in order to accomplish the goals of the institution. In this sense, it is directly linked to, and flows from, strategic human resource management decisions.

To ensure effective HR planning, the starting point is a public sector institution's mission statement and the corporate plan. Part of strategic planning is the formulation of strategies, goals, and objectives (goals being long-term broad purposes or aims, and an objective being short term and much more detailed). According to French, HR planning is an ongoing process within the context of overall strategic planning and the changing conditions both within and outside an institution (French 1994: 131).

This implies that the structure of the institution, the particular jobs to be performed, financial and technological resources needed, and the qualifications and numbers of people employed must always reflect the general institutional strategies and goals, as well as the HRM strategies and structural dimensions.

Hercus (1993: 405) summarises HR planning by stating that it is a management process involving the following elements:

- Forecasting workforce requirements for a public sector institution to execute its business plan;
- Forecasting human resources available for meeting these needs and doing a scan of the internal and external environments of the institution;
- Identifying the gaps between what will be needed and what will be available, and developing the necessary action plans; and
- Implementing and monitoring these action plans.

Although HR planning can be defined in various ways, the perspective taken here, in line with the viewpoint of the Department of Public Service and Administration, is that HR planning is a process of systematically reviewing human resource needs to ensure that the required number of public sector employees, with the required competencies, is available when they are needed. HR planning is also about ensuring that the composition of your staff gradually becomes more representative of society as a whole (Republic of South Africa 2002a: 5).

The government regards strategic planning as such a critical subset of the public sector's strategic PSHRM efforts that it is legally expected of public sector managers to get involved in the process. Both the Treasury Regulations of 2002 and the Public Service Regulations of 2001 emphasise the importance of strategic planning (which includes strategic HR planning) in the effective delivery of public services. In fact, the government refers to HR planning as integrated HR planning. Strategic planning, in other words strategic HR planning, is regarded as one of the key responsibilities of public sector managers. More specifically, Section 38 of the Public Finance Management Act 1 of 1999 and Section 7(3)(b) of the Public Service Act 103 of 1994 stipulate that strategic planning (including HR planning) is central to the effective, efficient, economic, and transparent use of resources.

The following are typical issues that an HR planning section will have to address (Republic of South Africa 1999b: 27; Republic of South Africa 2002a: 7):
- What is the strategic direction your public sector institution is taking?
  - Vision
  - Mission
  - Objectives
- What human resource challenges do you face (for example, workforce diversity, new legislative measures, organisational restructuring, HIV/AIDS, budgeting constraints, etc.)?
- How ready are current HR systems to cope?
- What can be done to improve the HR situation?

Other issues that may be addressed include the following:
- How many employees does the public sector institution currently employ?
- Where in the institution are these employees to be found?
- Will existing human resources meet the needs?

- How many employees leave the institution per year and in which job categories?
- In which areas (sections) of the institution do we tend to lose more employees?

DID YOU KNOW?

In 2008, The Public Service Commission (PSC) conducted an Audit of Selection Processes in selected state departments. This audit revealed that many state departments are unable to effectively implement selection processes and procedures. In this audit, the PSC found that the most important factors that inhibit the filling of positions are: scarce skills, unavailability of selection committee members, salaries that are not market related and inadequate delegations. The skills that were identified as scarce are the following:
- Engineering and planning;
- Artisan and technical skills;
- Health professionals;
- Veterinary and agriculture;
- Economic sciences;
- Information technology;
- Environmental management; and
- Social work.

Source: Republic of South Africa (2010: Online)

A failure to plan strategically for human resources can lead to significant financial costs for the public sector. For instance, an overstaffed public sector usually has negative consequences for the budget. Once a particular public sector institution becomes overstaffed in practice, an imbalance immediately arises between budgetary allocations and the different functions to be executed. In addition, overstaffing can cause redundancy. This may result in public sector employees feeling that their services are not really required by the institution. In turn, this can de-motivate them and lead to lower productivity or let them leave the institution (Van der Westhuizen 2000: 82). On the contrary, understaffing can have the result that certain work is not done. In some cases, especially in the medical profession, this can have serious repercussions that may lead to the death of patients. Understaffing can also result in temporary staff having to be employed. In most of the cases, temporary staff are not only expensive but are demanding in terms of training and additional requirements. In view of the above, one can say that HR planning is inevitable, especially in terms of the contribution it could make to reducing disturbances within the employment patterns of a large public sector institution. For this reason, the following factors are critical to the success of HR planning.

Integrated strategic HR planning

Integrated strategic HR planning implies that HR planning must be dealt with as an integral part of a public sector institution's corporate strategic planning process and also as part of the outcomes of the strategic PSHRM process. Those employees who are involved in HR planning must have a proper understanding of the overall corporate and HR strategic plan, vision, mission, objectives, values and the way that the environmental factors influence the process. In other words, there must be a definite link between corporate and business planning and HR planning. Figure 5.1 summarises this link.

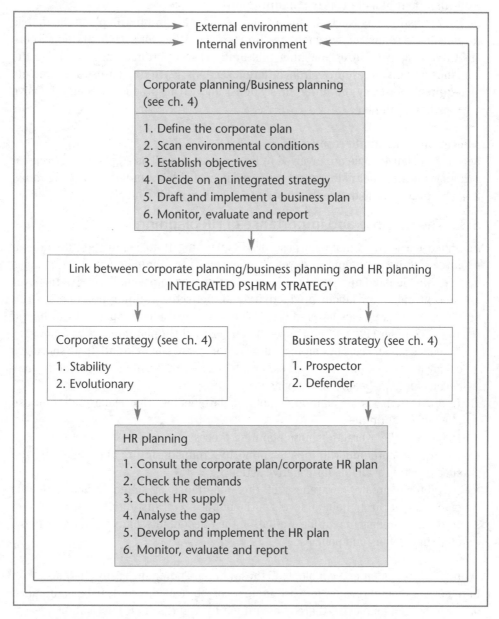

Figure 5.1   Link between corporate and business planning and HR planning

Commitment from senior management

It is essential that senior management must give the lead in emphasising the importance of human resources as a strategic asset and the way it links up with HR planning. Indeed, they should take the lead in the HR planning process.

Establishment of a central HR planning unit

In larger institutions such as the public service, a central HR planning that is responsible to senior management needs to be established for each institution. There are three objectives in establishing this unit: (1) to co-ordinate and reconcile the demands for human resources from different sections; (2) to standardise assessments of requirements from the different sections; and (3) to produce a comprehensive organisational HR plan.

Allocation of adequate resources

Because so many people are involved in the process, as well as a great deal of time, it is important that adequate resources be made available to undertake HR planning. It is also necessary to define the time span to be covered by the plan.

5.3   The purpose and importance of HR planning

As stated earlier, the main purpose of HR planning is to identify future human resource requirements and to develop action plans to eliminate any discrepancies between the demand and supply of labour that may be foreseen. Excessive turnover and absenteeism, low labour productivity and ineffective training programmes can be reduced and expenses lowered if HR planning is executed properly. According to Dolan and Schuler (1987: 42), the specific purposes of HR planning are as follows:

- To reduce labour costs by helping public sector management to anticipate shortages or surpluses of human resources, and to correct these imbalances before they become unmanageable and expensive;
- To provide a basis for planning employee development that makes optimum use of workers' aptitudes;
- To improve the overall business planning process;
- To provide more opportunities for minority groups in future and to identify the specific skills available (affirmative action);
- To promote greater awareness of the importance of sound human resource management throughout all levels of the public sector institution; and
- To provide an instrument for evaluating the effect of alternative human resource planning actions and policies.

With the aid of computer technology, all these aims are now more easily attainable than in the past. Computers allow for vast numbers of job-related records to be maintained on each job and employee, thereby creating a human-resource information system. Records could include information on employees' job preferences, qualifications, work experiences, performance evaluations, the job history of each employee in a public sector institution, and a complete set of information on the jobs or positions held in the institution or elsewhere. This can be used to facilitate HR planning in the interests of the individual as well as the institution.

DID YOU KNOW?

All HR functions in the public service are dependent on an effective management information system, as well as on reliable data within the system. A good human-resource information system is expected to improve government's administrative efficiency by providing updated information to support legal compliance, strategic planning processes, information security and management information.

To enable effective planning, management, and policy development, heads of department are in terms of regulation H of Chapter 1 of the Public Service Regulations of 2001 (National Minimum Information Requirements) required to collect information in the following major HR areas:

- Essential biographical information for all employees;
- Current rank and salary information for all employees;
- Education, training and development information for all employees;
- Career incidents within the public service;
- Disciplinary matters;
- Leave;
- Organisational and geographical information; and
- All posts on the fixed establishment.

Source: Republic of South Africa (2010: Online)

HR planning is thus important to public sector institutions for the following reasons (Anderson 1994: 36):

- Labour is a significant cost to an institution and planning allows greater control.
- Corporate planning is a key ingredient of institutional success, and financial and business planning must be augmented by HR planning.
- The labour supply is neither constant nor flexible, and people's social aspirations must be considered, especially in South Africa.
- Environmental changes (technological, political, social and economic) mean that HRM is becoming more complex and challenging, which makes planning essential.
- Changing service delivery demands have social implications for labour (ranging from redundancy to retraining), and planning can help to accommodate these demands.

5.4 Responsibility for HR planning

The responsibility for HR planning will depend to a large extent on variables such as the size of a public sector institution and the extent to which HRM is handled by specialists or has been devolved to other levels of management. For example, in very large public sector institutions, overall HR planning will normally be undertaken by a specialist section in the human resource department, with the necessary inputs from line function employees, while, in smaller public sector institutions, it may be carried out largely by the line function employees of the particular institution.

DID YOU KNOW?

According to the Public Service Regulations of 2001, heads of departments of executing authorities have to prepare a strategic plan for their department, which:

- States the department's core objectives, based on constitutional and other legislative mandates, functional mandates and the service delivery improvement programme mentioned in Regulation III C;
- Describes the core and support activities necessary to achieve the core objectives, avoiding duplication of functions;
- Specifies the functions the department will perform internally and those it will contract out;
- Describes the goals or targets to be attained in the medium term;
- Sets out a programme for attaining those goals and targets;
- Specifies information systems that: (1) enable the executing authority to monitor the progress made towards achieving those goals, targets and core objectives; (2) support compliance with the reporting requirements in Regulation III J and the national minimum information requirements, referred to in Regulation VII H; and
- Complies with the requirements in paragraphs 5.1 and 5.2 of the Treasury Regulations.

Read more about a strategic framework for the public service with specific reference to a human resource planning strategy for the public service for 2015 at [http://www.info.gov.za/view].

Large public sector institutions will probably have separate sections staffed by HR planning specialists, at a centralised level, focusing on the process of reconciling the number of available employees with the present and future demand for employees. One important issue to be considered in this process of reconciliation is the budget requirements of the institution concerned. The institution's budget will, to a large extent, determine whether decisions will be made on a centralised or decentralised level. In large public sector institutions, the usual practice is to monitor the HR planning process (once it has been designed by all the stakeholders) according to an approved plan. This may help ensure that head office keeps control over activities and that the institution as a whole continues to move towards stated goals. Different sections can then carry out the necessary HR planning, using the standard methods of deploying the workforce (for example, introducing flexible working hours and engaging contract employees and seasonal workers), to ensure the optimal utilisation of employees. In smaller public sector institutions, a centralised process of HR planning is recommended due to the smaller number of employees. The HR planning process could be decentralised should centralisation prove to be unsuccessful.

A general approach to HR planning would be to include all who are affected by the process. In the South African context, for example, it would be advisable to include employee representatives in this process. This could prove to be invaluable when the public sector institution is in a process of restructuring or re-engineering. A proper HR plan will not only assist in the smooth running of any necessary downsizing or adjustment in the institution, but the inclusion of employee representatives in the HR planning process could also assist in planning expansion and affirmative action programmes.

Due to concerns about the high level of staff turnover, particularly in the senior echelons (Senior Management Service) and among professional staff, a decision was taken to conduct a study into the causes and effects of mobility in the public service. An interesting argument of this study was that a high staff turnover in these positions impacts negatively on the public service's ability to deliver quality services. This is explained in more detail in Focus on Research 5.1.

FOCUS ON RESEARCH 5.1
Causes and effects of mobility amongst Senior Management Service and professional staff

The research results of this study highlighted the following:

- The greatest mobility at national level took place at the managerial level (68%) and a 4% mobility rate was recorded at the professional level. The comparable figures for provincial departments were 13% and 49%, respectively.
- The greatest mobility during the period under review was as a result of the internal movement of both SMS managers and professionals.
- Better and higher positions were cited as the main causes for mobility.
- Limited development of retention strategies and policies suggest that the importance of effective retention tools and strategies for addressing mobility has not been fully realised. The implementation of retention strategies was inhibited by an absence of guidelines and budgetary constraints that allowed for little flexibility.
- The retention tools that were most frequently utilised were the awarding of cash bonuses, external conferences and seminars, awarding of bursaries, managerial training and on-the-job training.
- Poor monitoring and an absence of management information in the area of mobility posed significant challenges to effective management of this aspect of human resources.

Source: Republic of South Africa (2010: Online)

The role that the line function employee plays in the HR planning process is crucial. It is accepted that the corporate plan and long-term strategic goals determine the direction of the institution. It is, therefore, the line function employees who must manage the employees who have been recruited to fill the identified posts within the structure. It is in the field that the plan must come together, where the success or otherwise of the plan will be demonstrated. The input of line managers into the HR planning process is therefore essential; they can provide feedback on such issues as the following:

- Whether there are enough and appropriate jobs to ensure the output;
- Whether there are enough and appropriate job categories;
- Whether the incumbents are performing in accordance with accepted standards;
- Whether there is a high labour turnover;
- Whether increased or different product output will necessitate more or different jobs; and
- Whether a change in product technology will change the job content with a concomitant change in training or recruitment requirements.

We believe, however, that all those affected (for example, line-function employees and employee representatives) should be included, although HR planning specialists in large public sector institutions may be responsible for driving the overall process. In smaller public sector institutions, the same approach holds true, should there be any HR specialists.

5.5 The HR planning process

The most fundamental task in the process of planning the workforce is to ensure that there is a clear link between the public sector institution's general strategic corporate plan, the formulated human resource management strategies and structures, and the HR plans as such. Cognisance must thus be taken of the institutional goals and, more particularly, of the human resource implications.

Once the external and internal factors have been considered, the supply and demand of current and new employees can be analysed.

The external factors include issues such as labour market conditions, government policies, and educational trends, while the internal factors refer to such issues as the number of employees leaving the institution who will have to be replaced, the number of employees retiring in the future, and the career progression of employees remaining in the institution. An important aspect to mention here is the impact of the Employment Equity Act 55 of 1998. Affirmative action target setting will have to be an integral part and major driving force behind HR planning. Other factors to consider include institutional reward systems, current work practices, the labour relations climate, technology and turnover targets. All of these issues are identified and analysed with the purpose of drafting and implementing a plan that can best utilise the implications these factors may have for the public sector institution. In other words, these factors must be incorporated into the HR plan to ensure that their influence on the institution is properly managed as the programme or plan is implemented.

For the remainder of this chapter, we shall discuss in detail the following five steps involved in the HR planning process:

- Step 1: Consulting the corporate plan
- Step 2: Gathering, analysing and forecasting workforce supply and demand data

- Step 3: Reconciling of demand and supply
- Step 4: Drawing up and implementing an HR plan
- Step 5: Monitoring, evaluating and reporting

5.6 Step 1: Consulting the corporate plan

HR planning starts with the corporate plan of the relevant public sector institution. The corporate plan is a detailed statement of the institution's vision, mission, objectives and values (see Chapter 4). Even more important is that all public sector managers should get hold of the corporate plan as soon as possible so that they can discover what course of action is being planned and what the strategic options for the future are – in this case, particularly from a human resource perspective. Actually, public sector managers at all levels are, in one way or another, supposed to participate in the institution's strategic planning processes. Therefore, they should have a copy of this plan in their possession (Foot & Hook 1996: 28; Van der Westhuizen 2000: 83). You will experience throughout the HR planning process that the emphasis is very much on the gathering of information as a basis for decision making. Therefore, you must make sure that information is gathered as comprehensively as possible so that you do not miss out on something that could have a serious impact. Most HR planning efforts imply forecasting of future actions. Hence, there will always be the possibility of potential developments that you may not have foreseen. Consider the potential developments that are likely to occur in the technological field over the next 20 years. Designing new technological systems and regulating them will fall at least in part to government (Denhardt 1995: 279). Because of all these changes, HR planning becomes a rolling process. This implies that an HR plan developed in 1997, for example, could not be followed slavishly until the year 2005 (Foot & Hook 1996: 28).

Consider the type of information that senior management in a state department (such as the Department of Health) will need to develop a corporate plan. Consider also the human resource implications. In these considerations, you will probably take account of a variety of factors. Your list may include the following:

- Changes in all kinds of legislation, regulations and instructions applicable to the Department of Health;
- Latest developments in medical technology;
- Changes in the needs (for example, the outbreak of a disease epidemic) of citizens/clients (patients);
- Extension of the department's medical services at regional and international level; and
- Economic conditions (in times of economic downturn, extensive employment and training programmes may have to be cut back).

Basically, all of the above factors have HR implications. For example, changes in legislation, regulations and instructions, and the latest developments in medical technology call for extensive training interventions. This is why it is so important that senior managers should involve HR specialists in the formulation of the corporate plan and business plan. It means that HR implications can be considered strategically and comprehensively and be integrated in the process, whereas the inputs of senior management can give direction to the corporate plan for greater success (Van der Westhuizen 2000: 84). The transfer of a certain section/s of a public service institution to a private sector company or companies could also have serious HR implications that need consideration in terms of planning. For example, Rand Airport Management Company indicated its intention to 'outsource' its gardening and security functions to different companies. Rand Airport Management Company distributed a letter to its employees, stating that their function 'will be outsourced in terms of Section 197 of the Labour Relations Act 66 of 1995'. This case is typically presented as a transfer of a service, and is covered in more detail in Spotlight on the Law 5.1.

SPOTLIGHT ON THE LAW 5.1
Transfer of a 'service'

In *SAMWU & others v Rand Airport Management Company* (2005) 26 ILJ 67 (LAC), affected workers were initially asked to apply for jobs with the proposed contractors. However, at a later date the workers were informed that they would be retrenched. The union approached the Labour Court for an interdict. The argument was held that the workers could not be retrenched because they would automatically transfer to the contractors. The Labour Appeal Court differed from this view. The Labour Appeal Court noted that a 'service' within an institution forms an integral unit, and the potential contractor takes over that unit. It was argued that the transfer of the service constitutes the transfer of part of an institution and is covered by Section 197 of the Labour Relations Act 66 of 1995. This case emphasises the fact that 'outsourcing' arrangements are no longer excluded from the effects of that provision. This implies that workers employed in the services concerned transfer automatically to the contractor.

Read about similar cases in *National Education Health & Allied Workers Union v University of Cape Town* (2000) 21 ILJ 1618 (LC) and *COSAWU v Zikhethele Trade* (2005) 26ILJ 1056 (LC).

Source: Deneys Reitz Attorneys (2010: Online); Grogan (2008: 249–250).

5.7   Step 2: Gathering, analysing and forecasting workforce supply and demand data

Step 2 entails the various important phases to be followed and the methods and techniques to be used to ensure the successful implementation of HR planning and programming. These phases are as follows:

- Phase 1: Forecasting
- Phase 2: Analysing the existing workforce in the public sector institution
- Phase 3: Workforce demand forecast
- Phase 4: Budget considerations
- Phase 5: Forecasting workforce supply

5.7.1 Phase 1: Forecasting

When forecasting is undertaken, the HR planner attempts to ascertain estimates of the supply and demand of various types of human resource in terms of the key performance areas that flow from the corporate plan. The primary goal is to predict areas in the public sector institution where there may be labour surpluses or shortages. Forecasting on both the demand and supply side can be done by judgemental and/ or statistical methods (see Phases 3 and 5 in this section). Statistical methods are used mainly to capture historic trends in a public sector institution's demand for labour and can, given the right conditions, provide much more accurate predictions than judgemental processes. In other circumstances, the judgemental approach is more appropriate, as in the absence of historical data regarding events occurring in the marketplace or in an institution. To achieve an appropriate and balanced result, workforce planners should ideally combine statistical and judgemental approaches when forecasting. Although many sophisticated forecasting techniques have been developed, forecasting is often informal and judgemental. Forecasting in stable public sector institutions is more accurate than in institutions in volatile environments. The value of a forecast should, however, be judged not so much on its accuracy but on the extent to which it forces public sector managers to think and consider alternatives.

The vacant positions in the public service currently are closely related to forecasting. The results of a 2008 Public Service Commission study into the vacancy rates at national and provincial level are reflected in Focus on Research 5.2.

FOCUS ON RESEARCH 5.2
Vacancy rates in the public service

The Public Service Commission reported on the vacancy rates as follows:

- The vacancy rate as at 1 August 2007 in the Public Service showed that the total number of funded posts according to PERSAL was 23%. National departments had the lowest vacancy rate of 16%.
- The vacancy rate according to information reported by departments was about 6%. This suggested a variance of about 18% as compared to information on PERSAL.
- The PSC concluded that it is safe to assume that, due to the inaccuracies in information on PERSAL, the actual vacancy rate is well below the rate of 23% as suggested by PERSAL.
- The highest number of vacancies was at salary levels 6 to 8 followed by salary levels 1 to 5.
- About 46% of the funded vacant posts had been advertised by departments and the selection process had commenced in respect of 28% of the posts.
- In response to the turnaround time in filling posts, the majority of departments indicated that the average turnaround time was two to three months.
- The most significant factors that impact negatively on the filling of posts were scarce skills and the unavailability of selection committee members.
- About three in four departments (72%) indicated that they had strategies in place to fill vacancies. Departments in some provinces were the least likely to have strategies in place to fill their vacancies. ▷

- There is a direct relationship between the retention of staff and job-hopping, where employees move between departments to higher posts and negotiate higher salaries on the basis of offers made by other departments.

Source: Republic of South Africa (2008(a): 12–28); Republic of South Africa (2010: Online)

5.7.2 Phase 2: Analysing the existing workforce in the public sector institution

This phase begins with an analysis of the inventory of the current workforce and the current jobs in a public sector institution. In more specific terms, it involves an assessment of the institution's existing human resource capacity. Its purpose is to assess your existing human resources by gender, race, disability, competencies, occupational category, organisational component and salary grade. Questions that need to be asked include the following:

- Does the existing workforce have the knowledge, skills and competencies that you need to deliver on your institution's mandate?
- Does the institution have the right number of employees at the right levels and at the right units to deliver the services required of it?
- Does the institution require more or less employees in a permanent or temporary capacity?
- Will the institution be in a position to re-skill current employees to deal with the changes faced in the internal or external environment (such as technological developments, public-private partnerships, economic conditions)?
- What is the situation regarding the representativeness of the institution's workforce in terms of the communities they serve?
- What are the obstacles that may be responsible for the under-representation of employees from designated groups? (Republic of South Africa 2002a: 11)

These are but a few of the questions that need to be answered. Ultimately, the main purpose for asking these questions is in helping the HR planner to conduct the kind of assessment envisaged in Part III.D(b) of the Public Service Regulations of 2001. According to the PSR, it is expected of public service institutions to assess existing human resources by race, gender and disability with reference to their competencies, training needs and employment capacities. In addition, the questions should also help to execute the analysis contemplated in Section 19 of the Employment Equity Act 55 of 1998 (see the box on pages 133-134). For more detailed guidance, consult the Code of Good Practice: Preparation, Implementation and Monitoring of Employment Equity Plans. Also consult the Code of Good Practice on Key Aspects of Disability in the Workplace. Both codes can be obtained from the Department of Labour at www.labour.gov.za.

It is also important to determine the characteristics of present jobs, how they are organised and structured, and the skills required to fill them. Organisational charts could, for example, be useful in this regard. Proper job analysis facilitates this part of the inventory. Much of the information in larger public sector institutions can be stored, adapted and retrieved from a human resource information system. You can also use the PERSAL system (the main database of the public service) to obtain statistical information in a variety of areas. Information on the reports that are available can be obtained from the PERSAL system on Sub-system 7: Management Information. If one needs more information on how the PERSAL system can assist one in analysing the existing workforce, go to http://PERSAL.gov.za. The importance of having updated records of all the jobs in a public sector institution cannot be overemphasised. Lately there seems to be a trend to regard rigid job descriptions and job specifications as outdated methods of determining the required skill levels in public sector institutions. The important issue, however, is not the method used but that the competency requirements at all levels in the institution should be known and determined by the requirements of the jobs and not by the characteristics of current incumbents. Many public sector institutions fail to produce credible HR plans because of the lack of accurate information on job requirements – in other words, job descriptions and specifications.

Some employment equity implications for conducting workforce analyses

Organisational variables

Every public sector institution is unique in terms of the way it is structured and will have to report to the Director-General (DG) of the Department of Labour about its existing structures, possible future changes to the existing structures, and any new methodologies in structuring job classifications, etc. The following aspects are relevant in the context of conducting workforce analyses that will form input for the Employment Equity Plan:

- Organisational structures;
- Job Evaluation system(s);
- Job categories broken down per discipline/department or division; and
- Number of positions per job category/occupational family.

Occupational analysis

It will also be important to analyse the situation with regard to the critical competencies and job entry requirement. Without appropriate information the DG will make certain assumptions with regard to the plans/targets the institution sets for itself – which may not be correct, and which could lead to further justifications being requested. The requirements of an occupational analysis include the following:

- Job skills/competencies/qualifications/experience required per job category;
- Identification of job categories/occupations that are critical to the overall success of the business;
- Summary of education/training and development institutions responsible for the development of the skills/competencies etc. identified as being of critical importance;
- Average cost estimates to acquire the required (critical) skills/competencies etc. (based on actual/historical training and development costs); ▷

- Average remuneration analysis and breakdown of benefits; and
- Average cost of employment to the institution (per job category and total).

Employee statistical analysis

This section is obviously very important as it will provide the DG with an overall profile of the distribution within the institution in terms of race, gender and people with disabilities. The following aspects are included here:

- Employee complement versus strength per occupational level;
- Employee strength by race and gender per occupation level;
- Employee strength in terms of disabled employees per occupational level (male/female);
- Comparative statistics for representatives per occupational group versus industry demographics, regional demographics, national demographics, or economically active population; and
- Statistics of suitably qualified persons available, both internally and externally.

Financial and economic factors

This section is important both with regard to the above, i.e. acquisition of skills and Section 27 of the Act, and in terms of Section 18 of the Act:

- Analysis of the total wage costs of the institution;
- Analysis of overheads associated with employment;
- Costs associated with recruitment, selection, and placement;
- Costs associated with training and development;
- Economic and financial factors relevant to the institution, sector or industry;
- Present and anticipated economic and financial circumstances of the institution; and
- Short/medium/long-term financial forecasts.

Another key aspect to be considered in HR planning (analysing the existing workforce), is that one needs to compile a workplace skills plan as required in terms of the Skills Development Act 97 of 1998. At the same time, one has to assess the training needs of one's employees. There are a number of sources that can assist one in this process. Obviously, the starting point would again be the Department of Labour. One can also obtain guidance from the SETA to which a specific public sector institution belongs. One institution that has been deeply involved in issuing guidelines in this regard is the PSETA. These guidelines are available at [http://www.labour.gov.za/services/setacontacts]. In practice, the training needs can be determined as follows: (1) One can conduct a detailed skills audit by comparing the existing skills of employees against the skills that are required at present and in the future. (2) One can determine the skills gap through interviews with key public sector managers in the relevant public sector institution, as well as through focus groups (the process is also referred to as 'training analysis' (Republic of South Africa 2002a; 12).

One extremely important area that needs to be considered in analysing the existing workforce for HR planning purposes is the threat the HIV/AIDS pandemic poses to the health and well-being of public sector institutions. Most significant is that one has to remember that HIV/AIDS are likely to result in more employees who are sick and more employees who die prematurely. Every public sector institution faces a fundamental issue concerning the management of HIV/AIDS. There is no doubt that, if the pandemic is not carefully planned for from an HR planning perspective, it might result in lower productivity, lower morale, higher staff turnover, and increased costs. Moreover, it should be clear from this that the end result would be a depleted ability to render efficient and effective services to the public. Various techniques can be used to estimate the HIV-infection levels of the current public sector workforce. These techniques could help to make some projections as to the impact of HIV-infections on aspects such as service delivery, productivity, morale and costs. The methods adopted include the following:

- Surveillance studies through voluntary counselling and testing; and
- HIV/AIDS projections.

DID YOU KNOW?

The number of posts filled and vacant in the public service as at October 2009 are as follows:
- Posts filled in national state departments and provincial departments totalled 1 170 044 (79%).
- Posts vacant in national state departments and provincial departments totalled 45 328 (21%). About 13% of the national state departments' posts were vacant.

Efficient and effective service delivery is dependent on the availability of the required human resource capacity and such a high vacancy rate should definitely be a cause for concern for the government.

Source: Republic of South Africa (2010: Online)

Other strategic steps to be taken in analysing the current workforce are as follows: (1) Consulting the Department of Health, the Department of Public Service and Administration, or the Department of Education on the approach that you should adopt. Of course, this depends on the relevant public sector institution you are part of. The above departments have conducted various studies on this matter and could provide you with useful information. These departments have also issued a range of policy guidelines on HIV/AIDS. In particular, the Department of Public Service and Administration has amended the Public Service Regulations of 2001 to provide for minimum standards in managing HIV/AIDS in the workplace. These amended regulations were issued in Government Gazette No. 7389 dated 21 June 2002 (Notice No. R.840). Take note that the Department of Labour has also published a Code of Good Practice in this regard. This code contains strategic information on the principles to be followed in managing the impact of HIV/AIDS in the public service. (2) Consulting your representative in the Interdepartmental Committee on HIV/AIDS. This Committee will also be able to provide one with useful HIV/AIDS information. (3) Visiting relevant HIV/AIDS websites. These include [www.labour. gov.za], [www. dpsa.gov.za], [www.redribbon.za], and [www.ilo.org/aids].

Another important challenge in completing your HR supply analysis is to determine the future supply of the human resources required for your public sector institution. This is perhaps the most important step, especially for those public sector institutions that are dependent on scarce skills. These institutions need to familiarise themselves with the availability of these skills. Take, for instance, the Department of Public Works which needs staff in specialised areas, such as engineers. One of the central concerns here is the under-representation of employees from designated groups, especially those who are qualified candidates. These people are usually in short supply. An analysis of these scarce human resources is essential, since it is expected of public sector institutions, in terms of Section III.D.2(a) to (d) of the Public Service Regulations of 2001, as part of HR planning, to develop and implement an affirmative action plan. This plan shall contain the following:

- A policy statement that sets out the institution's commitment to affirmative action and shows how the policy will be implemented;
- Numeric and time-bound targets;
- Annual statistics; and
- A plan for redressing numeric under-representativeness.

In addition, information on the supply of these scarce human resources can be obtained from public sector institutions such as the Department of Labour [http://www.labour.gov.za], Department of Public Service and Administration [http://www.dpsa.gov.za], Statistics South Africa [http://www.statssa.gov.za], and the Human Sciences Research Council [http://www.hsrc.ac.za].

What is also critical when analysing the existing workforce is the fact that employers often forget that employees frequently have skills that have not been utilised in their current positions. These skills could include facility in foreign languages, specialised computer knowledge, and interpersonal skills. Familiarising oneself with these latent skills is important because it makes no sense to embark on comprehensive recruitment efforts if employees in some work areas are underutilised. It may well be a possibility to re-deploy these employees to work in areas of greater need. Be aware that one must certainly expect incisive questions from union representatives should you embark on this approach.

5.7.3   Phase 3: Workforce demand forecast

The centrality of the workforce demand forecast can hardly be underestimated. It involves the assessment of the human resources that will be required in terms of skills and numbers of employees to achieve the strategic corporate objectives. The workforce demand forecast requires one to take into account the mandated functions, new functions, and abolished functions allocated to the public sector institution one is responsible for.

By asking questions like the above, thoughts in terms of human resource requirements will be stimulated. However, the information gathered through these questions will certainly not be enough. Therefore, corporate and business plans need to be broken down and the organisational structure has to be reviewed simultaneously. After all this has been done, strategic shifts have to be taken in a public sector institution's human resource requirements. The next step will normally be to determine a new organisational structure. Everyone agrees that, when giving consideration to a new organisational structure, the most important principle to bear in mind is that 'structure follows strategy'. This implies that you cannot design a new organisational structure (formal working arrangements and post structure) without having a clear understanding of what is expected in a broader sense.

One more aspect of the organisational structure is that it is depicted as an organisational chart. A complete organisational chart usually provides all the positions, reporting relationships, and lines of formal and informal communication. Various options for structuring a public sector institution are used today. The options that tend to have the most impact are the following:
- **Functional design:** The functional design options focuses on grouping work activities into manageable units according to similarity of function or process. This option has been used in a variety of fields, but it seems best to fit a work environment in which a high degree of specialisation is required or in which the nature of work demands formal rules and regulations.
- **Service programme or project structure:** This option groups work activities together according to the services that are rendered or according to major programmes or projects.
- **Matrix structure:** The matrix structure option is a mixture of the above options. In this structure, work groups or teams are formed as and when the need arises. The matrix structure gives team members the opportunity to get involved in various

projects, and they often report to more than one manager. However, despite being involved in different projects, team members remain members of their functional units as depicted on the organisational chart.

After the organisational review has been completed, you will be able to determine your human resource requirements. This brings us to the next step where you have to analyse all newly envisaged positions using the prescribed job analysis/evaluation system. Now you have to ask yourself, among other things (Van der Westhuizen 2000: 85):

- What tasks have to be performed?
- What knowledge, skills, and competencies are required to perform these tasks?
- How should tasks be grouped together?
- How many employees will be required to perform the tasks?
- What remuneration should be associated with the posts concerned?

The key to the above questions is job analysis.

5.7.3.1 Job analysis

As we have seen in the previous chapter, the most basic component of public sector institution's structure is the work and the various work units, such as positions created to facilitate the carrying out of that work. Objectives are achieved by means of people performing their work in the various jobs; it is therefore essential that, when jobs are designed, the utmost care should be taken with respect to the quantity and quality of people needed to execute the work. Job analysis is the key to this process, and a general description of this procedure is provided below.

Job analysis is a technical procedure which systematically explores the activities within a job (De Cenzo & Robbins 1994: 135).

In the job analysis process, the duties, responsibilities, and accountabilities of a job are analysed. The information gathered from a job analysis generates two outcomes – namely job descriptions and job specifications (see Figure 5.2).

Job descriptions define the nature of the job content, the environment, and the conditions under which employment is carried out. A job description is a written statement of the content of a job, which is derived from the analysis of the job. It states what the jobholder does, how it is done, under what conditions it is done, and why it is done.

Job specifications stipulate the minimum acceptable characteristics a jobholder must possess as a requisite to be able to perform the job. A job specification describes the attributes that an employee requires to carry out the job – that is, it identifies the knowledge, skills, level of education, experience, and abilities needed to do the job effectively.

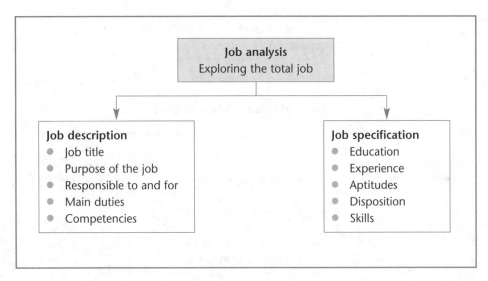

Figure 5.2   Job analysis

The job analysis process will also identify those competencies that are most important for the role of the relevant post. Most importantly, it identifies the level at which the potential job incumbent will need to demonstrate those competencies. These levels can be categorised as follows (Republic of South Africa 2002b: 5):

- **Basic:** Demonstrates the competency sufficient for adequate performance;
- **Developed:** Demonstrates the competency above adequate performance; and
- **Advanced:** Demonstrates the competency at the highest level.

5.7.3.2   Stages in the job analysis process

The job analysis process can follow various stages (see Figure 5.3). It is suggested that the following procedure be adopted:

- Determine the public sector institution's corporate and business strategy;
- Create a structure to identify the various jobs;
- Identify a target population to be analysed;
- Decide on a job analysis method to collect and verify job information;
- Compile the job descriptions and job specifications; and
- Ensure that the working group agrees that the job descriptions and job specifications accurately reflect the jobs concerned.

5.7.3.3   What job analysis can be used for

Job analysis can be used for a number of purposes (Cushway 1994: 41):

- HR planning ensures that the right number of employees, with the right skills, knowledge and experience, are available in the right places at the right time in an organisation. Objectives are set according to the corporate and business strategy, after which a plan must be devised to acquire the human resources necessary to

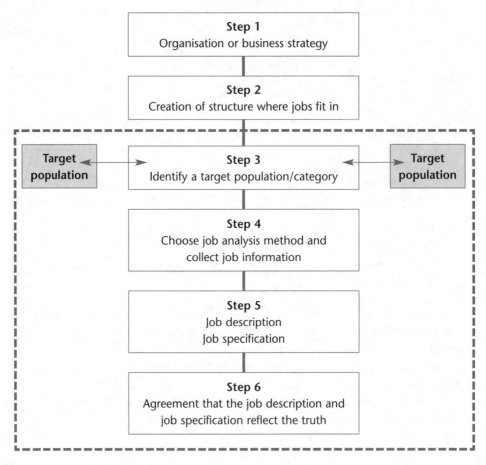

Figure 5.3 Stages in the job analysis process

meet the stated objectives. Institutional outputs required are derived from the objectives, and decisions must then be made on how many jobs are needed to achieve the various outputs. The implications of this may be that certain jobs should remain as they are, or that certain jobs should be slightly changed, or that completely new jobs should be designed. HR planning cannot be accurately undertaken without information about the different jobs.

- Selection can only take place if the job requirements have been clearly identified. With a job description and a job specification available, the qualifications, experience and personal attributes a potential candidate must possess are clear.
- Performance management cannot take place without proper job information. To measure job performance, it is necessary to compare the incumbent's performance with the standards set by the job. Without clear job objectives, proper performance management cannot take place.

- Labour relations may improve if every individual in a public sector institution knows what his or her responsibilities and reporting lines are. Proper job analysis helps to ensure that the chances of communication gaps are minimised.

5.7.3.4   Information to be obtained through a job analysis

Let us make a brief summary of the types of information to be obtained through a job analysis:

- One of the first tasks in the process of job analysis is to identify the job clearly – the job title, the department, and the number of employees doing the job.
- The reporting relationships must be identified. It is essential to provide the title of the job immediately superior to the job in question and to indicate clearly the co-ordination links and functional relationships between jobs.
- The job content must be defined; this includes the main purpose of the job, its boundaries, responsibilities and accountabilities, and the tasks and activities to be undertaken.
- The required performance standards and the way in which these are to be measured must be determined. The key performance areas (KPAs) or outputs of the job must be established, and the standard to which they should be performed must also be clearly indicated.
- Any constraints must be identified – the limits of authority and decision making must be established.
- Those aspects of the job for which the incumbent is responsible (such as budget, equipment, material) must be determined.
- The working conditions under which the incumbent must perform the job must be established.
- The necessary personal characteristics must be identified; these include the knowledge, skills, and experience required of the incumbent to meet the requirements of the job.
- Any other relevant information (for example training requirements or aspects of a temporary nature) must be included.

5.7.3.5   Job analysis methods

The following methods, among others, can be used to obtain the necessary job information (De Cenzo & Robbins 1994: 135):

- **Individual interviews:** Jobholders are identified and interviewed with the purpose of determining what the job entails. This will usually result in the preparation of a job description which will be confirmed by the manager. This is a time-consuming but effective method, and is commonly used. A significant drawback of this method is that people can inflate the importance of their jobs. It is also important that the interviewer prepares himself or herself properly for the interview.
- **Group interviews:** Some similar principles to those that apply to individual interviews apply to group interviews; the difference is that a number of jobholders

are interviewed simultaneously. Group dynamics may increase or decrease the effectiveness of this method; job assessments may be more accurate and time effective, but one has to be able to manage and utilise the group process properly.

- **Observations:** Observation involves watching public sector employees while they perform their duties. This can be done by means of direct observation or through videos. A negative aspect of this method may be the fact that employees do not perform as they normally do while knowing that they are being observed. A further problem is that certain aspects of jobs cannot always be observed all the time.
- **Structured questionnaires:** One of the methods most widely used to obtain information about jobs is the questionnaire. Employees are given a structured questionnaire on which they check or rate duties which they perform in the course of their work. This method is less time consuming and less costly than the interview, but exceptions may be overlooked and follow-up questions may not be asked or vague points not be clarified. The most common systems used are the Position Analysis Questionnaire (PAQ), and the Saville and Holdsworth Work Profiling System, which is a consulting service. The details of these methods, which are used worldwide as well as in South Africa, fall beyond the scope of this book.
- **Self-reports:** In the case of self-reports, jobholders are required to write their own job descriptions. It is, however, essential to provide the required training beforehand. Without the necessary guidance, the quality of the information received may be of no use. The success of this method also depends on the report-writing skills of the jobholder.

5.7.3.6 Writing job descriptions

When writing a job description, it must always be borne in mind why it is being written. The content of a job description will depend on the nature of the job, the organisation, and the environment. Job descriptions should contain such information as the following (see also the example of a job description in the box on page 143):

- Job title;
- Job identification details;
- Name of the current jobholder;
- Reporting lines;
- Main purpose of the job;
- Tasks and responsibilities (key performance areas);
- Context (optional);
- Relation to other positions;
- Subordinate positions;
- Financial and statistical data required to do the job;
- Working conditions;
- Knowledge, skills and experience required;
- Competencies;

- Other relevant information; and
- Signature and date.

A specimen is provided in Figure 5.4 of the job description for a senior personnel officer.

Post title:	Senior personnel officer: Recruitment
Summary:	Provision of human resource services where possible to line function personnel in the Department of Health. In general, the incumbent of this post is responsible for the recruitment, selection, and placement of personnel.
Purpose:	To ensure that well-trained and motivated personnel are obtained for the Department of Health.
Managerial responsibilities	(1) Responsible for two personnel officers and three responsibilities: personnel clerks. (2) Recruits, selects, places, evaluates, and disciplines the persons occupying the above-mentioned posts
Reports to:	(1) Reports to the Assistant Director: Personnel Provision. (2) Co-ordinates, controls, and plans the personnel provision section in conjunction with the Assistant Director.
Duties:	(1) Develops procedures for fair and equitable recruitment, selection, and placement. (2) Conducts interviews at the appointment of new human resource personnel. (3) Advises line function personnel on interviewing.
Qualifications:	Bachelor's degree in Human Resource Management.
Skills:	The incumbent must have at least two years' work experience in the principles, practice, methods, and techniques of personnel provision and must be conversant with legislation, regulations, and codes of instruction relating to recruitment, selection, and placement.
Salary scale:	R64 000 x 3 000 – 70 000 x 5 000 – 80 000

Figure 5.4   Job description for a senior personnel officer

5.7.3.7   Job specifications

The information necessary to compile a job specification is normally obtained during the process of job analysis and is often described as part of the job description document.

Job specifications are used primarily to facilitate the recruitment and selection process. Without a job specification, the characteristics of the ideal job incumbent are unknown and comparisons between job applicants cannot be made. The job specification should be related to the actual job requirements and must be consistent with the particular activities and duties of the job.

When a qualification is attached to a job, utmost care must be taken to determine whether that qualification is indeed necessary. Job specifications should be constantly monitored to determine whether the specifications are not too high or too low or whether the incumbent possesses the right profile. Cognisance must be taken of the possibility of indirect discrimination in job specifications due to preconceived and entrenched attitudes, prejudices, and assumptions.

All the information that flows from job analyses is eventually used for the purposes of workforce planning, recruitment and selection, training, and so forth. The first area, however, is workforce planning.

5.7.3.8   Job evaluation

When a job analysis of each post on the organisational chart has been completed, an evaluation of posts can be commenced. This is done so that a monetary value can be assigned to each post.

Job analyses and descriptions address the core of what is required in a job, and public sector managers should therefore realise how important a task the professional execution of job analysis and description is. Job analyses and descriptions form an inherent part of the means by which a public sector institution's work is designed and organised, and, to a large extent, they also impact on organisational structures. They will thus play a fundamental role in recruitment and selection policies and practices, as well as in training and promotion decisions. All of these decisions and practices are ultimately supposed to be linked to job analysis and description, and all of these have to be done in such a way that it is free of any form of unfair discrimination.

Employers should, when job descriptions and specifications are drawn up and decided upon, ensure that the inherent requirements of the job are very clearly spelled out.

Active steps must also be taken at this stage to ensure the promotion of affirmative action. An aspect high on the list here is work redesign. It may be necessary to reorganise work in such a way that the opportunities for women or disabled people as designated groups can be enhanced. In this regard, one may, for instance, consider work reorganisation in terms of more flexibility relating to time and place. Examples may be job sharing, part-time work, or even work-from-home. Rewriting job descriptions and specifications along such lines may help public sector institutions to achieve their employment equity targets.

From the above, it is clear that job analysis forms a strategic part of the workforce demand forecast. Now that one has familiarised oneself with the requirements of job analysis, let us briefly turn the attention to a few forecasting methods.

5.7.3.9   Forecasting methods

The accuracy of forecasts depends on the information available and on the predictability of events. Dolan and Schuler (1987: 50) distinguish between two classes of forecasting techniques to project an organisation's demand for employees, namely judgemental forecasts and conventional statistical projections. These are discussed on page 145.

Judgemental forecasts

- The Delphi technique is most commonly used in judgemental forecasts. This technique requires a large number of experts to take turns presenting forecast statements and assumptions (Schuler, Dowling, Smart & Huber 1993: 64). Each expert makes forecasts and the forecasts are then routed to the other experts, who then revise their own forecasts until a viable composite forecast emerges.
- The nominal group technique also entails using multiple inputs from several persons. The information can be obtained in a structured format and it is a structured variation of small-group discussion methods (Newstrom & Scannel 1980: 107). People sit around a conference table and independently list their ideas regarding the forecast on a sheet of paper. After a period of time, they take turns expressing their ideas to the group. Each member's ideas are recorded so that everyone can see all of the ideas and refer to them later on in the session.
- The managerial judgement technique involves public sector managers deciding, possibly in consultation with other staff, what their future activities are likely to be and what types of staff they will need to ensure success. This approach can be top-down or bottom-up (lower level managers who make estimates and pass them up) or a combination of the two (Cushway 1994).

Statistical projections

- Linear regression analysis can best be explained by the case of a perfect linear association between two variables, such as service delivery and employment (Babbie 1995). If a relationship can be established between the level of service delivery and the level of employment, predictions of future service delivery can be used to make predictions of future employment. However, although there may be a relationship between service delivery and employment, the relationship is often influenced by a number of factors; for example, if service delivery doubles, it does not mean that employment must be doubled – it could be achieved by better productivity arrangements.
- Multiple linear regression analysis is used to analyse those situations in which a given dependent variable is affected simultaneously by several independent variables. For example, instead of using only production to predict employment demand, productivity data and equipment-use data also may be used (Schuler *et al.* 1993: 65).
- The unit demand forecasting technique is a method whereby public sector managers provide certain labour estimates because they know what work activity will be performed by their units in the future. When the estimates for all units are added up, they form an overall forecast for the institution; this often differs from the institution's forecasted demands (as prepared by the workforce specialist).

Other statistical methods

According to Schuler *et al.* (1993: 66), other statistical methods may be helpful too, such as the following:

- **Productivity ratios:** Historical data are used to examine past levels of a productivity index (P):

$$P = \frac{Workload}{Number\ of\ people}$$ Where constant or systematic relationships are found, human resource requirements can be computed by dividing predicted workloads by *P*.

- **Personnel ratios:** Past personnel data are examined to determine historical relationships among the employees in various jobs or job categories.
- **Time series analysis:** Past staffing levels (instead of workload indicators) are used to project future human resource requirements.
- **Stochastic analysis:** The likelihood of landing a series of contracts is combined with the personnel requirements of each contract to estimate expected staffing requirements. This has potential application in government contracts and construction industries.

5.7.4   Phase 4: Budget considerations

A budget is a plan for controlling the use of funds over a period of time (Jarrell 1993: 86). By reconciling HR planning and budgeting, the whole exercise is placed into a financial perspective. Public sector managers have to indicate the need for additional personnel to fill posts in the future. The entire process is based on managers making accurate estimates. This forecasting method is highly judgemental, varying from a bottom-up approach (where the public sector manager determines his or her own needs) to a top-down approach where senior managers place constraints either in terms of budget allocations or numbers of employees. Managers are then required to plan their objectives within this framework (Cherrington 1995: 160). The workforce forecast must be expressed in terms of rand, and must be compatible with the institution's monetary objectives and overall budget limitations. The budget reconciliation process may also indicate that the budget has to be adjusted to accommodate the HR plan. This step provides the opportunity to align the objectives regarding the personnel of the institution with those of the institution as a whole.

In Part III.D/1(c) of the Public Service Regulations of 2001, it is spelt out that public service institutions have to do HR planning within the available budget funds. This planning needs also to be done for the remaining period of the relevant medium-term expenditure framework. More specifically, it is expected to be done in terms of recruitment, retention, deployment, and development of human resources.

5.7.5   Phase 5: Forecasting workforce supply

Forecasting supply can be derived from internal and external sources. The internal source is generally the most important and the most readily available. There are basically two categories of techniques to help forecast internal labour supply, namely judgemental and statistical.

5.7.5.1 Judgemental techniques

Replacement planning is a relatively short-term technique which uses replacement charts to show the names of the current incumbents of positions in the organisation, together with the names of likely replacements. Replacement charts make it clear where potential vacancies may occur based on the performance levels of the public sector employees in the current jobs.

It is important to note that such aspects as gender, race, and age should be omitted from these replacement charts to prevent these criteria from being used in making promotion decisions; this will avoid possible violations of the Labour Relations Act of 1995.

Succession planning is a longer term, more flexible method, which focuses on the development of managers or leader. An example is provided in Figure 5.5.

Management succession plan

Organisation: ....   Date: ....

Probability of vacancy:
A = within 1 year
B = after 1–3 years
C = beyond 3 years

Position incumbent	Readiness			Contingency plan
	A Now	B 1–3 years	C 3 years +	
J Cocker				

Source: Adapted from French (1994: 133)

Figure 5.5   Succession planning

The following differences can be identified between succession planning and replacement planning:
- Replacement planning covers a short time span (for example, up to 12 months), and the best candidate is chosen, while succession planning is more long term and the candidate with the best potential development is chosen.

- Replacement planning is very flexible but can be limited by the structure of the plan, while succession planning is perceived as being flexible but is intended to promote development and thinking about alternative candidates.
- In the case of replacement planning, the experience base of those managers to be considered is based on the judgement and observation of candidates, and this forms the basis of the plan; in the case of succession planning, the results of the plan are based on inputs and discussion involving a number of other public sector managers, and are thus a group effort.
- The development planning for public sector managers in replacement planning is normally informal, while for succession planning it is more formal and extensive. Specific long-term personal development plans for individuals are developed as part of succession planning.
- With replacement planning, the identified candidate will fill a vacant post, while, with succession planning, all candidates are considered to fill the post because a pool of candidates has been identified.

5.7.5.2 Statistical techniques

When statistical techniques are not widely used, it is usually because of inadequate databases, lack of software computer programs, and a shortage of trained professionals.

The following are examples of a few statistical methods (Schuler *et al.* 1993: 69):

- **Markov analysis:** This type of analysis projects future flows to obtain availability estimates through a straightforward application of historical transition rates. Historical transition rates are derived from analyses of personnel data concerning losses, promotions, transfers, demotions and, perhaps, recruitment.
- **Simulation (based on Markov analysis):** Alternative (rather than historical) flows are examined for effects of future human resource availabilities. Alternative flows reflect the anticipated results of policy or programme changes relating to voluntary and involuntary turnover, retirement, promotion, etc.
- **Renewal analysis:** Renewal analysis estimates future flows and availabilities by calculating vacancies as created by organisational growth, personnel losses, and internal movements, and the results of decision rules governing the filling of vacancies. Alternative models may assess the effects of changes in growth estimates, turnover, promotions, or decision rules.
- **Goal programming:** This type of programming focuses on optimising goals. Desired staffing patterns are established, given a set of constraints concerning such things as the upper limits on staff flows, the percentage of new recruits, and total salary budgets.

5.8 Step 3: Reconciling of demand and supply

The third step in the HR planning process will be to focus on the process of reconciliation necessitated by the mismatch between the quantitative and qualitative demand for public sector employees based on the future plans of the public sector institution and on current projections of employee availability – that is, the supply of employees. At first, this imbalance will be portrayed by a numerical shortfall or surplus in employees that is likely to occur in the future. Shortfalls in the institution may result in units running at overcapacity due to employee shortages and overtime work – with concomitant long-term problems. Surpluses of public sector employees may, on the other hand, lead to low productivity, financial losses and, if employees are not transferred or retrenched, to the eventual closing of the public sector institution. Proper HR planning is thus essential to maintain a proper balance in the number of employees required by the institution and to avoid the ill effects of employee problems or institutional readjustments. The supply forecast, once complete, can be compared with the workforce demand forecast to help determine action programming necessary to identify workforce talent and to balance the supply and demand forecast. It must, however, be borne in mind that most current forecasting of labour supply and demand is short range and is used for the purpose of budgeting and cost control. Because so many changes occur in the public service that may have an impact on personnel provision, it follows logically that the demand for human resources cannot be met on a continuous basis. To make matters even more complex, it follows logically that suitable human resources cannot always be found to meet the needs. Hence, there is a supply problem. Basically, you face three options in this regard: (1) supply equals demand, (2) supply is greater than demand, and (3) supply is less than demand. In those cases where supply equals demand, nothing needs to be done about the situation. The other two options are more complex to manage. If supply exceeds demand, HR plans have to be developed to get rid of excess employees. For example, one strategy would be redeployment, while others may include retirement packages or retrenchments. When supply is less than demand, HR plans have to be made to recruit new staff (Van der Westhuizen 2000: 92).

These gaps are determined by the difference between what was analysed in your workforce demand forecast in Phase 3 (see Section 5.7.3) and the workforce supply forecast in Phase 5 (see Section 5.7.5). If these forecasts have been made extensively, they will provide more than enough quantitative and qualitative data to make proper HR planning decisions. Quantitative data will include data on race, gender, and disability that have to be cross-referenced with, for example, the total number of employees within different occupations and the total number of permanent and temporary employees. Qualitative data, on the other hand, will highlight any weaknesses in procedures and practices such as retention strategies and remuneration policies. An example of a retention strategy question is: Do you have strategies in place which help to minimise the loss in investment that you make in developing your employees? An example of a remuneration policy question is: Does your public sector institution have a remuneration policy that indicates sensitivity to gender and race wage issues? (Republic of South Africa 1999b: 32). Two specific questions need to be asked here: (1) What are the gaps in numbers, competencies, and employment equity targets that need to be filled; and (2) To what extent does your existing human resource capacity match your future requirements? (Republic of South Africa 2002a: 14).

Once the gaps between demand and supply have been determined, you should summarise them in terms of the following:

- The competency levels of the employees;
- The number of employees that one will need at present and in the future and where one will utilise them;
- The areas of under-representation in the various occupational groups and salary levels of the institution in terms of race, gender, and people with disabilities; and
- The health profile of the institution (here the specific impact of HIV/AIDS should be highlighted).

5.9   Step 4: Drawing up and implementing of an HR plan

Drawing up and implementing an HR plan means developing a plan or strategy to address the gap between existing human resource capacity and future human resource requirements. Obviously, this needs to be done within the financial resources available – in other words, within the budget allocations. If one has been involved in HR planning before, and more specifically in the drawing up of HR plans, one may have asked pertinent questions about what one considers to be important. The range of questions that can be asked includes the following (Republic of South Africa 2002a: 15):

- What are the key actions one should embark on to ensure a better match between the human resource requirements and the available employees?
- How can we ensure that we have highly skilled employees in future to address the changing needs?
- How can we ensure that we attract employees with the right competencies in critical work areas?
- When oversupply of staff at certain levels occurs, how can this oversupply be re-directed to address other critical work areas? If redeployment or additional training is not an option, how can these staff be phased out?
- How can under-representation be addressed in the institution?
- How can the productivity of current employees be improved?
- What can be done to limit the impact of HIV/AIDS and other life-threatening diseases on the health and well-being of staff and the quality of services that is supplied?

Table 5.1 on page 151 provides a brief summary of some of the dimensions that might be considered in the HR plan with regard to filling the gaps that have been identified.

Table 5.1   Dimensions of an HR plan

Nature of gap	Options on bridging the gap
Skills deficits	• Conduct training needs analysis • Prioritise training needs ' • Identify most cost-effective training strategies • Identify possible training providers
Over-supply of certain skills	• Identify the employees that are surplus
Under-representation of employees from designated groups	• Assign responsibility for employment equity • Build a more productive and diverse workforce

Source: Adapted from Guidelines on Integrated HR Planning in the Public Service (Republic of South Africa 2002a: 17–19)

DID YOU KNOW? ?

The Department of Social Development in the Province of the Eastern Cape has developed its strategic plan for the period 2008–2011. Within this plan, the Department prioritised staff retention and training of a new social development cadre to tackle the next range of service delivery challenges, including poverty eradication. In order to implement this plan, it was imperative that a human resource plan be developed (to talk to the strategic plan of the Department) to ensure that the Department of Social Development has the appropriate human resource capacity to enable it to deliver on its mandate and achieve its strategic goals and objectives.

The HR plan aims to ensure that the department:
- Has the human resource capability to deliver on its mandate;
- Provides the workforce with the necessary skills and competencies to deliver on the strategic goals and objectives as outlined in the strategic plan;
- Recruits and retains the quality and quantity of staff that it requires;
- Promotes employment equity;
- Optimally utilises its human resources;
- Anticipates and manages shortages and surplus of staff;
- Progressively and continuously develops staff toward the developmental approach in order to meet the increasing and changing needs of clients and communities; and
- Develops leadership and creates a learning organization that values the importance of service delivery and hence putting people first.

The plan is available at http://www.socdev.ecprov.gov.za
Source: Republic of South Africa (2008(b): Online)

5.10   Step 5: Monitoring, evaluating and reporting

Public sector institutions should develop systems to review and evaluate their performance in all HR activities in order to ensure that there is feedback from this assessment into the corporate and business plan. This should be done on an annual basis, and it is important that, after it has been done, corrective steps should be taken where necessary. Possible criteria or standards for evaluating HR planning include the measurement of the following factors (Dolan & Schuler 1987: 59):

- Actual staffing levels against established staffing requirements;
- Productivity levels against established goals;
- Actual personnel flow rates against desired rates;
- Programmes implemented against action plans;
- Programme results against expected outcomes (such as improved applicant flows, reduced quit rates, improved replacement ratios);
- Labour and programme costs against budgets; and
- Ratios of programme results (benefits) to programme costs.

Monitoring and evaluation should involve an information system to provide one with information on how the plan is operating in practice. One can use the PERSAL and VULINDLELA (government financial information data source) systems respectively to the extent that they can provide some of the information that is required (Republic of South Africa 2002a: 20).

A final word about monitoring and evaluation is that one has to ensure that one will be able to report to the legislature on the results of the HR planning processes. In addition, reporting has to be done to the Department of Labour. The Public Service Regulations of 2001 outline what to consider when one is involved in the reporting process. The details of these reporting requirements can be obtained from the Department of Public Service and Administration [www.dpsa.gov.za]. Remember, one has to report on employment equity and skills development. These details can be obtained from the Department of Labour and from the Secretariat of the relevant SETA. (Contact details for SETAs are available at the SAQA website: [http://www.saqa.org.za]).

Every public sector institution should communicate the HR plan to all the employees and the public where it can be easily accessed, for example, via the intranet/Internet, notice boards, and boardrooms. Various methods of monitoring, evaluating and reporting have been done by the Department of Public Service and Administration with regards to the implementation of HR plans in the public service. One such method resulted in a study during 2006 entitled 'Development of interventions to improve the quality of human resource planning at departmental level in the public service'. The research results of this study are the subject of Focus on Research 5.3 on page 152.

FOCUS ON RESEARCH 5.3
Quality of HRM planning in the public service

RESEARCH

The results of the above study revealed, among others, the following:

- In some cases, it was reported that 'political pressure' was brought to bear on the human resource function, with little or no linkage to the 'real' human resource needs of the department.
- In many cases, the respondents indicated that they (the HR component) were not included in the departmental strategic planning processes. This resulted in a lack of appreciation by the other line managers of the role of the HR function in supporting the core business of the department.
- In general, the respondents felt disempowered and isolated from the core business of the departments. Additionally, it was found that the human resource function (in all its aspects) is not taken seriously enough by line departments. It is not seen as a strategic function, but rather as a 'pliable' support function.
- Respondents indicated *agreement* with the following statements: (1) HR planning is integrated with departmental business and financial plans (55%). (2) Linkages between the Public Service Act/Regulations and HR planning are communicated within the department (52%). (3) HR planning processes, roles, responsibilities and benefits are communicated to all stakeholders (managers, HR specialists, business planners, employees and unions) (52%). (4) There is a common framework for HR planning (51%).
- Respondents indicated *disagreement* with the following statements: (1) HR plans are shared between departments (53%). (2) Information from other departments relevant to HR planning is easily accessible (45%). (3) Good forecasting capacity is available (42%).
- When asked whether or not the Department of Public Service and Administration (DPSA) should have a role to play in HR planning for departments, 95% of the respondents indicated 'yes'. More specifically, this role should include, as indicated by 'yes' responses: (1) Develop an HR planning portal on the DPSA's website (100%). (2) Develop new competencies for the HR planning function (100%). (3) Provide HR planning training courses and workshops (100%). (4) Determine and communicate minimum requirements for reporting (97%). (5) Provide mentorship opportunities (98%). (6) Provide a framework for the accreditation of HR planners (98%). (7) Develop public service-wide communication plans that demonstrate the benefits of HR planning (96%).

Source: Republic of South Africa (2006: Online)

5.11   Review

In this chapter, we have discussed HR planning and the job analysis process. Job analysis is an integral part of HR planning, work design, and organisation design in that the total organisational structure and the different role responsibilities to govern work are established. We have discussed the stages in job analysis and various uses of this type of analysis, as in HR planning, recruitment and selection, training and development, compensation, and labour relations. We have considered the principles underlying job analysis and the methods used by job analysts, as well as the nature of job descriptions and job specifications.

The concept of HR planning was defined, followed by a discussion of its purpose and importance, and of the persons responsible for the process. The five steps in the HR planning process were also described in detail.

5.12   Self-evaluation questions

1. 'I don't need to know about any funny HR planning,' your public sector manager tells you. Explain why you agree or disagree with this statement.
2. Who is responsible for HR planning in a typical public sector institution? Give reasons for your suggestions.
3. Describe the steps of the HR planning process to a group of engineers who have just joined the public sector institution.
4. Why is it so important that HR specialists should be involved in the formulation of the overall corporate plan and the business plan of a public sector institution?
5. Discuss possible plans that can be developed to address both shortages and a surplus of employees in a public sector institution.
6. What is job analysis and how does it relate to HR planning?
7. Explain the differences between a job description and a job specification.
8. Describe the principles of job analysis and indicate how these principles contribute to institutional success.
9. Explain the various job analysis methods. What method would you recommend if approached to analyse: (a) the jobs of accountants who work in state departments; and (b) the jobs of ten computer analysts working in the Department of Health? Give reasons for your answer.
10. How would you draw up a job description and a job specification?
11. Explain the role of the budget in the HR planning process.
12. Discuss the implications of the Employment Equity Act on HR planning. Indicate clearly the areas that have to be considered, as well as the possible areas of direct and indirect discrimination in the process of attending to job analysis, job descriptions, job specifications, work design/redesign, and the drafting of HR plans.
13. How would one go about drawing up an HR plan?
14. Do monitoring, evaluating, and reporting on HR planning have to be a waste of time? Explain your answer.

Bibliography

Anderson, AH. 1994. *Effective personnel management: A skills and activity-based approach.* Oxford: Blackwell.

Babbie, E. 1995. *The practice of social research.* 7th edn. Harmsonburg, VA: Wadsworth.

Cherrington, DJ. 1995. *The management of human resources.* 4th edn. Englewood Cliffs, NJ: Prentice-Hall.

Cushway, B. 1994. *Human resource management.* London: Kogan Page.

De Cenzo, DA, & Robbins, SP. 1994. *Human resource management: Concepts and practices.* New York: Wiley.

Deneys Reitz Attorneys. 2010. Labour update. [http://www.deneysreitz.co.za].

Denhardt, RB. 1995. *Public administration: An action orientation.* Boston, MA: Wadsworth.

Dolan, SL, & Schuler, RS. 1987. *Personnel and human resource management in Canada.* New York: West.

French, W. 1994. *Human resource management.* 3rd edn. Boston, MA: Houghton Mifflin.

Foot, M, & Hook, C. 1996. *Introducing human resource management.* London: Longman.

Grogan, J. 2008. *Workplace law.* Cape Town: Juta.

Hercus, T. 1993. Workforce planning in eight British organisations: A Canadian perspective. In B. Towers (ed.), *Handbook of workforce management.* Oxford: Blackwell.

Jarrell, DW. 1993. *Human resource planning: Business planning approach.* Englewood Cliffs, NJ: Prentice-Hall.

Klingner, DE, & Nalbandian, J. 1985. *Public personnel management: Context and strategies.* Englewood Cliffs, NJ: Prentice-Hall.

McBeath, G. 1992. *The handbook of human resource planning: Practical manpower analysis techniques for HR professionals.* Oxford: Blackwell.

Newstrom, JW, & Scannel, EE. 1980. *Games trainers play: Experiential learning exercises.* New York: McGraw Hill.

Noe, R, Hollenbeck, JR, Gerhart, B, & Wright, PM. 1994. *Human resource management: Gaining a competitive advantage.* Boston, MA: Irwin.

O'Doherty, D. 1995. Towards human resource planning? In I Beardwell & L Holden (eds.), *Human resource management: A contemporary perspective.* London: Pitman.

Schuler, RD, Dowling, PJ, Smart, JP, & Huber, VL. 1993. *Human resource management in Australia.* 2nd edn. Melbourne: Harper Educational.

Sibson, RE. 1992. *Strategic planning for human resources management.* New York: AMACO

Swanepoel, B, Van Wyk, M, & Schenk, H. 2003. *South African human resource management: Theory and practice.* Cape Town: Juta.

Van der Westhuizen, EJ. 2000. *Public Human Resource Management. Study guide 1 for PUB303-F.* Pretoria: University of South Africa.

Acts of legislation

Republic of South Africa. 1994. The Public Service Act (Proclamation 103 of 1994). Government Printer. [http://www.polity.org.za/html/govdocs/legislation/1994]

Republic of South Africa. 1998a. The Employment Equity Act (Act 55 of 1998). Government Printer. [http://www.polity.org.za/html/govdocs/legislation/1998]

Republic of South Africa. 1998b. The Skills Development Act (Act 97 of 1998). Government Printer. [http://www.polity.org.za/html/govdocs/legislation/1998]

Republic of South Africa. 1999a. The Public Finance Management Act (Act 1 of 1999). Government Printer. [http://www.polity.org.za/html/govdocs/legislation/1999]

Government regulations

Republic of South Africa. 2001. Public Service Regulations of 2001. Government Gazette, 427 (21951).

Government reports

Republic of South Africa. 2006. Development of interventions to improve the quality of human resource planning at departmental level in the public service. Pretoria: Department of Public Service and Administration. [http://www.dpsa.gov.za/documents/hrp].

Republic of South Africa. 2008(a). Report on the audit on vacancy rates in national and provincial departments. Pretoria: Public Service Commission.

Republic of South Africa. 2010. Assessment of the state of human resource management in the public service. Pretoria; Public Service Commission. [http://www.psc.gov.za/docs/reports/2010/PSC].

Other government documents

Republic of South Africa. 2008(b). Province of the Eastern Cape. Department of Social Development. Human resources plan 2008–2010. Province of the Eastern Cape. Department of Social Development. [http://www.socdev.ecprov.gov.za].

Management guides

Republic of South Africa. 1999b. Baseline Implementation Guide. 22 June 1999. Department of the Public Service and Administration.

Republic of South Africa. 2002a. Guidelines on Integrated Human Resource Planning in the Public Service. December 2002. Department of Public Service and Administration.

Republic of South Africa. 2002b. Senior Management Service: Public Service Handbook. Department of Public Service and Administration [http:www.dpsa.gov.za/documents/sms/ publications/smshb2003].

Part 3

Obtaining suitable human resources for the public sector

WHEN public institutions are in a position to fill the available positions, they become fully involved in the hiring process, which basically consists of three components, namely recruitment, selection and orientation of the new employees. This is a very strategic process, and it lies at the heart of successful human resource management. It is not a simple task to secure a highly qualified and dedicated workforce. What makes it even more complex in nature is that, today, the hiring process takes place within the context of equal employment opportunity (EEO) requirements and affirmative action policy guidelines for the purpose of creating a representative bureaucracy. For several reasons, these requirements and policy guidelines create both obligations and constraints for all public sector managers and HR specialists. On the one hand, those involved in the hiring process are obliged to comply with the law (for example, the Employment Equity Act 55 of 1998), to protect employee rights (for example, off-duty rights such as sexual behaviour), and to deal with complaints of discrimination (for example, discrimination on the basis of race). On the other hand, constraints are imposed because traditional HR activities must now be executed in a different manner from that of the past. A good rule of thumb in this regard is that daily HR work needs to be conducted in such a way that it does not create barriers to equal employment opportunity.

To be effective, the hiring process should always be tied to the objectives of achieving and sustaining a workforce that is representative of the diversity of the society. On the downside, some public sector employers may see this as a huge constraint, and would therefore discount the ideas, perspectives and interventions of EEO and Affirmative Action (AA). Although employers may disagree with the specific applications of EEO and AA, compliance with the law is important because it is the right thing to do, and it simultaneously minimises potential financial and legal liability. You may also face a public relations nightmare if discrimination charges are publicised. The application of EEO requirements and AA policies is very much part of the daily work of public managers and HR specialists in the hiring process. Therefore, we have incorporated a chapter on equalising employment opportunities in Part 3 because this forms a strategic part of the hiring process. Thereafter we will move on to the more technical aspects of recruitment, selection and orientation.

6 Equalising opportunities by means of affirmative action

Purpose

The purpose of this chapter is to clarify the application of affirmative action as a means of equalising opportunities in the public service.

Learning outcomes

After you have read this chapter, you should be able to:
- Define, and differentiate from one another, the concepts affirmative action, reverse discrimination, equality of opportunity, formal employment equity and substantive employment equity.
- Describe sources of discrimination in South African society (past and present).
- Explain the organisational and employment equity plan.
- Explain which legislation and policies underlie affirmative action in the South African public service.
- Explain how public institutions could go about implementing affirmative action.

6.1 Introduction

The idea of a representative bureaucracy is well established in Public Administration discourse (see Muthien 1999: 207–224; Riccucci & Saidel 1997). The value of this idea lies mainly at the symbolic level. A representative bureaucracy demonstrates a legitimisation of government policies and programmes in the sense that diverse communities perceive a greater sense of fairness when officials at the point of service delivery are visibly representative.

Within the South African context, the pre-1994 public service was mainly characterised by its division on the basis of race and gender, and its lack of representativeness. As a result, the public service required legitimacy and credibility in the eyes of the majority of South Africans. Moreover, a continuation of its racial and gender composition would have contravened Section 195(1)(i) of the Constitution of the Republic of South Africa, 1996, which states that public administration 'must be broadly representative of the South African people [...]' (Republic of South Africa 1996: Section 195(1)(i)). Consequently, restoring legitimacy and credibility through the development of a broadly representative public service has become a major policy drive in the South African public service. Thus, affirmative action policies for the South African public service were introduced for the first time in 1994 (Republic of South Africa 1998: Chapter 1).

In order to analyse and clarify the application of affirmative action as a means of equalising opportunities in the public service, this chapter will be directed by the following key questions:

- What is the origin of affirmative action?
- Which concepts are related to the concept of affirmative action?
- What exactly is the nature of affirmative action?
- Which legislation and policies underlie affirmative action in the South African public service?
- How can an affirmative action programme be implemented in a public service?

6.2 What is the origin of affirmative action?

Affirmative action has its roots in the earliest efforts directed against unfair discrimination. The concept of affirmative action was first used in the United States of America in the Wagner Act of 1935. However, it was with the passing of the Civil Rights Act in 1964 that the foundation was laid (unintentionally, because the Act's objective was only to prohibit discrimination in the private sector) for the development of affirmative action law in the USA as we know it today. Whatever the intention was in 1964, by the time Congress enacted the Equal Opportunities Act of 1972, it clearly did intend to authorise preferential, results-orientated affirmative action. The most important federal legislation in the USA prohibiting discrimination in employment is Title VII of the Civil Rights Act of 1964. There were, however, several earlier efforts to make discrimination in employment unlawful. The modern history of these efforts starts in 1941 with President Roosevelt's Executive Order 8802, which prohibited discrimination based on race, creed, colour, or national origin by the federal government and by private employers in defence industries.

During and after World War II, the federal government tried to curb employment discrimination through the federal contract programme. Prior to the enactment of the Civil Rights Act in 1964, private employment relations remained beyond the reach of federal regulation and, despite the efforts of civil rights advocates, the issue of employment discrimination stayed off the national political agenda. The change in this political situation was heralded by the Supreme Court's decision in Brown v. Board of Education in 1954. Over time, the realisation grew that true equality requires more than the simple removal of existing discriminatory barriers, and it was left to the courts laboriously to reconstruct Title VII of the Civil Rights Act (dealing with discrimination in the workplace) to fit the ends dictated by these new insights.

One year after Title VII was enacted, President Johnson signed Executive Order 11246, which required federal contractors to 'take affirmative action to ensure that applicants are employed, and that employees are treated during employment, without regard to their race, colour, religion, sex or national origin'. The order left it to the Labour Department to define the specifics of affirmative action and its enforcement. The Labour Department's guidelines state that affirmative action applies to a wide range of minority groups and women and consists of 'results-oriented actions', such as goals, timetables, back pay, and retroactive seniority, designed to ensure equal employment opportunity. By 1968, the Labour Department had developed 'utilisation analysis'. The underlying assumption was that, in the absence of discrimination, persons from affected classes would be hired in roughly the same proportion as they were qualified and available. Based on this assumption, the Labour Department viewed disparate impact as strong evidence of discrimination. The Labour Department, the Equal Employment Opportunity Commission (EEOC) and the Office of Federal Contract Compliance (OFCCP) used such evidence to demand that goals and timetables be established to reduce the under-utilisation of affected groups. Now the government officially recognised discrimination as systemic (not necessarily intentional), and the results-oriented goal of proportional representation became part of US public policy.

Affirmative action in contract compliance was directed at collective social and institutional discrimination, rather than at acts of individual and/or intentional discrimination. This constituted a more direct and simpler form of promoting affirmative action in that it was based on disparate impact (and not on proof of intentional discrimination) and was thus not concerned with the legalities surrounding the meaning of unlawful discrimination, nor was proof of past discriminatory practices required to mandate affirmative action. The greater latitude to enforce affirmative action in the case of federal contracts is justified on the basis that employers are voluntarily seeking government contracts and the executive branch can impose conditions on participation which satisfy some legitimate public policy. In addition, the sanction for non-compliance could be termination of the contract based on the breach of a material term of the contract by the employer/contractor, thereby providing a strong incentive for employers to fulfil their affirmative action obligations in terms of the contract.

Title VII created a five-member EEOC, authorising it to receive complaints of discrimination from individuals, to investigate, and, upon determining that there was reasonable cause to believe that the charge was true, to seek to eliminate the alleged unlawful practice by informal negotiation, conciliation, and persuasion. If EEOC conciliation failed, the complainant could bring a civil action against the employer or trade union. This commission, with its very limited powers, played a surprisingly important role in the development of the notion of disparate impact under Title VII litigation. From the start, the EEOC's stance was that it had to investigate and conciliate not only individual complaints but also to investigate patterns of institutional discrimination, the effects of past discrimination, and disparate impact discrimination (as opposed to disparate treatment discrimination). The EEOC viewed Title VII as remedial and retrospective in nature, rather than as simply prospective, and measured its success in terms of numbers of minority group members in employment.

In the late 1990s, the opposition to affirmative action among the American public seemed to have grown to the extent that certain states (for example, California) adopted legislation to prohibit affirmative action, allowing only for protection against unfair discrimination. It is useful to bear in mind, when comparing the USA's experience with affirmative action to the situation in South Africa, that, whereas the beneficiaries of affirmative action in the USA are a minority (and hence politically non-dominant), the beneficiaries of affirmative action in South Africa are the politically dominant group. A major potential consequence of this political and demographic reality is that affirmative action in the South African context may be projected to remain a relatively permanent fixture of our social landscape.

6.3 Which concepts are related to the concept of affirmative action?

The concept of affirmative action is used together with many other concepts referring to various processes of making bureaucracies more representative of the societies that they are serving. Some of these concepts are equal opportunities, black advancement, black empowerment, reverse discrimination, social responsibility and managing diversity. These concepts and other related concepts play an important role in understanding the concept 'affirmative action' and other related concepts adequately, which is explained in Focus on Research 6.1.

 FOCUS ON RESEARCH 6.1
Concepts related to affirmative action

Two articles have been published 2005 and 2008 respectively, in which the concepts related to affirmative action and equal employment opportunities were discussed. In the first article entitled 'Equal employment opportunities: A conceptual puzzle' (Wessels 2005), a conceptual framework is offered to untangle the major transformation-related concepts in the public service. The second article entitled 'Transforming the public service to serve a diverse society: can representativeness be the most decisive criterion?' (Wessels 2008), it was concluded that equality and equal opportunities cannot be achieved for all members of a diverse South African society if representativeness is regarded as a sufficient condition for public service employment.

For the purpose of this chapter, we shall focus only on the concepts of affirmative action, equality of opportunity and reverse discrimination.

 DID YOU KNOW?

Affirmative action as a policy intervention is defined as a strategy for the achievement of employment equity through redressing imbalances, and a means of enabling the disadvantaged to compete competitively with the advantaged. So it appears to be a policy intervention intended to, among others, break down barriers to equality and equal employment (Wessels 2008: 28).

6.3.1 Affirmative action

The concept of affirmative action is used in many different guises and it is not always readily apparent what persons mean when employing it. The following comments regarding affirmative action are reproduced here to obtain a sense of what is generally understood by the concept.

- 'Affirmative action refers to specific steps, beyond ending discriminatory practices, which are taken to promote equal opportunity and to ensure that discrimination will not recur. The goal of affirmative action is to eliminate non-legal barriers to equal employment opportunity, including intentional discriminatory policies and practices and unintentional (structural or systemic) discrimination. Affirmative action is best understood as a diverse continuum of more or less severe responses that attempt to overcome discrimination. Some affirmative action programmes attempt to protect the individual against intentional discrimination, others are explicitly preferential (goals): [...] it is best to be clear that affirmative action involves some degree of preferential treatment, because not to do so is to beg the question – it is to force the most crucial issue into the background: the issue of whether preferential treatment for women and nonwhites can ever be morally justifiable' (Taylor 1991: 14).

- 'In its broadest meaning the phrase affirmative action is now generally understood to refer to the practice of favourably considering an individual's status as a woman, or as a member of a racial or ethnic minority group. Affirmative action is designed to aid those that have suffered historical and widespread mistreatment in the form of both de jure and de facto discrimination. Affirmative action may also be described as a temporary policy embraced by government, businesses and universities as a means of achieving true equal opportunity. Affirmative action policies are frequently used in awarding business contracts, in hiring and promotions, and in university admissions and granting of scholarships' (Starks 1992: 939).

- '[...] affirmative action is generally designed with three goals in mind: To eliminate existing discrimination against minorities and women; to remedy the lingering effect of past discrimination against these groups; and to prevent future discrimination against these groups' (Starks 1992: 940).

- 'Affirmative action in the South African context has extremely broad connotations, touching, as apartheid did and still does, on every area of life [...] affirmative action covers all purposive activity designed to eliminate the effects of apartheid and to create a society where everyone has the same chance to get on in life. In terms of the ANC draft Bill of Rights, all anti-discrimination measures, as well as all anti-poverty ones, may be regarded as constituting a form of affirmative action' (Sachs 1991).

- 'Affirmative action is not synonymous with quotas: 'quotas' reserve opportunities and benefits exclusively for qualified members of designated minority groups.'

- 'Preferential treatment, on the other hand, allows an individual's status as a minority to be considered as a positive factor among other factors when allocating opportunities and benefits' (Starks 1992: 942).

- '[Affirmative action] can be viewed as a pro-active development tool to overcome [...] constraints and more effectively mobilize latent resources in order to stimulate overall development' (Human 1993: 2).

- 'Affirmative action programmes can be broken down into judicially imposed; voluntarily enacted; and legislatively mandated. When affirmative action is judicially imposed a court orders a party to enact affirmative action policies as a remedy for proven discrimination. Voluntarily enacted affirmative action refers to the institutional practice of implementing affirmative action policies as a means of eradicating the effects of prior discrimination against minorities without being required to do so' (Starks 1992: 947).
- 'Affirmative action is thus a temporary intervention designed to achieve equal employment opportunity without lowering standards and without unduly trammelling the career aspirations or expectations of current organisational members who are competent in their jobs' (Human 1993: 3).
- '[A]ffirmative action is defined as the additional corrective steps which must be taken in order that those who have been historically disadvantaged by unfair discrimination are able to derive full benefit from an equitable employment environment' (Republic of South Africa 1998a: Chapter 1, v).

> For the purposes of this book, affirmative action is viewed as those proactive and remedial measures designed to bridge the gap between formal equality of employment opportunity and substantive equality of opportunity.

Viewed thus, affirmative action comes to the fore in a society in which the stage has been reached when the law does not discriminate, but societal discrimination is still prevalent. Affirmative action in the work environment is the last step towards the ideal of true employment equity. Logically and chronologically, a model of the steps from a state of employment inequity to employment equity will therefore follow the following sequence:

> 1. Discriminatory laws and societal discrimination exist (state of employment inequity).
> 2. Anti-discriminatory laws are enacted (state of formal equity in which societal discrimination is still present).
> 3. Affirmative action programmes and laws are enacted (state of striving towards true or substantive employment equity)

In the debate surrounding affirmative action, the participants are frequently labelled as falling into certain camps. Since some of this terminology is also used in this book, it may be expedient to provide a brief clarification of some of these terms.

- An egalitarian is someone who holds that the distribution of goods in a just society shall be according to the principle of 'equal shares' irrespective of differences among individuals in their respective contributions to the creation of a society's wealth (one could associate this view with communism or extreme forms of socialism).

- A libertarian is someone who contends that the distribution of social goods should be strictly according to merit and that the state's primary task is to protect the individual's freedom to pursue his or her own goals in life (capitalists, free marketers and individualists may be some labels associated with this school of thought).

- A liberal is one who holds that, while individuals should be left free to pursue their divergent ends, it should be recognised that an individual owes a debt to society and consequently that it is society's duty to distribute wealth more equally (thus wealth creation is protected but the distribution of wealth is not left entirely to the individual – social democrats or capitalists with a human face could be appropriate labels for this group).

6.3.2 Equality of opportunity

The title of this chapter refers to both affirmative action and equalising opportunities, thus implying that there is a difference between the two. The concept of equal opportunities was highlighted by the 1976 Race Relations Act in Britain – an Act making provision, among other things, for the promotion of equal opportunities in employment (Lee 1992: 141). Article 16 of the Constitution of India also provides for equal opportunity in employment (Tummala 1991: 383–411).

The aim of equality of opportunity is to provide special opportunities to members of specific groups, who are either absent from or under-represented in certain areas of work, so that they can catch up with applicants and employees in the more privileged groups. An equal opportunity programme therefore also aims at rectifying the wrongs of the past, but it differs from affirmative action in the means it applies to reach this ultimate goal.

For our purposes, equality of opportunity refers to that ideal state where everyone has an equal chance (all other things being equal, such as innate abilities) to compete with his or her peers for access to social goods, whereas affirmative action refers to those (fair) discriminatory interventions that are necessitated as a bridge between our apartheid past and our non-discriminatory future.

An equal opportunity programme acknowledges the value of objective employment standards and aims at advancing personnel to that standard. Equal opportunities can be made part of an organisation's management style by acknowledging the diversity of its personnel corps and by making provision for employee empowerment, employee advancement and enabling training (Wessels 1992: 46).

We live in a crossover phase of our history, during which discrimination and its very badges (such as gender and race) have to be employed to get past discrimination – there is no other way. This is the essential paradox inherent in affirmative action: to get past (unfair or invidious) discrimination, we have to discriminate, albeit fairly (unfair discrimination in the name of a good cause still remains just that, unfair, and exposes affirmative action to the often-heard charge of 'reverse discrimination'). The progress from employment inequity to true employment equity is depicted in Figure 6.1.

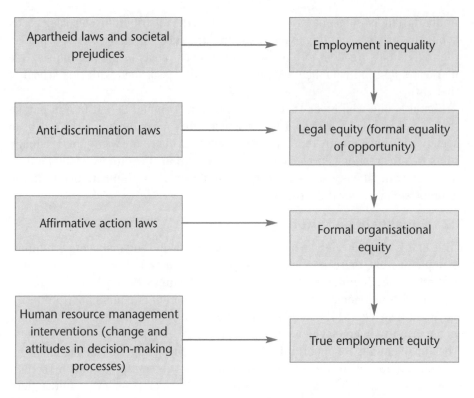

Figure 6.1   From apartheid to true or substantive employment equity

From Figure 6.1, it can be seen that anti-discrimination laws are not enough; although they do remove legal barriers to employment, they do not eradicate the historical inequalities which are still prevalent. Furthermore, even if affirmative action laws cause organisations to hire and promote historically disadvantaged people, the law cannot in itself remove non-legal or societal barriers arising from people's attitudes – for this, a concerted human resource management effort is needed. Thus, equality of opportunity is affirmative action in the narrow sense, that is, by prohibiting systems of legal privilege and disqualifications, thereby expanding the sphere of individual liberty. 'Formal' equality of opportunity is brought about by the enactment of anti-discrimination laws and the repeal of laws which allow for discrimination. 'True' or 'substantive' employment equity is, however, much more difficult to achieve, in that it requires a fundamental and honest change of heart among all relevant parties. This will entail a change of attitude and an acceptance of people, irrespective of their gender, culture, ethnicity or language.

6.3.3   Equality and affirmative action

The object of affirmative action within the South African context is the removal of inequalities. This, however, leaves some questions unanswered: 'equality for whom?', 'equality of what?', 'equality of means or equality of opportunities?' and 'how shall equality be measured?' These are highly complex issues which fall beyond the scope of this book, but it may be worthwhile for the reader to reflect on these questions. For example, the bland assertion that 'blacks or women should be treated equally' may be interpreted in a variety of ways, depending on what notion of equality the speaker has in mind.

All normative theories of the just society that have stood the test of time have one characteristic in common, namely that they demand equality of something, that something being central to a particular theory. Utilitarians demand that equal weight be given to the utilities of all; libertarians insist on equal enjoyment of civil rights and liberties for all; income and welfare egalitarians regard equal incomes and equal welfare levels, respectively, as indispensable for the just society. Therefore, to characterise the controversy over equality as one involving those who are against equality versus those who are for equality is 'to miss something central to the subject' (Sen 1992: ix). For instance, a libertarian would have no objection in principle to equal incomes, given a certain set of prevailing circumstances and provided that equal enjoyment of individual rights and liberties are not compromised.

Insisting on equality in respect of a particular variable that is central to a given theory of social justice necessarily entails tolerating inequalities in competing variables. For instance, a libertarian cannot demand equal enjoyment of rights and liberties and insist on the pre-eminence of the merit principle, while at the same time insisting on equality of income levels. Therefore, the dispute between egalitarians and libertarians, in truth, resides not in the concept of equality but in identifying the central social variable that should be given priority over competing socially desirable arrangements. Human diversity will inevitably result in equality in one respect giving rise to inequality in another. Ethical theories typically try to justify inequalities in the peripheral variables by pointing to equality in the focal variable, which it is proposed is the most important equality in terms of a particular ethical theory.

The concept of equality has, since the earliest times, been used in a variety of ways and normally in a context that implies that it is a fundamental element of justice. While justice has many manifestations, we are concerned with distributive justice when analysing the concept of equality. However, there seems to be little agreement as to what is meant by the concepts of equality and justice. One of the earliest definitions of justice holds that to treat equals equally and unequals differently encapsulate the essence of justice. But this simply begs the question, since one's system of classification of 'equals' and 'unequals', and the consequences of this classification, will determine the fairness of the awards and punishment attached to these classifications. For instance, to classify people as 'black' or 'white' may not be intrinsically reprehensible, but to make the distribution of social goods and civil liberties contingent upon the classification is certainly grossly unfair.

6.3.4 Reverse discrimination versus affirmative action

The difference between affirmative action and discrimination can be explained as follows: Affirmative action is not discrimination in reverse, nor is it appropriate to apply the same requirement of neutrality, applicable in the domain of antidiscrimination regulation, to affirmative action. This is so for two reasons. First, to equate affirmative action with discrimination is fallacious as the aim of discrimination is to exclude, whereas affirmative action's aim is to include. Second, affirmative action requires positive action to overcome systemic, institutionalised discrimination, whereas anti-discrimination laws are passive in the sense that they proscribe someone from indulging in certain types of behaviour (as opposed to mandating certain conduct, as is the case in affirmative action initiatives). Against a background of centuries of discrimination, anti-discrimination laws are perpetuating discrimination, rather than eliminating it. However, it should be noted that, depending on the modality of the affirmative action programme adopted (see Section 6.4.1), affirmative action may be unfair and indeed unconstitutional, irrespective of the good intentions and effectiveness of the programme. For example, an affirmative action programme amounting to 'no white males need apply' may, in all likelihood, be impugned as reverse discrimination.

6.4   The nature of affirmative action

Affirmative action has various dimensions and patterns. At its best, it remains a controversial policy option. In order to find an answer to the question 'what is the nature of affirmative action?' we will focus in this section on the diverse modalities and controversial nature of affirmative action.

6.4.1 Modalities of affirmative action

Affirmative action can take many forms. It is important to determine the type of affirmative action contemplated by the organisation's affirmative action policy, since not all types of affirmative action programme would be equally immune to challenges from persons who may feel aggrieved by such programmes. Another reason for this investigation of the permissible forms of affirmative action in terms of an employer's objectives (as contained in an affirmative action policy document) is that, if it can be shown that a form of preferential promotion was used that falls outside the ambit of the employer's objectives, such promotion could possibly be challenged as being unfair. This possibility is based on the argument that the fairness of preferential promotions is to be found in the employer's objectives.

Three modalities or forms of affirmative action can be distinguished: a strong, an intermediate and a weak form. In the strong variant, a person qualifies for preferential treatment solely on the grounds that he or she possesses an immutable characteristic (for example, an employee is promoted because she is a female, without satisfying the job specifications). In the intermediate/moderate variant of affirmative action, the person meets the minimum standards/qualification for the job and is given preference over another candidate who is better qualified, because of some immutable characteristic which he or she possesses but which the better qualified person does not. (As when the job specifies Matric as a minimum qualification, though preferably a bachelor's degree, and a black matriculant is promoted rather than the white male graduate candidate). In the weak variant of affirmative action, a black/female/handicapped/etc. employee is only promoted in preference to an able-bodied white male if both candidates are equally qualified for the job. While many South African employers would like to see only the weak modality of affirmative action adopted or mandated, it should be clear that such a policy will not be up to the task facing this country.

6.4.2   The controversial nature of affirmative action

'Affirmative action is a battleground for competing values, especially competing concepts of distributive justice' (Taylor 1991: xv). Libertarianism's claim that merit should be the universal principle of distributive justice can be questioned. First, there is the problem of defining merit, as well as the influence of culture on the definer of merit, which seems to make it a less than objective standard by which to allocate goods. Second, there is the inappropriateness of merit as a criterion of distribution in certain circumstances. Third, the question should be asked whether merit is a socially desirable criterion, since it may have undesirable societal consequences. Fourth, the criteria for defining the distributive values used to guide the allocation of social goods and resources are a further source of controversy. For some, prevailing standards are nothing more than collective, subjective preferences, and are, as such, suspect and open to the challenge that they are reflective of pervasive prejudice. Although there may be consensus about what value should serve as the basis of a distribution, there may be a considerable sense of injustice about the criteria that are used to define the value. Within a community, affirmative action may enjoy a generally high degree of acceptance, as a value in itself, on which to base job allocations, but there may exist an equally great resistance to the criteria used to identify the beneficiaries of affirmative action (for example, group-based criteria versus actual victims of past discrimination).

The incommensurability of the opposing sides in the affirmative action debate is based on fundamental disagreements about the meaning of such concepts as equality and justice; both sides proclaim their allegiance to the ideal of equality. Acceptance of competing views of the relationship between individuals and society can have profound implications for our view of such fundamental concepts as property rights, employment-related rights and duties, and equality. These topics are, however, so wide ranging that no attempt will be made to deal with them here, save for giving one example. By way of contrast with the orthodox libertarian conception of property rights, the modern tendency is towards a restriction of property rights in what has been referred to as the 'socialisation of property' (Rycroft & Jordaan 1992: 15). Rycrot and Jordaan (1992: 16–17) describe this process as follows:

'Socialisation' of law entails the adjustment of conflicting interests in society through the subordination of the individual's interests to those of society at large. In relation to property, it entails a shift away from an individualist 'and basically exploitive' perception of property rights towards the notion that property is a social responsibility. The underlying premise is that the institution of property is derived from and protected by society, i.e. it is a social institution and may be made to serve particular social objectives. This is accomplished through 'public law' regulation of the use and application of property resources. 'Absolute' rights are replaced by rights qualified to suit the needs of society best. [...] Legal rules do not exist in a vacuum but are tied to the social system within which they operate.

The above reasoning can therefore validly be used to justify further intrusions into managerial prerogative, for instance, to achieve the goals of affirmative action and equality.

6.5 How intense is the need for affirmative action in the SA public service?

Considering the fact that affirmative action has its roots in efforts directed against unfair discrimination, it makes sense to determine the extent of unfair discrimination in the South African public service which necessitates the introduction of affirmative action. For this purpose, we shall consider a brief historical overview of the recruitment, appointment and utilisation policies in the South African public service. This overview will be followed by a comparison between the composition of the South African population and the South African public service in order to determine the extent to which the public service reflects the composition of the country's population.

6.5.1 Historical overview of employment policies in the SA public service

The establishment of the Union of South Africa in 1910 serves as a logical point of departure for a brief historical overview of recruitment, appointment and utilisation policies in the South African public service. For this overview, the comprehensive research by Alan Sharpe, as documented in his thesis, 'The Policy Concerning the Employment of Non-Whites in the South African Public Service (1910–1981)', will be the main source of reference.

It seems that the South African public service over the period from 1910 to 1994 was an institution primarily for white people. Sharpe shows that, although the period between 1910 and 1924 saw an acute shortage of skilled manpower, 'non-whites' were employed only in the public service where whites were either unobtainable or 'no longer regarded particular types of work as becoming to themselves, for example the work of manual labourers'. Furthermore, it seems that 'non-whites' did not generally have the education and skills to be employed in administrative, professional, technical and clerical positions (Sharpe 1982: 20–21).

The traditional employment policy of the South African public service did not change during the period between 1924 and 1939. This policy was part of the government's general racial policy, which included job reservation and the separation of blacks and whites in the job situation. The effect of this policy was that 'non-whites' were not allowed access to all divisions of the public service. The educational facilities for 'non-whites' were still inadequate, with the result that there were no 'queues of qualified Non-Whites presenting themselves for appointment'. On the other hand, the supply of white candidates was such that there were long waiting lists for clerical and even lower graded posts (Sharpe 1982: 36–37).

During the period from 1939 to 1948, the public service experienced shortages of personnel, such as messengers and nurses. However, a strong anti-Indian feeling developed in Natal, which made it politically difficult to recruit Indians for the public service. As government policy regarding blacks was that they should live and work in their 'own areas' and that they were only temporary residents in the 'white areas', they were not seen as a solution for the shortages of personnel. In an attempt to relieve the shortage of messengers, white females were employed, while salary increases were given to white male messengers. In order to relieve the shortage of nurses, black female nursing assistants were appointed against the vacant (white) posts. The Social and Economic Planning Council of the Union of South Africa suggested in 1946 that white married women should be encouraged to rejoin the public service, on a temporary basis. Employment policies prior to 1961 did not permit married women to be employed permanently in the public service (Sharpe 1982: 59–61).

In 1961 the Public Service Joint Advisory Council proposed that women officials be retained in a permanent capacity upon marriage (Muthien 1999: 213–214). However, the possibility of employing 'non-whites' as substitutes for whites was not mentioned at all by the Council. In 1947, the government adopted a policy that each population group should, where possible, be served by its own people (Sharpe 1982: 59–61).

The National Party came into power in 1948, resulting in government policy that tended towards a separation of racial groups. The shortage of white manpower continued. The following steps were considered in order to relieve this shortage (Sharpe 1982: 70–71):

- Reducing the activities of government departments;
- Using the available resources sparingly;
- Relaxing appointment requirements;
- Granting salary increases;
- Appointing pensioners and other whites who did not meet the prescribed age limit, in a temporary capacity;
- Acknowledging previous experience for salary purposes; and
- Improving the fringe benefits.

The permanent employment of 'non-whites' in the (white) vacancies was seemingly not even considered (Sharpe 1982: 71). Sharpe (1982: 90) also points out that the Public Service Commission, during the period from 1948 to 1954, was reluctant to classify 'non-white' posts in a higher division in the public service than the General Division (non-prescribed). This practice was nothing other than job reservation, and was in step with the government's policy of racial segregation.

From 1948 to 1954, the government developed policies to the extent that 'non-whites' would not be allowed employment in the public service on equal terms with whites. 'Non-whites' would also not be placed in positions of authority over whites, despite the fact that severe shortages of white personnel were experienced at that time. In the case of messenger services, 'non-whites' were employed as temporary substitutes for whites who were unobtainable (Sharpe 1982: 114).

The emphasis during the period from 1954 to 1966 was still on creating opportunities for 'non-whites' to render a service to their own people. This resulted in the establishing of a Department of Coloured Affairs and a Department of Indian Affairs. Regarding black people, the intention of government was that they should be granted self-government in their own areas. The Public Service Commission was reluctant to afford 'non-white' personnel the same favourable conditions of service (such as membership of a pension fund) as were enjoyed by white personnel (Sharpe 1982: 149–152).

Although the shortage of (white) personnel in the public service worsened in the early 1970s (Brand 1982: 97), the government continued pursuing its policy that each population group should be served by its own people (Sharpe 1982: 210–212). Training and other endeavours to increase the supply of scarce human resources were hampered by statutory and administrative restrictions on the mobility of the 'non-white' workforce (Brand 1982: 100). Consequently, in 1972, both the government and the Public Service Commission came to the conclusion that 'non-whites' would of necessity have to be employed in the public service in fields of work which had hitherto been closed to them. In 1977, the Cabinet approved a policy on the basis of which 'non-whites' could be accommodated in the public service. The essence of this policy was that, where 'non-whites' were employed in the 'white' public service, it was done on an ad hoc basis to meet the needs of the moment (Sharpe 1982: 210–212). Dr. J.G. Garbers, then President of the Human Sciences Research Council, questioned the sense of these policies when he asked whether the government's policy was perhaps not hostile to the administration of the country (Garbers 1982: 118–119).

From 1966 to 1978, there was a gradual movement towards uniform posts and rank designations for whites and 'non-whites'. However, to ensure that each population group was served by its own people, the Public Service Commission amended the designations of posts which were open to 'non-whites' in general (Sharpe 1982: 210, 214).

From 1978 to 1981, 'non-white' posts were gradually classified in the same divisions as corresponding white posts and accorded the same designations. A decision was also made to narrow the wage gap between whites and 'non-whites' (Sharpe 1982: 248–250).

Resulting from this decision, the Commission for Administration reported in its annual report of 1987 that 'all disparities among population groups [would] be eliminated with effect from 1 March 1988' (Republic of South Africa 1988: 21). In its next annual report, the Commission stated that the following issues had been addressed by its office (Republic of South Africa 1989: 9–10):

- The more representative utilisation of all population groups in the public service, with special reference to the management echelon.
- The introduction of special training programmes for selected candidates of all population groups, with the additional purpose of making up circumstantially linked backlogs.
- The better utilisation of women in the public service, again with the emphasis on the management echelon.

Although women could compete freely with men for posts in the public service (Republic of South Africa 1990: 27), a gender breakdown of the public service indicates that women were largely confined to lower skill levels and to nurturing professions in the health and education sectors (Muthien 1999: 214). The number of women, especially in the senior ranks, was still low in the late 1980s. The Commission was concerned about that and was eager to remove hindrances to the upward mobility of women in the public service (Republic of South Africa 1990: 27).

The Transitional Executive Council (TEC), established to oversee the process of transition after the successful multi-party negotiations, decided to freeze all vacancies on both entry and promotion levels prior to the 1994 elections. Before any one of the various policies and legislation on affirmative action in the period following the 1994 elections came into force, the new government advertised 11 000 posts as part of a major affirmative drive (Muthien 1999: 216).

6.5.2 Comparison of the composition of the SA population and the composition of the public service

When the ANC government took office in 1994, it inherited a public service whose composition, specifically with regard to race and gender, did not reflect the composition of the South African population at large. Table 6.1 on page 174 illustrates the difference between the racial group composition of the South African population and the composition of the public service in 1995 to the same statistics 15 years later in 2010.

As a result of this cultural and racial discrepancy in 1995, the public service lacked legitimacy and credibility in the eyes of the under-represented part of the South African population (Republic of South Africa 1998a: 1.2). Consequently, affirmative action policies were introduced as early as 1994 in an attempt to change the demographic profile of the South African public service. These changes were especially visible in the composition of the management echelon of the public

Table 6.1   Comparison of the composition of the South African population and the public service by population group as a percentage in 1995 and 2010

Population group	South African population (%)		Public service (%)	
	1995	2010	1995	2010
African	76	79.6	64	80
Coloured	9	8.8	9	9
Indian	2	2.6	2	3
White	13	9.2	25	9

Sources: South Africa (1996b: Statistical Supplement, 9, 11); Republic of South Africa (2006: 86); Republic of South Africa (2010a)

service (see Table 6.2 below). However, by 2001, the composition of the management echelon was still not a reflection of the composition of the country's population.

According to Muthien (1999), a former member of the South African Public Service Commission, public policy programmes have been forced to recognise the importance of women in relation to citizenship rights and voting rights. Although it may seem that the gender distribution of the South African public service is fairly equal (Table 6.3 on page 175), Muthien points out that women are largely confined to lower skill levels and to nurturing professions in the health and education sectors, such as nursing, teaching, catering, social work and auxiliary health professions. She believes that women should be in the mainstream of the redistribution of status and power. Therefore, programmes of equity and redress should accordingly address the foundations of public institutions (Muthien 1999: 209–215).

Table 6.2   Managers at all levels, by population group, as a percentage of total managers in the SA public service: 1995–2002

Population group	South African population 1995 (%)	Managers in SA public service 1995 (%)	Managers in SA public service 1997 (%)	Managers in SA public service 2002 (%)	South African population 2002 (%)
African	76	30.0	38.2	51.1	79.0
Coloured	9	6.7	5.7	6.6	8.9
Indian	2	3.4	4.4	5.7	2.5
White	13	59.9	51.7	36.6	9.6

Sources: Combined information adapted from Annual Report of the Public Service Commission (1995, Statistical Supplement: 12); and Thompson & Woolard (2002) calculated from public service payroll information (PERSAL)

Table 6.3   Female managers at all levels, by population group, as a percentage of total managers in the SA public service per race group: 1995–2002

Population group	South African population 1995 (%)	Managers in SA public service 1995 (%)	Managers in SA public service 1997 (%)	Managers in SA public service 2002 (%)	South African population 2002 (%)
African	76	30.0	38.2	51.1	79.0
Coloured	9	6.7	5.7	6.6	8.9
Indian	2	3.4	4.4	5.7	2.5
White	13	59.9	51.7	36.6	9.6

Source: Adapted from Thompson & Woolard (2002), calculated from public service payroll information (PERSAL)

6.6   What legislation and policies underlie affirmative action in the SA public service?

Affirmative action programmes in the South African public service are determined by a variety of legislation and policy documents relevant to human resource management in the public service, such as the following:

- The Constitution of the Republic of South Africa, 1996;
- The White Paper on the Transformation of the Public Service, 1995;
- The White Paper on Public Service Training and Education, 1997;
- The White Paper on Human Resource Management in the Public Service, 1997;
- The Green Paper on a Conceptual Framework for Affirmative Action and the Management of Diversity in the Public Service, 1997;
- The Employment Equity Act of 1998;
- The White Paper on Affirmative Action in the Public Service, 1998; and
- The Public Service Regulations, 2001.

It is not possible to make a thorough study of affirmative action in the South African public service without reviewing this legislation and related policy documentation.

6.6.1   The Constitution of the Republic of South Africa, 1996

The Bill of Rights in the Constitution of the Republic of South Africa, 1996, sets the requirements for equality and representativeness in the workplace in general (Section 9), and specifically in the public service (Subsection 195(1)(i)). Subsection 9(1) rules that everyone is equal before the law and has the right to equal protection and benefit of the law. Subsection 9(2) follows on by declaring that equality includes the full and equal enjoyment of all rights and freedoms. In terms of this subsection, legislative and other measures may be designed to protect or advance certain people or categories of people.

In addition to the general ruling of Section 9, Subsection 195(1)(i) of the Constitution of the Republic of South Africa, 1996, is very explicit about the necessity of the public service being governed by the principle of broad representativeness and personnel management practices that are based on the need to redress the imbalances of the past. The Constitution rules that national legislation should ensure the promotion of these principles (Subsection 195(3)). In this regard, the Public Service Laws Amendment Act of 1997, the Employment Equity Act of 1998, and the Public Service Regulations of 2001 have come into effect.

6.6.2 The White Paper on the Transformation of the Public Service, 1995

The White Paper on the Transformation of the Public Service, 1995, focuses, among other things, on representativeness and affirmative action in the South African public service. This document can be regarded as the first of a series of official government policy documents on affirmative action. The point of departure for this document's chapter on representativeness and affirmative action is that 'representativeness is [...] a necessary precondition for legitimising the public service and driving it towards equitable service delivery' (Republic of South Africa 1995: 10). The main target groups for affirmative action programmes have been identified as black people, women, and people with disabilities. The following targets and time frames have been established by this white paper (Republic of South Africa 1995: Section 10.6):

> Within four years all departmental establishments must endeavour to be at least 50% black at management level. During the same period at least 30% of new recruits to the middle and senior management echelons should be women. Within ten years, people with disabilities should comprise two per cent of public service personnel.

This white paper requires each government department at national and provincial level to draw up detailed affirmative action plans, designed to meet the specific needs of black people, women and people with disabilities (Republic of South Africa 1995: Section 10.7). Enabling legislation, designed to ensure the active and correct implementation of affirmative action programmes, has also been envisaged in the white paper (Republic of South Africa 1995: Section 10.9).

6.6.3 The Public Service Laws Amendment Act of 1997

One of the first enabling acts of legislation that followed the White Paper on the Transformation of the Public Service was the Public Service Laws Amendment Act, Act 47 of 1997. Section 11 of the Public Service Act of 1994 (Promulgated under

Proclamation 103 of 1994) states that, 'In the making of appointments and the filling of posts in the public service due regard shall be had to equality and the other democratic principles enshrined in the Constitution'. This implies that the evaluation of persons shall be based, among other factors, on 'the need to redress the imbalances of the past to achieve a public service broadly representative of the South African people, including representation according to race, gender and disability' (Republic of South Africa 1997a: Section 8).

As the appointments of all public servants occur in terms of the Public Service Act of 1994, this amendment has made it legally possible to start with the implementation of the affirmative action targets as envisaged in the White Paper on the Transformation of the Public Service.

6.6.4 The White Paper on Human Resource Management in the Public Service, 1997

As human resource management is regarded as one of the strategic instruments of the transformation agenda for the public service (Republic of South Africa 1997b: Subsection 1.1.3), the White Paper on Human Resource Management in the Public Service was published in 1997. This white paper is based on the constitutional principles for the public service (see also paragraph 6.6.1 above).

One of the points of departure for this white paper was the perceived discriminatory nature of existing personnel management practices leading to a situation in which, although 79% of public servants were black, only 38% of staff in the management echelon (Director and above) were black (Republic of South Africa 1997b: Section 1.3.1). Furthermore, although the formal barriers to advancement for previously disadvantaged groups had already been removed in 1997, various levels of the public service were still 'effectively closed to external applicants' (Republic of South Africa 1997b: 1.3.3). This situation in 1997 did not comply with a vision of a diverse public service underpinned by such values as equity ensuring that human resource practices are free from discrimination, invisible barriers, and unjustness (Republic of South Africa 1997b: Section 2.3). Diversity seems to be one of the key principles of this white paper, not only to create a representative workforce, but to make a contribution to improved service delivery (Republic of South Africa 1997b: Section 3.3.1).

This white paper proposed the following main aims for a diversity management strategy (Republic of South Africa 1997b: Section 3.4.1):

- Identify and raise awareness of cultural differences within the workforce.
- Analyse the existing corporate culture and identity practices and behaviour which (a) support and (b) which undermine cultural diversity.
- Develop processes and behavioural norms to manage diversity which strengthen the positive and redress the negative aspects of the existing culture.
- Institutionalise diversity management by integrating it with the organisation's management practices.

Seven principles were also identified which were to be followed in the development of individual diversity management programmes (Republic of South Africa 1997b: Subsection 3.4.3). Selection and selection criteria can be regarded as fundamental in the application of any diversity management strategy. This particular white paper formulated four basic principles for recruitment and promotion by national departments and provincial administrations, namely the following of job-related selection criteria, fairness, equity, and transparency (Republic of South Africa 1997b: Section 4.7). Alongside these principles, national departments and provincial administrations are supposed to set targets for achieving specified employment equity objectives in order to achieve, among other things, the required race, gender, and disability balance (Republic of South Africa 1997b: Subsection 5.1.1). The white paper even contains prescribed principles for drawing up advertisements (Republic of South Africa 1997b: Subsection 5.1.2).

The white paper not only gives attention to the recruitment of personnel from outside the public service, but also to the position of existing public servants. One such example is the duty of managers 'in respect of employees who have been educationally disadvantaged, or women who are trying to combine a career with child-rearing responsibilities, or employees who are disabled' (Republic of South Africa 1997b: Subsection 5.10.2).

With regard to the implementation of the policies spelt out in this white paper, there are mainly two role players, namely national departments and provincial administrations, and the Department of Public Service and Administration. The Public Service Commission will monitor and evaluate the implementation of these two role players (Republic of South Africa 1997b: Section 7.1).

6.6.5   The White Paper on Public Service Training and Education, 1997

As the implementation of a diversity management strategy and a sound affirmative action policy depends on the availability of a skilled and well-equipped workforce, it follows that attention must be paid to the training and education of human resources. Therefore, it makes sense that the South African government has formulated policy on this function, as published in the White Paper on Public Service Training and Education, 1997.

The main aim of this white paper is to provide 'a new national strategic policy framework on training and education for public servants which contributes positively to the goals of public service transformation' (Republic of South Africa 1997c: 1.1.3). This document specifically refers to the importance of improving systems of pre-service training and education in order to ensure that the public service is able to attract and recruit high-quality personnel, 'particularly from those sectors of society that have been historically disadvantaged' (Republic of South Africa 1997c: 1.3.4).

This white paper identifies several key problem areas, of which the barriers to access and the so-called inflexible and discriminatory rules and regulations need to be mentioned in this discussion. It seems that, because bursaries for formal courses at the pre-tertiary level were not available until early 1997, the access of employees at the lower levels to effective training and education opportunities was restricted. This situation has in the meantime been rectified (Republic of South Africa 1997c: 2.2.6.1).

The white paper also points out that people with disabilities were effectively precluded from participating in the full range of training and education opportunities because they were confined to the status of temporary employees. The effect of their temporary status and subsequent lack of training opportunities was their restriction to occupational classes with little prospect for upward mobility (Republic of South Africa 1997c: 2.2.6.2).

With regard to recruitment and selection, the white paper makes the observation that current procedures overemphasise the importance of formal qualifications and experience, to the detriment of previously disadvantaged groups. Furthermore, the promotion prospects of formerly disadvantaged groups are, according to the white paper, impeded by the emphasis on seniority and formal qualifications, rather than on competency. These policies appeared to hamper the effective implementation of affirmative action programmes (Republic of South Africa 1997c: 2.2.7).

With these and other identified problems in mind, this white paper envisioned that, based on the principles of equality of access by all personnel at all levels to meaningful training and education opportunities and the empowerment of previously disadvantaged and marginalised groups, training and education can become an integral part of the process of increasing the representivity of the public service in terms of race, gender, and disability (Republic of South Africa 1997c: 3.1.4 & 3.1.3).

6.6.6 The White Paper on Affirmative Action in the Public Service, 1998

The first step taken by the post-1994 Executive Authority of South Africa in the direction of a comprehensive policy on affirmative action in the public service was the publication on 31 May 1997 of the Green Paper on a Conceptual Framework for Affirmative Action and the Management of Diversity in the Public Service (Republic of South Africa 1997d). This green paper was published by the Department of Public Service and Administration for general information, public comment, and discussion with stakeholders. According to this green paper, it is envisaged that affirmative action will 'facilitate the development of an equitable, service-orientated public service that is effective, efficient, accountable and affirming of the disadvantaged' (Republic of South Africa 1997d: Chapter 5).

Nearly a year later, on 23 April 1998, the White Paper on Affirmative Action in the Public Service was published in the Government Gazette by the Department of Public Service and Administration (Republic of South Africa 1998a). This white paper was a product of 'consultation with national departments, provincial administrations, organised labour of the central bargaining chamber of the Public Service, non-governmental organisations, disability organisations and experts in the field of affirmative action' as well as input received at public hearings held by the

Parliamentary Portfolio Committee of the Public Service and Administration (Republic of South Africa 1998a: Foreword). This white paper may be considered as the most important and comprehensive policy document regarding the implementation of affirmative action in the South African public service.

6.6.6.1 Purpose of the white paper

The purpose of the white paper is to convey the government's policy on the implementation of affirmative action programmes in the South African public service. This policy document sets out the mandatory requirements and provides guidance on the steps for national departments and provincial administrations to take in developing their affirmative action programmes. It also outlines the accountability, monitoring, reporting and co-ordinating responsibilities of various role players (Republic of South Africa 1998a: 1.1).

6.6.6.2 Scope of the white paper

The focus of this white paper is primarily on human resource management in the South African public service. It targets three groups, namely black people, women, and people with disabilities. For the sake of this white paper, the term 'black people' refers to African, coloured and Indian people (Republic of South Africa 1998a: 1.20).

6.6.6.3 The goal and objectives of affirmative action in the public service

The goal of affirmative action in the public service is spelt out in the white paper as follows (Republic of South Africa 1998a: 2.1):

> The goal of affirmative action in the public service is to speed up the creation of a representative and equitable public service and to build an environment that supports and enables those who have been historically disadvantaged by unfair discrimination to fulfil their maximum potential within it so that the public service may derive the maximum benefit of their diverse skills and talents to improve service delivery.

In order to reach this goal, three objectives have been formulated. The first is to enhance the capacities of the historically disadvantaged. The second is to inculcate a culture which values diversity and supports the affirmation of those who have previously been unfairly disadvantaged. The last objective is to speed up the achievement and progressive improvement of the numeric targets set out in the White Paper on the Transformation of the Public Service (Republic of South Africa 1998a: 2.2).

6.6.6.4 Mandatory requirements

This white paper suggests that affirmative action should be an integral element of every aspect of public institutions' management practices. National departments and provincial administrations should shape and manage their own affirmative action policies and programmes to reflect their own particular circumstances, in line with this white paper. Affirmative action programmes are thus the responsibility of every manager, supervisor, and human resource practitioner in the public service (Republic of South Africa 1998a: 3.1–3.2).

The following minimum requirements are set by the white paper for the affirmative action programmes in the public service (Republic of South Africa 1998a: 3.4–3.14):

- The broad numeric targets as set out by the White Paper on the Transformation of the Public Service must be translated by each department or administration into strategically prioritised, time-bound targets.
- Departments and administrations must keep and annually update accurate and comprehensive statistics on all personnel broken down by gender, race, and disability.
- The needs, priorities, and perceptions of all staff must be assessed annually by means of an in-depth affirmative action survey.
- The management practices of departments and administrations should be reviewed regularly to detect any possible barriers to the recruitment, retention, and advancement of members of the three target groups, and to identify any changes needed to enhance respect and appreciation for diversity.
- The performance assessment criteria for each employee must also measure the employee's implementation of and support for the organisation's affirmative action policies.
- A detailed affirmative action plan must be prepared, adopted, and promoted.
- The responsibilities of key role players within the department or administration for the institution's affirmative action plan must be clearly identified.
- The programme must also include a policy statement setting out the institution's commitment to affirmative action.

6.6.6.5   The role of the Department of Public Service and Administration

Although national departments and provincial administrations are, according to this white paper, primarily responsible for affirmative action programmes in their respective institutions, the Department of Public Service and Administration has an important supportive role to play. Its role consists of the following (Republic of South Africa 1998a: 4.3–4.7):

- A public service-wide communication campaign explaining the goals, objectives and principles of this white paper to public servants;
- The developing of practical guidelines for developing affirmative action programmes;
- The establishing of a network of affirmative action practitioners;
- The abolishing or amending of rules and regulations which unnecessarily restrict affirmative action activities and initiatives;
- The evaluation of the effectiveness of the policy set out in this white paper and the reporting on that to the Parliamentary Portfolio Committee on Public Service and Administration;

- Assist, co-ordinate or facilitate individual departments and provincial administrations in the developing of special affirmative measures needed to address specific forms of disadvantage that cut transversely across departments and administrations.

6.6.6.6 Accountability for implementation

The responsibility and accountability for drawing up and implementing affirmative action plans in the public service rests with the individual national departments and provincial administrations. Within these institutions, individual managers will ultimately be held responsible for the success of affirmative action (Republic of South Africa 1998a: 4.8).

Institutions such as the Public Service Commission, the Department of Labour, the Department of Public Service and Administration, and the Parliamentary Committee on the Public Service and Administration are supposed to monitor the progress of public institutions in this regard and to report to Parliament on the effectiveness of the policies (Republic of South Africa 1998a: 4.9–4.10).

6.6.7 The Public Service Regulations, 2001

The Public Service Regulations which came into operation on 1 January 2001 give further practical substance to the broad affirmative action policies discussed above. In this regard, Regulation III D1(c) of Chapter 1 stipulates that an executive authority (in other words, a national department or provincial administration) should plan, among other things, for the recruitment of human resources. Such a plan should include realistic goals and measurable targets for achieving representativeness, as well as specific plans to meet the training needs of persons historically disadvantaged (Republic of South Africa 2001: III D1(c) of Chapter 1).

Furthermore, the regulations determine that each 'executing authority' shall develop and implement an affirmative action programme, which shall contain at least the following (Republic of South Africa 2001: Regulation D2 of Chapter 1):

- A policy statement that sets out the department's commitment to affirmative action and the way in which that policy will be implemented;
- Numeric and time-bound targets for achieving representativeness;
- Annual statistics on the appointment, training, and promotion within each grade of each occupational category, of persons historically disadvantaged; and
- A plan for redressing numeric under-representativeness and supporting the advancement of persons who have been historically disadvantaged.

The outcomes of all these plans and programmes should also be communicated within the particular departments (Republic of South Africa 2001: Regulation D3).

The Public Service Regulations also stipulate that, from 1 April 2001, the annual report of each department and administration should include information on the progress made in implementing the institution's affirmative action programme, as well as race, gender, and disability statistics on recruitment, promotion, and termination of service by the particular institution (Republic of South Africa 2001: Annexure 1).

6.6.8   The Employment Equity Act 55 of 1998

The Draft Employment Equity Bill of 1997 was published during 1997 for general information and public comment. This was followed by the Employment Equity Bill, which was tabled in Parliament during 1998. After Parliament adopted it, the Employment Equity Act 55 of 1998 was signed by the President on 12 October 1998. The following commencement dates of various provisions of the Act apply:

- Establishment of the Commission for Employment Equity: 15 May 1999;
- Chapter II of the Act (anti-discrimination provisions): 9 August 1999;
- Chapter III of the Act (affirmative action provisions): 1 December 1999;
- Awarding of state contracts to employers who employ 150 or more employees: 1 September 2000; and
- Awarding of state contracts to employers who employ fewer than 150 employees: 1 April 2001.

In order to understand the architecture of the Act, it is important to know that the Act provides for two main pillars in its legislated structure to achieve employment equity:

- Chapter II deals with unfair discrimination and is applicable to all employers and employees (i.e., white males are also protected against unfair discrimination and all employers, irrespective of their size, are prohibited from unfairly discriminating against employees and job applicants).
- Chapter III deals with affirmative action and is applicable only to 'designated employers' and people from 'designated groups' (i.e., only employers who meet certain requirements are under a duty to implement affirmative action measures, and able-bodied white males cannot be the beneficiaries of affirmative action measures).

It is inevitable that a certain tension will prevail between these two pillars of the Act because anti-discriminatory measures protect and promote 'formal equality', whereas the affirmative action measures allow for unequal treatment that is deemed to be 'fair discrimination'. It is also inevitable that non-beneficiaries of affirmative action will seek support in Chapter II when claiming that an employer's affirmative action measures amounted to unfair discrimination against them, while employers and beneficiaries of affirmative action measures will seek to justify their actions on the permissible deviations from formal equality provided for under Chapter III of the Act. In this regard, see Section 6.3.4, in which a distinction was made between affirmative action amounting to fair discrimination and affirmative action measures that may amount to (unfair) reverse discrimination. In Figure 6.2 on page 184, the main provisions relating to these two pillars of the Act are depicted to provide an overall idea of the structure of the Act.

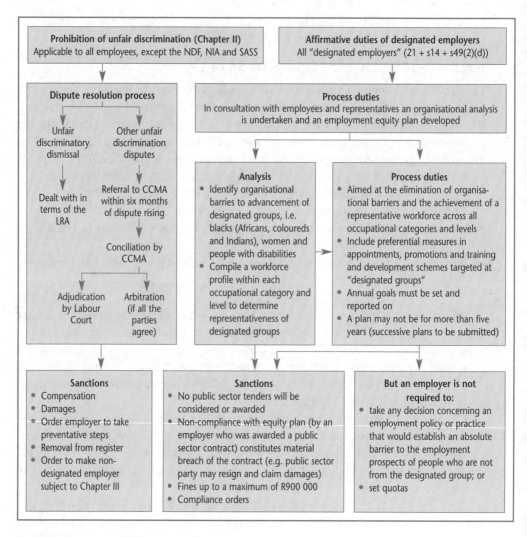

Source: *Du Plessis* et al. *(1998: 411)*

Figure 6.2   Overall structure of the Employment Equity Act

6.6.8.1   Purpose of the Act

From the preamble to the Act, it is clear that it aims to redress the present effects of South Africa's unfortunate past and that the Act recognises that anti-discriminatory measures would be insufficient to achieve this aim. It is also clear that it aims to bring about a 'diverse workforce' that is broadly representative of South Africa's demographics. This latter aim is not related to any historical injustices, and it reinforces the impression that a gender- and race-based form of affirmative action could potentially be viewed as a relatively permanent fixture of our labour market.

The two main aims of the Act, as stated in Section 2, are (1) to achieve employment equity by promoting equal opportunity and fair treatment in employment through the elimination of unfair discrimination, and (2) by implementing affirmative action measures, to redress the disadvantages in employment experienced by designated groups, in order to ensure their equitable representation in all occupational categories and levels in the workforce.

6.6.8.2 Scope of the Act

The only categories of employee that are wholly excluded from the Act are members of the South African National Defence Force, the National Intelligence Agency, and the South African Secret Service. These persons are not defined as 'employees' under the Labour Relations Act. However, they could bring unfair discrimination matters before the Constitutional Court, or lodge complaints with the Human Rights Commission. The anti-discriminatory provisions of the Act apply to all other employers and employees, whereas the affirmative action provisions apply only to 'designated employers' and members of 'designated groups'. The public sector in general and national departments and provincial administrations specifically are included in the scope of 'designated employers'.

6.6.8.3 Prohibition of unfair discrimination

In this section, the main provisions of Chapter II of the Act are briefly summarised. In terms of the Act, the following grounds for discrimination are prohibited: race, gender, sex, pregnancy, marital status, family responsibility, ethnic or social origin, colour, sexual orientation, age, disability, religion, HIV status, conscience, belief, political opinion, culture, language and birth.

By definition, harassment of an employee on any of the above-mentioned grounds is regarded as a form of unfair discrimination. The Act does not specify what constitutes 'harassment', but a 'Code of Good Practice on the Handling of Sexual Harassment Cases' was issued in 1998.

According to the Act, it will not be unfair discrimination to take affirmative action measures consistent with the purpose of the Act, or to distinguish, exclude, or prefer any person on the basis of an inherent requirement of a job.

Medical and psychological testing are made subject to very stringent requirements. Medical testing is prohibited, unless legislation permits or requires the testing or if it is justifiable in the light of medical facts, employment conditions, social policy, the fair distribution of employee benefits, or the inherent requirements of a job. Testing of an employee to determine that employee's HIV status is specifically prohibited unless such testing is determined to be justifiable by the Labour Court. Psychological testing and other similar assessments are prohibited unless the test or assessment being used has been scientifically shown to be valid and reliable, can be applied fairly to all employees, and is not biased against any employee or group.

Whenever unfair discrimination is alleged on one of the listed grounds, the burden of showing that the discrimination was fair shifts to the employer.

6.6.8.4 Procedure for resolving unfair discrimination disputes

First, it must be noted that, if an employee was dismissed for allegedly unfair discriminatory reasons, Chapter VIII of the Labour Relations Act applies. Therefore, these procedures apply only in cases other than dismissal cases, for example, the failure to appoint or promote a person for discriminatory reasons or in cases of alleged harassment. Second, in cases where a person alleges that he or she was subjected to an unfair labour practice that does not amount to unfair discrimination, the Labour Relations Act will apply. Since the time periods, remedies, and procedures differ for these three categories of offence (unfair discriminatory dismissals, unfair labour practices, and unfair discrimination), it is important to ascertain the exact basis of a person's claim against an employer.

The procedure for dealing with unfair discrimination disputes is basically that the applicant has six months within which to report the incident to the Commission for Conciliation, Mediation, and Arbitration (CCMA). The Commission must try to conciliate the dispute, failing which the dispute may be referred to the Labour Court for adjudication, or, if both parties agree, the dispute may be referred for arbitration.

6.6.8.5 Affirmative action

The following sections list some of the relevant stipulations of Chapter III of the Act.

General

As explained already, Chapter III deals with affirmative action and covers only 'designated employers' and people from 'designated groups'. Although the Act regards affirmative action as fair discrimination, one can foresee that there will be some tension between Chapter II and Chapter III of the Act, with non-members of designated groups (e.g., white males) challenging affirmative action programmes as being unfair. This is a healthy state of affairs, in that affirmative action measures will be kept in check by Chapter II, thereby preventing affirmative action from degenerating into 'reverse discrimination'.

Very broadly speaking, the Act requires an employer first to conduct an audit of its workforce composition in terms of race, gender, and disabilities, as well as employment practices and policies that may hinder the employment and/or advancement of people from designated groups. Once it has this data on the current situation, the employer must formulate an employment equity plan which is a blueprint of the way in which the organisation is going to promote the employment prospects of people from designated groups. This plan must include progressive targets for achieving employment equity in the organisation. Finally, the employer must submit annual reports (if it employs 150 or more employees) or bi-annual reports (if it employs fewer than 150 employees) to the Director-General of Labour to show, with reference to its employment equity plan, what progress the employer has made in achieving the targets. These three steps must all be done in consultation with the workforce and/or its representatives. These steps are dealt with in greater detail in subsequent sections.

Duties of designated employers

In terms of the Act, the duties of a designated employer are as follows:

- The employer must consult with its employees over the conduct of the employment equity analysis and its employment equity plan, as well as the progress reports that the employer must compile and submit to the Director-General.
- The employer must conduct an analysis of its employment policies, practices, procedures, and the work environment, in order to identify employment barriers which adversely affect people from designated groups, and it must include a profile of its workforce within each occupational category and level in order to determine the degree of under-representation of people from designated groups in various occupational categories and levels.
- The employer must prepare an employment equity plan.
- The employer must report to the Director-General on progress made in implementing its employment equity plan.

Affirmative action measures

In terms of the Act, affirmative action measures are measures designed to ensure that suitably qualified people from designated groups have equal employment opportunities and are equitably represented in all occupational categories and levels in the workforce of a designated employer. Note that this means that it will be insufficient to have senior positions filled by affirmative action appointees if these are restricted to only certain categories of occupation. Vertical as well as horizontal integration is required. Affirmative action measures implemented by a designated employer must include the following:

- Measures to identify and eliminate employment barriers, including unfair discrimination, which adversely affect people from designated groups;
- Measures designed to promote diversity in the workplace based on equal dignity and respect of all people;
- Measures to accommodate people from designated groups in order to ensure that they enjoy equal opportunities and are equitably represented in the workforce of a designated employer;
- Measures to ensure the equitable representation of suitably qualified people from designated groups in all occupational categories and levels in the workforce; and
- Measures to retain and develop people from designated groups and to implement appropriate training measures, including measures in terms of the Skills Development Act.

Quotas and reverse discrimination

The Act envisages that an employer's employment equity plan will include preferential treatment measures and numerical goals, but quotas are explicitly excluded. Nor is a designated employer compelled to take any decision concerning an employment policy or practice that would establish an absolute barrier to the prospective or continued employment or advancement of people who are not from designated groups. We can therefore conclude that the setting of quotas and affirmative action measures amounting to reverse discrimination are not part of the legislative intent.

The meaning of 'suitably qualified'

This is one of the most controversial provisions of the Act. For the purposes of the Act, a person may be suitably qualified for a job as a result of any one of, or any combination of, that person's formal qualifications, prior learning, relevant experience, or capacity to acquire, within a reasonable time, the ability to do the job. This is a very generous conception of 'suitably qualified' and – if the limitations placed on psychological testing and assessment, as well as the fact that an employer may not unfairly discriminate against a person solely on the grounds of that person's lack of relevant experience are taken into account – this aspect of the Act may well give managers some cause for concern.

Income differentials

This provision led to a heated debate between employer and labour representatives when the employment equity legislation was negotiated at NEDLAC. In the end, the position of labour prevailed, and the Act requires of every designated employer to submit, together with its report to the Director-General, a statement on the remuneration and benefits received in each occupational category and level of its workforce. If disproportionate income differentials are reflected, a designated employer must take measures to progressively reduce such differentials. These measures may include collective bargaining, compliance with sectoral determinations, applying the norms and benchmarks set by the Employment Conditions Commission, and/or relevant measures contained in the Skills Development Act.

Commission for Employment Equity

This Commission consists of a chairperson and eight other members appointed by the Minister of Labour to hold office on a part-time basis. The members of the Commission must include two people who represent organised labour, two people who represent organised business, two people who represent the State, and two people who represent the organisations of community and development interests.

The functions of the Commission are to advise the Minister of Labour. It may also make awards recognising achievements of employers in furthering the purpose of the Act. It researches and reports to the Minister on any matter relating to the application of the Act, including appropriate and well-researched norms and benchmarks for the setting of numerical goals in various sectors. The Commission must submit an annual report to the Minister of Labour.

Compliance, monitoring, enforcement and legal proceedings

General monitoring of an employer's compliance with the Act is left primarily to employees, shop stewards, trade unions, workplace forums, labour inspectors and the Director-General of Labour.

A labour inspector must request and obtain a 'written undertaking' from an employer if he or she has reasonable grounds to believe that a designated employer has failed to comply with its affirmative action duties.

A labour inspector may issue a compliance order to a designated employer if that employer has refused to give a written undertaking when requested to do so, or failed to comply with a written undertaking given by him or her. A compliance order must include the following:

- Those provisions of Chapter III with which the employer has not complied and details of the conduct constituting non-compliance;
- Any written undertaking given by the employer and any failure by the employer to comply with the written undertaking;
- Any steps that the employer must take, and the period within which those steps must be taken; and
- The maximum fine, if any, that may be imposed on the employer for failing to comply with the order.

A designated employer must comply with the compliance order within the time period stated in it, unless the employer lodges an objection with the Director-General within 21 days after receiving that order. If the employer is unhappy with the Director-General's decision, the employer can appeal against that decision to the Labour Court. If a designated employer does not comply with an order within the period stated in it, or does not object to that order, the Director-General may apply to the Labour Court to make the compliance order an order of the Labour Court.

Assessment of compliance

In determining whether a designated employer is implementing employment equity in compliance with the Act, the Director-General of Labour must take into account all of the factors listed in the Act.

Based on the Director-General's assessment of an employer's employment equity plan or the employer's non-compliance with the Act, the Director-General may make a recommendation to the employer. Should the employer fail to comply with the Director-General's recommendation, the Director-General may refer the employer's non-compliance to the Labour Court for adjudication.

6.7 Implementation of an affirmative action programme in the SA public service

The conditions have been set for affirmative action programmes in the South African public service by the various legislation and policy documents discussed in section 6.6 of this chapter. As each national department and provincial administration is supposed to formulate its own affirmative action programme (within the general statutory and policy framework), departments and provincial administrations will be held individually accountable for the successful implementation of these programmes. Institutions such as the Department of the Public Service and Administration, the Public Service Commission, and the Parliamentary Portfolio Committee on the Public Service and Administration, together with the Department of Labour, monitor and assess the implementation of these programmes. The following key questions direct this section:

- How does one measure the implementation of an affirmative action programme?
- Has the South African public service met its first affirmative action targets?
- Why do affirmative action programmes sometimes fail?

6.7.1 Measuring the implementation of an affirmative action programme

There will, perhaps, be general consent about the necessity of measuring the success of affirmative action programmes in the public service. To have the same consent about the result of the measurement exercise, it is imperative that the whole spectrum of the programme forms part of the scope of the evaluation. In her book Employers' guide to the Employment Equity Act, Simona Tinarelli (2000: 61–62) identifies three phases of an affirmative action programme, namely the preparation of the employment equity plan (phase 1), the implementation of the employment equity plan (phase 2), and the monitoring of the employment equity plan (phase 3). A valid measurement of the affirmative action programmes in the South African public service should thus take into consideration all three phases of the programme.

As discussed in the previous section, numerous policy and regulatory documents have been generated since 1994 giving direction to affirmative action programmes in the public service in one way or another. The formulation of these documents can be regarded as the preparation phase during which the implementation phase is planned. Tinarelli (2000: 61) identifies the following four steps in the preparation and planning phase:

- Step 1: Assigning responsibility and accountability to one or more senior managers;
- Step 2: Conducting communication, awareness, and training programmes;
- Step 3: Consulting with the relevant stakeholders; and
- Step 4: Analysing the existing workforce profile and relevant demographic information.

Applying the steps identified by Tinarelli (2000), the following is a brief assessment of the preparation phase for affirmative action in the South African public service:

Step 1: Assigning responsibility and accountability

The various policy documents show that the responsibilities for the development, implementation, and monitoring of the affirmative action programme for the South African public service have been assigned to the various responsible role players. As the public service consists of several national departments and provincial administrations, the assigning of responsibility occurs on two levels, namely the macro-institutional level and the institutional level. On the macro-institutional level, responsibility and accountability have been assigned to the Department of Public Service and Administration (see Sub-section 6.6.6.5 above) as well as the directors-general of the various national departments and provincial administrations. On the institutional level, directors-general or heads of departments and all managers, supervisors and human resource practitioners are held responsible for the success of affirmative action in the part of the institution for which they are individually responsible. The day-to-day responsibility for managing the programme is assigned to a designated person within the department (Republic of South Africa 1997b: 7.1; Republic of South Africa 1998a: 3.1–3.2; 4.2, 4.8).

Step 2: Communication, awareness and training programmes

As stipulated by the Code of Good Practice (Republic of South Africa 1999), it is expected of any employer to make its employees fully aware of its intentions regarding the preparation and implementation of an affirmative action programme in the workplace. In the South African public service, the Department of Public Service and Administration is responsible for a public service wide communication campaign, making public servants – as well as the public in general – aware of the rationale and purpose of the affirmative action programmes for the public service. It is acknowledged that openness and accountability are important for the involvement of the relevant stakeholders, as well as for the support for and acceptance of any affirmative action programme (Republic of South Africa 1997b: 7.2; Republic of South Africa 1998a: 2.8; 3.25–3.26; 4.3–4.7).

Step 3: Consulting with the relevant stakeholders

The development and monitoring of affirmative action programmes in the South African public service is shown to occur in consultation with the relevant stakeholders. The South African government's affirmative action policy for the public service is a product of consultation with various stakeholders, such as national departments, provincial administrations, organised labour of the central bargaining chamber of the public service, non-governmental organisations, disability organisations, and experts in the field of affirmative action (Republic of South Africa 1998a: Foreword). As part of the first monitoring project by the Public Service Commission, the Commission consulted and involved all the above-mentioned stakeholders, as well as the Department of Public Service and Administration (Republic of South Africa 2000: 11).

Step 4: Analysing the existing workforce profile and relevant demographic information

The South African public service, as a macro-institution, did indeed take this fourth step. The White Paper on Affirmative Action in the Public Service (Republic of South Africa 1998a: 1.8) contains a brief analysis of the workforce profile and relevant demographic information of the South African public service. It is also expected of individual departments and administrations to do the same.

The second phase identified by Tinarelli (2000: 62) is the implementation phase. This phase consists of an additional seven steps:
- Step 5: Setting objectives and corrective measures;
- Step 6: Establishing time frames;
- Step 7: Setting numerical goals;
- Step 8: Allocating resources;
- Step 9: Assigning responsibilities;
- Step 10: Agreeing on dispute resolution procedures; and
- Step 11: Communicating the plans.

The implementation phase of the affirmative action programme in the South African public service can be set out as follows:

Step 5: Setting objectives and corrective measures

According to the Code of Good Practice (Republic of South Africa 1999) an affirmative action programme should specify the broad objectives of the plan. In the case of the South African public service, these objectives have been identified as follows (Republic of South Africa 1998a: 2.2):
- To enhance the capacities of the historically disadvantaged;
- To inculcate a culture of diversity;
- To support the affirmation of those previously unfairly disadvantaged; and
- To speed up the achievement and progressive improvement of set numeric targets.

National departments and provincial administrations are also expected to state their commitment to affirmative action and to explain how they will implement their programmes (Republic of South Africa 2001: Regulation D2 of Chapter 1).

Step 6: Establishing time frames

Setting objectives (step 5) is, in practice, part and parcel of establishing time frames (step 6) and the setting of numerical goals (step 7). Both the Employment Equity Act (Republic of South Africa 1998c) and the Code of Good Practice (Republic of South Africa 1999) make provision for setting time frames for employment equity plans. The period included in such a time frame should allow an employer to make reasonable progress towards achieving the objectives of such a programme (Tinarelli 2000: 76).

The first time frame applicable to the South African public service ended in 1999 (Republic of South Africa 1995: 10.6). At the end of this four-year term, the results of the public service's affirmative action programme were evaluated by the Public Service Commission (Republic of South Africa 2000). New time frames were set for achieving full demographic representation; for example, the year 2005 has been set in the case of people with disabilities (Republic of South Africa 1998a: 3.5; Republic of South Africa 1999: 10).

Step 7: Setting numerical goals
Numerical goals constitute the third part of the measurable objectives of an affirmative action programme. According to Tinarelli (2000: 76), the purpose of numerical goals is to 'increase the representation of people from designated groups in each occupational level and category in the employer's workforce where under-representation has been identified', and to 'make the workforce reflect the relevant demographics'.

Numerical goals have been set for the South African public service (see Section 6.6.2 of this chapter) in the White Paper on the Transformation of the Public Service of 1995 (Republic of South Africa 1995). The White Paper on Human Resource Management in the Public Service (Republic of South Africa 1997b: 6.1.1) also stipulates that the recruitment policies and procedures of national departments and provincial administrations should set targets for achieving race, gender, and disability balance. This policy has been formally included in the Public Service Regulations (Republic of South Africa 2001: Regulation III D1(c) of Chapter 1).

Step 8: Allocating resources
The successful implementation of affirmative action programmes needs specific resources, such as funds separately budgeted for employment equity purposes, an affirmative action officer/manager, time allocated to role players, and infrastructure (Tinarelli 2000: 77).

In the case of the South African public service, it is part of the official policy that financial and other resources be allocated for achieving affirmative action objectives and targets (Republic of South Africa 1998a: 3.11). Furthermore, provision has been made for the appointment of a manager of the affirmative action programme in each department and administration (Republic of South Africa 1998a: 3.12). Special attention has also been given to the training infrastructure, whereas training and education have became an integral part of the process of increasing the representivity of the public service in terms of race, gender, and disability (Republic of South Africa 1997c: 3.1.4 & 3.1.3).

Step 9: Assigning responsibilities
The ninth step is to confirm the various responsibilities for the implementation and monitoring of affirmative action programmes, as assigned during the initial planning phase (Tinarelli 2000: 77). The White Paper on Affirmative Action in the

Public Service covered this step by identifying role players such as directors-general or heads of departments, line managers, heads of human resources and heads of training or human resource development (Republic of South Africa 1998a: 3.12).

Step 10: Agreeing on dispute resolution procedures

What will happen if government as an employer and its employees do not agree on the affirmative action programme and its implementation? The Employment Equity Act (Republic of South Africa 1998c) does not specify a dispute resolution procedure regarding the interpretation and implementation of such a programme (Tinarelli 2000: 77).

As stated in our discussion of the Employment Equity Act in section 6.6.8 above, the procedure for dealing with unfair discrimination disputes is that the applicant has six months within which to report the incident to the Commission for Conciliation, Mediation, and Arbitration (CCMA). The CCMA must try to conciliate the dispute. If unsuccessful, the dispute may be referred to the Labour Court for adjudication, or, if both parties agree, the dispute may be referred for arbitration.

The South African government, however, is not in favour of 'legalistic, confrontational procedures'. Its policy is that, where employees believe that their conditions of service have been infringed or that management has acted in a discriminatory manner, the employee is entitled to raise a grievance and to have it dealt with as promptly and objectively as possible (Republic of South Africa 1997b: 5.12).

Step 11: Communication plans

Communication and openness are not only necessary to involve stakeholders in the development of an affirmative action programme; they are also needed for the successful implementation of such a programme. Therefore, an affirmative action programme should be appropriately and comprehensively communicated to all employees and stakeholders (Tinarelli 2000: 78). According to the Employment Equity Act User Guide (Republic of South Africa 1999b) such communication should include details of persons responsible for the implementation of the programme, details of where information about the programme can be obtained, the objectives and duration of the plan, the dispute resolution procedures agreed to in step 10, and the roles and responsibilities of the role players tasked with ensuring the success of the programme. The accessibility of information to all levels of employees is of the utmost importance.

But what is the situation in the South African public service? The Department of Public Service and Administration realises the importance of commitment and support of staff throughout the public service for the implementation of effective and sustainable affirmative action programmes. Individual departments and administrations are therefore encouraged to develop a 'sustained, effective marketing and communication programme which enables staff to see affirmative action as a positive tool for achieving' their institution's core business goals. Departments and administrations are encouraged to include a two-way communication system in their programmes to ensure that staff at all levels are kept informed of plans and achievements, but also to take the views of staff members into account (Republic of South Africa 1998a: 3.25). According to the Public Service Regulations (Republic of South Africa 2001: Regulation III D3) national departments and provincial administrations (the so-called executing authorities) are compelled to communicate the outcomes of the planning process to staff members.

The last phase in the development of an employment equity plan, according to Tinarelli (2000: 62), is the monitoring of the plan. This phase has two steps:

- Step 12: Evaluation and review, and
- Step 13: Reporting.

Step 12: Evaluation and review

In the case of monitoring, evaluating, and reviewing affirmative action programmes, the Code of Good Practice (Republic of South Africa 1999a) requires the following from employers:

- Record keeping;
- Mechanisms for monitoring and evaluating affirmative action programmes;
- Regular evaluations;
- Adequate time to deal with these issues;
- Regular consultative meetings; and
- Reviewing and revising of affirmative action programmes.

It seems that the South African public service does comply with these requirements in the sense that it has to report on a regular basis to the Public Service Commission, the Department of Labour, the Department of Public Service and Administration, and the Parliamentary Portfolio Committee of the Public Service and Administration (Republic of South Africa 1998a: 4.8–4.11).

Step 13: Reporting

As the Department of Labour takes the responsibility for the implementation of the Employment Equity Act, Act 55 of 1998, this department receives the voluntary reports of all designated employers on their progress in the implementation of the Act. A specific form (EEA2) has been designed for this purpose.

6.7.2   The state of representativeness in the SA public service: The first targets

As discussed earlier in this chapter, the White Paper on the Transformation of the Public Service (Republic of South Africa 1995) supported by the White Paper on Affirmative Action in the Public Service (Republic of South Africa 1998a), sets definite targets for affirmative action in the public service. The first target date was the end of 1999. The logical step is to evaluate the extent to which these targets have been achieved. This evaluation was done by the Public Service Commission, which reported the results in 'the state of representativeness in the Public service', published in July 2000 (Republic of South Africa 2000). In analysing this report, the following questions are crucial:

- Does at least 50% of the management echelon of all departments and administrations consist of black employees?
- Are at least 30% of new recruits to the middle and senior management echelons women?
- What is the representation of disabled persons?

The Public Service Commission (Republic of South Africa 2000: 7) reports that 54.5% of the management echelon was black by the end of 1999 – 4.5% above the target set in 1995. With regard to the target set for the representivity of women, it reports that 18.28% of the members of the middle and senior management echelons are women. Unfortunately, the Commission's report takes the formulation of the target in this regard into consideration. The reader does not know how many individuals have been newly recruited to the management echelon from 1995 to 1999, and what percentage of them are women. The Commission reports that only 0.1% of all persons in the public service were disabled by the end of 1999. This falls short of the target of 2% to be achieved by the end of 2005. The Commission encourages departments 'that have not achieved the targets laid down, especially in respect of persons with disabilities' to 'vigorously embark upon a recruitment programme for this target group' (Republic of South Africa 2000: 30). The Public Service Commission (PSC) published another report on the implementation of Affirmative Action programmes in the South African Public Service (see Focus on Research 6.2 for more detail).

FOCUS ON RESEARCH 6.2
An audit of affirmative action in the public service

The Public Service Commission (PSC) published in 2006 a report entitled 'An audit of affirmative action in the Public Service'. This report is available on the PSC website [http://www.psc.gov.za/home_docs/Low-rez%20Document.pdf]. The project was undertaken to fulfil the Public Service Commission's mandate of promoting the Constitutional principles and values governing public administration as well as investigating, monitoring and evaluating the organisation, administration and personnel practices of the public service. The Ford Foundation provided funding, which the Institute for International Education (IIE) administered.

6.7.3 Why do affirmative action programmes sometimes fail?

Generally institutions that try a quick-fix route to affirmative action often find that their efforts are hampered by the following obstacles to success (Gerber *et al.* 1995: 205–206; Charlton & Van Niekerk 1994: 79–82):

- Strategic planning for affirmative action does not get implemented effectively. While commitment to affirmative action from the head of the institution is absolutely vital, the process requires support from all employees at all organisational levels for its successful implementation.
- People do not know how to implement affirmative action initiatives.

- Human resource planning is not carried out.
- Attitudes remain negative and rooted in the status quo. Control remains with white managers, and black employees are regarded as incapable of taking responsibility and accountability.
- Concerns are not clarified, and problems surrounding the programme are not addressed because of a failure to foster two-way communication.
- Formal training methods continue to be used although they are obsolete and do not equip people with the necessary skills to cope with the challenges of affirmative action (such as attitudinal reorientation, managing diversity, and empowerment). Furthermore, trainers are not equipped with the required skills and understanding of the issues to provide the necessary training.
- Line management eschews ownership of and responsibility for the programme.
- There is a lack of personal commitment by top management to invest sufficient time, effort, and public support in the programme. This (modelling) behaviour communicates the message that the failure to reach departmental targets in terms of the programme will be condoned because management itself is only going through the motions out of necessity.
- The programme lacks a clearly communicated objective and targets with timetables, which undermines its implementation and makes measurement of progress haphazard.
- Recruitment and selection methods are not adapted to attract and to screen suitable black people who can contribute to the success of the programme.
- Assumptions about the abilities and qualifications necessary to do a specific task are presumed to remain valid.

From the above, it should be evident that the removal of substantive employment inequalities is one problem that cannot be resolved by throwing money at it or hoping that it will go away. Programmes that are implemented without proper prior planning will prove to be costly and unproductive and will entrench negative stereotypes between groups. These will inevitably amount to a lose-lose outcome for the organisation and for the supposed beneficiaries of the programme, as well as for the non-beneficiaries. In the next section, a possible strategy for the successful implementation of affirmative action is outlined.

6.7.4 A strategic approach to affirmative action in public institutions

Because affirmative action forms such an integral part and key focus area of public human resource management in South Africa, it should be treated as a strategic priority by public institutions. In other words, the importance of the successful implementation of affirmative action for effective public service delivery by an institution must always be kept in mind. An affirmative action strategy should therefore be an integral part of the overall policy aims and human resource strategy of a public institution. The main purpose for a public institution is still to reach its

The challenge	Monitoring the affirmative action plan
• Society's needs for quality public services	• Evaluation and review
• Need for a legitimate public service	• Reporting
• The Constitution of the Republic of South Africa, 1996	
National legislative framework	**Implementing the affirmative action plan**
• The Public Service Act of 1994	• Corrective measures
• Institution-specific legislation	• Time frames
• The Employment Equity Act, Act 55 of 1998	• Numerical goals
• The Public Service Regulations, 2001	• Resource allocation
	• Assigning responsibility
	• Dispute resolution procedures
	• Communication plans
National policy framework	**Preparing the affirmative action plan**
• The White Papers on	• Assigning responsibility
– The Transformation of the Public Service, 1995	• Communication
– Public Service Training and Education, 1997	• Consultation
– Human Resource Management in the Public Service, 1997	• Analysis
– Affirmative Action in the Public Service, 1998	
Institutional business plan	**Institutional human resource plan**
• Vision, mission, and policy documents (e.g. white papers; strategic planning documents)	• Human resource strategy and workforce plan
• Strategic priorities and work programmes	• Identifying competencies and underpinning success
	• Determining the gap between supply and demand for human competence

Figure 6.3   A strategic approach to affirmative action in the public service

policy aims. Affirmative action needs to be implemented in such a way that it fosters those aims and increases public service delivery.

Compliance with the various legislations determining affirmative action in the South African public service should not be the primary aim of public managers. The rendering of high-quality public services to the people of the country is theprincipal aim. Affirmative action should therefore be seen as part of a strategic plan (see Figure 6.3) to make effective and efficient public services possible. Considering the earlier discussions in this chapter, we can construe a strategic approach to affirmative action in public institutions, consisting of eight distinguishable phases.

The first phase of this strategic approach to affirmative action in public institutions is to take cognisance of the fundamental challenge for public institutions. The challenge for public institutions is to fulfil society's need for public services - in other words, needs for protection of life, property, and other fundamental rights, as well as needs for assistance to attain the 'good life' (Loxton 1993: 60). This means that the state, by means of its various public institutions, is challenged to protect and promote in accordance with the principles set out in the Constitution of South Africa, 1996. The requirement of a broadly representative public service is fundamental to the rendering of public services.

The second phase of this strategic approach to affirmative action in public institutions consists of taking note of the prescriptive influence of the national

The third phase of a strategic approach to affirmative action in public institutions is to consider the implications of the national policy framework for the affirmative action of the specific institution. This framework includes the White Paper on the Transformation of the Public Service, 1995, the White Paper on Public Service Training and Education, 1997, the White Paper on Human Resource Management in the Public Service, 1997, and the White Paper on Affirmative Action in the Public Service, 1998.

SPOTLIGHT ON THE LAW 6.1
Individual rights

When implementing any affirmative system, you need to consider each individual's right to equality, dignity and fairness within the framework of the applicable policies and legislation of the country. These principles were specifically addressed in the ruling of the Labour Court when the case *Solidarity abo Barnard and Another v South African Police Services* (JS455/07) was considered. The court concluded as follows:

'[43.5] It is not apparent that consideration was given to the Applicant's right to equality and dignity. There appears to have been no consideration of her personal work history and circumstances... [43.6] As a separate conclusion and having regard to the facts the Respondent has failed to discharge the onus of showing that the proven discrimination was fair... [43.7] The failure to promote the Applicant was unfair and therefore not in compliance with the provisions of the Employment Equity Act.'

The fourth phase of a strategic approach to affirmative action in public institutions consists of developing an institutional business plan for the goal and the key functions of the institution. An integral part of this business plan should be the institution's plan for affirmative action. Consequently, this business plan should also take into consideration the previously mentioned phases in the process, as well as the vision, mission, and policy documents of the specific institution. The business plan should also contain the strategic priorities of the institution, as well as work programmes to achieve certain targets. The achievement of affirmative action targets should form part of these programmes.

The development of an institutional human resource plan can be regarded as the fifth phase of a strategic approach to affirmative action. This phase comprises a human resource strategy and workforce plan, the identification of competencies and underpinning success, and the determination of the gap between supply and demand for human competence. Although each public institution is responsible for its own plan, this plan is informed by the national policy framework for transformation of the public service, public service training, human resource management and affirmative action.

The preparation for the actual affirmative action plan in the public service is the sixth phase in the strategic approach to affirmative action. This phase consists of the actual assigning of responsibility and accountability to one or more senior managers, conducting communication, awareness, and training programmes, consulting with the relevant stakeholders, and analysing the existing workforce profile and relevant demographic information.

The seventh phase of the approach to affirmative action is the implementation of the affirmative action plan. This phase comprises the setting of objectives and corrective measures, establishing time frames, setting numerical goals, allocating resources, assigning responsibilities, agreeing on dispute resolution procedures, and communicating the plans. This phase is also informed by the national legislative and policy frameworks.

Monitoring affirmative action is the eighth phase in this strategic approach to affirmative action. An affirmative action plan is evaluated and reviewed during this phase. The institution is also supposed to report to the various monitoring institutions.

The final yardstick for the success of affirmative action is not simply whether all the numerical targets have been met. A strategic approach to affirmative action will determine whether society's needs for quality public services, rendered by a truly representative public service, have been met.

FOCUS ON RESEARCH 6.3
Diversity climate

Results of a recent study in the USA on the effect of diversity climate on professional employee of colour indicate that diversity climate affects organisational commitment and turnover intentions. The study also shows that when a diversity climate was perceived to be fair, racially aware respondents reported lower levels of psychological contract violation (Buttner, Lowe & Billings-Harris 2010: 239).

6.8 Review

Affirmative action in the South African public service cannot be evaluated properly without reflecting on the origin of the practice of affirmative action in the United States of America. The American history of this practice, as well as the application of various related concepts in the discourse on affirmative action, serves as a background to the discussion of the practice of affirmative action in the public service of South Africa.

We have shown that, due to the specific historical developments in employment policies in the South African public service, as well as a discrepancy between South Africa's population composition and the composition of the public service, a need has developed for the transformation of the public service. Hence, a variety of legislation and policies have been adopted to give strategic direction to affirmative action in the South African public service.

A strategic perspective on affirmative action in the public service reveals that it should not be an aim in itself. It should be seen as part of a bigger process of providing quality public services through a truly representative public service.

6.9 Self-evaluation questions

1. Briefly describe the origins of affirmative action.
2. Define the following concepts:
   • affirmative action
   • equality of opportunity.
3. Describe the relationship between affirmative action and equality.
4. Explain the different modalities of affirmative action.
5. What is an 'organisational audit and employment equity plan'?
6. Describe developments in and experiences of affirmative action in the South African public service.
7. Why do affirmative action programmes often fail?
8. Explain the implications of affirmative action for other HRM practices.

Bibliography

Arvey, RD. 1979. *Fairness in selecting employees.* Reading, MA: Addison-Wesley.

Asmal, K. 1992. *Affirmative action or not?* Paper delivered at the 5th Annual Labour Law Conference, Durban, 16–18 July, 1992.

Blanchard, FA, & Crosby, FJ. (Eds.). 1989. *Affirmative action in perspective.* New York: Springer.

Brand, SS. 1982. Vraag na en aanbod van mannekrag vir die openbare sektor. *SAIPA: Journal of Public Administration,* 17(3), 94–103.

Buttner, EH, Lowe, KB and Billings-Harris, L. 2010. Diversity climate impact on employee of color outcomes: does justice matter? *Career Development International,* 15(3): 239–258.

Castle, J. 1995. Affirmative action in three developing countries: Lessons from Zimbabwe, Namibia and Malaysia. *South African Journal of Labour Relations,* 19(1), 6–33.

Charlton, GD, & Van Niekerk, N. 1994. *Affirming action: Beyond 1994.* Cape Town: Juta.

Du Plessis, JV, Fouché, MA, & Van Wyk, MW. 1998. *A practical guide to the labour law.* 3rd edn. Durban: Butterworths.

Fullinwider, RK. 1980. *The reverse discrimination controversy: A moral and legal analysis.* Totowa, NJ: Rowman and Littlefield.

Garbers, JG. 1982. Moontlike strategieë ter verligting van die personeelvraagstuk in die openbare sektor. *SAIPA: Journal of Public Administration,* 17(3), 114–129.

Gerber, PD, Nel, PS, & Van Dyk, PS. 1995. *Human resources management.* 3rd edn. Halfway House: ITP/Southern.

Holloway, FA. 1989. What is affirmative action? In FA Blanchard & FJ Crosby (eds.), *Affirmative action in perspective.* New York: Springer.

Human, L. 1993. *Affirmative action and the development of people: A practical guide.* Cape Town: Juta.

Lee, YS. 1992. *Public personnel administration and constitutional values.* London: Quorum.

Loxton, A. 1993. A criteriological approach to the functional structure of central government administration in South Africa. Submitted in fulfilment of the requirements for the degree of Doctor Administrationis (Public Administration). University of Pretoria.

Muthien, Y. 1999. Race and gender inequalities in public administration. In JS Wessels, & JC Pauw (eds.), *Reflective public administration: Views from the South.* Cape Town: Oxford University Press.

Nkuhlu, W. 1993. Affirmative action for South Africa in transition: From theory to practice. In C. Adams (ed.), *Affirmative action in a democratic South Africa.* Cape Town: Juta.

Plaut, M. 1992. Ethnic quotas: Lessons from Malaysia. *Work in Progress,* 80, 42–43.

Ricucci, N, & Saidel, J. 1997. The representativeness of state-level bureaucratic leaders: A missing piece of the representative bureaucracy. *Public Administration Review,* 57(5), 423–430.

Rycroft, A, & Jordaan, B. 1992. *A guide to South African labour law.* 2nd edn. Cape Town: Juta.

Sachs, A. 1991. *Affirmative action and good government.* Alistair Berkeley Memorial Lecture, November, 14–15.

Schlei, BL, & Grossman, P. 1983. *Employment discrimination law.* 2nd edn. Washington, DC: American Bar Association, Section of Labour and Employment Law, the Bureau of National Affairs.

Sen, A. 1992. *Inequality re-examined.* New York: Oxford University Press.

Sharpe, AL. 1982. The policy concerning the employment of non-whites in the South African public service (1910–1981). Dissertation for the DPhil Degree. Pretoria: University of Pretoria.

Smith, N. 1992. Affirmative action: Its origin and point. *South African Journal on Human Rights,* 8(2), 234–248.

Starks, SL. 1992. Understanding government affirmative action and Metro Broadcasting Inc. v. FCC. *Duke Law Journal,* 41, 993–975.

Swanepoel, BJ. 1992. Affirmative action and employee empowerment in Namibia: Southern African research perspective on some pieces of the jigsaw puzzle. *South African Journal of Labour Relations,* 16(3), 23–36.

Swanepoel, B, Erasmus, B, van Wyk, M & Schenk, H. 2003. *South African human resource management: Theory and practice.* Cape Town. Juta.

Taylor, BR. 1991. *Affirmative action at work: Law, politics and ethics.* Pittsburgh, PA: University of Pittsburgh Press.

Thompson, K, & Woolard, I. 2002. Achieving employment equity in the public service: A study of changes between 1995 and 2001. Development Policy Research Unit Working Paper no. 02/61. University of Cape Town.

Tinarelli, S. 2000. *Employers' guide to the Employment Equity Act.* Pretoria: Van Schaik.

Tompkins, J. 1995. *Human resource management in government: Hitting the ground running.* University of Montana-Harper Collins.

Tummala, KK. 1991. Affirmative action: A status report. *International Journal of Public Administration,* 14(3), 383–411.

Van der Walt, S. 1992. Employment in the public sector of South Africa. *SAIPA: Journal of Public Administration,* 27(1), 3–33.

Weiner, M. 1993. Affirmative action: The international experience. *Development and Democracy (The Urban Foundation),* 4 May 1993, 1–15.

Wessels, JS. 1992. Training for equal opportunities in the public service. *SAIPA: Journal of Public Administration,* 27(1), 44–61.

Wessels, JS. 2005. Equal employment opportunities: A conceptual puzzle. *Politeia,* 24(2): 125–141.

Wessels, JS. 2008. Transforming the public service to serve a diverse society: can representativeness be the most decisive criterion? *Politeia,* 27(3): 21–36

Acts or legislation

Republic of South Africa. 1994. The Public Service Act (Proclamation 103 of 1994). Government Printer. [http://www.polity.org.za/html/govdocs/legislation/1994]

Republic of South Africa. 1996a. The Constitution of the Republic of South Africa of 1996. Government Printer.

Republic of South Africa. 1997a. The Public Service Laws Amendment Act (Act 47 of 1997).

Republic of South Africa. 1998a. The Employment Equity Act (Act 55 of 1998). [http://www.polity.org.za/html/govdocs/legislation/1998]

Government regulations

Republic of South Africa. 1998b. Public Service Regulations, 1998 and 2001. [http://www. gov.co.za]

Government white and green papers

Republic of South Africa. 1995. White Paper on the Transformation of the Public Service, 1995.

Republic of South Africa. 1996b. Green Paper on Employment and Occupational Equity. Pretoria: Government Gazette, 17303, 1 July 1996.

Republic of South Africa. 1997b. White Paper on Human Resource Management in the Public Service. Government Gazette, 390 (18594).

Republic of South Africa. 1997c. White Paper on Public Service Training and Education. [http://www.gov.co.za]

Republic of South Africa. 1997d. Green Paper on a Conceptual Framework for Affirmative Action and the Management of Diversity in the Public Service. [http://www.gov.co.za]

Republic of South Africa. 1998c. White Paper on Affirmative Action in the Public Service, 1998. [http://www.gov.co.za]

Government reports

Republic of South Africa. 1988. Commission for Administration: Annual report 1987. Seventy-fifth Annual Report of the Commission for Administration. RP 33-1988.

Republic of South Africa. 1989. Commission for Administration: Annual report 1988. Seventy-sixth Annual Report of the Commission for Administration. RP 30-1989.

Republic of South Africa. 1990. Commission for Administration: Annual report 1989. Seventy-seventh Annual Report of the Commission for Administration. RP 33-1990.

Republic of South Africa. 2000. The State of Representativeness in the Public Service. Pretoria: Public Service Commission. [http://www.gov.co.za]

Republic of South Africa. 2006. *An Audit of Affirmative Action in the Public Service*. Pretoria: Public Service Commission. Accessed online on 9 August 2010. [http://www.psc.gov.za/home_docs/Low-rez%20Document.pdf]

Republic of South Africa. 2010a. *Mid-year population estimates 2010*. P0302. Available online at: http://www.statssa.gov.za/PublicationsHTML/P03022010/html/P03022010.html. Accessed on 9 August 2010.

Management guides

Republic of South Africa. 1999a. Code of Good Practice for the Preparation, Implementation and Monitoring of Employment Equity Plans. Notice R.1394. Department of Labour.

Republic of South Africa. 1999b. The Employment Equity Act: User Guide. [http://www.labour.gov.za]

7 Recruiting potential public sector employees

Purpose

The purpose of this chapter is to enable the reader to understand the principles of recruitment in order to effect good recruitment practices within a public sector context.

Learning outcomes

After you have read this chapter, you should be able to:
- Demonstrate how human resource planning, job analysis and recruitment are related to each other.
- Prepare a recruitment policy.
- Identify the external and internal factors that have an influence on recruitment policy.
- Identify the right conditions of employment for the potential employee.
- Structure internal and external sources of recruitment.
- Choose the best possible recruitment method to attract a pool of candidates from which the ideal candidate can be selected.
- Conduct an effective recruitment process.
- Plan for the effective evaluation of recruitment.
- Identify the factors involved in strategic recruitment.

7.1 Introduction

Depending on how the work has been designed and structured and in terms of the HR plans, it may be necessary to recruit new public sector employees. In order to do this, certain activities must be performed to attract the necessary job applicants from whom the new employees will be selected (see Chapter 8).

By means of the recruitment process, the public sector institution aims to attract and to retain the interest of suitable applicants and to project a positive image of the institution to outsiders.

The recruitment process may be set in motion by the recognition of a need arising out of the HR planning process. It may also happen that vacancies arise from resignations, promotions or transfers. From time to time the public sector institution needs to attract job candidates with the required competencies and traits for the tasks to be performed. The response of potential employees depends on their attitude towards the work to be performed and towards the institution, as well as their perception of whether the necessary fit can possibly be established between them and the institution seeking to recruit them.

Traditionally, public sector institutions have done relatively little recruiting of potential employees. However, three factors are now changing the public sector's passive attitude towards recruitment into a more active one. First, many institutions are recruiting more aggressively to meet equal employment opportunity requirements and to comply with affirmative action policy guidelines. Second, because of increased delegation of hiring authority, more public sector institutions are now in a position to actively seek out the kinds of employee they need and want. Third, public sector institutions today find themselves in increasing competition with each other and with private sector employers for scarce qualified job applicants (Tompkins 1995: 184).

With these recruiting challenges in mind, this chapter deals with recruitment policy and procedures, the job choice a potential employee has to make, the sources and methods of recruitment, and the recruitment process in general. To conclude, we shall examine a strategic approach to recruitment.

7.2 Relationship between HR planning, job analysis, recruitment and selection

In Chapter 4, we saw how the HR planning process determines the specific number of posts to be filled. We also saw that job analysis forms part and parcel of the HR planning process. Job analysis gives one a clear understanding of the nature and requirements of the post to be filled. This means that, before any advertising campaign can be put into operation, one has to make sure that the posts are properly analysed to ensure that recruitment attempts are non-discriminatory and that recruiting takes place in line with the inherent requirements of the relevant post. Completion of the HR planning process and job analysis processes provide an overall impression of the post. In other words, one now has the job profile at your disposal. This job profile describes the post in terms of the task requirements (job descriptions) and the requirements for the person filling the post (see Chapter 5). When you have this broader picture of the post, the recruitment process can begin.

> Recruitment can be described as those activities in human resource management which are undertaken in order to attract sufficient job candidates who have the necessary potential, competencies, and traits to fill job needs and to assist the public sector institution in achieving its objectives.

Most people would agree that the processes of recruitment and selection are closely linked with each other. Therefore, they both form part of the hiring process. It is true that both these HR activities are directed towards obtaining suitably qualified public sector employees. However, the focus of the recruitment process is more on laying the groundwork for the selection process. In other words, the recruitment process provides the pool of applicants from whom the selectors may choose. Although the two activities are closely related, each requires a separate range of knowledge, skills, competencies, and expertise. In addition, each activity may in practice be executed by different staff members (Foot & Hook 1996: 53). Hence, each activity is discussed in a separate chapter of this book.

? DID YOU KNOW?

Research has shown that in a culturally diverse country such as South Africa, e-recruitment does not provide employers with access to all potential candidates. It has been found that Internet penetration into the labour market is less than 10%. What is interesting, however, is that certain categories of employees still choose to make use of traditional avenues such as newspapers and recruitment agencies only to find a job. Skilled candidates, on the other hand, prefer to establish a relationship with a professional recruiter who can act as a 'buffer' between them and potential employers.

Source: Singer (2010: Online)

7.3 Recruitment policy and procedures

The recruitment policy stipulates broad guidelines on the way in which a public sector institution intends to deal with recruitment. In very brief terms, the recruitment policy must indicate the institution's position concerning: (1) the general objectives of recruitment, and (2) the principle of equal job opportunities in recruitment (Van der Westhuizen 2000: 100). In keeping with these objectives, one has to undertake the following steps (Foot & Hook 1996: 53-54):

- Secure a pool of acceptable candidates for the vacancies.
- Ensure all recruitment efforts establish a positive image for the institution.
- Make sure that all recruitment activities are efficient and cost-effective.
- Conduct the recruitment process in a fair and equitable manner.
- Enable the institution to attract those potential employees who have the necessary knowledge, skills, and competencies relevant to the requirements of the post.

Obviously, the general objectives of recruitment imply that a number of HR decisions need to be taken on the way in which recruitment should be dealt with in the workplace. For example, what is meant by 'acceptable candidates' and who takes decisions about this? What types of recruitment action can be taken to influence a public sector institution's image positively? How can fairness be measured? The only way of ensuring that the recruitment process achieves these objectives is to develop and implement appropriate policies and procedures. A basic recruitment policy should, at the very least, give answers to the following questions:

- What are the objectives of recruitment in the public sector institution?
- What legal and regulatory prescriptions on fairness and discrimination should be taken into account? (for example, the Labour Relations Act 66 of 1995.)
- Which resolutions in collective agreements with public sector unions are applicable?

- Which targets in terms of employment equity are applicable, in particular for achieving race, gender, and disability balances?
- How can recruitment be carried out within budget limitations?
- How urgently should vacancies be filled?
- Which unit or person (designated title) will be responsible for the execution of the policy and procedure?
- What are the prescriptions of the HR planning and succession planning documents? For example:
  - Will promotions from within the institution take preference?
  - May relatives of existing public sector employees be employed?
  - Will handicapped persons be employed?
  - May part-time employees be employed?
  - May minors be employed?

DID YOU KNOW?

The Department of Public Service and Administration has complied a Consultation document on the Recruitment and Retention of People with Disabilities – A Strategy for the Public Sector (2006–2010). This document is available at: [http://www.dpsa.gov.za/documents/ee/JobACCESS].

?

Generally, most public sector employers would like to see that the 'employees in place' gets the first opportunity to apply for a post. The main consideration in such a case is whether the applicant is the most suitable candidate (Van der Westhuizen 2000: 100). It is important to be aware of the impact of such an approach because it may lead to entrenching any equal employment opportunity problems that occur. Therefore, clear guidelines on internal appointments must be contained in the recruitment policy. Over the years, certain trends developed in the public sector with regard to recruitment. These trends have resulted in the so-called career system. The career system strongly emphasised the notion of job security for public sector employees. Fortunately, with the passage of time, this approach has been done away with, and external appointments are being made more frequently, particularly where senior posts are involved.

Government policy and regulations are the most strategic recruitment factors to take into account in determining recruitment policy and procedures. There is already legislation in place, such as the Labour Relations Act 66 of 1995 and the Employment Equity Act 55 of 1998, which protects the interests of public officials during the recruitment process. Basically, there are two broad categories of discrimination, namely direct discrimination (unfair treatment related to, for example, an employee's sexual orientation) and indirect discrimination (unfair treatment by way of imposing a demand on an employee that is not objectively defensible). Spotlight on the Law 7.1 (*Stokwe v MEC Department of Education, Eastern Cape Province & another* (2005)

26 ILJ 927 (LC)) is a particularly crass example of unfair direct discrimination against a candidate during recruitment.

SPOTLIGHT ON THE LAW 7.1
Unfair discrimination

In the above case Ms Stokwe, a teacher, applied for a vacant post of principal of an Afrikaans-medium school. There was a difference of opinion between the interviewing committee and the school governing body on what merits the successful candidate should be appointed. She was ranked first by the interviewing committee, above a male candidate and the acting principal. In turn, the school governing body argued that the male candidate had more 'hands-on' experience. The Department of Education of the Eastern Cape Provincial Administration then intervened and set up a 'review panel' consisting of three white Afrikaans-speaking principals to take the matter further. They insisted that the interview:
- Should be conducted in Afrikaans. Ms Stokwe objected, whereafter the interview proceeded in English.
- Be translated by Ms Stokwe into Afrikaans.

The review panel ultimately told Ms Stokwe that she should not have applied for the post because she could not speak Afrikaans. In addition, she was also asked whether she was 'bold' enough to compete with men for this post. Ms Stokwe was not satisfied and lodged a complaint with the relevant department. Despite her complaint, the department decided to appoint the male candidate. Ms Stokwe took the case to court and the judge found that she had been discriminated against on the basis of race, sex, gender and language.

Read more about unfair discrimination in the workplace in *Swanepoel v Western Region District Council & another* [1998] 19 ILJ 1418 (SE) and *Du Preez v Minister of Justice & Constitutional Development & others* [2006] 27 ILJ 1811 (SE).

Source: Grogan (2008: 299–301)

Various factors influence recruitment policy. These may be divided into two broad categories, namely external and internal factors (Gerber, Nel, & Van Dyk 1992: 176). We shall briefly discuss these factors below.

7.3.1 External factors influencing recruitment

External factors are factors outside a public sector institution, such as labour market conditions, government policy and legislation, and trade unions.

7.3.1.1 Labour market conditions

If there is an abundance of qualified candidates who meet the job specification requirements, a limited recruiting effort may generate many applications. If the job market is tight, more creative and expensive efforts will be necessary. Skills shortages will require larger compensation packages to attract the right candidates. The Department of Labour has statistics available for different sectors of the labour market. Human resource specialists should remain abreast of current trends in the labour market to employ the right recruitment policy.

DID YOU KNOW?

?

The Adcorp Employment Index provides a quarterly update of those issues having a direct impact upon overall employment in the South African labour market. In their view these issues are: the global and local macro-economic situation, demand for labour, supply of suitable labour, and remuneration. According to the latest Index, employment is currently faced with, among others, the following trends:

- The overall environment for employment in South Africa has become negative – the quarter-on-quarter analysis has shown a decline of 12.9%. This downward turn is influenced by the substantial decline in macro-activity and a demand for labour that is down by 5.75.
- Based on the RSA Composite Leading Index, economic recovery can only be expected in the 1st or 2nd quarter of 2010.
- According to the International Labour Organisation Global Employment Trends Update, jobless people could grow by as many as 59 million people.
- The severity of job losses in South Africa is not that serious compared to other countries, mainly due to the large infrastructure development projects in the country.
- The recent release of the Ministry of Home Affairs' quota list of professional occupational classes, which government permits sourcing from abroad, has already resulted in the return of 39 000 South African emigrants.
- The sectors that are still employing are construction, government services, logistics, warehousing and communications.

Source: Smith, Boonzaaier, Schussler, Blair & Phillips (2009: Online)

7.3.1.2   Government policy and legislation

Government policy will in future play an increasingly important role in the determination of your internal recruitment policy, procedures, and practices. There are numerous measures prescribed by law to prevent discriminatory recruitment practices. The legal framework for recruitment is provided by the 1996 Constitution, the Public Service Act 103 of 1994, the Labour Relations Act 66 of 1995, the Employment Equity Act 55 of 1998, the Public Service Regulations of 2001, the White Paper on the Transformation of the Public Service of 1995, the White Paper on Affirmative Action for the Public Service of 1998, and the Senior Management Service: Public Service Handbook of 2003. Although white papers have no legal status, they should serve as a broad policy background. The only way in which requirements in white papers can be mandatory is when they are included as prescripts in legislation. In addition, the requirements can be included in regulations issued by the relevant minister. White papers can help you to understand the direction of thinking that the government takes in terms of general public administration affairs, as well as what is expected of you regarding PSHRM (Republic of South Africa 1999: 8).

Section 9 of the 1996 Constitution clearly stipulates that everybody is equal before the law and has the right to equal protection. More specifically, Section 9(2) provides that legislation and other measures may be introduced to benefit those who have suffered unfair discrimination in the past. In addition, Section 9(3) specifically outlaws discrimination against anybody on the grounds of race, gender, pregnancy, language, ethnicity, marital status, sexual preference, age, religion, and disability. A recurring question is: What are the implications for recruitment? Probably, the most important effect might be in the placing of advertisements. The major point here is that compilers of advertisements have a duty to formulate the wording of advertisements most carefully to ensure that no unlawful discrimination takes place. The Public Service Act 103 of 1994 takes the above provisions of the 1996 Constitution one step further. Section 11 of the Act prescribes the following:

(1) In the making of appointments and the filling of posts in the public service due regard shall be had to equality and the other democratic values and principles enshrined in the Constitution. (2) In the making of any appointment for the filling of any post in the public service: (a) all persons who qualify for the appointment, transfer or promotion concerned shall be considered; and (b) the evaluation of persons shall be based on training, skills, competence, knowledge and the need to redress the imbalances of the past to achieve a public service broadly representative of the South African people, including representation according to race, gender and disability.

As you already know, our legislation provides protection of the rights of persons seeking employment. For example, the Labour Relations Act 66 of 1995 (the LRA) expressly prohibits an employer from advantaging, or promising to advantage, a person seeking employment in exchange for that person's undertaking not to exercise any right conferred by the LRA (for example, joining a trade union, participating in protected strike action, or participating in workplace forums or in other procedures provided for in the LRA). This means that the LRA places certain important prohibitions on unfair discrimination in any employment policy or practice, which specifically include applicants for employment. This obviously holds direct implications for recruitment policy and practice. In addition, the Employment Equity Act 55 of 1998 states very clearly that no person may unfairly discriminate, directly or indirectly, against an employee on any of the various grounds (see chapter 6). Public sector institutions will thus have to change their recruitment policies, procedures, and practices to ensure that no unfair discrimination takes place and to promote affirmative action. According to Pons and Deale (1998: 18–28) advertisements for available positions should in no way indicate or imply an intention to discriminate unfairly against members of a particular group. The following are some examples:

- Subconscious discriminatory language, for example, the word 'she' is used when advertising secretarial positions.

- Inherent requirements of the job must be clearly spelt out to ensure that prerequisites or qualifications attached to the job are justifiable. For example, when a typist's job is advertised, the requirements would be for a person who can type and not for a person who has a certificate in typing. By requiring a certificate in typing, a group of people may be excluded from potential applicants.
- When using advertising media, advertisements should be placed where people from a particular race group are not excluded or disproportionately reduced.

The Public Service Regulations of 2001 include a plethora of strategic principles on which recruitment must be based. Some of these advertising requirements are provided in the box below. One key principle refers to that of increased open competition (Republic of South Africa 2003: 4). In practice, this means that positions will be filled through open, targeted, or internal competition. Open competition implies that positions are advertised nationally and are open both to existing public sector employees and external applicants.

DID YOU KNOW? ?

There are specific advertising requirements listed in the Public Service Regulations of 2001. These advertising requirements are, among others, the following:
- An executing authority shall ensure that vacant posts in the department are so advertised as to reach, as efficiently and effectively as possible, the entire pool of potential applicants, especially persons historically disadvantaged.
- An advertisement for a post shall specify the inherent requirements of the job, the job title and core functions.
- Any vacant post in the Senior Management Service shall be advertised nationwide.
- An executing authority shall advertise any other vacant post within the department as a minimum, but also advertise such post (a) elsewhere in the public service; or (b) outside the public service either nationwide or locally.
- The Minister may issue directives regarding the manner in which vacancies must be advertised within the public service.

Source: Republic of South Africa (2001: 26–27)

Targeted competition occurs when positions are advertised within a defined target area (for example, a specific geographical area such as Gauteng) or within a defined group (such as the engineering sector) and it is open to both existing employees and external applicants. Internal competition takes place when positions are advertised within a particular institution (such as the Department of Health) where expertise is only available within the public service (Republic of South Africa 1997: 34).

The White Papers on the Transformation of the Public Service of 1995 and Affirmative Action in the Public Service of 1998 lay down required guidelines for public service institutions on steps to be taken to implement employment equity and affirmative action in the workplace. These guidelines impose special requirements on PSHRM where recruitment is concerned. In considering these guidelines, proper planning will have to be done by HRM specialists in consultation with line-function employees on what posts have to be filled in terms of complying with employment equity and affirmative action requirements.

7.3.1.3 Trade unions

Many unions seek to persuade public sector employers to enter into agreements stipulating that only union members will be employed by the enterprise concerned; such agreements are referred to as closed shop agreements. Moreover, unions increasingly seek greater participation in recruitment processes and decision making, and they make known their approval or otherwise of selection criteria. Management should take cognisance of the influence of unions and adopt recruitment practices which are acceptable to all the stakeholders.

7.3.2 Internal factors influencing recruitment

Internal factors are those decided by the public sector institution such as strategic plans, institutional policy and recruitment criteria.

7.3.2.1 Strategic plans

Recruitment must not be seen as an isolated activity. The public sector institution's broad long-term plans are the basis for the detailed shorter term plans on which the recruitment efforts are based. It is essential that the human resource department should use the corporate plan (such as the government's vision, mission, and objectives) and the business plans of the relevant public sector institution to ensure strategic recruitment. A recruitment policy must be developed in line with the human resource strategy decided upon (see Chapter 5). The required number of vacancies and job titles for recruitment purposes is normally an outflow from the HR planning process.

7.3.2.2 Institutional policy

The public sector institution's recruitment policy must be clarified as soon as possible. If preference is given, for example, to affirmative action candidates or to promotion from within, or to employment of the handicapped, the policy must state this clearly, and certain procedures must be implemented to ensure the execution of the policy. It is, however, recommended that all the stakeholders in the organisation be included in the process of determining the institutional recruitment policy.

7.3.2.3 Recruitment criteria

Abnormally stringent criteria will hamper recruitment efforts. Accurate job descriptions and specifications will help to set realistic requirements to facilitate effective recruitment. Criteria must also be drawn up to avoid any discriminatory practices. In the public service, the head of the relevant public service institution, who is referred to as the 'Head of the Department' and is responsible for the administration and management of the institution, is also responsible for the recruitment programmes. In practice, however, there are basic criteria that have to be adhered to in designing and developing such a programme. These criteria that have to be reflected in the recruitment programme include the following:

- **Accessibility:** Recruitment should be aimed at reaching, as far as practically and financially possible the widest possible pool of available potential applicants.
- **Positive image:** A recruitment programme should be launched in such a way that the image of the public service in general, and a public service institution in particular, will be promoted, in order to foster the applicants' interest in the public service.
- **Equity:** All recruitment programmes must be underpinned by the guiding principle of employment equity.
- **Efficiency:** Recruitment activities must ensure the acquisition and retention of human resources with appropriate knowledge, skills, and competencies.

Berenice Kerr-Phillips and Adèle Thomas carried out a comprehensive inter-cultural study on talent management (recruitment) during 2009. The aim of the study was to explore the challenges presented in retaining South Africa's talent at both macro- (country) and micro- (organisational) levels. The research results of this study are the subject of Focus on Research 7.1 below.

FOCUS ON RESEARCH 7.1
Study on talent management

In their study, Kerr-Phillips and Thomas found that several factors are regarded as important to retaining employees. The following seven factors were regarded as critical to retention:

- Development according to merit and not race (80% of white male interviewees);
- Establishment of a high-performance work culture in which mediocrity and poor performers are not tolerated (100% across all groups);
- Personal growth associated with participating in leadership development programmes, including an international sabbatical at a Centre of Excellence (100% of black interviewees; 80% of white interviewees), and being part of a mentorship programme conducted by senior leaders who offer guidance on career progression (100% of black interviewees; 50% of white interviewees);
- Exposure to all aspects of the business (100% of black interviewees; 70% of white interviewees);
- Being valued for skills and ability (60% of white interviewees);
- Recognition for contribution to the organisation (100% of black interviewees; 60% of white interviewees); and
- Employment by an organisation with a respected employer brand (100% of black interviewees; 60% of white interviewees).

Source: Kerr-Phillips & Thomas (2009: 87)

7.4 The potential employee

Both the public sector employer and the person considering employment have a good deal at stake in the employment process. The applicant can be viewed as a person seeking a position that will provide him or her with both material and psychological rewards. For most people, the process of job choice begins long before they become aware of any recruitment efforts by public sector institutions. Recruiters must be aware of the factors influencing job choice, as this will enable them to give better advice and to make better choices when recruiting candidates. Job choice, for most people, consists of three components, namely occupational choice, job search and organisational commitment.

7.4.1 Occupational choice

During early childhood, an individual starts making choices about an occupation. This process continues through adolescence and adulthood and involves a number of decisions until an initial choice is made. During this process, psychological, economic and sociological factors influence the occupational interests of the individual. As occupational interests become more focused, the individual begins to seek employment that will best satisfy his or her particular interests. New research has shown that the entrance of Generation Y workers (those born between 1980 and 1994) into the workplace is shifting the traditional employer-employee power relations.

RESEARCH FOCUS ON RESEARCH 7.2
What attracts Generation Y go-getters?

The study sought to discover what attracts Generation Y workers to a particular institution and what their career and employment expectations were once employed in the institution. The study was done by Ms Gigliola Russo, a MBA student, and Dr Linda Ronnie, a lecturer from the University of Cape Town. The research report illustrated that Generation Y workers:

- Are young and 'tech-savvy', educated, informed, ambitious and determined to succeed;
- Have much to offer to the modern workplace and will become the most high-performing workforce in the history of employment;
- Enter the workplace with much more information in their heads and at their fingertips than is currently stored in the existing institutional memory; and
- Prefer employment practices that make provision for flexibility, work-life balance, mobility, career development opportunities, good ethical record by the employer, lifelong learning and social responsibility.

According to the two researchers, the following statement by one of the respondents captures the Generation Y workers' attitudes the best:

'... when I choose an employer I need to base my choice on how long am I going to work there, what am I going to learn, how are they going to teach me, and what can I do for them'?

Source: Russo & Ronnie (2010: Online)

According to the study, this trend has interesting recruitment implications for HR practitioners as Focus on Research 7.2 on page 214 reflects.

7.4.2 Job search

When designing a specific recruitment programme, one must consider the most preferred methods of job seeking used by candidates. There are both informal and formal methods, an example of the latter being the use of employment agencies. However, many candidates may prefer more informal recruitment methods, such as asking friends or responding to newspaper advertisements.

With this in mind, public sector management should design the recruitment drive around these preferred methods. We include a word of caution, however: should a public sector employer decide to encourage existing employees to refer friends and family, this could result in nepotism. This may influence other plans to redress the current cultural mix within an institution and hence it may lead to unfair discrimination.

7.4.3 Institutional commitment

The public sector recruiter plays a major role in gaining the prospective employee's commitment to the public sector institution right from the outset. Recruitment can play an important role in marrying the candidate's vocational and job-related needs with the institution's ability to satisfy them. Greenhaus (1987: 127) suggests that the recruiter should display the following desirable qualities in the initial interaction between candidates and the institution:

- Ensure that you are perceived as both knowledgeable and well prepared;
- Ask relevant questions;
- Discuss career paths;
- Produce positive responses from candidates; and
- Display warmth, enthusiasm, and perceptiveness.

DID YOU KNOW? ?

The 'new' HRM term used by employers to attract and retain talent is better known as 'employer value proposition (EVP)'. The EVP is regarded as a set of associations and offerings provided by the employer in return for the skills, capabilities and experiences an employee brings to the organisation. The EVP should answer the following questions:

- Why should the potential employee join the organisation?
- Why should the existing employee stay with the organisation?
- Why should the potential and existing employee gives his/her best for this particular organisation?
- Why should the potential and existing employee recommend this particular organisation as an employer?

Source: Minchington (2010: Online)

The public sector recruiter must not be afraid of providing realistic information, both positive and negative, as this will enhance commitment. Realistic information serves the following purposes:

- To prevent the formation of unrealistic expectations;
- To facilitate balanced and improved decisions regarding careers; and
- To allow individuals to feel that they have greater freedom of choice.

7.5 Recruitment sources

Once it has been decided that additional employees are needed, the public sector recruiter is faced with the decision of where to search for applicants. Two basic sources of applicants can be used: internal (current employees) and external (those not currently in the employ of the public sector institution).

7.5.1 Internal sources

The internal sources include the following:

- **Skills inventories:** If the employee shortage is for higher level public sector employees, a skills inventory system may be used to search for appropriate candidates. A skills inventory is simply a record system listing employees with specific skills (Singer 1990: 166).
- **Job posting:** Vacancies within the public sector institution are placed on notice boards or in information bulletins. Details of the job are provided and employees may apply.
- **Inside moonlighting:** In the case of a short-term need or a small job which does not involve a great deal of additional work, the public sector institution could offer to pay bonuses of various types to people not on a time payroll.

7.5.2 External sources

Examples of external sources include the following:

- **Employment agencies:** The public sector institution instructs the agency to recruit suitable candidates. The agency advertises or uses its placement database - that is, a database of persons who have provided curricula vitae to the agency which then seeks employment for them. The institution may elect to do its own selection or can leave this in the hands of the agency.
- **Postings:** Postings could be used to reach those communities that cannot normally be reached through the more traditional recruitment methods. In this case, public sector institutions could liaise locally with both public and private entities for the display of posters, brochures, and other recruitment material at places that are accessible to the local community. Recruitment material should be designed in the languages used in the area.
- **Radio advertising:** Radio advertising can also be used to reach rural communities. The benefit of radio advertising, when used in conjunction with posting, is that it can serve the purpose of announcing the localities where advertisements are posted.

- **Study aids:** The main aim with study aid is to recruit people in those fields of public sector employment where difficulty is experienced hiring suitably qualified candidates. Where candidates are drawn in for study aid they enter into a written agreement with the relevant public sector institution for employment upon successfully concluding their studies. It is essential that study aid schemes be advertised as broadly as possible so that all potential candidates have a reasonable opportunity to apply for bursaries (Republic of South Africa 2003: 9).
- **Walk-ins:** Often prospective employees will apply directly to the public sector institution in the hope that a vacancy exists or will complete application forms and send them to the person concerned. One third of employees obtain their first jobs in this manner (Singer 1990: 168).
- **Referrals:** This is a word-of-mouth technique in which present public sector employees refer candidates from outside the institution. This is an inexpensive technique which is effective in quickly finding candidates with specific skills.
- **Professional bodies:** Accounting, engineering and scientific institutes look after the interests of their members by allowing vacancy advertisements in their publications. Opportunities for networking are also afforded through academic and professional conventions.
- **Head-hunting/Skills search:** Top professional people are 'hunted' through specialised agencies. The individuals are approached personally with an offer to fill a vacancy. Alternatively, an advertisement is written with the specific person's CV in mind.
- **Educational institutions:** Schools, colleges and universities provide grass-roots level opportunities for public sector recruiters to pick the 'best of the crop'. This is especially important in areas of skills shortages and professional appointments. The recruiter normally makes a presentation to final-year students and invites desirable candidates to visit the public sector institution concerned. Once again, however, care should be taken not to approach only the traditionally 'white' universities. Specific efforts to recruit from tertiary institutions that traditionally cater more for people from designated groups may even form part of an institution's affirmative action drive.
- **Consultants:** Recruitment consultants or placement agencies have a broad network base and are exposed to management in action. It is important to make use of the following guidelines to ensure efficiency and sensitivity when dealing with consultants.
  - All applicants' personal details should be treated confidentially, and accepted professional recruitment procedures should be followed at all times. Professional bodies (such as the SABPP) may take disciplinary action if breaches occur among consultants/ professionals. To ensure client protection, a contract should be established with the agency or consultant. The client should also determine whether the consultant is experienced and is an expert in recruiting for a particular vacancy. Complete details of the job description should be

ascertained before the recruitment process begins. The consultant and client should agree on all the terms and the fee structure so that both parties can fully understand all the terms and what takes place in the recruitment process.

- The recruitment procedure may be established between the consultant and the client. This includes the number of required interviews, checking references, and determining how best to advise unsuccessful candidates. A consultant communicates the agreed procedure to candidates; the client is expected to adhere closely to the agreed procedure. Candidates will be briefed continuously on the progress of their applications. Unsuccessful candidates will be advised as quickly as possible. A candidate's current employer will not be contacted unless the candidate agrees.

Guidance in the utilisation of consultants can be obtained from 'A Guide to Managing Consultants' at [http://www.parliament.org.za./eupsp/consultants/ guide].

? DID YOU KNOW?

Today's talent has access to numerous online communication channels, and public service employers need to ensure that their recruitment efforts cut through the clutter of increasingly fragmented media options. Online channels that can be used include the following:
- Career websites;
- Social media pages;
- Job boards HTML e-mails;
- SMS job alerts;
- Webcasts;
- Podcasts;
- E-newsletters;
- Video testimonials;
- Videos on YouTube; and
- Digital television.

Source: Minchington (2010: Online)

7.6 Recruiting methods

Various recruitment methods can be used. We shall discuss some of the more important methods in this section.

7.6.1 Advertisements

The most popular method of recruitment is the advertisement. Whether in the daily newspaper, the weekend job supplement, or in periodicals, public sector institutions often advertise their vacancies in a carefully worded manner to attract as many right applicants as possible. Other media used are billboards, radio, the Internet and television. Professional publications are also used effectively to attract those in their respective professional fields.

Advertising has one basic underlying principle, and that is communication. The purpose of an advertisement is to gain the right person's interest and attention; this must then lead to action. The AIDA formula may be used to structure an advertisement:

- Attention;
- Interest;
- Desire; and
- Action.

7.6.1.1   Attention

An advertisement must attract attention. These aspects are important for this purpose.

- **Headings:** A meaningful heading can describe a potential job by making use of specific subject areas or by naming particular posts. Headings should be large and readable, and should also describe what is expected by the public sector employer. Headings should be specific, not ambiguous or misleading.
- **Visual layout:** The visual layout should have immediate impact on a potential applicant. The size and form of the advertisement may influence the extent of the reaction which it evokes. The position of the advertisement on a page is also important.
- **Variety:** Potential applicants may be attracted by various factors which make the advertisement stand out.
  - *Background differences:* The use of a dark background can serve to draw readers' attention.
  - *Colour:* Because of the high costs involved, only some newspapers make use of colour in recruitment advertisements. Research should be conducted to determine the influence of colour in attracting attention to advertisements.
  - *Outline:* Outlining is used to make an advertisement more prominent. The use of outlining may draw attention to an advertisement by emphasising it and contrasting it with competing advertisements. Neatness and unity are also emphasised.
  - *Imagery:* The use of imagery can serve to attract attention. Images may consist of people and faces, enlarged emblems, background images, and work situations.
  - *Style of lettering:* Various lettering styles may be used to make an advertisement easier to read and to differentiate it from other advertisements. Eye-catchers are especially black, broad letter types. The position which is being advertised is usually clear and large. Smaller lettering is usually used in subheadings and in the general content areas.

7.6.1.2   Interest

One of the most important elements of the interest factor is the public sector institution itself. Information about the institution may include a short description of its line of service delivery, its activities and goals, its growth potential, and its expectations for the future.

Information about the position being offered is also important and should be short, describing the responsibilities involved and what is expected of the successful applicant.

Last, the relevant requirements of candidates should also be included, limited only to information such as educational qualifications, experience, and other job-relevant attributes.

7.6.1.3   Desire/urge

In this context, desire refers to the wish of the reader of an advertisement to work for a particular public sector institution, but is not limited to a formal request for a post. The proposed salary may or may not be named; it may, however, serve as an important screening device.

- **Advantages of mentioning a salary:** If a salary is very attractive and competitive, this will be in the institution's favour. Possible candidates may desire such financial advantages and may thus be more eager to apply for the post.
- **Disadvantages of mentioning a salary:** Some potential applicants may resist applying for a post because they are receiving a lower salary at present. This will mean that the institution will not come into contact with such potentially successful candidates. Another disadvantage of advertising the salary offered is that other public sector institutions may raise their current salary levels in order to remain competitive. Employees may also feel dissatisfied if they are being paid less than the advertised salary.

?

DID YOU KNOW?

The second JobCrystal Happiness Indicator took a look at which South African employers had the happiest staff and are the best places to work for. Employers with the happiest employees:
- Auditor-General 72.6%
- Shell Oil 70%
- CSIR 69.8%
- Softline Pastel 69.8%
- Anglo Platinum 69.15%

Top employers to work for:
- KPMG 75%
- Sanlam 71%
- Pick n Pay 67.5%
- Momentum 67%
- PricewaterhouseCoopers 66%

Only two public sector employers have featured in the survey.

Available at: [http://www.jobcrystal.co.za/blog/post/JobCrystal/2010/04/Press_02]

7.6.1.4 Action

The placement of advertisements will be successful if it leads to applications from many 'right' candidates for the job. Each applicant should receive an indication of what is expected of him or her. The applicant should write his or her address clearly on the letter of application and should also include a telephone number so that more detailed information can be obtained if necessary. In this way, immediate arrangements may be made for an initial interview.

Sometimes applicants are required to fill in coupons or short job-request forms so that basic details can be obtained and a larger number of responses elicited by the advertisement.

See the box below for an overview of selected guidelines for the compilation of advertisements in the public service.

Selected guidelines for the compilation of advertisements

- An advertisement should not favour or prejudice any prospective candidate who has the necessary training, skills, competence, and/or knowledge. Advertisements should therefore be supportive of and in compliance with the 1996 Constitution, the Labour Relations Act 55 of 1996, the Public Service Act 103 of 1994 and the Public Service Regulations of 2001. Qualifications should not be defined primarily or solely in terms of educational attainment, but should include skills, relevant experience, and other criteria. Where educational requirements are considered to be essential, these must be set at the minimum level.
- An advertisement should be fully compatible with the valid post and person specifications for the post and should specify the inherent requirements of the job, the job title, and core functions. Do not include in an advertisement any requirements and/or skills that are not directly related to the applicant's ability to perform that specific job.
- Departments should consider using the relevant job title or domestic rank in advertisements in order to attract applicants with the ability to perform that specific job.
- Advertising should encourage competition between internal and external applicants to promote labour mobility and cross-fertilisation of energy and experience.
- Advertisements must in no way, either directly (race, gender, etc.) or indirectly (inordinate qualifications) discriminate against any potential candidate or discourage him or her from presenting his or her candidature.
- The requirements for additional health and security checks must be clearly stated in the advertisements.

Source: Adapted from Senior Management Service: Public Service Handbook (Republic of South Africa 2003: 13–14)

7.6.2 Special-event recruiting

Some public sector institutions stage open houses and visits to headquarters, and even son and daughter days. Others address specific groups of students on campuses.

7.6.3 Vacation work

Many public sector institutions hire students during their vacations. This allows the institution to get specialised piecework completed and simultaneously to identify prospective permanent employees. Students are also afforded an opportunity to experience working life, thereby eliminating unrealistic expectations. Sometimes, students take up a great deal of management time, and the work done is not always of the highest standard. Students may, however, become disillusioned when their initial expectations are not met, and on returning to their educational institutions, they may actually become reverse recruiters, having a negative effect on the institution's recruitment drive.

7.7 The recruitment process

The following steps in the recruitment process are usually followed, and can be used as a model approach to recruitment in the public sector. It should, however, be noted that, since public sector institutions have different needs, the recruitment process will have to be adapted to suit each institution's specific requirements.

Step 1: Determine the exact need
Before any action of recruitment is considered, it must be determined whether a genuine need exists for the post to be filled. Consider the circumstances under which the need for recruitment arose. Make sure that the decision can be substantiated with facts obtained from objective measurements or available valid management information. In the Public Service Regulations of 2001, it is recognised that HR planning should precede any recruitment action in the public service. Among other things, this involves forecasting the institution's HR needs, job analysis (unless it has been done before), and budgeting for the relevant posts. It is very important that departmental heads, HR specialists, and line function employees should be full partners in the process to verify the need for recruitment in cases where it has not been initiated by them. It is also important to consider the deployment or absorption of existing employees as an option. After deployment and absorption have been considered, and it has been established that it is impossible to fill the vacancy through such actions, the recruitment process can get started.

Step 2: Obtain approval to recruit in terms of the HR budget and level of appointment
Since employing a person is a major expenditure for a public sector institution (for example, an employee who is employed for ten years at an average salary of R100 000 per annum will cost the institution one million rand), the budget of the institution should be taken into account, as well as the corporate and business plans and guidelines for recruitment. Approval must be obtained from senior management. This will ensure that recruitment is compatible with the broad institutional and human resource plans. This step will also create the opportunity to reconsider the overall

recruitment strategy and to consider alternatives to recruitment, such as overtime and outsourcing. Public sector managers must be aware of the fact that a possible ad hoc restructuring may harm certain units in the institution and that recruitment must therefore be executed with the utmost care.

Step 3: Compile or update job descriptions and job specifications

We have already explained the role and nature of job descriptions and specifications. A job description and job specification comprise the point of departure for all recruitment activities, and it is thus essential that the job description should provide an accurate reflection of job activities. A job description will enable the public sector recruiter to determine the exact nature of the vacant job – that is, the purpose, duties, responsibilities, and position of the relevant job in the organisational structure. The job specification, on the other hand, helps the recruiter to profile the required jobholder, according to, for example, the necessary experience, qualifications, motivation, and communication abilities. Problems arise when job descriptions and job specifications have not been compiled and when job content has not been updated. As we have seen, the writing of job descriptions and specifications is often a cumbersome process which is often neglected in public sector institutions. The recruiter must, however, ensure that the correct job information is obtained.

Step 4: Determine the key result areas for the job

This step is a natural outflow of the previous step. Key result areas refer to those aspects of the job which are crucial for the success of the job, and they normally focus on outputs and not on job activities. This needs to be done objectively to provide the public sector recruiter and the person responsible for interviewing and selection with insight into actual job requirements. This may form part of a job description.

Step 5: Consult the recruitment policy and procedure (see Section 7.3)

The recruitment policy and procedure document will contain specific guidelines for recruitment, and should be consulted in the interest of consistency and in order to ensure the long-term efficiency of recruitment in the public sector institution. This document reflects the institution's views regarding the approach and procedures to be followed in the institution and could include steps in the recruitment process (as explained in this section). The policy and procedures document will indicate, for example, whether recruitment should be done internally or externally and will specify the cost limitations. This document is, however, a dynamic document and must be amended as and when required.

Step 6: Choose the source(s) (see Section 7.5)

When the public sector recruiter knows what type of person must be recruited for the job, the recruitment source can be selected. Historical data on the success rate of certain sources could be very useful in this regard. As mentioned in Step 5, the recruitment policy may give an indication of whether the person(s) should be recruited internally or externally, and, once this has been ascertained, the recruiter will make a choice of one or more sources (depending on the group or person required). It is good policy to try to recruit internally first of all and then, if a suitable candidate cannot be identified, to channel the recruitment effort externally. In certain cases, recruitment will have to be done externally – for example when a pool of new employees is required (such as new apprentices for possible technical training at a later stage or a specialised computer expert).

Step 7: Decide on a method of recruitment (see Section 7.6)
Recruitment methods which have traditionally proved successful must always be used, such as newspaper advertisements (which are very common) and internal succession planning. It is also important to consider previous experience with different methods, as well as factual data on the effectiveness of different methods in various geographical areas and in different job categories. The public sector recruiter must, however, select the best method or methods for recruitment. The possible source of recruitment may also be an indication of the methods to be used. Recruiters must also guard against being accused of discrimination through using one particular recruitment method to the exclusion of others. This could be the totally unintentional result of a traditional practice in the public sector institution – for example, advertising in only one newspaper which is circulated in only one particular area and in the process excluding potential employees from other areas in which the newspaper is not circulated.

Step 8: Implement the decision (apply the recruitment method)
In this step, the chosen recruitment method(s) must be applied. For example, in the case of a newspaper advertisement, the planned advertisement must be screened to prevent embarrassment to the public sector institution and to potential employees. When a recruitment agency is used, clear parameters of what is expected must be communicated well in advance.

An advertisement, for example, that is placed for a senior management post in the public service should specify the following (Republic of South Africa Public 2003: 15):

- Job title;
- Place to be stationed;
- Core functions and requirements of the post;
- All-inclusive package;
- Contact person to whom enquiries can be addressed;
- Closing date;
- Term of appointment, if this is to be specified; and
- Notice to the applicants that the successful candidate will be required to enter into an employment contract and a performance agreement.

Step 9: Allow sufficient time for response

The method used will dictate the time that should be allowed for responses. Set clear deadlines, but remain flexible to ensure the maximum number of responses.

Step 10: Screen responses

Potential employees will respond to the recruitment method used and the majority of the applicants will not be successful. Initial screening could be done telephonically as illustrated by the following example of a telephonic screening form. The applicants' particulars must at this stage be compared with what has been stipulated in the job description and specification. The unsuccessful candidates must be separated from those who may be considered for possible appointment. Screening should take place according to the initial criteria set for the job. Recruiters should guard against prejudice and subjective opinions that could lead to discrimination against applicants. Sometimes initial screening will lead to only some people receiving application forms. During this step, the recruiter may also screen applicants on the grounds of already completed application forms or CVs.

Step 11: Draw up an initial shortlist of candidates

During this step, a shortlist of possible successful candidates is drawn up. At this stage, telephonic screening can often help the public sector recruiter to obtain important information which can further eliminate unsuitable candidates. The shortlist of potentially suitable applicants must be forwarded and discussed with the relevant department or unit head before proceeding to the selection interviews. In summary, here are some of the basic requirements to be taken into consideration when compiling a shortlist (Foot & Hook 1996: 118):
- At least two people must be involved independently in compiling the shortlist.
- Each person must give a clear indication where applicants do not meet the requirements regarding knowledge, skills, and competencies.
- Each person must classify the applications into predetermined categories of 'acceptable', 'possibly acceptable', and 'unacceptable'.
- Each person must rank the acceptable applications in order of suitability.

- A specific choice must be made to determine which applicants will be invited for interviews.

Remember that the inputs made by the shortlisters constitute sensitive information and must be treated as confidential. The shortlist information should under no circumstances be discussed with colleagues (Van der Westhuizen 2000: 118).

Step 12: Advise applicants of the outcome

It is important to advise all applicants as soon as possible of the outcome of their applications. This will include those who were unsuccessful and those who may be invited for interviews. Great care must be taken to respond as soon as possible to ensure that the reputation of the public sector institution remains unblemished. The following guidelines can be used when communicating with unsuccessful applicants: (1) personalise the communication by using the applicant's first name/surname instead of addressing the person as 'Dear Applicant', and (2) make sure a member of senior management (preferably the human resource manager) signs the letter personally. When communicating via the Internet, make sure a senior manager's name appears in the message. Create the impression that the shortlisting was done after mature deliberation. Informing the successful applicants also requires a professional approach. When inviting successful applicants for an interview, it may prove useful to use the following guidelines (Van der Westhuizen 2000: 110):

- Candidates must be informed specifically (where, when, and for how long) that they are invited to an interview.
- Spell out all the requirements of the interview to the candidates (qualification certificates must be available, a medical examination must be undergone, selection tests must be written, etc.).
- Provide detailed information to the candidates about the payment of transport, subsistence allowance, what receipts should be kept for later payment, etc.
- Inform the candidates of actions to be taken when a problem arises (who to contact, what extension or cell phone number).

Step 13: Proceed to selection

Qualifying applicants are now invited for interviews. (See Chapter 8 for a detailed discussion of the selection process.)

7.8   Evaluation of recruitment

It should be borne in mind that recruitment is an expensive process that includes such costs as the following (Beardwell & Holden 1995: 208):

- Recruiters' salaries;
- Management and professional time spent on preparing job descriptions, job specifications, designing and placing of advertisements, and liaison activities;
- Costs of advertisements or other recruitment methods;

- Costs of producing supporting literature (such as brochures and placards);
- Recruitment overheads and other administrative expenses;
- Costs of overtime or subcontracting whilst the post remains unfilled; and
- Costs of recruiting unsuitable candidates for the forthcoming selection process.

Thus, it is essential that the recruitment process should be evaluated. It is relatively easy to evaluate the cost effectiveness of the public sector recruiter in terms of whether the recruitment target was reached. Another method of evaluation is to decide the number of interviews required per successful placement.

However, it is essential to evaluate the cost/benefit ratio of each method or of a combination of recruitment methods employed. When weighing up their cost effectiveness, factors such as external conditions in the labour market, time taken to fill the vacancy, and the nature of the job must be considered. Finally, the effectiveness of the recruitment strategy will impact on employee turnover statistics.

Table 7.1 outlines a general framework in terms of which a recruitment programme may be evaluated. The framework can produce useful information on the strengths and weaknesses of a specific programme; as well as useful ideas for improving the programme. It does not, however, provide a rands-and-cents evaluation.

Table 7.1   A framework for the evaluation of an overall recruitment programme

Stage of entry	Criteria
Pre-entry	● Ability of the organisation to recruit newcomers
Entry	● Initial expectations of newcomers

Post-entry	● Choice of organisation by the individual
	● Initial job attitudes such as:
	  – Satisfaction with the job
	  – Commitment to the organisation
	  – Descriptive statements about job expectations (to be compared with those held as an outsider)
	  – Thoughts about quitting
	  – Job performance
	● Job tenure and voluntary turnover rates

It is also important that an assessment should be made of the equal opportunity situation. The various applicants can, for example, be categorised in terms of their race, gender, religion, and disability status. A further list can be compiled in terms of the number of applicants for a particular position, the number who were unsuccessful, and the number of successful candidates, including the reasons for their success.

It is very important that the recruitment department should keep accurate records of each step in the recruitment process, including the relevant documents. This will enable the public sector institution to answer any possible questions which interested parties may have at any time during the selection process.

7.9 Notes on strategic recruitment

Recruitment approaches will have to change significantly to enable public sector institutions to move into a new era of international competition. There are various problems with the traditional recruitment methods because they are orientated to the past and the present. It must, however, be emphasised that, if the HR planning process has been executed properly, the reactive approach to recruitment will be largely eliminated. However, it is important that recruiters maintain a strategic approach to recruitment, which implies that job descriptions and job specifications, among other things, must be in line with the general strategic direction of the institution. If, for instance, it is of strategic importance to implement affirmative action more vigorously, recruitment efforts should support this.

?

DID YOU KNOW?

The Department of Public Service and Administration has issued a 'Toolkit on recruitment and selection' for the public service. This toolkit makes provision for, among others, the following HR activities:
- The importance of recruitment and selection;
- Where departments go wrong;
- Regulatory framework underpinning recruitment and selection;
- Important principles underlying recruitment and selection;
- Management of the recruitment and selection process; and
- Development of a departmental recruitment and selection policy.

Source: Republic of South Africa (undated: Online) [http://unpan1.un.org/intradoc/groups/public/documents/un/unpan]

According to Rothwell and Kazanas (1994), the following strategic approach to recruitment can be adopted:
- **Step 1:** Reconsider the purpose of the recruitment function in the context of the institutional strategy and human resource management strategy. What is it at present? What should it be in the future?
- **Step 2:** What are the present strengths and weaknesses of the institution's recruitment approach? Can present strengths be built on? Can present weaknesses be rectified?
- **Step 3:** What trends in the external and internal environments are likely to affect the recruitment function? Answer the following questions: To what extent will economic conditions make it easier to recruit certain kinds of talent in the future? To what extent will economic trends affect future labour supply outside the institution? Inside the institution? To what extent will technological change influence the kinds of talent needed? The appropriate sources to look for that

talent? To what extent will market conditions in the industry influence labour supply? To what extent will social changes affect public views about employer recruitment methods? How will those changes affect state-of-the-art practices?

- **Step 4:** What ranges of recruitment strategies are available?
- **Step 5:** What choice of recruitment strategy is appropriate considering other human resource management practices and strategies?
- **Step 6:** How is a new recruitment strategy implemented? Consider: What skills will be needed by public sector institution recruiters? By public sector managers? What rewards can be given to those who act in a manner consistent with new recruitment strategy?
- **Step 7:** What criteria should be used to evaluate recruitment?

7.10   Review

We initiated our discussion by stating that public human resource management activities cannot be effective unless suitable employees have been recruited. This process begins with the employee's occupational choice and job search, and culminates in his or her commitment to join the public sector institution.

Before a public sector institution can start recruiting, it must decide on a recruitment policy, taking various external and internal factors into consideration. Once these factors have been considered, the institution can utilise various employment sources such as skills inventories, job postings, employment agencies, and professional bodies. The second major decision that the public sector recruiter must make is which method of recruiting to employ, such as placing an advertisement above a special event promotion, or whether to use a combination of methods.

We have discussed the steps in the recruitment process, as well as the evaluation of recruitment, and we have concluded with a brief discussion on a strategic approach to recruitment.

7.11   Self-evaluation questions

1. Formulate an argument indicating the relationship between human resource planning, job analysis, recruitment, and selection.
2. Advise your human resource manager how to draw up a recruitment policy.
3. Discuss the way in which both internal and external factors can influence the recruitment policy in a public sector institution of your choice.
4. If you were a recruiter, what are the factors you would take into consideration in order to give better advice and to make better choices when recruiting potential candidates for a public sector institution?
5. Which recruitment sources should a public sector human resource manager use in the recruitment process?
6. What methods do you think should be used for recruitment in the public sector?

7. Compare the recruitment process discussed in this chapter with the recruitment process followed in a public sector institution of your choice. Describe any differences in the steps taken.
8. Draw up a recruitment advertisement for a chief financial officer.
9. Do you think it is necessary to evaluate the recruitment process? Give reasons for your answer.
10. Some authors claim that recruiters should maintain a strategic approach to recruitment in the current global era. Do you agree or disagree with this statement? Provide reasons for your answer.

Bibliography

Amos, T, Ristow, A, & Ristow, L. 2004. *Human resource management.* 2nd edn. Cape Town: Juta.

Beardwell, I, & Holden, L. 1995. *Human resource management: A contemporary perspective.* London: Pitman.

Dessler, G. 1984. *Personnel management.* 3rd edn. Boston, MA: Prentice-Hall.

Foot, M, & Hook, C. 1996. *Introducing human resource management.* London: Longman.

Gerber, PD, Nel, PS, & Van Dyk, PS. 1992. *Human resources management.* 2nd edn. Halfway House: Southern Books.

Greenhaus, JH. 1987. *Career management.* Orlando, FL: Dryden.

Grogan, J. 2008. *Workplace law.* Cape Town: Juta.

Hubbart, WS. 1993. *Personnel policy handbook: How to develop a manual that works.* New York: McGraw Hill.

Ivancevich, JM, & Glueck, WF. 1983. *Foundations of personnel/human resource management.* Revised edn. Plano, TX: Business Publications.

Kerr-Phillips, B, & Thomas, A. 2009. Macro and micro challenges for talent retention in South Africa. *SA Journal of Human Resource Management,* 7(1), 82-91.

Minchington, B. 2010. Communicate your EVP to attract and retain talent. *HR Future,* 6, [http://www.hrfuture.net].

Myers, IB, & McCaulley, MH. 1992. *A guide to the development and use of the Myers-Briggs Type Indicator.* Palo Alto, CA: Consulting Psychologists Press.

Pons, A, & Deale, P. 1998. *Labour relations handbook: A practical guide on effective labour relations policies, procedures and practices for South African management.* Cape Town: Juta.

Riley, DD. 1993. *Public personnel administration.* New York: Harper Collins.

Robinson-Hickman, G. 2001. *Managing personnel in the public sector.* New York: Wadsworth.

Rothwell, WJ, & Kazanas, HC. 1994. *Planning and managing human resources: Strategic planning for personnel management.* Amherst, MA: HRD Press.

Russo, G, & Ronnie, L. 2010. Study reveals what attracts Generation Y go-getters. *HR Future.* [http://www.hrfuture.net]

Singer, MG. 1990. *Human resource management.* Boston, MA: PWS Kent.

Singer, N. 2010. New dawn for recruitment: Role of recruiters in a technology enabled environment. *HR Future,* 6, [http://www.hrfuture.net].

Smith, W, Boonzaaier, J, Schussler, M, Blair, C, & Phillips, M. 2009. *The Adcorp Employment Index (AEI): Quarterly update.* Adcorp Holdings. [http://www.adcorp.co.za].

Swanepoel, B, Erasmus, B, Van Wyk, M, & Schenk, H. 2003. *South African human resource management: Theory and practice.* Cape Town: Juta.

Tompkins, J. 1995. *Human resource management in government: Hitting the ground running.* University of Montana-Harper Collins.

Van Der Westhuizen, EJ. 2000. Public Human Resource Management: Study guide 1 for PUB302- F (Public Administration). Pretoria: University of South Africa.

Wanous, JP. 1980. *Organizational entry: Recruitment, selection, and socialization of newcomers.* Reading, MA: Addison-Wesley.

Wingrove, T. 1993. *Affirmative action.* Randburg: Knowledge Resources.

Acts of legislation

Republic of South Africa. 1994. The Public Service Act (Proclamation 103 of 1994). Government Printer. [http://www.polity.org.za/html/govdocs/legislation/1994]

Republic of South Africa. 1995a. The Labour Relations Act (Act 66 of 1995). Government Printer. [http://www.polity.org.za/html/govdocs/legislation/1995]

Republic of South Africa. 1996. The Constitution of the Republic of South Africa (1996). Government Printer. [http://www.polity.org.za/html/govdocs/legislation/1996]

Republic of South Africa. 1998a. The Employment Equity Act (Act 55 of 1998). Government Printer. [http://www.polity.org.za/html/govdocs/legislation/1998]

Government regulations

Republic of South Africa. 2001. Public Service Regulations of 2001. Government Gazette, 427 (21951).

Government white papers

Republic of South Africa. 1995b. White Paper on the Transformation of the Public Service. 24 November 1995. Government Gazette, 365 (16838).

Republic of South Africa. 1997. White Paper on Human Resource Management in the Public Service. Government Gazette 390 (18594).

Republic of South Africa. 1998b. White Paper on Affirmative Action in the Public Service. 23 April 1998. Government Gazette, 564 (18800).

Government circulars

Republic of South Africa. 2010. National Minimum Information Requirements (NMIR). Department of Public Service and Administration. [http://www.dpsa.gov.za/documents/acts&regulations/nmir.pdf]

Management guides

Republic of South Africa. 1999. Baseline Implementation Guide. Department of Public Service and Administration.

Republic of South Africa. 2003. Senior Management Service: Public Service Handbook. Department of Public Service and Administration. [http://www.dpsa.gov.za/documents/sms/ publications/smshb2003]

Republic of South Africa. 2004. A Guide to Managing Consultants. SA Parliament. [http://www.parliament.gov.za./eupsp/consultants/guide]

Republic of South Africa. Undated. A toolkit on recruitment and selection. Department of Public Service and Administration. [http://unpan1.un.org/intradoc/groups/public/documents/un/unpan]

8 Selecting, appointing and orientating public sector employees

Purpose

The purpose of this chapter is to analyse and clarify the principles that guide the selecting, appointing and orientating of new employees in the public sector.

Learning outcomes

After you have read this chapter, you should be able to:
- Write out a primary aim and objectives for selection.
- Design a selection policy and procedures to guide those that are involved in the selection process.
- List the various steps that can be taken in the selection process.
- Apply selection strategies to manage the process of a selection in a more confident manner.
- Explain how to conduct a preliminary interview.
- Demonstrate a variety of selection methods with which to improve the effectiveness of the collection and assessment of selection information.
- Describe the various employment tests that can be used in the selection process.
- Plan and conduct an interview and formulate the appropriate questions for the applicant.
- Conduct reference checks.
- Demonstrate the ability to make a selection decision, justify your selection decision, and provide feedback to unsuccessful applicants.
- Practise the steps in placing and orientating the new public sector employee.

8.1 Introduction

The purpose of recruitment is to gather a large pool of good quality applicants from which to select and appoint the most suitable employees. Another important facet of human resource management is to select, appoint, and orientate public sector employees.

It is not always possible to draw a distinct line between the steps of the recruitment and the selection process. This is the case because selection flows naturally from the recruitment process.

However, it can be said that the selection process commences after the closing date of the advertisement. The selection process is successfully concluded after a candidate has been given a job offer and accepts it.

Personnel selection is based on individual differences between human beings – that is, on the fact that attributes differ greatly from person to person, each individual possessing unique traits and abilities.

Selection can be defined as the process of trying to determine which individuals may best match particular jobs in the public sector institutional context, taking into account individual differences, the requirements of the job, and the institution's internal and external environments.

Essentially thus, selection is the prediction of future performance in terms of individual differences. Selection requires information about the job or work in question and about the knowledge, skills, and abilities needed to do the job successfully. Selection decisions therefore require one to know how such knowledge, skills, and abilities can be assessed, which makes the proper use of predictors in selection very important. Obviously this is not an easy task. In view of the complexity of the task, public sector employers need to take it most seriously. Therefore, appropriate investment needs to be put into the selection process beforehand to avoid possibly enormous and incalculable costs due to faulty employee selections. This implies that the selection process should be strategically planned. This can be achieved as follows:

- Create an awareness of the essential nature of the selection task and its underlying constraints.
- Set clear definitions of the criteria for effective work performance by having a comprehensive job analysis system in place.
- Conceptualise the meaning and understand the implications of reliability and validity for employee selection.
- Become aware of the range of possible methods, their value, and their potential predictive capabilities.
- Get public sector selectors involved in the training for the selection process; for example, training in interviewing skills.
- Incorporate a follow-up system in the selection process to see whether predictions (appointments) that have been made have turned out well in practice.

This chapter focuses on the selection process, the value of the different selection devices, assessment centres, and the importance of fairness in selection decisions. A brief overview of the appointment and induction (or orientation) of newly appointed public sector employees makes up the final part of this chapter.

8.2   The aim and objectives of selection

The primary aim of selection is usually expressed as 'selecting the best candidate for the post'. During the selection process, selectors try to determine a candidate's future work performance and the value, knowledge, skills, and competencies that can be added to the public sector institution. Of equal importance is that public sector selectors must make sure that the relevant post is acceptable so that the candidate does not leave the institution after a short period of employment (Foot & Hook 1996: 78; Van der Westhuizen 2000: 113). Most writers agree that the following objectives will lead to the achievement of the primary aim:

- Collect as much relevant information about the candidate as possible.
- Organise and evaluate collected information by having proper systems in place.
- Assess each candidate as objectively as possible by taking into consideration equal employment opportunity requirements and affirmative action policies so that predictions about future work performance can be made.
- Provide the collected information to successful candidates so that they can be in a position to decide whether to accept an offer of employment.

DID YOU KNOW?

It is actually unacceptable to ask candidates to attach a photo to their application form. Such requests can entail a candidate's gender and race, for instance, becoming known. Potentially it could give rise to unfair discrimination against that person during the selection process.

8.3   Selection policy and procedures

As we have seen above, the selection task is complex in nature. In the absence of clear guidelines, selection becomes even more difficult, and, in the process, the selector may be left in the dark. In so many instances in the past, it has happened that appointments have been made based on the judgements formed by public sector managers on very short acquaintance with the candidate. In most of these cases, the interview has been used as the only selection method. Within a few minutes, selection decisions are made based on a single method without taking into consideration the bigger picture; this means that other selection method options, which are also available, have not been used. In many of these cases, it appears that the successful candidate was not the right one. Because of this overconfidence and subjectivity in public sector selectors, interviews are no longer highly rated as a selection method. With this background, we can now say that every effort should be made by public sector employers to design and implement appropriate policy and procedure measures for selection. Obviously, good selection policies and procedures will provide guidance to those involved in the selection process and make them confident that they are following the tenets of best practice (Foot & Hook 1996: 79).

Good selection policies and procedures should include the following:

- Prescribed selection principles;
- Set entry requirements;
- Prescribed qualifications for appointment;
- Steps, methods, and techniques to be used;
- Personnel to be involved in assessing candidates; and
- The relevant administrative procedures (for example, record keeping).

A selection policy that does not include specified selection principles runs the risk of being confronted legally. A variety of principles should be taken into account to ensure that the whole field is covered.

DID YOU KNOW?

?

Entry requirements for appointment in the public service are prescribed in Part VII.B1 and B3 of the Public Service Regulations of 2001 (Section 10 of the Public Service Act 103 of 1994) and the White Paper on Human Resource Management in the Public Service (1997: 38–39). These may include:

- **Merit:** Every effort should be made to ensure that the public service appoints people of the highest calibre. An important component of a merit approach to selection is to make sure that the applicant being offered the job is best suited in terms of skills, experience, abilities, personal attributes and competencies.
- **Fairness:** To ensure that everyone has a fair opportunity to participate in the selection process, there should be no discrimination against any applicant on the grounds of race, culture, colour, marital status, belief, gender, sexual orientation, pregnancy, disability, domestic circumstances, age, religion or any other arbitrary criterion.
- **Equity:** This principle derives from the fact that all candidates should be measured against the same objective criteria. Naturally, you also have to take into consideration the need for representativeness. Equity is also related to other requirements; for example, it is suggested that all applicants who apply for a particular post should be assessed by the same selection panel.
- **Transparency:** Selection policies and procedures should also demonstrate transparency. This means that easily accessible written records should be kept of: (1) criteria used in selecting interviewees; (2) criteria used in selecting the most suitable candidate; and (3) evaluation records of individual candidates.
- **Citizenship:** The public service has adopted an employment policy of requiring those who work for them to be South African citizens, including those who have legally acquired citizenship. Furthermore, it is stipulated that non-South African citizens may be employed on fixed-term contracts for up to a maximum of five years. However, there is the possibility of extending contracts beyond five years, provided that prior approval is given by the head of the relevant public service institution.
- **Age:** The age limit for employment in the public service ranges between 16 and 60 years.
- **Health:** A central feature of the health requirements of the public service is that they should solely relate to the inherent nature of the duties to be undertaken. One of the implications of this ruling is that no pre-employment health checks will be undertaken unless the inherent requirements of the post call for particular physical attributes. Another health requirement is directed towards disabled applicants. A major issue of concern in this regard is that disabled persons may not be discriminated against simply because the relevant public service institution lacks facilities, and reasonable steps should be taken to accommodate them. If a post has demands that require certain health or physical requirements, the appropriate requirements should be clearly specified in advertisements. ▷

- **Good character:** One major issue that public service employers face is the screening of applicants on the basis of whether they meet entry requirements in terms of good character. In short, one has to determine whether applicants are law-abiding and prepared to conform to the high standards of conduct set in the Code of Conduct for Public Servants. One approach is to require potential employees to provide information about past criminal convictions.
- **Security clearance:** Candidates applying for positions that deal with sensitive information, where the security of the State is at stake, may be subjected to security clearances. In these instances, where a security clearance is a requirement, this should be clearly stated in the advertisement.

8.4 The selection process

The selection process consists of several phases, which should include those indicated in Figure 8.1 on page 237. These phases are typical of most public sector institutional selection procedures. After each phase, the applicant can either be rejected or accepted.

8.4.1 Phase 1: Deciding on a selection strategy

As with most of the HR activities, selection is an enormously complex task. A practical expression of this complexity is presented in the fact that selection requires predicting future work performance based on information that comes from the past. A considerable segment of work performance is determined by the so-called hard skills, such as technical knowledge of job-related abilities. Another component of work performance lies in the so-called soft skills, which include such variables as interpersonal relations and motivation. Every aspect of the selection process is directed at deciding which determinants of work performance to measure and which selection techniques to use. Whichever measurements or selection techniques are utilised, these choices require the adoption of a deliberate selection strategy. There are basically eight selection strategies to choose from:

- **Knowledge, skills, and abilities (KSA) strategy:** This strategy is commonly regarded as synonymous of most selection processes in the public sector. Primarily this strategy involves a review of the applicant's educational background and work history. This type of information is gathered from the application form or personal résumé. In addition, this strategy may also include the testing of applicants for specific knowledge, skills or abilities. The disadvantage of this strategy is that it reveals very little about the 'soft skills' of an applicant.
- **Track record strategy:** This strategy, of course, relies on the belief that work performance in the past is the best predictor of future performance. Basically there are two ways this strategy can be constructed. These include reviewing of the application forms that have been submitted and interviewing of candidates. The apparent objective of both these strategies is that they seem to determine whether specific results have been produced in similar work environments. Indeed, the

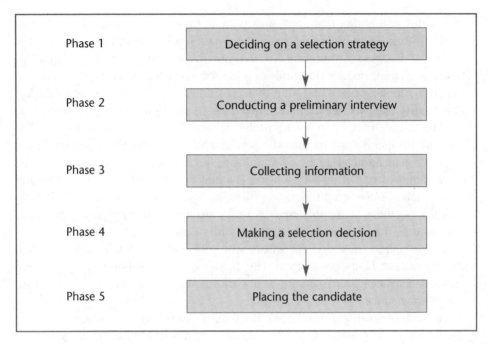

Figure 8.1   The selection process

implementation of this strategy poses particular considerations. You need to remember that work experience gained at a previous workplace is not the same thing as demonstrated performance during an interview. Likewise, educational knowledge may indicate little more than the ability of a candidate to do well in an academic environment. In addition, technical skills do not guarantee high work performance, and employment tests do not always measure effort. Selectors should note that using this strategy for the filling of entry-level posts is not appropriate. It would be fair to use it for more senior level posts where applicants have had sufficient opportunity to establish track records.

- **Learning/Intelligence strategy:** In short, this strategy makes use of employment tests, such as intelligent tests, that measure general mental abilities. The most common criteria used for measuring these abilities include such factors as reasoning ability, visualising ability, verbal comprehension, memory, and numerical ability. This strategy has enormous potential, but, because there are doubts about the validity of intelligence tests, it is seldom used in the public sector. There is also a major concern over the potential adverse affect it could have on minority applicants.

- **Aptitude strategy:** As with the learning/intelligence strategy, the aptitude strategy makes use of a test (in this case, the aptitude test) to measure certain traits of individuals. The main objective here is to determine what kind of work an applicant is best suited for. With the aptitude strategy, the public sector selector makes the assumption that applicants with an interest in or aptitude for certain kinds of work are more highly motivated to perform well than those who are not interested. Because the aptitude test does not give an exact indication of efficient future work performance this strategy is not top of the league in the public sector. Generally, applicants are placed in those positions for which they have applied.

- **Personality trait strategy:** This strategy focuses on the use of standardised tests in order to construct a personality profile of candidates (see Section 8.4.3.3). The tests are also supported by interviews to determine a candidate's personality in terms of such characteristics as forcefulness, flexibility, tolerance for uncertainty, self-confidence, and need for security. The aim of this strategy is to understand a candidate's inner qualities rather than to determine knowledge, skills, and abilities. Needless to say, this strategy relies heavily on the interpretations of the test results. This is why so much attention is directed towards the role of the interviewers and those HR specialists who interpret the test results. Although test results can be assessed accurately, this strategy is seldom employed in the public sector because personality traits are relatively poor predictions of future work performance.

- **Work sample strategy:** Another strategy used in the selection process, namely the work sample strategy, involves the measuring of a candidate's performance on some of the job's basic tasks. For example, an applicant applying for a secretarial position may be instructed to complete a typing test. This strategy is increasingly receiving more attention because it predicts future work performance more accurately and, at the same time, gives a high degree of validity to the process.

- **Networking strategy:** The networking strategy was originally established in the private sector. It has been used less frequently in the public sector. Typically this strategy includes the encouraging of current employees to identify potential candidates who they believe will make a good contribution and add value to a public sector institution. Integral to this strategy is its potential to form an important part of a public sector institution's employment equity programme. The recommendations made by knowledgeable employees can sometimes result in the appointment of very capable candidates. Unfortunately if managed wrongly this strategy can have the opposite effect. For instance, the networking strategy will often be used to select individuals with similar backgrounds. This is a matter of imposing a homogeneous group of individuals' ideas on others, which produces inbreeding for the public sector as a whole. One example of this is the forming of 'old-boy networks' that circumvent the merit system. These actions will automatically deny equal employment opportunities to others.

- **Situational strategy:** In this strategy critical behaviours are identified as necessary to successful job performance. By making use of tests or interviews, it is determined whether an applicant is capable of exhibiting such behaviours; in other words, how he or she would respond to particular work situations. During a structured interview, a candidate can be asked to respond to a job-specific situation. For example, an accountant may be given an accountancy problem. The situational strategy is widely viewed as a valid measure of determining future work performance if pursued with care. However, it remains questionable whether the candidate will behave in the same way on the job as was the case during the interview (Tompkins 1995: 187–192).

8.4.2 Phase 2: Conducting a preliminary interview

Although one has to decide on a specific selection strategy, the selection process actually starts with the preliminary interview, which is short and concise. The main purpose of a preliminary interview is pre-selection and the elimination of applicants who are obviously not qualified for the job. Straightforward questions are asked around such areas as qualifications, experience, and salary. This is normally done once people have responded to initial recruitment efforts. It usually happens over the telephone and can, in a certain sense, also be viewed as part of the recruitment process (see Chapter 7).

DID YOU KNOW? ?

Foreign nationals need valid work permits to be employed in the South African public service. In respect of the quota category of work permits as envisaged in Section 19(1) of the Immigration Act 13 of 2002, the Director-General of the Department of Home Affairs may issue a work permit to specific occupational categories but also with numerical quotas attached thereto. Specific deadlines are also set for foreign nationals. For example, in terms of Regulation 16(3) to the Act, the holder of a quota work permit must, within 90 days of admission to the country, submit to the Director-General of Home Affairs a written confirmation of having secured employment within the particular category in which they have applied.

It is also important to note that Section 49 of the Act does make provision for serious penalties against employers who do not comply with the provisions of the Act. It is therefore of the utmost importance that HR practitioners keep an effective diary system in place to warn employers in time of impending deadlines in respect of these requirements.

Read more about a study done by Mulenga & van Lill (2007: Online) entitled 'Recruitment and selection of foreign professionals in the South African job market: Procedures and processes'. The study investigated procedures and processes used in the selection of prospective foreign applicants by recruitment agencies.

Source: Pokroy (2010: Online)

8.4.3 Phase 3: Collecting information

Although almost every public sector employer includes interviews as part of the selection process, it is definitely not the only method one can use collecting information on candidates. There are many different ways in which the collection and assessment of information can be dealt with. In this section, we shall look at the most commonly used methods of selection, which are the following:

- Reviewing letters of recommendation;
- Reviewing biodata;
- Setting up employment tests, sometimes in the form of an assessment centre;
- Interviewing the candidates;
- Conducting reference checks; and
- Conducting physical examinations.

8.4.3.1   Reviewing letters of recommendation

Although letters of recommendation are generally not highly related to future work performance, they should not be totally eliminated as a selection method. Normally, these letters are written in a highly positive manner and cannot always be regarded as a positive indicator of work performance. It is important that consideration should also be given to a poor letter of recommendation because it may be predictive of future work performance (Gómez-Mejía et al. 1998: 160).

8.4.3.2   Reviewing biodata

Biographical details (biodata) can be obtained through an application blank, biodata form, curriculum vitae (CV), and a portfolio of evidence.

An application blank is a form that is completed by the applicant providing information such as education, work history, some personal data, medical history, hobbies, etc.

This information gives an indication of an applicant's suitability for a job. The use of past behaviour to predict future performance continues to form part of the selection process and, as a result of research, application blanks have become more scientific, and, to some extent, more predictive because of the refinements.

Studies have shown that the application blank is a valid predictor of job performance and of length of service (Heneman, Schwab, Fossum, & Dyer 1986: 315). A major concern regarding the usage of application forms is whether the questions/statements provide accurate and reliable information. Studies conducted in England have found that 20% to 50% of job applications contain information that is not a true reflection of what happened in the past. Consequently, it appears that a substantial number of applicants tend to exaggerate their previous work records. For example, it was found that slightly more than 50% of the applicants overestimated their duration of previous employment and the previous salary earned. The verification of qualifications forms an important HR activity during the selection process. During the early 2000s, the Minister of Public Service and Administration announced that the qualifications of all public officials would be verified. Since then, the Public Service Commission has completed two studies to assess the qualifications of employees at senior and middle management levels. Focus on Research 8.1 gives the results of these studies.

FOCUS ON RESEARCH 8.1
Qualifications audit of managers in the public service

The first study was completed in 2001 and focused verifying the qualifications of senior management. The study found that of the 2 376 senior managers (about 80%) were found to have misrepresented themselves. The study also determined that, although senior managers were found to be well qualified, it was suggested that they lack specific and fundamental management training.

The second study focused on the verifying the qualifications of middle managers and was completed in 2005. The research results revealed that 8 123 middle managers submitted 24 604 qualifications for verification. Of these qualifications, 22 021 (89%) were verified. Further responses indicated that, of the 22 021 verified qualifications, 21 973 qualifications from a pool of 7 541 middle managers were positively verified. It also became very clear from the study that middle managers in the public service were qualified from a technical perspective and were operating in functional roles.

Read more about the verification of qualifications in the public service in a report published by the Public Service Commission entitled 'Oversight report on the verification of qualifications in the public service'. This report is available at: [http://www.info.gov.za/otherdocs/2007/psc_verification-qualifications].

Source: Republic of South Africa (2001b: Online); Republic of South Africa (2005: Online)

Compared to the above percentages, one can undoubtedly say that information on qualifications provided by senior managers in the South African public service is a true reflection of what happened in the past. Generally, it is very important to verify information provided in application blanks, especially in those cases where there is suspicion. Unfortunately this may become a very costly exercise.

The design of an application blank may continuously change because of future court judgements, but there are some basic items that are universally relevant. These are listed below:

- Applicant's name;
- Applicant's home address (wherever possible only the postal address), telephone number, cell phone number, fax number, and e-mail address. It may also be necessary in some instances to obtain work particulars if this information is not too sensitive;
- Date of birth;
- Nationality;
- Educational, developmental level and experience required for the specific post;
- Applicant's work history (dates, salary progression, duties and responsibilities and reasons for leaving previous employment);
- Information to determine whether the applicant will meet certain post requirements, such as having to work over weekends; main current interests and achievements outside the workplace;
- Health condition;

- Court convictions;
- Membership of professional associations;
- Referees; and
- Information required for personal records.

In the context of employment equity and affirmative action, public sector managers will also have to scrutinise their institution's application forms to ensure that these do not lead to unfair discrimination claims. For example, items relating to age, gender, race, religion, health, disability and an applicant's criminal record will have to be handled with circumspection. Only if one is confident that this information is really necessary to select a suitable person for the job in question should these be retained. For example, should the application form require an applicant to disclose that he or she is HIV positive and the vacancy carries no risks for other people should the incumbent be thus afflicted, this may form the basis of alleged unfair discrimination. On the other hand, it may indeed be justifiable to include items relating to gender and race on the application blank – for instance, to assist in the initial screening process with the aim of promoting affirmative action. If a public sector institution has set certain targets for the active promotion of women, it will, for instance, be very difficult to pursue this route actively without knowing from the completed application forms which applicants are male and female.

A more recent variation of the traditional application blank is the biodata form. The biodata form is a more detailed version of the application blank, in which candidates are asked to complete a detailed form that examines their background, experiences, preferences, and aspects of their personal lives. When forms are completed, points are allocated to certain information or to certain achievements by candidates. Sample questions may include: How willing are you to travel while on the job? What leisure activities are you involved in? How much experience do you have with computers?

> The CV is an account of the applicant's career history and enables the applicant to present himself or herself to a prospective employer without first securing a face-to-face discussion.

The curriculum vitae (CV) plays a vital role in the selection process. Therefore, it is necessary for selectors to make sure that they acquire the right information from CVs. Flood (2000: 15) provides the following definition of a CV:

Basically, the CV provides the public sector employer with an overview of potential candidates for the relevant post. It also gives the interviewer an idea of the applicant's educational level, knowledge, skills, and experiences obtained. In other words, it informs the interviewer of what to expect from the applicant. In addition, the CV, because it is a written document, gives the interviewer an opportunity to test the accuracy of it and establishes whether or not the applicant is honest.

Traditionally, CVs were used by applicants to include a large amount of detail of their work history. As a result of this, many applicants tend to over-market themselves, which can have a negative effect on employment prospects. In recent years, however, the tendency is to use a more modern approach to compiling CVs. One of the reasons for this is that the training focus in South Africa has moved to what is termed 'outcomes-based training'. The National Qualifications Framework has been established to regulate this new phenomenon (see Chapter 11). What this means is that, in making a selection decision, interviewers should now focus on what applicants can do rather on what they have learned. A second reason is that there has been a change in the environment that prescribes employment conditions. New legislation makes it unnecessary for applicants to provide certain information. The Constitution of the Republic of South Africa, 1996, the Labour Relations Act 66 of 1995, and the Employment Equity Act 55 of 1998 are focused on doing away with discrimination in all its forms. In terms of these Acts, certain information no longer needs to be disclosed. The following information needs to be provided (Flood 2000: 15):

- Identity number;
- Address;
- Age;
- Date of birth;
- Place of birth;
- Gender;
- Marital status;
- Spouse's employer and occupation;
- Children's detail;
- Health;
- Disability;
- Hobbies;
- Sport; and
- Transport.

The portfolio of evidence provides a more amplified and expanded record of an applicant's experience and abilities. Flood gives the following description of a portfolio of evidence:

> The portfolio of evidence is a document that explains what the applicant can do as a result of their training and experience.

There is consequently a good reason for using a portfolio of evidence in gathering biographical details. The need for this has arisen through a change in legislation. When the government introduced the National Qualifications Framework of outcomes-based training, the idea was that people should benefit from attending particular training courses. In fact, the portfolio of evidence looks back a long way into the life of an applicant. For example, while at high school, the applicant may have played cricket for the first team. They may also have captained the team. The public sector selector can use this information by considering what a cricket captain does in the playing field. Below is a list of some of the actions a cricket captain is involved in.

1	At the toss, make a decision as to whether the side will bat or bowl.
2	Consult the coach on what they believe the decision should be.
3	Decide who will bowl or in what order they will bat.
4	Encourage the bowler or batsman.
5	Keep the players informed of what the status is.
6	Discuss tactics with the side.
7	Motivate the side to achieve its goal.
8	Give advice to fellow players.
9	Set an example for the team to follow.
10	Decide at what stage to declare the innings.

Source: Flood (2000: 19)

When the public sector selector closely analyses the information presented above, the following are revealed (Flood 2000: 19):

- Points 1, 3 and 10 show that you must have the ability to make decisions.
- Points 2, 5 and 6 show that you must have the ability to communicate.
- Points 4 and 7 show that you have the ability to motivate a group of people.
- Point 8 shows that you have the ability to encourage others.
- Point 9 shows that you have leadership skills.

8.4.3.3 Setting up employment tests

Once the applicants have been screened by means of the application blank, the next step is for the successful candidates to undergo employment tests.

An employment test is an instrument which is used to obtain information about personal characteristics.

It is really not an easy task to construct an employment test. As you already know, the Employment Equity Act 55 of 1998 requires selection instruments (employment testing and other similar instruments) to be scientifically shown to be reliable, objective, and valid. Reliability, objectivity and validity predictors are thus prerequisites for fairness in selection. There are three major concerns that public selectors need to understand in this regard:

- An employment test must be reliable. Reliability in this context refers to the consistency and trustworthiness of a measure. This means that a test can be regarded as reliable if the same candidates are tested repeatedly and the results are consistent and do not vary with time, place, or different subjects – that is, test and retest reliability. If there are vague questions in the test, this will often make it unreliable.
- Employment tests must also be objective. An objective test is one which truly measures whether a candidate has the technical skills, mental abilities, and other qualities required to occupy a post successfully. To avoid the aspects that might deprive a test of its objectivity, you have to make sure that it is not influenced by external factors such as race, religion, allegiance to a particular political party, gender and age.
- An employment test must also comply with the requirements of validity. This implies that the test should measure what it purports to measure. It is very difficult to achieve this. For example, if you test the cognitive ability of a candidate by making use of an intelligence test, you will find that the test results may be providing consistent results. Unfortunately, the results may tell us very little about how well this candidate will perform as a police officer or social worker.

There are many different employment tests that may be used in the practice of employee selection. These are listed below.

Cognitive ability (intelligence)
The measurement of intelligence is a popular ability test for selection. An intelligence test gives an indication of general intelligence by means of a single score.

DID YOU KNOW?

?

The following intelligence tests are used in South Africa:
- The South African Wechsler Individual Intelligence Scale for Adults;
- The Mental Alertness Scale of the National Institute for Personnel Research (NIPR);
- The New South African Group test; and
- The senior and junior South African Individual Intelligence Scale (for use with children).

Although intelligence tests have traditionally been part of the selection process in the public sector, they have lost their popularity because they are not always free from cultural influences.

Aptitude
Aptitude measurement is used, among other purposes, for the selection of job applicants. Most aptitude tests, such as the High Level Scales and the Senior Aptitude Test (SAT), are based on Thurstone's primary group factors such as verbal ability

word fluency memory deductive reasoning, inductive reasoning, numerical ability, perceptual speed, form perception, spatial aptitude and co-ordination.

Personality tests

The majority of authors agree that the individual's personality has an influence on work performance. The aim of personality questionnaires is to identify personality traits. People are aware of their own behaviour and are able to make valid assessments of themselves. The following are examples of personality tests used in South Africa:

- Projective techniques;
- The Thematic Apperception Test (TAT);
- The Rorschach Test;
- The Structured Objective Rorschach Test (SORT);
- Self-report questionnaires;
- The 16 Personality Factor Questionnaire (16PF);
- The Jung Personality Questionnaire (JPQ);
- The South African Personality Questionnaire (SAPQ); and
- The Occupational Personality Questionnaire (OPQ).

Performance

The purpose of performance tests is to assess the applicant's performance on specific tasks that are representative of the actual job. As performance tests are designed for a specific job, there are many different versions. Examples would be a typing test (for typists), mechanic tool identification, editing skills, etc.

Performance tests are good predictors of job success, and studies have revealed that these tests are more valid than written tests (Scarpello & Ledvinka 1988: 340).

Interest

Interest is also regarded as an important determinant in choosing an occupation. Interest is related to an individual's motivation and satisfaction. The basic premise in measuring interest, is that people will be happy in a job if they like the activities involved. The following are examples of tests:

- Strong Vocational Interest Blank;
- Kuder Interest Questionnaires;
- Field Interest Inventory; and
- Self-Directed Search.

Assessment centres

Another well-known selection method is the assessment centre, which is a technique that uses multiple approaches to test for knowledge, skills, and competencies that are needed in a post. Applicants are asked to perform within a simulated work environment. Trained assessors then measure the applicants' job behaviours with the aid of various instruments. Assessment centres are most often used in the selection of public sector managers or other personnel required to plan, guide, control and make decisions about operations. Generally, assessment centres include exercises such as simulations, stressful decision-making situations, small group activities that test leadership skills, in-basket exercises that require certain managerial skills such as delegation of authority, and assignments that test communication skills.

A particular purpose of assessment, as with all the other employment tests, involves reducing the number of applications received to an appropriately sized list of candidates to be invited for the interview. However, assessment in a divided society, such as South Africa, will also be a complex HR matter. An example of such as case is given in Focus on Research 8.2.

FOCUS ON RESEARCH 8.2

Competency testing in a divided society

In 2005, in the small twin-island Republic of Trinidad and Tobago in the West Indies, the government – in a radical departure from the old method of selection based primarily on seniority – introduced competency testing in order to fill the newly established positions of deputy permanent secretaries. This new method of selection, however, has been fraught with a number of problems such as charges of cultural bias and allegations that there was inadequate time to prepare for these tests. One of the more pressing complaints levelled against the new method of selection was that while it was supposed to allow for transparency and impartiality, this did not take place.

It was also suggested that the lack of transparency was an indication that this method of competency testing was merely a façade by which the government ensured that its supporters maintained top positions in the public service. This study, using an old model proposed by Fred Riggs in 1966, suggests that while a new model may be applied as a result of either ideological or global pressures, what actually emerges is that it may prove to be unsuccessful because the old attitudes, beliefs, values and mistrust are still prevalent in that society. In addition, while the trappings of the 'new' fads are imposed, it is not accompanied by the basic culture to support its introduction. A number of issues emerged from the interviews conducted:

- All the applicants were ill-prepared for the kind of testing they had to undergo.
- The tool that was used was not geared to the West Indian experience but rather was directed to the Canadian public sector.
- There was a high level of distrust with the tool that was introduced.
- The East Indians perceived that they were the victims of racial discrimination as far as selection was concerned.

The study suggests that (1) certain basic elements should have been put in place including the need to make the process transparent; (2) the preparation of applicants before hand by way of training opportunities in the new system; (3) the administration of employment tests which were more in keeping with the reality of the country; and finally (4) the establishment of clear criteria for selection. The researcher also found that it was clear that before introducing a system of competency testing, there should have been some attempt ▷

to first change the 'old' behaviours and patterns of the public service. Accompanying what psychologists have termed 'behaviour modification' through counselling, should have been other supporting mechanisms, such as transparency processes, where the short list should have been displayed and selection the criteria clearly specified.

In addition, before the introduction of a new 'tool' for selection, the existing regulations have to be modified. Applicants should also have had some basic exposure to the new process, and while it was true there had been training for the top level managers, this in no way prepared them for the kind of testing they were now required to undergo. The bottom line, though, is that such introductions should not have been implemented without the proper planning and the foundation to support the new measure.

Source: Bissessar (2010: Online)

8.4.3.4 Interviewing the candidates

One of the most common assessment tools used for selecting employees is the employment interview. The aim of the interview is to determine an applicant's degree of suitability for a job by matching the information given by the applicant to the job requirements. The applicant may be interviewed by a combination of human resource specialists, or senior management within the public sector institution, a potential public sector manager, worker representatives (such as shop stewards), and special affirmative action committee members.

Types of interviews

Interviews usually range from unstructured to structured. The unstructured interview refers to the coincidental, poorly organised type of interview where there is no attempt to explore specific areas for information about the applicant. It is usually left to the interviewer to mention topics which he or she considers to be important. Although it is not necessarily detrimental to concede such freedom to an interviewer, this method can give rise to a lack of validity if the interviewer has no training in conducting interviews. In the hands of an untrained and incompetent person, this method might not differentiate accurately between applicants with high or low potential.

Structured interviews are characterised by two essential features: careful, systematic planning of the interview and exclusive use of technically skilled interviewers. It is to be expected that a systematic approach to any problem would normally produce better results than coincidental, random procedures. Naturally, an interview is planned according to the requirements of the job for which the selection is taking place. The reason for conducting the interview is therefore to obtain precise job-related information about the applicant.

Planning and preparation for an interview

Somebody once wrote the following about interviewing: 'a lack of preparation is tantamount to preparing for failure'. This indicates how important it is that the interviewer should be prepared for an interview. We shall now discuss ten steps that can be taken in preparing for this.

Step 1: Appointing a selection committee

Group and panel interviews require the appointment of a selection committee. In the public service, selection committees should consist of at least three members who are managers of a salary grading equal to or higher than the grading of the post to be filled. The committee can also include persons from outside the public service. Additional requirements are as follows:

- The chairperson of a selection committee should be a manager of a grading higher than the post to be filled.
- In the event that the manager of the unit within which the vacant post is located, is graded lower than the vacant post, such a manager may be included as a member of the selection committee.
- A selection committee shall, where possible, include adequate representation of historically disadvantaged persons.
- Managers of a grading which is lower than the grading of the post to be filled may provide secretarial or advisory services during the selection process (Republic of South Africa 2001c: 21).

Step 2: Establishing a job one knows

Ensure you know the required knowledge, skills, aptitudes and personal characteristics. Study the job description and job specification carefully in this regard.

Step 3: Scrutinising all written material

Carefully scrutinise such documents as letters of recommendation, application blanks, biodata forms, CVs, portfolios of evidence and reference checks.

Step 4: Planning the opening of the interview and the type of interview

If a panel interview is used, the introduction should include the name and job title of each interviewer. A nameplate can also be put in front of the interviewers. The interviewer should also give an idea of the degree of formality expected by using (or not using) first names. Once this has been decided, it is important to establish rapport. In this regard, the atmosphere must be friendly and relaxed. Most people experience the employment interview as stressful. The interviewer is primarily responsible for putting the applicant at ease. Establishing rapport can be seen as the process of creating a harmonious relationship between the interviewer and the applicant in order to develop the applicant's confidence in the interviewer to such an extent that he or she begins to talk spontaneously (Fear & Chiron 1990: 46).

Once rapport has been established, the purpose of the interview should be explained. In this regard, the applicant should be told that you want to find out more about his or her previous experience, training, background, interests, goals, and values. The applicant, in turn, will be told more about the public sector institution and the job in question. The applicant should also be invited to ask questions.

Step 5: Preparing questions in advance
Guidelines for questioning are provided below (Fear & Chiron 1990: 57–68):
- Make use of open-ended questions. This will enable the applicant to talk freely. Use phrases like 'to what extent', 'how do you feel about', etc. to make questions open-ended.
- The interviewer must make use of follow-up questions in order to ensure that the applicant meets critical job requirements.
- The interviewer should clarify the true meaning of the applicant's casual remarks. Where the interviewer is concerned about an applicant's remarks, such as his or her dislikes, the interviewer should establish the extent of these dislikes by means of further questioning.
- The interviewer must search for evidence which substantiates hypotheses established earlier. Interviewers often observe clues to an applicant's behaviour early on in the discussion, and a hypothesis is then established. Further questions should be asked to determine whether or not there is support for such a conclusion.
- Emphasise the present rather than the past; concentrate on real job experiences.
- The interviewer should also be careful not to be too direct in the questioning; it is important not to lose rapport.
- Questions must be work related. To avoid issues which may be regarded as unfairly discriminatory, interviewers must ensure that the questions that they ask are job related. Try to obtain only the necessary information which is required to determine whether or not the applicant will be successful on the job.

Certain specific guidelines also need to be followed when questions are asked during the interview. The following are some guidelines:
- Questions must be job related.
- Ask all the different groups of people the same questions.
- Avoid asking questions out of curiosity.
- Avoid asking females questions such as their plans for marriage or children.
- Do not ask questions that can be seen as unfairly discriminatory against older people, the disabled, etc. Such factors should not be taken into account unless they can be shown to be job related.

Avoid asking questions such as the following:

- How old are you?
- Are you living with anyone?
- Do you have any plans for marriage? Have you been married in the past? How long have you been single?
- Are you considering having any children in the future?
- What is your religion?
- How can you be sure that you will be reliable given the fact that you have small children who still need care?
- Which sport do you play or to what country clubs do you belong?
- Have you ever been a member of a trade union?
- Will you be joining the union active in the company should you be successful in your application?

Interviewers should be aware of culturally related issues during the interview situation. Interviewers must understand that cues such as body language (for example, eye contact) assertiveness (women often tend to phrase their responses less assertively), and differences in verbal fluency or in the choice of words and intonation, may be irrelevant to the job if viewed from a cultural diversity point of view.

Step 6: Setting up a timetable
Another important step, which is often neglected by interviewers, is the preparation of a realistic timetable. It would be useful to allow sufficient time for each interview, allow sufficient time to consider each candidate, give time breaks for candidates to freshen up between interviews and allow sufficient time for the interviewers to discuss the day's events.

Step 7: Determining realistic and measurable criteria
It is of the utmost importance that interviewers determine realistic and measurable criteria before the interview starts. This will ensure that all applicants are treated in an equitable and comparable manner. In this regard, interviewers should take care to eliminate any prejudice when candidates are assessed. For example, in the public sector workplace, it is sometimes expected of an employee to possess a motor vehicle in order to complete the work successfully. In this situation, one should take care not to attach higher value to a candidate who possesses a Mercedes Benz than to one who owns a Ford Fiesta.

Step 8: Making arrangements to receive the candidate
Always remember the old saying: 'First impressions are lasting.' An important action here is that somebody (usually the HR manager's secretary) should receive the candidate face to face. Make sure this person is informed about the names of all the candidates and their times of arrival, and instruct this person to see that

refreshments are provided and that the chief interviewer is notified when the first candidate arrives.

Step 9: Preparing a private room

Usually one must prepare a private room for the interview so that no disturbances will occur. Make sure there are enough chairs and other furniture and ask the secretary to put flowers in the room.

Step 10: Closing the interview

Public sector interviewers must remember that the applicant will also have to ask certain questions in order to make sure that this is the right job for him or her. The interviewer should at least give the applicant enough information to make an informed decision. The applicant should also be given an indication of when an answer may be expected from the organisation regarding the outcome of the application.

DID YOU KNOW?

Section 20 of the Employment Equity Act states that a candidate may be considered 'suitably qualified' for a job as a result of any one or combination of that person's:
- Formal qualifications;
- Prior learning;
- Relevant experience; and
- The capacity to acquire, within a reasonable time, the ability to do the job.

Other guidelines for professional interviewing

The interview is not rated highly as a selection instrument because of its low validity. Recent research findings have, however, revealed a more optimistic view of the predictive capability of the interview – two studies found average validities in the 0.40 to 0.50 range (Landy, Shankster-Cawley, & Moran 1995).

It appears that structured and panel interviews make a significant difference (Smith, Gregg, & Andrews 1989: 46). Validity of structured interviews can reach the same level as that of ability tests (Huffcutt & Woehr 1995: 10). Two types of structured interview, namely the situational interview and the patterned behavioural description interview (PBDI), are described here.

The situational interview deals with samples of work behaviour. The applicant's response to situations which are typical of the job and crucial to the successful performance of the job is tested (Singer 1993: 26).

In the PBDI, the applicant is expected to recall an incident similar to the situation described and to relate how he or she reacted in that situation (Singer 1993: 26).

The panel interview gives more people the chance to assess the applicant. The fact that more people are involved in the selection process leads to a fairer assessment.

There should not be too many interviewers involved – only, for instance, a chairperson, the line function employee, and the human resource specialists.

So the effectiveness of the interview can be improved by doing the following:

- **Eliminate prejudice towards older persons**. To illustrate this, in a study completed by Rosen & Jordec (in Beardwell & Holden 1995: 246–247), it was found that business management students displayed the following prejudices towards older people, namely that they are: (a) more change resistant; (b) more rigid and less creative; (c) less inclined to take risks; (d) have less physical ability than younger workers; and (e) are disinclined to learn.

- **Avoid generalisations**. Generalisations vary in nature, and the major problem is that they may result in skilled candidates being turned down for such reasons as: (a) men who wear suede leather shoes; (b) obese persons; (c) thin persons; (d) short men; (e) too much makeup on women; (f) old-fashioned apparel; (g) the candidate's laughter; (h) candidates who live in certain areas; (i) men who wear earrings; and (j) young unmarried men.

8.4.3.5 Conducting reference checks

Reference checks are conducted after the employment interview to find out more about an applicant's employment record, education and training, and behavioural patterns. These details are used to predict the expected competence of a particular applicant for the job in question. Reference checking is important for the following reasons (Kieffer 1991):

- Input is obtained from a number of people.
- There is useful feedback on the strengths and weaknesses, achievements, and failures of individuals.
- The organisation receives a verbal report on an individual's performance.

Guidelines for checking references

A popular way of checking references is by telephone. Candidates are required to furnish the names and contact numbers of previous employers and other people who may be contacted for this purpose. References are useful if they satisfy the following four requirements (McCormick & Ilgen 1987: 195):

- The person providing the reference must have observed the candidate in a relevant situation (such as during work).
- The person providing the reference must be capable of assessing the candidate's performance.
- The person must be prepared to express his or her forthright opinion.
- The person must express himself or herself in such a way that his or her opinion is not misinterpreted.

Although all of these requirements are important, the honesty with which an opinion is expressed is probably the point on which most references fail, as people are often reluctant to state a negative opinion.

The person following up references may also ask about the candidate's job title, employment period and salary and whether his or her previous institution would consider rehiring him or her. As a general guideline, only the references of serious candidates are worth checking. The validity of the information provided must be checked, the candidate should be informed that the references he or she has provided will be checked, and the questions to be asked should be formulated in such a way that information about the candidate's qualifications, skills, work habits, sense of judgement, and performance level will be obtained. Recent reports of widespread fraud in respect of educational qualifications, such as fake degrees from certain institutions, show that it is also important to check and ensure that all educational particulars are verified as valid.

8.4.3.6 Conducting a physical examination

Before the successful applicant is appointed, he or she may be required to undergo a physical examination. The purpose is to determine the applicant's physical suitability for the position for which he or she has been selected. Public sector institutions must also be careful when specifying a physical qualification to ensure that it is job related and that the employee would not otherwise be able to do the job properly.

SPOTLIGHT ON THE LAW 8.1
Medical testing for HIV/AIDS

In *Irvin & Johnson Ltd v Trawler & Line Fishing Union & others* [2003] 5 BLLR 475 (LC), the Labour Court found that medical testing is not itself an act of discrimination. It was argued that Section 7 of the Act is a pre-emptive measure designed to reduce the risk of discrimination on the grounds of a medical condition. A contravention of Section 7 is not stated by the Act to be a criminal offence. It thus appears that a dispute concerning medical testing cannot be referred to the CCMA nor can a contravention of Section 7 be visited with a fine or an order for damages or compensation.

What then is the consequence of a violation or threatened violation of Section 7? Where testing is compulsory and is not objectively justifiable (under Section 7(1)) or, in the case of HIV testing, has not been authorised by the Labour Court (under Section 7(2)), an employee would be entitled to approach the Labour Court for an order declaring that the compulsory testing is prohibited and interdicting same. The judgement made it very clear that a person who does not wish to be tested and who is not required to undergo testing would have no need for the protection of a declaratory order and an interdict. However, a person who volunteers for testing would in the nature of things not seek redress. The Labour Court finally held that employers need not apply for permission to conduct tests for HIV/AIDS if the employees have consented and the tests are voluntary and anonymous.

In addition, there is no obligation for a public-sector employer to pay for medical tests. However, it is advisable that in severe medical conditions, employees should be allowed to attend the local health centre, which can offer assistance.

Source: Grogan (2008: 306); Southern African Legal Information (2010: Online)

Generally, medical testing of public officials for employment is prohibited. However, if permitted by legislation or justifiable in the light of the medical facts, employment conditions, social policy, the fair distribution of employee benefits or the inherent requirements of a job, as stated in Section 7(1) of the Employment Equity Act 55 of 1998, then it is acceptable. During 2003, Irvin and Johnson Ltd wished to arrange for the voluntary and anonymous HIV testing of 1 100 workers in its trawling division. This particular employer believed that it required information on HIV prevalence in its workforce to assess, among others, the potential impact of HIV/AIDS on the workforce and to enable them to engage in appropriate manpower planning so as to minimise the impact of HIV/AIDS mortalities and HIV/AIDS-related conditions on its operations. However, Trawler & Line Fishing Union & others was of the opinion that the employer's act was based on discriminatory grounds and the case landed in the Labour Court. The court decision of this case is set out in Spotlight on the Law 8.1 on page 254 which indicates some of the issues involved in medical testing.

8.4.4 Phase 4: Making a selection decision

After the last candidate has been interviewed, the interviewer and the selection committee must reach consensus on the most suitable candidate for the post. It is important that this recommendation/decision should be supported by a wide range of evidence. Therefore, it is necessary to make use of as many selection methods as possible. When making a final selection decision, one must make sure that the following aspects are considered (Republic of South Africa 2001c: 24):

- Information used is based on reliable, objective, and valid selection methods.
- Criteria utilised are free from any bias and discrimination.
- The knowledge, skills and competencies necessary to meet the inherent requirements of the post are clear.
- The institution's need for developing human resources is understood.
- The representativeness of the unit where the post is located is considered.
- The institution's affirmative action programme is considered.
- The information provided by the candidate is verified (this includes information pertaining to the candidate's educational qualifications, citizenship, and experience).
- The candidate is subjected to a security clearance if the nature of the post requires it.

Also, when it is decided to turn down a candidate, the following are important, especially from an equity point of view:

- Keep written records indicating why applicants have been rejected. In the event of a claim of unfair discrimination, such records will be necessary to prove that no unfair discrimination took place. Normally, reasons need not be provided when a person is informed that his or her application has been unsuccessful.
- However, should a candidate ask for reasons for having been turned down, the major reason (or two) should be provided and particular care should be taken to ensure that the reason(s) given are based strictly on objective criteria. Such

reason(s) should preferably be given in writing (even in the case of internal applicants to whom verbal explanation had already been given at the time of the request) in a succinct, public sector manner to avoid any possible future disputes. Reasons should normally not be given verbally to outside job applicants.

? DID YOU KNOW?

It is important that the potential employee is clearly informed about the particular job requirements, such as:
- The need to travel;
- Working overtime;
- Working night shifts;
- Working long hours; and
- Working during weekends and in the evenings.

The employee should also be made aware that to perform these tasks is an inherent requirement of the job.

Source: Israelstam, Healy, Hayward, Randall, Jackson, Squire, Molefi & Meyerson (2004: Online)

Another step that can be taken is to expose the candidate physically to the work environment before a final decision is made.

8.4.5 Phase 5: Placing the candidate

The last stage of the selection process is the placing of the candidate. Once a selection decision has been made, an offer of employment can be made to the successful candidate. Basically, there are four steps one can follow when placing a candidate.

8.4.5.1 Offering the position

A soon as the final selection decision has been reached it is usual practice to discuss a provisional offer with the prospective employee. Initially, a telephone call is made, giving the main details. In principle, a verbal telephonic agreement can be regarded as an employment contract. However, most employees prefer to commit the contract to a full written document because it is safer for both parties to do so. In fact, the White Paper on Human Resource Management in the Public Service (Republic of South Africa 1997b: 32) stipulates that all employees in the public service should have a written contract. If the candidate wishes to negotiate any details of the employment contract, such negotiations have to start immediately, especially if you need the services of the candidate urgently.

8.4.5.2 Confirming employment particulars in writing

A soon as agreement is reached a letter of employment is given to the candidate. Because PSHRM is influenced by an increasingly fast-changing environment at present, the content of the employment contract will be shaped by all these changes. Therefore, the public service requires flexible contractual options.

DID YOU KNOW?

The White Paper on Human Resource Management in the Public Service of 1997 makes provision for one of the following types of employment contracts:

- **Continuous employment contract:** This contract enables an employee to be engaged to the public service for an unspecified period. Those employees entered into continuous contracts can expect to remain in the public service until retirement age. However, there are two distinctions here. First, continued employment will depend on the employee's work performance over a certain period of time. Second, an employment contact will be continued if the employee's skills and potential match the institution's operational requirements according to Section 189 of the Labour Relations Act 66 of 1995.
- **Fixed-term employment contract:** This contract is especially designed for times when public service institutions are experiencing fluctuating or rapidly changing operational requirements. An important feature of fixed-term contracts is that an employee is engaged for work of a limited duration. Normally, fixed-term contracts are offered for a period of one to three years. In addition, the contract may not be longer than five years and will be individually negotiated with the relevant employee.
- **Temporary employment contract:** This contract is ideally suited to short-term and ad hoc work requirements. The primary feature of this contract is that it may not extend beyond a period of 12 months.

Source: Republic of South Africa (1997b: 32)

There are a number of elements that need to be considered when compiling a letter of employment or employment contract. Most of the basic elements can be found in employment law, such as the Basic Conditions of Employment Act 75 of 1997. At the minimum, the following elements should be included in such a letter or contract (Van der Westhuizen 2000: 149–150):

- **Particulars of the candidate's post:** Title and duties, and the name and position of the immediate manager;
- **Remuneration:** Commencement salary, salary adjustment dates, deductions, and bonuses;
- **Hours of work:** According to the Act regulating occupational health and safety: time structure of the day normal working hours, overtime, lunchtime, resting periods, work on Sundays, night shifts, and public holidays;
- **Leave:** Annual leave arrangements, payment for annual leave, sick leave, disability leave, leave associated with occupational accidents or diseases, maternity leave, leave to meet family commitments, leave on public holidays;
- **Medical benefits:** Rules and requirements for membership of a medical aid scheme;
- **Outside work:** Rules and regulations pertaining to outside work;
- **Pension benefits:** Membership arrangements;

- **Personnel evaluation:** Details about purpose, frequency and procedures of personnel evaluation, and about the probationary period;
- **Termination of service:** Notice, payment, severance pay and certificate of service;
- **Confirmation:** The candidate accepts the conditions of employment by signing the letter of appointment and requests that the following documents be returned:
  - Income tax form (IRP 2);
  - Proof of age (copy of identity document);
  - Bank particulars;
  - Driver's licence (where applicable);
  - Firearm licence (where applicable).

The exact particulars of the format of an employment contract can be found in Annexures 1 and 2 of the Public Service Regulations of 2001 (Republic of South Africa 2001a).

8.4.5.3 Entering into a probationary period

Obviously, there is no better way to determine whether public sector employees can do a job than to have the person actually execute the duties allocated to the post. One way to assure that an employee performs in a way that is consistent with the requirements of a post is to let the person undergo a period of probation. In other words, the probationary period allows public sector managers to determine how an employee fulfils assigned duties before a long-term commitment is made (Dresang 2002: 219-220). The length of a probationary period varies with the nature of the post. It can be accepted that lower level jobs will require shorter probationary periods and that professional and managerial jobs that require a high level of skill may require longer periods of probation. Normally these periods vary between three and six months. However, there are exceptions, especially at the higher level jobs, where the probation period may require two or more years. According to Part VII.E of the Public Service Regulations of 2001, the following requirements for managing the probationary period are applicable in the public service, namely that the probationer must:

- Be familiar with performance requirements for obtaining confirmation of probation;
- Receive written feedback on a quarterly basis on the performance level acquired;
- Receive training (including induction training), counselling, or other assistance when needed;
- Receive written confirmation of appointment at the end of probationary period; and
- Be afforded the opportunity for defence if dismissed as a result of poor performance.

8.4.5.4 Orientating the new public sector employee

The orientation programme is aimed at gradually (but as soon as possible) introducing the new employee to the public sector institution, the work unit in which he or she will be working, the particular work, and the people and things with which he or she will have to work.

It is basically a structured process that involves welcoming, receiving, and introducing the newly appointed public sector employees, providing them with the necessary information, and making them feel at ease so that they can settle down as soon as possible.

The process is therefore aimed at making the newcomer feel at ease and involves the following:

- Reducing anxiety/tension;
- Creating a feeling of security as soon as possible;
- Creating realistic expectations on the part of the employee;
- Creating a foundation for the integration of personal and institutional objectives (creating the match or fit); and
- Making the employee productive as soon as possible.

Part of the orientation involves introducing the employee to the public sector institution itself. This entails providing the employee with information about such aspects as the following:

- A brief overview of the institution – its history, functions, services, organisation structure, and the senior management team;
- Conditions of employment and benefits, such as normal hours of work, holidays, medical and pension schemes, group life insurance;
- Remuneration policy, pay scales, when paid and how, payroll administration;
- Work rules and standard procedures;
- Human resource and labour relations management policy;
- Disciplinary code and procedure;
- Grievance procedure;
- Relationships with employer organisations;
- Trade union-related arrangements – which unions, recognition agreements, consultative structures;
- Training and development policy and facilities;
- Employee health policy;
- Medical and first aid infrastructure;
- Restaurant facilities;
- Social responsibility policy;
- Community involvement policy;
- Procedures for internal and external telephone system and correspondence;
- Procedures relating to travelling and subsistence expenses; and
- Issues relating to confidentiality of certain institutional information.

8.5   Review

Selection is the process of making decisions about the matching of individuals to jobs, taking into account individual differences and the requirements of the job. The selection process consists of five steps, and the success of the whole process can be improved by continuously improving each step. The first step is deciding on a selection strategy, the purpose of which is to give direction to the whole selection process. Second, a preliminary interview is conducted, where unqualified candidates are eliminated. The third step involves the collecting of information. This step entails such methods as reviewing letters of recommendation and biodata, setting up employment tests, and interviewing the candidate. The fourth step is making a selection decision. The selection decision must be made on information that is based on reliable, objective, and valid selection methods and on criteria that are free from any bias and discrimination. To improve the fairness of selection decisions, the whole selection process should be based on job relatedness and on specific links between the requirements of the job and the personal characteristics required to do the job. The fifth step is the placing of the candidate, whereby the post is offered to the candidate, employment particulars are confirmed in writing, the candidate is entered into a probationary period, and the new employee familiarises himself or herself with the new working environment.

8.6 Self-evaluation questions

1. What is personnel selection? Explain how it may differ between a small and a large public sector institution.
2. Distinguish between the primary aim and the objectives of selection.
3. Why is it so important to have a public sector selection policy and procedures in place and what principles should be incorporated in policy manuals?
4. Outline the steps in the selection process.
5. What are some of the selection strategies one can adopt to direct the selection process?
6. What methods would you suggest one can use for collecting information on potential candidates? To which of these methods would you give top priority? Provide reasons for your answer.
7. What role would the interviewing of candidates play in the selection process? Give reasons for your answer.
8. What is the real purpose of reference checks?
9. What would you suggest should be taken into consideration when making a final selection decision?
10. How would you go about placing and orientating a new employee who has been selected for a particular position in the public sector?

Bibliography

Arvey, RD, & Faley, RH. 1988. *Fairness in selecting employees.* New York: Addison-Wesley.

Beardwell, I, & Holden, L. 1995. *Human resource management: A contemporary perspective.* London: Pitman.

Bissessar, AM. 2010. The challenges of competency testing in a divided society. *Public Personnel Management,* 39 (2), 97–116 [http://www.ipma-hr.org].

Bragg, A. 1990. Checking references. *Sales and Marketing Management,* 142, 68–70.

Byars, LL, & Rue, LW. 1987. *Human resource management.* Homewood, IL: Irwin.

Cascio, WF. 1991. *Applied Psychology in Personnel Management.* Englewood Cliffs, NJ: Prentice-Hall.

Cayer, NJ. 2004. *Public personnel administration.* New York: Thomson Wadsworth.

Cooke, R. 1988. Human resource management: A case for reference-checking. *Credit Union Management,* 11(10), 28–29.

Dresang, DL. 2002. *Public personnel management and public policy.* New York: Longman.

Einhorn, LJ, Bradley, HP, & Baird, JE. 1982. *Effective employment interviewing.* Glenview, IL: Scott Foresman.

Erasmus, P, & Arumugam, S. 1998. Psychometric testing is dead. *People Dynamics,* 16(9), 39–41.

Falcone, P. 1992. Reference checking: Revitalize a critical selection tool. *HR Focus,* December 1992, 19.

Fear, RA, & Chiron, RJ. 1990. *The evaluation interview.* New York: McGraw Hill.

Flood, F. 2000. *Write your own CV.* Cape Town: Ampersand.

Foot, M, & Hook, C. 1996. *Introducing human resource management.* London: Longman.

Gatewood, RD, & Feild, HS. 1987. *Human resources selection.* New York: Dryden.

Gómez-Mejía, LR, Balkin, DB, & Cardy, RL. 1998. *Managing human resources.* Upper Saddle River, NJ: Prentice-Hall.

Grogan, J. 2008. *Workplace law.* Cape Town: Juta.

Guion, RM. 1966. Employment tests and discriminatory hiring. *Industrial Relations,* 5, 20–37.

Heneman, HG, Schwab, DP, Fossum, JA, & Dyer, LD. 1986. *Personnel/human resource management.* Homewood, IL: Irwin.

Huffcutt, AI, & Woehr, DJ. 1995. A further analysis of employment interview validity. Paper presented at the 10th Annual Meeting of the Society for Industrial and Organisational Psychology, Orlando, Florida.

Israelstam, I, Healy, T, Hayward, Randall, L, Jackson, D, Squire, D, Molefi, N, Meyerson, D. 2004. *Labour law for managers practical handbook.* Northriding: Fleet Street Publications [http://www.fsp.co.za].

Kaplan, RM, & Saccuzzo, DP. 1993. *Psychological testing.* Belmont, CA: Wadsworth.

Kemp, N. 1999. Psychometric testing is not dead. *People Dynamics,* 17(3), 14–17.

Kieffer, M. 1991. The reference check: What you need to know. *Health Care Executive,* 6(6), 18–19.

Kriek, HJ. 1991. Die bruikbaarheid van die takseersentrum: 'n Oorsig van resente literatuur. *Tydskrif vir Bedryfsielkunde,* 17(3), 34–37.

Kriek, HJ, Hurst, DN, & Charoux, JAE. 1994. The assessment centre: Testing the fairness hypothesis. *Journal of Industrial Psychology,* 20(2), 21–25.

Landy, FJ, Shankster-Cawley, L, & Moran, SK. 1995. Advancing personnel selection and placement methods. In A. Howard (ed.), *The changing nature of work.* San Francisco: Jossey-Bass.

McCormick, EJ, & Ilgen, D. 1987. *Industrial and organizational psychology.* Englewood Cliffs, NJ: Prentice-Hall.

Momberg, JP, & Langenhoven, HP. 1974. *Die indiensnemingsonderhoud in die Suid-Afrikaanse bedryf.* Bloemfontein: University of the Orange Free State.

Mulenga, CN, & Van Lill, B. 2007. Recruitment and selection of foreign professionals in the South African job market: Procedures and processes. *SA Journal of Human Resource Management,* 5 (3), 30–37. [http://sajhrm.co.za/index.php/sajhrm].

Munchus, G. 1992. Check references for safer selection. *HR Magazine,* 1992, 75–77.

Owens, WA. 1976. Background data. In MD Dunnette (ed.), *Handbook of industrial and organizational psychology.* Chicago: Rand McNally.

Peel, M. 1988. *Ready-made interview questions.* London: Kogan Page.

Plug, C, Meyer, WF, Louw, DA & Gouws, LA. 1986. *Psigologiewoordeboek.* Johannesburg: McGraw Hill.

Plumbley, P. 1991. *Recruitment and selection.* Worcester: Billing and Sons.

Pokroy, J. 2010. Foreign nationals need valid work permits. *HR Future.* [http://www.hrfuture.net].

Scarpello, VG & Ledvinka, J. 1988. *Personnel/human resource management.* Boston, MA: PWS-Kent.

Schultz, DP & Schultz, SE. 1986. *Psychology and industry today.* New York: Macmillan.

Schultz, DP & Schultz, SE. 1994. *Psychology and industry today: An introduction to industrial and organisational psychology.* New York: Macmillan.

Singer, MC. 1990. *Human resource management.* Boston, MA: PWS-Kent.

Singer, M. 1993. *Fairness in personnel selection.* Aldershot: Avebury.

Smith, M, Gregg, M & Andrews, D. 1989. *Selection and assessment: A new appraisal.* London: Pitman.

Smither, RD. 1988. *The psychology of work and human performance.* New York: Harper & Row.

Southern African Legal Information Institute. 2010. South Africa: Labour Court. [http://www.saflii.org/za/cases/ZALC/].

Sylvia, RD. 1994. *Public personnel administration.* Belmont, CA: Wadsworth.

Taylor, HC & Russell, JT. 1939. The relationship of validity coefficients to the practical effectiveness of tests in selection: Discussion and tables. *Journal of Applied Psychology*, 23, 565–578.

Tompkins, J. 1995. Human resource management in government: *Hitting the ground running.* University of Montana-Harper Collins.

Van der Westhuizen, EJ. 2000. Public Human Resource Management: Only study guide for PUB302-F. Pretoria: University of South Africa.

Weitzul, JB. 1992. *Evaluating interpersonal skills in the job interview.* New York: Quorum.

Acts of legislation

Republic of South Africa. 1994. The Public Service Act Proclamation 103 of 1994. Pretoria: Government Printer. [http://www.polity.org.za/html/govdocs/legislation/1994]

Republic of South Africa. 1995. The Labour Relations Act (Act 66 of 1995). Government Printer. [http://www.polity.org.za/html/govdocs/legislation/1995]

Republic of South Africa. 1996. The Constitution of the Republic of South Africa (1996). Government Printer. [http://www.polity.org.za/html/govdocs/legislation/1996]

Republic of South Africa. 1997a. The Basic Conditions of Employment Act (Act 75 of 1997). Government Printer. [http://www.polity.org.za/html/govdocs/legislation/1997]

Republic of South Africa. 1998. The Employment Equity Act (Act 55 of 1998). Government Printer [http://www.polity.org.za/html/govdocs/legislation/1998]

Government regulations

Republic of South Africa. 2001a. Public service regulations of 2001. Government Gazette, 427 (21951). Government Printer.

Government white papers

Republic of South Africa. 1997b. White paper on human resource management in the public service. Government Gazette, 390 (18594). Government Printer.

Government reports

Republic of South Africa. 2001b. Verification of qualifications of senior managers in the public service. Public Service Commission. [http://www.psc.gov.za].

Republic of South Africa. 2005. The verification of qualifications of middle managers on levels 11 and 12 in the public service. Public Service Commission. [http://www.psc.gov.za].

Management guides

Republic of South Africa. 2001. Senior management service: Public service handbook. Department of Public Service and Administration. [http://www.dpsa.gov.za/documents/ sms/publications]

Part 4

Utilising and developing public sector employees

SO FAR, we have concentrated on those public sector human resource activities that are directed at the strategising and planning of human resources (Part 1), and on the defining, analysing, evaluating and filling of posts (Parts 2 and 3). Sooner or later we will be confronted with the task of finding out whether the people we've selected and appointed are performing well enough to deliver efficient and effective services. In other words, in Part 4, the emphasis will be on how to manage employee performance effectively, whereas in Parts 2 and 3, the focus was on the managing of positions.

In Parts 2 and 3, we have seen that obtaining suitable and competent employees is essential for effective PSHRM. But it is also clear that those employees who staff the offices of the public sector should be responsive to the public. Being responsive to the public means that employees need to be appraised, promoted, trained, disciplined, and even demoted. All of these HR activities need to be done to ensure that the quality of the individual worker's performance is at a high level. In Part 4, we shall learn how appraising, career management and structuring learning programmes for public officials are vital to the effective utilising and developing of public sector employees.

9 Appraising and managing work performance

Purpose

The purpose of this chapter is to offer insight into the appraisal and management of work performance to practise it effectively in a public sector-wide context.

Learning outcomes

After you have read this chapter, you should be able to:
- Define the concept of 'performance appraisal' in practical terms.
- List the purposes of performance appraisal.
- Understand the integrated nature of performance appraisal.
- Know the regulatory framework for performance appraisal and the demands it places on the human resource function.
- Explain the typical problems that may be experienced with performance appraisal systems and identify possible solutions.
- Design an effective performance appraisal system by following basic steps.
- Distinguish various appraisal techniques and discuss the limitations of each.
- Outline the requirements for conducting effective appraisal interviews.

9.1   Introduction

In previous chapters, we have emphasised that measuring and assessing is an activity that is applied in virtually all the human resource management functions. In this chapter, we shall see that individual performance, as the outcome of work activities, must also be subject to measurement. In the course of their daily managerial activities, public sector managers should continuously assess how well their subordinates are doing their work on an informal basis. Such informal assessment enables the individual manager to make the necessary decisions regarding the most effective use of staff, motivating those who perform well, and rectifying employees who provide substandard performance.

Informal appraisal, which usually results in an overall impression of worker efficiency and effectiveness, often operates satisfactorily in small public sector institutions where the management knows and interacts with all employees. However, even though it may be argued that effective public sector managers continually provide informal feedback to their subordinates (Robbins 1995: 229), the information generated through an unsystematic informal evaluation has limited value for making valid and justifiable human resource management decisions in a large institutional context. In such a context, accurate performance data obtained through standard processes is required for activities such as HR planning, training and development, compensation, career development and succession planning. Therefore, most public sector institutions have a need for a formal performance appraisal system, and the human resource specialist has to play a leading role in the areas of the development, implementation, maintenance and utilisation of such systems.

In this chapter we shall explore this role, together with the current human resource management technology available for providing public sector institutions with meaningful formal appraisal systems.

9.2 Definition and objectives of performance appraisal

Cardy & Dobbins (1994: 2) define performance appraisal as a formal and systematic process by means of which the job-relevant strengths and weaknesses of employees are identified, observed, measured, recorded, and developed.

The essential components of the above definition may be amplified as follows:
- **Identification:** Determining the performance dimensions to be examined;
- **Observation:** Observing all appraisal aspects sufficiently for accurate and fair judgements to be made;
- **Measurement:** Translating the public sector appraiser's observations into value judgements about the ratee's performance;
- **Recording:** Documenting the outcomes of the performance appraisal process; and
- **Development:** Focusing on the future and the improvement of individual performance (appraisal is not simply an assessment of the past).

In establishing the role of performance appraisal within human resource management, we need to consider the typical purposes for which appraisals can be used and the relationships that may exist between the appraisal system and other human resource management functions in a public sector institution.

Many uses and objectives of performance appraisal have been advanced. Generally performance appraisal may be used for the following objectives (Foot & Hook 1996: 213–224; Republic of South Africa 1997: 42):
- To ensure that public sector employees know what is expected of them;
- To inform public sector managers whether the employee's performance is delivering the requested set objectives;
- To identify poor performance;
- To improve poor performance;
- To recognise and reward outstanding performance;
- To increase motivation;
- To identify training needs;
- To aid in career planning; and
- To provide information for HR planning.

9.3 The integrated nature of performance appraisal

Performance appraisal, when applied correctly, links up with most of the other HRM activities. This implies that performance appraisal should be used in an integrated and co-ordinated manner in order to accomplish institutional goals effectively. First, from an integrated perspective, notice how performance links up with the following activities:

- **Human resource planning** (see Chapter 5): In part, HR planning involves an understanding of the strengths and weaknesses of the existing workforce. This means that HR planning decisions, to a greater or lesser extent, are based on the performance levels of public sector employees.
- **Probation and promotion:** It would be impossible for any public sector employee to pass the probationary period successfully or be promoted without undergoing evaluation of his or her current work performance.
- **Merit pay increases:** One of the most common uses of performance appraisal is in the situation where remuneration depends on work performance. The current work performance of a public sector employee is often the most significant consideration for determining whether to give an employee a salary increase or not.

DID YOU KNOW? ?

Money isn't everything when it comes to recognition for meritorious performances. The following are a few examples of what can be offered by HR specialists and line function managers to reward employees:
- Public recognition (for example, their photo on the notice board);
- Mention achievements in the office newsletter;
- Provide family incentives;
- Offer time off;
- Award specially branded clothing to achievers;
- Provide new office equipment;
- Hold lunches when a team performs well; and
- Offer status symbols for up-and-coming managers (for example, use of the company's box at sports events or concerts).

Source: Labour Bulletin (2010: Online)

- **Employee training and development:** When it is determined that there are weaknesses in the performance levels of employees, performance appraisals can give an indication of where and when training and development interventions should be made.
- **Dismissals:** Performance appraisal information can also provide needed input for determining where to terminate (dismiss) the services of public sector employees (Dresang 2002: 173).

Second, apart from managing performance appraisal in an integrated manner with other HR activities, it also involves a co-ordinated effort between HR specialists and line function employees. Although a great deal of performance appraisal work can be devolved to line function employees, there is also an important role for HR specialists. On the one hand, the responsibilities of HR specialists are as follows:

- To design and implement performance appraisal systems;
- To train line function employees in conducting performance appraisals;
- To monitor the effectiveness of performance appraisal procedures; and
- To maintain performance appraisal records.

On the other hand, the responsibilities of line function employees are the following (Byars & Rue 1997: 284):

- To evaluate the performance of employees;
- To ensure that performance appraisal forms are completed and returned; and
- To review the appraisals with the employees.

9.4 Regulatory framework for performance appraisal

In order to ensure purposeful action, uniform guidelines have been introduced for performance appraisal. These guidelines have been embodied in statutes such as the Public Service Act 103 of 1994, the Public Service Regulations of 2001, and the White Paper on Human Resource Management in the Public Service, 1997.

9.4.1 The Public Service Act 103 of 1994

Section 3(5)(c) of the Public Service Act 103 of 1994 clearly indicates that performance appraisal should be provided for in the public service. Section 7(3)(b) of the above Act goes even further and specifically stipulates that a head of a public service institution shall be responsible for the effective management and administration of his or her institution/department/section. Although this section does not directly refer to performance appraisal, 'management and administration' reflects every public service activity, meaning that performance appraisal is included here.

9.4.2 The Public Service Regulations of 2001

The Public Service Regulations (PSR) of 2001 (Republic of South Africa 2001) provide for the establishment of three performance appraisal systems in the public service. Part VIII, paragraph B1 of the PSR and Section 1.5 of the 'Senior Management Service: Public Service Handbook' (Republic of South Africa 2003) indicates that a public service institution shall determine different systems for performance appraisal for the following categories of staff, namely: (1) heads of departments, (2) senior managers, and (3) all other staff. 'Heads of departments' refers to the incumbents of posts mentioned in the second column of Schedules 1 or 2 of the Public Service Act 103 of 1994. This includes those staff members operating as heads of national state departments and provincial administrations. They are respectively referred to as 'directors-general' and 'heads of provincial departments'. The Senior Management Service (SMS) cadre consists of employees who are remunerated on grade 13 and higher. They are referred to as 'senior managers'. In addition, Chapter 4, paragraph A, of the PSR of 2001 states that the performance of all members of the SMS will be managed through a performance agreement.

9.4.3 White Paper on Human Resource Management in the Public Service of 1997

This White Paper makes provision for the following principles regarding performance appraisal in the public service (Republic of South Africa 1997):

- **Results orientation:** Results orientation implies that a public service employee's performance should be assessed on the basis of a work plan. This work plan must cover a specific period explaining the employee's responsibilities as well as the objectives to be achieved. In addition, the work plan must be mutually agreed between the employee and his or her immediate manager.
- **Training and development:** One of the key objectives of performance appraisal is to help identify the strengths and weaknesses of employees and the HR interventions that are needed to manage these. In more practical terms, these interventions refer to various training and development options.
- **Rewarding good performance:** The primary orientation of performance appraisal is developmental and for recognising outstanding performance. This area of performance appraisal entails the awarding of incremental increases in salary.
- **Managing poor performance:** Part VIII, paragraph D, of the PSR is very specific on performances that have not met the requirements of the work plan. It is clearly stated that employees should be informed in writing where the performance is unsatisfactory and of the reasons for that assessment. To avoid conflict, mutual agreement should be reached on the steps that need to be taken to effect improvement. These steps may include such interventions as career counselling, coaching, mentoring, retraining, and redeployment. If these interventions have been implemented and the desired improvement has not been effected, dismissals may be considered.

DID YOU KNOW?

Traditionally, assessment of work performance in South African institutions has been viewed as judgmental and anxiety provoking. However, this situation has changed with the implementation of the National Qualification Framework (NQF). The NQF (policy document), like other legislation, such as the Labour Relations Act 66 of 1995, the Employment Equity Act 55 of 1998 and the Skills Development Act 97 of 1998; has two core objectives that are basically political and economic in nature. From a political perspective, these policy guidelines and legislation support the acquisition of skills and the improvement in quality of life of previously disadvantaged people. The economic incentive is to grow South Africa's skills base in line with international standards, so as to place the country in a position to compete effectively in the global market.

Source: Saunders (2000: 176)

- **Openness, fairness and objectivity:** Failure by the manager to apply the principles of openness, fairness, and objectivity can have a negative effect upon the results of performance appraisal, as it can make them seem untrustworthy. Employees may see the manager as acting in a dishonest manner if he or she is not open, fair, and objective. Therefore, it is important that every employee should be given a copy of the written assessment. In addition, the employee should be given the opportunity to comment on the results of the assessment. If it appears that the assessment seems to be unfair, employees should also be given the right to appeal. Another way of ensuring objective reporting is to task the reporting manager's immediate manager to review the written assessment.

9.4.4 Public Service Coordinating Bargaining Council Resolution No. 13 of 1998

A fundamental determinant of Resolution No. 13 of 1998 is that it provides for a framework for senior managers in the public service to agree to individual performance agreements. This Resolution prescribes the following five items that must be included in a performance agreement (Republic of South Africa 1998):
- Key duties and responsibilities;
- Output targets for the performance agreement period;
- Dates for performance review;
- Dispute resolution mechanisms; and
- Date on which salary increments will come into effect and mechanisms for the managing/awarding of salary increases.

9.4.5 Public Service Coordinating Bargaining Council Resolution No. 9 of 2000

Resolution No. 9 of 2000 is complementary to Resolution 13 of 1998. As we have already indicated, performance appraisal serves as an important tool in providing for salary increases if performance exceeds the standard that is expected. This Resolution provides for the structuring of remuneration packages to be translated to a more transparent total cost-to-employer and inclusive flexible remuneration package system (Republic of South Africa 2000).

9.5 General problems in performance appraisal

The literature abounds with reasons why appraisal systems fail and, in practice, many problems are experienced.

9.5.1 Problems related to appraisal system design

It would be safe to state that there is not a single method or format of performance appraisal that is not subject to some limitations. Indeed, the very fact that there are so many different formats of varying complexity from which to choose is a direct result of trying to overcome deficiencies of previously conceived formats. Such deficiencies in the design of performance appraisal instruments are mostly related to concerns about their reliability and validity as basic psychometric requirements for any measuring instrument.

Reliability in assessment refers to the consistency and stability of the measurement process. Szilagy and Wallace (1990: 535) suggest four approaches for improving reliability in performance measures:

- Increasing the number of items in the rating instrument that measure the same performance dimension;
- Using more than one evaluator in order to obtain multiple observations;
- Increasing the frequency of observations; and
- Standardising the administration of the appraisal process.

There are two indisputable facts when using assessment centres to promote employees based on work performance: (1) they predict managerial performance; and (2) they are expensive. More controversial is the issue of whether the economic benefits of the assessment centre methods justify their costs. In this regard, a study was done in the Texas Police Department (City of Dallas) during 2006 to examine the economic utility of an assessment centre as a part of the promotional examination of candidates for promotion to the position of sergeant. Utility analysis is a systematic process of examining the economic gain to an institution from an investment in a HRM intervention. It involves an analysis of several variables that contribute to the costs and benefits of an intervention. When applied to promotional procedures, utility analysis involves a consideration of the relative validities of a new and an old procedure, the number of persons assessed, the percentage of candidates selected, costs and, most important, the variability of job performance of incumbents expressed in dollar units. The research results of the above study are presented below in Focus on Research 9.1.

FOCUS ON RESEARCH 9.1
Is the cost of an assessment centre worth it?

RESEARCH

In summary, the study found that the assessment centre conducted for promotion of candidates into the position of sergeant in the Texas Police Department was expensive, but it paid off in terms of economic utility. The total cost to assess 208 candidates was $158 970 – a cost per candidate of $764. At the same time, utility analyses clearly demonstrated that the economic benefits far outweighed these costs. Using reasonable assumptions about the validity of the assessment centre, the validity of a common alternative used in other jurisdictions along with its costs, length of service of persons promoted to the position, and the benefit of effective persons in the position, various levels of economic utility were calculated. High estimates show utility of $4 187 per candidate, $18 861 per person promoted, and $870 963 for the total utility. Low estimates show utility of $1 995 per candidate, $12 442 per person promoted, and $414 943 for the total utility. Even the lowest estimates of utility show that investment in the assessment centre resulted in economic gains. ▷

The cost of running the assessment centre is greater than the cost of conducting panel interviews, but the increase in information yielded by the assessment centre justifies the added costs. Assuming that there is variation in performance among sergeants on the job that yields benefits to the city, the analyses demonstrate clearly that using the assessment centre will result in substantial additional benefits to the city.

Conclusion: This assessment centre was expensive, but well worth it!

Source: Thornton, & Potemra (2010: 67–68)

Validity of assessment addresses the questions of 'what' and 'how well' an instrument measures; that is, whether it really measures what it is supposed to measure.

In terms of format design, the use of irrelevant performance criteria or reliance on personality trait measures may compromise validity, while certain rater biases may detract from validity during the evaluation process. The most common of these biases or errors are discussed individually in the sections that follow.

9.5.2 Problems related to rater errors

Performance appraisal requires the public sector manager/rater to observe and judge behaviour as objectively as possible. Since both these processes are conducted by humans, the appraisal process is necessarily prone to distortions and biases which confound any attempts at total objectivity.

In order to evaluate the effectiveness of an employee's behaviour, the rater must first have observed such behaviour. Unless the rater is able to observe his or her subordinates continuously and to provide regular evaluative feedback, annual appraisal judgements will have to be based on a limited sample of observed performance events (those which the manager still remembers). Since many managers may simply not have the time or the inclination to practise 'management by walking around' and observing their subordinates at work, sampling errors such as the recency effect and infrequent observations may lead to invalid and subjective evaluations (Aamodt 1999: 320–322).

- The **recency effect** refers to the tendency to emphasise recent behaviours rather than the individual's performance over the entire review period. Good performers who may have slacked towards the end of the rating period may thus be penalised unfairly.
- The error of **infrequent observations** usually manifests itself in ratings based on non-representative samples of behaviour and unsubstantiated inferences.

Apart from the obvious advantages that continuous performance management may hold in this regard, the use of multiple public sector raters may alleviate the problem somewhat. Some commonly encountered judgemental biases or rater errors are outlined below.

- **Leniency and strictness error:** This is the tendency of some public sector evaluators to assign either mostly favourable ratings or mostly very harsh ratings to all employees.

- **Central tendency:** This is the tendency to assign all ratings towards the centre of all scales, thus evaluating all workers as 'average'.
- **Halo error:** This is the tendency to allow the rating assigned to one performance dimension to excessively influence, either positively or negatively, the ratings on all subsequent dimensions.
- **Same-as-me and different-from-me errors:** This refers to the tendency to assign more favourable ratings to employees who are perceived by the rater to be similar to, or to behave in a similar way to, the rater or, alternatively, to rate less favourably those workers who demonstrate traits or behaviours different from those of the rater.
- **Contrast error:** This is the tendency to allow the rating of an individual to be positively or negatively influenced by the relative evaluation of the preceding ratee. Thus, an average performer may receive a poorer rating than would otherwise have been the case if his or her appraisal follows that of the organisation's star performer.

9.5.2.1   Overcoming rating errors

Three basic approaches can typically be followed in trying to combat rating errors (Birkenbach 1984; Jourden & Heath 1996).

- The first approach focuses on the statistical correction of ratings by for instance, converting all ratings to some type of standard score or by using a forced distribution of ratings in terms of the requirements of a normal curve. In the latter case, the assumption of a normal distribution of employee performance ratings (that is, that there are certain percentages of excellent, average, and poor employees in every group) may be a fallacy, since star performers and underperformers may already have been promoted or dismissed out of the group. Similarly, a group may, for example, consist entirely of top performers due to excellent selection and training.
- The second approach follows the traditional route of addressing appraisal problems, namely that of developing new, more sophisticated techniques and formats that incorporate design features and procedures aimed at minimising the risk of subjectivity.
- Finally, the third approach comprises the training of raters in three important areas (Latham & Wexley 1994: 137–167):
  - training aimed at eliminating or at least lessening rating errors and biases;
  - training aimed at promoting better observational skills in raters; and
  - training aimed at improved interpersonal and communication skills during appraisal interviews.

9.5.3   Problems related to the human interaction process

The very notion of evaluation – as well as the appraisal process itself – may often be a highly emotional issue for both raters and ratees alike.

Public sector raters who feel uncomfortable about any confrontation with subordinates may, for instance, assign average ratings where poor ratings would have been appropriate; ratees facing even the most accurate and objective criticism may resist or trivialise findings if they perceive the assessment as a blow to their self-esteem.

In addition, many situational factors (such as stress, sexual and racial biases, leadership style, etc.) have been implicated in contaminating accurate and valid ratings (Cascio 1991: 97–91).

Clearly, not even the most advanced and complex technique could possibly hope to control all such possible interactional problems. Evidence shown in Focus on Research 9.2 would support the view that performance appraisals often result in problems, particularly between managers and their subordinates.

RESEARCH

FOCUS ON RESEARCH 9.2
The limitations of performance appraisals

This research by Maley focused on the major factors that influence the inpatriate manager's (Australia) experience of performance appraisals during 2009. It was found in this study that, although performance appraisals were widely used, they were for the most part performed inadequately. This study revealed three core problems that represent major influences on the performance appraisal process: there was (1) limited face-to-face contact between the managers and subordinates; (2) lack of feedback from the managers; and (3) absence of appraisal follow-ups by the managers.

Typical views of the situation were as follows:

'When I go there I don't get much time with F. Well, the last time I hardly saw him. I run around like a headless chicken, with so many people to see.'

'For the last three years my appraisal has been over the phone. It's as though he doesn't have the courage to face me. It's really a joke. I find the whole process farcical.'

'After he has finished the appraisal, well, that's it for another year. I can guarantee that we will never talk about what we discussed until the same time next year. It's like an annual ritual, a bit meaningless and it really doesn't fit with the real business.'

Source: Maley (2009: 104–105)

9.6 Steps in the development of a successful appraisal system

While the foremost requirement for any effective appraisal system would be a tailor-made design and process that fits the specific needs, environment, and culture of the public sector institution, there are five basic steps common to any successful system. In the sections that follow, we shall consider the typical strategic choices or questions to be addressed at each development step to ensure an appropriate customised appraisal system. Since this book is mainly focused on management level, we will deal with each of these steps as it relates to the senior manager's responsibilities and role with regard to performance appraisal. The five basic steps in the development of an appraisal system are listed below:

- Step 1: Designing a policy framework
- Step 2: Developing the system

- Step 3: Signing a performance agreement
- Step 4: Measuring performance
- Step 5: Managing the outcomes of performance appraisal

9.6.1 Step 1: Designing a policy framework

The pertinent questions to be addressed during the policy-making phase relate directly to the typical problems and fundamental system requirements, for example:

- What is the regulatory framework (see Section 9.4)?
- What are the categories of staff to be involved?
- Who should be involved in developing the policy framework? All staff (line function employees, HR specialists, trade unions, and staff in general) can make valuable contributions to the development, design, and implementation of a performance appraisal system.
- Should an off-the-shelf system or tailor-made system be developed?
- Who should drive the process? The classical approach to performance appraisal indicates that active involvement of senior management will play a crucial role in the development, design, and implementation of the performance appraisal system. The type of involvement refers to activities such as overseeing the process, setting an example, problem solving, and improvement of the system.
- Should assessments be individual or group based?

9.6.2 Step 2: Developing the system

During this phase, appropriate solutions need to be found to such questions of design such as the following:

- What is to be appraised (quantitative outputs, traits, etc.)?
- How is it to be appraised (choice of format)?
- Who is to appraise whom?
- How often must it be appraised?
- How will the results be linked to improving, developing, and rewarding performance?

These questions translate into the following essential activities to be performed by the HR department.

9.6.2.1 Obtaining basic job information

The gathering of job-related information is done through appropriate job analysis techniques (see Chapter 5) and it results in the writing of job descriptions. Analysing job duties and responsibilities should be part of manager-employee interaction, and HR specialists should only provide expert advice and the necessary training in writing job descriptions in the style or format chosen by the institution. Agreement must be reached between manager and subordinate on the job requirements.

9.6.2.2   Establishing performance standards and performance criteria

Performance standards describe the conditions for totally satisfactory performance. Performance standards should be mutually agreed upon and should provide details as to the following:

- The worker action or output that will be assessed;
- The criteria to be used for the assessment; and
- The way in which performance will be measured.

Criteria are the measures of 'what a person has to do to be successful at performing his or her job' and may be obvious in certain jobs, as, for example, in the number of arrests and number of cases solved for policemen. (Note that these criteria may not be appropriate if the strategic emphasis of the policeman's job is on community relations and involvement.)

DID YOU KNOW?

The extension of a probation period allows a public-sector employer more time to assess the general suitability as well as the overall *performance* of the employee. The Labour Relations Act 66 of 1995 (Section 8 of the Code of Good Practice: Dismissal) provides that 'an employer may require any newly hired employee to serve a period of probation before the appointment of the employee is confirmed'. It is only when the employee's performance is adjudged to be at the requisite standard, that the employer would then confirm the appointment. In the case of an employee not complying with the required standard, this reason would be accepted during the probation period, whereas such reason would not be acceptable after completion of the probation period as valid and compelling reason to dismiss. HR specialists can make decision-making easier for employers by following this principle.

Source: The Business Blue Book of South Africa (2008: unnumbered)

9.6.2.3   Choosing the format and the sources of appraisal information

Decisions on the format of the appraisal instrument and the sources that should generate the ratings (that is, the direct manager, peers, subordinates, consultants, etc.) must again be the outcome of thorough deliberation on many factors, such as the overall objectives, potential advantages and disadvantages, and public sector institution-specific circumstances.

9.6.2.4   Preparing documentation

Once the above-mentioned decisions have been made, the appraisal forms have to be designed and appraisal techniques must be chosen. Numerous performance appraisal techniques have been developed over the years. Below, we shall discuss those techniques that are both commonly used and legally defensible.

Relative rating techniques

The relative ranking techniques can be classified as ranking, paired comparisons, and forced distribution.

- **Ranking:** Straight ranking entails simply the rank ordering of individuals, according to overall merit or according to other performance factors, from the best performer through to the worst performer. This is a very basic evaluation procedure, and it is suggested that its use should be limited to cases in which:
  - Only small numbers of individuals are to be rated;
  - Only the 'better than' is important and not the 'how much better than';
  - Employees will not be compared across groups; and
  - The evaluation is not aimed at feedback to employees (Singer 1990: 213).
- **Paired comparisons:** This procedure requires the public sector evaluator to compare each worker separately with each other worker. The eventual ranking of an individual is then determined by the number of times he or she was judged to be better than the other worker. The number of comparisons required may be calculated by the formula where N refers to the number of individuals to be ranked. The more workers to be ranked, the more unwieldy the method becomes. Limitations are similar to those identified for ranking.
- **Forced distribution:** When using this technique, the public sector evaluator is required to assign certain portions of his or her workers to each of a number of specified categories on each performance factor. The forced distribution chosen can specify any percentage per category and need not necessarily comply with the requirements of a normal curve. Whilst this format controls rating errors such as leniency and central tendency, the forced distribution chosen may differ substantially from the performance characteristics of the ratees as a group.

Absolute rating techniques

The key absolute rating techniques are the essay method, critical incidents, behavioural checklists and graphic rating scales.

- **Essay method:** The public sector rater is required to write a report on each employee, describing individual strengths and weaknesses. The format of the report may be left entirely to the discretion of the rater, or certain specific points of discussion may have to be addressed. This is generally a time-consuming method, the success of which is very much dependent on the writing skills of the raters. If done well, however, it may prove valuable as a feedback tool for the ratees.
- **Critical incidents:** This technique requires the public sector manager continuously to record actual job behaviours that are typical of success or failure, as they occur. Whilst this method focuses on behaviour rather than on traits as a basis of appraisal and thus has the potential for meaningful feedback, the recording of incidents is both time consuming and burdensome for managers.
- **Behavioural checklists:** This format provides the public sector rater with a list of descriptions of job-related behaviours which have to be marked if they are

descriptive of the individual being rated. In a variant of this format, the summated ratings method, the behavioural statements are followed by a Likert-type scale of response categories, each of which is weighted, for example 'strongly agree' = 5 to 'strongly disagree' = 1. The weights of the checked response for each item are then summed and represent the overall performance score of the individual.

- **Graphic rating scales:** As this is a very popular format, many variations of graphic rating scales can be found. Basically a scale for a specific trait or characteristic consists of a continuum between two poles on which the rater indicates to what degree the ratee possesses that characteristic. The variations on this basic format stem from:
  - The dimensions on which individuals are to be rated;
  - The degree to which the dimensions are defined; and
  - The degree to which the points on the scale are defined.
- **Behaviourally anchored rating scales (BARS):** In essence, BARS are a variation of graphic rating scales with the difference that performance dimensions are defined in behavioural terms, and the various levels of performance are anchored by examples of critical incidents. Behaviourally anchored rating scales are job specific and require a high level of participation from public sector managers. The development of BARS is a complex process, the details of which are beyond the scope of this chapter. Rudimentary details regarding the various steps in the construction of BARS are provided below:
  - Behavioural statements/incidents describing effective, average and ineffective behaviour are gathered from job knowledgeable employees and supervisors.
  - Public sector managers classify the statements in terms of performance dimensions (for example, motivation and know-how) and reject those that are ambiguous.
  - A different group of judges then retranslates each statement by rating it on a scale ranging from outstanding to poor performance.
  - Specific statements are then chosen as anchors on the final scale, with the calculated average of the judges' ratings determining where on the scale the statement will feature.

Other appraisal techniques

There are other performance appraisal techniques as well. Two appraisal techniques referred to in this section – management by objectives and assessment centres – did not originate as appraisal techniques, although they may be utilised as such.

- **Management by objectives:** Management by objectives (MBO) is a management philosophy that focuses on the motivation of individual performance, but which, due to its process, can also be used for evaluating performance. This method typically entails:
  - Public sector managers and employees mutually establishing and discussing specific goals and formulating action plans;
  - Public sector managers aiding their employees to reach their set goals; and

- Each public sector manager and employee reviewing at a preset time the extent to which objectives have been attained.
- **Assessment centres:** An assessment centre is a procedure originally adopted to assess managerial potential. It is an assessment method that consists of a standardised evaluation of behaviour, based on multiple raters and multiple measures such as in-basket exercises, paper and pencil ability tests, leaderless group discussions, simulations, and personality questionnaires. In the South African context, assessment centres enjoy a relatively high level of popularity. The application of the technology is monitored through an Assessment Centre Study Group in terms of professional guidelines adapted from international standards (Spangenberg 1991: 29–32), and a substantial body of evidence has already been amassed to confirm the value and utility of the technique (Kriek 1991: 34–37).
- **360-degree appraisals:** Another approach that has gained increasing popularity is the so-called 360-degree performance appraisal technique. This is a multiple rater/multiple source approach to the assessment of an individual's work performance. In South Africa, more and more public sector institutions are making use of (or considering switching to) this method.

The method involves gathering and processing performance assessments on individual employees from a broad range of interested parties. These include customers (both internal and external to the organisation), suppliers, peers and team members, superiors, and subordinates, as well as the person assessed. The data collection process normally includes such elements as formal and structured interviews, informal discussions, surveys, and observations. The assessment information is used as feedback to the employee and provides important inputs for career development and management, and training development. Because of the use of multiple sources, a broader perspective can be developed of an individual's strengths and weaknesses. This enhances self-insight in the process of developing to one's full potential.

9.6.3 Step 3: Signing a performance agreement

According to Chapter 4, Part IIIA of the PSR of 2001, the performance of a person appointed to a post on senior management level shall be managed in accordance with a performance agreement. This performance agreement shall apply for a particular financial year and shall be reviewed on an annual basis. The process does not end with the signing of the performance agreement, as the performance of a senior public sector manager must be reviewed on a quarterly basis. There is also an understanding that such reviews may be verbal if the manager's performance is satisfactory. Of particular importance is that a minimum of two formal reviews must be done during the course of a performance cycle (Republic of South Africa 2003: 15). The entering into a performance agreement should be reached through a series of stages (Stredwick 2000: 240–241). We shall examine each of these stages in the following sections.

9.6.3.1 Linking the performance agreement to the corporate plan and business plan

An effective performance agreement should enable and empower public sector managers to implement the strategy and objectives of the institution successfully. This means that all performance agreements in the public service should be based on the overall corporate plan and business plan of the institution. See Chapter 4 for a detailed discussion on making a corporate and business plan operational.

9.6.3.2 Entering into an individual performance agreement

The performance agreement for each senior public sector manager shall (Republic of South Africa 2001: 49):

- Assist the relevant person to define her or his key responsibilities and priorities;
- Encourage improved communication between that member and the person she or he reports to; and
- Enable the person to whom that member reports to assess his or her work and provide appropriate support.

The 'Senior Management Service: Public Service Handbook' (Republic of South Africa 2003) states that the performance agreement should consist of the following six elements:

- Description of the purpose of the job;
- Identification of key result areas and agreement on the standards for measuring core management criteria;
- Monitoring the performance of senior public sector managers against the criteria and standards of the performance agreement;
- Agreement on a personal development plan;
- Specification of mechanisms for dispute resolution; and
- Consideration of annual remuneration package adjustment and performance-related rewards.

We shall now examine these six elements in detail.

1. Description of the purpose of the job

To a large extent, the purpose of the job should be based on two sources of information. First, information can be obtained from the job profile. Second, the business plan should also be consulted for information on what is expected of the job holder.

2. Identification of key result areas and agreement on the standards for measuring core management criteria

Any performance appraisal scheme is unlikely to succeed if the criteria upon which the performance of an employee is to be assessed are not clearly determined in the performance agreement. In order to provide for this, the Department of Public Service and Administration identifies two components of criteria that must be contained in the performance agreement. The criteria to be assessed consist of key result areas (KRAs) and core management criteria (CMCs). KRAs cover the main areas of work of a senior public sector manager and describe the key actions and activities that will ultimately assist the particular public service institution in performing effectively. One way to capture these KRAs in a clear and concise manner is to include them in a work plan. The work plan makes provision for different aspects of the work, such as specific tasks that the public sector manager should execute to ensure that the objectives are achieved, as well as duties and responsibilities related to provision of advice and support. Because KRAs cover the main areas of work of a senior public sector manager, they will account for 80% of the final assessment. An example of a performance work plan is provided in Figure 9.1.

Key result area	Performance standards	Resource requirements	Enabling conditions

Source: Department of Public Service and Administration Circular 1/2/1/P (Republic of South Africa 2002)

Figure 9.1   Example of a performance work plan

DID YOU KNOW?

The Department of Public Service and Administration has identified the following CMCs for senior managers in the public service:
- Strategic capability and leadership;
- Programme and project management;
- Financial management;
- Change management;
- Knowledge management;
- Service delivery innovation:
- Problem solving and analysis:
- People management and empowerment:
- Client orientation and customer focus;
- Communication; and
- Honesty and integrity.

Core management criteria must also be concerned with generic standards. It is important to note here that these core criteria and generic standards are related to how senior public sector managers do their jobs – they do not describe the results that should be achieved. Figure 9.2 is an example of the way in which two core criteria – strategic capability and leadership, and programme and project management – relate to generic standards for effective performance.

Core management criteria	Description	Generic standards
1. Strategic capability and leadership	Provides a vision, sets the direction for the institution and/or unit, and inspires others to deliver on the organisational mandate.	● Gives direction to team in realising the institution's strategic objectives. ● Develops detailed action plans to execute strategic initiatives. ● Assists in defining performance measures to evaluate the success of strategies.
2. Programme and project management	Plans, manages, monitors, and evaluates specific activities in order to deliver the desired outputs and outcomes.	● Establishes broad stakeholder involvement and communicates the project status and key milestones. ● Defines roles and responsibilities for project team members and clearly communicates expectations. ● Balances quality of work with deadlines.

Source: Adapted from Department of Public Service and Administration Circular 1/2/1/P (Republic of South Africa 2002)

Figure 9.2   Example of core criteria and generic standards

The most common way of reaching an agreement is that every senior public sector manager should be assessed against all those CMCs that are applicable to his or her post. For example, not all posts in the public service have the same level of managerial responsibility. A person operating as a scientist may not have any employees under his or her control. Therefore, 'people management and empowerment' should not be included as a core management criterion for a scientist. In most cases, CMCs will not be equally important for the same post, or they may apply in different ways to different posts. When determining the specific CMCs for a specific job context, the assessing public sector manager, together with his or her immediate manager, will need to: (1) decide which of the CMCs apply to the job holder's post; (2) weigh each relevant criterion; and (3) adapt the generic standards to the demands and context of the post. Whereas the KRAs account for 80% of a senior public sector manager's assessment score, CMCs cover 20%. The weighing of all the KRAs and CMCs should add up to 100%.

3. Monitoring the performance of senior public sector managers against the criteria and standards of the performance agreement

Most prominent in the signing of a performance agreement is the matter of determining arrangements for the monitoring of the performance of senior public sector managers. Senior public sector managers must comply with the dates for quarterly and mid-term reviews and annual appraisals to ensure that objectives are achieved, as these may lead to modifications to the performance agreement (Republic of South Africa 2002).

4. Agreement on a personal development plan

A more inclusive version of signing a performance agreement embraces the designing of a developmental plan. This plan reflects the developmental requirements of a senior public sector manager through the using of a self-assessment tool produced by the Department of Public Service and Administration. (This self-assessment tool is available on the Internet at [http://www.dpsa.gov.za/ docs/ policy/ index.htm].) For best results, steps should be agreed upon to address the developmental gaps and the date at which a review of progress will be undertaken. Thus, the development plan forms part of the performance agreement, and a personal development plan is required for every senior public sector manager. An example is provided in Figure 9.3.

Competency to be assessed	Proposed actions	Responsibility	Time frame	Expected outcome

Source: Adapted from Department of Public Service and Administration Circular 1/2/1/P (Republic of South Africa, 2002)

Figure 9.3   Example of a personal development plan

5. Specification of mechanisms for dispute resolution

Another aspect to be dealt with when entering into a performance agreement is to specify mechanisms for resolving disputes. In this regard, we may consider the following actions:

- Develop mechanisms for dispute resolution that include any differences that may arise out of the assessment.
- Agree on a mutually acceptable person to resolve disputes. Preferably a person within the public service should be considered first.
- If possible, involve the selected person in the conclusion of the performance agreement. Involvement of this person at this stage will enhance his or her understanding of the contents of the performance agreement. This person's involvement may even prevent possible disputes from arising.
- Select this person on the basis of his or her functional expertise and people skills and not his or her legal qualifications. The reason for this is that dispute resolution is an informal process.

6. Consideration of annual remuneration package adjustment and performance-related rewards

The signing of an annual performance agreement implies that a senior public sector manager may be considered for performance-related pay increases and/or rewards, based on the outcome of the performance appraisal. Failure to sign a performance agreement may result in disciplinary action.

9.6.4   Step 4: Measuring performance

Once the performance agreement has been finalised, public sector raters must make sure that they will be prepared to assess actual performance against the required level of performance. The only way to be successful in this activity is to give attention to the following primary concerns.

9.6.4.1   Establish an assessment instrument

Part VIII.C.1 of the Public Service Regulations of 2001 determines that separate instruments for different occupational categories or levels of work should be established. Therefore, a particular performance assessment instrument has been developed for the performance of senior public sector managers. Although this instrument prescribes certain basic requirements, institutions may customise it to suit their particular needs.

9.6.4.2   Decide on the frequency of appraisal

Many issues may arise when deciding on the frequency of appraisals. Of course, too many appraisals can easily result in a situation in which an individual employee is over-managed. Another possible outcome is that insufficient appraisal is undertaken. In this case, an employee is basically ignored in the appraisal process (Bezuidenhout,

DID YOU KNOW?

The performance assessment instrument provides for the following:
- Personal details, such as period under review, surname, job title, probation, permanent, etc.;
- Comments by rated senior public manager prior to appraisal;
- Actual performance appraisal that includes ratings on KRAs and CMCs;
- Scoring;
- Provision for development, training, coaching, guidance and exposure needed;
- Recommendations by rater, manager himself/herself, comments by chairperson of moderating committee, and decision by institution; and
- Confirmation/extension/termination of probation.

Garbers, & Potgieter 1998: 177). In order to overcome these problems, it has been decided that senior public sector managers in the public service will undergo regular performance reviews and an annual performance appraisal.

Performance reviews

In its simplest form, the performance review is used to provide an opportunity for senior public sector managers to receive feedback on how they are performing. In other words, a performance review can be used to serve as important feedback sessions and it takes place at regular intervals during the performance cycle. It should be emphasised that, apart from the formal annual performance appraisal, at least one performance review should take place annually (preferably in the middle of the performance cycle). The type of performance review form that can be used may differ from institution to institution. However, the following basic information should be included (Republic of South Africa 2002: Annexure C):
1. Personal details;
2. Particulars on deployability/transferability;
3. Action points from performance review discussions;
4. Self-assessment against work plan;
5. Self-assessment against core management criteria;
6. Performance assessment by reporting officer (manager);
7. Assessment of potential; and
8. Signature.

Annual performance appraisal

Basically, the annual performance appraisal process involves two activities.

1. Assessment of the achievement of results as outlined in the work plan

Each KRA and CMC as listed in the work plan (see Section 9.6.3.2) should be assessed according to the extent to which the specified standards have been met. When assessing the performance of each individual senior public sector manager, an indicative rating should be provided for each KRA and CMC on the following five-point scale:

- **Level 5:** Outstanding performance. (85% and higher) In this case, the performance is regarded as far exceeding the standard that is expected of a senior public sector manager at this level. Decisions to be made when a manager falls on Level 5 of the scale are: (1) confirmation of probation; (2) allocation of between 6% and 8% of the total remuneration package as a performance bonus; (3) progression to next higher package in the remuneration band; and (4) access to training and development opportunities which are in line with promotion along the career path.
- **Level 4:** Performance significantly above expectations. (80% to 84%) Here performance is seen as significantly higher than the standard expected in the job. Decisions to be made on Level 4 include: (1) confirmation of probation; (2) allocation of between 3% and 5% of the total remuneration package as a performance bonus; (3) progression to next higher package in the remuneration band; and (4) access to training and development opportunities to bring about improvement in those areas of less outstanding performance which are in line with promotion along the career path.
- **Level 3:** Fully effective. (65% to 79%) On Level 3, performance is regarded as having fully met the standard expected in all areas of the job. Typical decisions on Level 3 include: (1) confirmation of probation; (2) progression to next higher package in remuneration band; and (3) access to training and development opportunities to bring about improvement in those areas of less outstanding performance which are in line with promotion along the career path.
- **Level 2:** Performance not fully adequate. (50% to 64%) A rating on Level 2 indicates that performance in key areas is below the standard required for the job. Decisions appropriate on Level 2 are: (1) confirmation of probation (in exceptional cases, the probation period can be extended); (2) agreement on performance improvement measures and identification of responsibility for remedial action; and (3) agreement on a programme for supporting and monitoring performance improvement.
- **Level 1:** Unacceptable performance. (49% and lower) This level reflects performance that does not meet the standard expected for the job. There is a choice between two decisions in this situation: probation can be extended, or employment can be terminated. It is important that prescribed incapacity procedures should be followed when unacceptable performance has been determined.

2. Using the Assessment Rating Calculator to provide a final score.

An overall rating should ultimately be done. In this regard, a spreadsheet utility, the Assessment Rating Calculator, may be used to add the scores and calculate a final KRA score, based on the 80% weighting allocated to the KRAs. The same should be done to calculate a final CMC score, based on the 20% weighting allocated to the CMCs. Figure 9.4 is an illustration of the Assessment Rating Calculator. (This assessment utility is available at [http://www.dpsa.gov.za/ documents/sms/ publications/assessment].)

Senior Management Service
Department:
Annual Performance Assessment
Assessment Rating Calculator

Name:
Year:

KRA	Weight	Rating	Score	CMC	Weight	Rating	Score
1	20%	3	0.6	1	20%	4	0.8
2	30%	3	0.9	2	50%	5	2.5
3	30%	3	0.9	3	30%	5	1.5
4	20%	3	0.6	4			
5				5			
6				6			
7				7			
8				8			
9				9			
10				10			
11				11			
	100%		60		100%		96
KRA weight:			80%	CMC weight			20%
KRA score:		48%	CMC score:			19%	
FINAL SCORE:							67%

Source: Department of Public Service and Administration Circular 1/2/1P (Republic of South Africa, 2002: Annexure E)

Figure 9.4   Illustration of the Assessment Rating Calculator

Follow the guidelines below for using the Senior Management Service Assessment Rating Calculator (guidelines available at [http://www.dpsa.gov.za/documents/ sms/ circulars/PMDSAnnexe.pdf]):

For the KRAs

1. For each KRA, fill in the weighting that you have allocated to it. Ensure that the weighting adds up to 100. Note that space is made for 11 KRAs. But you may have only 5 or 6. Fill in whatever number of KRAs is relevant to you.
2. Rate each KRA according to the extent to which performance has met the criteria specified in the standards and indicators. Use the five-point scale described in the guidelines.
3. The assessment rating calculator will automatically calculate a score for each KRA by multiplying the weighting by the rating.
4. The calculator will then automatically calculate a total score for the work plan by adding up the scores and multiplying this total by the 80% weighting allocated to the KRAs.

For the CMCs

5. For each relevant CMC, fill in the weighting that you have allocated to it. Ensure that the weighting adds up to 100. Note that there are certain CMCs that are compulsory for SMS members with managerial responsibilities.
6. Rate each CMC according to the extent to which performance has met the specified standards. Use the five-point scale described in the guidelines.
7. The assessment rating calculator will automatically calculate a score for each CMC by multiplying the weighting by the rating.
8. The calculator will then automatically calculate a total score for the CMC by adding up the scores and multiplying this total by the 20% weighting allocated to CMCs.

For the overall rating

9. The assessment rating calculator will provide a final appraisal score by adding the totals obtained for the KRAs and the CMCs.

9.6.5   Step 5: Managing the outcomes of performance appraisal

According to Part VIII.D.1 of the Public Service Regulations of 2001, the senior public sector manager shall inform him/her in writing of the outcome of the assessment and, if the employee's performance is unsatisfactory, of the reasons for that assessment. In practice, this implies that there are two basic outcomes that follow from an effective performance appraisal process and that need to be managed: satisfactory performance and unsatisfactory performance.

9.6.5.1   Managing satisfactory performance

Irrespective of the approach used, those involved in the performance appraisal process must realise that there are basically three ways of giving recognition to good performance: pay progression, performance bonuses, and non-financial rewards.

Pay progression

Very generally pay progression refers to an upward progression in remuneration from a lower remuneration package to a higher remuneration package. If a senior public sector manager achieves a score of 65% and above (see Section 9.6.4.2) he or she becomes eligible for progression to the next higher package in the remuneration band. We shall look more closely at remuneration issues in Chapters 12 and 13.

Performance rewards
See Section 9.6.4.2 above for a summary of the cut-off points and maximum percentages that will apply for the awarding of performance bonuses for senior public sector managers in the public service.

Non-financial rewards
Non-financial rewards require you to devise more creatively conceived rewards for performance. Among the most common that could be applied are:
- Increased autonomy to organise one's own work;
- Acknowledgment and recognition of performances in official publications or other publicity material; and
- Recognition of specific achievements or innovations in public.

9.6.5.2 Managing unsatisfactory performance

Part VIII.E of the Public Service Regulations (PSR) of 2001 is very specific on the way in which to manage unsatisfactory performance. It is stated here that, in the case of such performance, systematic remedial or developmental support should be provided to assist the relevant senior public sector manager to improve his or her performance. In short, this means the implementing of corrective measures. Under the same regulation, it is specified that, if the performance is so unsatisfactory as to be poor and the desired improvement cannot be effected, steps should be considered to discharge the manager for unfitness or incapacity to carry out his or her duties. As one can see from the stipulations in the PSR, there are two options for managing unsatisfactory performance. One option focuses on implementing corrective measures, and the section option deals with terminating the services of the employee. The latter part will be dealt with in Chapter 17.

Implementing corrective measures involves various options. These include such options as training/re-training, counselling/coaching, setting clear work performance standards, provision of enabling working facilities and resources, and designing of a personal development plan. The Labour Relations Act 66 of 1995 requires a proper investigation before action is taken against an employee for poor work performance. An investigation is essential because it may well be determined afterwards that an employee's poor work is attributable to factors such as inadequate equipment or institutional problems, which is many times outside the control of the employee (Grogan 2008: 213). How narrow the dividing line may be, is illustrated by a case in which employees were dismissed for failing to attain production goals. Many employers dismiss poor performers unexpectedly or prematurely, while others wait too long before taking action. One key reason for unnecessary delays in dismissals is the employer's fear of being taken to the Commission for Conciliation, Mediation and Arbitration (CCMA) and being forced to reinstate the employee and/or to pay punitive amounts in compensation. Item 9 of the Code of Good Practice: Dismissal of the Labour Relations Act 66 of 1995 states that 'any person determining whether a dismissal for poor work performance is unfair should consider:

- Whether or not the employee failed to meet a performance standard; and
- If the employee did not meet a required performance standard, whether or not:
  - The employee was aware, or could reasonably have been expected to be aware, of the required performance standard;
  - The employee was given a fair opportunity to meet the required performance standard; and
  - Dismissal was an appropriate sanction for not meeting the required performance standard.'

Items 8(2) and 8(3) of the abovementioned Code provide that:
'(2) ... an employee should not be dismissed for unsatisfactory performance unless the employer has:
(a) Given the employee appropriate evaluation, instruction, guidance, training or counselling; and
(b) After a reasonable period of time for improvement, the employee continues to perform unsatisfactorily.
(3) The procedure leading to dismissal should include an investigation to establish the reasons for the unsatisfactory performance and the employer should consider other ways, short of dismissal to remedy the matter.'

The onus at the CCMA falls entirely on the employer to bring solid proof:

- That it followed the procedural guidelines quoted above; and also
- That, regardless of the procedure followed, the dismissal decision itself was appropriate under the circumstances.

An example of the obstacles in managing unsatisfactory performance is illustrated in Spotlight on the Law 9.1.

SPOTLIGHT ON THE LAW 9.1
Managing unsatisfactory performance

In the case of *White v Medpro Pharmaceuticals (Pty) Ltd* [2000], 10 BALR (1182), the employee White was dismissed for consistently failing to meet her performance targets. The employer justified its dismissal decision by stating that achieving the performance targets was a crucial requirement expected of the employee. Medpro also alleged that, had the employee made the targeted number of client calls, the performance targets would have been achieved. However, the employer brought no proof of its allegations and did not prove that its decision to dismiss was fair. The arbitrator held that the employer had the onus of proving that the performance standards set were applied in affair manner. As the employer failed to do so, the arbitrator found the dismissal to be both procedurally and substantively unfair. ▷

In *Robinson v Sun Couriers* [2003], 1 BALR (97), the CCMA commissioner blamed the employer for the employee's failure to meet the required performance targets and reinstated the unfairly dismissed employee. While the targets set may have been reasonable the arbitrator held that 'it is not only the employee who is responsible for achieving the desired results'.

In *Duff v McGregor (Pty) Ltd* [2004], 1 BALR (21), the arbitrator again blamed the employer for the employee's poor work performance because the employer could not prove that the targets set were appropriate and attainable. Again, the dismissal for poor performance was found to be both substantively and procedurally unfair.

The above laws and findings make it clear that every employer in the public sector must:
- Draw up attainable work performance targets for each and every employee;
- Induct every employee as to these targets; and
- Keep proof that the above has been done.

Source: Israelstam (2010: Online)

9.7 Appraisal interview (See Chapter 8)

Although a continuous, or at least regular, interaction process is advocated by the performance management process, the formal appraisal interview at the end of a review period remains a prominent feature of most performance appraisal systems.

Irrespective of the appraisal techniques or methods used, appraisal results need to be communicated to public sector employees in a constructive way in order to achieve the aims of providing feedback, motivating and counselling the individuals, and rectifying poor performance.

Despite the fact that the interviews are the responsibility of line function employees, it will most probably be the HR specialist's job to ensure the effectiveness of this process by training public sector managers how to plan and conduct appraisal interviews properly.

9.8 Review

The effective management of individual performance is the central requirement for the attainment of institutional goals. If line function employees are to achieve strategic objectives, accurate information regarding the performance levels of their team members is essential. This is the reason why most public sector institutions insist on a formal and systematic process whereby such information may be gathered and recorded.

An effective performance appraisal procedure is the hub of any integrated public sector human resource management system, and the information that it generates is utilised for many purposes. However, despite their extreme importance as a human resource function, the effectiveness of appraisal systems has traditionally been plagued by a variety of awkward problems related to technical and human obstacles.

On a macro-level, the continuous performance management approach has been advanced as a potentially promising solution while, on the micro-level, several categories of general problems and their possible remedies have been identified. These may serve as the basic background against which the HR specialist can develop and implement a performance appraisal system which is most likely to achieve its stated purpose and is least likely to flounder on the many possible obstacles.

Fundamental requirements for effective appraisals may sometimes be mutually exclusive and decision making during the development process may therefore require trade-offs regarding the utility of the many available choices of appraisal techniques and procedures. The importance of proper implementation procedures and evaluator training has been stressed throughout, since even the best conceived systems and techniques will be ineffective in the hands of an incompetent manager.

Performance appraisal is a vital component of the process of managing human resources in the public sector with the aim of achieving employee and institutional goals, and it will remain a key concern for South African public sector HR specialists and line function employees alike.

9.9   Self-evaluation questions

1. Define performance appraisal.
2. Give at least nine purposes of performance appraisal.
3. How does performance appraisal link up with other human resource management activities such as human resource planning, promotion, remuneration, training and development and dismissals?
4. 'Performance appraisal involves a coordinated effort between line function employees and human resource specialists.' Discuss this statement.
5. What instructions are stipulated in the South African public service regulatory framework for performance appraisal?
6. What are some of the major problems related to many performance appraisal systems?
7. Write an essay detailing the steps in developing a successful appraisal system.
8. What guidelines can you provide regarding the successful conduct of a performance appraisal interview?

Bibliography

Aamodt, MG. 1999. *Applied industrial/organizational psychology.* 3rd edn. Belmont, CA: Wadsworth.

Ancona, D, Kochan, TA, Scully, M, Van Maanen, J, & Westney, DE. 1999. *Managing for the future: Organizational behavior and processes.* Cincinnati, OH: South-Western.

Anthony, WP, Perrewé, PL, & Kacmar, KM. 1999. *Human resource management: A strategic approach.* 3rd edn. Orlando, FL: Dryden.

Atwater, L, & Waldman, D. 1999. Accountability in 360-degree feedback. *HR Magazine,* 43(6), 96–104.

Bezuidenhout, MC, Garbers, CJ, & Potgieter, S. 1998. *Managing for healthy labour relations: A practical guide for health services in southern Africa.* Pretoria: Van Schaik.

Birkenbach, RC. 1984. Halo, central tendency and leniency in performance appraisal: A comparison between a graphic rating scale and a behaviourally based measure. *Industrial Psychology,* 10(1), 15–34.

Boverie, PE, & Smuda, JF. 1999. Spinning wheel: In what direction is your 360-degree feedback process headed? Paper presented at the 1999 annual conference of the American Society for Training and Development, Atlanta, Georgia.

Berman, EM, Bowman, JS, West, JP, & Van Wart, M. 2001. *Human resource management in public service.* London: Sage.

Butler, JE, Ferris, GR, & Napier, NK. 1991. *Strategy and human resource management.* Cincinnati, OH: South-Western.

Byars, LL, & Rue, LW. 1997. *Human resource management.* 5th edn. Chicago: Irwin.

Cardy, R, & Dobbins, G. 1994. *Performance appraisal: Alternative perspectives.* Cincinnati, OH: South Western.

Cascio, WF. 1991. *Applied psychology in personnel management.* 4th edn. Englewood Cliffs, NJ: Prentice-Hall.

Cascio, WF. 1998. *Managing human resources: Productivity, quality of work life, profits.* 5th edn. New York: McGraw Hill.

Dresang, DL. 2002. *Public personnel management and public policy.* 4th edn. New York: Longman.

Foot, M, & Hook, C. 1996. *Introducing human resource management.* London: Longman.

Grogan, J. 2008. *Workplace law.* Cape Town: Juta.

Israelstam, I. 2010. What is poor work performance. Paper delivered at a seminar entitled 'Changes and dangers in labour law'. [http://www.skillsportal.co.za].

Jourden, FJ, & Heath, C. 1996. The evaluation gap in performance perceptions: Illusory perceptions of groups and individuals. *Journal of Applied Psychology,* 81(4), 369–379.

Kreitner, R, & Kinicki, A. 1995. *Organizational behavior.* 3rd edn. Homewood, IL: Irwin.

Kriek, H. 1991. Die bruikbaarheid van die takseersentrum: 'n Oorsig van resente literatuur. *Journal of Industrial Psychology,* 17(3), 34–37.

Labour Bulletin. 2010. 19 Incentives to reward and motivate employees. Fleet Street Publications. [http://www.fsp.co.za].

Latham, GP, & Wexley, KN. 1994. *Increasing productivity through performance appraisal.* 2nd edn. Reading, MA: Addison-Wesley.

Lockett, J. 1992. *Effective performance management.* London: Kogan Page.

Maley, JF. 2009. The influence of performance appraisal on the psychological contract of the inpatriate manager. *SA Journal of Human Resource Management,* 7 (1), 100–109.

McLean, GN. 1997. Multirater 360-degree feedback. In LJ Bassi and D Russ-Eft (eds.), *What works: Assessment, development and measurement.* Alexandria, Vancouver: ASTD.

McGregor, D. 1957. An uneasy look at performance appraisal. *Harvard Business Review,* 35(3), 89–94.

Nankervis, AR, Compton, RL, & McCarthy, TE. 1996. *Strategic human resource management.* 2nd edn. Melbourne: Thomson.

Rice, B. 1996. Performance review: The job nobody likes. In GR Ferris & MR Buckley (eds.), *Human resources management.* 3rd edn. Englewood Cliffs, NJ: Prentice-Hall.

Robbins, SP. 1995. *Supervision today.* Englewood Cliffs, NJ: Prentice-Hall.

Robbins, SP. 1998. *Organizational behavior: Concepts, controversies, applications.* 8th edn. Upper Saddle River, NJ: Prentice-Hall.

Saunders, E. 2000. *Assessing human competence: Practical guidelines for South African managers.* Randburg: Knowledge Resources.

Singer, MG. 1990. *Human resource management.* Boston, MA: PWS-Kent.

Spangenberg, H. 1991. New guidelines and ethical considerations for assessment centre operations. *IPM Journal,* June, 29–32.

Spangenberg, H. 1993. A managerial view on performance management. *People Dynamics,* 11(12), 30–34

Spangenberg, H. 1994. *Understanding and implementing performance management.* Cape Town: Juta.

Spangenberg, HH, Esterhuyse, JJ, Visser, JH, Briedenhann, JE, & Calitz, CJ. 1989. Construction of behaviourally anchored rating scales (BARS) for the measurement of managerial performance. *Journal of Industrial Psychology*, 15(1), 22–27.

Stredwick, J. 2000. *An introduction to human resource management.* Oxford: Butterworth Heineman.

Swan, WS. 1991. *How to do a superior performance appraisal.* New York: Wiley.

Sylvia, RD, & Meyer, CK. 2002. *Public personnel administration.* New York: Thomson Wadsworth.

Szilagy, AD, & Wallace, MJ. 1990. *Organizational performance and behavior.* 4th edn. Glenview, IL: Scott Foresman.

The Business Blue Book of South Africa. 2008. Newsletter. Questions and answers. 2 (10), unnumbered.

Thornton, GC, & Potemra, MJ. 2010. Utility of assessment center for promotion of police sergeants. *Public Personnel Management,* 39 (1), 57–68.

Tompkins, J. 1995. *Human resource management in government: Hitting the ground running.* New York: Harper Collins.

Tyson, S, & York, A. 2000. *Essentials of HRM.* 4th edn. Oxford: Butterworth Heineman.

Vecchio, RP. 1996. *Organizational behavior.* 3rd edn. Orlando, FL: Dryden.

Veldsman, TH. 1999. Profiling the high performance, high commitment, high flexibility organisation. Paper presented at the Best Human Resource Practices in Southern Africa conference of the Institute for International Research, Johannesburg.

Acts of legislation

Republic of South Africa. 1994. The Public Service Act (Act 103 of 1994). Government printer. [http://www.polity.org.za/html/govdocs/legislation/1994]

Government regulations

Republic of South Africa. 2001. Public Service Regulations (promulgated under Section 41 (1) of the Public Service Act 103 of 1994.) Government Gazette, 427 (21951). Government Printer.

Government white papers

Republic of South Africa. 1997. White paper on Human Resource Management in the Public Service. 31 December 1997. Government Gazette, 390 (18594). Government Printer.

Management guides

Republic of South Africa. 2002. Performance Management and Development System for the Senior Management Service (SMS). Department of Public Service and Administration. Circular 1/2/1P of 28 March 2002.

Republic of South Africa. 2003. Senior management service: Public service handbook. Department of Public Service and Administration. [http://www.dpsa.gov.za/documents/ sms/publications/ smshb2003]

Collective agreements

Republic of South Africa. 1998. Public Service Coordinating Bargaining Council Resolution No. 13 of 1998. Department of Public Service and Administration. [http://www.dpsa. gov.za/documents/ scbc/1998/13]

Republic of South Africa. 2000. Public Service Coordinating Bargaining Council Resolution No. 9 of 2000. Department of Public Service and Administration. [http://www.dpsa.gov.za/ documents/ scbc/2000/9]

10 Career management in the public sector

Purpose

The purpose of this chapter is to expose the reader to a range of factors related to the management of public sector employees' careers.

Learning outcomes

After you have read this chapter, you should be able to:
- Describe the concepts of career, career development, career planning, and career management.
- Discuss the career choice theories of Holland and Super.
- Explain the purpose of career management.
- Define the term 'career anchor' and discuss the various anchors.
- Describe the various career patterns.
- Describe the various kinds of plateaued performer.
- Discuss possible solutions to career plateauing.
- Define 'obsolescence'.
- Name certain actions that can be taken by organisations to prevent obsolescence.
- Describe the different forms of career movement.
- Define 'job loss' and explain how employees who have lost their jobs can be assisted.
- Define a 'working couple' and explain its effect on the career movement of one or both members of the couple.
- Discuss career management in the public sector.

10.1 Introduction

Public officials worldwide face an ever-changing milieu. The environment in which they function has become increasingly complex, bringing varied and growing challenges in service delivery. One of these challenges is the growing pressure on public institutions to be flexible and to render more and better services with fewer, but multi-skilled, staff members. Globally, the structures of public institutions have become flatter. They increasingly use self-directed work teams, and they have become more knowledge based. These changes have wide-ranging implications for careers, such as the following:
- Careers are becoming more cyclical and lateral rather than upward in structure (Hall & Mervis 1995: 333);

- Individuals take ownership of their careers, while the organisation plays a supportive role (Hall & Mervis 1995: 334);
- Continuous learning and development are essential in order to live up to the new expectations (Schein 1993: 54);
- New kinds of employment relationship are emerging as more people are becoming freelance providers of skills and services (Rousseau & Wade-Benzoni 1995);
- Employability rather than employment becomes a source of security (Kanter 1990: 322); and
- Career development is becoming more holistic in its focus.

In the light of the above, the individual is expected to take control of his or her career, while the institution plays more of a supportive role in this self-management process. Information about opportunities in the public service and the provision of techniques to facilitate the career planning process are two important sources of assistance in this process.

10.2   Career concepts

An indication of the changes currently taking place in institutions is that, according to Hall & Mervis (1995), careers should become more 'protean', which means having the capacity to change and adapt. The term 'protean' derives from the name of the Greek god Proteus who could change shape at will (Hall & Mervis 1995: 322). Besides the concept of the protean career, there are also other relevant concepts to take note of, namely career development, career planning, and career management.

- A protean career is defined as 'a process which the person, not the organisation, is managing. It consists of all the person's varied experiences in education, training, work in several organisations, changes in occupational field and so forth. The protean career is not what happens to the person in any one organisation. In short, the protean career is shaped more by the individual than by the organisation and may be redirected from time to time to meet the needs of the person' (Hall & Mervis 1995: 332).
- Career development can be defined as an 'ongoing process by which individuals progress through a series of stages, each of which is characterised by a relatively unique set of issues, themes or tasks' (Greenhaus, Callanan, and Goldshalk 2000: 13).
- Career planning is described as 'the process by which employees obtain knowledge about themselves (their values, personality, preferences, interests, abilities, etc.) and information about the working environment, and then make an effort to achieve a proper match' (Schreuder & Theron 2001: 21).
- Career management is described as follows by Greenhaus, Callanan, and Goldshalk (2000): '[An] ongoing process in which an individual (1) gathers relevant information about himself or herself and the world of work develops an accurate picture of his or her talents, interests, values and preferred lifestyle; as well as alternative occupations, jobs and organisations develops realistic career goals based on this information and picture

▷

develops and implements a strategy designed to achieve the goals and obtains feedback regarding the effectiveness of the strategy and the relevance of the goals.'
- Career management can also be defined as 'the process that plans and shapes the progression of individuals within an organisation in accordance with the organisational needs and objectives, employees' performance potential and their preferences (that is, the integration of the individual's objectives with those of the organisation)' (Republic of South Africa, 2000: 6).

10.3   Career choices

A discussion of career choice cannot take place without considering the context of the individual's preferences, orientation, and aspirations, as well as the context of economic conditions and sociological factors such as family and education (Schreuder & Theron 2001: 37). Over the last fifty years, many different theories of career choice have been formulated to explain how individuals choose careers. These theories can be divided into the so-called content theories – which describe career choice in terms of specific factors, such as individual characteristics or the psychological phenomena that are involved in choice – and the so-called process theories, which describe career choice as a dynamic process that evolves over stages of development (Schreuder & Theron 2001). Career choice may be better understood with the help of two theories, namely Super's process theory and Holland's content theory.

DID YOU KNOW?   ?

The concept *work volition* refers to 'an individual's ability to freely make career choices, including the initial job choice when first entering the work world and any subsequent career decisions' (Duffy & Dik 2009: 30).

10.3.1   Super's process theory

According to Super, career choice refers to a whole series of related decisions that are made during a development process covering five life stages from childhood to old age. The following career stages are identified (Super 1992):
- **Growth** (birth to puberty, from 0 to about 14 years): Although, during childhood, careers have not yet become a relevant factor, it is now generally believed that the instinct of curiosity makes children explore their environment, all the while gathering information, particularly through contact with adults whom they adopt as role models. During this time, they ought to develop certain concepts of their future roles as adults, their autonomy, self-esteem, a perspective on the future, and a feeling of being in charge of their lives. Once they have developed interests through fantasy, experience, and feedback, they are able to plan for the future. As they gradually become aware of the opportunities that life offers them, their interests become more closely linked to reality.

- **Exploration** (adolescence, from about 14 to 25 years): While the only type of systematic exploration during this stage is provided by schools and other organisations, an adolescent's social exploration is stimulated by his or her parents and peer group. This may lead to the first tentative attempts at career exploration, which later become more focused. If, however, an adult has set an adolescent career goal, his or her career exploration may be too narrowly focused, which may lead to unhappiness and frustration later in life.
- **Establishment** (early adulthood, from about 25 to 45 years): As early adulthood is reached, some individuals stabilise as far as their career exploration is concerned, while others continue to change careers, their field of activity, and their level of employment throughout their lives. It has been found, however, that children of well-educated parents tend to be well-educated themselves and to be employed at higher levels than the children of people with a low level of education. Young adults also tend to pass through a stage of trying out various careers in their late twenties, followed by stabilisation in their thirties and early forties. This is followed by a period of consolidation and advancement, without which the individual usually becomes frustrated, causing him or her either to stagnate in a career or to change careers.
- **Maintenance** (middle age, from about 45 to 65 years): Those adults who have previously stabilised in a career now attempt to maintain their position in the workplace in the face of competition from younger people whose more up-to-date training may pose a threat to the career advancement of their older counterparts. Those who fail to advance tend to stagnate and become disillusioned. They now avoid opportunities to learn new skills, and they develop a passive approach to their work instead of actively acquiring and applying new knowledge. The more motivated keep up to date in their career fields, while the innovators are constantly exploring new avenues.
- **Decline** (old age, from about 65 years onwards): As people age, they often grow to resent their physical and mental decline and the implications that this has for their future. In fact, the process of decline already begins around the age of 25. This is particularly apparent in physically oriented careers, as in sports. As older people become aware of their declining powers, they tend to slow down, sometimes disengaging themselves from some areas of life. Others continue to work long past retirement age. Indeed, for many people, retirement is a negative experience, while, for some, it means a wealth of new opportunities, flexibility, a feeling of being wanted, and the excitement of returning to the explorative stage.

10.3.2 Holland's theory

One of the most widely used approaches to guide career choices is the theory of John L Holland. According to Holland (1973), personality (including values, driving forces, and needs) is an important determinant of career choice. Holland (1973) says that the choice of career is in fact an expression of personality. He states that there is an interaction between personality and the environment, so that individuals are drawn towards environments which correlate with their personal orientation. Holland found it necessary to categorise people according to their personality types, and to associate these personality types with specific environmental models. He identified six basic personality types, and, according to him, each person shows a degree of similarity to one of these types. The greater the degree of similarity, the more an individual will exhibit behaviour patterns typical of a certain personality type. With regard to the environmental models, he distinguishes between six similar types, and, by integrating the individual and the environment, conclusions can be made regarding career choice, career stability, career performance, personal capabilities, and social behaviour. Holland (1973) based his theory on four primary points of departure:

- In our culture, most people can be categorised as one of six types: realistic, investigative, social, conventional, enterprising and artistic. Each type is established through a unique interaction between various socio-cultural, personal and physical environmental factors. Each individual belongs primarily to one of these personality types, but may also exhibit characteristics of the other types. In this way, a profile is derived which could indicate that individual's personality pattern.
- There are six corresponding environmental types: realistic, investigative, social, conventional, enterprising and artistic. In each environment, there are individuals of similar personality type. Each environment also has certain limitations, and individuals of the same personality type group together according to the same environmental models.
- People seek out environments which will allow them to practise their capabilities and abilities, to express their attitudes and values, and to accept problems and roles. This pursuit takes place in various ways, and has the result that a realistic person will, for example, find the biggest potential for self-expression in a realistic environment, and the social person in a social environment.
- A person's behaviour is determined by the interaction between a personality and an environment. Being aware of an individual's personality pattern and the type of environment he or she prefers could facilitate a prediction with regard to career choice, career stability, career performance, and educational and social behaviour.

10.3.2.1 Personality types

Holland (1973: 14–17) describes the characteristics of the personality types as follows.

- The **realistic personality type** develops a preference for the clear and orderly manipulation of aspects such as tools, machinery, and animals, through which mechanical, electrical, technical, and manual skills, for instance, could be acquired. This personality type prefers realistic careers, such as craftsman, farmer, and so forth, and avoids socially oriented careers such as barman, social worker, etc. This person values concrete things, such as money, and personal characteristics such as status and power.
- The **investigative personality type** develops a preference for the observation and creative investigation of physical, biological, and cultural phenomena, with the

aim of understanding and controlling these phenomena. This personality type prefers investigative careers in such fields as economics, engineering, psychology, veterinary science, computer programming, tool making, and so forth, and avoids situations of an enterprising nature. This person regards himself or herself as learned and has a high regard for scientific knowledge.

- The **social personality type** develops a pattern of behaviour preferences which includes the manipulation of people by means of activities such as training and assistance. This type of person usually prefers socially oriented careers, such as social worker, teacher, and so forth, and avoids realistic careers, such as mechanical engineer, plumber, etc. This person regards himself or herself as being well equipped to help other people, to understand and to educate them, and he or she also places a high priority on social and ethical matters.

- The **conventional personality type** displays a pattern of preference for orderly, systematic jobs, such as keeping records, filing, and so forth, through which clerical and accountancy skills, for example, are acquired. This type of person prefers conventional careers such as record keeper and typist and avoids careers in the arts such as photographer, musician, etc. This individual sees himself or herself as conforming and orderly and as having clerical and numerical skills, and has a high regard for business and economic achievements.

- The **enterprising personality type** develops a pattern of preference for activities which entail the manipulation of people in the pursuit of organisational objectives or economic advantages, through which leadership and interpersonal and persuasive skills are acquired. This type of person prefers careers and situations which demand an enterprising nature, such as banker, estate agent, and so forth, and avoids careers requiring analytical skills such as economist, actuary, etc. This personality type regards himself or herself as aggressive, popular, full of self-confidence, and blessed with leadership and communicative skills, and has a high regard for economic achievements.

- The **artistic personality type** develops a pattern of preference for free, unsystematised activities which involve the manipulation of human, physical, and verbal material, and the acquisition of skills in the fields of language, art, music, drama, and writing. This type of person prefers a career in the arts such as language teacher, dramatist, etc., and avoids conventional activities such as typist, accountant, and so forth. This individual regards himself or herself as creative, nonconforming, independent, organised, and blessed with artistic and verbal skills such as writing, communicating, and acting, and has a high regard for the aesthetic.

10.3.2.2 Environmental types

Holland (1973: 29–33) describes the characteristics of the six corresponding environmental types as follows:

- The **realistic environment** is characterised by the domination of environmental demands and opportunities involving the orderly and systematic use of tools, machinery and animals, and is also marked by a population consisting mainly of realistic personality types.

- The **investigative environment** has dominant characteristics such as the observation and the symbolical, systematic, and creative investigation of physical, biological or cultural phenomena.
- The **social environment** is distinguished by a population consisting mainly of social personality types.
- The **conventional environment** is characterised by the dominance of environmental demands and opportunities involving the orderly and systematic manipulation of data, such as record keeping, filing, reproducing documents, compiling data according to a prescribed plan, and working with business machines and data processors. This environment is dominated by conventional personality types.
- The **enterprising environment** is characterised by demands and opportunities from the environment regarding the manipulation of other persons in order to achieve personal or organisational goals, and is also marked by the presence of especially enterprising personality types.
- The **artistic environment** is dominated by demands and opportunities including ambiguous, free and unsystematised activities and skills to create art and art products, and consists mainly of a population of artistic personality types.

When an individual is faced with a career choice, his or her characteristics are compared with the above-mentioned types, with the aim of determining with which type he or she displays the most similarities. A person's personality type is the primary determinant of career choice, in that an enterprising type, for example, would most probably select an enterprising career. The first and second sub-personality types will determine the individual's second and third choices. The vocational guidance tutor who works according to this approach will concentrate on determining the individual's personality style and on the selection of a suitable career environment.

10.3.2.3 Environmental influences on career choice

Thus far we have only discussed individual differences which influence career choice. There are, however, also a number of environmental influences which play a role in career choice. These are described as non-psychological factors (Crites 1969: 79).

The family undoubtedly plays an important role in career choice, as, even at an early age, children identify with their parents and often prefer the careers which their parents hold in high esteem. It is often believed that the family, through its economic interests, affiliations, and values, determines the careers of family members. A South African study by Van Rooyen (1969: 180) indicated that the higher the career structure and educational level of the parents, the higher the aspirations of their children. Hall (1976: 22) asserts that the background and attitudes of the parents have a greater influence than those of friends, teachers, and other influential people in society. According to Crites (1969: 88), the school, second to the family, exerts the biggest influence on career choice.

Sometimes an individual finds himself or herself in a career which he or she did not purposefully pursue, but is appointed in a position due to coincidence and unplanned, unforeseeable circumstances. These are normally referred to as the chance factors which influence a person's career choice (accident theory) (Crites 1969: 79).

 FOCUS ON RESEARCH 10.1
External influences that affect career decision-making

In a study on external influences that affect career decision making, it has been found that family expectations and needs, life circumstances, spiritual and religious factors, and social service motivation can be considered as constraints or motivators, depending on the particulars of the situation of circumstance (Duffy & Dik 2009: 39).

10.4   The purpose of career management

The theories on career choices discussed above focus primarily on the choices made by the individual. Career management, on the other hand, focuses mainly on the actions of employing institutions. Career management programmes usually incorporate a large number of human resource practices aiming at assisting employees to improve their performance, clarifying available career options, and aligning the aspirations of employees with organisational objectives (Republic of South Africa 2000: 6).

Career management programmes are developed by employers to involve employees in setting their own goals and recognising their strengths and weaknesses. They assist employees with the identification of skills and other qualities required for current and future jobs. Furthermore, they seek to improve the matching of jobs with the right employees. Why would employers bother with career management practices such as the rotating and transferring of employees? The obvious answer is mainly to improve their institution's effectiveness (Republic of South Africa 2000: 6–7).

 DID YOU KNOW?

The word *career* can be used as different concepts (meanings). When the word *career* is used as a qualifier (career choice or career decision-making) it means 'any process related to work or working'. But when it is used as a noun (the course of an individual's career), it means 'a series of paid or unpaid occupations a person holds throughout his or her life' (Duffy & Dik 2009: 31).

10.5   Career anchors

Career anchors are developed during the early stages of an individual's career, that is, during the establishment and achievement stages. Nevertheless, it is quite possible for an individual only to become aware of his or her career anchors much later.

What is a career anchor? Although a new employee may be appointed to a position for which he or she has been trained, this does not mean that he or she will be able to meet the present and future requirements of his or her job and potential career. New employees will not know whether they will like the new work or whether their values will fit those of the organisation. During the initial period of employment, the organisation and employees get to know each other. This allows individuals to acquire more information about the career they have embarked on. New employees gradually gain more knowledge about themselves and develop a clearer self-concept. This self-concept comprises the following three components, which, according to Schein (1978), together form employees' career anchors. Schein (1978: 125) describes a career anchor as follows:

- Self-perceived talents and abilities based on actual successes in many work settings;
- Self-perceived motives based on opportunities for self-testing and self-diagnoses in real situations and on feedback from others; and
- Self-perceived values based on actual encounters between self and the norms and values of the employing organisation and work setting.

According to Schein (1978, 1990), a career anchor consists of the individual's talents, motives and values, as perceived by themselves, which the individual uses to delimit motives and stabilise their career. If an employee is not aware of their career anchor, they could land up in a work situation in which they lack job satisfaction. As an individual is likely to make job selections that are consistent with their self-image, career anchors can serve as a basis for career choices (Schein 1990).

Is there more than one type of career anchor? Schein (1990: 58–60) identifies eight career anchors, which we shall examine in the following sub-sections.

10.5.1 Technical/functional competence

Employees for whom technical/functional competence is a career anchor attempt to find ways in which they can use skills to improve their competence. They are self-confident and enjoy challenges. Such employees are usually competent leaders in their own fields of specialisation, but tend to avoid general management because this usually involves leaving their field of expertise. As the working environment becomes increasingly technologically complex, the need for technical/functional expertise will grow. However, the rapid advances in technological development means that such experts must constantly keep up to date and abreast of the progress being made in their particular fields (Schein 1996: 83).

10.5.2 Managerial competence

Employees for whom general managerial competence is a career anchor like to coordinate the activities of other employees and want to be seen to be making a positive contribution to the success of the organisation or department for which they work. A person with this type of anchor is compelled to be a manager as he or she must give expression to interpersonal skills (influencing and controlling people), analytical skills (identifying and solving problems in uncertain situations), and emotional stability (stimulation by emotional and interpersonal crises, rather than experiencing them as tiresome). Schein (1996) foresees that the need for general management will increase and will permeate the lower levels of organisations. Greater co-ordination and integration at lower levels will be required as work becomes more technically complex.

10.5.3 Autonomy/independence

Employees for whom autonomy/independence is a career anchor like to carry out their work in their own way. They enjoy variety and flexibility, but are unsuited to strictly regulated jobs or jobs that require them to exercise control over others. If forced into such positions, they may well decide to start a business of their own. As the working environment is changing rapidly, such employees often find the world an easier place to negotiate. Schein (1996: 820) puts it as follows: 'The autonomy anchored is aligned, at least for the present, with most organisational policies of promising only employability.' Self-reliance, which is important for future career survival, is already inherent in these employees, and they may become the role models for others in future (Schein 1996).

10.5.4 Security/stability

Employees for whom security/stability is a career anchor consider both financial and job security to be important. They like to settle at a company and are prepared to employ their skills in any manner required of them. If such an employee changes from one organisation to another, he or she always chooses a similar type of organisation and a similar type of work. At present, these employees are experiencing the most severe problems due to the current shift from 'employment security' to 'employability security' which is taking place in organisations. This means that employees can only expect from employers the opportunity to learn and they should become dependent on themselves (Schein 1996).

10.5.5 Entrepreneurial creativity

Employees for whom entrepreneurial creativity is a career anchor would jump at the opportunity of creating a business of their own. They want to show the world that they can create a business that is the result of their own efforts. These people often work for a company initially to gain the experience that they need in order to go out on their own. Current developments in the working environment are convincing more and more people that they can develop their own business. The opportunities for people who are anchored in entrepreneurial creativity will probably be greatly increased in future.

10.5.6   Lifestyle

Employees for whom lifestyle is a career anchor like to find a compromise between their personal needs, family needs, and the requirements of their career. Schein (1990: 60) explains this as follows: 'You want to make all of the major sectors of your life work together toward an integrated whole and you therefore need a career situation that provides enough flexibility to achieve such integration.' Sometimes such employees have to sacrifice certain aspects of their careers (for example, they are often reluctant to accept transfer to another city or country). They define success in broader terms than simply career success, and their identity is more dependent on the way in which they live their total life. Schein (1996: 82) states that, since his original research of the 1960s and 1970s, this anchor has shown the most change. As social values are moving towards more autonomy and concern for self, people are becoming more preoccupied with lifestyle. Just as in the United States, the current trend in South Africa is for executives to shift from the technical/functional or general management category or career anchor to the lifestyle career anchor.

10.5.7   Sense of service/dedication to a cause

Employees for whom service/dedication is a career anchor are always prepared to do something to improve life in general, whether to upgrade the state of the environment, or to promote peace, for example. These employees may even change employers in order to carry on doing this kind of job, and do not accept any promotion unless the new position meets the requirements of their value system. Schein (1996: 85) reports that the number of people with this anchor is increasing. He states that not only young people but people of middle age are expressing this need to do something meaningful in a larger context.

10.5.8   Challenge

Employees for whom pure challenge is a career anchor enjoy undertaking difficult tasks and solving complex problems. They never choose the easy way out of a problem and like to 'achieve the impossible'. They tend to grow bored quickly when the job holds no challenge for them. Schein (1996: 85) is of the opinion that the number of people with this career anchor is growing. However, he is uncertain whether this is the result of more people with this predisposition entering the labour market or the result of an adaptation to the present-day changing and challenging working environment.

10.6   Career patterns

Just as career success and advancement can indicate whether or not an individual's career is oriented around a specific career anchor (Schein 1993), so too can these factors be indicative of the career patterns that individuals follow (Brousseau 1990).

For some, success may mean promotion, and for some it is recognition in a field of expertise, while others seek to live a life of social contribution or to move frequently from one challenge to another. Driver (1979) has developed a model which suggests that individuals possess unique views about the way in which their careers should develop. This model can be used to identify an individual's preferred career pattern and also to provide a basis for career decisions. The following four career patterns describe different types of career and provide a means of describing the ideal career. Each career pattern is based on underlying motives (Brousseau 1990).

10.6.1 The linear career pattern

Employees who prefer a linear career pattern like to progress within the organisational hierarchy and be rewarded with promotion and instant recognition, as well as with financial rewards such as high salaries, perks and incentive schemes. They are usually in managerial positions and hold power, achievement, status and money in high regard.

10.6.2 The expert career pattern

These employees work within their chosen career field for their entire careers. They identify themselves with their fields of expertise, and aspects such as expertise, security, and stability are strongly correlated with this pattern. Their emphasis is on the acquisition of special skills. Examples of this career pattern are medical practitioners, engineers, and lawyers. These people prefer to be rewarded by speciality assignments and skills training. They prefer recognition for their expertise in a specific field.

10.6.3 The spiral career pattern

Employees who prefer a spiral career pattern tend to change their career fields periodically. These changes are major and entail a change from one field to another, thus allowing them to acquire new skills and capabilities while using their previous experience. Motives such as self-development and creativity are highly regarded by the spiral career person.

10.6.4 The transitory career pattern

Employees with a transitory career pattern tend to change career fields every two to four years. This pattern has been referred to as a 'consistent pattern of inconsistency'. They are independent and like variety in life. Their most favoured rewards are immediate financial rewards, flexible working hours, job rotation and autonomy.

10.7 Career plateaux

Career plateauing happens to just about everyone in the course of a career. It is 'the point in a person's career when there is no longer any opportunity to progress in the organisational hierarchy' (Leibowitz, Kaye, & Farren 1990: 28).

A distinction can be made between structural and content plateauing. Structural plateauing refers to a situation in which opportunities for promotion are restricted by the structure (pyramid) of the organisation. Only a few employees can make it to the top. Content plateauing occurs when an employee knows the job too well and no challenges are left. The challenge for managers is at least to address the problems of content plateauing, as it is the easier one to avoid (Leibowitz *et al.* 1990: 28).

10.7.1 Plateaued performers

Four kinds of plateaued performer are identified by Leibowitz *et al.* (1990: 30), namely productively plateaued, partially plateaued, passively plateaued and pleasantly plateaued.

- **Productively plateaued:** These employees experience job satisfaction because they feel that they have achieved their ambitions. They are loyal to the organisation because they feel that the organisation supports them in achieving their personal goals, and recognises their contributions. They are productive high performers, but occasionally require motivation.
- **Partially plateaued:** Employees who are partially plateaued feel that the organisation does not do much for them, but they usually have an interest that maintains job involvement. These people are usually specialists in a certain field, but feel that their jobs lack excitement and that their organisation does not support them enough in acquiring new skills. They value any opportunity to acquire new skills.
- **Passively plateaued:** Employees who are passively plateaued feel that they have been in their jobs for too long and know them too well. They lack challenge and display no interest in additional training in their fields. However, they also feel unable to change their situations.
- **Pleasantly plateaued:** These employees who are pleasantly plateaued do not aim for promotion and change, but prefer to remain where they are. They are unlikely to be innovative, and usually stay with one organisation.

10.7.2 Dealing with plateauing

Certain actions can be taken to address the problem of plateauing. The following are possible solutions (Allen, Poteet, Russel, & Dobbins 1995: 15–18; Leibowitz *et al.* 1990: 32):

- Change the structure of the organisation.
- Pay for performance.
- Set up job rotation programmes to create lateral movement and broaden skills.
- Give candid feedback.
- Establish a career plan and goals.
- Provide individual career planning opportunities (for example, career planning workshops and self-assessment of skills).
- Encourage career exploration.
- Encourage further education.

10.8 Obsolescence

Obsolescence refers to the extent to which employees lack the up-to-date competencies necessary to maintain successful performance in either their current or future work roles. This simply means that an individual is becoming outmoded and outdated.

How does one deal with worker obsolescence? Worker obsolescence illustrates the continuous process in which the balance between the employee and the job is upset, either by technological factors such as computerisation or by organisational factors such as restructuring, or even by an action on the part of the employee. Once the balance has been upset, symptoms such as frustration, hostility, or resistance to change may result. Once the symptoms have been identified, treatment in the form of training courses, organisational changes, or career counselling may follow to restore the balance between the worker and the job, until the cycle is repeated (Bracker & Pearson 1986).

A paradigm shift by managers and employees from once-off learning to lifelong learning is probably the most sustainable solution to this challenge (Wessels 2000: 315). This shift implies that individual employees should start taking responsibility for their own learning by adopting a learning approach to life, drawing on a wide range of resources to enable them to support their lifestyle practices. Public officials need to refresh and supplement their knowledge on a regular basis in order to meet the challenge of a constantly changing work and world environment.

Managers can take certain actions to prevent worker obsolescence and to reduce feelings of obsolescence. These include the following:

- Providing training and education;
- Encouraging continuous learning;
- Providing challenging initial work;
- Encouraging people to attend conferences and to subscribe to professional journals;
- Stimulating employees to stay up to date with new techniques; and
- Creating a culture of growth and development.

10.9 Career movements

Careers, by their very nature, are not static. As mentioned in Section 10.2, the concept of the 'protean career' illustrates the changing inherent nature of careers. There can be various reasons for career moves by individuals, both within and outside a particular organisation. Employee dissatisfaction may cause a career move – and such dissatisfaction may arise from various factors such as technological and work design changes, changing employee values, attitudes, or objectives, career plateaus, behavioural issues (such as interpersonal dynamics between employees), or work performance-related problems.

Career movements within organisations usually take on the form of lateral, vertical or even diagonal moves within the organisational structure. Typical lateral movements are transfers. When an employee is transferred it is a horizontal move from one job to another – at a similar job level, with similar level duties, responsibilities, status, and remuneration.

10.9.1 Lateral career movement

Transfers are often accompanied by such aspects as re-skilling (when an employee's new job is in a different field that requires some different competencies) or geographical relocation (especially in the case of large organisations with geographically dispersed units). With organisational structures becoming flatter, it is becoming more and more common for employees to make such lateral career moves.

10.9.2 Vertical career movement

Vertical career movement within an organisation usually takes the form of demotion or promotion. Moving into a job of a higher level is known as promotion. Promotions typically entail such aspects as higher level responsibilities, more complex work, greater competency demands, and better remuneration. In South Africa, promotion has been and will increasingly be a contentious issue, due to such factors as employment equity, affirmative action, and the concept of merit.

Because promotion decisions are traditionally based on such factors as work performance history and 'meritorious work-related grounds', and because the flatter organisational structure limits promotion opportunities, it is to be expected that promotion decisions will lead to a good deal of debate and even discontent. In the context of employment equity and affirmative action, the following should be kept in mind in the case of promotion decisions within public institutions:

- All employees should be provided with information regarding promotion opportunities.
- The standards that will apply in promotions must be clearly communicated to all employees.
- Unsuccessful candidates must be provided with feedback on the reasons for their failure to be promoted. Furthermore, suggestions must be made regarding ways in which they can supplement deficiencies in their competency profiles (for example, suggesting particular training courses).
- Employees from designated groups must be groomed for promotion.
- All employees must be provided with career paths and with supplementary training, experience, and skills necessary at each stage in their career paths in order to be considered for promotion.
- Promotion decisions must be made on the basis of aspects such as competencies, not merely on paper qualifications, and must also take into consideration prior learning and relevant experience.
- Job specifications must be reassessed to determine whether these are really in line with essential and inherent requirements of the job.
- The use of promotion selection panels that are representative of all important stakeholders (for example, trade union representatives and current and prospective

supervisors) must be considered for making promotion decisions, rather than leaving them in the exclusive domain of managerial prerogative.

- Psychometric testing must be used carefully and only in line with the Employment Equity Act (see also Chapters 6 and 8). This will mean not basing one's decision exclusively on psychometric results, but viewing such valid and reliable test results only as one source of information in the decision-making process. Such tests must also have cross-cultural validity and reliability, and preference should be given to tests that measure potential and competencies rather than constructs that may be unduly influenced by differences in candidates' formal education.
- The organisation's affirmative action programme and goals must be taken into account in the final decision on whom to promote from the list of candidates who satisfy the minimum job specifications.

With regard to the last point, it is suggested that the following guidelines may be considered for adoption as policy regarding promotional issues:

- In 'same merit' situations, 'designated' employees may be promoted over equally qualified white male employees;
- Unqualified 'designated' employees may not be promoted over qualified white male employees; and
- If 'designated' employees are qualified, they may be promoted over better qualified white male employees.

It is important that such decisions should not be made on an ad hoc basis. All such policy guidelines should be formalised and all employees should be well informed of what they are.

Finally, we have to emphasise that it is necessary to reassess the importance of relevant past experience as a consideration in making promotion decisions. If in-organisation experience in a particular job is included in an employer's merit or performance evaluation system, this may taint promotions with discrimination. This form of discrimination is called 'the present effects of past discrimination', and it does not matter that the actual discriminatory practices which precluded protected group members from acquiring the requisite experience took place prior to the enactment of discriminatory legislation. Now that prospective employees are protected against discrimination by our legislation, organisations that have experience requirements may be exposing themselves to unfair labour practice (discriminatory promotion) claims. For instance, employees who were previously barred from certain jobs by job reservation or organisational policy, or who have been appointed as temporary employees for indefinite periods for which they have received no seniority recognition, may claim that they are being unfairly discriminated against and file a dispute. The employer's defence in such cases will have to be based on the 'inherent requirements of the job' rationale (that is, that the prescribed experience is absolutely essential for the job in question).

Demotion is basically a downward career move within an organisation. This is typically when an employee is put into a lower level job, with fewer responsibilities, lower status, and fewer competency requirements. It is indeed very rare that an employee would prefer and initiate a demotion. This may perhaps happen when an employee has realistic career views and realises that he or she was maybe promoted to a level beyond his or her capability or potential to acquire the ability (known as the Peters principle). However, demotion may under certain circumstances be the only real option to an employee, and this usually comes about through an employer-focused decision. For instance, it may be that, due to organisational restructuring, a certain position becomes redundant and no similar level positions are vacant within the organisation. The employee may then be afforded the opportunity to choose between being laid off (see Chapter 17) or accepting a lower level position within the organisation. With the scarcity of work in the form of formal job opportunities in South Africa, the chances are that opting for a demotion may be more viable than normally expected. Alternatively, a situation may arise due to employee misconduct or poor work performance, when the only option short of dismissal may be for the employee to agree to be demoted.

It is important to note, however, that an employee may in general not be demoted by a unilateral decision by the employer. Demotion has to be a voluntary acceptance by the employee in question. It should also be noted that demotion need not always be accompanied by an immediate reduction in employee remuneration and benefits. In particular, it is advisable that, should demotion become the only alternative to a no-fault termination of the employment relationship (as in the case of retrenchment), an attempt should be made to keep the remuneration and benefits at existing levels for as long as is practically possible. In any event, it should also be remembered that any downward career move, in particular if it is caused by no fault on the employee's part, involves certain delicate dynamics (such as psychological adjustment) that have to be managed properly.

10.9.3 Diagonal career movement

Diagonal career movement refers to the movement of employees not only up or down the career ladder but also across disciplines. An example is the case where an employee who used to be an operations/production manager is promoted to a senior financial manager position within the organisation.

10.9.4 Horizontal career movement

Outward career movement generally refers to the situation in which a person's career change entails moving outside the public service. This generally entails employee separation – in other words, when the paths of an employee and his or her employing organisation separate. This may be the case, for instance, when an employee decides to resign or go on early retirement. However, this may also happen involuntarily – as in the case of 'job loss'.

Job loss may be defined as any involuntary separation from an organisation's workforce. It can occur at any career stage, but if it happens during the later stages it could be more traumatic.

It is well known that an individual's emotional well-being can be most adversely affected by the loss of a job. It is even more traumatic if any of the following conditions are present (McKnight 1991):

- If it appears unlikely that the individual will find alternative employment;
- If the individual lacks multiple skills;
- If the individual has worked for only one employer; and
- If the employee perceives himself or herself to be unemployable.

Job loss can be caused by a multitude of factors, including organisational restructuring efforts such as downsizing, rightsizing, re-engineering, and the outsourcing of certain organisational functions. As Stevenson (1998: 40) says:

> Not a week goes by without one of the national newspapers reporting on South African companies downsizing, restructuring or laying off staff. Reasons put forward include re-emergence of international competition, affirmative action, the lack of growth in the economy or, as more frequently appears to be the case, mergers, acquisitions and buy-outs.

He then goes on to illustrate the importance of such aspects as career transition counselling and outplacement when job loss occurs:

> [Although] an employer's responsibility is primarily to those who remain, it would be wrong of them to ignore those who must go. It is most definitely in the employer's interest to help the leavers retain their self-esteem and dignity, and to assist them in establishing themselves on a new career path (Stevenson 1998: 43).

Such an approach will fit in well with the more holistic approach to career development proposed by Boden (1998: 24–25):

> The recent economic decline has contributed to a renaissance of career support activities by employers. [...] Instead of creating loyalty which, by association, implies longevity in the partnership between employer and employee, staff need to become more entrepreneurial, committed to lifelong learning. [...] Career development is about work and life balance and therefore life management.

From the above, it should be quite clear that, due to all the changes in organisational environments, career movements and the management and development of careers require a much more holistic and flexible approach in which employability, rather than employment, becomes the focus and anchor.

Managers can thus take a number of steps, such as the following, to assist people who have lost their jobs due to reasons beyond their control:

- Introduce training programmes which teach workers who have been laid off how to manage stress and take control of the future.
- Help people to overcome the initial shock of job loss and provide advice on career moves (professionals can be used in this regard).
- Give them entrepreneurial and small/own business management skills.

10.10 The effect of working couples and work-family conflict on career movements

- A working couple can be defined as 'any two people in an ongoing, committed relationship, where both partners work, where there may or may not be children, and where decisions (family and work) are influenced by the working situation of each partner' (Guterman 1991: 169).
- Working couples are more likely to experience work-family conflict than couples in which only one partner works.
- Work-family conflict can be defined as 'a form of inter-role conflict in which the role pressures from the work and family domains are mutually incompatible in some respect' (Greenhaus & Beutell 1985: 77).

Three types of work-family conflict have been identified (Greenhaus & Beutell 1985: 88):

- **Time-based conflict** develops when time that is devoted to one role cannot be devoted to another. Time-based conflict would occur when time pressures in one role make it impossible to satisfy the expectations of the other role. Inflexible work schedules, excessive overtime, and work involvement can be related to work-family conflict.
- **Strain-based conflict** occurs when performance in one role is adversely affected by the stress that is experienced in another. For example, a crisis in the family can cause fatigue, which results in poor performance at work.
- **Behaviour-based conflict** occurs when certain patterns of role behaviour are in conflict with expectations of behaviour in other roles. For example, a male manager is expected to be self-reliant, emotionally stable, and somewhat aggressive, while the manager's family expects him to be warm and caring.

Conflict between work and family roles can, for instance, be created by the following work-related factors:

- Number of hours worked;
- Lack of control over the decision to work overtime;
- An inflexible work schedule;
- Irregular starting time; and
- Psychologically demanding work.

On the basis of current research, Schreuder and Theron (1997: 152) suggest the following action to balance family and work needs:

- More organisational sensitivity for home life;
- The introduction of flexible benefits to assist employees with family needs such as child care and the care of sick children;
- The introduction of flexible work hours and work-at-home programmes;
- The revision of relocation policies to make provision for the needs of the modern worker; and
- The introduction of alternative career paths – not all employees want to climb the corporate ladder.

The diversity of today's workforce underscores the need for flexible policies to accommodate the personal responsibilities, aspirations, and needs of employees.

10.11 Career management in the public service

The South African Public Service Commission reported in 2000 that career management programmes had been implemented in only three national departments out of the 26 national departments and eight provincial administrations that were investigated by the Commission. These three departments are the South African National Defence Force (SANDF), the South African Police Service (SAPS), and the Department of Public Works (Republic of South Africa 2000: 10). Since then, the Gauteng provincial government has commenced with the development of a career management programme. In analysing these programmes, it is necessary to determine who the various role players are, what the major elements of the programmes are, and which practices support the programmes.

10.11.1 Role players

An analysis of the programmes of public institutions shows that the role players involved in the development of the career management programmes differ among the various institutions. For example, the human resources components were responsible for the career management programmes in the SANDF and the SAPS, while this responsibility was vested in the training component of the Department of Public Works. These role players, in turn, consulted other role players, such as:

- Line managers, including senior management;
- Line functionaries;
- Employee organisations (where departmental bargaining chambers existed);
- Educational institutions;
- Other departments (for example, the DPSA and the Department of Labour);
- The private sector (in the case of the SANDF); and
- International training and development organisations (in the case of the SANDF).

10.11.2   Elements of career management programmes

Although many public institutions worldwide develop and implement career management programmes, it is commonly accepted that these programmes differ in various respects. However, Baron and Greenberg (1990: 320) identify a few characteristics that have been shown to be typical to most of these programmes. These general characteristics are as follows:

- Helping employees to assess their own career strengths and weaknesses;
- Setting priorities and specific career goals;
- Providing information on various career paths and alternatives within the organisation; and
- Offering employees yearly reviews of their progress towards these goals by managers who have received training in conducting such assessments.

The South African Public Service Commission suggests the following process for the public service (Republic of South Africa 2000: 36–38):

- Assessment of an employee's performance;
- Discussion between employee and supervisor about employee's performance;
- Identification of needs for development;
- Determination and assessment of the career goals of the employee;
- Identification of attainable career goals;
- Indication of employer's expectations and needs by means of an organisational needs audit;
- Agreement on possible career paths for employee within the institution;
- Identification of employee's needs for career development;
- Development of a personal career development plan for each employee; and
- Consideration of the effect of rotation of staff on addressing requirements regarding specific work fields.

In order to assist employees and their supervisors to go through the process of career planning and career management, the Public Service Commission suggests the application of a pro-forma instrument. It is suggested by the Commission that this instrument be amended by individual institutions to comply with the unique circumstances that apply to departments and provincial administrations. Separate instruments can also be used for different occupations. However, a characteristic of highly specialised occupations (such as engineers and medical doctors) might allow limited scope for progression within the public service outside the defined field of specialisation (Republic of South Africa 2000: 38–39).

10.11.3   Practices that support career management programmes

A career management programme in a public institution is part of the broader human resource management system. It is thus supported by other practices, such as performance management (see Chapter 9), institutional skills audit (see Chapter 11), training (see Chapter 11), and affirmative action (see Chapter 6).

10.11.3.1   Performance management

It makes sense to synchronise activities relating to career planning with feedback on performance. An employee's performance in his or her current position has a deciding impact on management's perceptions regarding his or her potential for further progression. In fact, one can argue that sustained high-quality performance is the key to an employee's aspirations for higher positions. It is therefore necessary to determine the requirements for an employee to improve his or her performance in his or her current position. Proper feedback by management to employees is therefore necessary to enable employees to improve their performance (Republic of South Africa 2000: 39).

10.11.3.2   Institutional skills audit

On the institutional level, it is necessary for the employer to know which competencies (knowledge, skills and values) are needed by the employees in order to meet the challenges of their changing milieu. What competencies are required to equip public officials within their milieu? The White Paper on Public Service Training and Education (Republic of South Africa 1997: Appendix C) suggests at least ten possible public service competencies, which include leadership (including teamwork), thinking skills, communication, and action management. These competencies are not time-, technology-, or knowledge-specific with the risk of becoming obsolete (Wessels 2000: 319).

Consequently, the Public Service Commission suggests in its report on career management in the public service that departments 'should on an annual basis assess their needs in respect of specific skills'. For this purpose, the Commission recommends the conducting of a skills audit by individual departments and provincial administrations (Republic of South Africa 2000: 40). A skills audit implies more than it says, namely an investigation to determine the actual competencies of the current workforce of an institution in order to define the skills gaps and the real skills requirements of the institution. It may happen that specific employees are identified with the necessary competencies to address the skills gaps. The careers of these employees may subsequently be redirected in order to utilise their competencies to the benefit of both the institution and the individuals. In cases where the skills audit shows that particular employees lack certain competencies needed by the institution, learning opportunities should be provided by the employer in order to fill the gap.

10.11.3.3   Training

Due to the size of the public service, it seems not always practical to address the development needs of employees on an individual basis. That is why training interventions are usually identified and scheduled in a coordinated way.

Most public institutions have training components that are responsible for co-ordinating training interventions. In order to support the career management programmes of departments, the training components are usually assigned the duty of developing a career development programme. The Public Service Commission suggests that these programmes 'should take the line functional needs of departments into consideration and could comprise the development of a set of standard courses which employees at different levels and occupations in the department can attend on an annual basis'. It is, however, imperative that the contents of these training interventions be updated continuously to make provision for the changing needs of the particular institution (Republic of South Africa 2000: 39–40).

10.11.3.4 Affirmative action

A public institution's affirmative action programme is supposed to be closely integrated with its career management programme. The two programmes depend on each other for their respective success. A department's career management programme is expected to support the affirmative action objectives of the particular institution. Posts that have been targeted for filling with a view to promoting representativeness should be identified, and all supervisors should be informed accordingly. It is essential that the requirements attached to such posts should be taken into consideration in the career planning of employees of the under-represented population groups. It is also imperative that all these programmes be executed in fairness to all role players in order to prevent a situation in which a court action rules against the particular department (see Spotlight on the Law 10.1, which discusses such a court action).

SPOTLIGHT ON THE LAW 10.1
Court dismisses SAPS case against white cops

The Labour Court ruled against the SA Police Service on Friday in a case involving ten white policemen who were overlooked for promotion because of their race.

Judge Adolf Landman on Friday dismissed with costs an application for leave to appeal by the SAPS against his ruling in November last year that the inspectors, all members of the bomb squad, be promoted to captain. Police spokesman Superintendent Mohabi Tlomatsana said on Friday the judgment would not affect the SAPS' affirmative action programme. Landman found that the SAPS had denied the men promotion for two consecutive years simply because they were white males and because the police had a policy in place to promote only 'designated groups in effect everybody but white males'. According to the 1998 Employment Equity Act, members of designated groups include blacks, coloureds, Indians, all women and any disabled person. The purpose of the law was to change the racial profile of the workplace from white dominated to broadly representative of the country's demographics.

On Thursday, the SAPS attempted to convince the court that it grant the service an appeal which would allow it to dispute the promotions order in the Labour Appeal Court. But on Friday, Landman, in a three-page written judgment, said the police had not convinced him that their grounds for appeal held any merit or that their appeal would succeed before ▷

another court. 'It is not permissible for me to decide the application on any basis other than the grounds upon which the applicants (the police) rely. The result is that I am precluded, by the applicant's grounds for leave to appeal, from sending a matter of undoubted public importance for consideration by a higher court,' Landman ruled. 'In the result the application for condonation and with it the application for leave to appeal, fails and is dismissed with costs,' he told the police legal team, which included its head of legal services, Commissioner Linda Pienaar. Pienaar declined to comment on the case outside court, referring journalists' questions to a spokesman. Tlomatsana said the police would now study the judgment before briefing top management on a suitable course of action.

Two choices remained: The police could promote the men, as ordered, or could petition the Judge President for leave to appeal. They had eight days to do the latter. Counsel for the ten policemen, Sakkie Prinsloo, was exuberant, praising the judgment as 'correct' and 'excellent'. 'Justice was done and was seen to be done,' Prinsloo told Sapa. He also called on the police to now implement the judge's ruling. Two of the policemen were also present for the judgment and were visibly delighted with the outcome.

Source: Soldeer 49 (2003)

10.12 Review

In this chapter, we have examined various factors related to the management of employees' careers, and we have briefly discussed the implications of recent developments taking place in organisations worldwide. We have considered the concept of 'career' as defined within the context of the adaptive organisation: 'The new career is about experience, skill, flexibility and personal development. It does not involve predefined career paths, routine ticket punching, stability or security' (Hall & Mervis 1995: 330).

We have considered a model that depicts career management as an ongoing process whereby the individual develops realistic career goals and a strategy for achieving these goals. The process of career choice has been illustrated by different theories.

Although career management is primarily the responsibility of the individual, the institution has a role to play in helping the individual to make better career decisions. This can be achieved through in-house career workshops, career centres, the provision of career workbooks and counselling.

Career issues such as plateauing, job loss and working couples are the order of the day. We have looked at suggested actions that organisations can take to manage these issues.

Career management in a public service, such as the South African public service, is characterised by its distinct set of role players, tailor-made career management programmes for each public institution, and distinct practices that support these programmes.

10.13   Self-evaluation questions

1. Do individuals have a responsibility to manage their own careers? Explain your answer.
2. How would you describe the employer's responsibility in career management?
3. Would you agree that career choice is a single event which usually occurs in the early twenties? Give reasons for your answer.
4. What is a career anchor? With which anchor do you associate best?
5. How would you utilise the concept of career anchors in career management?
6. Describe briefly what appears to you to be the ideal career.
7. How would you distinguish between a structural and a content career plateau?
8. Define a 'working couple'.
9. Discuss career management in the public service.

Bibliography

Allen, TD, Poteet, ML, Russel, JEA, & Dobbins, GH. 1995. Influence of learning and development factors on perceptions of plateauing. Paper presented at the Tenth Annual Meeting of the Society for Industrial and Organisational Psychology, Orlando, Florida.

Baron, RA, & Greenberg, J. 1990. *Behavior in organizations: Understanding and managing the human side of work.* Boston, MA: Allyn & Bacon.

Boden, A. 1998. Career development: What works and what doesn't? *Management Today,* 14(4), 24–26.

Bracker, JS, & Pearson, JN. 1986. Worker obsolescence: The human resource dilemma of the 80s. *Personnel Administrator,* 31(12), 113.

Brousseau, KR. 1990. Career dynamics in the baby boom and baby bust era. *Journal of Organizational Change Management,* 3(3), 47–58.

Court dismisses SAPS case against white cops. 2003. *Soldeer 49.* [http://www.solidarity.co.za]

Crites, JO. 1969. *Vocational psychology.* New York: McGraw Hill.

Cronbach, LJ. 1970. *Essentials of psychological testing.* New York: Harper & Row.

Dalton, GW, Thompson, PH, & Price, RL. 1986. *Innovations: Strategies for career management.* Glenview, IL: Scott Foresman.

Dessler, G. 1988. *Personnel management.* Englewood Cliffs, NJ: Prentice-Hall.

Driver, JJ. 1979. Career concepts and career management in organisations. In *Behavioral Problems in Organizations,* CL Cooper (ed.), 79–139. Englewood Cliffs, NJ: Prentice-Hall, Inc.

Duffy, RD and Dik, BJ. 2009. Beyond the Self: External Influences in the Career Development Process. The *Career Development Quarterly,* 58(September 2009): 29–43.

Erwee, R. 1991. Accommodating dual-career couples. *IPM Journal,* 9, 29–34.

Feldman, DC. 1988. *Managing careers in organisations.* Boston, MA: Scott Foresman.

Ginzberg, E, Ginsberg, SW, Axelrad, S, & Herman, JL. 1951. *Occupational choice: An approach to a general theory.* New York: Columbia University Press.

Ginzberg, E. 1984. Career development. In D. Brown & L. Brooks (eds.), *Career choice and development.* Washington, DC: Jossey-Bass.

Greenhaus, JH, & Beutell, NJ. 1985. Sources of conflict between work and family roles. *Academy of Management Review,* 10, 77.

Greenhaus, JH, Callanan, GA, & Goldshalk, VM. 2000. *Career management.* 3rd edn. Fort Worth, TX: Dryden.

Guterman, M. 1991. Working couples: Finding a balance between family and career. In JM Kummerow (ed.), *New directions in career planning and the workplace.* Palo Alto, CA: Davies Black.

Gutteridge, TG, Leibowitz, ZB, Shore, JE. 1993. When careers flower, organizations flourish. *Training and Development,* 47(1), 14–29.

Hall, DT. 1976. *Careers in organisations.* Pacific Palisades, CA: Goodyear.

Hall, DT, & Mervis, PH. 1995. Careers as lifelong learning. In A. Howard (ed.), *The changing nature of work.* San Francisco: Jossey Bass.

Harris, TG. 1993. The post-capitalist executive: An interview with Peter F. Drucker. *Harvard Business Review,* May/June, 115–122.

Holland, JL. 1973. *Making vocational choices: A theory of careers.* Englewood Cliffs, NJ: Prentice-Hall.

Kanter, RM. 1990. *When giants learn to dance.* New York: Simon & Schuster.

Kaufman, HG. 1974. *Obsolescence and professional career development.* New York: AMACON.

Leana, CR, & Feldsman, DC. 1988. Individual responses to job loss: Perceptions, reactions and coping behaviours. *Journal of Management,* 14(3).

Leibowitz, ZB, Kaye, BL, & Farren, C. 1990. Career gridlock. *Training and Development Journal,* April 1990, 29–35.

Levinger, B. 1996. *Human capacity development across the lifespan.* Newton, MA: Educational Development Center.

Mcknight, R. 1991. Creating the future after job loss. *Training and Development,* 45, 69–72.

Otte, FL, & Hutcheson, PG. 1992. *Helping employees manage careers.* Englewood Cliffs, NJ: Prentice-Hall.

Rousseau, PM, & Wade-Benzoni, KA. 1995. Changing individual-organisational attachments: A two-way street. In A. Howard (ed.), *The changing nature of work.* San Francisco: Jossey-Bass.

Schein, EH. 1978. *Career dynamics: Matching individual and organisational needs.* London: Addison-Wesley.

Schein, EH. 1990. *Career anchors: Discover your real values.* San Diego, CA: University Associates.

Schein, EH. 1993. *Career survival: Strategic job and role planning.* London: Pfeifer.

Schein, EH. 1996. Career anchors revisited: Implications for career development in the 21st century. *Academy of Management Executive,* 80–88.

Schreuder, AMG, & Theron, AL. 2001. *Careers: An organisational perspective.* Cape Town: Juta.

Stevenson, M. 1998. Career transition counselling. *People Dynamics,* 16(10), 40–46.

Super, DE. 1992. Toward a comprehensive theory of career development. In DH Montross & CJ Shinkman (eds.), *Career development: Theory and practice.* Springfield, IL: Charles Thomas.

Uys, JS. 1993. The organisation of the future. Paper presented at the SATBT Congress, Grahamstown.

Van der Walt, S. 1982. *Work motives of women in the retail business.* Pretoria: Human Sciences Research Council.

Van Rooyen, MS. 1969. Aspekte van die beroepskeuse struktuur van 'n generasie standaard X leerlinge. Ongepubliseerde MA-verhandeling. University of Port Elizabeth.

Wessels, JS. 2000. Equipping public officials for the challenges of responsible governance: A South African perspective on lifelong learning. *International Review of Administrative Sciences,* 66, 311–324.

Government reports

Republic of South Africa. 2000. Report on career management in the public service. Public Service Commission. [http://www.psc.govz/docs/reports/2000/career]

11 Structuring learning programmes for public sector employees

Purpose

The purpose of this chapter is to allow the reader to reflect on the structuring of learning programmes necessary to equip public sector employees for their changing milieu.

Learning outcomes

After you have read this chapter, you should be able to:

- Explain why traditional education and training are unsuitable for preparing public sector employees for an ever-changing environment.
- Explain why lifelong learning is essential for the maintenance of the desired level of competence of public sector employees.
- Analyse the philosophy and practice of outcomes-based education.
- Explain why it is necessary to do competency modelling for a public institution.
- Evaluate the advantages and disadvantages of on-the-job learning and off-the-job-learning.
- Explain the advantages of e-learning from an employer's perspective.
- Assess an existing learning programme for public sector employees.
- Develop a model for systematic learning for a public institution.

11.1 Introduction

Change, and more specifically the unpredictability of change, can be regarded as a key characteristic of the milieu of contemporary public officials. For many officials, change and transformation are perhaps the only permanent fixtures of their daily reality. It is commonly accepted that a major task of any system of public human resource management is to ensure that public officials are competent to understand and respond effectively to their ever-changing milieu. It is therefore appropriate to question the extent to which traditional education and training assist in meeting the requirements of professional competence in the workplace.

In this chapter, we shall see how traditional education and training have become unsuitable in preparing public officials for the challenges of an ever-changing professional milieu. Lifelong learning will be proposed as an alternative to the traditional paradigm. We shall investigate the practice of outcomes-based education (OBE), especially within the South African context, and the chapter will conclude with a suggested model for systematic learning for public officials.

11.2 The unsuitability of traditional education and training

Most public officials have a qualification obtained from a university or technicon. Many public officials are still studying part time. Numerous officials attend in-service training courses on a regular basis. Most, if not all, of these interventions can be described as traditional in nature. In other words, some people possess all the knowledge while others lack knowledge. Those who are knowledgeable train those who are not.

It is therefore appropriate to ask whether traditional education and training really assist in meeting the requirements of professional competence by public officials. In answering this question, it is necessary to reconsider the concepts professional and competence. The professional element focuses attention on unique skills, based on a distinct corpus of knowledge and theories (Larson 1977; Louw 1990; Pauw 1995; Wessels 2000: 313). The idea of competence extends the focus by referring to 'what a person knows and can do under ideal circumstances', embracing the structure of knowledge and abilities (Messick, in Eraut 1994: 179). According to Gonzi (in Eraut 1994: 178) the competence of professionals derives from their possessing a 'set of relevant attributes such as knowledge, skills and attitudes'. These attributes are often referred to as competencies which can be improved through training and development (Wessels 2000: 313).Training and development interventions are thus part of a process of transforming an individual employee into a professional. This process is amply described by Dall'Alba (2009: 37) as the 'transformation of the self through embodying the routines and traditions of the profession'. Another concept that recently has became important in the learning discourse, is 'enactivism'. Li, Clark and Winchester (2010: 405) define this concept as 'a philosophy based on two important premises: cognition and environment are separable, and 'systems' enact with each other from which they 'learn'.' This implies that learning 'is through the learner's acts and is acted upon the world and understanding is embedded in doing' (Li, Clark & Winchester 2010: 413).

It is commonly accepted that the 'expert knowledge' of a profession is provided through academic study at higher education and often postgraduate level (Edwards 1997: 95). Completion of academic education is commonly regarded as an indication to other professionals that the qualifying student has undergone adequate intellectual preparation, including a proper initiation into the values and tradition of the profession (Aronowitz & DiFazio 1994: 209). To the world outside the profession, education and training seem to give professionals a degree of autonomy, control, and power – the power that results from knowledge (Clapper 1999: 141). Although professions are characterised to a large extent by the best available technology and knowledge, in reality it is the skills, the 'tricks of the trade', and aptitude that distinguish professions from non-professions (Pauw 1995: 8; Wessels 2000: 313).

In a recent scholarly article Dall'Alba (2009: 35) argues that the purpose of professional education programmes can be understood as developing 'ways of being the professionals in question'. The crucial question for public human resource managers is: Does the conventional pattern of education and training contributes to develop public officials into being the professionals which they are supposed to be by providing the skills and ethos that make public officials not only competent to discharge their professional responsibilities, but being professionals? The answer to this question is most probably negative. There are three reasons for this answer.

First, the traditional adult education and training paradigm, also known as the 'instruction paradigm', is based on an assumption that some people have and retain superior knowledge in relation to others. Furthermore, it is based on the assumption that knowledge which is imparted through formal instruction has a long lifespan. These assumptions ignore the rapidly changing nature of the world and the rate at which knowledge can become outdated.

Second, as criteria to determine the success of training programmes, this paradigm uses resources, quantity and quality of students entering programmes, and methods of instruction. These criteria, however, focus on the inputs in the training process and do not necessarily imply the results of education and training – that is, the learning that has occurred.

Third, the instruction paradigm places emphasis on specific teaching and training structures such as comprehensive study materials, evaluation of learning within classes by lecturers, and end-of-course (instead of continuous) assessment. It is generally not open and responsive to the frequent changes and new challenges that face officials (Barr & Tagg, 1995: 16–17; Wessels, 2000: 314).

11.3   Lifelong learning

With the unsustainability of the instruction paradigm becoming increasingly evident, different discourses on the learning society have led to what is known as the learning paradigm. The purpose of learning, according to this paradigm, is as follows:
- To produce learning, and not merely to provide instruction;
- To elicit learner discovery and construction of knowledge, rather than just to transfer knowledge to learners;
- To create powerful learning environments, as opposed to offering courses and programmes; and
- To improve the quality of learning, rather than instruction (Wessels 2000: 315).

The learning paradigm applies the following criteria to determine the success of learning:
- Learning and students' outputs (not inputs);
- The quality of exiting (not entering) students;
- The quality and quantity of outputs and outcomes (not resources);
- The aggregation of learning growth and efficiency (not of number of officials enrolling for courses); and
- The quality of learners (not lecturers) and the quality of learning (not instruction) (Wessels 2000: 315).

Learning in terms of the learning paradigm is characterised by teaching and learning structures such as the following (Barr & Tagg 1995: 16–17; Wessels 2000: 316):

- Cross-disciplinary or interdepartmental collaboration;
- Specified learning results (not complete study packages);
- External (not internal) evaluation of learning; and
- Pre/during/post assessment of learning (not just at the end of a course).

The shift to the learning paradigm implies a process of lifelong learning for public officials, in which various providers of learning are involved, such as universities, technikons, and PALAMA (Public Administration Leadership and Management Academy). Edwards (1997: 79) identifies what he calls a 're-differentiation of the boundaries' between various formal providers of learning opportunities (those institutions whose sole task is to organise the provision of education and training); between formal and non-formal providers of learning opportunities (institutions, groups, and organisations that provide learning opportunities as part of their function); between learning organised by institutions for others and informal learning organised by individuals and groups for themselves; and between learning as a dedicated activity, as well as incidental learning which takes place as a result of other activities. These arrangements, as well as the shift of control from the provider (for example, University, Technikon, PALAMA, or a departmental training component) to the learner (the public official), imply also a shift from the classroom to practice (Zuber-Skerritt 1993: 53; Wessels 2000: 316).

The shift described above brings a very important concept to the fore, namely praxis, which involves a movement away from critical thinking as problem solving (the traditional classroom activity) to critical thinking as a process in which knowledge and action are dialectically related through the process of critical reflection (Van Aswegen 1998: 279). The process of critical reflection leads to authentic knowledge (knowledge not produced from textbooks) and autonomous action (action not prescribed in detail in procedural manuals). Critical reflective practice is that form of practice that 'seeks to problematise many situations [...] so that the practitioner can continue to learn, grow, and develop in and through their practice' (Van Aswegen 1998: 281). Critical reflection and learning within the context of application are thus crucial elements of effective lifelong learning (Wessels 2000: 316).

Why is it necessary for learning to occur within the context of application, whether in industry, government, or society more generally? Implicit in lifelong learning is the need for student discovery and construction of knowledge (Barr & Tagg 1995) to be concentrated on real issues and problems under authentic conditions (Zuber-Skerrit 1993: 46) in order to solve specific problems. In order for the learning that occurs to be useful, it makes sense that learning material and methods of tuition need to enhance relevant learning (Wessels 2002: 190).

Another, and perhaps equally important, perspective on the necessity of contextualised learning is the enhancement of the understanding of learners. It has been found that understanding requires activity that relates new information to previous knowledge, connecting facts and weaving bits of knowledge together. This research confirms the notion that learning within the context of application – in other words, a real-life experience – illuminates what a learner has previously read but not understood.

Therefore, the following requirements apply to any structured learning programme in the work environment (Wessels 2002: 190):

- It should make provision for learning experiences essential to successful performance in the various life roles of the learner.
- It should connect to learners' own experiences and reality to create personal relevancy.
- It should have a problem-based approach, instead of a discipline-based (textbook-based) approach.

11.4 Outcomes-based education (OBE)

The ascendancy of the learning paradigm directly concerns what is currently a hotly debated matter in South Africa: outcomes-based education (OBE). OBE has its origin in the significance of the intended outputs as opposed to the inputs which feature prominently in the instruction paradigm. In this regard, Spady (1992: 7) describes an outcome as follows:

[An outcome is] a culminating demonstration of the entire range of learning experiences and capabilities that underlie it, and it occurs in a performance context that directly influences what it is and how it is carried out. These defining elements clearly tell us that an outcome is not simply the name of the learning content, or the name of a concept, or the name of a competence, or a grade or test score, but an actual demonstration in authentic context.

> Outcomes are demonstrations of competence – what learners can do and what they know – in settings that embody a variety of challenges.

In the learning paradigm, outcomes occupy the same position as 'objectives' do in the instruction paradigm.

The following list compares the characteristics of outcomes with the characteristics of objectives (Republic of South Africa 1997: 27):

- Outcomes focus on what the learning official will do; objectives focus on what the teacher or instructor will do.
- Outcomes describe the results of learning; objectives describe the intent of teaching.
- Outcomes emphasise how learning is used in new areas; objectives focus on opportunities provided for learning.
- Outcomes require flexible allocation of time; objectives involve estimating the amount that can be learned in a given period of time.

OBE for public officials implies that their learning will be designed directly around the intended learning demonstration that is necessary for them to cope with the challenges of a learning milieu (Republic of South Africa 1997: 24). This is why curriculum developers work backwards from agreed desired outcomes, which are supposed to state clearly what the learner should be able to demonstrate, to understand, or to apply (Republic of South Africa 1997: 25). Learning programmes are designed to help learners to achieve these outcomes (Wessels 2000: 317).

OBE for public officials fits into the broader scheme of the National Qualifications Framework (NQF), which is a framework for providing and funding lifelong learning opportunities. The learning outcomes for public officials have been formulated as part of unit standards for Public Administration and Management by Standards Generating Bodies (SGBs). This process is overseen by SAQA.

SAQA has formulated two categories of generic outcomes, applicable to all learning, namely the critical cross-field education and training outcomes (the 'critical outcomes'), and the developmental outcomes. The critical outcomes are as follows:

1. Identify and solve problems in which responses demonstrate that responsible decisions using critical and creative thinking have been made.
2. Work effectively with others as a member of a team, group, organisation or community.
3. Organise and manage oneself and one's activities responsibly and effectively.
4. Collect, analyse, organise and critically evaluate information.
5. Communicate effectively using visual, mathematical and/or language skills in the modes of oral and/or written presentation.
6. Use science and technology effectively and critically, showing responsibility towards the environment and health of others.
7. Demonstrate an understanding of the world as a set of related systems by recognising that problem-solving contexts do not exist in isolation (developing a macro-vision).

The developmental outcomes are as follows:

1. Reflect on and explore a variety of strategies to learn more effectively.
2. Participate as responsible citizens in the life of local, national and global communities.
3. Be culturally and aesthetically sensitive across a range of social contexts.
4. Explore education and career opportunities.
5. Develop entrepreneurial opportunities.

It is clear that these outcomes are conceived to prepare learners not only for their careers, but also for success in their personal, civic, and economic lives. The emphasis is on the complete person. Contrary to what some people may fear, these outcomes are open and are not time and context specific. Also, unlike the learning of theories, facts, and procedures which will quickly become obsolete, they are supposed to remain valid for all learners, regardless of their present or future careers, and despite changes in their milieu (Wessels 2000: 319).

What competencies are required to equip public officials within the present and future context? The White Paper on Public Service Training and Education (Republic of South Africa 1997: Appendix C) suggests at least ten possible public service competencies, including leadership (and teamwork), thinking skills, communication, and action management. Once again, these competencies are also not time, technology, or knowledge specific with the risk of becoming obsolete. Table 11.1 presents the list of possible competencies.

Table 11.1 Illustration of possible public service competencies

Characteristics	Frontline	Supervisor	Middle manager	Director	Chief Director	Deputy Director General
Basic literacy (8), Numeracy, and Communication skills (5)	Required	Required	Assumed	Assumed	Assumed	Assumed
Judgement, Integrity, Self-confidence, Flexibility, Initiative, Perseverance, Creativity (1 & 3)	Required	Required	Required	Required	Required	Required
Leadership (2)	Teamwork	Teamwork and motivating	Providing challenge	Employee development	Organisational influence	Creating vision and values
Thinking skills (1, 4 & 7)	Empowered to innovate where necessary	Operational problem solving	Problem formulation and anticipation	Integration	Strategic perspective	Extracting meaning
Organisational awareness (10)	Being part of the culture and purpose	Same, plus knows how to use the system	Same, plus develops linkages	Organisational know-how	Building support	Political acumen
Interpersonal relations (2)	Supportive	Same, plus sensitivity	Same, plus handling group situations	Managing sensitive interpersonal situations	Diplomacy	Interpersonal versatility
Communication (5)	Required	Required	Briefing	High-impact communi-cation	Strategic communi-cation	Instilling communi-cation
Action management (3, 9, & 6)	Best results come from team work	Co-ordination	Planning	Direction/ Delegation	Orchestration action	Sustaining
Knowledge (8)	Required	Required	Required	Required	Required	Required

(Numbers indicate SAQA outcomes)

DID YOU KNOW?

SAQA's role is to:
- Advance the objectives of the NQF;
- Oversee the further development of the NQF; and
- Co-ordinate the sub-frameworks.

You can get the most recent information regarding SAQA on their website at http://www.saqa.org.za.

Table 11.2 Curriculum design matrix

		Outcomes (SAQA)	Career	Entrepre-neurial (12)	Civic (6 & 9)	Personal (6 & 9)	Learner (11)
Essential technical skills?		Problem or information-based decision making (1 & 4)					
Essential interpersonal skills?	Relational	Effective teaming/ collaboration (2)					
	Commu-nication	Effective communicating (5)					
Essential management skills?	Self	Organising and managing oneself (3)					
	People	Participating in the life of local, national, and global communities (9)					
	Things	Using science and technology effectively (6)					
Essential life orientations?		Broad systems thinking (7); Cultural/aesthetic sensitivity (10)					
Essential knowledge?		Learning strategies (8)					

It makes sense that the providing of learning opportunities for current and future public officials is programmed. By doing that, different programmes may be offered for different contextual or occupational needs.

According to Spady *et al.* (1999), the ten outcomes in the framework form a hierarchy, with the life-role applications being the most complex and super-ordinate component. The outcomes of underlying abilities provide a basis for and directly support the life-role applications. The same also holds for the 'thinking enablers'.

In structuring a learning or development programme for public officials, it is necessary to organise one's thinking around a matrix (see Table 11.2). The columns in the matrix respond to the question: What are the various life roles of a public official? Each column determines a separate life role, namely the role as official (career role), entrepreneur, citizen, private person, and learner, with each representing one of the complex and super-ordinate life roles already identified (Wessels 2000: 321).

The rows of the matrix comprise the underlying abilities and the thinking enablers. Only one of the nine rows relates to knowledge – the foundational competence.

11.5   A model for systematic learning (professional development) for public sector employees

One of the main reasons why lifelong learning and professional development fail is probably that institutions lack a systematically developed learning or professional development model. Where the principal aim of training is to contribute to an organisation's overall objectives, the principal aim of an institutional learning model is to develop public officials professionally and to prepare them to be lifelong learners. A systematic approach to learning is outlined in Table 11.3. The Competency framework for the Senior Management Service of the South African Public Service will be used as an example (Republic of South Africa 2001). Three phases are shown in this model: the competency modelling phase, the learning phase, and the learning assessment phase.

11.5.1   The competency modelling phase

Successful professional development begins with a competency framework, defining the competencies that are important for the individual public official and for the Public Service as an institution to be successful. The components of the competency framework for the Senior Management Service (SMS), for example, can be seen in Table 11.3.

Table 11.3 Components of the SMS Competency Framework

Competency name (competency modelling phase)	Name used to identify the senior manager's behaviour or groupings of behaviour.
Competency definition (learning phase)	General description of behaviours and activities that must be demonstrated by senior managers to achieve the desired competency. ▷

Competency level (learning assessment phase)	Description of the degree to which a senior manager has mastered the criteria of a competency. The competency scale classifies observable and measurable behaviours (behavioural indicators) sequentially. Individual progresses through the hierarchy by developing the knowledge, skills, behaviours, or outcomes required at the specific level.

The following are examples of competencies which are viewed as being critical for high performance in the senior manager's role:

- Strategic capability and leadership;
- Programme and project management;
- Financial management;
- Change management;
- Knowledge management;
- Service delivery innovation (SDI);
- Problem solving and analysis;
- People management and empowerment;
- Client orientation and customer focus;
- Communication; and
- Honesty and integrity.

Can a structured learning or professional development programme correct a performance deficiency or improve the competency level of an official? Below is a set of critical questions to aid in competency modelling. The questions address aspects of deficiency in performance or competency.

Quick reference checklist
- What is the performance discrepancy?
  - What is the difference between the level of what is being done and the level of what should be done?
  - What is the evidence and is it reliable?
- Is the discrepancy important?
  - What is it costing?
  - Will the problem grow?
  - Is it worth fixing?
- Is it a skill/knowledge lack?
  - Could they do it if their lives depended on it?
- Did they know how to do it in the past?
  - Have they forgotten?
  - Is the skill used often?
  - Do they get regular feedback on how they are doing? ▷

- Is there a simpler way?
  - Can the job be simplified?
  - Could job aids be used?
  - Can they learn by being shown instead of training?
- Do they have the potential to do the job well?
  - Are they physically fit?
  - Have they the mental potential?
  - Are they over/under qualified?
- Is the correct performance being punished?
  - Do they perceive performing correctly as penalising?
  - Is not doing the job rewarding?
  - Is there some reward for non-performance (less work or worry, more attention)?
- Does correct performance really matter?
  - Is there a favourable outcome for performance?
  - Is there any status/job satisfaction connected with the job?
- Are there any obstacles to performing?
  - Are the resources available (time, equipment, tools, space)?
  - Are there any other barriers (policy, culture, ego, systems, conflicting time demands)?
- What is the best solution?
  - Are there any solutions which are unacceptable to the organisation?
  - Are the solutions beyond the resources of the organisation?

11.5.1.1   The Workplace Skills Plan

The competency modelling phase is strongly influenced by the Skills Development Levies Act of 1999 (South Africa 1999). This Act makes provision for the development of a Workplace Skills Plan by employer institutions. According to Coetzee (2002: 95), the Workplace Skills Plan (WPSP) refers to the strategic human resource training and development aim of developing the workforce skills capacity and thereby achieving the institutional goals contained in the policies and business plan of the specific institution. Developing a workplace skills plan is a systematic process which entails the following:

- Proper workplace planning;
- Proper job analyses as an input to the workforce planning process;
- Identifying and defining the skills requirements of the organisation as derived from the workforce planning process;
- A skills audit to determine the actual skills of the current workforce;
- Defining skills training priorities as derived from the skills audit;
- Identifying skills programmes to address the skills training needs;
- Implementing the workplace skills plan;
- Monitoring, evaluating, and reporting of the workplace skills plan; and
- Establishing a quality assurance system to ensure effective and value-added skills training and development.

The following information should be contained in the WPSP of an institution:

- Number of persons in each occupational group who received training during the year ended as specified in the regulations;
- Strategic skills development priorities for the levy grant for the period as mentioned in the regulations;
- Qualitative information relevant to skills planning (referring to the recruitment and filling procedure);
- Training skills needs for the required period referred to in the regulations; and
- Issues relating to quality assurance with reference to staff education, training, and development.

A skills audit plays a crucial role in a workplace skills plan. A skills audit is an investigation which is undertaken to determine the actual skills of the current workforce in order to define the skills gaps and real skills requirements of the organisation (Coetzee 2002). The ultimate aims of a skills audit are to establish the following (Coetzee 2002):

- What skills actually exist within the organisation;
- How these compare with the organisational skills requirements as determined through the workforce planning and job analyses process;
- What the skills development priorities are (per occupational group, levels and demographic profile);
- How and when the skills development priorities may best be addressed through a systematic plan;
- What the key success indicators/measures of the workplace skills plan will be;
- How to implement, track, and monitor progress; and
- What to report to management and the relevant SETA.

A skills audit requires time, money and expertise. Unfortunately, many institutions undertake training without making the essential preliminary investment. Often there is no systematic plan to predict future skills development needs in order to determine whether perceived skills development requirements can be addressed by training or any other structured learning programme. It is therefore necessary for employer institutions to formulate clear learning outcomes, additional to the critical cross-field outcomes discussed earlier in this chapter. These outcomes should be based on the needs established during this phase. The outcomes approach encourages the use of an end result. This end result is a product of a learning process in which knowledge is obtained through participation and transparency (Erasmus & Van Dyk, 1999: 140). An outcome statement should cover the following elements (Van der Horst & McDonald, 1997: 64–65):

- Indicate who is to perform;
- Indicate the learner's performance in terms of observable, demonstrable and assessable performance;

- Specify action verbs, be clear and unambiguous; involve more than mere isolated tasks or skills;
- Refer to knowledge, skills and attitudes/values (abilities);
- Spell out what task is to be performed;
- Be clear on what conditions apply (if any); and
- Indicate what the minimum response is that will indicate mastery of the task.

11.5.1.2 The Public Service Sector Education and Training Authority (PSETA)

Within the South African Public Service, the PSETA plays a crucial role in the creation of a model or system for systematic learning. The PSETA was established in accordance with Sections 9 & 13 of the Skills Development Act, Act 97 of 1998, and it was promulgated by the Department of Labour on 20 March 2000. The PSETA develops Sector Skills Plans and submits them to the Department of Labour. It also trains and registers both national and provincial Skills Development Facilitators to develop their Work Place Skills Plans, which are expected to reflect both the individual needs and departmental strategic objectives. Furthermore, it gives advice to departments on the Sector Skills Plan and the development of workplace skills plans.

FOCUS ON RESEARCH 11.1
Skills and career progression

RESEARCH

The Public Service Commission has recently published their 'Report on the Assessment of the Public Sector Education and Training Authority's Contribution Towards the Development of Skills and Career Progression' available online at
http://www.psc.gov.za/docs/reports/2010/

11.5.2 The learning phase

Once the learning needs have been determined and outcomes have been formulated, learning programmes are developed to achieve the stated outcomes. Various institutions play a role in this phase, of which the PSETA is probably the most prominent. The PSETA is responsible for the implementation and fostering of a culture of lifelong learning in the South African Public Service. In addition to the registering of national and provincial Skills Development Facilitators, the PSETA is also responsible for the identification of appropriate learnerships for the following categories of employee in the public service:

- Senior managers;
- Middle managers;
- Senior and junior clerks; and
- General assistants.

11.5.2.1   Off-the-job learning

If learning takes place outside the direct field of application – in other words, in a programme designed by a university, technicon, or other providers of learning – the learning programme needs to be designed to transfer learning to the job situation. If this does not happen, the programme will be ineffective.

Learning theorists recommend these ways of maximising the transfer of learning:

- Connect the learning situation to the learner's own experience, as adults already possess a great deal of knowledge and experience on which they can rely.
- Connect the learning of new concepts and skills to their application in the job situation by focusing on present problems and learning about those things that have immediate use.
- Maximise the similarity between the learning situation and the job situation.
- Ensure that learners take responsibility for themselves and their learning.
- Make sure that general principles are understood.
- Design the learning content so that the trainees can see and experience its applicability.

After each learning event, learners should be encouraged to assess their own learning against the expected outcomes of the learning experience.

Some of the ways in which learning programmes can be structured, especially for learners who are already in managerial positions, are the following:

- **Sensitivity training:** This includes techniques such as laboratory, T-group training, communication workshops, and outward-bound trips. The purpose of sensitivity training is to make employees more aware of their own behaviour and the way in which their behaviour is perceived by others. It also increases the participants' awareness and acceptance of the differences between them. Small groups of eight to fourteen individuals who are strangers to each other are normally grouped together and assisted by a trainer. During the discussion, employees discuss themselves, their feelings, and frequent changes derived from this training include a more favourable self-perception, reduced prejudice, improved scores on tests of interpersonal relations, and changed interpersonal behaviour as observed by others, all of which are particularly relevant in South Africa.
- **Team building:** Team building focuses on intact work groups and strives to develop the ability of managers to work together with them on the types of task they face each day. Team building is also an important organisational development technique. The first phase is normally a data collection phase, followed by questionnaires or interviews with team members. This phase addresses information about how the group works together, what problems exist, and what norms are followed and sought. Typical activities in a team-building exercise include goal setting, development of interpersonal relations, and role analysis to clarify roles and responsibilities. A summarised version of the information is fed back to the group so that they can take an objective look at their functioning. The facilitator helps

the team to understand the feedback and develop action plans for improving group processes. Team building attempts to use high interaction among group members to increase trust and openness.

- **Behavioural modelling training:** This process holds that most human behaviour is learned by observing others and then modelling one's behaviour when appropriate. Learning from others reduces the need to learn from failure. A fixed sequence of steps is normally followed (Latham 1989; 269–273). First, the trainer introduces a single interpersonal skill. Second, trainees view a videotape of a supervisor performing the skill correctly. During this process, the learning points should be highlighted. Third, trainees practise the skill by role-playing with other trainees. Finally, trainees get feedback on the effectiveness of their role-playing behaviour.

- **Case study:** In a case study, a trainee is presented with a written description of an actual or hypothetical problem in an organisational setting. The trainee is required to read the case, identify and discuss the problem, and recommend possible solutions. The purposes of a case study are as follows (De Cenzo & Robbins 1994: 269):
  - It shows trainees that there is usually no easy solution to complex organisational problems.
  - Trainees realise that different perspectives and solutions to the same case may be equally valid.
  - Case studies help managerial trainees develop their problem-solving skills. The case study provides stimulating discussion and opportunities for individuals to defend their analytical and problem-solving abilities. It is an effective method of improving decision-making abilities within the given contracts.

- **Simulation:** By using simulation methods the work setting in which the trainee will have to perform is replicated for the trainee to try out different behaviours or strategies. The objective is for trainees to learn from their own actions, and from the group discussion that follows the simulation. Various forms of simulation are used, for example:
  - In-basket exercises;
  - Role plays;
  - Leaderless group discussions;
  - Large-scale behavioural simulations; and
  - Computerised business decision-making games.

11.5.2.2 On-the-job learning

On-the-job learning (OJL) is conducted at the work site and focuses on the actual job. There are several advantages of on-the-job learning (Bird McCord 1987: 356; French 1994: 290; Piskyrich 1993: 262):

- The transfer of learning to the job is maximised.
- A full-time facilitator and separate training facilities are avoided.

- Learner motivation remains high because what employees are learning is relevant to the job and provides a sense of satisfaction.
- The employee is assimilated more quickly into the organisation.

An OJL programme should be planned as carefully as any other learning programme. OJL should be designed to form part of the total learning effort in an institution.

For managers, a great deal of learning takes place on the job. Fisher, Schoenfelt, and Shaw (1993: 395) discuss several recent studies of managerial learning and skill development in the USA as a result of on-the-job experience. This research suggests that managers learn the most from assignments that are very difficult and challenging. A learning programme for managers should include assignments and job rotating plans that stretch them to their limits. The general on-the-job management learning events are briefly discussed below.

- **Coaching:** Experienced managers guide the actions of less experienced managers to help them develop their delivery. The advantage of coaching is that it provides immediate feedback on performance. A possible disadvantage is that it maintains the present values, since the less experienced manager may adopt the same values and approaches as the coach (Fisher *et al.* 1993: 395).
- **Committee assignments:** Junior executives are assigned to committees where they can observe more experienced managers in action because a good deal of organisational work takes place in committees. The purpose of this method is to use normal committees as training instruments, in which the inexperienced manager will be helped to participate. The major reason for his or her presence, however, is to observe the proceedings, such as the interpersonal processes, agreements and disagreements, decision-making processes, negotiations, and successes and failures of the committee.
- **Job rotation:** This method entails moving from one job assignment to another within the same organisation and can take four to six months. The inexperienced manager will gain insight and broad understanding of the organisation, and the method therefore allows specialists to become generalists. This is true for senior management who must obtain an overall perspective of the organisation especially, and who must spend more and more of their time managing the total organisation and less and less time managing on the micro-level. Job rotation is a means of broadening individuals' exposure to company operations, reducing boredom, and stimulating new ideas. A further advantage of job rotation is that people are prepared to assume greater responsibility at the higher levels. A disadvantage, however, is that it can demotivate intelligent and aggressive employees who seek specific responsibilities and can eventually produce a number of employees with limited specific job knowledge (De Cenzo & Robbins 1994: 272).
- **Understudy assignments:** A person who acts as an assistant to someone else may be termed an understudy. Understudying is similar to coaching, but this method is a full-time mentor-understudy arrangement in which coaching is only periodic.

The understudy works with the mentor on a daily basis to learn how the job is done. In the manager's absence, the understudy performs the role of the manager in non-critical activities and develops valuable managerial skills. A disadvantage of this method is that managers may feel threatened by understudies and may not assist them as they should.

DID YOU KNOW?

?

PALAMA has the statutory responsibility for arranging or overseeing management and development training for the South African public service in national, provincial and local government.

More information is available on their website at http://www.palama.gov.za/

11.5.2.3   E-Learning

E-Learning is a valuable tool for providing learning opportunities to public officials. It is not new; it has been around in one form or another for the past ten years. However, interest is rapidly growing. A quarter of all learning is expected to take place electronically in five years' time. The government of India, for example, has announced the inclusion of Information Technology (IT) as a compulsory component in the curricula of all Polytechnics and Engineering Colleges to meet the needs of the country (More 2002).

E-learning or online learning refers to a mode of learning in which the learning resources are provided electronically. The learning topics and material are stored in the form of databases, slide shows, or other presentation formats on the computer. The most common forms of e-learning are computer-based training products available through CD-ROMs and audio/videotapes, and web-based training services provided by online learning portals (More 2002).

In its broadest form, e-learning is undertaken at the following two levels:

- The provision of information via information or communication technologies in a very accessible and immediate way that can enable individuals to refresh or extend their knowledge and improve their performance; and
- The provision of interactive learning materials and packages designed to facilitate skills or wider personal development. The actual courses currently provided via e-learning focus mainly on IT skills and, to a lesser extent, on softer skills (people-to-people training) such as general management skills, or more specific aspects of management such as interviewing, negotiation, conducting meetings, etc.

At a third level of application, e-learning is multidimensional and embraces both the above levels in a wider performance support framework. This is coupled with processes to administer and monitor learning provision and outcomes, and to provide learners with various forms of support from experts and peers. In terms of administration, e-learning can provide access to learning resources, including previews, registration, and tracking of user history. This can be done to a greater or lesser extent, either through passive portals or simply through learning management systems (Pollard & Hillage 2001).

11.5.2.4 Advantages and disadvantages of using computers as training tools

The following advantages and disadvantages are applicable when using computers:

Advantages
- Self-paced learning is facilitated, and immediate feedback and reinforcement are provided.
- Computers are interactive, which makes learning very flexible and allows for learner control.
- Computer-assisted instruction can be conducted from remote sites, on all shifts. It can be fitted into lulls in the work schedule that would otherwise be unproductive.
- Managers and supervisors can be trained in their offices so that they are available to deal with job-related problems if necessary.
- Transportation and lodging costs for trainees are nonexistent, and overall training costs can be reduced once the system has been developed.
- There is consistent quality of instruction over time and from group to group and subjectivity is eliminated.
- Disruptions during instruction due to unexpected trainer problems (such as illness) are excluded.
- Updates and changes can be disseminated very quickly to all training points.
- Retention of learning content is at least as good as in other instructional methods.
- Slow learners have a greater chance of success than in classroom training.
- Customised instruction can be developed according to each learner's needs.

Disadvantages
- Computers require motivated learners, and students must be familiar with computer operations before they can learn.
- Systems are costly to develop.
- Computer technology is changing rapidly, and an effort will have to be made to keep abreast of the latest changes.
- There is still widespread computer illiteracy and an effort has to be made to help employees overcome obstacles.

11.5.3 The learning assessment phase

The last phase is the learning assessment phase. Many people refer to this phase as the evaluation phase. It goes without saying that, as assessment provides the necessary feedback for effective learning, it directly affects learning. Assessment is done by means of tasks and situations in which learners are given opportunities to 'demonstrate their understanding and to thoughtfully apply knowledge, skills, and habits of mind in a variety of contexts' (Marzano, Pickering, & McTighe 1993: 13).

The assessment of learning is often done poorly or not done at all. One reason for this is that the preferred outcomes and the measurement criteria have not been formulated specifically enough. Another reason is that it is generally assumed that learning programmes will work, and those who initiated the learning programmes fear that an objective assessment will prove otherwise.

The basic approach to assessment should be to determine the extent to which the learners have met the learning outcomes and the performance criteria. For example, the competence to be learned could be 'working in a team', and the outcome for the learning could be 'good working relationships are maintained and colleagues readily co-operate'. In this case, some of the performance criteria against which the assessment of learning can be done may be as follows (South Africa 1997: Appendix G): The learner:

- Is open, honest, and courteous in dealing with colleagues and readily offers information and assistance when necessary;
- Appreciates team goals, understands the work of immediate colleagues, and is able to cover for them when necessary;
- Shares knowledge and experience with team members;
- Is committed to equal treatment and fairness for all staff;
- Handles differences with colleagues diplomatically and knows when to seek advice from the line manager; and
- Takes responsibility for own mistakes and is prepared to speak up when he or she spots errors and discrepancies.

Planning for the assessment should commence at the same time that the planning for the learning programme begins. In other words, the performance criteria should be formulated together with the outcome for each competency to be learned.

Within the training paradigm, Kirkpatrick (in Cascio 1992: 253–254) suggests four levels of evaluation. His evaluation model can be adapted as follows to fit the requirements of the learning paradigm:

Level 1: Reaction
The first level is the reaction level, or the participants' feelings about the programme. If learners have enjoyed a programme, it does not imply that they have reached the learning outcomes, but unpopular programmes may be cancelled due to a lack of interest. A questionnaire is normally used to obtain the information during or immediately after the programme. Typical questions to be answered are 'Are you satisfied with the programme arrangements?' 'Are the learning outcomes clear to you?'

Level 2: Learning
Learning measures the degree to which learners have mastered the learning outcomes as measured by the various performance criteria. Learning is assessed continually,

during, and/or at the end of the learning programme, with paper-and-pencil tests, assignments, portfolios, and practical demonstration of performance and behaviour, as well as examinations.

Level 3: Behaviour
In the learning paradigm, behaviour is included in the learning assessed on Level 2.

Level 4: Results
The impact of the learning programme on the work group or organisation as a whole is assessed objectively. The appropriate objective measures to use depend on the learning outcomes and performance criteria for each outcome. A successful learning programme should lead to an improvement of public service delivery and the saving of public expenditure (cost savings), higher productivity, better quality, less accidents, lower turnover of staff, and positive employee attitudes.

So how can we evaluate training? Well, we can apply the evaluation model shown below in Table 11.4.

Table 11.4   Evaluation matrix

Degree	I	II	III	IV
What we want to know	• Are the learners happy? If not, why not?	• Do the learners learn the predetermined competencies? If not, why not?	• Are learning experiences relevant to the 'real world'? If not, why not?	• Do the learning experiences positively affect the institution? If not, why not?
What might be measured	• Learners' reaction during workshop	• Learners' performance during workshop support	• Learners' performance at end of workshop	• Assignments • Ongoing management
Measurement dimensions	• Relevance • Ease of learning	• Perceived 'worth' • Application	• Understanding • Reflection	• Analysis • Results
Sources of data	• Learners' comments • Questions about exercises • Questions about concepts	• Learning time • Performance on exercises • Presentation • Use of tools on exercises	• Results • Discussions	• Results • Discussions ▷

Degree	I	II	III	IV
Data-gathering methodology	• Observation • Interview • Questionnaire	• Observation • Review • Questionnaire	• Interview • Questionnaire • (Critical incidents)	• Interview • Questionnaire • (Critical incidents)

11.6   Review

If it is true that the unpredictability of change is a key characteristic of the milieu of contemporary public officials, it will also be true that the task of public human resource management in ensuring that public officials are competent to understand and respond effectively to their ever-changing milieu, becomes more and more challenging. In this chapter, we have seen that the traditional forms of education and training have become unsuitable in preparing public officials for the challenges of an ever-changing professional milieu.

Lifelong learning has been proposed as an alternative to the traditional paradigm. Lifelong learning in South Africa is supported by an educational system called outcomes-based education. In order to make provision for successful learning programmes for the staff of a public institution, it is necessary for public human resource managers to have a broad picture of the way in which learning for public officials can be understood and implemented systematically.

11.7   Self-evaluation questions

1. For what reasons are traditional forms of education and training inadequate in the ever-changing environment of today?
2. What is meant by the concept of lifelong learning?
3. Explain the philosophy of outcomes-based education.
4. What is the purpose of competency modelling in a public sector institution?
5. Describe the method of undertaking a skills audit according to the principles of outcomes-based education.
6. List the various types of on-the-job learning that may be provided by an organisation.
7. Write an argument in favour of your organisation implementing e-learning for its trainee staff.
8. Explain the purpose of the learning assessment and describe the basic approach that should be taken in preparing such an assessment, according to the principles of outcomes-based education.

Bibliography

Aronowitz, S, & DiFazio, W. 1994. *The jobless future: Sci-tech and the dogma of work.* University of Minnesota Press.

Barr, RB, & Tagg, J. 1995. From teaching to learning: A new paradigm for undergraduate education. *Change: The Magazine of Higher Learning*, 27 (6, November/December), 12–25.

Bird McCord, A. 1987. Job training. In RL Craig (ed.), *Training and development handbook.* 3rd edn. New York: McGraw Hill.

Cascio, WF. 1992. Managing human resources: *Productivity, quality of worklife, profits.* New York: McGraw Hill.

Clapper, VA. 1999. Ethics and public administration and management in the twenty-first century. In JS Wessels, & JC Pauw (eds), *Reflective public administration: Views from the South.* Cape Town: Oxford University Press.

Coetzee, M. 2002. *Getting and keeping your accreditation.* Pretoria: Van Schaik.

Dall'Alba, G. 2009. *Learning Professional Ways of Being: Ambiguities of becoming. Educational Philosophy and Theory,* 41 (1): 34–45.

De Cenzo, DA, & Robbins, SP. 1994. *Human resource management: Concepts and practices.* Toronto: Wiley.

Edwards, R. 1997. *Changing places? Flexibility, lifelong learning and a learning society.* London: Routledge.

Erasmus, BJ, & Van Dyk, PS. 1999. *Training management in South Africa.* Halfway House: ITP.

Eraut, M. 1994. *Developing professional knowledge and competence.* London: Palmer Press.

Fisher, CD, Schoenfelt, LF, & Shaw, JB. 1993. *Human resource management.* Boston: Houghton Mifflin.

French, WL. 1994. *Human resource management.* Boston, MA: Houghton Mifflin.

Larson, MS. 1977. *The rise of professionalism: A sociological analysis.* Berkley, California: University of California Press.

Latham, GP. 1989. Behavioral approaches to the learning process. In IL Goldstein (ed.), *Training and development in organizations.* San Francisco: Jossey-Bass.

Li, Q, Clark, B and Winchester, I. 2010. Instructional design and technology grounded in enactivism: A paradigm shift? *British Journal of Educational Technology,* 41(3): 403–419

Louw, J. 1990. *Professionalizing psychology.* Pretoria: Human Sciences Research Council.

Marzano, RJ, Pickering, D, & McTighe, J. 1993. *Assessing student outcomes: Performance assessment using the dimensions of learning model.* Alexandria, VA: ASCD.

More, S. 2002. E-learning: A new tool of education in YCMOU. Paper read at the XV Annual Conference of the Asian Association Open Universities (AAOU), New Delhi, India, 21–23 February 2003.

Morrison, M. 1993. *Professional skills for leadership: Foundations of a successful career.* St. Louis, MN: Mosby.

Pauw, JC. 1995. Kan universiteitsonderrig beroepsgerig én wetenskaplik wees? Intreerede gelewer met die aanvaarding van die amp van hoogleraar in die Departement Publieke Administrasie aan die Universiteit van Suid-Afrika op 21 Augustus 1995. Pretoria: University of South Africa.

Piskyrich, GM. 1993. *ASTD handbook of instructional technology.* New York: McGraw Hill.

Pollard, E, & Hillage, J. 2001. *Report 376: Exploring e-learning.* [http://www.employment-studies co.uk]

Spady, WG. 1992. *Outcome-based education: Critical issues and answers.* Arlington, VA: American Association of School Administrators.

Van Aswegen, EJ. 1998. Critical reflective practice: Conceptual exploration & model construction. Unpublished dissertation submitted in accordance with requirements for the degree of Doctor of Literature and Philosophy in the subject Nursing Science at the University of South Africa, Pretoria.

Van der Horst, H & McDonald, R. 1997. *Outcomes-based education: A teacher's manual.* Pretoria: Kagiso.

Wessels, JS. 2000. Equipping public officials for the challenges of responsible governance: A South African perspective on lifelong learning. *International Review of Administrative Sciences,* 66(2), 311–324.

Zuber-Skerritt, O. 1993. Improving learning and teaching through action learning and action research. *Higher Education Research and Development,* 12(1), 46–57.

Acts of legislation

Republic of South Africa. 1998. The Skills Development Act (Act 97 of 1998). Government Printer. [http://www.polity.org.za/html/govdocs/legislation/1998]

Republic of South Africa. 1999. The Skills Development Levies Act (Act 9 of 1999). Government Printer. [http://www.polity.org.za/html/govdocs/legislation/1999]

Government regulations

Republic of South Africa. 2001. Public Service Regulations (promulgated under Section 41 (1) of the Public Service Act 103 of 1994). Government Gazette, 427 (21951). Government Printer.

Government white papers

Republic of South Africa. 1997. The White Paper on Public Service Training and Education. Department of Public Service and Administration. [http://www.dpsa.gov.za/docs/policy/ white-papers/pservice]

Part 5

Compensating and caring for public sector employees

IN REFERRING to its staff as 'human resources', a public institution clearly indicates that its employees are regarded as 'assets' of the institution. The 'human' part indicates that this 'asset' has a freedom of choice. This freedom of choice implies that staff can decide unilaterally to leave the employment of the particular institution for another one. In order to retain their employees, especially those who can be regarded as 'assets' to the institution, public institutions need to compensate them adequately for the service they render to the institution, and also to care for them in various other ways.

In this part of the book, we shall focus on the basic wage and salary structure (Chapter 12), as well as incentives and other benefits (Chapter 13), as means of compensating public officials. In Chapter 14, we shall consider the non-material ways of caring, namely the health and safety of officials, as well as counselling.

We believe that sound compensation programmes are of critical importance to public institutions as well as to public officials. Special care must therefore be taken in the design and administration of these programmes to ascertain employees' commitment to the objectives of public service delivery. Part of these programmes is the great variety of incentive systems and benefit programmes, including a wide variety of financial incentive plans that link the pay of employees more closely to their performance. Although benefits nowadays comprise a substantial component of employees' total compensation, they are not normally linked to performance. Despite the fact that benefits are seen as part of the conditions of employment, most of the wide array of possible benefits are provided by employers in an attempt to attract and retain employees, and thus to remain competitive in the labour market. Efficient administration plays a major role in ensuring the success of a benefits programme.

Finally, we regard the comprehensive field of employee wellness promotion as very important. In Chapter 14, we shall examine the necessity of a holistic and proactive approach to promoting and maintaining the complete well-being of a public institution's personnel.

12 Compensating public sector employees: Basic wage and salary structures

Purpose

The purpose of this chapter is to facilitate learning about the compensation of employees in the public sector.

Learning outcomes

After you have read this chapter, you should be able to:
- Define compensation and distinguish between different types of institutional reward.
- Explain the objectives of compensation systems.
- Distinguish between the external and internal factors influencing the design of compensation systems.
- Discuss the various quantitative and non-quantitative methods of job evaluation.
- Demonstrate your understanding of the fundamental mechanics of the major job evaluation systems in use in South Africa.
- Explain how to design a basic pay structure.
- Discuss some process issues affecting the implementation of compensation systems.

12.1   Introduction

The most basic dimension of any employment relationship is the economic dimension. This dimension revolves around the exchange transaction between employees and the organisation that employs them. An important part of human resource management is therefore concerned with this economic dimension, relating specifically to the compensation of employees as part of the exchange transaction.

Compensation has thus always been central to any employment relationship. This relationship, in its simplest form, is usually based on an economically motivated process in which certain inputs (physical and mental work behaviour) are exchanged for certain outputs (rewards) that are considered to be desirable in satisfying individual needs or goals. The use of rewards can therefore be a very important and powerful tool for shaping and determining work behaviour aimed at attaining the strategic objectives of an institution.

Rewards such as the pay and benefits that people gain from an employment relationship are highly important to individuals, since they can meet many needs. Satisfaction of needs can range from the most basic human needs for food and shelter to those signs of achievement, status, and power (such as luxury cars, or overseas vacations) that may be bought if sufficiently high levels of remuneration are received. Self-esteem needs may also be addressed, because levels of pay usually indicate an individual's worth to the institution.

From the institution's perspective, compensation is of equally critical importance, since employee compensation is often the single largest cost item for an institution. The total cost of the overall compensation and reward system can have a decisive bearing on an institution's competitive position; effective management of the cost, nature and distribution of rewards therefore demands careful attention.

A multitude of possible rewards can be included in an overall reward system and these rewards may be classified in various categories.

Common categories include extrinsic versus intrinsic rewards, financial versus non-financial rewards, and performance-related versus membership-related rewards. Naturally, rewards may be classified in other ways, and certain rewards can fit equally well in more than one category.

12.1.1   Compensation defined

The extrinsic-intrinsic typology illustrated in Figure 12.1 is especially useful for defining the domain of compensation management.

Intrinsic rewards are self-administered rewards that are associated with the job itself, such as the opportunity to perform meaningful work, experience variety, and receive feedback on work results.

Although certain human resource management-related decisions may focus on intrinsic rewards (such as flexible working schedules, job enrichment and job rotation), the fact that these rewards have to be given by employees to themselves leaves little scope for direct control by management. As Bernardin and Russell (1993: 420) rightly point out, if you feel little or no satisfaction from completing a challenging assignment, there is not much that the institution can do about it.

Extrinsic rewards, on the other hand, include all those rewards an employee receives from sources other than the job itself. An institution has a large degree of control over the nature and monetary cost of the extrinsic rewards with which it intends to compensate the efforts of its employees, and it can therefore manipulate the use of these external rewards to affect employee behaviour.

In the light of the above, compensation may be defined as the financial and non-financial extrinsic rewards provided by an employer for the time, skills, and effort made available by the employee in fulfilling job requirements aimed at achieving institutional objectives.

Concepts that are sometimes used as more or less equivalent to compensation management are reward management, remuneration management, salary and wage administration or pay administration.

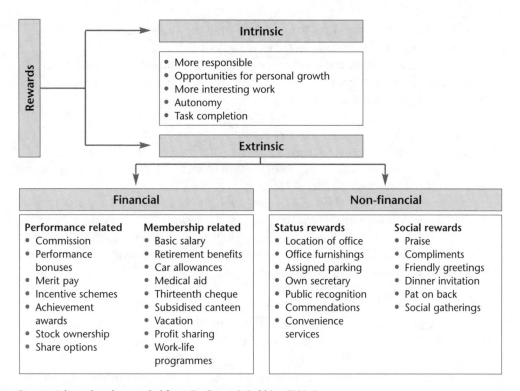

Source: Adapted and expanded from De Cenzo & Robbins (1994)

Figure 12.1   Types and structure of rewards

12.1.2   Compensation management: An overview

Compensation management has become a complex and specialised HR function, and it must be emphasised from the outset that there is no one 'best' reward system that will work for every institution.

In designing an appropriate compensation system, two challenges typically have to be met to link the compensation strategy to the organisation's overall business strategy (Gomez-Mejia, Balkin, & Cardy 2001: 235):

▪ The system must enable the organisation to achieve its strategic objectives; and
▪ It must be shaped to fit the institution's unique characteristics and environment.

In choosing from the large variety of available design options, the compensation manager must always consider the overall reward strategy, to ensure that design features are congruent and fit well with other human resource practices and with the institution's business strategy (Lawler 1987: 270; McNally 1996: 312).

The following three issues have to be addressed in this design planning process:

- What should be the overall objectives of the system?
- What external and internal influences exist, and what impact may they have on specific design decisions?
- What policies should govern the system?

The consideration of these issues constitutes the first part of this chapter. The second set of design issues focuses on the essential elements or 'nuts and bolts' of a compensation system. Such aspects as job evaluation, pay surveys, and pay structure are examined in the second part of the chapter.

As Steers and Porter (1991: 487) note, even the best designed reward systems can go awry in producing their intended results because of the manner in which they are implemented. In view of this, we shall discuss some important issues of implementation or process, such as communication policies and decision-making practices, in the final part of the chapter.

12.2 Compensation objectives

Compensation objectives are those guidelines that determine the nature of a reward system. They also serve as standards against which the effectiveness of the system is evaluated (Cascio 1991: 42).

The classical objectives of any compensation system are to attract, retain and motivate employees. Many more objectives may be formulated to ensure that the compensation system contributes to the institution's overall objectives. The following are some common objectives of an effective reward system (Biesheuvel 1985).

12.2.1 Attracting the right quality of applicants

Generally, institutions that give the greatest rewards tend to attract the most applicants and can therefore recruit the best qualified staff. In order to maintain a competitive pay-level strategy an institution needs some knowledge of the going rate in the labour market. Salary surveys are typically utilised for this purpose.

12.2.2 Retaining suitable employees

To encourage valuable staff members to remain, the compensation system must provide sufficient rewards for these employees to feel satisfied when they compare their rewards with those received by individuals performing similar jobs in other institutions.

12.2.3 Maintaining equity among employees

In the context of compensation, the concept of equity relates to the perception of fairness in the distribution of rewards. It is generally considered to be one of the most important objectives of any compensation system.

Different types of equity can be distinguished: external, internal and individual.

- **External equity** concerns comparisons of rewards across similar jobs in the labour market. Pay surveys are usually used for information regarding external equity.
- **Internal equity** deals with comparisons of rewards across different jobs within the same institution. It addresses the issue of the relative worth of, for example, an engineer versus an accountant working for the same employer. The techniques of job evaluation and pay structuring are to establish internal equity. The issue of 'income differentials' (in terms of the Employment Equity Act) is thus very relevant here.
- **Individual (or procedural) equity** is concerned with the extent to which an employee's compensation is reflective of his or her contribution and the fairness with which pay changes such as raises are made. Changes may be based, for example, on individual performance, on competencies, or according to fixed increments or seniority (Cherrington 1995: 412; Kerr 1997: vii).

12.2.4 Rewarding good performance and providing incentives for desired behaviour

An institution can structure its reward system to encourage employee behaviour directed towards improving corporate performance and achieving specific aims. (We do not have public service examples of this practice.)

12.2.5 Maintaining cost-effectiveness

The compensation system often constitutes the single largest operating cost of an organisation and should therefore be designed and assessed from a cost-benefit perspective. A systematic pay structure is therefore needed to prevent undue expense and possible over- or underpayment of employees.

12.2.6 Complying with legal requirements

Compensation design faces certain legal constraints and must comply with legislative regulations and collectively bargained agreements.

12.2.7 Providing for flexibility and administrative efficiency

Design should be flexible enough to prevent bureaucratic rigidity and allow for dealing with alterations in relative market rates and individual differences in terms of merit. In addition, it should be simple enough to explain, understand, and operate.

12.3 Compensation policies

Compensation policies are formalised guidelines for compensation-related decision making by management.

12.3.1 Compensation policy areas

The areas in which compensation policies need to be formulated include the following (Anthony, Perrewe & Kamar 1999; Armstrong & Murlis 1988):

- **Pay level:** This area concerns external competitiveness and is expanded upon in Section 12.3.2. The policy question will be: Should the level of pay be above, below, or at the prevailing market rate?
- **Equity:** To what degree is the institution going to strive for internal equity, and by what means are internal relativities between jobs to be established?
- **Performance-related rewards:** How should achievement be rewarded, and what role should incentive and bonus schemes play?
- **Market rate policy:** To what extent should market rate pressures (for example, scarce and highly regarded skills) be allowed to affect or possibly distort the salary structure?
- **Salary structure:** Is a formal structure required and, if it is, what type of structure is necessary to ensure consistent and equitable, yet flexible, administration of salaries? (See Section 12.10 for a definition and discussion of this aspect.)
- **Control:** What is the amount of freedom given to individual managers to influence the salaries of their staff?
- **Total package:** What is the best reward mix of basic pay, benefits, and incentives for the various categories of employee?
- **Communication:** How much information about the compensation system should be made freely available to employees or their representatives, and what degree of pay secrecy should be enforced?

?

DID YOU KNOW?

The compensation of South African public servants is explained extensively in a booklet on salaries and benefits in the Public Service, released by the Department of Public Service And Administration (DPSA). The purpose of this booklet is to explain the salaries and benefits that government is offering to public servants. The booklet is available online at the DPSA web site [http://www.dpsa.gov.za/documents/rp/2009/salaries.pdf]. All other documents relevant to the compensation of South African public servants are available online at http://www.dpsa.gov.za/r_documents.asp#incentives.

A further important design decision concerns the relative emphasis that is to be placed on the different policy areas (Milkovich & Boudreau 1994: 553). For example, the aims of pursuing internal equity may be compromised if external competitiveness takes precedence in certain cases in which job offers exceed the pay ranges stipulated by the institution's internal pay structure. This could lead to a problem of compression; that is, the reduction of pay differentials between jobs or levels of jobs due, for instance, to the pay rate for jobs filled from outside the institution increasing faster than the pay rate for job incumbents within the institution.

(There may be other causes for pay rate compression, but the problem typically occurs when employees in a particular job grade perceive that there is not a sufficient difference between their level of compensation and that of the employees in the next lower job grade.)

12.3.2 Pay level policy

Essentially an institution's pay level policy refers to the way in which its average pay rate for a specific group of jobs compares to that of its competitors. This policy is of particular importance, since it has a direct impact on an institution's ability to attract and retain appropriately qualified and competent employees and maintain its competitive position in its market; that is, the level of external equity it maintains. In positioning itself in its prevailing external labour market, the institution can choose between three broad pay level policy options:

- Lead policy;
- Match policy; and
- Lag policy.

A lead policy implies that the employer pays at a higher rate than its competitors for comparable jobs, a match policy means paying at the average market rate, and a lag policy obviously means paying below the market average.

Many of the influencing factors identified in the next section will have a bearing on the institution's pay level policy, and the optimum policy is dependent on the employer's unique set of circumstances. For example, an employer that wishes to attract only the best candidates, pursues an image of prestige, and tries to limit labour turnover would probably need to consider a lead policy.

A match policy is the most common, and in practice this would mean that the employer pays at the market median or 50th percentile; in other words, that salary value where 50% of the market sample earns more than this salary and 50% earns less (FSA-Contact: 1999). Implementing a lead policy could, for example, be achieved by either redrawing the market line at a higher level or paying at the 75th percentile or higher.

12.4 Influences on compensation policies

There are various interacting factors that have an impact on the design of the compensation system. Some of these are external forces, while others are a function of the internal conditions of the institution.

12.4.1 External factors

- The Constitution of the Republic of South Africa, 1996;
- The Labour Relations Act 66 of 1995;
- The Basic Conditions of Employment Act 75 of 1997;
- The Employment Equity Act 55 of 1998;

- Skills Development Act 97 of 1998;
- The Skills Development Levies Act 9 of 1999;
- The Income Tax Act 58 of 1962, as amended – in particular also Schedule 7 of this Act, which pertains to fringe benefit taxation;
- The Public Service Act promulgated under Proclamation 103 of 1994, as amended;
- The Public Service Regulations of 2001;
- The Correctional Services Act 111 of 1998; and
- The Defence Act 44 of 1957.

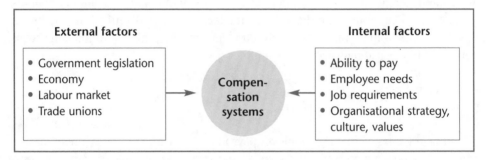

Figure 12.2   Major influences on compensation systems

- **Economy:** Broad economic conditions such as high levels of inflation, recessionary periods, differences in the cost of living in different parts of the country, general level of employment, and competitiveness in the local or international product market can greatly affect the general level of compensation.
- **Labour market:** Compensation levels may often vary according to the forces of supply and demand in terms of general labour or specific skills. Unions. Organised labour can have a significant impact on the determination of wage levels and benefits by means of collective bargaining and other mechanisms (see Chapter 3).

12.4.2   Internal factors

- **Ability to pay:** An institution's ability to pay has a great impact on its general level of compensation. Its level of productivity its profitability its size, and its competitors are all determinants of its ability to generate revenues for paying its human resources (Sherman & Bohlander 1992: 314; Mondy Noe, & Premeaux 1999: 379).
- **Employee needs:** Employees differ in terms of what they prefer to receive as compensation. For example, younger employees may have a higher cash need than older employees, and highly compensated executives' needs differ from those of general workers. There may thus be a need to build choices into the system.
- **Job requirements:** Requirements in terms of the average skill level of employees may impact on the pay level that the institution will be able to set and still be able to obtain sufficient numbers of qualified employees.

- **Strategy, culture and values:** As previously emphasised, pay policies should be supportive of the institution's strategic objectives. In addition, institutional values such as decision-making style, openness regarding communication, and social responsibility may have a bearing on compensation policies. (For example, institutions valuing a competitive, achievement-driven climate will probably opt for performance-related rather than fixed increment pay increases, while companies that are sensitive to the needs of female employees may adopt policies of fully paid extended maternity leave.)

12.5   Pay system design

The traditional and predominant pay system design is job-based compensation. This means that we pay jobs or, in other words, an employee who holds a job just happens to get the salary that is assigned to that position (De Cenzo & Robbins 1996: 368). The amount paid to each job is based on an assessment of its internal and external importance and worth. Because not all jobs are equally important to an institution, the compensation system's primary objective is to allocate pay in a systematic manner to ensure that the most important jobs are paid the most (Gomez-Mejia *et al.* 2001: 335). Internal worth is established through the use of job evaluation systems, and external worth is determined through market surveys. A pay structure is established to set boundaries on pay, based on the results of the job evaluation and market survey. Movement takes place within the pay structure based on merit or on time spent by the individual in the job category (seniority).

The emerging alternative to the job-based pay system is an employee-based system such as skills-based pay.

Skills-based pay (also termed knowledge-based or competency-based pay) is an unconventional compensation scheme in which employees are paid at a rate that is based on their range, depth, and types of skill in which they demonstrate capability, irrespective of the job they are assigned to (Newstrom & Davis 2002: 154).

Three dimensions of skill are usually identified in skills-based pay (Heneman, Ledford, & Gresham 2000: 212):

- **Depth of skill,** indicating increased knowledge of one technical speciality. An example would be apprenticeship systems for workers in the skilled trades;
- **Breadth of skill,** meaning increased knowledge of a variety of tasks or jobs. For example, factory workers may be rewarded for learning all the job skills in their work team; and
- **Vertical skill,** which refers to self-management skills. For example, team members are given an increase if they can operate without direct supervision.

In this approach, organisations create various skill steps that are aligned with the specific process requirements of their organisation. Pay is then related directly to the total number of skill dimensions in which an individual has demonstrated capability. The basic assumptions behind linking base pay to skills acquisition are that employees become more efficient and capable as their competency profile broadens, and that a group of multi-skilled employees can perform greater quantities of work in a more flexible manner (Bremen & Coil 1999).

Endorsement of this approach is mixed. Despite advantages such as flexibility, reduction of competition between workers, broadbanding possibilities, and decrease in supervisor cost, disadvantages such as high development and maintenance cost and continued payment for skills that are no longer used routinely make skill-based pay a potentially high-risk endeavour (Anthony *et al.* 1999; Bremen & Coil 1999; Ivancevich & Matteson 2002).

Gomez-Mejia *et al.* (2001: 330) suggest that skill-based compensation systems may be suitable in organisational environments that have the following characteristics:

- Employee participation and teamwork are applicable;
- Opportunities for upward mobility are limited;
- Opportunities exist for learning new skills;
- The technology and organisational structure change frequently;
- A relatively educated workforce exists with both the willingness and ability to learn different jobs; and
- Cost of turnover and absenteeism in terms of lost production are high.

The most common job-based pay methodology is the time-based system, in which the individual is paid in accordance with the amount of time he or she spends on the job; in other words, hours worked for hourly paid jobs, or a monthly fraction of an annual rate of pay for salaried staff. Since such job-based pay systems dominate the South African compensation scene in general and are still supported most widely in terms of job evaluation and salary survey services, the sections that follow are aligned to the job-based approach.

12.6 Essential elements of a compensation system

Having planned and established the overall objectives, the desired design features, and the guiding policies of the compensation system, compensation specialists can now set out to put the plans into practice and construct the system. To achieve this aim, four basic tools or technical elements of the compensation system design should be utilised:

- Job analysis;
- Job evaluation;
- Pay surveys; and
- Pay structuring.

Due to the complexity of some of these elements, each will be discussed separately in Sections 12.7 to 12.9 that follow.

12.7 Job analysis

As in so many other human resource management functions, the process of job analysis and the resulting job descriptions constitute the basic building blocks for compensation system design. Job analysis has been discussed fully in Chapter 5, but, in the context of compensation system design, it has the following twofold purpose (Cascio 1991: 429):

- To identify the important characteristics of each job so that job evaluation can be carried out; and
- To identify, define, and weigh the compensable factors; that is, all those shared characteristics of jobs that provide a basis for judging job value.

These factors are typically linked to the specific job evaluation plan, for example, decision making (Anglo American 1994) or know-how, problem solving and accountability (Hay Management Consultants 1993) (see Section 12.8.2).

12.8 Job evaluation

Job evaluation may be defined as a systematic process of determining the value of each job in relation to other jobs in the institution.

The purpose of this process, as discussed in Chapter 4, is to rank jobs within a hierarchy that reflects the relative importance or worth of each job within the institution.

Job evaluation is concerned with the relative worth of jobs as such, and not with the worth of the job incumbents. The latter issue is addressed by performance appraisal, which has already been discussed in Chapter 9.

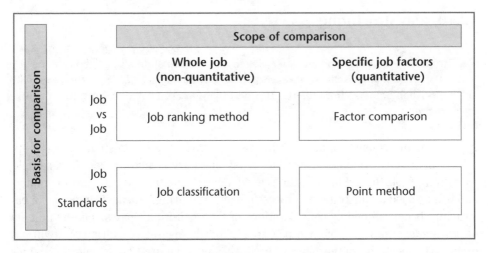

Figure 12.3   Basic job evaluation methods

Job evaluation is essentially a process of comparisons (comparisons with other jobs, comparisons against defined standards, or comparisons of the extent to which common factors are present in different jobs) and it is these various comparisons that form the foundation of the various job evaluation methods (Aamodt 1999: 91–93; Armstrong & Murlis 1988: 74). See Figure 12.3 on page 357.

12.9 Pay surveys

Once jobs have been graded by means of job evaluation, the next step in the development of a compensation system is the determination of a pay rate for the grades. The compensation tool used to set the monetary worth of jobs or grades of jobs is the pay/compensation survey. A pay survey provides information on the way in which other employers compensate similar jobs and skills in an institution's labour market. The labour market for a specific job category may be defined as that area from which employees are drawn or to which they are lost (Auld 1991: 17–21). Having identified the appropriate labour markets in which he or she is competing for human resources, the survey user can determine the relative position of his or her own pay rates against those of competitors. Pay surveys therefore enable an institution to maintain external equity.

An institution can obtain pay survey data by conducting or commissioning its own pay survey that is designed according to its specific informational needs, or it can subscribe to various comprehensive external surveys that are conducted on a regular basis by large consultancies such as FSA-Contact, P-E Compensation Services, International Compensation, or Hay Management Consultants. Access to the data of these surveys is usually limited to subscribing companies who pay a fee and are obliged to submit input details for the surveys to receive the resulting survey reports.

12.10 Pay structuring

Pay structuring refers to the process whereby the information obtained from the job evaluation exercise (that is, the relative worth of jobs within the institution) is combined with the information obtained from the pay surveys (that is, market values of jobs) to establish a pay structure.

A pay structure consists of an institution's pay scales relating to single jobs, groups of jobs or grades. Among the various types of salary structure (see, for example, Armstrong & Murlis 1988: 117), the graded salary structures are the most common, and will be used to illustrate the process of pay structuring. The development of a pay structure is determined by considerations of the institution's pay slope, the number of pay grades, the range of each pay grade, and the degree of overlap between pay grades. The meanings of these terms are illustrated in Figure 12.4 on page 359, which represents a simple pay structure.

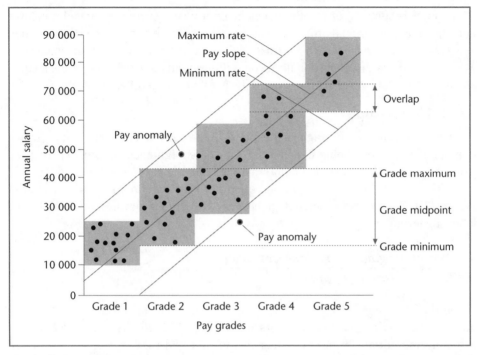

Figure 12.4   A basic pay structure

The compensation system of the South African Public Service consists of three remuneration scales, with distinct grades and remuneration bands (with commensurate job evaluation weights). As an example, the remuneration bands for the Senior Management Service in the South African Public Service are listed below.

Structure of the compensation system of the South African Public Service

1. Senior Management Service Grade A
   - Remuneration band A
   - Equate job weight of 695 points to 790 points
2. Senior Management Service Grade B
   - Remuneration band B
   - Equate job weight of 747 points to 842 points
3. Senior Management Service Grade C
   - Remuneration band C
   - Equate job weight of 800 points to 895 points
4. Senior Management Service Grade D
   - Remuneration band D
   - Equate job weight of 896 points to 1 000 points.

Source: Republic of South Africa (2003)

In terms of Section 27 of the Employment Equity Act, every designated employer must include in its annual affirmative action report a statement on the remuneration and benefits received in each occupational category and level of that employer's workforce. Where disproportionate income differentials are reflected, a designated employer must take measures to progressively reduce such differentials.

12.10.1   Pay slope

The pay slope refers to the angle or steepness of the pay curve. The pay curve (which is a curve due to pay being exponential) can be straightened by transforming the pay data (that is, the dispersion of job salaries in all the pay grades) into logarithmic form. The pay slope can be expressed quantitatively in ratio form, as indicated in Figure 12.4. The pay slope percentage between two grades may be calculated by the following formula:

$$\frac{Pay\ rate\ for\ grade\ 2\ -\ Pay\ rate\ for\ grade\ 1}{Pay\ rate\ for\ grade\ 1}\ \times\ 100$$

While the percentage size of the pay slope is dependent on variables such as the number of grades and economic factors, a pay slope of 15–20% between pay grades is generally appropriate for most circumstances (Auld 1990).

12.10.2   Number of pay grades

The various jobs in an institution are usually classified into pay grades with all jobs falling within a given pay grade receiving the same pay rate (with individual differences based on factors such as seniority or merit). A pay structure based on the Paterson job evaluation plan will have 11 pay grades, and a structure based on the Peromnes system will have 21 pay grades.

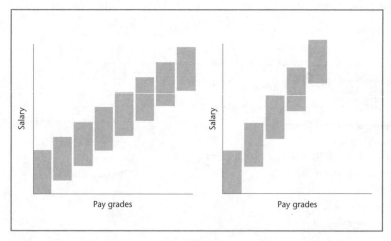

Figure 12.5   Pay structures with different numbers of grades

As can be seen from Figure 12.5, the fewer pay grades a structure has, the steeper the pay slope will have to be, and vice versa. Too few pay grades (with a resulting very steep pay slope) may create internal inequity and employee morale problems because jobs with significantly different job content and responsibilities may be paid at the same pay rate.

On the other hand, an excessive number of pay grades will result in very similar pay differentials among different jobs.

Reduced numbers of pay grades may result from changes in institutional design, such as the recent trend to de-layer institutional hierarchies to yield flatter structures (Hay Management Consultants 1993).

The problem of too many grades may arise, for example, from such practices as multi-skilling and skill-based compensation systems where the assigning of sub-grades for each group of skills would result in severe difficulties in differentiating between the many categories and maintaining internal equity (Bussin 1993: 26–27).

A method of compensation administration that has emerged as a tool for determining the optimum numbers of grades in changing institutional circumstances is the concept of broadbanding. Essentially, this is a process aimed at decreasing the number of job grades by collapsing the number of original grades into broader bands, but without compromising accurate job measurements within these broad bands. The concept is illustrated in Figure 12.6.

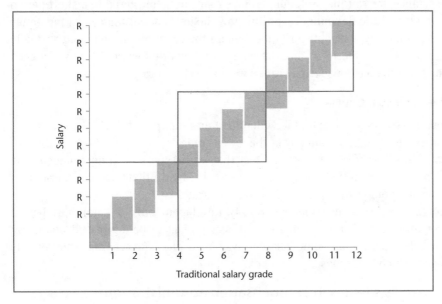

Figure 12.6   A broadbanded salary structure

The three 'bands' (that is, the large boxes) in a broadbanded pay structure replace four or more traditional salary grades. Another example of broadbanding would be to place all managers into one band, all technicians into a second band, all clerical employees into a third band, and all part-time employees into a fourth band (Ivancevich & Matteson 2002: 208).

12.10.3 Pay ranges

The pay range refers to the difference between the minimum and maximum for each pay grade. It therefore reflects the width of a pay scale. In determining the optimum width of a pay range, two factors need to be considered (Lewis 1980: 22):

- The relative emphasis to be placed on promotion and performance; and
- The nature of the jobs within a particular grade.

A narrow pay range is appropriate if the company wishes to encourage employees to seek promotion. In order to increase his or her basic pay, an employee is obliged to compete for promotion to the next grade.

A wide pay range, on the other hand, is appropriate if performance is to be encouraged within the context of the employee's current job. A wide range allows for the accommodation of greater variations in employee performance.

The width of a pay range is also determined by the nature of jobs; that is, the length of the learning phase before a job can be performed at an acceptable standard and the extent of variation in individual performance.

For instance, for routine, well-defined jobs that can be mastered in a short period of time and have little flexibility regarding how the job is done, a narrower pay range is justified. Similarly, for managerial jobs where the learning phase is longer due to the many tasks to be mastered and the wide variations that can exist between good and poor performance, a wider pay range would be appropriate.

12.10.4 Grade overlap

Grade overlap refers to the extent to which the minimum pay of the higher pay grade is overlapped by the maximum pay of the lower grade.

Such an overlap acknowledges the fact that an inexperienced newcomer to the higher job grade may initially be of lesser value to the institution than an experienced, well-performing employee in the next lower job grade.

Once the pay structure has been fully developed, only a small number of implementation considerations or process issues need to be addressed before we have our fully operational compensation system in place (apart from the benefits component, which is discussed in the next chapter).

12.11 Process issues in compensation administration

The process by which compensation systems are implemented and administered in institutions is often considered to be just as important as the technical soundness of the design itself (Steers & Porter 1991: 482).

Lawler (1990: 221) contends that process issues are closely linked to the perceptions that employees have about a compensation plan. Irrespective of whether these perceptions are justified or not, they may have a powerful influence on the effectiveness of the pay system.

Some of the more important process issues that will be discussed briefly are:

- Performance appraisal and its link to reward administration;
- Decision-making practices; and
- Communication policies.

12.11.1   Performance appraisal

If a compensation system is designed to distribute rewards in relation to differences in performance, it is absolutely essential that the institution should have an effective system in place for assessing the relative quality and quantity of employee performance. If such an appraisal system is unreliable or is perceived to lack validity, it is unlikely that the rewards distributed on the basis of that system will have any positive effect on levels of performance and productivity.

The profound influence exerted by this issue is illustrated by the research of Spangenberg (1994) into South African performance management practices, which led the researcher to question the expediency of actually linking performance appraisal results to the reward system. Spangenberg states that it is not advisable to establish such a direct linkage, unless a strong supportive culture, good job designs, and adequate manager-employee relationships exist (Spangenberg 1994: 233).

12.11.2   Decision-making practices

Traditionally, compensation design and administration decisions have been made in a top-down manner with no input from line management or other employees. This approach is still valid for institutions in which the management style suits the hierarchical decision-making process, but higher levels of employee participation in compensation design and administration can result in significant benefits for institutions that have a culture of open communication and employee involvement (Lawler 1990: 221–242).

Such participation can involve employees in co-determining compensable factors and choosing their own mix of benefits in a flexible compensation system.

Although employee involvement is an obvious way of ensuring that rewards take greater cognisance of specific employee needs, indications are that this approach is not practised widely in the South African context (Horwitz & Frost 1992: 32).

12.11.3   Communication policy

The question of how much information about the compensation system should be communicated to employees is not an easy matter to resolve. While the practice of pay secrecy is probably more the rule than the exception, it is generally a matter of the degree to which pay policies are open. The institution may, for instance, provide full disclosure of the way in which pay rates are set, but divulge no information on individual pay levels. Relevant stipulations in labour legislation regarding information disclosure are obviously very important in this regard.

Ivancevich and Matteson (2002: 200) point out that research on the issue has produced mixed findings, and they outline the following factors that appear to be necessary for an open system to succeed:

- Measures of performance must be objective.
- The pay-performance link must be apparent to employees.
- Workers' attitudes towards pay secrecy must be established.
- There should be no blatant pay inconsistencies between employees with comparable jobs.

12.11.4 Compensation management and information technology

While the advances in computer technology and software applications have for some time provided indispensable tools for payroll administration, salary package modelling, and scenario planning during wage negotiations for example, many new applications are continuously being developed as aids to professional compensation management.

Dessler (1997: 440) highlights the streamlining of the often cumbersome manual job evaluation process by means of CAJE – computer-aided job evaluation. Such CAJE systems typically feature electronic data entry computerised checking of questionnaire responses, and automated outputs of job evaluation. These are seen rather as an enhancement than a replacement of the traditional job evaluation system, which is usually still needed for initial analysis of benchmark jobs. A computerised version of the popular Peromnes system is currently being introduced in the South African job evaluation market.

For participation in salary surveys and utilising survey data, information technology provides useful tools for compensation specialists and managers. Not only can survey information be submitted electronically, but packages such as RemNet, which is operated by FSA-Contact, allow subscribers access to a database of survey data and to manipulate and project such data, produce graphs, etc.

Self-service by employees is becoming a growing trend in the application of IT. Intranet-based self-serve human resource systems typically replace paper documents with electronic transactions, freeing human resource staff from routine information request and benefits-related transactions. At British American Tobacco South Africa (BAT SA), for example, the objective of the employee self-service system is to enable employees directly to update certain personal details on the human resource database, to file administrative documentation (such as leave forms) electronically, and to view and print personal details on company records, including pay slips (Ciucci 2001).

The Internet also provides various sites for access to useful compensation and salary survey information. Useful sites are those of the South African Reward Association (SARA), [http://www.sara.co.za], the American Compensation Association, [http://www.acaonline.org], and the Society for Human Resource Management, [http://www.shrm.org] or [http://jobsmart.org/ tools/salary/].

12.12 Review

Sound compensation programmes are of critical importance to institutions because the way they are designed and administered can have a significant influence on employees' behaviour and on their commitment to achieving institutional objectives. Of the many types of reward available to an organisation for compensating the productive efforts of its employees, pay remains the most important extrinsic reward. Therefore, the effective utilisation of monetary resources for rewarding and motivating workers constitutes a major part of the manager's role of 'managing his or her people'.

Compensation systems can be designed in many ways, and the challenge for the institution lies in the development of a system that is best suited to its own particular objectives with regard to such factors as cost-effectiveness, motivational ability, equitable distribution of rewards and administrative efficiency. In this chapter, we have identified the various external and internal influences that may impact on the design options and policies an institution may wish to implement.

The compensation system mechanics of job analysis, job evaluation, pay surveys, and pay structuring have been explored in some detail, with the aim of systematically leading up to a fully operational pay structure. Finally, we have briefly considered performance appraisal linkages, communication policies, and decision-making practices as important considerations in the implementation and administration of pay systems.

Compensation management involves some complex topics, not all of which could be adequately explored within the scope of this chapter. Two important aspects that form an integral part of a comprehensive compensation system are benefits administration and incentive compensation practices; these topics are discussed in the next chapter.

12.13 Self-evaluation questions

1. 'Compensation has always stood at the heart of any employment relationship.' Discuss this statement critically.
2. By making use of a diagram, differentiate between different types of reward.
3. Explain the objectives of compensation management
4. Write brief notes on compensation policies and aspects that influence them.
5. Describe the basic elements of a compensation system.
6. Write an essay on the topic of job evaluation. Pay particular attention to major job evaluation systems used in South Africa. What are some recent trends regarding job evaluation within the context of new approaches to work design?
7. Explain what 'pay structuring' entails.
8. Describe the role of the following process issues in compensation administration:
   • Performance appraisal;
   • Decision-making processes; and
   • Communication and information disclosure.
9. Contrast the benefits and limitations of job-based and person-based compensation systems.

Bibliography

Aamodt, MG. 1999. *Applied industrial/organizational psychology.* 3rd edn. Belmont, CA: Wadsworth.

Anglo American Corporation. 1984. *Paterson job evaluation handbook.* Johannesburg: Personnel Systems Department.

Anthony, WP, Perrewé, PL, & Kacmar, KM. 1999. *Human resource management: A strategic approach.* 3rd edn. Orlando, FL: Dryden.

Armstrong, M, & Murlis, H. 1988. *Reward management: A handbook of salary administration.* London: Kogan Page.

Auld, D. 1990. Compensation. In JA Slabbert, JJ Prinsloo, & W Backer (eds.), Managing industrial relations in South Africa. Pretoria: Sigma. 1991. Compensation surveys. *IPM Journal*, October, 17–21

Barling, J, Fullagar, C, & Bluen, S. (Eds.). 1986. *Behaviour in institutions.* Johannesburg: McGraw Hill.

Bernadin, HJ, & Russell, JE. 1993. *Human resource management: An experiential approach.* New York: McGraw Hill.

Biesheuvel, S. 1985. *Work motivation and compensation.* Vols. 1 & 2. Johannesburg: McGraw Hill.

Bremen, JM, & Coil, M. 1999. Comparing alternative base pay methods: Which one meets your organization's need? *ACA News*, June, 21–28.

Bussin, M. 1993. Broadbanding, multiskilling, skill-based pay: Any correlation? *HRM*, July, 26–27.

Butler, JE, Ferris, GR, & Napier, NK. 1991. *Strategy and human resource management.* Cincinnati, OH: South-Western.

Cascio, WF. 1991. *Applied psychology in personnel management.* 4th edn. Englewood Cliffs, NJ: Prentice-Hall.

Cherrington, DJ. 1995. *The management of human resources.* 4th edn. Englewood Cliffs, NJ: Prentice-Hall.

Cogill, C. 1988. The Paterson way: Does it pay? *HRM*, September, 32–34.

Cuicci, P. 2001. E-remuneration: Dawning reality or myth, a BAT case study. Paper delivered at Pay Con 2001 Conference, Sandton.

De Cenzo, DA, & Robbins, SP. 1996. *Personnel/human resource management.* Englewood Cliffs, NJ: Prentice-Hall.

Dessler, G. 1997. *Human resource management.* 7th edn. Upper Saddle River, NJ: Prentice-Hall.

FSA-Contact. 1995. TASK compensation survey. Johannesburg

FSA-Contact. 1998. Paying for performance: A special survey of trends in performance-based pay strategies, May 1998.

FSA-Contact. 1999. Peromnes compensation survey, March.

Gómez-Mejía, LR, Balkin, DB, & Cardy, RL. 2001. *Managing human resources.* 3rd edn. Upper Saddle River, NJ: Prentice-Hall.

Hay Management Consultants. 1993. Institutional broadbanding report, June.

Heneman, RL, Ledford, GE, & Gresham, MT. 2000. The changing nature of work and its effects on compensation design and delivery. In SL Rynes & B Gerhardt (eds.) *Compensation in organisations: Current research and practice.* San Francisco: Jossey-Bass.

Horwitz, F, & Frost, P. 1992. Flexible rewards: Critical success factors. *People Dynamics*, June, 27–33.

Incomes Data Services. 1994. *Multiskilling: Study* 558, 1–32.

Ivancevich, JM, & Matteson, MT. 2002. *Organizational behaviour and management.* 4th edn. Chicago: Irwin.

Kerr, S. (Ed.). 1997. *Ultimate rewards: What really motivates people to achieve.* Boston, MA: Harvard Business School Press.

Lawler, EE. 1987. The design of effective reward systems. In JW Lorsch (ed.), *Handbook of institution behaviour.* Englewood Cliffs, NJ: Prentice-Hall.

Lawler, EE. 1990. *Strategic pay: Aligning institutional strategy and pay systems.* San Francisco: Jossey Bass.

Leap, JL, & Crino, MD. 1993. Personnel: Human resource management. 2nd edn. New York: Macmillan.

Lewis, WM. 1980. *The design of basic pay structures.* Pers 315. (CSIR special report) Pretoria: National Institute for Personnel Research.

Lundy, O, & Cowling, A. 1996. *Strategic human resource management.* London: Routledge.

McNally, KA. 1996. Compensation as a strategic tool. In GR Ferris & RM Buckley (eds.), *Human resource management: Perspectives, context, functions and outcomes.* Englewood Cliffs, NJ: Prentice-Hall.

Milkovich, GT, & Boudreau, JW. 1994. *Human resource management.* 7th edn. Homewood, IL: Irwin.

Mondy, RV, Noe, RM, & Premeaux, SR. 1999. *Human resource management.* 7th edn. Upper Saddle River, NJ: Prentice-Hall.

Newstrom, JW & Davis, K. 2002. *Organizational behavior: Human behavior at work.* 11th edn. New York: McGraw Hill.

Retief, A. 1995. Job evaluation: The heat is on. *Human Resource Management*, 10(10), 28–34.

Sherman, W, & Bohlander, GW. 1992. *Managing human resources.* 9th edn. Cincinnati, OH: South-Western.

Singer, MG. 1990. *Human resource management.* Boston, MA: PWS-Kent.

Spangenberg, H. 1994. *Understanding and implementing performance management.* Cape Town: Juta.

Steers, RM, & Porter, LW. 1991. *Motivation and work behaviour.* 5th edn. New York: McGraw Hill.

Stone, RJ. 1998. *Human resource management.* 3rd edn. Brisbane: Wiley.

Management guides

Republic of South Africa. 2003. Senior Management Service: Public Service Handbook. Department of the Public Service and Administration.

13 Providing incentives and benefits to public sector employees

Purpose

The purpose of this chapter is to discuss incentive compensation rewarding outstanding efforts aimed at achieving institutional goals and benefits which are intended to improve the quality of work life for employees.

Learning outcomes

After you have read this chapter, you should be able to:
- Explain why it is often difficult to relate pay to performance.
- Discuss the basic principles for establishing effective incentive systems.
- Distinguish between various types of incentive schemes and discuss their relative merits for the public service.
- Explain the importance of benefits in the overall compensation system.
- Describe different benefit arrangement strategies and explain the principles guiding the choice of strategy.
- Discuss the importance of the elements of choice, flexibility, and administrative delivery for successful benefits programmes.
- Evaluate the inclusive compensation package of the Senior Management Service in terms of the various benefit arrangement strategies.

13.1 Introduction

In the previous chapter, we explored the development of a fundamental compensation system and we noted that, apart from a basic wage and salary structure, the typical overall compensation system also comprises an incentive and a benefits component.

Incentive compensation differs from other forms of compensation in that it constitutes an additional reward for outstanding efforts aimed at achieving institutional goals. It is usually monetarily based, and its widespread use stems from the general belief that pay is able to motivate individuals or groups of employees to exceed minimum performance requirements and increase institutional effectiveness.

Benefits, on the other hand, are linked to employment rather than to performance, and may be described as an indirect form of compensation that is mainly intended to improve the quality of work life for an institution's employees. A wide array of possible benefits may be incorporated in a total compensation package. While the provision of some of these benefits (such as a retirement plan and accident and death insurance) is required by law, the possible range of employer-provided benefits is bound only by the creative limits of compensation specialists.

13.2 Incentive compensation

The generally recognised problem of low productivity rates in South Africa continuously challenges managers and compensation specialists to devise compensation structures that will motivate employees towards increased levels of performance. Although the basic salary structure discussed in the previous chapter can motivate and reward superior work effort by increasing an individual's pay within the salary range or by promoting the individual into a higher pay grade, such rewards are usually provided only on an annual basis. Due to such delays, the recipients of such rewards often do not perceive them to be directly linked to performance.

Incentive compensation schemes are devised essentially as an attempt to link rewards to superior performance in a direct and prompt way. They usually function in addition to basic pay, and are specifically aimed at the achievement of specified results, outputs or productivity targets.

The following are typical reasons for introducing incentive compensation plans:

- To increase the institution's competitiveness in the labour market in attracting and retaining talent;
- To stimulate individual, team or institutional performance by making incentive rewards dependent on agreed targets or work;
- To encourage employee identification with the institution's objectives and values, including the company policy; and
- To control fixed compensation costs by putting a portion of pay at risk if certain agreed objectives are not achieved (Stone, 1998; Munchinsky, Kriek, and Schreuder 2002: 268).

In this section, we shall explore the nature, requirements, types and applications of incentive compensation schemes within the South African context.

13.2.1 Linking pay to performance

Over the last decade, South African compensation specialists have consistently reported a trend towards relating rewards to performance (Stacey 1991; Gathercole 1992; Bussin 1992). This 'paying for performance' trend has also been confirmed by recent national surveys of South African compensation practices (FSA-Contact 1993; 1995; 1998). From such surveys, it would appear that many South African institutions are designing reward systems that reduce the guaranteed component of pay packages and increase the portion of pay at risk by means of the introduction of incentive systems.

However, despite the widespread support for and the intuitive appeal of linking pay to performance, there is also extensive evidence of many performance-related pay systems more often than not failing to produce the expected positive effects (Horwitz & Frost 1992; Spangenberg 1993). Even strong proponents of performance-related compensation such as Edward Lawler, agree that the design of an effective pay-for-performance programme is a difficult undertaking that should be approached with circumspection (Lawler 1990: 70–131).

13.2.1.1 Problems with pay for performance

In Chapter 9, we discussed the problematic nature of performance appraisal. This very same set of problems can generally be said to represent many of the underlying obstacles in effectively relating pay to performance. The often subjective nature of performance assessment and the difficulties in eradicating the resulting inconsistencies create the risk of pay differences that cannot be justified.

The following common problems are often responsible for the failure of performance-related pay systems:

- The lack of objective, quantitative performance measures for many jobs and the resulting reliance on subjective performance ratings;
- A poorly perceived link between performance and pay, usually due to systems ignoring the principle of immediate reinforcement by linking performance to the reward only at the end of the year;
- Failure to relate aspects of performance that are rewarded to the overall strategic performance objectives, thus encouraging 'wrong' kinds of behaviour (for example, a production bonus scheme that rewards according to levels of output could encourage workers to take short cuts in quality assurance procedures);
- Inadequate communications about the objectives, procedures, and benefits of the pay scheme;
- The level of the performance-based portion of pay not being perceived as proportionate to the additional efforts required; and
- Union resistance to performance-based schemes and to change in general.

FOCUS ON RESEARCH 13.1
Pay for performance

Research by Weibel, Rost and Osterloh undertaken in 2010 reveals the following:

Pay for performance has a strong, positive effect on performance in the case of non-interesting tasks. Pay for performance, however, tends to have a negative effect on performance in the case of interesting tasks. The vignette study reveals (1) why pay for performance sometimes undermines performance; and (2) how pay for performance produces hidden costs, which also need to be accounted for.

Their findings suggest the following five reasons for the modest success of pay for performance in the public sector:

First, it seems that in the public sector high intrinsic motivation is at stake [...] Second, public funding is clearly more limited than private sector funding. As a result the price effect of pay for performance in public management tends to be rather small. Third, pay for performance might reduce investments in policy expertise and select the wrong type of employees [...] Fourth, the so-called multitasking problem [...] can pose an additional difficulty for implementing pay for performance in the public sector [...] Fifth, from a politico-economic perspective, the application of performance-contingent rewards also carries the danger of political manipulation.

13.2.2 Requirements for effective incentive compensation plans

While the literature on compensation management is replete with lists of 'success criteria' for incentive systems, it should be borne in mind that each institution considering the implementation of pay-for-performance plans will be faced with a unique set of issues and problems for which it will have to find its own specific solutions. As public institutions are usually not aimed at profit making but at public service delivery, it is also not so easy to develop an effective incentive compensation plan for public servants. The type of department and job will determine the plan to be developed.

However, although there is no single recipe for selecting the most appropriate design and implementation procedure for a successful incentive scheme, there are a number of generally accepted guiding principles that are relevant to all schemes (see, for example, Gupta & Shaw 2000: 147–152; Dessler 1997: 488; Bussin 1994: 19–26; Spangenberg 1994: 233–241; Lundy & Cowling 1996: 313–314; Bartol & Locke 2000: 124). These guidelines are described in the sub-sections that follow.

13.2.2.1   Establish a pay-for-performance work culture

The effectiveness of compensation systems is linked to the extent to which such systems are appropriately matched to their institutional context. In order for an incentive scheme to achieve its desired results, the organisational culture must therefore be generally conducive to the principles of individual merit and performance. Considering that so many South African attempts at comprehensive performance management are thwarted by a lack of a work culture of productivity and quality, this requirement probably poses the biggest challenge to South African managers and compensation specialists (Spangenberg 1993: 30–34).

There are two important considerations in creating an appropriate performance-orientated work culture; measuring of performance and establishing determinants of performance (Bernadin & Russell 1993: 480–481; Ivancevich 1998: 352).

The first consideration entails the development of performance evaluation systems that are regarded as meaningful and equitable by both management and employees (see Chapter 11 for guidelines). Spangenberg (1994: 233) cautions that the link between a newly designed performance appraisal system and the pay system should not be established until such time as employees and managers have developed the trust needed to conduct participative performance discussions. The second consideration entails the establishment of an environment or climate that is conducive to the following worker-related determinants of performance:

- Employees' views regarding the value of money relative to other rewards;
- Employees' ability to control the rate of performance;
- Employees' ability to increase their performance;
- Employees' belief that increased performance will be rewarded; and
- Employees' perception of the size of the reward as sufficient to warrant increased effort in their work.

13.2.2.2 Ensure employee acceptance

Employees and their representatives, such as trade unions, must accept the incentive scheme, and it should be welcomed by all those employees covered by it. Employee acceptance may be fostered by effectively communicating the benefits of the scheme, by establishing a highly visible and clear connection between employees' incentive payments and their performance, and by encouraging employees to participate in administering the scheme.

13.2.2.3 Ensure a clear line of sight

The concept of line of sight refers to the degree to which employees can see a clear connection between their behaviour and the payout from an incentive system. For example, rewards for corporate performance in the private sector (profit sharing or share options) may have a weak line of sight. Employees at lower levels of a large public institution may find it difficult to believe that they can influence the incentive payouts because they do not see how they can affect the overall performance of the institution. In private companies by contrast, individual or team-based incentives such as sales commissions or production bonuses have a clear line of sight and therefore often stronger motivational effects (Heneman, Ledford, & Gresham 2000: 209).

13.2.2.4 Set high but attainable standards of performance

Performance targets should be attainable, but not too easily attained. They should become progressively more difficult to achieve as the levels of potential reward increase. Incentive payments should never be permitted to be seen as guaranteed.

13.2.2.5 Establish clearly defined and accepted performance standards

Performance standards or output targets should be based on objective, preferably quantified, measures and should be agreed upon with each individual or group.

13.2.2.6 Ensure a simple and understandable design

The incentive scheme should be sufficiently simple to enable all employees to understand its operation so that they can easily calculate their rewards.

13.2.2.7 Provide for flexibility and review

Schemes should be sufficiently flexible to allow for adjustments that may be called for by changes in the business environment. The effectiveness of the scheme should be monitored on an ongoing basis. Typical areas that need regular review are:

- Whether the performance factors that determine the level of payments still reflect the institution's operational realities and are still relevant to the strategic business objectives;
- Whether the scheme is losing motivational value due to employees taking the incentive payments for granted; and

- Whether the scheme needs re-communicating and repackaging to revitalize interest and improve performance.

13.2.2.8 Ensure effective administration

The ongoing success of an incentive scheme is often determined by the efficiency of the administrative support structures and procedures associated with the scheme. The following are some vital administrative issues:

- Effective ongoing communication and procedures for addressing questions and complaints;
- Consistent and fair application of the rules within each group and across groups;
- Sufficient budget provision and full and timely payment in accordance with the rules; and
- Congruence with the overall compensation system, for example incentive schemes should not be used to make up for deficiencies in the basic salary structure.

13.2.3 Types of incentive schemes

Incentive schemes are usually categorised according to whether the system is applied on an individual, group, or institution-wide level. Further distinctions are sometimes made according to the category of employees involved, for example sales personnel, non-managerial workers and executives.

In general, the choice between individual or group-based incentive plans is dictated by whether performance is a function of individualised or collective effort and

---

Types of incentive scheme

Individual schemes

- Production
  - Piece-rate plans
  - Standard-hour systems
  - Individual bonuses
  - Suggestion systems
- Sales
  - Commission plans
  - Merit awards
  - Merchandise & travel incentives
- Management
  - Bonuses based on work unit performance
  - Deferred compensation
  - Share options
  - Supplementary benefits

Group/organisational schemes

- Bonuses based on group performance
- Gain sharing, for example Scanlon & Rucker plans
- Profit sharing (ownership plans)
- Suggestion systems

Source: Adapted and expanded from Byars & Rue (1991: 352); Gomez Mejia, Balkin & Cardy (2001: 366)

---

whether the institution can readily evaluate individual versus group performance. It is, however, not uncommon for the same employee or group of employees to be covered by various types of incentive scheme at any given time. For example, a miner at an Anglo American gold mine may, for instance, currently receive a drilling bonus based on individual performance and also be covered by institution-wide profit-sharing and employee share-ownership schemes.

13.2.3.1 Individual incentive schemes

Individual incentive schemes can take several forms, but they all share one primary advantage – employees can distinctly see the relationship between what and how much they do and what they get.

This advantage is, however, often the cause of some unwanted effects. For example, an institution may 'only get what it pays for', since employees will be likely to concentrate their efforts only on those activities of their total job outcome that are being measured and rewarded (for example, a commission system that is based only on sales volumes may encourage employees to neglect the customer-care aspect of their jobs). Furthermore, the increased competition among employees may become dysfunctional due to workers becoming reluctant to share knowledge or ideas that can lead to overall improved productivity, or due to work groups imposing informal ceilings on outputs and enforcing these less than optimal productivity levels by means of peer pressure.

Popular individual incentive approaches include piece-rate plans, standard-hour plans, commission plans, and individual bonuses.

Piece-rate plans

Under piece-rate plans, individual pay is directly linked to the number of units produced. Straight piece-rate plans usually pay an employee a set wage (minimum wage, for example) for an expected minimum level of output (the standard) and a piece-rate incentive for all production above the standard. This standard is determined by job analysis and work study techniques, and is often adjusted by collective bargaining.

Differential piece-rate plans are a common variation, according to which the employer pays a smaller piece rate up to the standard and a higher piece rate for production above the standard.

Standard-hour plans

Standard-hour plans are similar to piece-rate plans, with the exception that the productivity standard is not measured in terms of output units, but is set in terms of time units needed to complete a particular task. Employees who complete such tasks in less than the standard time qualify for incentive payments on the basis of the time saved.

By way of illustration, suppose that, at Louis Motors, an oil change has been calculated as requiring 30 minutes to complete (standard time). A mechanic earning R50 an hour will earn R25 to complete the job, irrespective of whether he used more or less time than the allotted 30 minutes (0.5 standard hour R50). Should he manage to complete three oil changes within one hour, he would consequently be paid R75 (1.5 x R50) under a time-bonus system where the full benefit of the time saved goes to the employee.

Commission plans

The competitive and largely independent nature of sales work demands a sustained high level of motivation and enthusiasm from salespeople and therefore makes financial incentives well suited to this category of employee. Most salespeople are usually rewarded according to some form of commission plan based at least partially on their sales volume.

Types of plan range from a straight commission to various combinations of salary plus commission and/or sales bonuses. Under a straight commission plan, pay is entirely determined by volume of sales, whereas, under combination plans, the salesperson is paid a guaranteed basic salary plus a (usually smaller) commission on sales. In addition to, or sometimes instead of commission, companies often also pay sales bonuses for sales that exceed a specific predetermined quota. Another variant is the draw plan, which is often implemented to counter the negative effect of fluctuating earnings caused by periodic changes in business climate and is typically associated with straight commission plans. Essentially, this involves the payment of a basic salary which is deducted from future commissions.

Examples of commission plans

	Straight commission plan	**Salary plus commission**
Formula	1% of total monthly sales	R300 per week + 0.7% of total monthly sales
		4 × R300 = R1 200
Pay	1% × R400 000 = R4 000	0.7% × R400 000 = R2 800
		= R4 000

	Draw plan	**Salary plus bonus**
Formula	1% of total monthly sales less R400 weekly draw	300 per week + 2% of sales in excess of quota of 2 600 units
Pay	total draw already advanced:	4 × R300 = R1 200
	R1 600	
Commission[1] still owing:	R2 400	2% × R140 000 [2] = R2 800
	R4 000	R4 000

[1] R4 000 – R1 600
[2] 1 400 excess units @ R100
(Based on sales of 4 000 units at R100 each)

Individual bonuses

A bonus is an additional one-off reward for high performance. It is a discretionary payment; that is, it is not guaranteed and it does not become part of the recipient's basic salary as in the case of a merit pay increase. Bonuses may be based on a variety of performance measures, such as performance ratings or the achievement of specific objectives, or, in the case of executives, a percentage of total profits or return on shareholders' investments.

Care should be taken not to allow a bonus to become a virtual extension of basic salary due to its payment becoming practically guaranteed, as has happened in the case of the typical South African annual bonus ('13th cheque'). During 1993, an FSA-Contact survey indicated that 92% of respondent companies offered a general annual bonus, and that almost all these respondents (95%) had paid all their employees the bonus, despite the prevailing recessionary climate (FSA-Contact 1993). It is only recently that South African surveys have indicated a strong decline in 13th cheque bonuses and a switch to incentive-based bonus options previously reserved for senior management staff (Heard 2001).

In the case of executives, a bonus payment may sometimes take the form of shares or options to buy shares in the institution. A bonus payment may also be deferred until a set future date (for example retirement) in order to realise income tax savings. Deferred bonus payments may also serve as 'golden handcuffs' with which an institution may attempt to retain the services of valuable senior personnel and sustain managerial performance (Horwitz & Frost 1992: 32).

13.2.3.2 Group and organisation-wide incentive schemes

Group or team-based incentive schemes provide incentive pay to all group members, based on the performance of the entire group. Such schemes are most applicable under the following conditions (Gómez-Mejía, Balkin and Cardy 2001: 375):

- Work tasks are so intertwined that it is difficult to single out individual contributions (for example, research teams in research and development (R&D) laboratories).
- Jobs are interdependent (for example, assembly lines).
- Co-operation is needed to complete a task or project.
- The measurement of individual output is difficult.
- The objective is to foster entrepreneurship in self-managed work groups.

Another determining factor is the value that is placed on individualism. Dominant collectivist cultures place greater emphasis on the individual as an element of the team than do typical Western orientations towards individualism, and the prevalence of collectivism in an organisation will ease the implementing of team-based incentive systems (Nelson and Quick 2002: 178).

In the South African context, indications are that, at the operational level, team-based incentive schemes are more applicable than individual-based schemes. However, a benchmarking study on team management and measurement conducted by the Saratoga Institute in 1997 found that there was no consensus regarding recognition or rewards for teams, and that the issue of individual versus team rewards was equally undecided. The recommendation is made that rewards and recognition should align with and complement the cultural norms of the institution, unless, of course, there is a conscious desire to change the culture (Saratoga 1998: 19). Trade union positions on pay linked to productivity and collective bargaining agreements no doubt also exert tremendous influence in this regard. In the case of the South African public service, the Minister for the Public Service and Administration determines service benefits, compensatory practices, work facility practices, and allowances for employees through the collective bargaining process. For employees who fall outside the Labour Relations Act, these are determined directly (Republic of South Africa 2001: Chapter I, Part V, E.1).

Suggestion systems

A suggestion system is an incentive scheme under which employees receive rewards for useful ideas on reducing costs, improving safety or product quality, or generally increasing institutional effectiveness. Such systems typically utilise forms that employees can use to write out their suggestions and deposit them in conveniently placed boxes for submission and evaluation by management or a special committee.

Marx (1992: 3) cautions against the informality of suggestion boxes and sets the following criteria for a formal suggestion scheme:

- Accepted suggestions must relate to specific or potential problems or opportunities to improve processes or situations.
- A suggestion must provide a solution or possible strategy; complaints do not qualify.
- Suggestions should be in writing and must be signed by the employee. Written suggestions must be received and registered by the suggestion office.
- The scheme must be recognised and accepted by top management.

In the South African context, a National Association of Suggestion Systems (SANASS) has been active since 1990 in the promotion of this type of incentive scheme.

Incentive compensation in South Africa

In a survey on human resources practices covering 551 companies, Grobler (2001) found variable pay and performance-related pay as the most common option in place for managers in 71% of the companies. Group bonuses being offered ranged from 49% of the companies offering them at managerial level to 42% at manual worker level. Profit sharing also had a wide coverage, with 43% of companies offering this option to managerial staff and 14% to manual workers.

A special survey on performance-based pay strategies by FSA-Contact in 1998 produced the following findings (FSA-Contact 1998; Grobler 2001):

- 77% of institutions showing consistent profit growth over three years have short-term incentives.

- Of all respondents, 62% have short-term incentives and 50% operate share schemes.
- Time necessary for developing and implementing incentive schemes ranges between two and 24 months, with an average of nine months.
- Review intervals for schemes are very short, probably due to the pace of change in the RSA.
- Excess profits are the most common source of funding for incentive pools, followed by share of total profit and then financial ratios.
- In 29% of companies with subsidiaries, loss-making divisions could earn bonuses on reduction of losses.
- South African practices in the arena of short-term incentives do not differ widely from those of European countries, but, in terms of average payments, the United States sets the pace.

13.3   Employee benefits

Benefits are indirect forms of compensation which, like direct compensation, are intended to aid the achievement of the human resource objective of attracting, retaining and motivating employees.

Both in South Africa and abroad, benefits form a very substantial portion of total compensation expenditure. In the first place, this section examines the major reasons behind the existence of benefits, as opposed to direct cash remuneration. Second, we shall consider a benefits classification, detailing the most common benefits offered by South African institutions.

The degree to which the benefit arrangement offered by an institution aids the achievement of the human resource objectives of attracting, retaining, and motivating employees is largely determined by the benefit arrangement strategy followed by the institution. This section, therefore, also deals with various benefit arrangement strategies and the merits of providing the elements of choice and flexibility within such strategies.

Well-structured and appropriate benefits are, however, not enough to ensure the success of an institution's benefit programme. We shall therefore conclude by detailing a number of important considerations aimed at ensuring the successful administrative delivery of benefits to an institution's employees.

13.3.1   Reasons for providing employee benefits

The extent and nature of the benefits commonly offered by institutions within a particular country are largely determined by the country's specific circumstances and the country's laws. In South Africa, for example, the need to travel long distances, together with the lack of adequate public transport, has contributed significantly to the fact that company cars are a very common benefit.

A country's laws also exert a profound influence. A number of the benefits offered by South African institutions are mandated by law. Some of these are:

- Minimum leave provisions stipulated by the Basic Conditions of Employment Act 75 of 1997, for example:
  - Annual leave (21 consecutive days' annual leave);
  - Sick leave (six weeks' paid sick leave in every cycle of 36 months);
  - Maternity leave: four consecutive months; and
  - Family responsibility leave: three days during each annual leave cycle.
- Paid public holidays as stipulated by the Public Holidays Act 36 of 1994; Unemployment insurance benefits as stipulated by the Unemployment Insurance Act 30 of 1996; and
- Compensation for injuries or diseases contracted while working, as stipulated by the Compensation for Occupational Injuries and Diseases Act 130 of 1993.

In addition to these, it may be expected that the Employment Equity Act will also gradually lead to institutions considering the provision of benefits that may otherwise not have been provided. The case of an institution employing a significant number of working mothers may, for instance, lead to the provision of child-care facilities.

The tax laws of a country, in particular, contribute very significantly to the extent and nature of benefits commonly offered. In a country like the United States, where the marginal tax rates are relatively low, most of the compensation package is given directly as cash. In South Africa, on the other hand, marginal tax rates are relatively high, and benefits, despite the introduction of benefit taxation, are still generally conservatively taxed. This results in a significant portion of compensation packages being given indirectly in the form of benefits. This practice is particularly common at managerial levels in South Africa.

13.3.2   Types of benefits

South African institutions, like many institutions elsewhere in the world, provide a truly amazing range of benefits. They are available to employees while on the job (such as shift allowances and coffee breaks) as well as off the job (such as private use of company cars and vacation payments). In addition, benefits are also provided to the families and dependants of employees (for example medical aid and life insurance).

Benefits can be categorised in a number of ways. A popular way is to categorise benefits into cash and non-cash benefits. Non-cash benefits are then typically further subdivided into current benefits (that is, those enjoyed immediately) and deferred benefits (that is, those enjoyed at some future date). A list of the most common benefits offered in South Africa is provided below in terms of this benefit classification.

Classification of common benefits offered in South Africa

Cash benefits
- Bonuses
  - Fixed annual bonus
  - Incentive/performance bonus
- Allowances
  - Entertainment allowance
  - Car allowance
  - Shift allowance
  - Stand-by allowance
  - Tool allowance
  - Abnormal working conditions
  - Acting allowance
- Other
  - Overtime pay
  - Commission
  - Payment for time not worked (leave)

Non-cash benefits
- Current
  - Transport/travel
    - Company car
    - Second company car
  - Free or subsidised transport to and from work
    - Free or subsidised rail/bus/sea/air fares
    - Free or subsidised parking
    - Overseas travel allowance
  - Accommodation
    - Housing subsidy
    - Housing loan
    - Free or low rental accommodation
    - Holiday accommodation
- Deferred
  - Pension fund
  - Deferred compensation
  - Provident fund

- Group life cover
- Disability cover
- Accident insurance
- Accumulated leave
- Share options
- Other
  - Interest-free or low interest loan
  - Free or cheap services
  - Free or cheap company products
  - Educational assistance
  - Telephone account payment
  - Newspapers and periodicals
  - Meals and refreshments
  - Club fees
  - Professional fees
  - Medical Aid/health-care benefits
  - Encashable leave
  - Incentive award
  - Long-service award
  - Share purchase
  - Computer and faxes at home
  - Cell phones

Source: Grogan (2008: 306); Southern African Legal Information (2010: Online)

The nature and range of benefits that employers offer often reflect the changing trends of the contemporary labour force (De Cenzo & Robbins 1996: 384; Luthans 1998: 71). For example, an institution employing a significant number of working mothers may be obliged to provide on-site child-care facilities to retain the services of this sector of its staff complement. Realities such as the nature of modern urban life, the emergence of dual-career families, and globalisation have led to innovative new benefits and so-called work/family benefits.

The following are examples of such benefits:

- On-site child-care facilities or elder-care facilities or transportation to such centres;
- Convenience benefits such as on-site dry-cleaning services, ATMs, etc.;
- Health promotion benefits such as on-site or subsidised membership to commercial fitness centres, company-provided flu shots, or stress management programmes;
- Comprehensive relocation and extended settling-in programmes;
- Leave/time-off policies and pay-back for unused days off;
- Alternative work schedules and telecommuting;
- Sick child care and back-up child care; and
- Legal and financial planning, tuition reimbursements, and casual day programmes.

The exact nature and range of benefits provided will be influenced by the changing labour market trends, legislative changes, and the benefit arrangement strategy followed by a particular institution. For example, the nature of a company car or car allowance benefit offered under an add-on benefit arrangement strategy will differ significantly from a company car or car allowance benefit offered under a flexible benefit arrangement strategy.

13.3.3   Benefit arrangement strategies

13.3.3.1   Strategy alternatives

In return for their services, South African institutions typically offer their employees a basic salary to which a number of benefits are added. Eligibility for such benefits generally tends to be based on an employee's length of service or job level. There is also a tendency for the value of such benefits to increase with increase in length of service or rise in job level.

Typically, these benefits are also managed and reviewed in relative isolation from each other (and from basic salary) and the employee is tied to a cash/benefit mix as defined by the institution. This relatively isolated management of benefits very often results in employees not being aware of their total earnings, inclusive of the institution's expenditure on benefits.

The benefit arrangement strategy described above is often referred to as the add-on benefit arrangement strategy. The term 'add-on' refers to the nature of the employment agreement between employer and employee which, as described above, offers the employee a basic salary to which a number of benefits are added.

The local opposite of the add-on benefit arrangement strategy is the pure flexible benefit arrangement strategy (Greene 1990: 26–28).

Instead of a basic salary plus benefits, the employee now receives a total package value in return for his or her services. Each employee's compensation is managed and reviewed in terms of a single entity, namely total package value, as opposed to the relatively isolated management and review of basic salary and individual benefits.

Under the pure flexible benefit arrangement strategy, individual employees also have full discretion over the cash/benefit mix of their own total package value. Essentially, an institution will determine the total package cost it is prepared to spend in employing each of its different employees. It will then compile a list of the types of benefit that it is prepared to offer an employee. From this 'menu' of benefits, each employee can choose those benefits which best suit his or her individual needs. The cost to the institution of providing the particular mix of benefits is then added up and is deducted from the total package value in order to calculate the net cash salary of the employee.

Although the pure flexible benefit arrangement strategy serves a very useful purpose as a theoretical opposite to the add-on benefit arrangement strategy, it is seldom implemented in its pure form. The most important reason for this is that institutions wish to safeguard themselves from possible adverse consequences arising from particular employee choices.

An example would be where the institution has to inform the widow of an employee that no funds will be payable to her, as her late husband opted out of group life cover and pension benefits and converted these into improved company car benefits.

One can obviously argue that employees and their families have to live with the consequences of their own decisions. Many, if not the majority, of institutions would, however, prefer to design their benefit arrangements in a way that precludes the possibility of events similar to the above example. This is achieved through a flexible benefit arrangement that includes so-called core benefits. As opposed to the other benefits under a flexible benefit arrangement strategy, which are optional, employee participation in so-called core benefits is compulsory. In practice, employees are obliged to channel specified minimum portions of the total packages offered to them into these defined core benefits. The range of core benefits should ideally include basic retirement, death, disability, and major medical expense (for example surgery or hospitalisation) benefits.

The most common advantages and disadvantages of flexible benefit arrangements are summarised below.

Advantages of flexible benefit arrangements

- Flexible benefits promote a clearer understanding for employers and employees of the real costs associated with benefits and the way in which they contribute to the total package values.

- Employers have improved control over the compensation expenditure, since package values are not driven by changing external factors or fluctuations in employee utilisation of specific benefits (for example medical aid).
- Fairness and internal equity are enhanced, since differences in total package values typically result only from differences in performance and job complexity and not from differences in personal circumstances. (For example: under a non-flexible system, two employees with the same entitlement to a housing subsidy benefit and a fully maintained company car benefit may end up with substantial differences in the value of the benefits if one of them rents a flat and lives close to work, while the other has a large bond on his or her house and travels a long distance to and from work.)
- Employees are permitted to choose benefits most suited to their individual needs and also to structure their package in the most tax-efficient way.

Disadvantages of flexible benefit arrangements
- Flexible systems are more complex to set up and to administer. Despite the availability of computer software that can address the complexities of the payroll administration and the financial modelling of optimum package mixes, additional resources are usually needed for providing individual advisory and counselling services for each employee in the system.
- The problem of adverse choice may sometimes be encountered. This relates to the situation in which those employees who have a specific and immediate need for a particular benefit select that option more often than the average employee, thus causing an inordinate rise in the cost of such a benefit. (For example: employees close to retirement may attempt to buy as many additional retirement benefits as possible, or an employee with a serious medical condition may attempt to buy as much medical and group life insurance as possible.) The inclusion of compulsory core benefits can, however, often address this problem. Unions may sometimes offer resistance to flexible benefit schemes if previously negotiated benefit improvements or the loss of control over a benefit programme are at stake.

13.3.3.2 Choosing a suitable benefit arrangement

The choice between particular arrangement strategies should take account of certain fundamental compensation principles in order to ensure a benefits system that not only addresses particular institutional needs and circumstances, but will also be in line with the objectives of the overall compensation strategy. These principles are detailed in the list that follows on page 384.

Compensation principles

The following compensation principles should be considered when choosing a benefit arrangement strategy:

- **Cost control:** Limit the exposure of compensation packages to unpredictable cost factors over which the institution has very little or no control.
- **External equity:** The positioning of compensation levels inside the institution relative to comparable remuneration levels in the broader labour market should be done on the basis of total package values.
- **Internal equity:** Differences in the total package values of individual employees should only be due to differences in job complexity (as measured by the job evaluation process), in skill premiums payable to certain occupational groupings (as measured by remuneration surveys), and in job performance (as measured by a performance appraisal system).
- **Flexibility:** Individual employees should be given the opportunity to select a cash/benefit mix that satisfies their personal needs without adding to the total compensation expenditure of the institution.
- **Simplicity:** Benefit arrangements should be simple to administer and easily understood by the employees to whom they apply.

Generally, it would appear that a flexible benefit arrangement strategy has a greater potential for satisfying the fundamental compensation principles mentioned above, and it is therefore not surprising to find an ever-increasing number of South African institutions of all sizes following the international trend towards greater flexibility in benefit agreements.

13.3.3.3   Successful delivery of benefit arrangements

Well-structured and appropriate benefits are not enough to ensure the success of an institution's benefit programme. The administrative delivery of the benefits to the institution's employees must also be on time and as contracted before the benefits programme can be regarded as a success. Of particular importance in this regard is the integration of effort across functional lines within the institution and the issue of benefit programme communication.

13.3.3.4   Integration of effort

The administrative delivery of a benefits programme seldom involves only one functional area within the institution. Responsibility for this delivery often spans the human resources, financial, and information technology functions. Given the diversity of these functions, a significant potential exists for important responsibilities to 'get lost' between these areas.

Where more than one functional area is responsible for the administrative delivery of a benefits programme (which is almost always the case), it is advisable for these areas to clarify and document their respective responsibilities. A co-ordination committee with representation from all the functional areas responsible for the administrative delivery of the benefit programme is also advisable. Benefit arrangements are seldom, if ever, static, and such a body can play a very important role in realigning the administrative infrastructure whenever changes are made to the institution's benefit arrangement.

13.3.3.5 Benefit programme communication

Compensation affects employees directly and personally. It is therefore imperative that they fully understand the processes and personal responsibilities associated with the institution's benefit programme. The proper communication of this is of the utmost importance. Inadequate communication could quite easily result in employer and employee having different perceptions as to what has been contracted.

Under a flexible benefit arrangement strategy benefit programme communication becomes even more vital. A flexible benefit arrangement always means transferring at least some responsibility for the structuring of individual compensation packages from the employer to the employee. The employee has to know and accept this responsibility.

Booklets, presentations, workshops, and videos are among the most popular means for ensuring understanding and acceptance of the processes and personal responsibilities of the institution's benefit programme.

13.3.4 Structure of the compensation package for the Senior Management Service in the SA public service

The structure of the remuneration system for the Senior Management Service (SMS) of the South African public service, in terms of distinct grades and remuneration bands, has been discussed in Chapter 12. This section will focus in greater depth on the structure of the inclusive compensation package in the public service.

The inclusive compensation package of South African public servants consists of a basic salary, the employer's contribution to the pension fund, and a flexible portion. The basic salary consists of 60% of the total compensation package (although, in exceptional cases, the percentage is 62% or 74%) (Republic of South Africa 2003: 31).

The flexible portion of the compensation package for members of the Senior Management Service of the South African public service may be structured into the following items (Republic of South Africa 2003: 31–32):

- A car allowance to a maximum amount of 25% of the total package per annum;
- A 13th cheque equal to one twelfth of the basic salary;
- Contribution to a medical aid scheme;
- A housing allowance;
- An entertainment allowance;
- A newspaper and periodical allowance;
- A computer allowance; and
- A non-pensionable cash allowance.

Examples of the structure of inclusive packages for the Senior Management Service are provided in Table 13.1 (Republic of South Africa 2003).

Table 13.1 Examples of the structure of inclusive packages

Inclusive compensation package per annum	Basic salary	Employer's contribution to the pension fund	Flexible portion per annum	
(1) R100 000	R60 000	R9 000	Total: R31 000	
			Motor car allowance:	R14 000
			Service Bonus:	R0 000
			Medical assistance:	R8 000
			Housing allowance:	R5 000
			Entertainment allowance:	R0 000
			Newspaper and Periodical Allowance:	R0 000
			Computer allowance:	R4 000
			Non-pensionable Cash Allowance:	R0 000
(2) R200 000	R120 000	R18 000	Total: R70 000	
			Motor car allowance:	R40 000
			Service Bonus:	R0 000
			Medical assistance:	R8 000
			Housing allowance:	R5 000
			Entertainment allowance:	R2 499
			Newspaper & Periodical Allowance:	R2 400
			Computer allowance:	R4 000
			Non-pensionable Cash Allowance:	R8 101
(3) R300 000	R180 000	R27 000	Total: R93 000	
			Motor car allowance:	R40 000
			Service Bonus:	R15 000
			Medical assistance:	R8 000
			Housing allowance:	R19 101
			Entertainment allowance:	R2 499
			Newspaper & Periodical Allowance:	R2 400
			Computer allowance:	R6 000
			Non-pensionable Cash Allowance:	R0 000

▷

Inclusive compensation package per annum	Basic salary	Employer's contribution to the pension fund	Flexible portion per annum		
(4) R500 000	R300 000	R45 000	Total: R155 000		
			Motor car allowance:		R120 000
			Service Bonus:		R6 000
			Medical assistance:		R10 000
			Housing allowance:		R0 000
			Entertainment allowance:		R2 500
			Newspaper & Periodical Allowance:		R2 400
			Computer allowance:		R6 000
			Non-pensionable Cash Allowance:		R8 100

FOCUS ON RESEARCH 13.2
Employee benefits cost control strategies

Roberts (2001) did research on employee benefits cost control strategies in municipal government (US) and came to the following conclusion:

The provision of a quality compensation programme entails a balance of competitive wages and attractive benefits. A balanced benefits package is critical for addressing employee health and safety needs and for improving the balance between the work and personal lives. Employee benefits are costly, however, and organisations are under pressure to reduce benefits expenditures. An effective benefits cost control process is based on a systematic needs assessment, labour-management co-operation and comprehensive prevention programmes. Most municipal governments rely on short-term displacement strategies that are negatively associated with an effective benefits package. The key is to implement a balanced set of long-term structural and targeted short-term displacement strategies that rationally allocate scarce benefits dollars. Effective and balanced cost reduction programmes provide the opportunity for the simultaneous achievement of attracting and retaining high-quality employees with an acceptable expenditure of scarce public funds.

Source: Roberts (2001)

13.4   Review

Incentive systems and benefit programmes usually form an integral part of an overall compensation system. A wide variety of financial incentive plans are used in an effort to link the pay of employees more closely to their performance. This link is not always easily established, since the success of an incentive system not only depends on the sound mechanics of the plan but also on a variety of determinants such as the institutional climate, employee acceptance, effective administration, and suitability to particular institutional needs and circumstances.

In achieving the common goal of fostering increased performance or output, incentive schemes utilise a variety of approaches in terms of the class of employees to be covered, the measures of performance utilised, the types of behaviour or areas of performance to be encouraged, the institutional level of performance to be rewarded, and the nature of the rewards themselves. These differences in options must be carefully considered when deciding what type of incentive plan will be the most appropriate in addressing the particular needs and compensation objectives of an institution.

Benefits usually comprise a substantial component of employees' total compensation. Other than incentive payments, however, benefits are not normally linked to performance, but are mostly regarded as entitlements; that is, they are seen as part of the conditions of employment. While some benefits are mandated by labour legislation, most of the wide array of possible benefits are provided by employers in an attempt to attract and retain employees and thus remain competitive in the labour market. In devising a suitable benefits programme, various benefit arrangement strategies may be utilised, the most common of which are the add-on strategy and the flexible benefit strategy. The latter has become increasingly popular in the South African context in line with a trend towards greater choice and flexibility in accommodating differing employee needs.

Efficient administration plays a major role in ensuring the success of a benefits programme.

Incentive compensation and benefits programmes, together with the basic salary structure, are equally important components of an overall compensation system. The challenge for effective reward management lies in finding the optimal balance between these components and their congruence with the strategic objectives of the institution, and, in particular, the human resource management strategies that are decided upon.

13.5 Self-evaluation questions

1. What is incentive compensation?
2. List at least five reasons why it is important to have incentive schemes.
3. Discuss the important principles that underlie the process of establishing incentive systems.
4. Differentiate between and compare the merits of individual- and institution-based incentive systems.
5. Discuss the nature and potential of 'ESOPs'.
6. Explain the rationale for and different types of benefits that can be provided to employees.
7. Briefly explain the compensation principles to be considered when a benefit arrangement strategy has to be chosen.
8. How can one go about successfully delivering benefit arrangements?
9. Evaluate the inclusive compensative package of the Senior Management Service in terms of the various benefit arrangement strategies.

Bibliography

Armstrong, M. 1993. *Managing reward systems.* Buckingham: Open University Press.

Armstrong, M, & Murlis, H. 1988. *Reward management.* London: Kogan Page.

Bartol, MB, & Locke, EA. 2000. In SL Rynes & B Gerhart (eds.), *Compensation in organizations: Current research and practice.* San Francisco: Jossey-Bass.

Bekker, D. 1995. Profit sharing: Friend or foe? *HRM*, 11(4), 22–23.

Bernadin, JH, & Russell, JE. 1993. *Human resource management: An experiential approach.* New York: McGraw Hill.

Biesheuvel, S. 1985. *Work motivation and compensation.* Vol. 2. Johannesburg: McGraw Hill.

Bird, A. 1988. ESOPs: Part of a strategy to smash democracy. *SA Labour Bulletin*, 13(6), 44–50.

Brehm, N. 1988. Incentive schemes: Taking over from fringe benefits. *HRM*, May, 10–13.

Burgess, LR. 1989. *Compensation administration.* 2nd edn. Columbus, OH: Merrill.

Bussin, M. 1992. Performance appraisal, remuneration and strategic performance management. *People Dynamics*, March, 23–28.

Bussin, M. 1994. Incentives as a strategic lever. *People Dynamics*, April, 19–26.

Byars, LL, & Rue, LW. 1994. *Human resource management.* 4th edn. Boston, Massachusetts: Irwin.

Cherrington, DJ. 1995. *The management of human resources.* 4th edn. Englewood Cliffs, NJ: Prentice-Hall.

Croome, B. 2001. Structuring your remuneration packages. Unpublished paper presented at PayCon 2001 Conference, 26 September, Sandton.

De Cenzo, DA, & Robbins, SP. 1996. *Human resource management: Concepts and practices.* 4th edn. New York: Wiley.

Dessler, G. 1997. *Human resource management.* 7th edn. Upper Saddle River, NJ: Prentice-Hall.

FSA-Contact. 1993. Peromnes remuneration survey, September 1993.

FSA-Contact. 1995. Peromnes remuneration survey, September 1995.

FSA-Contact. 1998. Paying for performance: A special survey of trends in performance-based pay strategies, May 1998.

Gathercole, J. 1992. Flexibility in institutional and employment practices. *People Dynamics*, February, 8–12.

Gómez-Mejía, LR, Balkin, DB, & Cardy, RL. 2001. *Managing human resources.* 3rd edn. Upper Saddle River, NJ: Prentice-Hall.

Greenblo, A. 1989. In praise of ESOPs. *Finance Week*, March 23–29, p. 4.

Greene, MH. 1990. Flexible benefits. *Superfunds*, August, 26–28.

Grobler, PA. 2001. *Report on human resource management practices in South Africa.* Pretoria: Department of Business Management, University of South Africa.

Gupta, N, & Shaw, JD. 2000. Let the evidence speak: Financial incentives are effective! In FH Maidment (ed.), *Human resources annual editions*, 10th edn. Guilford: Dushkin/McGraw Hill.

Heard, J. 2001. Annual bonus: Are you getting yours? *Business Times*, 2 December 2001.

Heneman, RL, Ledford, GE, & Gresham, MT. 2000. The changing nature of work and its effects on compensation design and delivery. In SL Rynes & B Gerhart (eds.), *Compensation in organizations: Current research and practice.* San Francisco: Jossey-Bass.

Horwitz, F. 1988. Ownership issues: How employee share participation schemes can be made to work. *Finance Week*, February, 4–10, 27.

Horwitz, F, & Frost, P. 1992. Flexible rewards: Critical success factors. *People Dynamics*, June, 27–33.

Ivancevich, JM. 1998. *Human resource management.* 7th edn. Homewood, IL: Irwin.

Lawler, EE. 1990. *Strategic pay.* San Francisco: Jossey-Bass.

Lidstone, J. 1992. *Beyond the pay packet.* London: McGraw Hill.

Lundy, O, & Cowling, A. 1996. *Strategic human resource management.* London: Routledge.

Luthans, F. 1998. *Organizational behavior.* 8th edn. Boston, MA: McGraw Hill.

Maller, J. 1987. Employee share ownership: South Africa's new capitalists? *SA Labour Bulletin*, 12(8), 59–59.

Marx, AE. 1992. *A practical guide on implementing suggestion systems*. Cape Town: Juta.

Mohamed, Y. 1989. Worker participation: A Trojan horse? *SA Labour Bulletin*, 14(5), 93–100.

Muchinsky, P, Kriek, HJ, & Schreuder, D. 2002. *Personnel psychology*. 2nd edn. Cape Town: Oxford University Press.

Nelson, DL, & Quick, JB. 2002. *Understanding organisational behavior: A multimedia approach*. Cincinnati, OH: South-Western.

Roberts, GE. 2001. Employee benefits cost control strategies in municipal government. *Public Performance and Management Review*, 24(4): 389–402

Saratoga Institute (South Africa). 1998. South African human resource effectiveness report. Cape Town.

Sherman, AW, & Bohlander, GW. 1992. *Managing human resources*. 9th edn. Cincinnati, OH: South-Western.

Snelgar, RJ. 1988. Rewarding participation. *IPM Journal*, July, 4–8.

Spangenberg, H. 1993. A managerial view on performance management. *People Dynamics*, October, 30–34.

Spangenberg, H. 1994. *Understanding and implementing performance management*. Cape Town: Juta.

Stacey, K. 1991. Remuneration trends: 1991 and onwards. *IPM Journal*, February, 21–26.

Stone, RJ. 1998. *Human resource management*. 3rd edn. Brisbane: Wiley.

Weibel, A, Rost, K & Osterloh, M. 2010. Pay for performance in the public sector – benefits and (hidden) costs. *Journal of Public Administration Research and Theory*, 20(2): 387–412.

Government regulations

Republic of South Africa. 2001. Public Service Regulations of 2001. Government Gazette, 427 (21951).

Management guides

Republic of South Africa. 2003. Senior management service: Public service handbook. Department of Public Service and Administration. [http://www.dpsa.gov.za/documents/ sms/publications/ smshb 2003]

Establishing and maintaining public sector employee wellness: Health and safety at work

Purpose

The purpose of this chapter is to focus on the various approaches in eliciting, enhancing, and maintaining optimal states of wellness that are beneficial to both the employees and the organisation.

Learning outcomes

After you have read this chapter, you should be able to:
- Describe what is meant by employee wellness.
- Give a brief overview of the statutory regulations governing occupational health and safety in South Africa.
- Explain what is meant by 'a proactive and holistic approach' to employee wellness.
- List and describe the nature and importance of at least seven specific issues in proactive, holistic health and safety management.
- Explain what is meant by occupational mental health.
- Discuss the issue of work-related stress.
- Describe the nature and importance of employee assistance.
- Write an essay on the topic of 'Occupational diseases, hazards, accidents and injuries'.
- Explain the challenges facing South African organisations as a result of the HIV/AIDS threat.
- Describe how to deal with employees who are HIV positive or who have AIDS.
- Name the different stakeholders or role players in occupational health and safety and briefly describe the role of each.

14.1 Introduction

Management's efforts should be directed at eliciting from employees the behaviour and performance that will best achieve the organisation's mission and objectives. Apart from attracting and appointing high-quality staff and deploying strategies and practices that unlock the potential of employees, management may also need to show that they care for or look after their employees. In addition to the provision of remuneration and fringe benefits, it is important also to promote and maintain the overall general state of well-being of the organisation's employees. All other things being equal, an employee who is generally well will usually perform better than one who is generally not well. The idea is thus to improve and maintain 'employee wellness'. As Matlala (1999: 24) states: 'failure by organisations to adopt employee wellness into their culture will inevitably lead to the escalation of sickness and the deterioration of organisational performance'.

Employee wellness refers to the employees' state of optimised social, physical, and mental health and well-being. It entails a holistic approach to looking after the physical, psychological, and social state of well-being of the employees of an organisation. The absolute minimum requirement in this respect is to provide a working environment that is safe and that complies with all legal requirements.

RESEARCH FOCUS ON RESEARCH 14.1
A general overview of research

Employee wellness is a well-research field and covers a wide variety of topics as reflected by the following scholarly publications:

Toxic workplaces and toxic emotions at work
Frost, PJ. 2003. *Toxic emotions at work: How compassionate managers handle pain and conflict.* Boston, Massachusetts: Harvard Business School, 251.

Emotionally anorexic workplaces
Fineman, S. 1993. Organizations as emotional arenas. In S. Fineman (Ed.), *Emotion in organizations.* London, Thousand Oaks, New Delhi: Sage, 9–35.

The personal cost for those exposed to redundancies and downsizing
Stein, HF. 1998. *Euphemism, spin, and the crisis in organizational life.* Westport, Connecticut and London: Quorum.

Stein, HF. 2001. *Nothing personal, just business: A guided journey into organizational darkness.* Westport, Connecticut; London: Quorum.

Vickers, MH. 2002. 'People first – Always!': Values rhetoric to enhance betrayal – A downsizing case study. *Employee Responsibilities and Rights Journal,* 14(2), 207–217.

Bullying and violence at work
Barron, O. 2002. Why workplace bullying and violence are different: Protecting employees from both. In M Gill, B Fisher & V Bowie (Eds.), *Violence at work: Causes, patterns and prevention.* Cullompton, Devon, UK: Willan, 151–164.

Mann, R. 1996. Psychological abuse in the workplace. In P McCarthy, M Sheehan & W Wilkie (Eds.), *Bullying: From backyard to boardroom.* Sydney: Millennium, Beyond Bullying Association, 83–92

Quine, L. 1999.Workplace bullying in NHS community trust: Staff questionnaire survey. *British Medical Journal,* 318(7178), 228–232.

Randall, P. 1997. *Adult bullying: Perpetrators and victims.* London and New York: Routledge.

Rees, S. 1995. Greed and bullying. In S Rees & G Rodley (Eds.), *The human costs of managerialism: Advocating the recovery of humanity.* Sydney, Australia: Pluto, 197–210.

Vickers, MH. 2001. Bullying as unacknowledged organizational evil: A researcher's story. *Employee Responsibilities and Rights Journal,* 13(4), 207–217.

Vickers, MH. 2006. Towards employee wellness: Rethinking Bullying Paradoxes and Masks. Employees Responsibilities and Rights Journal, 18: 267–281

Alienating workplaces
Blauner, R. 1964. *Alienation and freedom: The factory worker and his industry.* Chicago and London: The University of Chicago Press. ▷

Braverman, H. 1994. The degradation of work. In H Clark, J Chandler, & J Barry (Eds.), *Organisation and identities: Text and readings in organisational behaviour.* London and Glasgow: Chapman & Hall, 385–387.

Fromm, E. 1963/1994. Alienation. In H Clark, J Chandler, & J Barry (Eds.), *Organisation and identities: Text and readings in organisational behavior.* London, Glasgow, New York, Melbourne: Chapman & Hall, 391–396.

La Bier, D. 1986. *Modern madness: The emotional fallout of success.* Sydney: Addison-Wesley.

Abusive workplaces

Perrone, J, & Vickers, MH. 2004. Emotions as strategic game in a hostile workplace: An exemplar case study. *Employee Responsibilities and Rights Journal,* 16(3), 167–178.

Powell, GN. 1998. The abusive organization. *Academy of Management Executive,* 12(2), 95–96.

The traumatised worker

Vickers, MH. 2004. The traumatised worker: A concern for employers and employees. *Employee Responsibilities and Rights Journal,* 16(3), 113–116.

The work-home conflict

Thomson, D, & Dunstan, D. 2002. Examining the relationship between and the effect of litigation on an injury. In: *Occupational Stress Conference, PPL Education Services,* Sydney, 20 November, 43–60.

Vickers, MH. 1998. Life at work with 'invisible' chronic illness (ICI): A passage of trauma – Turbulent, random, poignant. *Administrative Theory and Praxis,* 20(2), 196–210.

Vickers, MH. 1999. 'Sick' organisations, 'rabid' managerialism: Work-life narratives from people with 'invisible' chronic illness. *Public Voices,* 4(1), 59–82.

Vickers, MH. 2001 *Work and unseen chronic illness: Silent voices.* London and New York: Routledge.

Vickers, MH, Parris, M, & Bailey, J. 2004. Working mothers of children with chronic illness: Narratives of working and caring. *Australian Journal of Early Childhood,* 20(1), 39–44.

Although some types of work are generally more dangerous than others, a common-law duty rests on all employers to provide their employees with safe working conditions. South African courts have often endorsed the common-law principle that requires employers to take reasonable care of the health and safety of their employees. Apart from the common-law requirements, there is specific legislation in South Africa which focuses on the health and safety of employees.

Although legislation is only a very basic starting point when it comes to promoting and maintaining employee wellness in the workplace, this chapter begins with a brief introduction to some of the important aspects relating to health and safety legislation in South Africa. Of course, taking good care of an organisation's employees goes far beyond simply keeping within the requirements of the law. A much more constructive and proactive approach is required to elicit, enhance, and maintain optimal states of wellness that are beneficial to both the employees and the organisation. This chapter therefore focuses largely on the elements of such a holistic approach which fall, to a large extent, beyond the scope of the law.

14.2 The legislative framework governing health and safety at work

14.2.1 General

Apart from the common law and the Bill of Rights (in the Constitution), there are two pieces of legislation with refined legal requirements regarding employee health and safety, namely the Occupational Health and Safety Act (OHSA) 85 of 1993 and the Mine Health and Safety Act 29 of 1996.

The overall aim of the OHSA is to provide for the health and safety of employees at work (including such aspects as health and safety hazards and the safety of plant machinery and equipment). The OHSA is also applicable to public officials: the Public Service Regulations of 2001 stipulate that 'a head of department shall establish and maintain a safe and healthy work environment for employees of the department' (Part VI,D). Certain employers and employees are, however, specifically excluded from the ambit of the OHSA. These include parties covered by the Merchant Shipping Act and people employed in mines, mining areas, or any works as defined in the Mine Health and Safety Act 29 of 1996.

Because the mining industry still forms the bedrock of the South African economy, and because it is in mining in particular that major health and safety problems occur, it is important to take note of health and safety regulations in terms of the Mine Health and Safety Act. Before taking a brief look at this legislation, let us illustrate why we regard this as such an important topic in the mining industry.

Hermanus (1991: 17) points out that, between 1900 and 1991, over 68 000 mineworkers died through accidents on South African mines, and more than one million workers were permanently disabled. Statistics generally bear testimony to the fact that mining is a very hazardous occupation: In 1989 alone, 735 workers died in accidents on mines and a further 10 000 were injured; in 1993, 578 miners died in accidents; in 1994 there were 483 deaths due to mining accidents and 7 852 injuries (Hermanus 1991: 17; Brase 1995: 24; Spearing 1996: 21). In 1986, a fire at Kinross mine near Secunda in Gauteng claimed the lives of 177 workers, and, in 1995, 104 workers died due to an accident involving a locomotive that fell down a mine shaft at Vaal Reefs gold mine (Jones 1996). Gleason (1996) observes:

'SA gold mines have always been deep, dark and dangerous places. More than 80 000 lives have been taken in accidents since the discovery of gold in 1886. The men who work in them accept a precarious working lifestyle as part of the deal.'

14.2.2 The Mine Health and Safety Act 29 of 1996: Objects of the Act

Historically in South Africa, the concern for the health and safety of workers arose from the dangers inherent in mining. Apart from the common-law right to work in a safe environment, safety in the mining industry was regulated by industry-specific statutes, the earliest of which was the Mines and Works Act of 1911. The latest statute in this regard is the Mine Health and Safety Act 29 of 1996. The objects of the Act are as follows (Section 1 of Act 29 of 1996):

- To protect the health and safety of persons at mines;
- To require employers and employees to identify hazards and eliminate, control, and minimise the risks relating to health and safety at mines;
- To give effect to the public international law obligations of the Republic that concern health and safety at mines;
- To provide for employee participation in matters of health and safety through health and safety representatives and the health and safety committees at mines;
- To provide for effective monitoring of health and safety conditions at mines;
- To provide for enforcement of health and safety measures at mines;
- To provide for investigations and inquiries to improve health and safety; and
- To promote: (1) a culture of health and safety in the mining industry; (2) training in health and safety in the mining industry; and (3) co-operation and consultation on health and safety between the State, employers, employees, and their representatives.

Employees in the mining industry who are injured in the performance of their duties or who suffer from occupational diseases are compensated in terms of the Occupational Diseases in Mines and Works Act 78 of 1973 (ODMWA) in a similar manner to which workers in other industries are compensated for occupational diseases or work-related injuries in terms of the Compensation for Occupational Injuries and Diseases Act 130 of 1993 (COIDA).

14.2.3 The Occupational Health and Safety Act 85 of 1993: Provisions of the Act

14.2.3.1 General

As we indicated earlier, the Occupational Health and Safety Act 85 of 1993 (OHSA) forms the legislative framework in respect of health and safety issues in most South African organisations and specifically institutions in the South African public sector. The OHSA makes the following provisions for the achievement of its objectives:
- Establish an Advisory Council for Occupational Health and Safety.
- Every employer (including every head of a public institution) must provide and maintain, as far as is reasonably practicable, a working environment that is safe and without risk to the health of his or her employees, as well as other people affected by the operations of the business.
- Every supplier or manufacturer of items used in a workplace must ensure that such items do not pose a safety or health risk.
- Every employer must inform his or her workforce (and the appointed health and safety representatives) of hazards at the workplace.
- Every employee must:
  - take reasonable care for the health and safety of himself or herself and of other persons who may be affected by his or her acts or omissions;

- carry out any lawful order given to him or her, and obey the health and safety rules and procedures laid down by his or her employer;
- report any unsafe or unhealthy situation which comes to his or her attention; and
- report any incident which may affect his or her health or which has caused an injury to himself or herself.

- The appointment of health and safety representatives. The Act provides that every employer who employs more than twenty employees at any workplace must appoint health and safety representatives.
- The establishment of one or more health and safety committees in each workplace where two or more health and safety representatives are designated.
- Certain incidents must be reported to an inspector.
- Occupational diseases must be reported to the chief inspector.
- Wide powers of inspection, entry enquiry and seizure are held by inspectors.
- A wide range of acts of omission and commission are declared offences and can incur criminal penalties.

14.2.3.2 Health and safety representatives and committees

An employer must provide the agreed-upon facilities, assistance and training that the health and safety representative reasonably requires for the performance of his or her functions. A health and safety representative shall not incur any civil liability by reason of the fact only that he or she failed to do anything which he or she may do or is required to do in terms of the Act.

Functions of health and safety representatives

A health and safety representative may perform the following functions in respect of the workplace or section of the workplace for which he or she has been designated:

- Review the effectiveness of health and safety measures;
- Identify potential hazards and potential major incidents at the workplace;
- In collaboration with his or her employer, examine the causes of incidents at the workplace;
- Investigate complaints by any employee relating to that employee's health or safety at work;
- Make representations to the employer or a health and safety committee on matters arising from his or her performance of the preceding functions;
- Make representations to the employer on general matters affecting the health or safety of the employees at the workplace;
- Inspect the workplace with a view to the health and safety of employees, at such intervals as may be agreed upon with the employer;
- Participate in consultations with inspectors at the workplace and accompany inspectors on inspections of the workplace;
- Receive certain information from inspectors; and

- In his or her capacity as a health and safety representative attend meetings of the health and safety committee of which he or she is a member, in connection with any of the above functions.

In order to perform the above functions, a health and safety representative is entitled, in respect of the workplace or section of the workplace for which he or she has been designated to do the following:
- Visit the site of an incident at all times and attend any inspection *in loco*;
- Attend any investigation or formal inquiry held in terms of this Act;
- Inspect any document which the employer is required to keep in terms of this Act, in so far as it is reasonably necessary for performing his or her functions;
- Accompany an inspector on any inspection;
- Be accompanied by a technical adviser on any inspection with the approval of the employer (which approval shall not be unreasonably withheld); and
- Participate in any internal health or safety audit.

Functions of health and safety committees
- Make recommendations to the employer or, where the recommendations fail to resolve the matter, to an inspector, regarding health or safety matters;
- Discuss any incident at the workplace in which any person was injured, became ill or died, and may in writing report on the incident to an inspector; and
- Perform such other functions as may be prescribed.

14.2.3.3 Reporting duties

In the event of an incident in which a person died, or was injured to such an extent that he or she is likely to die, or suffered the loss of a limb or part of a limb, no person may, without the consent of an inspector, disturb the site at which the incident

Reporting of certain incidents to an inspector

The following must be reported to an inspector: each work-related incident or incident in connection with the use of plant or machinery, in which, or in consequence of which:
- Any person dies, becomes unconscious, suffers the loss of a limb or part of a limb or is otherwise injured or becomes ill to such a degree that he or she is likely either to die or to suffer a permanent physical defect or likely to be unable for a period of at least 14 days either to work or to continue with the activity for which he or she was employed or is usually employed;
- A major incident occurred;
- The health or safety of any person was endangered and where a dangerous substance was spilled, the uncontrolled release of any substance under pressure took place, machinery or any part thereof fractured or failed resulting in flying, falling or uncontrolled moving objects, or
- Machinery ran out of control.

occurred or remove any article or substance involved in the incident. This provision, as well as the provisions relating to the reporting of incidents, does not apply in respect of a traffic accident on a public road, an incident occurring in a private household (provided that the householder reports the incident to the South African Police), or an aviation accident.

14.3 Employee wellness: Managing health and safety

14.3.1 General

Traditionally, management has not always been proactively altruistic: if it is anticipated that there is no real benefit to be derived from a particular investment of resources (in other words, to offset the outlay), the investment may well be made elsewhere. Management has thus tended to adopt a follow-the-rulebook policy in matters of health and safety.

In more recent times, however, with the spiralling costs of medical care, as well as the growing realisation that absenteeism costs a lot of money and that labour productivity must be improved, management has been considering alternatives that may yield results superior to the reactive, minimum-legalistic approach. There has thus been an increasing awareness of the direct and indirect costs that can be associated with such a negative approach. According to one expert ('Healthcare needs total company management' 1993), the 'direct costs of healthcare financing through medical aid have been escalating at 50% above the CPI for several years'. Santhey (1993: 14–15) indicates that medical costs rose beyond control over the period 1985–1990, with medical aid premiums having risen by 34%. Organisations have thus begun to realise that the costs linked to maintaining their medical schemes (some estimate it at more than 7% of their monthly wage bills) can no longer be afforded.

As Taylor (1992) points out: 'If every employee takes 10 days' paid sick leave per year, the cost to the company is just over 4% of payroll'. Obviously, not all absenteeism cases are related to poor physical health – some are also attitudinal. Attitudinal problems – although the whole spectrum of human resource management activities and practices and a host of other external factors can play a role – can also, however, often be related to the social, psychological, or mental well-being of a person.

It has therefore become increasingly common for managers to consider the potential benefits of a system focused on proactively promoting and maintaining the mental and physical well-being of employees rather than dealing with health and safety problems as they occur. Such an approach has various characteristics.

14.3.2 A strategic and holistic focus

It has already been stated that a holistic approach requires that care be taken of the 'whole person or employee'. This means that the focus is not only on safety or on the provision of medical aid assistance but also on the acknowledgement that any person coming to work comes there as a whole person. One cannot detach the worker from the human being. It can almost be said that what needs to be taken care of proactively is thus 'body mind, and soul'. This means that even the broader social and domestic dynamics of employees, such as those related to personal and family lives, must be taken into account. In this respect attention must, for instance, be paid to a well-balanced work and family life.

In addition, and linked to such a holistic approach, is the strategic focus that is required. Part of a strategic approach to managing employment relationships will be the need for functional strategies. One particular sub-strategy relates to drawing up some kind of organisational employee wellness strategy, plan, and programme. A policy document (based on the strategy) should therefore ideally be drawn up, spelling out at least what the organisation's philosophy is in respect of promoting and maintaining the physical, mental, and social well-being of employees. Formulating such a strategy and policy should obviously be developed as part of an inclusive process in which all the stakeholders are involved and take ownership. The plan should contain a vision and mission statement and some general principles, as well as specific objectives in respect of employee wellness.

14.3.3 Specific issues in proactive, holistic health and safety management

The old adage that prevention is better than cure can be taken one step further in the context of employee wellness: it has been proven that not only is prevention better than cure, it is also cheaper than cure (Jensen 1987: 4). A preventative approach entails a number of factors to be incorporated in the strategies, policies, and action plans or programmes.

14.3.3.1 Ergonomics and workplace design

Ergonomics have to do with matching the physical work environment to the worker. If the work environment is ergonomically satisfactory, it will enhance the general state of health and safety as well. Hattingh (1992: 55) puts it as follows:

> The purpose of ergonomics is to ensure that a person's abilities are utilised efficiently and that the equipment being used will not endanger his health or safety ... if the job is ergonomically satisfactory, then the worker will work and apply safety measures.

Care should thus be taken right from the outset at the point of workplace design – including the design of buildings and infrastructure.

In 1989, research conducted in the USA indicated that 30% of all buildings in America suffer from what is known as the sick building syndrome (Erwee 1993). In 1982, the World Health Organisation officially accepted this concept, which they define as a building in which a significant percentage of workers show symptoms such as headaches and fatigue, and eye, nose, and throat irritations.

Sick-building syndrome in South Africa

In 1992, an opinion survey conducted in South Africa under the auspices of the American organisation, Healthy Buildings International, showed that South African employers cannot afford to be complacent about the 'sick building syndrome'.

The researchers visited 800 office buildings and interviewed 500 office workers from Johannesburg and Cape Town. Of those interviewed, 66% were of the opinion that there was scope for improving their office environments. More than 80% were dissatisfied with the temperature control in their offices and would have preferred to control it themselves. Sixty-five per cent indicated that they regularly stayed away from work to recover from symptoms that can be related to sick-building syndrome. The symptoms most commonly experienced by these people included fatigue or tardiness (42%), listlessness (26%), headache (39%), itchy and tired eyes (26%), dry eyes (22%), runny nose (22%) and dry throat (24%). According to the Director of Healthy Buildings International, 75% of these sick building syndrome symptoms in South African office buildings can be ascribed to polluted air, poor ventilation, and insufficient filter systems in air conditioners. The research showed that almost 50% of the office buildings had filters that were dirty and contaminated.

Source: Erwee (1993)

14.3.3.2   Health screening and safety auditing

Traditionally, health screening was often viewed as a perk earmarked for senior management and especially executive employees. This situation is, however, gradually changing, with some organisations offering such a service to all levels of employees. Health screening or assessment tests are basically medical investigations that do not arise from an employee's request to be assessed with regard to a specific health-related complaint. It is a proactive intervention to make an early identification of any diseases from which an employee may be suffering and to diagnose an employee's general state of health.

By conducting such assessments, health-related problems can be detected at early stages and a health status baseline can be developed; from this a programme of lifestyle improvement can be designed. Comprehensive health screening interventions may furthermore go beyond assessing concrete health measures (such as coronary heart disease, respiratory disease, blood pressure, cholesterol levels, etc.). Aspects such as habits, knowledge, and attitudes may also be screened in such comprehensive health screening interventions. Other tests may include stress level tests, hearing and vision tests, urine tests, blood tests, and fitness tests. Nutritional assessments can also be conducted to collect information on such aspects as food intake and eating patterns to detect how healthy an employee's lifestyle is. Determining the nutritional status of employees should be an important component of holistic health assessment interventions in South African organisations.

Safety audits, on the other hand, are aimed at establishing the quality of an organisation's safety policies, programmes, procedures, and practices. This may include conducting safety attitude surveys to determine the extent to which workers are sensitive and knowledgeable about a safety-driven environment.

These assessments and audits are necessary to identify and detect in good time potential threats to the establishment of an environment conducive to employee wellness. These evaluations therefore have to be conducted on a regular basis.

14.3.3.3 Sensitisation and education

If an organisation wishes to establish a work environment of employee wellness, it is essential to launch aggressive campaigns to promote the philosophy that employee health, safety, and general well-being are important and beneficial to both the employee and the organisation.

This begins with a process of awareness creation by means of methods such as posters, leaflets, talks, competitions, videos, demonstrations, or advertisements in internal/in-house newspapers. The idea is, however, not only to sensitise employees or to create awareness. At the end of the day, the efforts to promote such an environment require employees to be proactive and to do something about their own health and safety. The idea is to import information to explain the importance of health and safety and to persuade employees to become more serious about these aspects in their day-to-day lives and in the workplace. Such efforts should thus include workshops where employees can learn from others (co-employees preferably) how to go about being more safety conscious and leading a more healthy lifestyle. An important component of a healthier lifestyle is looking after fitness and relaxation.

14.3.3.4 Fitness programmes and recreation facilities

Research has shown that proper physical exercise and general fitness can not only enhance a person's quality of life but can also prolong it. Promoting exercise and the improvement of the fitness of employees is therefore an important component of a holistic, proactive approach to the establishment of employee wellness. Being fit is important for the healthy functioning of the cardiovascular system, the endocrine system, and the musculoskeletal system. It helps to control weight and to reduce stress, thereby making a positive contribution to a person's general feeling of well-being – and thus to his or her state of mental health. Fit employees are generally regarded as being more energetic and as better workers. Such employees will usually be happier and more productive, and absenteeism will, in all likelihood, decrease.

There are various ways of promoting exercise and fitness. Sport as a recreational activity often forms part of the lifestyle of fit people. As Jensen (1987: 58) points out:

> Many people get their exercise from participating in sports, so recreational activities can form an important component of a complete wellness system ... Sports can be an effective release valve for stress that originates with the individual or the organisation.

Organised recreational activities such as sports events can have the additional benefit of enhancing the social dimension of the work environment. Some informal gatherings lead to constructive interaction and communication, which can create a sense of togetherness and team spirit among employees.

Improving physical fitness through organised recreation and sports events (such as soccer, cricket, tennis, golf, etc.) can thus improve morale and cooperation among employees. Apart from team sports, there are also outdoor activities such as hiking, backpacking, sightseeing and fishing and cultural activities such as going to art and musical festivals. Obviously not all of these contribute positively to physical fitness, but they do have the potential to act as stress relief valves. Exercise can take various forms, such as gymnasium work, aerobics, jogging, cycling, squash, swimming, tennis, walking, etc.

It is up to the management of an organisation to decide what premium they put on the physical fitness of their employees. If fitness is seen as beneficial, free fitness assessments may be offered, and it may be decided to provide recreation and exercising facilities on the organisation's own premises.

14.3.3.5 Work and family life interactions

Research has shown that conflicts between family and working life are related to aspects such as increased health risks for parents, poor morale, depression, reduced life satisfaction, absenteeism, poorer work performance, and decreased productivity (Covin & Brush 1993).

Job-family conflict is becoming an increasingly important issue within the context of human resource management. Because our workforces are becoming more and more diverse, with the female/male ratio increasing and with an increasing number of two-career couples, the chances of employing individuals who experience job-family conflict are greater. This phenomenon is, however, not limited to female employees. Any employee who experiences the dual pressure of having to comply with the competing requirements and expectations of work and family life may suffer from the conflict.

Various options are available to organisations to prevent job-family conflict levels which are so high that they impact adversely on employee mindsets and on performance and productivity. These range from providing child and elder (parent) care facilities to more flexibility in terms of time, working place and leave, and to the involvement of spouses and children in certain recreational, fitness, and other social activities and facilities of the organisation. An organisation may even, as part of their management development initiatives for instance, occasionally involve the spouse of the trainee in the development programme. Part of the performance incentive scheme of an organisation may be to award 'family breakaways' for high achievers. Some refer to these efforts holistically as work-life programmes (Martinez 1993).

It seems that one of the most popular and feasible options is flexibility. This may include various possibilities such as work schedule adaptations, flexitime, job sharing, flexi-place and telecommuting. Such arrangements may provide employees with the necessary scope and flexibility to attend to family-related issues like caring for sick children or attending school activities such as an athletics meeting or a rugby or soccer match.

FOCUS ON RESEARCH 14.2
Working mothers of children with chronic illness

In an article 'Working mothers of children with chronic illness: Narratives of working and caring' published in 2004 in the *Australian Journal of Early Childhood*, 20(1): 39–44, Vickers, Parris and Bailey conclude as follow on their research:

'The role of mothers as primary carers of children remains despite the shift of many women to the full-time workforce. These stories reflect a familiar theme: women juggling full-time work against competing and conflicting demands at home. [...] However, the stories presented here are of grave concern.

'These women reported 'doing it all' as they bear the additional burdens of caring for their child with chronic illness. Alongside the demands of full-time employment, these women are often the first point of call for their child's needs, whether at home, at school, or with medical requirements such as doctors' visits and hospitalisation. Furthermore, they may often shoulder the main responsibility for both the daily physical and emotional care of their chronically ill child. For childhood educators relating with these women, an understanding of these competing, and often overwhelming, demands is essential in establishing rapport and working together for optimal benefits for their children.

'The women in this study also spoke of the frustrations and challenges in endeavouring to foster their child's development, while at the same time having responsibility for the healthy functioning of their entire family. These demands often create a sense of uncertainty and fear about the future. Again, in working with these women and their families, recognition of these stresses and fears is paramount when determining ongoing strategies.

'These exploratory stories flag a very serious problem in our communities, homes and workplaces. On the strength of the findings presented in this paper, and other emergent themes, we would recommend a larger, more generalised study of the concerns experienced by these respondents. If women are expected to shoulder the burden for all this, then it is inevitable that their children and families will suffer, especially those in greatest need – their children with chronic illness.'

An increasingly important aspect is the need for employers to show concern about childcare (Bryant 1990). Options in this area are also quite diverse. One option is that of providing resource and referral services. An official is appointed or an agency is contracted to provide employees with consultation on childcare and to make lists available regarding childcare options. The employer may even establish an on-site day-care facility, or it may purchase slots in existing community facilities which are then reserved for the children of the organisation's employees. Other options are to enter into some joint venture with other nearby organisations or to appoint an official of the organisation to organise and supervise a day-care network of caregivers in the neighbourhood.

Irrespective of the way in which organisations go about dealing with potential work-family conflict, it is essential that they should be fully aware of the importance and potential value of this aspect of human resource management. As the human resource director of one company points out (Martinez 1993: 38): 'When companies are willing to recognise that blood is thicker than water, it shows employees that their employer really cares about them – and that galvanises loyalty.'

14.3.3.6   Nutrition programmes

An essential component of a healthy lifestyle is a good balanced diet. Unfortunately, we live in an era in which junk food is extremely popular. Many of the health problems plaguing our society, such as cancer and cardiovascular disorders, can possibly be linked to unhealthy lifestyles and poor eating habits. It is estimated, for instance, that 35% of the risk of developing cancer is related to diet (Wheeler 1984: 294). In addition, many people today are overweight, which can sometimes be a threat to a person's health and can also be linked to diet deficiencies and poor eating habits. Nutrition programmes are basically aimed at improving the eating habits of individuals and at encouraging them to follow a more balanced diet.

Some workplace nutrition programmes are very basic and aim simply at informing employees about the potential disadvantages and risks associated with poor nutritional habits and the potential benefits of following a good diet. This may include increasing staff awareness by means of leaflets, booklets, and posters, or even group sessions involving short presentations using visual aids such as videos or films. Other programmes are much more intervening by nature and aim at preventing or even treating diet-related health problems through weight control and diet modification. Such interventions will normally form part of a holistic wellness programme that includes fitness exercises, stress-control elements, and anti-smoking programmes (discussed in the next section).

In such nutrition programmes which involve behaviour change, assessments will be done to identify the employee's eating habits and the quality of his or her diet. This may include physical examinations (for example mass, height, blood pressure) and screening the usual intake of fats, carbohydrates, protein, vitamins, minerals, sugar, etc. It may also include an investigation into the perceptions and attitudes of the employee regarding eating and nutrition. After determining the employee's dietary habits and particular needs, an individualised programme is worked out that may include food choice combinations, meal planning guidelines, and guidelines regarding meal preparation and general eating habits. These programmes will typically also be longer term, including some kind of ongoing monitoring, feedback, and support system.

Although such comprehensive intervening workplace nutrition programmes may be very expensive and not entirely appropriate for all South African public institutions, some institutions may well find them worth considering as part of their promotion of holistic employee wellness.

14.3.3.7 Smoking policies

It is common knowledge today that smoking causes health problems. These problems can basically be categorised into two groups:
- The health implications for the employee who smokes; and
- The health and other implications for non-smoking employees who become passive smokers as a result of their colleagues' smoking habits.

The health risks associated with smoking are generally well known. Smoking is, for instance, a major contributing factor in chronic respiratory diseases. It is estimated, for example, that nine out of ten lung cancer deaths are attributable to smoking (Humphrey & Smith 1991: 137). In addition to this, research has shown that smoking is an important contributory factor in coronary heart disease. With regard to the latter, Jones and Kleiner (1990: 29) state that 'recent studies have shown that approximately 46% of total coronary disease and 54% of non-fatal heart attacks in women are attributed to cigarette use.'

The implications of smoking for organisations are thus abundantly clear. According to American Lung Association reports, each year smokers are absent from work more than 81 million more days than non-smokers (Jones & Kleiner 1990: 29) (bearing in mind, of course, the size of the total American workforce). Jones and Kleiner (1990: 29) make the following assertion:

> Since the employer directly, through paying sick leave, or indirectly through lost production, pays for the cost of absenteeism, employers are becoming increasingly aware of the cost of having employees who smoke. In addition, with company paid medical plans, the cost of increased illnesses among smokers is ultimately borne by the business.

Apart from the implications for the smoker, there are also major implications for non-smoking employees and for the organisation as a whole (as illustrated above). It follows that, if cigarette smoke is a health risk for the smoker, it must also be so for the non-smoker. The breathed-out smoke contains the same harmful ingredients (such as carbon monoxide and recognised carcinogens – in other words, chemicals that cause cancer) to which the smoker is exposed. Smoking often bothers non-smokers, causing conflict, hostility, negative feelings and deteriorating interpersonal relations – all of which may impact negatively on workforce morale and productivity.

Smoking is thus an issue affecting health in the holistic sense: physical, mental, and social well-being. It is therefore essential for organisations to tackle the issue of smoking in the workplace. In this regard, Araujo (1996: 39) gives the following general advice:

> There is no single approach and policy for all organisations. The general principles, however, are that a working party should be established, the issue should be raised, the workforce should be consulted and the policy must then be formulated and implemented. One should try to avoid allowing this to become a management/subordinate issue and turn it into a health matter. It is in the interest of good industrial relations to work out an agreed policy between the company, employees and their representative trade union (if any), taking into account the interests of smokers and non-smokers, rather than merely imposing an immediate and total ban.

With regard to balancing the interests of smokers and non-smokers, one of the areas in which smoking causes the most discomfort is that of open-plan offices. While unrestricted and uncontrolled smoking can cause a great deal of discomfort to non-smokers in open-plan areas, it is also true that a complete ban on smoking in such areas could be counterproductive – especially if smokers leave their workstation every now and again to go and smoke. A more meaningful approach would thus be to take into consideration the interests of both groups of employees.

Smoking imposes certain costs on an organisation, such as those linked to absenteeism and productivity, as well as cleaning costs and medical retirements. The control of smoking in the workplace through a professional process of formulating and implementing an appropriate non-smoking policy will enhance the healthiness or wellness of both smoking and non-smoking employees. This, in turn, can result in major positive benefits for the organisation. It may even be possible for the organisation to negotiate an improved benefit premium deal with its medical aid company.

In summary, Araujo (1996: 40) asserts: 'Because implementation of a non-smoking policy is relatively inexpensive, it represents a good investment for health promotion.'

14.3.3.8 Being prepared for emergencies

Part of a proactive approach to managing employee health and safety at work is to draw up contingency plans and to have the necessary infrastructure to deal with any emergencies. There are many types of emergency situation that can arise in the work situation and that can threaten the life, safety, or general well-being of employees. A distinction can be made between natural and man-made disasters. The former refer to situations like floods, storms, earthquakes, and epidemics, while the latter include riots and serious labour unrest, bomb threats, and fires.

Apart from constantly ensuring that all the necessary emergency equipment such as fire appliances and equipment (fire extinguishers and fire alarms) are at the right places and in working order, it is important to ensure that adequate emergency escape routes exist and that these are easily visible and clearly marked.

Although all employees should be trained to observe the housekeeping rules so that emergency situations such as fire outbreaks can be prevented, emergency procedures covering all kinds of eventuality should be well established, and all employees should be thoroughly drilled in the way in which to deal with any kind of emergency situation.

The emergency infrastructure should include the necessary first-aid facilities such as a first-aid room and first-aid equipment and material. Certain employees, who are specifically designated as first-aiders, should receive special training in first aid. Often, these employees are trained by outside experts – especially if the organisation does not have the necessary internal expertise. Furthermore, all employees should receive at least some very basic, introductory first-aid training.

As already mentioned, one of the most important elements of a proactive attitude towards employee safety and health is to establish adequate contingency or emergency plans and procedures that can cater for a variety of eventualities such as fires, bomb scares, or explosions. Obviously, contingency plans will depend largely on the nature of the workplace. The evacuation process would, for instance, differ radically between a gold mine, an open-core coal mine, a chemical factory, or a large retail store. Regardless of the exact nature of these infrastructural elements, plans, and procedures, it is essential not to neglect these aspects, as they form an essential component of also proving to employees that the organisation's management values employee safety and health.

Part of any such emergency plan is to appoint a person who will be the emergency controller. This person will have the responsibility of drafting the emergency plan and organising the emergency training. In order to do this, he or she will require the following (Acutt 1992: 168–169):

- A plan of the whole site, together with a floor plan of the buildings indicating all entrances and the different areas;
- The floor plan must indicate main electricity boards, hazardous substances, inflammable materials, gas cylinders, etc.;
- All fire extinguishers, first-aid boxes, and emergency equipment, including rescue equipment, must be indicated on this chart;
- Updated lists of names, addresses, and telephone numbers of all emergency personnel, senior management, and local emergency services;
- An effective communication system;
- An identification system for emergency personnel;
- An emergency transport system; and
- An efficient evacuation system.

Other aspects to be catered for relate to security, an emergency command centre, the structuring and framing of rescue, fire control and first-aid teams, transport, and detailed plans to protect buildings, material, plant, equipment, stock, and especially the employees of the organisation.

14.3.4 Other special issues regarding health and safety in the work environment

14.3.4.1 Occupational mental health

Occupational mental health (OMH) as an applied field of clinical and abnormal psychology deals with the maladjustment or adjustment of employees in the work or organisational context (Bergh 1992: 194). This is an extremely important and specialised topic, to the extent that it is a separate branch of Industrial Psychology as a field of study. For the purposes of this chapter, a brief introduction to some of the topics and issues that fall within the field of OMH will suffice.

The first question one may wish to ask relates to what constitutes an adjusted or maladjusted employee. In other words, what criteria are used to evaluate psychological adjustment (or maladjustment) in the work environment? In this regard, there are many relevant criteria, and these can be classified in many different ways. It must be emphasised, however, that a person's behaviour at work, and the meaning of that behaviour, must always be compared with certain criteria in the context of his or her actions (Bergh 1992: 197). Some of the general categories of criteria, within which more specific criteria can be set, include the following (Bergh 1992: 201):

- Attitudes towards and observations of one's own personality (self), which include accurate observation of one's self-image, attitudes towards one's own personality (self), and an understanding of one's identity;
- Growth, development, and self-actualisation, where the level of development and the person's usefulness in a role are evaluated;
- Integration, which refers to the individual's ability to assimilate and cope with influences from the environment;
- Autonomy, which implies the ability to act effectively by means of internal powers without the unnecessary domination of external influences;
- The observation of reality, which implies the accurate assessment of the external environment in terms of internal psychological needs;
- Interpersonal efficiency, which refers to the establishment of interpersonal relationships;
- Affective conditions, which include emotional manifestations such as manic depression, anxiety, fear, etc.;
- Specific pathological conditions, both physical and psychological, for instance schizophrenia, neuroses, brain syndromes, etc.; and
- Adjustment and adaptability; in other words, the person's ability to meet the demands of the environment in terms of his or her personal capabilities.

A complex web of potential factors may, separately or in various combinations, influence the state of OMH of an employee either positively or negatively. Before we briefly look at these, it is important to take note of certain types of psychological work-adjustment problem that may be encountered by employees in organisations.

Some psychopathological conditions relate to stress-based disorders, others to anxiety, some to personality disorders or to psychosomatic, narcotic, and organic conditions, and still others to mental retardation.

Stress-related adjustment problems can, for instance, occur immediately or at some time after a very traumatic experience such as a disaster; for example, after an explosion in a factory or a rock slide in a mine. Emotional disorders such as fear, anger, or depression may follow, which may in turn lead to poor concentration or absenteeism. On the other hand, neurotic conditions are characterised by internal emotional states such as anxiety, which can directly have a negative effect on work behaviour. As far as personality problems are concerned, it is important to note that some experts believe that general personality disorders need not affect the work personality (the work personality is the personality of a person in the work or production situation). Some people, for instance, have a negative perception of work and of their roles as employees – possibly because they were brought up in an environment in which work was over emphasised to the extent that it could be equated to something akin to slavery. For some, work may arouse feelings of fear, discomfort, or tension – for instance, if they doubt their abilities or are handicapped.

Psychosomatic disorders refer to cases in which physical symptoms and psychological states are closely interlinked. Thus, for instance, negative emotions such as anger, worry, and anxiety can contribute to the formation of stomach ulcers. As soon as the physical symptoms are identified, the person begins to worry all over again. Bergh (1992: 233) observes that 'psychosomatic problems are among the major work-related problems encountered among managers. In severe cases these conditions can result in death, early retirement, disability, hospitalisation or poor health which leads to losses for both the individual and the organisation.' Organic conditions refer to the negative emotional, intellectual, and behavioural implications that brain damage can cause. When there is mental retardation due to underdeveloped intellectual functioning, behavioural problems may also arise in the workplace.

All these types of disorder may have effects that lead to such problems as absenteeism, accidents, underachievement, poor productivity, and staff turnover. There are also other psychological work adjustment problems such as workaholism, burnout, and work alienation.

Work alienation occurs when an employee has a feeling of being detached from his or her work, which seems to have lost its meaning and value. Workaholism, on the other hand, is a kind of addiction to work. The person's workload does not decrease at all, and there is a compulsion to work continuously. Some may suffer from these symptoms because they have an intense need to be successful, while others may do so to withdraw from unpleasant domestic situations such as an unhappy marriage relationship. Burnout refers to the situation in which a person eventually becomes listless, ineffective, inefficient, and unproductive due to a prolonged period of work overload which has negatively impacted on the physical and mental health of the employee. Such incapacity at work can in turn lead to stress and such behaviour as increased use of alcohol and increasing conflict with co-employees.

The potential spectrum of causes is wide, varied, complex, and often interlinked. Some factors are unique to the individual (such as personality type, intellectual ability, needs, values, attitudes, self-image, occupational concepts, and psychiatric problems such as psychotic or neurotic conditions). Sometimes the causes may form part of the work environment itself, for example certain managerial processes and practices (such as retrenchments or job re-design) and physical factors (such as workload, toxic substances, working hours, temperatures, noise, and physical dangers in the workplace). Other factors that may play a role in psychological work adjustment can be categorised as being external to the employee or the organisation. These include such aspects as family life, traumatic external events such as war or major political change, ecological factors like housing and pollution, and economic conditions such as a depression.

Irrespective of the actual problems or their underlying causes, it is essential for organisations to be aware of the importance of OMH. Organisations must strive continually to create a situation in which the employees experience, as far as is possible, optimal states of OMH.

14.3.4.2   Stress and work

A topic that has been receiving increasing attention in the area of occupational health over the last three decades is that of work-related stress. As the world around us – and especially the world of work and business – has become increasingly subject to fast-changing forces such as increased competition, the pressure for quality innovation, and an increase in the pace of doing business, the demands on employees have grown equally dramatically. This creates stress within employees, which has led some to refer to 'the pressure cooker of work' (Jaire, Leon, Simpson, Holley, & Frye 1989: 92–95). Apart from the stress that arises from the work situation, other sources of stress may relate to personal factors such as relationships with others and the use of free time.

But what is stress?
Stress can be defined as the arousal of mind and body in response to an environmental demand (the stressors).

What is a stressor to one person may not be regarded as such by another, simply because people differ in the amounts of arousal they need to act and the amounts that they can take before the situation becomes personally distressing. Arousal patterns therefore differ from person to person. As human beings, we require additional energy as soon as we have to face up to a particularly difficult and stressful situation (the stressor). Thus, as we think of all the things that we have to do (as we worry and plan) energy is released. Sometimes, however, it becomes bound within us, building up in areas of the body, for example the neck and shoulders, and then we develop tension headaches and tensed shoulders. This can become even worse, leading to physical problems such as ulcers, a lowering of the immune system, and even heart problems. It is therefore essential to develop ways of managing stress. Smit and Venter (1996) propose a process approach to the management of stress. The first step is to identify the sources or causes of the stress by tracing whether any symptoms of stress are present. Below is a list of symptoms of stress that one can use as a checklist to determine whether one suffers from stress.

Symptoms of stress

Mental symptoms
- Feeling wound-up; anxious;
- Excessive worry;
- Irritability;
- Easily frustrated;
- Aggressive outbursts;
- Poor concentration;
- Forgetfulness;
- Depression;
- Lack of fun in life;
- Poor motivation;
- Wanting to be alone always;
- Poor self-esteem; and
- Feeling out of control.

Physical symptoms
- Headaches;
- Spastic colon;
- Indigestion;
- Ulcers;
- High blood pressure;
- Palpitations'
- Hyperventilation;
- Asthma'
- Stiff, sore muscles;
- Trouble sleeping;
- Change in appetite;
- Change in sexual drive; and
- Decreased immunity (easily ill).

Other symptoms
- Increased smoking;
- Increased alcohol intake to try to cope better; and
- Increased intake of medication to try to relieve stress-related symptoms.

Source: Smit & Venter (1996: 11)

The next step is to assess whether the stress is justified and whether one's health can sustain the stress. If it justifies the end result and one can sustain it, there is no need to change anything. If the response to either of these two is negative, one needs to deal with it by working on eliminating the sources, and doing things deliberately to relieve the symptoms. This may include relaxation techniques, hobbies, shrugging off things that you cannot change or cope with, regular exercise, getting sufficient sleep, and possibly eliciting help from outside, for example a psychologist, occupational therapist, or an addiction clinic (in the case of substance dependence).

One aspect that has been proven to be closely related to stressfulness is the personality type of an individual. Type A and Type B personalities are relevant in this regard. Type A people have an intense drive to achieve, an eagerness to compete, the need to accelerate the execution of all physical and mental activities, an extraordinary mental and physical alertness, and a persistent need for recognition, and they are constantly involved in many things with deadlines. These people are prone to higher stress levels than Type B people who are basically the opposite.

Although stress management remains the responsibility of each individual employee, it is important for organisations to provide the necessary assistance and support. In this regard, research undertaken by an American life insurance company led to the ten recommendations listed below (Milkovich & Boudreau 1994: 727–729).

Recommendations on handling workplace stress

- Allow employees to talk freely with one another. 'Employees thrive in an atmosphere where they can consult with colleagues about work issues and defuse stress with humour.'
- Reduce personal conflicts on the job. Employers should resolve conflicts through 'open communications, negotiations, and respect'. Two basics: 'Treat employees fairly'; 'Define job expectations clearly'.
- Give employees adequate control in the way in which they do their jobs. 'Workers take greater pride ... are more productive and better able to deal with stress if they have some control and flexibility' in the way they do their jobs.
- Ensure adequate staffing and expense budgets. 'Many organisations are facing the economic reality of smaller budgets', but 'a new project may not be worth taking on if staffing and funding are inadequate'.
- Talk openly with employees. 'Management should keep employees informed about bad news as well as good news' and should 'give employees opportunities to air their concerns to management'.
- Support employees' efforts. By regularly asking employees how their work is going, listening to them, and addressing issues that are raised, 'stress levels are significantly reduced'.
- Provide competitive personal and vacation benefits. 'Workers who have time to relax and recharge after working hard are less likely to develop stress-related illnesses.'
- Maintain current levels of employee benefits. Cuts in pension, health insurance, vacation benefits, and sick leave invite employee stress. Employers must weigh potential savings against the high costs of employee burnout.
- Reduce the amount of red tape for employees. 'Employers can lower burnout rates if they ensure that employees' time is not wasted on unnecessary paperwork and procedures.'
- Recognise and reward employees. 'A pat on the back, a public word of praise, a raise or a bonus' for accomplishments and contributions can pay 'big dividends in higher employee morale and productivity'.

14.3.4.3 Substance abuse and employee assistance

Employee assistance (EA) essentially concerns social services offered to troubled employees who need professional treatment for varying kinds of personal problems with which they cannot cope and which may have a potentially negative impact on their work performance and personal lives.

Historically employee assistance has been linked to alcohol dependency. Other chemical dependencies today fall into the same category. It is well known that a chemically dependent employee can cost an organisation a good deal of money not to mention the negative effect it has for family and personal life. According to Fisher (1999: 10), a chemically dependent employee costs an organisation approximately 25% of his or her salary in terms of aspects such as absenteeism and poor productivity. Some research results about substance abuse in South African organisations are provided below.

Drug trafficking, substance abuse and the South African workplace

According to a recent report, a by-product of South Africa's transition from apartheid to a post-apartheid society has been an increased exposure to drug trafficking and its concomitant problems. (This is partly ascribed to such global aspects as the re-introduction of the country into the world economy and an increase in tourism.) South Africa now, for instance, boasts a population of more than half a million cocaine addicts and has become a major trafficking centre for mandrax, heroin, LSD, and cocaine. Marijuana and alcohol are the drugs of choice in the South African workplace. It has been found that up to 89% of males and up to 77% of females in South Africa drink alcoholic beverages, that 20% of psychiatric admissions to mine-based hospitals have been for chemical dependency, and that 72% of mine employees drink alcohol - with 44.5% of these indicating that they have lost the ability to control their drinking.

The high rate of alcohol consumption on South African mines also contributes to other health and psychosocial problems among mineworkers, such as enuresis and sexually transmitted diseases.

Source: Maiden (1999: 41–51)

As mentioned, employee assistance programmes (EAPs), as a health management intervention, have specific historic links with alcoholism rehabilitation. The scope of such programmes is, however, much broader nowadays. It covers treatment for all sorts of substance dependence, abuse, or addiction, as well as therapy and counselling for personal problems such as marital problems, stress and depression, and financial problems.

Substance abuse and dependence can have ripple effects that impact negatively on various areas of people's lives. Alcoholism, for instance, causes a person to neglect his or her diet, and in this way the nutritional value of food intake deteriorates, which can in turn destroy stress-coping skills, leading to more drinking. This eventually results in more stress and a deterioration of cognitive processes, emotional problems like depression, lack of motivation and aggression, a deterioration in personal affairs (as in family life), poor work performance, and absence from work. Finally, serious physical health problems and even death can result. It is widely recognised that alcoholism is a disease that needs professional treatment rather than condemnation. Employee assistance programmes specifically include alcoholism rehabilitation interventions.

Managers should be very sensitive about substance abuse by their subordinates. They are in an ideal position to play a proactive role. Fisher (1999: 10) provides guidelines to assist managers in this role, as listed below.

Dealing proactively with substance abuse-related issues in the workplace

Focus on attendance, production, and interpersonal dynamics to identify the following potential problems:

Attendance
- Absenteeism and lateness, especially on Mondays and Fridays;
- Repeated and suspicious minor illnesses; and
- Unusual though convincing excuses

Production
- Complaints from colleagues;
- Unreliability, negligence, forgetfulness, poor judgement, inability to complete tasks; and
- Erratic performance patterns

Interpersonal relationships
- Unusually sensitive to advice or constructive criticism;
- Irritability and resentment towards colleagues and management; and
- Anxiety and depression

If a problem is suspected, a number of do's and don'ts may apply

Do
- Document everything, make notes on discussions and any disciplinary procedure;
- Discuss each incident and explain how it should improve;
- Be firm and supportive; and
- Liaise closely with and follow the instructions of the treatment centre or counsellor – your support demonstrates your sincerity and enhances treatment outcomes.

Do not
- Be drawn into an argument;
- Discuss drinking/drugging or alcoholism/addiction;
- Make idle threats – find your bottom line and stick to it;
- Be misled by periods of apparent sobriety – self-recovery is unlikely; and
- Dismiss the employee before help has been offered through the EAP or community resources, if at all possible.

Source: Adapted from Fisher (1999: 10)

An even more proactive approach to working towards employee wellness would be the inclusion in EA programmes of elements that are aimed at the not-so-troubled employees – those who abuse chemical substances such as alcohol from time to time but not to the extent that it may overtly impact negatively on work behaviour and performance. If such people are not helped in time, the situation may well become more serious. In this regard, educational interventions run by experts from inside or outside the organisation can be very helpful. In general, health awareness campaigns should also include substance abuse warnings.

Although EA programmes may require substantial amounts of money, this should be viewed as an investment with longer term returns. However, from a management point of view, it is important regularly to evaluate the quality of such programmes and to undertake cost-benefit analyses.

One aspect that requires consideration is whether to opt for the internal or external models of EA programmes. The internal model involves the employment of EA professional staff in the organisation. This may be more cost-effective, but poses the problem of confidentiality – especially in the eyes of those who need to make use of the service, often causing them to shy away from using it. In the external model, use is made of professionals from outside the organisation. This may be more expensive, but aspects like credibility and confidentiality may be viewed more positively. Bews and Bews (1988) also list other factors which must be considered when a choice has to be made in this regard, namely accessibility, availability of expertise, acceptance by employees, unions, and management, comprehensiveness of the services, and ease of monitoring the programmes.

Regardless of which model is chosen, it is important – if one wants to create a caring environment – to provide one or another form of employee assistance. Management should make a policy decision in this regard, and when the policy is formulated, it is important to acknowledge that employees must also be willing to help themselves.

14.3.4.4 Occupational diseases, hazards, accidents, and injuries

Occupational diseases

In practice, it is often very difficult to distinguish between so-called occupational diseases and non-occupational diseases. This is because the causal relationships between any person's ill health and hazards in his or her work or private life are very complex and interconnected. The World Health Organisation, however, provides a clear definition of an occupational disease (Metz 1992: 91):

> Occupational diseases are defined as diseases which are solely or principally caused by factors which are peculiar to the working environment and are therefore 'arising out of and during work', with the qualification that the actual manifestation, i.e., the disease, may well arise 'after work'.

In the Compensation for Occupational Injuries and Diseases Act 130 of 1993 (COIDA), it is stated that 'an occupational disease is any disease mentioned in the first column of Schedule 3 of the Act, arising out of and contracted in the course of an employee's employment' (Mischke & Garbers 1994: 88). Schedule 3 of the Act lists the relevant diseases in the first column and the work which gives rise to those diseases in the second column. It is specifically stated that, if a worker has performed any work involving the handling of or exposure to any of the listed substances in use in the workplace, and he or she contracts the corresponding occupational disease, it is presumed that the disease arose out of and in the course of that workers' employment – unless the contrary is proved.

Various occupational diseases can be identified, such as anthrax, occupational dermatitis, occupational asthma, tuberculosis of the lung, and hearing impairment. What is thus more important is to focus on the occupational hazards that may lead to occupational diseases.

Occupational hazards

Occupational hazards can cause harmful effects to employees in various ways, such as when certain hazardous substances are inhaled, swallowed, or even absorbed through the skin. One can distinguish between various categories of occupational hazard, including chemical, mechanical, biological, physical, and psychological hazards.

Chemical hazards include gases, vapours, fumes, and dust. Mechanical hazards relate mainly to the over-exposure of an employee to machine-related vibrations (for example, turbines and pressure drills). Employees who work with animals and other people can be exposed to biological hazards such as viral, bacterial, or fungal infections. Physical hazards include exposure to radiation, sound and noise, lighting, extreme temperatures, and abnormal atmospheric pressures. Psychological hazards relate directly to OMH, and may include such aspects as the risks and dangers involved in a particular job and the way in which work is designed (meaningfulness versus alienation, work overload, and other factors that can cause work stress).

Accidents and injuries

Workplace safety revolves around creating a work environment in which the chances for and effects of accidents and injuries are minimised and personal security maximised. Hattingh (1992: 33) defines an accident as follows:

A sudden, uncontrollable, unplanned, undesirable happening which disrupts the normal functions of persons and causes or has the potential to produce or cause unintended injury, death, or property damage and/or business interruption.

There are various types of accident and injury. Injuries that result from accidents occurring during the course of work can be minor (requiring only some first-aid treatment) or more serious (causing temporary total disablement). In extreme cases, permanent disablement that may be partial, total, or fatal may occur. Accidents can be officially classified as follows (Hattingh 1992: 34–35):

- Being struck by falling objects;
- Being caught in, on, or between objects;
- Stepping on, striking against, or being struck by objects;

- Falling from a different level (for example from a ladder);
- Falling on the same level (for example slipping on a wet floor);
- Electrical exposure or contact;
- Strain, over-exertion, or strenuous movements (pushing, pulling, picking up); and
- Exposure to or contact with harmful substances through inhalation, ingestion, or absorption.

Accidents may be caused by various factors that involve unsafe conditions and/or unsafe behaviour or acts. Unsafe conditions can be caused by equipment deficiencies or inadequacies or by unsafe working environments. Unsafe behaviour and acts result from the human error factor. Factors that can play a role include employee fatigue and boredom, employees' levels of experience, and certain social, psychological, and physiological factors. Poor eyesight or hearing may lead to accidents and so can certain attitudinal and emotional conditions. In the social context, alcohol usage is often linked to accidents and injuries. Measures to prevent unsafe acts, behaviour, and conditions include the following:

- Create a safety infrastructure with control mechanisms and processes.
- Establish safety standards.
- Plan and design the work and workplace with safety in mind.
- Install safety committees and representatives.
- Carry out regular inspections to ensure that safety standards are adhered to.
- Establish who is accountable and responsible.
- Train all employees to be safety conscious.
- Ensure that employees are aware of and alert to safety issues.
- Develop and run accident prevention programmes.

To ensure the success of accident prevention programmes, management must lead by example, creating safe, healthy working environments and conditions and inculcating a culture of safe working habits and practices. This calls for management commitment (particularly in terms of resources) right from the top down to the lowest supervisory levels. It also requires the maintenance of day-today discipline, as well as a system of rewards and recognition for those who live by the policy of safety first.

14.3.4.5 Workplace bullying and sexual harassment

A relatively new phenomenon that affects employee wellness in the work environment is workplace bullying. Stone (2002: 660) says that workplace bullying 'includes persecuting or ganging up on an individual, making unreasonable demands or setting impossible work targets, making restrictive and petty work rules, constant intrusive surveillance, shouting, abusive language, physical assault and open or implied threats of dismissal or demotion'. Sexual harassment, on the other hand, may include unwanted physical contact, indecent sexual comments, language, or references, making unwelcome sexual advances to fellow employees, and even the display of sexual material. Sexual harassment is unlawful in South Africa, and the EEA (see Chapter 6) deals with the topic. Workplace bullying, as can be gathered from the description above, can manifest in various situations, such as constructive dismissal or unfair labour practice claims.

14.3.4.6   HIV/AIDS in the workplace

People in the Western world first became aware of HIV/AIDS in the early 1980s. Although the medical profession soon realised the potential for the disease to develop into a worldwide pandemic, governments were slow to act. This inertia is generally ascribed to the fact that HIV/AIDS was seen as a problem affecting already marginalised groups such as homosexuals and drug users. However, as the disease presented itself increasingly in the heterosexual population, and the social, medical, and economic implications became clear, the search for a cure gathered momentum. Slowly people came to realise that we are all, or will be, affected by the disease, whether we are infected or not, and irrespective of our choice of lifestyle.

It is estimated that in 2001 no fewer than 14 000 people were infected with HIV every day and that, over the next 20 years, 68 million people will die of HIV/AIDS in the 45 worst-affected countries (this is a five-fold increase compared with the preceding 20 years). There can therefore be little doubt that the world is faced with a pandemic and that societies as a whole will be affected by it, and no one will be left untouched, either as an employer, an employee, a child, a parent, or a relative. Furthermore, around 95% of the global total of HIV infections occurs in the developing world, with 70% in the sub-Saharan Africa.

The magnitude and impact of the problem

Most experts on the subject agree that, as we enter the new millennium, HIV/AIDS will transcend most other problems in South Africa. This is borne out by the fact that

HIV/AIDS in South Africa
- Between 3 and 8 million South Africans are carriers of the HI-virus.
- Approximately 22% of all pregnant women examined at prenatal clinics are HIV positive.
- The highest incidence and the fastest increase in HIV/AIDS take place among teenagers (21% are infected) and people between 20 and 29 years old (nearly one in three).
- More than 6 000 babies are born annually who are infected with the virus.
- At least 1 600 South Africans are infected every day (more than million new HIV carriers per year).
- The incidence of HIV/AIDS in South Africa increased fourteen fold over the past six years.
- The incidence of HIV/AIDS is highest in KwaZulu-Natal where one in three of all pregnant women is infected.
- It is estimated that in the next two years between 2.5 and 3 million children in South Africa will either be infected with HIV or left orphaned when their parents die of AIDS.

Source: Reconstruct (1999) & Hudson (1999)

at present it is estimated that between three and eight million South Africans are carriers of the HI-virus. In 2001, the South African Medical Research Council issued a report in which it was stated that, by 2000, HIV/AIDS was the leading cause of death in South Africa. The highest mortality occurs between the ages of 20 and 54 years for males and between the ages of 15 and 49 years for females. The implications for the economy and employers are clear: not only are we losing people in whom a substantial amount has already been invested in terms of schooling and training (i.e., a net loss to society) but, by 2020, the labour force in South Africa will be 17% smaller than it was in 2000.

The ILO report mentions that HIV/AIDS-related illnesses and deaths of workers will affect employers by increasing costs and reducing revenues. Employers will be required to spend more on health care, burial, and the training and recruitment of replacement employees. There will be a reduction in revenues due to absenteeism related to illness, attendance at funerals, time spent on caring for the ill, and training of replacements.

It is estimated that 15% of all South Africans aged between 20 and 64 are currently infected and that these levels could rise to 27% by 2010. It is also estimated that another 1 000 people are infected with HIV every day and that an expected three million South Africans will die of HIV/AIDS over the next 20 years, if behaviour patterns do not change or effective treatment is not developed (Editorial 1997: 2). The box below shows the magnitude of this epidemic in South Africa, clearly illustrating

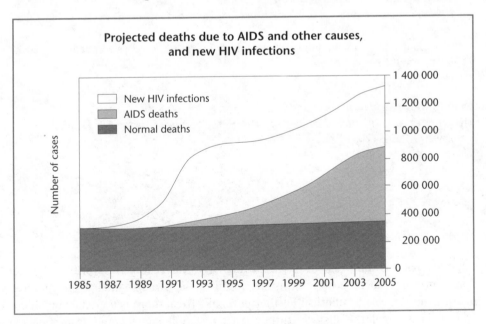

Source: Actuarial society of South Africa AIDS Model, AIDS Analysis Africa (1997: 4)

Figure 14.1   Projected new HIV infections and deaths due to AIDS and other causes

that the disease will affect many economically active people and have a profound impact on the business sector in South Africa. In addition to this, most South African employees can expect a reduction in the value of their employee benefits (medical aid cover, retirement funding, etc.) because of the increased financial burden that their funds will have to bear due to HIV/AIDS.

The AIDS Committee of the Actuarial Society of South Africa has developed a demographic model to project the impact of HIV and AIDS on South Africa (AIDS Analysis Africa 1997: 4). Using this model, the projected deaths due to HIV/AIDS and other causes, as well as new HIV infections, are depicted in Figure 14.1 on page 419.

Since 1982, when two HIV/AIDS cases were reported in South Africa, the incidence of the disease has increased alarmingly. According to some estimates, one in five adults will be infected by the year 2005, with 1% of GNP lost due to direct health costs. The epidemic is so serious that, in March 1999, the Minister of Health made HIV/AIDS a reportable illness in order to protect health workers and the sexual partners of infected persons. South Africa has the largest number of infected people in the world according to a report in *The Star* of 3 August 2002. Accompanying this report, some other alarming statistics are provided on HIV/AIDS in South and Southern Africa (see the box below).

Facts about HIV in Southern Africa

In South Africa

- 64.3% of men treated for sexually transmitted diseases test HIV positive. Half of female sex workers test HIV positive.
- Fewer children attend school than before. In 2001, 20% fewer pupils enrolled in KwaZulu-Natal schools than in 1999.
- 56% of truck drivers tested at five truck stops were HIV positive.

In neighbouring countries

The number of pregnant women testing HIV positive at government facilities are:

- Botswana 44.9% (2001)
- Lesotho 42.2% (2000)
- Zimbabwe 35% (2000)
- Swaziland 32.3% (2000)
- Namibia 29.6% (2000)
- South Africa 24.8% (2001)

What compounds the problem in Africa relative to the rest of the world is the fact that ours seems to be a more resistant strain of the virus than that encountered in, for instance, North America. Furthermore, in Africa, there is a greater incidence of transmission of the disease through heterosexual contact and from infected mothers to their unborn children. There also seems to be some resistance to the use of condoms.

Countering the threat of HIV/AIDS

Although research over the past two decades has led to the discovery of new or improved treatments for people living with HIV/AIDS, the most promising treatment regime so far is a cocktail of drugs that attacks the virus on multiple fronts.

Since the major cause of transmission of the disease is through voluntary conduct, behaviour modification on a large scale, if this could be achieved, would be very efficient in reducing the threat of HIV/AIDS. For example, abstaining from casual sex or taking precautions when engaging in sexual encounters (by insisting on the use of a condom) or by distributing free needles to drug users or assisting drug users to rehabilitate, could go a long way in countering the spread of the disease. In this, employers can play an important role by sponsoring HIV/AIDS awareness programmes, by training employees how to avoid being infected, and by emphasising the low risk of contracting the disease from a co-worker. Resources expended in this manner would be justified not only by altruistic motives, but, given the speed with which the disease spreads, enlightened employers could also save themselves huge amounts in increased medical aid contributions and the costs associated with replacing experienced employees. It should be remembered that the people most at risk are those who are in the most productive phase of their lives.

South African organisations' reaction to the problem

A survey conducted in 1994 among South African organisations regarding their HIV/AIDS policies and practices found that the majority of organisations have not prepared themselves adequately to deal with the issues raised by the spread of HIV/ AIDS (Bracks & Van Wyk 1994). The researchers concluded their report with the following two interesting observations. First, although HIV/AIDS will probably affect most organisations and although most of the larger organisations have taken steps to protect their employees against discrimination by the implementation of appropriate policies, research has shown that the majority of the organisations have generally tended not to implement such policies. Second, despite the vigour and tenacity with which the unions have criticised racial discrimination, they do not seem to make any effort to voice their opposition to discrimination based on HIV/AIDS. The reason for this can be assumed to be the prejudices of their own members against infected people, or the fact that HIV/AIDS has not yet taken on proportions significant enough to justify union attention.

As the disease spreads, the probability is increasing that employers will sooner or later be confronted with HIV- and AIDS-infected people in employment. The economic impact of the disease in organisations will be manifested in a loss of productivity as a result of employees absenting themselves from work for treatment, and later dying. This would also result in an increase in the cost of medical aid and pension schemes. Employees could also be discriminated against in the group life policies of organisations because they suffer from HIV/AIDS.

In the decade since the study by Bracks and Van Wyk, not much has changed, with the notable exception of some large employers in the mining industry. It is estimated that about 20% of Anglo American's 125 000 employees in South Africa are HIV positive, and it is encouraging that the giant corporation made public in 2002 that it intends to tackle the problem. De Beers also announced an even more comprehensive plan to face up to the HIV/AIDS challenge. In 2002, Gold Fields announced a R90 million-a-year HIV/AIDS initiative as part of a wellness management programme for its employees. Gold Fields has more than 13 000 HIV-positive employees, or more than one in four of its 50 000 workforce.

Discrimination against HIV/AIDS sufferers

Despite the steps being taken to protect HIV/AIDS-infected employees, research literature has shown that, in the face of pressure from co-workers, a third of the organisations will discriminate against the infected employee. The problem is exacerbated by the fact that no distinction is drawn between those employees who have tested HIV positive and those who have AIDS (full blown). The difference is based on the fact that the former could still be alive and well for the next five to 15 years. Discrimination against infected employees, whether with HIV or AIDS, places them at a disadvantage; the significance of this has been highlighted in various articles written on the subject, both in South Africa and the USA.

Discrimination against employees who are HIV/AIDS infected can take on various forms, for example:

- Compulsory medical screening at pre-employment level and of employees at any stage of employment;
- Denial of employment to potential employees who admit to being HIV positive;
- Disciplining of employees who inform their employers that they have HIV/AIDS;
- Demotion or transfer of employees who test HIV positive or who admit to having AIDS;
- Workers forcing the employer to have an employee tested because he or she is suspected of suffering from HIV/AIDS;
- The testing of foreigners who enter the country to seek employment;
- Suspension with salary of HIV-infected employees;
- Variation of the conditions of employment (changing the work area); and
- Dismissal.

Except in a few situations in which discrimination may be justified (such as an HIV-positive health care worker), there can be no justification for discrimination in the workplace. Many eminent writers on the subject have condemned the practice of discrimination in the workplace because, at present, medical consensus is that HIV (the human immunodeficiency virus) is transmissible essentially through body fluids – that is, blood or semen. The prime risk is for the virus to be transmitted from an HIV-positive person to another person during either homosexual or heterosexual intercourse, or when an abrasion or excoriation occurs with resultant exposure of capillaries or cells, involving also the factor of mucosal spread. Blood transfusions pose a threat if the blood or equipment used for the transfusion is contaminated. Based on the above, none of the ways in which infection takes place is directly connected with most work situations as such, or with the social and occupational contact which employees ordinarily have with one another in the workplace. In exceptional cases, there may be a relatively minor risk of infection in the work situation. One such situation is in the operating theatre if a doctor fails to take the necessary precaution of wearing surgical gloves, and accidentally cuts himself with a scalpel while operating on an HIV-infected individual. Consequently, the spread of HIV at the workplace is very unlikely. This, however, will not guarantee an HIV/ AIDS-free workplace, since, judging from the statistics, one or more employees will be infected sooner or later, forcing management to face the question of how to deal with HIV-positive employees.

Protection of employees who are HIV positive

In terms of Section 6 of the Employment Equity Act (see also Chapter 6 of this book), unfair discrimination against an employee or the harassment of that employee due to his or her HIV status is explicitly prohibited. Should such an employee be dismissed because of his or her HIV status or be forced to resign because of being HIV positive (the so-called constructive dismissal scenario – see Chapter 17), such a dismissal would also automatically be an unfair dismissal in terms of the Labour Relations Act. Likewise, the unfair treatment of an employee or job applicant because of his or her HIV status would in all likelihood be categorised as unfair.

In addition, medical testing is made subject to very stringent requirements in the Employment Equity Act, which will make it more difficult for an employer to justify the testing of employees or job applicants for their HIV status. As usual, in cases in which the nature of the job is such that an unacceptable risk will ensue if the job incumbent were to be HIV positive, the escape clause could be used by an employer to show that the discrimination against an HIV-positive person amounted to fair discrimination.

Dismissal of employees who have AIDS/are HIV positive

Although dismissal will be dealt with in detail in Chapter 17, a brief explanation of those aspects relevant to HIV/AIDS is essential here. All employees have the right not to be unfairly dismissed (Section 185 of the Labour Relations Act of 1995). This principle does not allow for any exceptions and is equally applicable to the individual who has AIDS or who is HIV positive. As will be seen in Chapter 17, one may only terminate the services of an employee if it can be justified on the basis of the employee's conduct or capacity or for reasons relating to the operational requirements of the organisation. Failure on the part of the employer to justify the dismissal in terms of one of these grounds will render it unfair. Furthermore, should the dismissal be regarded as discriminatory, it will amount to an 'automatically unfair dismissal' in terms of Section 187 of the Labour

Relations Act. The same principles apply in the case of the employee who suffers from AIDS or who is HIV positive. In dismissal cases, it is especially important for employers to distinguish between the case of the employee who is in the later stages of the disease (that is, who is suffering from full-blown AIDS) and the employee who is HIV positive (that is, who is a carrier of the disease but who does not present any symptoms). In the former case, dismissal may be justifiable on the basis of the person's inability to perform his or her duties (as is the case with any employee suffering from a debilitating disease rendering him or her incapable of doing his or her job). In the latter case, it may be more difficult to justify the dismissal and to evade the charge of unfair discrimination, since the employee would normally still be perfectly capable of performing his or her duties. In the following paragraphs, the dismissal of infected employees on the basis of one of the three grounds that may be offered as justification is examined in greater detail (see also Chapter 17).

- **Misconduct:** This justification would in most instances not be available to the employer. The mere fact of having contracted the disease would obviously not constitute misconduct. Conceivably an infected employee who knowingly and wilfully exposes a co-worker or customer of the employer to infection could fall under this category.

- **Incapacity:** An investigation into the employee's alleged incapacity is required, and this should be done by conducting a fair hearing. During this investigation, certain factors may be taken into account, such as the experience of the employee or the type of work concerned. However, when it is evident that an employee has become incapable of doing the work properly, his or her long service record as such will be to no avail. It should also be established whether the employee's particular disability, such as poor eyesight, could create a dangerous situation for co-workers (or, for that matter, for anybody else) (Brassey, Cameron, Cheadle, & Olivier 1987: 445). The fact that HIV/AIDS is communicable is irrelevant because, according to the current knowledge of the aetiology of the disease, there is virtually no risk of communication of the disease in the work situation. What would clearly be decisive would be the degree to which the disease itself, or a secondary condition caused by it, makes the employee unfit to do the required job (which may be manifested by such factors as absenteeism, debility, lack of concentration, confusion, or general unproductiveness). When the employee's incapacity has indeed been proved (or admitted), alternative employment (and not dismissal) should be considered; the employer should consult with the employee in this regard (Brassey *et al.* 1987: 446). Because the condition of a person with HIV/AIDS may deteriorate rapidly (in the last stage, the body's defences collapse and bacterial and viral infections which are normally harmless become life threatening), it would seem that the possibility of alternative employment may often not be feasible.

- **Operational reasons:** Under this heading, the so-called commercial rationale for dismissal may be put forward. What this justification amounts to is that the employee's continued presence in the employer's workforce frustrates the employer's legitimate objective of being in business to make a profit. A dismissal for being HIV positive may be fair, provided that it can be shown that the news of an employee's HIV-positive status is the direct and only cause of an appreciable decline in business, and all alternatives to the dismissal of the employee have been exhausted (Cameron 1992: 3). It should be cautioned, however, that the commercial rationale as a justification for dismissal is a very tenuous one and may well be found to be unfair, unless the employer has done whatever could reasonably be expected to remedy the situation, short of resorting to the dismissal of the employee. The same applies where co-workers of an infected individual refuse to work with him or her. To dismiss the infected person would most definitely be unfair, unless it is resorted to as a measure of absolute last resort.

Pre-employment testing

As justification for testing, organisations have argued that an organisation requires a healthy workforce which will be productive and not result in a high labour turnover. HIV-infected people have been seen as a high risk. This argument is irrelevant, since organisations do not test for any other life-threatening diseases in particular. Furthermore, available statistics clearly show that more and more people could become infected with the disease while being employed, making an HIV/AIDS-free work environment virtually impossible.

Another reason why pre-employment testing is unjustifiable is that the way in which the disease is identified does not clearly indicate whether a person is HIV positive or HIV negative when he or she is tested, first because the disease can be dormant for a long time in the person's system, and second, because, as a result of human error, a person who is HIV negative could be diagnosed as HIV positive, thereby disqualifying the person unfairly from possible employment opportunities.

Pre-employment testing could result in serious social problems. Tests carried out on a wide scale are expensive, and thousands of people will be unemployed while they are capable of being employed. This means that all these skills (if they are skilled employees) would be lost to the economy.

Managers need to be aware of the impact of tests on employees, and should carry the responsibility of their testing policy by providing necessary support and counselling to those tested. The rejection of an employee solely because he or she has tested HIV positive is unwarranted, since statistics have shown that, in South Africa, the period between testing positive and developing full-blown AIDS is from five to ten years. During this period, those who tested HIV positive could fulfil most of their responsibilities in a position. To reject employees with HIV/AIDS has an impact not only in the workplace but also on society, since, while an employee with HIV/AIDS continues to work, that person is a productive member of society and does not have to rely on the state for support. Realistically, the employee contributes to the economy and saves the state money because it will not have to make special provision for the employee.

Our labour legislation extends the right to fair treatment and the protection against unfair discrimination to prospective employees. This means that the rejection of a job applicant because he or she was shown to be HIV positive by the pre-employment test will amount to unfair discrimination unless the employer can show that the job in question requires a person not to be a carrier of the infection and that no reasonable precautionary measures could be taken to adjust the work content or process to accommodate the person. For instance, a medical doctor who is HIV positive may still be gainfully employed provided that he or she wears protective clothing and is prohibited from doing certain duties. It should be noted that employers may find themselves in a difficult position because by law they are required to provide employees with a safe working environment, and they could furthermore be held vicariously liable should a member of the public be infected by an employee during the course of his or her duties. However, these risks should be rare in the case of HIV and, should it not be reasonably possible to safeguard co-workers or members of the public due to the nature of the job, an employer will not be guilty of unfair discrimination in refusing to employ an infected job applicant.

Code of good practice: Key aspects of HIV/AIDS and employment

This code was published on 1 December 2000. It contains useful guidelines and legal requirements for employers, trade unions, and employees who grapple with the HIV/AIDS pandemic.

14.3.4.7 People with disabilities

In terms of the Employment Equity Act, 'people with disabilities' means people who have a long-term or recurring physical or mental impairment which substantially limits their prospects of entry into, or advancement in, employment. The Act places a duty on designated employers to provide reasonable accommodation for people with disabilities, such as modifying or adjusting a job or the working environment that will enable persons with disabilities to have access to or participate or advance in employment, in order to ensure that they enjoy equal opportunities and are equitably represented in the workforce of a designated employer. What is 'reasonable accommodation' will be determined by the size and resources of the employer, the nature of the job, and the nature and degree of the disability in question.

14.3.4.8 Health and working time

The arrangement of working time may have a direct impact on the health and safety of employees. This is especially true in the case of night work and shift work. In recognition of the fact, a code of good practice on the arrangement of working time has been issued under the Basic Conditions of Employment Act 75 of 1997. The object of this code is to provide information and guidelines to employers and employees concerning the arrangement of working time and the impact of working time on the health, safety, and family responsibilities of employees.

14.3.4.9 Pregnant and post-natal employees

Bearing in mind that there is a duty on employers not to discriminate against women on the basis of pregnancy (which includes intended pregnancy, termination of pregnancy, and any medical circumstances related to pregnancy) as well as a duty to provide a safe working environment, a code of good practice on the protection of employees during pregnancy and after the birth of a child was issued under the Basic Conditions of Employment Act 75 of 1997. The objective of this code is to provide guidelines for employers and employees concerning the protection of the health of women against potential hazards in their work environment during pregnancy, after the birth of a child, and while breastfeeding.

14.4 Role players in occupational health and safety

As we have emphasised throughout this chapter, the promotion and maintenance of health and safety is important for the well-being of the individual, for the success of organisations, and for the general success of the country. Individual employees and their representatives such as trade unions thus form one stakeholder group, and employers (and managers as their representatives in the workplace) form another group with a vested interest in employee health and safety. The state or government is, however, also an important stakeholder in the sense that healthy and safe working environments and employees who enjoy a general state of well-being make up crucial building blocks of any society striving for stability and prosperity. Each of these stakeholder groups thus has a certain role to play.

The government's principal role lies in the realm of promulgating and enforcing legislation such as those Acts which were briefly discussed at the beginning of this chapter. The general duty imposed on employers by the Occupational Health and Safety Act (Section 8(1)) is to provide and maintain, as far as is reasonably practicable, a working environment that is safe and without risk to the health of employees. Furthermore, the OHSA (Section 14) imposes the general duty on every employee at work to take reasonable care of the health and safety of himself or herself and of other employees who stand to be affected by his or her behaviour. In general, the OHSA encourages the parties (employers and employees) to regulate and promote health and safety in the workplace themselves and to co-operate in this regard. To this end, the roles and duties of safety representatives and committees are spelt out in detail in the OHSA (Sections 18 and 20). The OHSA furthermore facilitates the policing of the enforcement of the Act's provisions by means of the creation of an inspectorate, which is part of the Department of Labour. The inspectorate is headed by a chief inspector (appointed by the Minister of Labour) who is in charge of other inspectors – all of whom are charged with the administration of the OHSA's provisions and regulations. The inspectorate has continuously to monitor compliance with the OHSA's provisions and regulations. The Department of Labour also has a chief directorate of Occupational Health and Safety. This directorate has, in addition, a number of different directors, each charged with the administration of certain delimited areas and aspects of health and safety. Each of the Department of Labour's regional and satellite offices in the country also has a deputy director responsible for matters of occupational health and safety, who is in charge of controlling inspectors who in turn have authority over the ordinary inspectors. The Act also contains provisions for investigations and inquiries that have to be conducted when accidents occur at work.

Another important role player is the National Occupational Safety Association (NOSA), a not-for-gain incorporated association that is partially funded by the State Accident Fund. The National Occupational Safety Association was established in 1951 as a joint venture of the then Workmen's Compensation Commissioner and employers through their employer organisations.

The overall purpose of NOSA is basically to provide occupational health, safety, and environmental services. NOSA's aims are as follows (NOSA 1995):

- To promote the prevention of occupational accidents and diseases and to endeavour to eliminate their causes and results in industry and commerce;
- To act as a national body encouraging and promoting health and safety, and to carry out occupational health and safety publicity;
- To deal with all matters and questions pertaining to occupational health and safety; and
- To act as a general advisory body on all occupational health and safety matters.

Although the state and NOSA are important role players, the bulk of the responsibility for promoting and maintaining health and safety at work lies with the primary role-playing parties: employers and employees.

As explained already, the OHSA spells out a number of duties and prohibitions imposed on employers. These stipulate how the employer must treat employees in order to promote health and safety at work. The chief executive officer of an organisation is made responsible for ensuring, as far as is reasonably practicable, that there is compliance with the employer's duties imposed by the Act. An officer who delegates responsibility, as he or she is well entitled to do, is not absolved (either that chief executive officer himself or herself or the employer) from the ultimate responsibility of ensuring compliance with the duties of employers in terms of the OHSA.

Thus, although the chief executive officer may make it part of the job of lower level line management to manage aspects of health and safety, in the eyes of the law he or she will remain responsible.

It is thus clearly evident how important health and safety matters in the workplace are for the government and for employers in general. Every manager responsible for other employees under his or her authority should thus have a key performance area dealing with aspects of health and safety promotion and maintenance. Because of the importance of this aspect, however, senior or top management will most likely also want to employ specialists to help ensure that health and safety matters are attended to in a professional way.

Because health and safety have to do with the human dimension of organisations, it is largely the responsibility of the human resource department to initiate and finally draft and oversee, in collaboration with line management, the implementation of the organisation's health and safety policy, procedures, programmes, etc. Obviously, as stated before, this process ought ideally to be an inclusive one, involving all other role players and stakeholders – especially all other employees (management and non-management) and their representatives such as trade unions.

The horizons of occupational health and safety have broadened to such an extent, however, that in most cases it is no longer possible or feasible for one individual to be responsible for the whole spectrum of employee wellness promotion and maintenance. The need for various specialist skills has thus developed gradually over time. The overall role of the HR specialist in this regard is summarised below (Saunders 1992: 63).

Table 14.1   General role of HR specialists in health and safety

Task	Specific activity
Accident investigator	Carry out investigations into all accidents and dangerous occurrences in order to establish contributory factors.
Advocate	Establish health and safety as a priority within the organisation and secure its recognition at board level. Secure sufficient resources.
Auditor	Carry out regular examinations of current health and safety policy, procedures, practice and programmes to ensure satisfaction.
Leader	Know and understand the workforce and lead by example. Motivate workers and develop schemes and plans to change attitudes and behaviour.
Planner	Plan, implement, monitor, and evaluate remedial measures designed to reduce or prevent accidents from happening.
Provider	Issue protective clothing and/or equipment. A knowledge of the legal requirements is necessary. Expert help is sought where necessary.
Trainer	Provide on-the-job training, safe systems of working, indoctrination, workplace rules and regulations, and employee responsibilities.

Source: Saunders (1992: 63)

As we have previously seen, various other specialist role players may be involved in the promotion and maintenance of employee wellness in the organisation. These may include medical doctors, occupational nurses, dentists, physiotherapists, psychologists, social workers, ergonomists, and safety officers.

14.5 Review

In this chapter, we have seen how comprehensive and important the field of employee wellness promotion and maintenance is. We have seen that a reactive approach to employee health and safety is no longer applicable or sufficient. What is needed is a holistic and proactive approach to promoting and maintaining the complete well-being of an organisation's personnel. These are areas that have to be attended to professionally in order to ensure an environment in which employees feel and know that they are being cared for, because they are such valuable resources.

14.6   Self-evaluation questions

1. 'Employee wellness is something more comprehensive and important than is realised by many South African managers.' Critically evaluate and discuss this statement.
2. Write concise notes on the nature and managerial implications of the following:
    *   The Mine Health and Safety Act 29 of 1996;
    *   The Occupational Health and Safety Act 85 of 1993.
3. Describe the role of health and safety representatives in terms of the OHSA.
4. 'Ergonomics and work design hold no implications for employee wellness.' Do you agree with this statement? Provide reasons for your answer.
5. Describe the general nature and importance of health screening and safety auditing. Explain the problems related to HIV/AIDS in this regard.
6. 'Smoking is a personal issue and holds no organisational or managerial implications.' Critically discuss this statement.
7. Write brief notes on the nature and importance of being prepared for emergencies in organisations.
8. What does 'occupational mental health' entail?
9. Discuss the challenges posed to management by the following:
    *   Work-related stress;
    *   Work alienation;
    *   Work and family life;
    *   Substance dependency such as smoking and alcohol abuse;
    *   Personal problems of employees.
10. Differentiate between occupational diseases and hazards and cite examples of them.
11. Write brief notes on the following topic: 'Workplace safety and accidents and injuries at work: Their meaning, nature, and managerial implications.'
12. How do South African organisations generally deal with the problems related to HIV/AIDS? What advice would you give to these organisations' managers in this regard? (Refer specifically to discrimination against HIV/AIDS sufferers, pre-employment testing, and the dismissal of employees who have AIDS or who are HIV positive.)

Bibliography

Acutt, J. 1992. Emergencies and disaster planning. In AJ Kotzé (ed.), *Occupational health*. Cape Town: Juta.

AIDS Analysis Africa. (Southern African Edition), Dec 1996/Jan 1997, 7(4).

Araujo, JP. 1996. The introduction of a no-smoking policy. *People Dynamics*, 13(12), 39.

Bergh, ZC. 1992. Psychological adjustment of the worker in the work environment. In AJ Kotzé (ed.), *Occupational health*. Cape Town: Juta.

Bews, N, & Bews, C. 1988. Employee assistance programmes: Internal or external model? The options considered. *IPM Journal*, 7(2), 22.

Bracks, R, & Van Wyk, MW. 1994. The position of HIV/AIDS employees in South African companies: A legal and empirical survey (unpublished MBL research report, Graduate School of Business Leadership, University of South Africa).

Brase, N. 1995. How safe is safe? *People Dynamics*, 13(1), 24.

Brassey, M, Cameron, E, Cheadle, H, & Olivier, M. 1987. *The new labour law*. Cape Town: Juta.

Bryant, W. 1990. Child care options for employers. *IPM Journal*, 9(1), 17–21.

Cameron, E. 1992. *Comments: Aids and HIV in employment*. Andrew Levy News, 1(7).

Covin, TJ, & Brush, CC. 1993. Attitudes toward work-family issues: The human resources professional perspective. *Review of Business*, 15(2), 25–29.

Editorial. *AIDS Analysis Africa* (Southern African Edition), Dec 1996/Jan 1997, 7(4).

Erwee, C. 1993. Koors, hoofpyne en spierpyne dalk 'siek' gebou se skuld. *Beeld*, 29 Januarie, 13.

Fisher, S. 1999. Company alcohol and drug policy and intervention. *Management Today*, 15(2), 10.

Gathiram, V. 1999. The age of the great Aids plague. *The Mercury*, July 15, 9.

Gleason, D. 1996. Fighting for survival in a shrinking market. *Financial Mail*, 4 October, 22.

Harper, T. 1999. Employee assistance programming and professional developments in South Africa. *Employee Assistance Quarterly* 14(3), 1–18.

Hattingh, S. 1992. Occupational safety. In AJ Kotzé (ed.), *Occupational health*. Cape Town: Juta.

Healthcare needs total company involvement. 1993. *Human Resource Management*, May, 27.

Hermanus, M. 1991. Occupational health and safety: A NUM perspective. *IPM Journal*, 9(9), 17.

Hudson, M. 1999. AZT: Alles of niks. *Insig*, Junie, 30–31.

Humphrey, J, & Smith, P. 1991. *Looking after corporate health*. London: Pitman.

Jaire, SA, Leon, JS, Simpson, DB, Holley, CH, & Frye, RL. 1989. Stress: The pressure cooker of work. *Personnel Administrator*, March , 92–95.

Jensen, DW. 1987. *Worksite wellness*. Paramus, NJ: Prentice-Hall.

Jones, B. 1996. Poor pay keeps mine safety inspectors away. *Sunday Times*, 14 April, 6.

Jones, TH, & Kleiner, BH. 1990. Smoking and the work environment. *Employee Relations*, 12(6), 29.

Lewis, P, & Jeebhay, M. 1996. The Mines Health and Safety Bill 1996: A new era for health and safety in the mining industry. *Industrial Law Journal*, 17, 429–447.

Maiden, RP. 1999. Substance abuse in the new South Africa: Implications for the workplace. *Employee Assistance Quarterly* 14(3), 41–60.

Martinez, M. 1993. Family support makes business sense. *HR Magazine*, January, 38–43.

Matlala, S. 1999. Prioritising health promotion and employee wellness. *People Dynamics*, 17(6), 22–25.

Metz, JT. 1992. Occupational medicine and occupational diseases. In AJ Kotzé (ed.), *Occupational health*. Cape Town: Juta.

Milkovich, GT, & Boudreau, JW. 1994. *Human resource management*. 7th edn. Homewood, IL: Irwin.

Mischke, C, & Garbers, C. 1994. *Safety at work*. Cape Town: Juta.

Muller, J. 1988. Employee assistance programmes: A new approach to workplace productivity? *IPM Journal*, 6(12), 21.

NOSA. 1995. NOSA information brochure.

Reconstruct. 1999. Supplement to *Sunday Independent*, 13 June.

Santhey, C. 1993. Medical costs: Optimise your diagnosis. *People Dynamics*, 11(7), 14–15.

Saunders, R. 1992. *Taking care of safety*. London: Pitman.

Smit, A, & Venter, E. 1996. Life in a pressure cooker. *Productivity SA*, 22(1), 10–12.

Spearing, S. 1996. Mining safety: Put your fingers away. *Productivity SA* 22(3), 21.

Stone, RJ. 2002. *Human resource management*. 4th edn. Milton Qld: John Wiley & Sons.

Sunday Times Supplement: Primary Health. 1994. Alcohol and drugs exact their grim toll, 24 March, 10.

Taylor, G. 1992. The cost of absenteeism. *People Dynamics* 10(12), 31.

Wheeler, BJ. 1984. Nutrition programs. In PO O'Donnell & TH Ainsworth (eds.), *Health promotion in the workplace*. New York: Wiley.

Yadavalli, L. 1999. Labour problems in the next century. *Management Today*, 15(4), 25–27.

Acts of legislation

Republic of South Africa. 1993. The Occupational Health and Safety Act (Act 85 of 1993). Government Printer. [http://www.polity.org.za/html/govdocs/legislation/1993]

Republic of South Africa. 1996. The Mine Health and Safety Act (Act 29 of 1996). Government Printer. [http://www.polity.org.za/html/govdocs/legislation/1996]

Republic of South Africa. 1997. The Basic Conditions of Employment Act (Act 75 of 1997). Government Printer. [http://www.polity.org.za/html/govdocs/legislation/1997]

Part 6

Managing public-sector employee relations

IN GENERAL, the reasoning thus far in this book has been that, if certain HR activities are executed in an efficient and effective manner, the probability is good that a public sector institution will accomplish its goals. This statement sounds logical if PSHRM is strategically planned for in a timely and accurate way, competent people are hired, the appraisals for work performance are managed correctly, employees' learning needs are catered for properly, and employees are remunerated in a fair and equitable manner. Of course, all these HR activities are interdependent and interrelated to each other. But there is one major threat: a public sector institution will not operate effectively unless it has constructive and mutually advantageous relations among its employees and between labour and management (Tompkins 1995: 298). If such relations are not in place, superior work performance cannot be expected and the situation will inevitably lead to high staff turnover, poor attendance, lack of involvement and other negative results of unsatisfactory work performance.

Part 6 presents a PSHRM approach towards dealing with labour relations at the level of a public sector institution. It reviews the history of labour relations in the public sector and describes the management processes of collective bargaining, negotiation, dispute resolution, industrial action and resolving of labour conflicts in such areas as grievances, discipline and dismissal. It also evaluates diversity management, sexual harassment and communication as key contemporary processes closely related to labour relations.

15 Understanding public sector labour relations

Purpose

The purpose of this chapter is to introduce the nature and the foundations of public sector labour relations in order to establish a sound understanding for its application in the workplace.

Learning outcomes

After you have read this chapter, you should be able to:
- Present and interpret the historical developments of labour relations in the public sector since 1912.
- Define the nature of an employment relationship as the basis of all public sector labour and employee relations.
- Describe the roles, duties, and rights of the parties involved in public sector labour relations.
- Explain the nature, functioning and role of trade unions within the public sector context.
- Explain the impact of legislative changes that have been implemented and how they affect labour relations in the public sphere.

15.1 Introduction

Managing the relationship between public sector employers and their employees has become a very specialised but complex function in the HR field. Any relationship in the workplace is formed within the broader context of many roles, rights, expectations, obligations, and duties. What makes this relationship even more difficult is that these roles, rights, expectations, obligations, and duties may either be individualised or managed in group terms. When a group is formed as one party in the relationship that has shared interests, the situation becomes even more complex. In such a situation, these roles, rights, expectations, obligations, and duties need to be managed on a collective basis (Foot & Hook 1996: 139). This implies that you may need to formally negotiate and reach agreement on certain issues. It will also require active involvement and participation by the employees to ensure that their voices are heard and inputs are made. Obviously, public sector employers have to listen to employees to understand what they are saying and experiencing. In order for this to happen, structures and processes need to be formalised for collective bargaining and dispute resolution. All of these are found in the various statutory provisions that are on the table. Chapter 15, therefore, presents an overview of the many facets of public sector labour relations in order to create a better understanding of the employment relationship and the broader environment within which it takes place.

15.2 History and development of labour relations in the public sector

This discussion of the history and development of public sector labour relations begins with a description of developments in public service representative, management, and advisory bodies between 1902 and 1947. The second part of this history deals mainly with the period of intense change in legislation, management, and representation that affected public service labour relations during the decade from 1984 to 1994.

15.2.1 Public sector labour relations between 1902 and 1947

Although post office clerks in Cape Town were the first to establish a staff association in 1902, namely the Cape Postal and Telegraph Clerks' Association, the formal management and co-ordination of public sector labour relations began with the formation of a central personnel agency in 1912 under the name 'Public Service Commission' (PSC) (Cloete 1997: 213). This was two years after South Africa was declared a largely independent unitary nation state within the British Empire in 1910. No staff associations were allowed to organise labour relations during these times and, since 1912, the PSC managed all aspects of the employer-employee relationship. This included, among other things, the determination of wages and conditions of service, disciplinary measures, and grievance procedures (Adler 2000: 7).

Bargaining with public service employees over conditions of service had started in 1920 after the then Public Service Act provided for the recognition of staff associations in the public service. But bargaining was done on a limited scale since only one staff association, namely the Public Service Association, was then established, which represented white (almost exclusively male) permanent public servants (Macun & Psoulis, in Adler 2000: 95). The question of how healthy relations might be established between the public servants and the government occupied the minds of practitioners through these times. This led ultimately to the establishment of the Public Service Joint Advisory Council in 1947. This was a purely advisory body which the PSC consulted on labour relations issues.

15.2.2 Public sector labour relations between 1948 and 1994

No significant developments in labour relations occurred in the public sector for the period 1948 to 1980. While there were other staff associations, such as the Medical Association of South Africa (MASA), the only staff association that was recognised by the government of the time was the PSA. The apartheid National Party

(NP) government treated the public service as a vast pool of patronage for white party loyalists. This resulted in a range of discriminatory practices. Black people were denied citizenship rights, excluded from industrial relations legislation, and repressed by security forces and employer hostility. Generally, they were largely excluded from the racialised patronage networks within the public service. A new public service system was created in which blacks were given independence under separate administrations (the so-called TBVC states and self-governing territories). This development further entrenched the organising of labour relations along racial lines. As a result, it had a negative impact on public administration practices because resources were not utilised efficiently and effectively. One HR issue that was seriously affected was that of remuneration. Because of the top-down approach followed by the then NP government, no serious collective bargaining took place. This contributed to the allocation of a bewildering array of bonuses and allowances and the creation of massive wage gaps characterised by high levels of inequality on the basis of race and gender (Adler 2000: 8).

In 1979, the Wiehahn Commission recommended the extension of union recognition and collective bargaining to the public service. Unfortunately, the NP government ignored the Wiehahn Commission's advice and opted for a non-adversarial model on a racial basis. Because the labour relations situation was dictated by the government, trade unions were not allowed into the public service. This resulted in the expansion of more staff associations such as the Public Service League (PSL), the Public Service Union (PSU), and the Institute of Public Servants (IPS). These associations were mainly racially based. They could not operate independently from the state as employer, and could not get involved in industrial action (Macun & Psoulis, in Adler 2000: 96).

In 1984, the PSC (formed, as we have seen, in 1912) was renamed as the 'Commission for Administration' (CFA) during a major restructuring programme of the public service. Wider HR responsibilities were now allocated to the CFA, including the co-ordination of employment in the public service, regulation (or policymaking) of the HR function, and management of the employer-employee relationship.

The mid-1980s saw the beginning of a new era in the public service. It was referred to as the 'transitional period'. During this period, a massive restructuring of the state took place that included the streamlining of state departments and commercialisation of state enterprises. In labour relations terms, it entailed retrenchments, a freeze on new employment, and attempts to reduce wages. In addition, a Directorate of Labour Relations was established in 1988 in the office of the Commission for Administration (CFA) to undertake research and evaluate the state of labour relations in the public service. This was a last effort signalling that change in the labour relations structural framework was inevitable. But it was already too little too late. The situation was very complex because it became both a political and administrative matter. Black public servants' administrative grievances against the discriminatory policies in the workplace merged with their broader political ideals against the social policies of apartheid. In this context, the government was faced with a dual onslaught against apartheid (politically) and against the apartheid public service employer administratively).

Against this background, a new union movement led by affiliates of the Congress of South African Trade Unions (COSATU) began to make inroads into the public service.

In 1993, the Commission for Administration was renamed as the PSC. In 1994/1995, the allocation of HR functions was reviewed, and it was decided this time to remove the regulation (policymaking) functions and management functions and transfer them from the PSC to the Department of Public Service and Administration (DPSA) (Republic of South Africa 2000c: 6–7). According to Section 196(4)(a) to (f) of the 1996 Constitution, the PSC is now mainly involved in an investigative, monitoring, and advisory role.

15.2.3 Public sector labour relations from 1994 onwards

Political power changed hands in April 1994 when the ANC-dominated Government of National Unity took over. We were now moving towards a constitutional democracy – an era with its own expectations and challenges in the field of labour relations. This was the era of transformation in labour relations and democratisation of worker rights and collective bargaining. The following key issues have been addressed since 1994.

15.2.3.1 Transformation

A White Paper on the Transformation of the Public Service was introduced in 1995, which entailed a strategic framework for change with eight specified transformation priorities and processes. These priorities and processes were as follows:

- Rationalisation and restructuring of the public service;
- Institution building and management;
- Representativeness and affirmative action;
- Transformation of service delivery;
- Democratisation of the state;
- Human resource development and training;
- Promotion of a professional service ethos; and
- Employment conditions and labour relations.

In order to address employment conditions and labour relations, the government introduced the following related measures:

- Introduction of a phased increased adequate minimum wage from R900 to R1 500 a month over a three-year period commencing in 1994;
- Implementation of equal pay and benefits for work of equal value;
- Reduction of differentials in pay and benefits in line with international norms;
- Development of appropriate career paths;
- Reduction of the number of salary grades; and
- Improvement of the conditions of women and people with disabilities.

15.2.3.2 Democratisation of worker rights and collective bargaining

The Public Service Labour Relations Act of 1994 was repealed by the Labour Relations Act 66 of 1995 (LRA) which provides for labour relations in the private sector as well as in the public sector. The LRA provides, among other things, for: (1) bargaining councils in the public service; (2) workplace forums; and (3) labour courts. These matters are dealt with in greater detail in section 15.6.2 of this chapter.

15.2.3.3 Transferral of management authority

Since 1996, the labour relations function has been transferred from the PSC to the Department of Public Service and Administration (Republic of South Africa 2001: 2). The Department of Public Service and Administration has been established to provide policy-making support to the Minister of Public Service and Administration. Chapter 11, Section 3(2)(a)(iv) of the Public Service Act 103 of 1994 entrusts the Minister with the powers and duties to make policy on an HR function such as labour relations. Probably one of the most significant collective agreements concluded in the Public Service Bargaining Council (PSBC) – the single overarching structure for collective bargaining in the public service – is Resolution 9 of 2000: Senior Management Service. This resolution provides a framework for senior public sector managers to enter into individual performance agreements (Republic of South Africa 2000b).

15.3   The employment relationship

An employment relationship is essentially one of exchange which comes into being when a person is employed by someone else to be available to work in exchange for some form of remuneration. Without this employment relationship, there can be, by definition, no labour, employee, or industrial relations in the public sector. It is an inherently complex relationship, exhibiting a simultaneous need for co-operation between non-management and management employees (due to mutual interests) and a natural state of conflicting interests, perceptions, and needs.

This employment relationship is complex partly because of its multidimensional nature. The economic dimension of this relationship derives from the fact that the primary parties are engaged in a relationship of exchange. Public sector employees give their energy, knowledge, skills, abilities, and productive time in return for some sort of reward from the public sector employer, which includes an economic or financial aspect. Money, as the exchange medium, is thus central to the employment relationship.

The legal dimension derives from the fact that the parties enter into a legally binding agreement and that there are specific laws and formal rules which have an official bearing on the relationship between employer and employee in the public sector. Some legalities pertain to the individual dimension of the employment relationship – in other words, to the relationship between an individual employee and his or her employing institution as a single legal entity. In this regard, we may consider the common law (law of contract) which forms the basis of the contract of employment between an employee and an employer.

DID YOU KNOW?

If your employer doesn't have an officially recognised trade union, employees can still join a union in their personal capacity. Employees also have the right to:

- Attend union meetings;
- Represent other employees in disciplinary meetings;
- Be represented by a trade union representative (shop steward);
- Take part in protected strikes;
- Participate in the election of shop stewards, office bearers or officials; and
- Stand for election and be eligible for appointment as a shop steward, office bearer or official.

Source: Labour Bulletin (2010: Online)

On the other hand, collective labour law ensures some sort of formality in the relationship on the collective dimension – in other words, between labour as a group (including trade unions) with their representatives, on the one hand, and the employer(s) (or their representative public sector institutions) on the other. This would include legislation relating to collective bargaining (including dispute settlement and industrial action). The legal dimension can therefore also be referred to as the formal dimension of the employment relationship because it forms the basis of the formal rights and duties of the parties.

The social dimension gives the employment relationship its informal character; it revolves around the interaction and behaviour between people associated with human activity of employment or work. The social or informal dimension, thus, refers essentially to human behaviour in public sector institutions within the context of the collective dimension (in a group context, which may include labour unions), and the individual dimension (in an individual and interpersonal context). Human beings as individuals and as group members all have certain feelings, needs, attitudes, and perceptions, and therefore they bring to the employment relationship the dynamics which flow from these social and psychological phenomena. This dimension can also be referred to as the 'soft dimension' of the employment relationship.

15.4 The parties involved in labour relations: Roles, duties and rights

The labour relations system in any country is made up of three parties which exist in a tripartite relationship: The two primary parties are employers (and management as their representatives) and labour (and their representatives such as trade unions); the third (secondary) party is the government in its regulatory role (as opposed to its role as an employer). This tripartite relationship is a prerequisite for sound labour relations and for the socio-economic stability and prosperity of any country, and the government's primary concern, therefore, is to provide a suitable statutory framework within which the primary parties can conduct their relationship in an orderly fashion.

15.4.1 Role of the government

The role of the government as third party is thus to create and enforce the legal framework which can regulate the rights and duties of the two primary parties. In this sense, it plays the role of master and referee in that it also has to enforce all those laws pertaining to the different dimensions of labour relations in the country. However, it also plays the role of servant in that it can offer the necessary assistance to enable the primary parties to conduct their relations in a sound and mutually acceptable manner. The government can, for example, provide the parties with relevant information and guidance regarding labour relations procedures, structures, institutions, systems, developments, and the like. The government, therefore, as protector of the public interest, has a natural interest in overseeing and guiding the conduct of all the parties in order to ensure that the nature and the quality of labour relations do not have a negative impact on the country's inhabitants. The government is also an employer; therefore, in labour relations in the public sector, the government also becomes a primary party.

15.4.2 Role of the employer

Public sector employers or management form one of the primary parties in the tripartite labour relations system of a country. Employers want their institutions to be successful; public sector management must therefore see to it that the right things are done in the right way to ensure the achievement of the institution's objectives. Public management's role is traditionally to make the necessary decisions regarding the optimal utilisation of all the institutional resources.

Public management's interests in labour and employee relations (and thus in collective bargaining) are therefore quite obvious. Public sector managers have to engage in collective bargaining and related labour relations dynamics in such a way that it ultimately serves the interests of the employer of the institution. Once non-management employees (workers) are at work, the concerns of management employees revolve around getting the employees (as individuals or as group members) to respond in a positive way to the work situation. They seek ways to control the work process and work-related behaviour and performance so that the objectives of the public sector institution can be achieved. The responsibilities of management in the public sector, thus, include the following:

- Protecting and serving the interests of employers;
- Determining objectives;
- Arranging for the optimal utilisation of the institution's resources (including the human resources);
- Ensuring customer satisfaction;
- Ensuring that the necessary standards of service quality are maintained; and
- Ensuring that all operations of the institution are conducted in a cost-effective and efficient manner, which will include the control of labour costs.

15.4.2.1   Duties of the employer (management)

It is the particular duty of public sector management to see to it that the quality of public sector labour relations ultimately contributes to the success of the institution. This will obviously include management's duty to respect and uphold the basic rights of workers. In this regard, the duties of public sector management include the following:

- Keeping employees in the service of the institution and not dismissing them arbitrarily;
- Paying employees for their work and for services rendered;
- Allowing employees to join trade unions;
- Negotiating with the employees and/or their representatives;
- Providing safe and healthy working conditions; and
- Ensuring that all aspects related to the human activity of employment are dealt with within the bounds of the law.

15.4.3   Role of public sector employees

The other primary party in any public sector labour relations system consists of the employees and their representative bodies (such as trade unions). It is the duty of public sector employees to hire out their labour potential (energy, skills, knowledge, abilities, etc.) to perform certain work on behalf of the employer, under the control of management, and ultimately to further the interests of the institution. Public sector employees therefore have a particular role to play, which includes duties such as:

- Behaving in the required manner at work;
- Performing their work as required;
- Remaining obedient and loyal to the employer (and management);
- Complying with reasonable rules and instructions; and
- Exercising the right to associate, bargain, and strike in a responsible manner.

According to a study by Brewer & Gilbert, there is evidence to suggest that public sector employment continues to attract individuals with different values and expectations to those who choose a career in the private sector. In this study (see Focus on Research 15.1), the Rahim Organizational Conflict Inventory (ROCI-II) was administered to a total of 107 Hong Kong Chinese accountants from the Treasury Department and a large private accounting firm, to test whether the same interpersonal conflict handling strategies would be used in conflict situations with a manager.

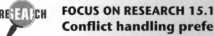

FOCUS ON RESEARCH 15.1
Conflict handling preferences in the public and private sector

The study of Brewer & Gilbert indicated that public and private sector employees are similar in their overall approach to conflict resolution. However, public employees favoured more strongly the integrating, problem-solving approach, which requires information exchange, looking for alternatives and reaching a solution acceptable to all. These findings are interpreted in relation to the Hong Kong public sector's well-established principles of procedural due process and formal dispute-resolution mechanisms. The study indicated that the public-private distinction continues to exist and it is not appropriate to apply universally private sector strategies to personnel management in public organisations.

Source: Brewer & Gilbert (2009: 9–10)

15.4.3.1   Public sector employees' rights

The rights of South African public sector employees have broadened in the last decade as the government has enacted laws giving employees specific protections in the workplace.

A right is the ability to engage in conduct that is protected by law or social sanction, free from interference by another party (such as an employer) (Gómez-Mejía, Balkin, & Cardy 1998: 424).

The rights of public sector employees can be categorised as the following: (1) statutory rights; (2) contractual rights; and (3) other rights.

Statutory rights
Statutory rights are protected by law enacted by the government. Public sector employees' key statutory right is protection from discrimination based on race, gender, sex, pregnancy, marital status, ethnic or social origin, colour, sexual orientation, age, disability, religion, conscience, belief, culture, language, and birth as stipulated in Chapter 2 (dealing with the Bill of Rights) of the 1996 Constitution. Another important anti-discrimination law which reserves protected status for certain employees is the Employment Equity Act 55 of 1998 (see section 15.6.5). The Commission for the Promotion and Protection of the Rights of Cultural, Religious, and Linguistic Communities and the Commission for Gender Equality also have the power to monitor, investigate, research, educate, lobby, advise, and report on issues concerning the respective rights of gender equality and of cultural, religious, and linguistic communities. According to Section 23 of the 1996 Constitution, employees have the legal right to form, join, and participate in trade union activities.

Contractual rights

Contractual rights are based on the law and the context of employment contracts. An employment contract spells out the terms of the employment relationship for both the employer and the employee, and is legally binding (Gomez-Mejia *et.al* 1998: 44). As we have seen in Chapter 8 (selection) all employees in the public service must be provided with a written contract of employment that specifies the terms and conditions.

Other rights

Apart from statutory and contractual rights, public sector employees often expect other rights as well. Normally these rights are not included in legally bound laws or contracts. Therefore, public sector employees cannot opt for legal recourse if they feel that these rights have been violated by the employer. Public sector employers choose to extend these rights because employees expect to be treated fairly and ethically in return for providing their employer with a fair and reasonable amount of work. This concern or expectation has resulted in the use of the so-called psychological contract. Using the principles of a psychological contract, public sector employers undertake to create a climate of fairness and ethical behaviour through the example and tone they set in the workplace. We present this not as a philosophical theory, but really as a way of inspiring public sector managers to commit themselves to the following principles of behaviour (Gómez-Mejía *et al.* 1998: 426):

- Take deliberate actions that develop trust by sharing useful information with employees and making commitments on certain issues in the workplace.
- Act consistently at all times by making decisions in such a way that employees are not surprised.
- Demonstrate integrity by honouring confidentiality of discussions with employees and showing concern for fellow workers.
- Deal fairly, professionally, and equitably with all employees.
- Demonstrate respect towards employees by showing open commitment to their optimal development, motivation, and utilisation.
- Co-operate fully with all employees to advance the public interest.
- Be truthful by never abusing employees' authority.

DID YOU KNOW? ?

One way of getting the psychological contract operational is to develop and publicise a code of conduct. In order to give practical effect to the relevant constitutional provisions relating to the public service, all public officials are expected to comply with the Code of Conduct provided for the public service. The Code acts as a guideline to employees as to what is expected of them from an ethical point of view – both in their individual conduct and in their relationship with others – and to enhance professionalism and help to ensure confidence in the public service.

Read more about the Code of Conduct for the public service at
http://www.dpsa.gov.za/acts&policies.asp.

15.5 Overview of trade unions

Trade unions have played an important role in transforming the country from an apartheid society to a democracy, but they also remain major stakeholders and role players in the governance of the country today. In this part of the book, the focus falls on the nature of trade unions as institutions in their own right.

15.5.1 Anatomy of trade unions: A brief overview

Although collective bargaining as a process can thus be highlighted as a particular means through which trade unions get involved in representing the interests of their members, there are also other processes that may be used for this purpose. In this regard, more co-operative processes such as joint problem solving, indirect participation in decision making through consultation, and even processes of co-determination may form part of the way in which trade unions serve the interests of their members within public sector institutions and society at large.

15.5.1.1 Why trade unions exist

From what we have seen in this chapter so far, it should be quite clear why trade unions exist: they are formed to serve the interests of their members – the employees. The question arising from this is why certain public sector employees want to belong to a trade union. In essence, it can be stated that trade unions exist simply because certain groups of public sector employees do not feel satisfied with their employment relationships. With the advent of the Industrial Revolution, the nature of employment relationships changed considerably, due to the rise of mass production, factories, and capitalism. The focus was on outputs only, and the needs of employees were often grossly neglected. Some groups of employees thus experienced (and many still do today) certain discrepancies between what they felt they were actually getting out of their employment relationships relative to others and what they felt they ought to get (in such aspects as job satisfaction, freedom to make decisions for themselves in the workplace, working conditions, remuneration, and fringe benefits). Broadly speaking, therefore, the primary purpose of trade unions is to restore and maintain some sort of balance or equity in employment relations, as well as in society as a whole. This is especially so when one considers the imbalances in power and the inequalities between certain classes of people in society – most notably between the working class and those who own the productive institutions such as business enterprises and government institutions. In practice, these imbalances and inequalities largely involve the relationship between two groups, namely public sector managers (employees who are appointed to represent the interests of the real employers in the workplace) and the so-called non managerial employees – the employees or labour. From this, we can derive many different generalised objectives of trade unions:

- They want to promote the establishment of merit systems and the prevention of politically-based hiring and firing.
- They try to improve the working conditions of their members as well as their terms of employment.

- They want to ensure that employees are treated fairly at work.
- They strive to ensure that employees get a fair share of the wealth generated by organisations.
- They aim at improving social security.
- They want to achieve greater democracy in the governance of individual organisations, industries and society by taking part in decision-making processes.
- They aim in particular at getting greater control over the management of employment relationships within institutions.
- They strive to do away with class structures in societies where some have a great deal while others have very little and many are not employed at all.

In order to achieve their objectives, trade unions have to operate both efficiently and effectively.

15.5.1.2 How trade unions operate: Structures and methods

Just as public sector institutions have to be managed in order to achieve their objectives, trade unions – as institutions in their own right – also have to be managed. They have to plan and set objectives, they have to be structured (or organised), leadership is essential, and control has to be exercised. The topic of how to manage a trade union falls beyond the scope of this book. However, it is necessary to develop a general understanding of the way in which trade unions operate, and we shall thus focus on the overall structuring and methods employed by these institutions.

Although details regarding the structuring of unions may differ in accordance with such variables as type, size, policy, and affiliation to a federation, we can sketch a general structural pattern. In contrast with most public sector institutions, the power of a trade union is vested in its membership and not so much in its top hierarchy. Trade unions are democratic institutions, and employees usually join them voluntarily. Under the old laws, a trade union had to prove that more than 50% of the employees in the institution were members of that particular union in order to be legally representative. However, under the current labour law system it is far easier for a trade union to pass the 'representivity test' and to win organisational rights. Unfortunately, the law is not clear what 'sufficient representation' means. In practice, the new laws have not replaced the 50% yardstick. Instead, the law leaves it up to the arbitrating Commissioners at the CCMA to determine the cut-off percentage required in each case. In many cases so far the CCMA has allowed trade unions with far less than 50% membership the right to demand (Israelstam, Healy, Hayward, Randall, Jackson, Squire, Molefi & Meyerson (2004: Online)):

- Access to the workplace;
- Deduction and pay-over of union fees; and
- Leave for union activities.

An example of a CCMA arbitration judgment regarding union membership is given in Spotlight on the Law 15.1 on page 448.

SPOTLIGHT ON THE LAW 15.1
Union membership

In the CCMA arbitration judgment *HOSPERSA & Zuid Afrikaans Hospital*, [1997], (GA637) partial organisational rights were given to the HOSPERSA trade union even though it had only 24.6% membership in the workplace. The issue in dispute between the parties, and the subsequent referral to arbitration, concerned whether or not the applicant had sufficient representation within respondent's work force for the purposes of applicant obtaining the organisation rights referred to in Section 18 of the Labour Relations Act 66 of 1995, namely:

'18 Right to establish thresholds of representativeness:

(1) An employer and a registered trade union whose members are a majority of the employees employed by that employer in a workplace, or the parties to a bargaining council, may conclude a collective agreement establishing a threshold of representativeness required in respect of one or more of the organisational rights referred to in Sections 12, 13 and 15.

(2) A collective agreement concluded in terms of subsection (1) is not binding unless the thresholds of representativeness in the collective agreement are applied equally to any registered trade union seeking any of the organisational rights referred to in that subsection.'

Read more about cases with regard to union membership in *Jeremiah v National Sorgum Breweries* [1999] 20 ILJ 1055 (LC) (1058A), *Western Cape Workers Association v Gansbaai Marine* (J190/99) [1999] ZALC 127 (19 August 1999) and *Equity Aviation Services (Pty) Ltd v South African Transport and Allied Workers Union and Others* [2009] 20 (10) SALLR 1 (LAC) at [http://www.saflii.org/za/cases/ZALC/1999].

Read more about the collection and payment of trade union fees in *National Entitled Workers Union v Sithole & others* [2004] 25 ILJ 2201 (LAC) at [http://www.saflii.org/content/south-africa-index].

The members elect shop stewards to act as the link between the union, the members, and the management of institutions. Often, the elected shop stewards form shop steward committees within the institutions in which they act as representatives of the employees. These shop steward committees thus make up the next structural layer (above the membership base) of the trade union. Typically, the next structural level is formed by the trade union's branch offices, which usually include full-time union officials (full-time employees of the trade union) and members of the shop steward committees (or other shop stewards duly elected by the committees).

Should a trade union's membership be significant, it may be necessary to create regional structures in the form of regional union offices. Full-time union officials and branch level members may also be involved at this level.

At the next level, there is the national committee and national executive. This structural level usually consists of a president of the trade union or a chairperson, a vice chairperson, a general secretary, and a treasurer. These officials are appointed or elected, and their roles are determined in accordance with the constitution of each individual trade union. The roles of president and vice-president are normally filled by union members who are shop stewards. Full-time union officials usually take on the roles of treasurer and secretary. The task of the national committee –and in particular the national executive – is to implement the policies of the trade union and also to act and speak on its behalf. Overall responsibility for the smooth functioning of the trade union rests with these structures.

Unions are democratic institutions. All union policy decisions are made at the level of the national congress. The national congress represents grassroots membership and elects the executive. The overall management of trade unions thus rests with the executives at the various structural levels.

15.5.2 Rights relating to trade unionism in South Africa

In South Africa, trade unionism has been entrenched in the country's 1996 Constitution, and the rights that stem from this have been defined by the Labour Relations Act 66 of 1995 (henceforth referred to as the Act). These rights are founded on the right to freedom of association which every South African enjoys. Because of this right, trade unions can legitimately be formed, and their rights have accordingly also been spelt out in the Act. (It should be noted that, although the focus in this section is on trade union rights and duties, most of these also apply to employers' institutions.)

15.5.2.1 Freedom of association

Section 4 of the Act grants employees the right to participate in the formation of a trade union or a federation of trade unions and, subject to the union's constitution, to join that trade union. Union members have the following rights:

- To participate in the lawful activities of their union;
- To participate in the election of any of its office bearers, officials, or trade union representatives;
- To stand for election and be eligible for appointment as office bearer or official and, if elected or appointed, to hold office; and
- To stand for election and be eligible for appointment as a trade union representative and, if elected or appointed, to carry out the functions of a trade union representative in terms of the Act or in terms of any collective agreement.

Section 5 of the Act further protects freedom of association by prohibiting discrimination, victimisation, and so-called yellow-dog contracts of employment. No person may compel or threaten to compel an employee or job applicant to be or to become, or not to become, a member of a trade union or a workplace forum, or to give up membership of a trade union or workplace forum.

It should be noted that Sections 6 and 7 of the Act extend the right to freedom of association and protection against victimisation to employers.

According to Section 8 of the Act, a trade union has the right to the following:

- To determine its own constitution and rules;
- To hold elections for its office bearers, officials, and representatives;
- To plan and organise its administration and lawful activities;
- To participate in the formation of a federation of trade unions or a federation of employers' institutions;
- To join a federation of trade unions or a federation of employers' institutions, subject to its constitution, and to participate in its lawful activities; and
- To affiliate with, and participate in the affairs of, any international workers' institution or international employers' institution or the International Labour Organisation, and contribute to, or receive financial assistance from, those institutions.

Disputes arising from any alleged interference with freedom of association or from victimisation may be referred for conciliation to a bargaining council or to the Commission for Conciliation, Mediation and Arbitration (CCMA). (Note that, whenever the phrase 'bargaining council or the CCMA' is used in this chapter, it is used in the following context and as shorthand to describe the following process: The Act encourages labour and capital to establish their own structures and procedures; thus, if there is a functional bargaining council which has jurisdiction, that council will deal with the dispute. Only in the absence of such a council will the CCMA be required, as the default option, to deal with a matter.) Should the dispute remain unresolved, it may be referred to the Labour Court for adjudication.

15.5.2.2   Organisational rights of trade unions

The freedom to associate would have had little meaning in practice had the rights of the institutions with whom one may associate not also been catered for in the legislation. Depending on how many employees a union represents – its so-called level of representativeness – it will enjoy certain statutory organisational rights. At this point, it may be instructive to note the four different types of trade union representativeness encountered in the Labour Relations Act 66 of 1995 as a whole, along with their attendant rights. The various circumstances under which a trade union may become entitled to organisational rights are listed below:

- When a union enjoys majority support (50% plus one) in the workplace.
- When a union is 'sufficiently representative' in the workplace. The Act does not attempt to define 'sufficiently representative', but we may accept that it does mean a significant membership, albeit falling short of an outright majority.
- When a non-majority union meets the thresholds as determined for specific organisational rights in a collective agreement between the majority union and the employer.
- When an employer has conferred upon a union certain organisational rights in terms of a collective agreement.
- When a union is a member of a bargaining council or a statutory council.

Understanding public sector labour relations

- When a recognition agreement concluded in terms of Act 28 of 1956 that is still in force confers some organisational right on a union.

15.5.2.3 Trade union registration and relevant statutory requirements

A simplified registration procedure is provided for in the Act. Of great importance is the fact that, although the process for registration has been made very simple, all rights in terms of the Act are now granted only to registered trade unions. The Act makes no provision for a dual system such as that which prevailed under the old Act. (It should be noted that all the provisions referred to in the text that relate to the rights and duties of trade unions, except those relating to shop stewards, also apply in essence to employers' institutions.) Unregistered bodies would not be recognised under the new Act, although, in keeping with the principle of voluntarism, there is no direct compulsion to register in terms of the Labour Relations Act. Any trade union may apply for registration provided that it has adopted a suitable name, its constitution meets the statutory requirements, it has an address in South Africa, and it is independent. The last requirement is an expression of the legislator's disapproval of the practice of some employers in setting up trade unions as their puppets in opposition to 'difficult' or 'radical' trade unions in order to divide the loyalty of the workforce and thus to undermine the independent trade union(s). In terms of the Act, a trade union is independent if it is not under the direct or indirect control of any employer or employers' institution and it is free of any interference or influence of any kind from any employer or employers' institution. With the exception of the independence requirement, the same provisions apply to employers' institutions that wish to register.

15.5.2.4 Prominent public sector trade unions

The activities of trade unions in the public sector tend to differ from those of their counterparts in the private sector. This can mainly be attributed to the fact that the main purpose of the public sector is not directed at profit making. Because of the absence of the profit-making principle in the public sector, funds for wage increases need to be obtained from the taxpayers, of whom public sector employees form a part. Therefore, public sector employees would have to bear the consequences of such wage increases (Finnemore & Van Rensburg 2000: 192). One consequence of the absence of the profit-making principle is that different types of organisations have been created to represent workers in the public sector.

DID YOU KNOW?

?

Basically, three types of trade unions can be identified:
- **Staff associations:** These associations are involved in advisory forums, consultation and full-scale negotiations. Examples of staff associations in the South African public service include the Public and Allied Workers Union of South Africa (PAWUSA), the United National Public Servants Association of South Africa (UNIPSA), the Public Servants Association of South Africa (PSA), and the Public Service Union (PSU). ▷

- **Professional associations:** Professional associations have been established to represent the interests of highly skilled employees. They are mainly concerned with the regulation of entry into professions through certification procedures and training requirements. Examples of professional associations include the South African Medical Association (SAMA), the Democratic Nursing Organisation of South Africa (DENOSA), and the Hospital Personnel Trade Union of South Africa (HOSPERSA).
- **Trade unions:** Trade unions have a more militant approach than staff associations and professional associations and have a clear commitment to negotiations on behalf of their members. Examples are the National Education, Health, and Allied Workers Union (NEHAWU), the South African Democratic Teachers Union (SADTU), and the South African Police Union (SAPU) (Adler 2000: 103).

Source: Adler (2000: 103)

15.6 The legal context of public sector labour relations

The history of labour relations law since the 1980s can be seen as a deliberate balancing act by government to address the deficiencies of the contractual approach to the employment relationship. We may observe that modern South African labour law is characterised largely by its legislative implications. In this regard, government has tried to balance the employment relationship by enacting legislation that is aimed at: (1) determining the rights, duties, and responsibilities of public sector employers; (2) recognising and promoting the collective dimension of labour relations – referring to trade unionism, collective bargaining and employee participation; and (3) protecting the individual employee by requiring the employer to comply with at least certain minimum standards concerning working conditions and the general treatment of employees in the workplace (Bezuidenhout, Garbers, & Potgieter 1998: 39). This section deals with a discussion of the various laws enacted from the 1990s and onwards.

15.6.1 Constitution of the Republic of South Africa, 1996

In Chapter 2 of the 1996 Constitution, we find a Bill of Rights protecting the rights of employers and employees in the workplace. Section 23 of the 1996 Constitution deals with labour rights. These include the following:

- Everyone has the right to fair labour practices.
- Every worker has the right:
  - To form and join a trade union;
  - To participate in the activities and programmes of a trade union; and
  - To strike.
- Every employer has the right:
  - To form and join an employers' organisation; and
  - To participate in the activities and programmes of an employers' organisation.
- Every trade union and every employers' organisation has the right:
  - To determine its own administration, programmes, and activities;

- To organise; and
- To form and join a federation.
- Every trade union, employers' organisation, and employer has the right to engage in collective bargaining. National legislation may be enacted to regulate collective bargaining. To the extent that the legislation may limit a right in this Chapter, the limitation must comply with Section 36(1).
- National legislation may recognise union security arrangements contained in collective agreements. To the extent that the legislation may limit a right in this Chapter, the limitation must comply with Section 36(1).

An analysis of Section 8(1) of the 1996 Constitution reveals that the Constitution has a direct impact on the public sector employment relationship. According to Section 8(1) of the Constitution, the Bill of Rights binds the legislature, the executive, and the judiciary, and all other organs of the state. This implies that all the rights listed in the Bill of Rights are directly applicable to the employment relationship between the state as employer and its employees. This allows the individual public sector employee to rely directly on these constitutional rights in those cases where an employer infringes upon them.

The 1996 Constitution also has a possible indirect impact on other legislation (Bezuidenhout, Garbers, & Potgieter 1998: 40). Most of the rights referred to in Section 23 of the Constitution are also regulated in other parts of ordinary legislation such as the Labour Relations Act 66 of 1995. If, for example, a public sector employer forbids an employee to participate in union activities, the employee has the right not only to rely on Section 23(2)(b) of the Constitution, but on the provisions of Sections 4–10 of the Labour Relations Act as well. These Sections allow every public sector employee the right to participate in the activities and programmes of a trade union.

15.6.2 Labour Relations Act 66 of 1995 (LRA)

The underlying principle of the LRA is to promote the right to fair labour practices in the public sector workplace. In particular, it gives public sector employers, employees, unions, and employer institutions the following rights and obligations:

- Freedom of association (Sections 4–10);
- Organisational rights (Sections 11–22);
- Unfair dismissal (Sections 185–197);
- Unfair labour practice (Schedule 7, Part B); and
- Strikes and lockouts (Sections 64–77).

The LRA is applicable to every public sector employee in South Africa, excluding members of the National Defence Force, the National Intelligence Agency, and the South African Secret Service. The main point of course, is that the LRA is an attempt to move away from the traditional adversarial system of labour relations to a more inclusive one.

The Act provides for forums to be established by the parties (bargaining councils, statutory councils, and workplace forums) on which employers' representatives and employees' representatives can interact on matters of mutual interest and prevent or resolve disputes which may arise between them. In addition, the Act grants recognition and strong rights to shop stewards (called trade union representatives in the Act). The Act also provides for the establishment of the Commission for Conciliation, Mediation and Arbitration (CCMA) and specialist courts (the Labour Court and the Labour Appeal Court) to adjudicate and resolve certain labour matters. In addition to the Labour Relations Act, we must take regard of the National Economic, Development and Labour Council Act 35 of 1994 which provides for the establishment of a national economic, development, and labour council (NEDLAC).

 DID YOU KNOW?

A number of 'Codes of Good Practice' have been published under the provisions of the LRA. Examples are the following:
- Code of Good Practice on the handling of sexual harassment cases; and
- Code of Good Practice on key aspects of HIV/AIDS and employment.

15.6.2.1 Code of Good Practice on the handling of sexual harassment cases

We may ask why a Code of Good Practice on the handling of sexual harassment cases is necessary, but the answer is quite obvious. In a survey done in 1990, it was found that 76% of career women in South Africa had been harassed in some or other way in the workplace. Prior to this Code, there were no clear guidelines for public sector employers on the way in which to manage cases of sexual harassment (Finnemore & Van Rensburg 2001: 524).

Women are now protected legally. Sections 10 and 14 of the 1996 Constitution stipulate that sexual harassment is viewed as an infringement upon a person's right to privacy and dignity. Sexual harassment is also strictly forbidden in terms of Section 6(3) of the Employment Equity Act 55 of 1998 (EEA). The Code of Good Practice on the handling of sexual harassment provides specifically for the elimination of sexual harassment in the workplace. The Code is very specific on the forms of sexual harassment, and it also provides for appropriate procedures to deal with the problem and prevent its recurrence. Probably the most important provision in the Code is that public sector employers are encouraged to develop and implement policies on sexual harassment that will serve as a guideline for the behaviour of all public sector employees. However, the provisions in the Code are also very clear on existing policies and agreements. It is clearly stated that the Code is not intended to serve as a substitute for collective agreements. What should an employer do if a claim of sexual harassment has been brought to its attention? Section 60 of the EEA clearly states that the employer must consult with the relevant parties, take reasonable steps to address the matter and prevent recurrence. In terms of the EEA an employer is liable only if (Grogan, Jordaan, Maserumule & Stelzner, 2009: 105):

- The conduct complaint of was perpetrated by one of its employees;
- It constituted sexual harassment;
- The harassment occurred while the employee was at work;
- It was immediately brought to the attention of the employer; and
- The employer failed to consult all relevant parties, or to take reasonable steps to prevent the harassment, or take steps to eliminate it.

An example of a sexual harassment case that landed in the Labour Court is shown in Spotlight on the Law 15.2.

SPOTLIGHT ON THE LAW 15.2
Sexual harassment

In *Potgieter v National Commissioner of the SAPS 7 another* [2009] 30 ILJ 1322 (LC) the applicant reported to her employer that she had been kissed by a male police officer. As a result of this incident, the offending police officer was fine for sexual harassment. However, the applicant decided to resign, claiming that she suffered post-traumatic stress. She was also of the opinion that the case was not dealt with in a satisfactory manner by the employer. In the Labour Court the applicant claimed that the employer had failed to comply with the provisions of Section 60 of the EEA in that:

- The employer delayed to deal with the complaint;
- Her report was not kept confidential;
- The perpetrator was not removed immediately after the incident was reported;
- The sanction imposed by the chairperson of the perpetrator's disciplinary hearing was too lenient; and
- She was not timeously referred for assistance.

The Labour Court held that:

- It was common cause that the incident constituted sexual harassment;
- The incident occurred at the workplace during working hours; and
- That the employer had taken action against the perpetrator.

However, in sum the Labour Court decided that the applicant failed to demonstrate that the employer had failed to do what was required by Section 60 of the EEA.

Source: Grogan, Jordaan, Maserumule & Stelzner (2009: 105–106)

15.6.2.2 Code of Good Practice on key aspects of HIV/AIDS and employment

Vincent (in Mitchell 2002: 269) writes that approximately 15% of all South Africans between the age of 20 to 64 are HIV (Human Immunodeficiency Virus) positive. Moreover, this percentage is set to rise to 23% in the year 2005 and 27% in 2010.

Approximately 50% of these people acquire HIV before they turn 25. It is further estimated that over 50% of this group of people will die of AIDS (Acquired Immune Deficiency Syndrome) before the age of 35.

These figures have serious repercussions for employers, both in the public sector and the private sector. The illness will affect every workplace through prolonged staff illness and absenteeism as well as deaths. As a result, it will impact on productivity, employee benefits, occupational health and safety, and staff morale. Therefore, it is essential that public sector management and labour should co-operate to find proactive and holistic solutions for the problem at hand. In this regard, the government has acted in advance with a Code of Good Practice on key aspects of HIV/AIDS with the following goals:

- To eliminate unfair discrimination practices in the workplace that are related to an employee's HIV status;
- To promote a non-discriminatory workplace in which employees with HIV/AIDS are in a position to reveal their status without fear of stigma or rejection;
- To develop and promote effective ways of managing HIV/AIDS in the workplace;
- To ensure that there is a balance between the rights and responsibilities of all parties involved in the workplace; and
- To make an effort to give effect to the regional obligations prescribed by the Southern African Development Community.

It is important that the Code should be read in conjunction with certain provisions of the 1996 Constitution, the Employment Equity Act 55 of 1998 (Sections 6(1)7(2) and 54(1)(a) – prohibition of unfair discrimination), the Labour Relations Act 66 of 1995 (Section 187(1) – no dismissal on the grounds of HIV/AIDS), the Occupational Health and Safety Act 85 of 1993 (Section 8(1) – safe workplace), the Compensation for Occupational Injuries and Diseases Act 130 of 1993 (Section 22(1) – infection with HIV as a result of occupation exposure: benefits), and the Basic Conditions of Employment Act 75 of 1997 (Section 22(2) – sick leave). In its broadest sense, the Code refers to the following:

- Measures to deal with HIV/AIDS in the workplace (for example, development of policies and programmes);
- Prohibition of unfair discrimination within the broader employment relationship, including recruitment procedures, advertising and selection criteria, appointments, job classification, and grading;
- Mechanisms to promote acceptance and openness towards HIV/AIDS in the workplace;
- Emphasis on providing support for employees infected by HIV/AIDS; and
- Grievance procedures and disciplinary measures to deal with HIV/AIDS-related complaints in the workplace.

15.6.3 Basic Conditions of Employment Act 75 of 1997

The primary objective of the Basic Conditions of Employment Act is to give effect to and regulate the right to fair labour practices conferred by Section 23(1) of the 1996 Constitution. Therefore, the Act sets out minimum provisions for basic conditions of employment for all public sector employees working in South Africa, except members of the National Defence Force, the National Intelligence Agency, the South African Secret Service and unpaid volunteers working for charitable organisations.

DID YOU KNOW? ?

The minimum provisions for employment provided for in the Basic Conditions of Employment Act 75 of 1997 are as follows:
- Hours of work, including night work;
- Overtime and overtime payment;
- Meal intervals and rest periods;
- Pay for work on Sundays and public holidays;
- Annual and sick leave, maternity leave and family responsibility leave;
- Written particulars of employment;
- Remuneration details and severance pay;
- Termination of employment;
- Prohibition of child and forced labour; and
- Variations of basic conditions of employment.

15.6.4 Occupational Health and Safety Act 85 of 1993

Consider the following statistics: In just the year 2000, the Department of Labour was involved in the investigation of 5 950 incidents in which health and safety standards were violated. Of these figures, 493 were fatalities. During 2000, 10 060 inspections were done, which resulted in a total of 6 970 contraventions of the Health and Safety Regulations and 649 contraventions of the Act (Taljaard, in Mitchell 2002: 188).

These statistics make it clear that adherence to the requirements of the Occupational Health and Safety Act is not negotiable. This brings us to the main purpose of the Act, and that is the regulating and ensuring of health and safety standards by public sector employers as well as public sector employees. It is of vital importance to note that not only are employers and employees covered by the Act, but the public is also protected from hazards emanating from work-related activities. The Act covers four main principles:
- It imposes certain roles, duties, functions, rights, and powers on employers and employees to ensure a healthy and safe working environment. That includes safe systems of work, plant, and machinery.
- It requires a system of self-regulation through which health and safety representatives have to be appointed. Broadly speaking, the safety representatives

should monitor the effectiveness of health and safety methods, identify potential hazards, and investigate incidents.

- It provides for a system of consultation, as a health and safety committee must be established. The safety committee may have to make recommendations to
- the employer concerning occupational health and safety and report on any accident or incident in which anyone is killed or seriously injured, or becomes seriously ill.
- It requires a system of policing, as a chief inspector and other inspectors may be appointed by the Minister of Labour to enter premises, question persons, and conduct inquiries into any reportable incidents, for example.

15.6.5 Employment Equity Act 55 of 1998

An important aspect on which the Employment Equity Act focuses is discrimination – past and present. The overall objectives of the Act include the elimination of employment discrimination, the promotion of equal employment opportunities, and the implementation of affirmative action to redress the effects of discrimination and to achieve a representative workforce. Again, the Act is not applicable to members of the National Defence Force, the National Intelligence Agency, or the South African Secret Service. Although we have, by now, discussed many parts of the Act, we shall nevertheless recap in general terms. Generally speaking, the Act comprises two main parts: (1) Chapter II concerns prohibition of discrimination, and (2) Chapters III, IV, and VI deal with affirmative action and the ways in which it is to be put into operation and enforced in the workplace (Rautenbach, in Mitchell 2002: 123).

There are several provisions in the Act that public sector employers have to comply with, of which the following are the most important:

- Active steps must be taken to promote equal opportunities by eliminating unfair discrimination in employment policies and practices.
- Direct or indirect discrimination against employees or job applicants on the grounds of race, gender, sex, pregnancy, marital status, family responsibility, ethnic or social origin, colour, sexual orientation, age, disability, religion, conscience, belief, political opinion, culture, language, birth, or HIV status is at all times prohibited.
- Medical testing of employees is prohibited unless legislation permits or medical facts justify such testing. Limitations are also placed on psychological testing.
- Employers must consult with employees on affirmative action policies.
- Employment equity plans must be prepared containing specific affirmative action measures to achieve equitable representation.
- An employment equity manager must be appointed.
- Reporting must be done to the Department of Labour.
- Employment equity measures must be established subject to the guidance of the Minister on advice given by the Commission for Employment Equity.
- Labour inspectors must be allowed to enter, question, and inspect the workplace.

15.6.6 Compensation for Occupational Injuries and Diseases Act 130 of 1993

The above Act provides for compensation in cases where losses are experienced due to occupational injuries and diseases at the public sector workplace. The Act applies to all public sector employees including members of the permanent force of the South African National Defence Force. The more significant principles are as follows:

- No-fault compensation is to be provided for employees who are injured in accidents while they are on duty or who contract occupational diseases.
- Employees are prohibited from instituting a claim of damages against the employer, manager, or any other person involved in the incident for the damage suffered.
- The Act is administered by a Compensation Commissioner who is also responsible for the Compensation Fund. Employers contribute to the Compensation Fund and these payments are used for compensation and administrative costs.
- National and local authorities may obtain a certificate of exemption from the Compensation Commissioner. In such an event, they are classified as 'employers individually liable'.
- Benefits are payable to employees who suffer temporary disability, employees who are permanently disabled, and dependants of employees who have died as a result of their injuries or illness. In cases of temporary disability, employers have the obligation to pay employees' compensation for the first three months of absence from work.
- Payment of medical aid is also required when employees are temporary or permanently disabled.

15.6.7 Protected Disclosures Act 26 of 2000

According to the preamble to this Act, every public sector employer and public sector employee has the responsibility to disclose criminal and other irregular conduct in the workplace. The Act also emphasises that a public sector employer has the responsibility to take the necessary steps to protect employees who disclose such information from any reprisals as a result of such disclosure. (Employees who disclose such information are generally referred to as 'whistle blowers'.) The objects of the Act are: (1) to protect an employee, whether in the private or the public sector, from being subjected to an 'occupational detriment' on account of having made a protected disclosure; (2) to provide for certain remedies in connection with any occupational detriment suffered on account of having made a protected disclosure; and (3) to provide for procedures in terms of which an employee can, in a responsible manner, disclose information regarding improprieties by his or her employer.

According to Sections 5 to 8 of the Act, public sector employees can make protected disclosures to legal advisers, employers, members of the Cabinet or Executive Councils, and such bodies as the Public Protector and the Auditor General. The Act prohibits an employer from subjecting an employee to what is called an 'occupational detriment' (see the objects of the Act above). An occupational detriment is described by the Minister of Justice and Constitutional Development as any of the following to which a public sector employee may be subjected (Mitchell 2002: 583):

- Any disciplinary action;
- Dismissal, suspension, demotion, harassment, or intimidation;
- Transfer against his or her will;
- Refusal of transfer or promotion;
- A term or condition of employment or retirement which is altered to that person's disadvantage;
- Refusal of a reference, or provision of an adverse reference;
- Denial of appointment to any appointment, profession, or office; and
- Adverse effects in respect of employment, profession, or office, including employment opportunities and work security.

15.7   Review

In this chapter, we have looked at certain historical developments of labour relations in the South African public sector. We have seen that the employment relationship forms the basis of labour relations, and that it determines the basic roles, duties, and rights of the various role players. We have also examined the prominent role that trade unions play in the employment relationship.

The basic labour relations-related statutory requirements that have been discussed in this chapter provide only the basic framework within which the public sector employment relationship is managed. This will now form the foundation for Chapter 16, in which we shall examine certain managerial aspects of labour relations.

15.8   Self-evaluation questions

1. What did the evolution of public sector labour relations since 1912 teach you?
2. What is an 'employment relationship'? Do you think it is important to have an employment relationship?
3. Who are the parties involved in labour relations? What are their respective roles, duties, and rights?
4. What is meant by a 'psychological contract'? In what way can public sector employers put the psychological contract into operation? Explain by means of an example.
5. Explain why and how trade unions exist and operate.
6. What are the basic rights of trade unions in terms of the 1996 Constitution and the Labour Relations Act 66 of 1995?
7. The changes in South African labour relations law are profound. What impact do these changes have on labour relations in the public sector?

Bibliography

Adler, G. 2000. *Public service labour relations in a democratic South Africa.* Johannesburg: Witwatersrand University Press.

Bendix, S. 1996. *Industrial relations in the new South Africa.* 3rd edn. Cape Town: Juta.

Bezuidenhout, MC, Garbers, CJ, & Potgieter, S. 1998. *Managing for healthy labour relations: A practical guide for health services in southern Africa.* Pretoria: Van Schaik.

Cloete, JJN. 1997. *Personnel administration and management.* Pretoria: Van Schaik.

Brewer, B, & Gilbert KY. 2009. Conflict handling preferences: A public-private comparison. *Public Personnel Management,* 38 (3), Fall, 1–14.

Du Plessis, JV, Fouché, MA, Jordaan, B, & Van Wyk, MW. 1996. *A practical guide to labour law.* 2nd edn. Durban: Butterworths.

Finnemore, M, & Van der Merwe, P. 1996. *Introduction to labour relations in South Africa.* 4th edn. Durban: Butterworths.

Finnemore, M, & Van Rensburg, R. 2001. *Contemporary labour relations.* Durban: Butterworths.

Foot, M, & Hook, C. 1996. *Introducing human resource management.* London: Longman.

Gómez-Mejía, LR, Balkin, DB, & Cardy, RL. 1998. *Managing human resources.* New Jersey: Prentice-Hall.

Grogan, J, Jordaan, B, Maserumule, P, & Stelzner, S. 2009. *Juta's annual labour law update 2009.* Cape Town: Juta.

Israelstam, I, Healy, T, Hayward, Randall, L, Jackson, D, Squire, D, Molefi, N, Meyerson, D. 2004. *Labour law for managers practical handbook.* Northriding: Fleet Street Publications [http://www.fsp.co.za].

Labour Bulletin. 2010. Trade unions and your employees' rights. Fleet Street Publications. [http://www.fsp.co.za].

Levy, A & Associates. 1995. *Annual report on labour relations in South Africa: 1995–1996.* Johannesburg: Andrew Levy and Associates.

Levy, A & Associates. 1996. *Annual report on labour relations in South Africa: 1996–1997.* Johannesburg: Andrew Levy and Associates.

Mitchell, L. 2002. *Business blue book of South Africa.* Cape Town: National Press.

Rosenbloom, DH, Goldman, DD, & Ingraham, PW. 1994. *Contemporary public administration.* New York: McGraw Hill.

Salamon, M. 1992. *Industrial relations: Theory and practice.* 2nd edn. New York: Prentice-Hall.

Tompkins, J. 1995. *Human resource management in government: Hitting the ground running.* New York: Harper Collins.

Acts of legislation

Republic of South Africa. 1993a. The Occupational Health and Safety Act (Act 85 of 1993). Government Printer. [http://www.polity.org.za/html/govdocs/legislation/1993]

Republic of South Africa. 1993b. The Public Service Labour Relations Act (Act 102 of 1993). Government Printer.

Republic of South Africa. 1993c. The Compensation for Occupational Injuries and Diseases Act (Act 130 of 1993). Government Printer. [http://www.polity.org.za/html/govdocs/ legislation/1993]

Republic of South Africa. 1994. The Public Service Act (Act 103 of 1994). Government printer. [http://www.polity.org.za/html/govdocs/legislation/1994]

Republic of South Africa.1995. The Labour Relations Act (Act 66 of 1995). Government Printer. [http://www.polity.org.za/html/govdocs/legislation/1995]

Republic of South Africa. 1996. The Constitution of the Republic of South Africa (1996). Government Printer. [http://www.polity.org.za/html/govdocs/legislation/1996]

Republic of South Africa. 1997. The Basic Conditions of Employment Act (Act 75 of 1997). Government Printer. [http://www.polity.org.za/html/govdocs/legislation/1997]

Republic of South Africa. 1998. The Employment Equity Act (Act 55 of 1998). Government Printer. [http://www.polity.org.za/html/govdocs/legislation/1998]

Republic of South Africa. 2000a. The Protected Disclosures Act (Act 26 of 2000). Government Printer. [http://www.polity.org.za/html/govdocs/legislation/2000]

Government white papers
Republic of South Africa. 1995. White Paper on the Transformation of the Public Service. 24 November 1995. Government Gazette, 365 (16838).

Government reports
Republic of South Africa. 2000c. Public service review report for the year 1999/2000. Department of the Public Service and Administration. [http://www.dpsa.gov.za/docs/reports]

Republic of South Africa. 2001. Annual Report of the Department of Public Service and Administration for the year 2001. Department of the Public Service and Administration. [http://www.dpsa.gov. za/docs/reports/annual]

Other government documents
Republic of South Africa, Undated. We resolve by negotiations, lets negotiate: A 10-year review of the PSCBC. Lyttelton: Public Service Co-ordinating Bargaining Council.

Collective agreements
Republic of South Africa. 2000b. Resolution 9 of 2000: Senior Management Service. Department of Public Service and Administration. [http://www.dpsa.gov.za/documents/pscbc/2000/09]

16 Managing public sector labour relations

Purpose

The purpose of this chapter is to analyse the importance of establishing sound labour relations in the public sector workplace.

Learning outcomes

After you have read this chapter, you should be able to:
- Discuss the formalising of the union-management relationship.
- Describe how to establish sound union-management relations using processes such as collective bargaining.
- Discuss best practice in the handling of disputes.
- Explain the most appropriate types of industrial action in the handling of strikes.
- Identify critical success factors in communicating with employees.
- Describe the appropriate principles and procedures underlying grievance handling.
- Outline a ten-step procedure to make objective decisions regarding disciplinary measures.

16.1 Introduction

In this chapter, the focus shifts to those aspects that are more directly related to the management of labour and employee relations at the level of the public sector institution. The emphasis is therefore on how public sector managers can deal with certain aspects in the workplace which relate to labour and employee relations. With regard to the establishing of union-management relations, the emphasis is on handling initial trade union contact in order to formalise the relationship. As far as collective bargaining is concerned, the primary focus is on the negotiation process. It has to be accepted that, from time to time, negotiations may end in differences of opinion between the employer (employer institutions) and employees (trade unions), and therefore this chapter also deals with dispute resolution. Because a breakdown in relations can always occur, we shall also discuss the issues involved in the handling of strikes. With regard to the individual employee, we shall conclude the chapter by examining detailed aspects of employee relations, including communication, grievance handling, and the disciplining of staff.

16.2 Establishing sound union-management relations

Because trade unions play such an important role in South African public sector institutions today, it is essential for public sector management to be professional in its dealings and interactions with such employee representative bodies. No matter how much attention is paid to the individual dimension of employee relations – in other words, to ordinary human resource management practices and to one-on-one employee relations – negligence in respect of the collective dimensions (particularly as far as trade unions are concerned) can have serious negative consequences for a public sector institution's quest for success.

DID YOU KNOW?

The South African Labour Guide is a private company providing assistance on HRM matters. It focuses on real issues in the workplace that relate to labour and employee relations. More particularly, guidance is provided in terms of labour law. Areas in the HR field that are covered include, among others, conditions of employment, constructive dismissals, a leave guide, alcoholism in the workplace, warnings and procedural fairness. Read more about the South African Labour Guide at http://www.labourguide.co.za/index.

16.2.1 Handling initial trade union contact

At some point, a trade union may approach or contact public sector management for the first time. This initial contact may be in the form of a letter or by means of a telephone call. In some instances, it may be a direct person-to-person contact between a management representative and a union official or a person who says that he or she has been elected as shop steward. The issue at hand may be a request for recognition as the ongoing representative of a group of public sector employees, or it may entail a once-off representation of an employee regarding an issue such as a grievance, the alleged unfair dismissal of another employee, or the need to negotiate improved wages or working conditions for employees.

The purpose of the first meeting should involve getting to know each other better. It is therefore imperative to make it clear that, in order to have a fruitful first meeting, the parties should be willing to exchange certain information.

DID YOU KNOW?

Not all trade union demands for recognition will necessarily be successful in their attempts to register as a trade union at the Department of Labour. For a trade union to be successful in gaining organisational rights, it should comply with the following three criteria:

- It should be registered with the Department of Labour and should show the employer the registration certificate.
- Its constitution should allow it to represent and recruit members employed at the particular employer.
- It should have enough signed-up members to claim representivity (Section 21 of the Labour Relations At 66 of 1995).

Source: Israelstam, Healy, Hayward, Randall, Jackson, Squire, Molefi & Meyerson (2004: Online)

16.2.2　Formalising the union-management relationship

Formalising the relationship with a trade union usually involves some kind of an agreement between the parties. The process of formalisation will often depend to a large extent on the level of the union's representativeness in the public sector institution and will include the following steps:

- The trade union will be required to present proof of its membership. This normally includes the submission of signed and correctly completed union membership forms that have to be verified.
- Management will have to inform the trade union of its approach regarding the type of representativeness required before a trade union will be recognised as an official representative body of the institution's employees, or of some of them. In terms of the current dispensation, public sector management will have to be guided by the principles laid down in the Labour Relations Act 66 of 1995 (the LRA). It seems that the LRA has subordinated the importance of bargaining units to the notion of majoritarianism in the workplace.
- Both parties will have to decide on the type of recognition agreement. A written recognition agreement may take the form of a skeletal agreement or a full agreement (Bendix 1996: 289–290). While the former simply states the broad principles involved, the latter is a comprehensive agreement containing detailed procedures and providing for most eventualities.

In terms of the LRA, management and a trade union may opt to enter into so-called closed shop agreements or agency shop agreements. Public sector management and a majority trade union may conclude an agreement in terms of which all public sector employees covered by the agreement are compelled to become members of that trade union. This is known as a closed shop agreement and is very controversial because of its compulsory nature and, as some allege, the curtailment of the freedom of association as a basic human right. This makes it somewhat uncertain as to whether the closed shop provision would survive a constitutional challenge. It is therefore not surprising that the drafters of the LRA found it necessary to build in various checks and balances (for example, a mandatory ballot must be held in which at least two thirds of employees must vote in favour of the closed shop agreement) in an effort to protect the closed shop from possible constitutional challenge.

An agency shop agreement is an agreement between a public sector employer and a trade union in terms of which the employer is compelled to deduct from the wages of employees within the bargaining unit who are not trade union members an amount equal to or less than (and in lieu of) the membership fees paid by the trade union members. It may be regarded as morally questionable to require someone to belong to a trade union against his or her wishes (as is the case where a closed shop agreement prevails). The requirements for validity of collective agreements are the same as for those of ordinary contracts, such as employment contracts. Apart from failure to comply with formal requirements, a collective agreement may be challenged, for example, by breach by the other party, duress and vagueness. For an example of the validity of a collective agreement, see Spotlight on the Law 16.1.

SPOTLIGHT ON THE LAW 16.1
Validity of collective agreements

In *National Education Health and Allied Workers Union v Public Health and Welfare Sectoral Bargaining Council and others* [2002] ZALC 5 23 ILJ 509 (LC) employees had gone on strike (and unlawfully occupied state buildings) in protest over the failure of the provincial administration to adjust their salaries. A representative of the Department of Health signed an agreement with the employees' union in terms of which the provincial administration undertook to implement adjustments in the salaries of qualified personnel. The departmental representative later testified he had to sign the contract under duress to prevent the collapse of health services. However, the provincial administration decided to reverse the adjustments made in terms of the agreement. An arbitrator held that the adjustments were unlawful because, among other things, the collective agreement had been signed under duress. On review of the decision, the Labour Court decided that the pressure exerted on the department's representative by the strikers was improper and accordingly vitiated the collective agreement.

Source: Grogan (2007: 107–108)

16.2.3   Entering into collective bargaining/negotiations

After the collective agreement (normally a full procedural agreement) has been finalised, the next step is collective bargaining/negotiation. Collective bargaining/ negotiation results in numerous forms of negotiation and takes place in certain structures promoted by the Labour Relations Act 66 of 1995.

Although some may hold the view that negotiation and bargaining as concepts have different meanings, Pienaar and Spoelstra (1991: 5) argue that these terms can be used in much the same way, implying that they have much the same purpose and meaning and follow the same methods. This does not mean, however, that collective bargaining and negotiation are synonymous concepts.

Collective bargaining and collective negotiation are, however, used interchangeably in this book. The qualification 'collective' indicates that the negotiations are conducted by representatives on behalf of a particular group of people – the group of employees who are union members and the group designated as management, which represents the interests of the employer at the bargaining table.

16.2.3.1   Distributive negotiation

In this type of bargaining, the parties are generally antagonistic and display little reasonableness in the process. Focusing on positions and using power are seen as central elements of this type of negotiation. Trade unions usually view management as exploiters of all workers and as fully controlling the labour or work process.

Likewise, management often negotiates from the assumption that the trade union is an unnecessary intruder, making management's life difficult and serving no real economic purpose as it simply causes labour costs to rise. This type of negotiation is associated with the collective side of employment relations, with the result that the collective bargaining process is traditionally viewed as being of an adversarial, win-lose nature.

We can identify three phases or stages of the process of distributive negotiation: the pre-negotiation phase, the interactive phase and the post-negotiation phase.

Phase 1: The pre-negotiation phase

During the pre-negotiation phase topics can vary from procedural aspects such as grievance, disciplinary, staff-reduction, or dispute-settling procedures to substantive aspects such as working hours, wages, leave, job evaluations, bonuses, equal opportunities, health and safety, and so on.

It is also important to appoint competent negotiation teams during this phase, to train them, and to synchronise their efforts. A negotiating team prepares all the issues by prioritising them in terms of relative importance, establishing opening positions, and working out bargaining ranges with ideal and fall-back positions.

Phase 2: The interactive phase of negotiation

In this phase, the two parties face each other and systematically try to persuade each other to change points of view regarding their respective positions.

Knowledge and particular skills play a major role during this stage. Below is a list of some potentially useful guidelines to help during the interactive phase of negotiations.

- Keep to the agenda as far as possible.
- Maintain order at all times.
- Stick to the facts and do not discuss people as such (separate the problems from the people).
- Take note of and use body language and gestures effectively.
- Listen more and talk less (two ears, one mouth) – ask a lot of appropriate questions, in the right way to get the right information.
- Remain alert all the time.
- Regularly confirm when you have understood, and get confirmation that others understand.
- When in doubt or uncertain about anything, call for a caucus.
- Take your time and never talk, act, or make decisions too hastily.
- Be pleasant, true, and decent all the time.
- Treat everyone else with due respect.
- Be sensitive to cultural and language differences.
- Make careful notes and keep looking for alternatives and inaccuracies in information and arguments.

- Offer various possible choices of option to the other party and make sure that everything is understood within the context of the real interests at hand.
- Be emotionally stable – do not become unnerved by militant action or provocation. Let a colleague talk when you are angry.
- Regularly check progress and summarise where the process stands – seek confirmation of common understanding on this.
- Always keep some flexibility in your negotiation positions or stances and always remind others of the interests at hand.
- The negotiator should not only be concerned with what the other party says and does, but must constantly find out the real interests and the reasons underlying these positions or stated problems.
- If something is not well understood, ask for a thorough explanation.
- Respect the importance of face-saving for the other party and be graceful. Allow other parties the necessary dignity.
- Be constantly alert to the real intents of the other party, not only with respect to objectives and positions but also to priorities and real interests.
- Build a reputation for being fair but firm.
- Make each negotiation decision in relationship to the other decisions – that is, link all interests into a whole.
- Pay close attention to communication, do not interrupt and listen with interest to what is being said and what is not said. Never hesitate to make sure that you understand things as they are meant to be understood.
- Remember that collective negotiations in the labour area should essentially be a process of compromise. There is no such thing as winning or getting your own way in everything.
- Try to understand the people on the other side of the table – their personalities, fears, interests, perceptions, needs, concern, and so forth; it could bear fruit during negotiations.
- Always consider the impact of the current negotiations on future negotiations – remember that collective bargaining revolves around long-term relationships.
- Remain positive and assertive.
- Sanctions may be used but not misused.
- Pay close attention to the wording of each clause of agreements negotiated. Words and phrases (or expressions) are often the source of valuable information.
- Read agreements carefully before signing and do not ignore the fine print.
- Close the negotiations by summarising key, agreed points and by breaking the eye contact – then get up and shake hands in a pleasant, decent manner.

The final stage of this interactive phase – that is, agreeing on solutions, recording the agreements, and summarising the bargains that have been struck – should be sought on a continuous basis. The interactive phase usually concludes with some sort of agreement (or contract) which is usually put in writing.

Phase 3: The post-negotiation phase

The post-negotiation phase usually refers to the total validity period stated in agreements. During this period the parties make sure that all role-players abide by the agreed-upon procedures and substantive issues (such as wages and other conditions of service). The role of the grievance and disciplinary procedures applied during this phase is, of course, extremely important.

During this phase, the role of the junior public sector managers and shop stewards is of equally crucial importance.

DID YOU KNOW?

It is essential that those people participating in the negotiation process have the necessary competencies and characteristics. Below is a list of some of the essential characteristics of successful negotiators, they have to:
- Be well trained and knowledgeable in the intricacies of negotiations;
- Possess good social interpersonal skills;
- Deal with people, especially in difficult circumstances;
- Be good planners and thus need good information-processing skills;
- Show a positive approach towards mutual gains and should not be greedy and egocentric;
- Be good communicators, able to listen sincerely and express themselves clearly;
- Need a lot of persuasive abilities;
- Be very alert and perceptive to what is happening around them (and what is not);
- Show high-quality discretionary judgement and analytical skills;
- Be patient and should possess good stress tolerance;
- Be able to control their emotions (keeping cool under heated circumstances); and
- Show good conceptual abilities to relate aspects and continually to see the bigger picture.

Sources: Salamon (1992); Kniveron (1974); Bendix (1996) and Alfred (1984)

16.2.3.2 Integrative negotiation

The parties to negotiation sometimes wisely recognise and emphasise the fact that there is indeed common ground between trade unions and public sector management. According to this approach to bargaining, the parties explore the possibilities of creating win-win situations. Although they acknowledge the basic conflict in perceptions, goals, and interests, the parties deliberately channel their energies towards enlarging the areas of common concern. They thus concentrate on interacting in such a way that the outcomes of the negotiation process eventually lead to overall mutual gains. More emphasis is placed on trust, openness, information sharing, constant meaningful two-way communication, and joint problem solving. The parties emphasise the fact that they have to solve problems jointly in order to reach optimum solutions. Negotiation is thus not viewed as a fixed-sum game. An analysis of the literature (Fisher & Ury 1981; Fisher & Brown 1988; Höck 1991/92;

and Power 1991) reveals that there are certain approaches or styles that can be used to bring about or facilitate more integrative types of negotiation. Two such styles are interest negotiation and target-specific negotiation.

Interest negotiation

One of the key ideas of this approach is that parties who engage in collective bargaining should focus on the interests which motivate the parties and their claims rather than on the claims themselves. For example, if a trade union's claim is a 20% across-the-board wage increase, the question ought to be asked: Why? Similarly, if an organisation's position is an offer of 2%, the question ought to be asked: Why? As the parties explore these underlying questions, they will most likely discover that the reasoning behind the claims or bargaining positions represents the interest range of the parties, and that, for every interest range, there is normally more than one possible settlement position which could satisfy the interest underlying the initial position. In this way, they are more likely to identify common ground or interests which are compatible. These interests are explored during pre-bargaining meetings, even before letters of demand are tabled by the union.

Another important element of interest negotiation is to separate the people from the problems. Thus, although a party may be hard on defending its interests (not its positions as such), it will be soft on the people – that is, the other party's negotiators. Parties should thus be prepared to try to understand each other's needs and concerns, the fact that people are people (all with different personalities, emotions, feelings, fears, needs, etc.) and that, at the end of the day, the failure to reach workable agreements could be to the detriment of all.

Target-specific negotiation

This approach of integrative negotiation is based on the idea of changing the bargaining process to one which is actually productive for both parties, through the use of valid information and with the aim of generating less confrontation. As an approach, it is claimed to fall somewhere between win-win and win-lose types of bargaining, and extensive use is made of a mediator.

Power (1991: 16–20) describes a seven-step process which structures the target-specific negotiation approach.

- Step 1 is a problem-seeking process during which both public sector management and the union go back to their members (constituents), where they meet in small groups to record, in a uniform format, all problems and issues, their symptoms, and their causes or sources.
- Step 2 is a procedural step in which each party lists its problems (including the symptoms, reasons, etc.) and lodges the list with a central source. This information is kept confidential at this stage.
- Step 3 has two stages. Each party goes separately to the mediator with whom it reviews its list of problems. The mediator asks questions, probes into reasons,

points out potential inconsistencies or duplications, and helps each party to finalise its list. Stage 2 of this step commences when the management and trade union teams come together to exchange lists and clarify uncertainties.

- Step 4 commences with each party clearly understanding the nature of each problem and its perceived causes. The parties now move to a situation of joint ownership of the problems, in which they decide jointly what information will be needed to address each specific problem listed by the two sides.
- Step 5 is the final pre-negotiation meeting where the parties, with the aid of the mediator, jointly set the 'bargaining agenda by sequencing the order of discussion by groupings of classifications' (Power 1991: 16).
- Step 6 sees the beginning of the actual negotiation process; the joint problem-solving processes are now constructively facilitated by the mediator.
- Step 7 revolves around the ratification and follow-up processes. The parties go back to their members and present them with the agreed-upon solutions.

16.2.4   Structures for collective bargaining/negotiation

The Labour Relations Act 66 of 1995 provides for specific structures within which collective bargaining/negotiation must take place in the public sector.

16.2.4.1   The National Economic Development and Labour Council (NEDLAC)

The National Economic Development and Labour Council is governed by an executive council and consists of the following four chambers:
- A public finance and monetary policy chamber;
- A trade and industry chamber;
- A labour market chamber; and
- A development chamber.

DID YOU KNOW?

The objectives of NEDLAC are as follows, namely to:
- Strive to promote the goals of economic growth, participation in economic decision making, and social equity;
- Seek to reach consensus and conclude agreements on matters pertaining to social and economic policy;
- Consider all proposed labour legislation relating to labour market policy before it is introduced in Parliament;
- Consider all significant changes to social and economic policy before it is implemented or introduced in Parliament; and
- Encourage and promote the formulation of co-ordinated policy on social and economic matters.

It can be expected that NEDLAC will have (and indeed has already had in its short history) a telling influence on the development of economic policy labour laws, and our system of industrial relations. Through the Labour Relations Act 66 of 1995, NEDLAC also has a direct role to play, in that the LRA confers on it the following responsibilities:

- Demarcation of the sector and area in respect of which a bargaining council is to be registered;
- Nominating members to the governing body of the CCMA;
- Preparing Codes of Good Practice relating to industrial relations at the workplace for publication in the Government Gazette;
- Advising the Judge President on the appointment of judges to the labour courts;
- Facilitating consultation between the Minister of Labour and the Minister of Public Service and Administration and NEDLAC on matters concerning the LRA; and
- Monitoring of socioeconomic issues giving rise to protest action.

16.2.4.2 Public Service Co-ordinating Bargaining Council (PSCBC)

The Labour Relations Act 66 of 1995 provides for a single overarching structure, the Public Service Co-ordinating Bargaining Council (PSCBC), which should regulate and co-ordinate collective bargaining/negotiation across the public service. In the PSCBC, all negotiation councils will negotiate collectively. More specifically, they will negotiate on such aspects as uniform rules, norms, conditions of service, and general policy matters applying to the whole of the public service. The National Defence Force, the National Intelligence Agency, and the South African Secret Service are excluded from the PSCBC. At present, the negotiation councils for national departments and provincial administrations and for sectoral councils covering the police (SSSBC), health and welfare (PHWSBC), educators (ELRC) and core general public service and administration (GPSSBC) are represented in the PSCBC. These negotiation councils operate separately and collectively and have the task of dealing with matters relating to these specific sectors.

The most important powers and functions conferred on bargaining councils are listed below:

- To conclude collective agreements;
- To enforce those collective agreements;
- To prevent and resolve labour disputes (mainly through mediation/ arbitration);
- To establish and administer a fund to be used for resolving disputes;
- To promote and establish training and education schemes;
- To establish and administer pension, provident, medical aid, sick pay, holiday, unemployment and training schemes or funds or any similar schemes or funds for the benefit of one or more of the parties to the bargaining council or their members;
- To develop proposals for submission to NEDLAC or any other appropriate forum on policy and legislation that may affect the sector and area;

- To determine by collective agreement the matters which may not be an issue in dispute for the purposes of a strike or a lock-out at the workplace; and
- To confer on workplace forums additional matters for consultation.

16.3 Handling disputes

Although the Labour Relations Act 66 of 1995 promotes collective bargaining/negotiations, it has to be accepted that, from time to time, bargaining may break down. This is why one of the objects of the Act is also to facilitate and promote effective and efficient dispute resolution. Disputes often arise in public sector labour relations, and it is therefore important to understand what labour disputes entail.

DID YOU KNOW?

One can distinguish between a dispute of right and a dispute of interest.

?

16.3.1 Types of labour dispute

Although the concepts dispute of right and dispute of interest cannot be found in the Labour Relations Act, the distinction between these two types of dispute is fundamental to the philosophy informing the dispute resolution procedures of the Act.

16.3.1.1 Dispute of right

A dispute of right is a dispute about the interpretation of an existing right. The parties are not in disagreement about the existence of the right, only over whether the right has been infringed or not by one of the parties. For example, in an alleged unfair dismissal dispute, the public sector employer does not maintain that the employee does not have the right not to be unfairly dismissed; the employer asserts that the employee was fairly dismissed and therefore that his or her right not to be unfairly dismissed has not been infringed. Rights disputes typically involve dismissal disputes or disputes over the interpretation of a collective agreement. It should be evident that these disputes are of a legal nature and therefore that the best way to resolve them would be to make use of a judicial or quasi-judicial process such as arbitration. Section 64 of the Labour Relations Act 66 of 1995 specifies that a union or its members can strike over an issue of mutual interest when that issue remained unresolved for 30 days at the relevant bargaining council. In addition, every employer has the recourse to lock-out if the issue in dispute has been referred to a council or to the Commission as required by this Act, and a certificate stating that the dispute remains unresolved has been issued. In the case of a proposed strike, at least 48 hours' notice of the commencement of the strike has been given to the employer in writing.

With regard to the above stipulation in the Act, two disputes for conciliation were referred to the CCMA, one in respect of a matter of mutual interest and the other over a dispute of right. The case finally landed in the Labour Court and the hearing is affirmed in Spotlight on the Law 16.2 on page 474.

SPOTLIGHT ON THE LAW 16.2
Dispute of right

In *SA Transport & Allied Worker Union & others v Platinum Investments (Pty) Ltd t/a Transition Transport* [2008] 29 ILJ 1742 (LC) there were two disputes between the trade union and the employer. The one dispute concerns organisational rights and the other one was about the employer's use of a labour broker. The first dispute was pending before the CCMA and the second one was referred to the National Bargaining Council for the Road Freight Industry (NBCRFI). The trade union members embarked on a strike and were then called to a disciplinary hearing for participating in an unprotected strike. The members refused to attend the hearing and they were dismissed. The dispute remained unresolved for more than 30 days and was referred to the Labour Court. The Labour Court found that the strike was about a dispute of mutual interest regarding the use of labour brokers and not organisational rights. The Labour Court was also of the opinion that the notice of the strike was not defective and did not specifically refer to the grievance which was the subject of the proposed strike.

Source: Grogan, Jordaan, Maserumule & Stelzner (2009: 81–82)

16.3.1.2   Dispute of interest

Disputes of interest are disputes over issues of mutual interest between the public sector employer and public sector employees where neither party has a right to that which it wants. In contrast to disputes of right, a dispute of interest is not over an existing right, but over the creation of a new right. An example would be a wage dispute. The union is not asserting that it has a right which it wishes to enforce (there is no right to a wage increase), but it wishes to create a right to a new (higher) wage. In such disputes, it is appropriate that the outcome should be determined by power play, because there is no 'right' or 'wrong' answer in the sense that a third party can interpret an existing agreement or legal provision. Only in cases where the parties agree to refer an interest dispute to arbitration, or where policy considerations (for example, the social and economic costs to society in general of industrial action in essential services), prohibit recourse to industrial action, will disputes of interest be resolved through arbitration.

16.3.2   Mechanisms for dispute resolution

The Labour Relations Act 66 of 1995 also provides for the resolution of disputes through formal mechanisms, especially in those cases where conflicts arise and cannot be solved. More particularly, the Act foresees the resolution of disputes through the Commission for Conciliation, Mediation and Arbitration (CCMA), the Labour Court, and the Labour Appeal Court.

16.3.2.1   Commission for Conciliation, Mediation and Arbitration (CCMA)

The Labour Relations Act provides for the establishment of the CCMA, which is to be independent of the state, any political party, trade union, employer, employers' institution, federation of trade unions, or federation of employers' institutions. The CCMA is governed by a governing body, consisting of a chairperson and nine other members (labour, employers, and the state, represented by three persons each), each nominated by NEDLAC and appointed by the Minister to hold office for a period of three years, and the director of the Commission.

Functions of the CCMA

The functions of the CCMA can be broadly grouped into three categories.
1. The CCMA must:
   * Attempt to resolve, through conciliation, any dispute referred to it in terms of the Act;
   * If, after conciliation, a dispute still remains unresolved, arbitrate the dispute if the Act requires arbitration and any party to the dispute has requested that it be resolved through arbitration, or all the parties to a dispute in respect of which the Labour Court has jurisdiction consent to arbitration by the Commission;
   * Assist in the establishment of workplace forums; and
   * Compile and publish information and statistics about its activities.
2. The CCMA must further:
   * If asked, advise a party to a dispute about the procedure to follow in terms of the Act;
   * Assist a party to a dispute to obtain legal advice, assistance or representation;
   * Offer to resolve a dispute that has not been referred to it;
   * Accredit councils or private agencies (see below);
   * Subsidise accredited councils or accredited agencies;
   * Conduct, oversee or scrutinise any election or ballot of a registered trade union or registered employers' institution if asked to do so by that trade union or employers' institution;
   * Publish guidelines in relation to any matter dealt with in this Act; and
   * Conduct and publish research into matters relevant to its functions.
3. The CCMA may provide, on request, employees, employers, registered trade unions, registered employers' institutions, federations of trade unions, federations of employers' institutions, or councils with advice or training relating to the main objectives of the Act, such as the following issues:
   * The establishment of collective bargaining structures:
   * The design, establishment, and election of workplace forums and the creation of deadlock-breaking mechanisms;
   * The functioning of workplace forums;
   * The prevention and resolution of disputes and employees' grievances;

- Disciplinary procedures;
- Procedures in relation to dismissals;
- The process of restructuring the workplace;
- Affirmative action and equal opportunity programmes; and
- Sexual harassment in the workplace.

Resolution of disputes under the auspices of the CCMA

As should be clear by now, the general route that any dispute would follow is first conciliation, failing which, arbitration (or, in a few cases, adjudication). We shall consider details of these three levels of dispute resolution below.

- **Resolution of disputes through a Dispute Resolution Committee:** The Labour Relations Act provides that the Minister for the Public Service and Administration must, after consultation with NEDLAC and the Public Service Collective Bargaining Council, establish a Dispute Resolution Committee under the auspices of the CCMA. The Minister must appoint to the Dispute Resolution Committee persons who have knowledge and experience of labour law and labour relations in the public service. If a dispute remains unresolved, any party involved in the dispute may request that the dispute be resolved through arbitration.

- **Resolution of disputes through conciliation:** When a dispute has been referred to the CCMA, it must appoint a commissioner to attempt to resolve it through conciliation (no provision is made, as is the case in arbitration, for the parties to request a specific commissioner to be appointed to perform the conciliation function). The appointed commissioner must attempt to resolve the dispute through conciliation within thirty days of the date the CCMA received the referral; the parties may, however, agree to extend the thirty-day period. At the end of the thirty-day period, or any further period agreed between the parties, the commissioner must issue a certificate stating whether or not the dispute has been resolved.

- **Resolution of disputes through arbitration:** A dispute may be resolved through arbitration if the following conditions apply:
  - It is a dispute about a matter of mutual interest;
  - The Act requires settlement through arbitration;
  - A commissioner has issued a certificate stating that the dispute remains unresolved; and
  - Any party to the dispute has requested that the dispute be resolved through arbitration.

- The commissioner tasked with arbitrating the dispute may be the same commissioner who attempted to resolve the dispute through conciliation. Provision is also made for the appointment of a senior commissioner to arbitrate in a matter at the request of any party to the dispute. When considering whether the dispute should be referred to a senior commissioner, the director of the commission must hear the party making the application, any other party to the dispute, and the commissioner who conciliated the dispute. The Act expressly provides that commissioners must 'determine the dispute fairly and quickly, but must deal with the substantial merits of the dispute with the minimum of legal formalities' (emphasis added). In addition, the Act specifies that, within fourteen days of the conclusion of the arbitration proceedings, the commissioner must issue an arbitration award with brief reasons, signed by that commissioner (the director may extend the period within which the arbitration award and the reasons are to be served and filed).

Special provisions for arbitrating certain disputes

The Labour Relations Act 66 of 1995 makes special provisions for disputes in, for example, essential services. These provisions are outlined below.

- **Arbitrating disputes in essential services:** The LRA provides specifically for essential services that are defined as '[...] a service the interruption of which endangers the life, personal safety or health of the population or the Parliamentary service or the South African Police Service'. The Act also requires an Essential Services Committee to be established under the auspices of the CCMA to decide what services should be designated as essential services.
- **Arbitrating disputes about dismissals for reasons relating to conduct or capacity:** If the dispute being arbitrated is about the fairness of a dismissal and a party has alleged that the reason for the dismissal relates to the employee's conduct or capacity, the parties are not entitled to be represented by a legal practitioner in the arbitration proceedings unless: (1) the commissioner and all the other parties consent; or (2) the commissioner concludes that it is unreasonable to expect a party to deal with the dispute without legal representation.
- **Consent to arbitration under the auspices of the CCMA:** Provision is made in Section 141 of the LLA for all the parties to agree to arbitration under the auspices of the CCMA of disputes which, but for that agreement, a party would have been entitled to refer to the Labour Court for adjudication.

Arbitration awards

An arbitration award is final and binding, and may be made an order of the Labour Court unless it is an advisory arbitration award. An arbitration award may only be amended or rescinded if: (1) it was erroneously sought or erroneously made in the absence of any party affected by that award; or (2) if the award contains an ambiguity, obvious error, or omission; or (3) if the award was granted as a result of a mistake common to the parties to the proceedings.

Mediation

Sometimes the parties cannot reach an agreement on their own. When such a stalemate is reached, the parties could, of course, decide to strike (trade union action) or to lock employees out (employer action). However, it may happen that neither of the parties is willing to take the risk of such drastic forms of industrial action because the potential losses or costs are too high. In such a case, the parties can agree to use an objective outsider (the so-called third party) to mediate their negotiations.

DID YOU KNOW?

The negotiating parties may decide to use a mediator in the following circumstances:
- Both parties have much to lose should their inability to reach an agreement result in direct conflict, but they are nonetheless unable to settle the dispute.
- Negotiations reach a deadlock and neither party are prepared to concede.
- The positions initially taken by the two parties are so far removed from each other that the difference first has to be reduced before an agreement can be reached (here the mediator can assist the parties in making their demands more realistic).
- It is necessary to help one or both of the parties to change its point of view without losing face in the eyes of its interest group.

The following are some features of mediation:
- Mediation is a voluntary process of settling disputes.
- The mediator has no decision-making powers.
- The conflict, communication, and people-handling skills of the mediator are of paramount importance (rather than legal or technical expertise). The mediator has to be completely impartial, show understanding of the parties' points of view (be empathetic), and treat confidential information as such. The mediator's primary task is to promote constructive communication and to moderate any aggression and personal acrimony between the parties. The mediator should never take credit for an agreement – the credit must go to the parties.
- The mediation process begins when the parties agree to use mediation. After the mediator has been appointed and a date fixed for the first meeting, the parties compile written submissions about the dispute, which are sent to the mediator so that he or she can determine the nature and extent of the dispute.

16.3.2.2   Labour Court and Labour Appeal Court

The Labour Relations Act provides for the establishment of the Labour Court as a open court of law with jurisdiction in all the provinces of South Africa. The Labour Court is a court of record and has the same powers and status as a provincial division of the Supreme Court. The Court is presided over by a Judge President, a Deputy Judge President, and as many judges as the Judge President may consider necessary, acting on the advice of NEDLAC and in consultation with the Minister of Justice and the Judge President of the Labour Court. The Labour Court may make any appropriate order or fulfil certain functions, including, amongst others, the following: (1) to grant an interdict; (2) to grant a declaratory order; (3) to award compensation; (4) to order compliance with any provision of this Act; and (5) to make any arbitration award or any settlement agreement, other than a collective agreement, an order of the Court.

A new court of appeal in labour matters is instituted by the Act. The Labour Appeal Court is a court of law and equity. The Labour Appeal Court is the final court of appeal in respect of all judgements and orders made by the Labour Court in respect of the matters within its exclusive jurisdiction. In relation to matters under its jurisdiction, the Labour Appeal Court has the same power and status as the Appellate Division.

16.4 Handling strikes

No matter how much is done by management to improve the quality of public sector employee and labour relations in a public sector institution, conflict always forms an inherent part of the employment relationship. The aim of public sector management will, however, always have to be to manage conflict levels to facilitate better chances of the overall success of the public sector. Sometimes this does not happen, and it may then lead to the manifestation of serious forms of organised, collective labour-management conflict such as strikes. Strikes can take on various forms, such as go-slows, work-to-rule, sympathy striking, and overtime bans (lock-outs are a form of action taken by the employer).

16.4.1 The nature and content of a 'strike' and 'lock-out'

According to the literature, a strike constitutes the following elements:
- **Concerted action:** This implies, first, that one public sector employee cannot go on a strike (two or more employees are needed), and, second, that the refusal to work, etc., must be the result of some form of collusion or understanding between the employees (two or more employees independently refusing to work do not constitute a strike as defined).
- **Type of action:** The action constituting a strike may be a refusal to work or the retardation or obstruction of work (thus go-slows and sit-ins could qualify as strikes as defined).
- **Purpose:** This is the crucial and defining constituent element of a strike. Only strikes in support of a demand in respect of a matter of mutual interest between public sector employer and employee will qualify as strikes in the legal sense.

Only if all three of the above elements of a strike are present can one talk of a strike in the defined sense. The Labour Relations Act 66 of 1995 Act defines a lock-out as follows:

[T]he exclusion by an employer of employees from the employer's workplace, for the purpose of compelling the employees to accept a demand in respect of any matter of mutual interest between employer and employee, whether or not the employer breaches those employees' contracts of employment in the course of or for the purpose of that exclusion.

It is important to note that a lock-out will only be recognised as such if the conduct and intent satisfy the definition. Two elements need to be present simultaneously for it to be a lock-out in terms of the Labour Relations Act: (1) a particular course of action on the part of the employer; and (2) which is accompanied by a certain intent. The Labour Court has the power to determine the true nature of a dispute between the employer and the trade union (or other relevant parties) despite the CCMA commissioner's categorisation of it. For example, if a dispute arises whether or not a strike is protected, the entry in the certificate of non-resolution is merely a guide for the relevant parties unto the next step. An example of how one can determine where the authority lies when there is a dispute in relation to a strike is discussed Spotlight on the Law 16.3.

SPOTLIGHT ON THE LAW 16.3
Dispute in relation to a strike

In *Lesedi Local Municipality v SA Municipal Workers Union obo Members* [2008] 29 ILJ 2780 (LC), the trade union referred a mutual-interest dispute regarding salary adjustments and increase to the South African Local Government Bargaining Council (SALGBC). The SALGBC decided on the following procedure:

- The dispute was conciliated.
- A certificate was issued indicating that the matter should be referred to arbitration.

The trade union then wrote a letter to the CCMA requesting that the error should be corrected of referring the dispute to arbitration. The relevant commissioner subsequently issued another certificate and indicated that the dispute could be resolved by a strike or lock-out. The trade union gave the municipality 48 hours' notice of the commencement of a strike. This action by the trade union was based on the provisions of the second certificate. However, the municipality contended that the second certificate was not valid since due process was not followed and was issued without considering its objection to the variation.

With this argument in mind, the municipality sought to interdict the proposed strike. The case was referred to the Labour Court and the judge held that whether a strike is protected or not cannot be determined by the mere entry in the certificate of non-resolution. The Court said that this was not determinative of the true nature of the dispute. Finally, the Court declared the proposed strike protected.

Source: Grogan, Jordaan, Maserumule & Stelzner (2009: 85–86)

16.4.2 Status of strikes and lock-outs in terms of the LRA

Statutorily speaking, strikes and lock-outs can be categorised as prohibited, protected, or unprotected. There is also another category, namely specific types of statutory industrial action.

16.4.2.1   Prohibited strikes and lock-outs

These are strikes and lock-outs that are absolutely prohibited. These usually occur under the following circumstances:

- If a collective agreement is in force that prohibits industrial action in respect of the issue in dispute;
- If the issue in dispute is subject to compulsory arbitration;
- If the issue in dispute is one to which a party has the right to refer to arbitration or to the Labour Court in terms of the Act;
- If the employee is employed in an essential service (see following sections);
- If the employee is designated as a maintenance employee;
- If the issue in dispute is in the first year of a wage determination made in terms of the Wage Act that regulates such issue; and
- If a binding arbitration award or a ministerial determination has been made that regulates the issue in dispute.

Public sector employees participating in a prohibited strike are guilty of misconduct and may be dismissed, provided that a fair procedure is followed.

16.4.2.2   Protected strikes and lock-outs

These are strikes or lock-outs that conform to the procedural requirements stipulated in the Act. The most important legal consequence of a protected strike is that the strikers may not be dismissed for participating in it.

Procedure for protected industrial action

Every public sector employee has the right to strike and every public sector employer the right to lock-out, provided that certain procedural requirements are met. In essence, these procedures require a dispute to be referred to a council (or, if there is no council with jurisdiction, to the CCMA), which has thirty days to resolve the dispute through conciliation, failing which, the trade union or the employer may give 48 hours' written notice of its intention to strike or lock-out. After the expiry of the notice period, the strike or lock-out will be protected (provided, of course, that the prohibited circumstances are not applicable). Deviations from the above general procedure are applicable under the following circumstances:

- **Strike/lock-out procedure in a collective agreement:** If there is a collective agreement containing a procedure for strikes and/or lock-outs, then a strike or lock-out that conforms to that procedure will be protected industrial action. The Act in effect allows the parties to contract out of the provisions of the statutory strike law in favour of their own (self)-regulated agreed procedure.
- **Defensive strike/lock-out in reaction to unprocedural industrial action by the other party:** If the strike or lock-out is in response (a so-called defensive strike or lock-out) to an unprocedural strike or lock-out, then the defensive strike or lock-out will be protected under the Act.

- **Constitution of a council:** If the parties to the dispute are members of a bargaining council or a statutory council that has dealt with the dispute in terms of its constitution, then the industrial action will be a protected strike or lock-out under the Act.
- **Unilateral alterations of employment conditions by the public sector employer:** If the employer has unilaterally altered a term or condition of employment or intends to do so, and if the trade union or employee who has referred the dispute to a bargaining council or statutory council or the CCMA has at the same time sent a copy of the referral, giving forty-eight hours' notice to the employer not to proceed or to reverse the unilateral alteration, and the forty-eight hour period has ended without the employer having retracted the change (whether implemented or intended), then the strike in reaction to this unilateral action will be protected even though it does not comply with the general procedural requirements set out at the beginning of this section.
- **Refusal to bargain:** If the issue in dispute concerns a refusal to bargain, an advisory award must have been made by the CCMA before the forty-eight hours' notice of the start of the proposed strike/lock-out can be given. A refusal to bargain includes a refusal to recognise a trade union as a collective bargaining agent; or a refusal to agree to establish a bargaining council; or a withdrawal of recognition of a collective bargaining agent; or a resignation of a party from a bargaining council; or a dispute about appropriate bargaining units, levels, or subjects.
- **Essential services and maintenance services:** In terms of Section 65, no person may take part in a strike or a lock-out if that person is engaged in an essential service or a maintenance service. Disputes in these services must first be resolved through conciliation, and, should that fail to settle the dispute, through arbitration. The only exception to the no-strike rule in essential services is where the parties to a dispute have previously provided for the maintenance of minimum services in a designated essential service by way of a collective agreement which has been ratified by the Essential Services Committee (ESC).
- **Scab labour:** A public sector employer may not make use of replacement labour under the following two circumstances: first, to continue or maintain service delivery during a protected strike if the whole or a part of the employer's service has been designated a maintenance service; or, second, for the purpose of performing

? DID YOU KNOW?

According to labour legislation, an employer can deduct money from employees' salaries for losses suffer, but no more than 25% of their weekly/monthly earnings. The employer should also ensure that a fair procedure was followed before deducting the money and the employee has to agree in writing to these deductions. Unfortunately, for the employer this is where a dispute may arise, as it is almost guaranteed that the employees will not agree to the deductions.

Source: Labour Law for Managers (2010)

the work of any employee who is locked out, unless the lock-out is in response to a strike. Replacement labour includes persons engaged through the services of a temporary employment service or an independent contractor.

16.4.2.3 Unprotected strikes and lock-outs

These are strikes or lock-outs that fall outside the procedures of the Act. The most important legal consequences are that the Labour Court may interdict such strikes or lock-outs, and order any just compensation for losses attributable to such strikes or lock-outs. In addition, strikers participating in an unprotected strike may be dismissed for striking, provided that their dismissal is procedurally and substantively fair.

16.4.2.4 Specific types of statutory industrial action

Thus far the focus has been on strikes as a form of industrial action in the South African public sector. The Act, however, caters for various types of industrial action, including lock-outs, as we have already seen.

Secondary strikes

The Labour Relations Act 66 of 1995 defines a secondary strike as '[...] a strike, or conduct in contemplation or furtherance of a strike, that is in support of a strike by other employees against their employer but does not include a strike in pursuit of a demand and referred to a council if the striking employees, employed within the registered scope of that council, have a material interest in that demand.'

A secondary strike must therefore qualify as a strike as defined and, in order to qualify as a protected industrial action, the primary strike must itself be a protected strike (in other words, both the secondary and the primary strikes must be in conformity with the Act).

Picketing

Picketing may be described as a public expression by employees of their grievances in order to make their cause known to, and to elicit support from, the general public and other relevant constituencies.

Picketing typically involves some form of public protest directed at the public sector employer and in the near vicinity of the employer's place of service delivery, as well as efforts to dissuade the general public and suppliers from normal service delivery dealings with the targeted employer and to persuade other workers to stop working and to join the picket.

Protest action

'Protest action' is defined in the Act as '[...] the partial or complete concerted refusal to work, or the retardation or obstruction of work, for the purpose of promoting or defending the socioeconomic interests of workers, but not for a purpose referred to in the definition of strike.'

It has, of course, to be admitted that what constitutes socioeconomic interests of employees is not amenable to precise definition. For instance, whereas protest action against proposed new legislation on labour matters or taxation or against the government's intended privatisation of state assets (in so far as job security may be affected) would clearly fall within the ambit of socioeconomic interest of employees, a stay-away for or against the reinstitution of the death penalty or a political party should not be regarded as permissible protest action. The Labour Court can interdict protest action that does not comply with the laid-down prerequisites or grant a declaratory order in respect of such action.

Lock-outs

The lock-out is the employer's economic weapon during the collective bargaining process to compel workers to accept its offer or proposal.

The following three points amplify the definition of a lock-out:

- Lock-out dismissals are, in terms of Section 187, regarded as automatically unfair dismissals ('a dismissal is automatically unfair if [...] the reason for the dismissal is [...] to compel the employee to accept a demand in respect of any matter of mutual interest between the employer and employee'). Thus, not only are lock-out dismissals not regarded as lock-outs any more, they are in fact stringently censured as constituting an 'automatically unfair dismissal' (see Chapter 17).
- Employees who go on strike in response to a unilateral change in their conditions of employment will be protected even if they have not complied with the prescribed procedures relating to protected strikes.
- The total or partial discontinuance by the employer of his or her business is no longer regarded as a form of lock-out.

Once it has been established that the action taken by the employer constitutes a lock-out, as defined, it remains to be determined whether the lock-out conforms to the requirements of the Act. The requirements are, with the necessary changes, the same as those applicable to strike action. Likewise, the consequences of a protected lock-out and an unprotected lock-out, respectively, are similar to the consequences that follow respectively upon a protected and unprotected strike.

16.4.3   Strike management phases

Strike management entails more than strike handling. Strike handling refers specifically to the active phase of strike management – the phase when all the plans and preparations are activated and implemented. Strike management, on the other hand, includes strategic preparation and contingency planning, as well as post-strike restoration and recovery procedures.

16.4.3.1   Pre-strike or preparatory phase

The best way to manage a strike is to engage in management practices that prevent strikes. However, no public sector management team can be totally sure that they will never have to deal with any form of industrial action. The basic steps of managing the pre-strike phase include the following:

- **Objective setting:** The primary objective of management must be to handle the situation in such a way that public sector employees become productive again as soon as possible. The idea is to minimise the disruption of operations and to restore order and the normal working processes in the shortest possible time.

- **Preparatory action:** Through preparatory actions such as drawing up a strike-handling and contingency plan, management should be more able, when a strike does take place, quickly to identify and address the real causes of the conflict, to relieve unproductive conflict levels, to prevent any form of damage to property or injuries to people, to arrive at mutually acceptable settlements in the shortest possible time, and thus to minimise the disruptions to the normal service delivery processes. Management must appoint a strike-handling team and ensure that all team members are fully informed and sufficiently competent to fulfil their tasks. With regard to the organising of a strike-handling team, it is always necessary to appoint a strike-handling leader. This person should ideally hold a very senior position in the public sector institution and must have the responsibility and mandate to make all final decisions regarding the strike situation

The members of the negotiating team will, as a rule, be responsible for negotiating with the representatives of the strikers. Such a team will obviously have to include some of the most competent and experienced negotiators in the institution. On the other hand, the operations team will consist of senior persons who have the best knowledge of the core operations, activities, and processes of the institution, as well as the most important support personnel. A group of special consultants (internal or external) may also form part of the strike management team. The particular members of this sub-team will vary in accordance with the nature of the strike and the strikers' demands. Normally, the sub-team will include experts in the legal field, language experts, media experts, security specialists, and also key personnel who are experts on the administrative and financial implications of any decisions and actions which may be considered during the course of the strike-handling phase. The HR procurement specialist should also be a team member to give the necessary inputs on the procurement of human resources to help ensure continued operations.

? DID YOU KNOW?

As part of the contingency plan, it is also necessary to train the role players and even to arrange strike-handling exercises. Furthermore, it is necessary to organise the physical infrastructure. This includes aspects such as a strike monitor, and a control room with the necessary equipment (such as telephones, fax machines, photocopy facilities, radio communication devices and megaphones). Evacuation procedures must also be available should the situation get out of control. Lists with contact details of important parties (for example, the police, customers, suppliers, the Department of Labour, the CCMA, and the relevant bargaining council) must also be available. Other facilities may include normal stationery, flip charts (for brainstorming and discussion sessions), and tape recording and video equipment. It is also advisable for management to negotiate (as part of the recognition and procedural agreement) a code of conduct to be applicable in strike situations. This code can spell out the rules for behaviour during strikes.

16.4.3.2 Active phase of strike management

As soon as any suspicions develop that a strike may be looming, the appropriate member of the strike management team must be informed. This person may then analyse the information and, if necessary, assemble the strike management team.

The strike management team will collect and analyse all the information, discuss possible courses of action, and commence with their functions as stipulated in the strike-handling plan. The negotiating sub-team will, for example, get together to analyse relevant information and to prepare their negotiating strategies and tactics.

One of the most important things to be done throughout any strike episode is to record accurately all relevant events which take place during the strike. Use is often made of a so-called strike diary. With the objectives of strike handling in mind, it is obviously extremely important to open up communication with the representatives of those on strike in order to identify the grievances and the real causes of the industrial action. Although a policy of 'no work, no pay' is advisable, management must always try to get the employees productive again as soon as possible, and a deviation from the 'no work, no pay' rule can be used as a trade-off in return for those who resume normal work promptly.

Whatever the strike-handling team decides to do, however, the need to encourage dialogue and to reach the set objectives must always be addressed. The sting of a strike is often eased by the spirit in which management deals with the demands, the anger (sometimes the violence), and the people with whom management negotiates. Although strictness and discipline are always important, it is also necessary to show an understanding of the emotions of those involved in the strike.

16.4.3.3   Post-strike phase

After an episode of serious industrial conflict, it is important to take certain steps immediately in order to rebuild the relationship between the parties. These include the following:

- Ensure that all undertakings (agreements and promises) relating to the negotiations during the strike episode are fulfilled.
- Work at restoring relations. Without restoring communication between all parties concerned, the quality of the relationships cannot be expected to return to normal.
- Acknowledge that serious conflict and a breakdown in relations has occurred.
- Ensure that all the normal procedures and processes (such as disciplinary and grievance procedures) are confirmed as operative and applied.
- Adhere to all relevant legal requirements.
- Attend to the so-called 'industrial action post mortem'. In this, the whole incident is reviewed, and special attention is paid to the process of strike handling, the effectiveness of the strike handling and contingency plans, mistakes that were made, the competence of the strike management team members, and the lessons to be learned from the strategies and tactics followed by the parties.
- Ensure that appropriate media liaison take place. Normalising the relations with customers, suppliers, and the general public can be facilitated by a proper media release on the incident.

16.5   Establishing sound public sector employee relations

Regardless of whether or not public sector employees belong to trade unions, public sector managers have to see to it that the relations between themselves and their subordinates, between the subordinates themselves, and between the employees and their work are maintained at a standard that is conducive to a generally more successful public sector institution. The activities and practices in managing public sector employee relations can be viewed as those aimed at improving co-operation and optimising conflict levels among various categories of employee, irrespective of the presence or absence of trade unions.

16.5.1   Communicating with public sector employees

One of the most important things all public sector managers have to do is to communicate with their subordinates. Whatever the form of communication, the aim remains the transmission of a message to a receiver so that he or she can understand the intended meaning of the sender's message. It is important to focus briefly on some of the methods used for communication with employees in the workplace.

16.5.1.1   Methods of communicating with public sector employees

A variety of methods can be used to communicate with employees.

Formal letters or memoranda

A general letter or memorandum can, for example, be distributed by the HR department to all the members of the institution's medical aid scheme when some of the conditions of membership change.

Notice boards

Frequently, management wants to make information of a general nature available to those who may be interested, while not bothering those who may not be interested. Notice boards can, for example, be used to put up notices of vacancies elsewhere in an organisation – for those who may be interested in a career or job change.

In-house newspapers/journals

As a general rule, such publications are produced and distributed to all public sector employees free of charge. Such a publication is usually published quite regularly (on a monthly or two-weekly basis) and normally contains interesting and important general information about the institution and its employees. It can, for example, be used to recognise employees' achievements (both in and out of work), to inform the staff of important new appointments or staff movements, to advertise internal vacancies, to inform the readers of service delivery developments, and so forth.

Electronic mail (e-mail)

In the current era of information technology, there are many opportunities to use computer technology to transmit information to public sector employees. Important and urgent messages can, for example, be sent to certain managers via an electronic mail system; they can then pass the necessary information on to their subordinates if not all the employees have access to the system. If, for example, there is a strike and labour unrest in particular areas of a public sector institution, public sector managers in other areas can constantly be kept informed of developments in order to monitor the chances of the unrest spreading. The Intranet is a very common communication medium in today's public sector institutions, especially in the large ones.

Committees

The establishment of formal committees, where representatives of management and non-management public sector employees (including, but not limited to, union representatives) get together to deal with certain issues in a formalised manner, can be viewed as a method of securing more employee involvement, participation, and thus (hopefully), identification with and commitment to the institution's objectives.

Workplace forums

A workplace forum may be established in any workplace that comprises more than 100 public sector employees. Any representative trade union may apply to the CCMA for the establishment of a workplace forum. The applicant must satisfy the CCMA that a copy of the application has been served on the employer. Once the CCMA receives the application, it has to ascertain whether there are 100 or more public sector employees employed at that workplace, whether the applicant is a representative trade union, and whether there is no functioning workplace forum already established in terms of the Act. Thereafter, the CCMA must appoint a commissioner to assist the parties to establish a workplace forum by collective agreement or, failing that, to establish a workplace forum in terms of the Act. The commissioner must convene a meeting with the applicant, the employer, and any registered trade union that has members employed in the workplace, in order to facilitate the conclusion of a collective agreement between those parties, or at least between the applicant and the employer. If a collective agreement is concluded, the role of the commissioner regarding the establishment of a workplace forum is completed. If a collective agreement is not concluded, the commissioner must once again try to convene a meeting between the relevant stakeholders (or at least between the applicant and the employer), with a view to reaching agreement on a constitution for the workplace forum in accordance with the Act. If agreement is not reached on a constitution, the commissioner must establish a workplace forum and determine the provisions of the constitution in accordance with the Act. After the workplace forum has been established, the commissioner must set a date for the election of the first members of the forum and appoint an election officer to conduct the election.

The Act specifies that there must be regular meetings of the workplace forum, and it specifies three different types of regular meeting: (1) meetings between the employer and the workplace forum; (2) meetings between the workplace forum and employees; and (3) meetings between the public sector employer and employees at a workplace. At these meetings, the employer must present a report on its financial and employment situation, its performance since the last report, and its anticipated performance in the short term and in the long term, and it must consult the workplace forum on any matter arising from the report that may affect employees in the workplace.

Except where a collective agreement determines otherwise, a workplace forum is entitled to be consulted by the employer about proposals, amongst others, relating to any of the following: (1) restructuring the workplace, including the introduction of new technology and new work methods; (2) changes in the organisation of work; (3) partial or total plant closures; and (4) mergers and transfers of ownership, in so far as they have an impact on the employees.

Current literature states that trade unions and collective bargaining are thriving in the public sector. Experience has also shown over the last few years, and more particularly during the 2010 financial year, that trade unions have negotiated significant gains for their members. However, according to research done by

Kearney (2010: 105), serious hurdles must be cleared if public employee unions and collective bargaining are to progress and prosper in future. Focus on Research 16.1 provides more detail on this study.

RE EA CH **FOCUS ON RESEARCH 16.1**
Challenges for public sector unions

According to Kearney (2010: 105), trade unions in the public sector environment operate today in a challenging environment. The decline of private sector trade unions hangs like a black cloud over the heads of unions in the public sector. In the light of this, the main findings of the study are summarised as follows:

- The debt compiled by governments and the recession of 2008–2010 portend reductions in employment levels at all levels of government and little funds for wage increases in the next few years.
- The level and scope of benefits, particularly health insurance, are at risk. It was found that substantial reductions through increased premiums, deductibles and co-payments will be in the order of the day during the next few years.
- Mandatory defined contribution retirement plans for new public officials will likely be widespread throughout the public sector.

Although this study was done in the United States of America, much of the above trends are also visible in the South African public sector. These trends, mixed together, do not make a recipe for harmonious labour-management relationships in the years ahead. Against this background, it is evident that trade unions must demonstrate their relevance to present and prospective dues-paying members. Privatisation and outsourcing of traditional public service functions must be resisted and trade unions everywhere need to contend with the changing demographics and technologies of the workplace. It is also important that positive public opinion must be nurtured.

Source: Kearney (2010: 89–90)

16.5.2 Handling public sector employee grievances

When a public sector employee is unhappy or dissatisfied with something in the workplace, he or she may ultimately decide to terminate the relationship by resigning if the matter is not resolved. However, before such a drastic, final step is taken, there should be an opportunity to address the relevant issue(s) in a formalised manner through grievance handling.

Grievance handling refers to the process whereby public sector management formally deals with the officially presented complaint(s) of employees relating to the employment relationship (excluding disciplinary matters). A grievance must, however, be distinguished from an employee complaint or problem. A public sector employee may experience a problem that is not work-related, but which may eventually have an influence on the employment relationship, such as personal financial difficulties, family problems, or drug addiction problems. These are not grievances because they are not directly related to the employment relationship. On the other hand, an employee may be dissatisfied with something directly related to the employment relationship, but the dissatisfaction may simply be expressed in an informal way, by complaining to somebody else, for example. Such a case does not involve a grievance as such because the issue has not been formalised or fed into the official grievance procedure.

Public sector employees' work-related complaints can be formalised as official grievances by means of a grievance procedure. By formally presenting such a complaint to management, the employee communicates to management the fact that there is either a real or a perceived breach of the psychological or employment contract. The grievance procedure can therefore be viewed as a method of (mostly) upward communication in the workplace.

16.5.2.1 Principles underlying grievance handling

A number of important principles (some of which have already been referred to in the preceding paragraphs) form the basis of grievance handling. In this regard management must:

- Acknowledge the fact that public sector employees may from time to time be dissatisfied with aspects of the employment relationship;
- Accept the responsibility for addressing and settling all legitimate employee grievances in a fair manner;
- Solve grievances as promptly and as close as practically possible to the point of origin;
- Ensure that public sector employees who air grievances enjoy guaranteed protection against any form of discrimination, victimisation, or prejudice whatsoever;
- Accept the fundamental right of employees to make use of the help of representatives (either union or otherwise) in the process of airing and handling grievances;
- Ensure for the smooth operation of the public sector institution; although grievance handling is extremely important, the utilisation of the grievance procedure should not unnecessarily disrupt (but rather facilitate) the operation of the institution;
- Spell out time-specified and progressive procedural steps, from the lowest to the highest level, in order to arrive at the point where a grievance is solved to the optimum satisfaction of all parties concerned; and
- Acknowledge the right of public sector employees to pursue channels of dispute resolution beyond the institution in cases where grievances cannot be solved through the grievance procedure must be recognised.

16.5.2.2 Grievance procedure

An employer's grievance procedure is normally made available in a document which spells out the stages or steps to be followed when employees (as individuals as well as in a group context) have grievances. Nonetheless, certain steps can be outlined by way of example.

Step 1 occurs when the aggrieved person verbally informs the immediate manager about the complaint. In this way, the grievance is made official, and it can therefore be recommended that the event (if solved) be recorded in some way. At this stage it may not yet be necessary for any third party involvement (for example, in the form of a worker representative). However, if the issue involves or relates to the immediate manager, the grievance procedure normally stipulates the first step to be the referral of the issue to the next higher level of management. If the issue is not resolved within a reasonable time (for example, within twenty-four hours) Step 2 will follow.

Step 2 generally entails putting the grievance in writing (usually in triplicate), involving a third party such as a shop steward (if so wished), and presenting it to a higher level of management (that is, to the superior of the immediate manager). One copy is kept by the employee and the other is normally handed to the industrial relations or HR officer. If the grievance is not resolved within a reasonable time (say another twenty-four hours) Step 3 will follow.

Step 3, the last stage, depending on the institutional characteristics, will involve consideration of the issue by an even higher level of management or a formal grievance investigation led by a grievance committee. As a rule, such an impartial committee consists of a labour relations/human resources specialist, employee representatives, a senior public sector manager, and any other experts who may be of particular value in regard to the specific issue at hand. The outcome of the grievance committee's investigation has to be announced in writing to all relevant parties. If the issue is not solved, the process of external dispute resolution may be put in motion.

16.5.3   Disciplining employees

The aim of discipline therefore, according to Salamon (1992: 592), is to ensure that all employees conform to the performance and behavioural standards and criteria necessary for the successful operation of the institution. From a positive point of view, discipline is therefore a constructive element of public sector management designed to facilitate learning and opportunities for personal growth, as well as the achievement of institutional objectives.

The process of disciplining public officials entails both informal and formal aspects. The informal part of discipline forms an integral part of managing the performance and behaviour of employees on a continuous basis. Employees are supposed to be taught not simply to conform to minimum requirements related to performance and behaviour, but actually to display superior behaviour and work performance. The first stage of disciplining employees is therefore informal by nature.

At times, however, some public officials fail to adhere to the basic minimum standards and requirements. This is normally where the formal dimension of discipline comes into play. It is therefore advisable for public employers to have a system for formally disciplining those employees who fail to comply with the institution's requirements. Apart from a formal policy statement regarding discipline, this formal disciplinary system usually consists of a written disciplinary code and procedure which has to be applied by management.

16.5.3.1   Disciplinary procedure

As a general rule, a disciplinary procedure is drafted to assist public employers in the identification of offences warranting formal disciplinary measures and to help ensure consistency in disciplinary matters. Therefore, such a procedure usually contains a list of possible offences and the concomitant sanctions to be considered by management. Due to the fact that the nature of various offences may differ in terms of seriousness (ranging, for instance, from minor, to moderate, to very serious), some form of progressive discipline is usually built into the disciplinary procedure dealing with the penalty guidelines connected to the various types of offence.

DID YOU KNOW?   ?

If a public official is charged with misconduct that could possibly lead to dismissal, management must act in line with the fundamental rights of employees regarding procedural fairness in discipline. As a general rule, these rights may include the following:
- The right to be told the nature of the offence or misconduct with relevant particulars of the charge;
- The right to a timely hearing;
- The right to be given adequate notice prior to the enquiry;
- The right to some form of representation;
- The right to call witnesses;
- The right to an interpreter;
- The right to a finding (if found guilty, the employee has the right to be told why);
- The right to have previous service considered;
- The right to be advised of the penalty imposed (for example, verbal warnings, written warnings, termination of employment); and
- The right of appeal, for example to a higher level of management (which is usually the case).

Disciplining: Step 1

The first step in the disciplinary procedure is to assess the seriousness of the alleged misconduct. The following rules apply in the public service for determining an act of misconduct (this list is not intended to be exhaustive):

Acts of misconduct
- Fails to comply with or contravenes an Act, regulation, or legal obligation;
- Wilfully or negligently mismanages the finances of the state;
- Without permission possesses or wrongfully uses the property of the state, or that of another member/employee and/or visitor;
- Wilfully, intentionally, or negligently damages and or causes loss of state property;
- Endangers the lives of self or others by disregarding safety rules or regulations;
- Prejudices the administration, discipline, or efficiency of a department, office, or institution of the state; ▷

- Misuses his or her position in the public service to promote or to prejudice the interest of any political party;
- Steals, bribes, or commits fraud;
- Accepts any compensation in cash or otherwise from a member of the public or another member/employee for performing his or her duties without written approval from the department;
- Fails to carry out a lawful order or routine instruction without just or reasonable cause;
- Absents or repeatedly absents himself or herself from work without reason or permission;
- Commits an act of sexual harassment;
- Discriminates against others on the basis of race, gender, disability, sexuality, or other grounds outlawed by the 1996 Constitution;
- Performs poorly or inadequately for reasons other than incapacity;
- Without written approval from his or her department, performs work for compensation in a private capacity for another person or institution either during or outside working hours;
- Without authorisation, sleeps on duty;
- While on duty, is under the influence of an intoxicating, illegal, unauthorised, habit-forming, and/or stupefying drug, including alcohol;
- While on duty, conducts himself or herself in an improper and unacceptable manner;
- Contravenes any prescribed Code of Conduct for the public service;
- Assaults, or attempts or threatens to assault, another member/employee or person while on duty;
- Incites other personnel to unprocedural and unlawful conduct;
- Displays disrespect towards others in the workplace or demonstrates abusive or insolent behaviour;
- Intimidates or victimises fellow members/employees;
- Prevents other members/employees from belonging to any trade union or body; and
- Operates any money-lending scheme for members/employees for own benefit during working hours or from the premises of the public service;

Source: Republic of South Africa (2003: 107–108)

Disciplining: Step 2

The second step in a formal disciplinary procedure is normally corrective counselling. Here public sector managers must bring the misconduct to the employees' attention. Now that the employee has some grounding in what happened the reasons for the misconduct need to be determined. Simultaneously the employee must be given the opportunity to respond to the allegations.

Disciplining: Step 3

If corrective counselling does not help and the misconduct warrants a verbal warning, the third step for the public sector manager is to give a verbal warning. The verbal warning must also go with a further warning that if the act of misconduct continues more serious disciplinary action will follow. These warnings should be recorded – the verbal warning is valid for three months.

Disciplining: Step 4

If the act of misconduct does not change after the first verbal warning, the public sector manager, as a fourth step, may give the employee a written warning.

The public sector employee must sign receipt of the written warning. If the employee refuses to sign, the manager must hand the written warning to the employee in the presence of another employee. In this instance, the employee must sign in confirmation that the written warning was conveyed to him or her. The written warning must be kept on the employee's personal file for six months, after which it must be removed and destroyed. If there is an objection to the written warning, the employee has the right to direct an appeal within five working days.

Disciplining: Step 5

If the public sector employee still ignores the written warning, the fifth step is to give a final written warning. In those cases where an employee was given a number of final warnings for recurrent violations, without any constructive action from the employer, the other employees may begin to suspect that, no matter how badly they behave, they will never be dismissed. It is general practice that disciplinary codes provide that written and final written warnings remain in force for a specific period.

SPOTLIGHT ON THE LAW 16.4
Final written warning

In *Shoprite Checkers (Pty) Ltd v Ramdaw NO & others* [2000] 21 ILJ 1232 (LC), the Labour Court ruled that '... the fact that a person no longer has a final warning hanging over his head no more extinguishes prior misconduct than the lapsing of a suspended prison sentence extinguishes the conviction from a person's criminal record'. However, on appeal, the Labour Appeal Court found that the relevance of lapsed disciplinary warnings depends on the policy adopted by the employer. In addition, an arbitrator has held that expired warnings may not be taken into account with the aim of imposing progressive discipline. It was argued that expired warnings may serve as evidence that the employee was aware of the rule.

A second case, *NUMSA & others v Atlantis Forge (Pty) Ltd* [2005] 26 ILJ 1984 (LC), shows that reliance on lapsed disciplinary warnings may be dangerous if the applicable code provides that the employer may not do so. In this case, the employers' disciplinary code provided that lapsed warnings must be destroyed in the presence of the employee. The ruling of the Labour Court stated that a symbolic destruction of a lapsed warning served to underscore the fact that the employer may not rely on expired warnings.

In a third case *SACTWU v Novel Spinners (Pty) Ltd* [1999] 11 BLLR 1157 (LC), it was held by the Labour Court that serious disciplinary action should only be applied where the employee committed an offence similar in character to one for which he or she received a written or final written warning. In this particular case the Court decided that it was unfair to dismiss employees for 'collective misconduct', such as an illegal strike or stay-away, on the basis of prior warnings for individual misconduct.

Source: Grogan (2008: 99–101)

The courts held that this period should be applicable so that employees' offences should not be held against them in perpetuity. It is not clear from previous decisions of the Labour Court if a lapsed warning can be taken into account when considering a penalty for a later offence (Grogan 2008: 100). The notion of a final written warning is illustrated in Spotlight on the Law 16.4.

Disciplining: Step 6
Some acts of misconduct may require a sixth step, namely a disciplinary enquiry. In order for the enquiry to be effective public sector managers should adhere to some commonly accepted guidelines concerning the proper administering of the process. The disciplinary enquiry process begins with a notice that must be given to the employee at least five working days before the date of the hearing. Again, if the employee refuses to sign receipt of the notice, a fellow employee needs to be present who shall sign in confirmation that the notice was conveyed to the guilty party.

Disciplining: Step 7
The seventh step in the disciplinary procedure is the option of precautionary suspension. This aspect of the disciplinary procedure requires special attention. In effect, with precautionary suspension, a public sector employee may be suspended on full pay or transferred under the following conditions: (1) when the employer is of the opinion that the employee has committed a serious offence; and (2) when the employer believes that the presence of the employee on the premises might jeopardise any type of investigation or put the well-being of any person at risk.

Disciplining: Step 8
The eighth step in the disciplinary procedure is to conduct the disciplinary hearing. To reduce any delay, the disciplinary hearing must be held ten working days after the notice referred to in step six. These hearings must be chaired by a person on a higher grade than the representative of the public sector employer. In those instances where interpretation is necessary, the services of an interpreter may be obtained for the hearing. Although the disciplinary procedure could have legal implications, neither the employer nor the employee may be represented by a legal practitioner, unless the employee is a legal practitioner.

When a public official fails to attend the hearing, the natural assumption is that there is a reason for the absence. However, if the chairperson determines that the employee did not have a valid reason for being absent, the hearing may proceed without the employee being present. Therefore, the chairperson will read the notice for the record and start hearing the alleged misconduct. The employer's representative, whose task it is to prove the employee's guilt, will lead evidence on the alleged misconduct during the hearing. Both the employer's representative and employee's representative will have the opportunity to question and cross-examine witnesses. If the chairperson is satisfied that sufficient facts are on the table and that the employee has committed misconduct, the employee must be informed of the finding and the reasons for it. A chairperson of a disciplinary hearing should also be aware that, before a sanction is decided on, the employee must be given an opportunity to present relevant circumstances in mitigation. Simultaneously, the employer's representative may present aggravating circumstances. After the disciplinary hearing, the chairperson must communicate the final outcome to the employee within five working days after the conclusion of the disciplinary enquiry. In addition, the outcome must be recorded on the employee's personal file.

Disciplining: Step 9

If the chairperson finds a public official has committed misconduct, he or she, as a ninth step, must pronounce a sanction or penalty. The chairperson takes a final decision on the appropriate disciplinary sanction after considering such aspects as the nature of the case, the seriousness of the misconduct, the employee's previous record, and any mitigating or aggravating circumstances. Sanctions may include the following:

- Counselling;
- A written warning;
- A final written warning;
- Suspension without pay, for no longer than three months;
- Demotion;
- A combination of the above; and
- Dismissal.

Disciplining: Step 10

Finally, if the public sector employee is not satisfied with the sanction, he or she may appeal the sanction by completing a notice of appeal.

The appeal authority usually consists of a member who has not been involved in the decision to institute the disciplinary enquiry and who has a rank that is on a higher grade than that of the chairperson of the disciplinary hearing. Basically, the appeal authority has three options, and may: (1) uphold the appeal; and/or (2) reduce the sanction; or (3) confirm the outcome of the disciplinary hearing. It is expected of the employer immediately to implement the decision of the appeal authority.

Before actually implementing the outcome of the appeal authority's decision, there is an additional stage, which is that the employee retains the right to utilise dispute-handling mechanisms (see section 16.3) provided under the LRA.

16.6 Review

In this chapter, the focus has been on the management of various aspects of public labour and employee relations at the institutional level. Establishing sound labour and employee relations at the level of the workplace is certainly one of the most important challenges facing South African public sector institutions. This is the case largely due to the historical development of this country, with the resultant huge trust gaps existing between labour and management in many public sector institutions. Even though legislation may go a long way in facilitating sounder and more constructive industrial relations in the country, it is ultimately up to the primary parties to work hard at building relationships of trust and co-operation at the institutional level.

In this regard, we have focused on union-management relations, dispute resolution, collective bargaining/negotiation, and the handling of strikes. We have also considered the means by which sound public sector employee relations could be established. In this regard, we have discussed communication, grievance handling, and the disciplining of employees. We have also examined workplace forums as structures for co-operation and worker participation.

16.7 Self-evaluation questions

1. Assume you are the manager responsible for labour relations in a public sector institution where a new trade union has recently been established. Compile a list of actions you should take in handling initial contact with the union.
2. What do we mean by 'formalising the union-management relationship'? What requirements, procedures, and agreements influence this?
3. Compare and contrast 'distributive negotiation' and 'integrative negotiation'.
4. The Labour Relations Act 66 of 1995 provides extensively for collective bargaining structures. Identify and elaborate on these structures.
5. From time to time, the employment relationship is characterised by the occurrence of disputes which call for action. What are some of the formal mechanisms, according to the LRA, that parties can use to solve disputes in the workplace?
6. Conflict may sometimes arise in the workplace and may result in serious actions such as strikes. Under what conditions do public sector employees have the right to strike? Distinguish between specific types of strike and elaborate on the means by which public sector managers can deal with these strikes.
7. Explain at least six methods of communicating with public sector employees.
8. List the principles underlying the handling of employee grievances and related procedures in the public sector.
9. The disciplinary procedure consists of ten steps. Discuss management's role in the disciplinary procedure, and describe the components of each step.

Bibliography

Alfred, N. (Ed). 1984. *Bargain, don't fight!* Johannesburg: Thompson.

Anstey, M. (Ed). 1990. *Worker participation.* Cape Town: Juta.

Anstey, M. 1990. Worker participation: Concepts and issues. In M. Anstey (ed.), *Worker participation,* Cape Town: Juta.

Anstey, M. 1997. *Employee participation and negotiation forums.* Cape Town: Juta.

Bendix, S. 1992. *Industrial relations in South Africa,* 2nd edn. Cape Town: Juta.

Bendix, S. 1996. *Industrial relations in the new South Africa,* 3rd edn. Cape Town: Juta.

Bezuidenhout, MC, Garbers, CJ, & Potgieter, S. 1998. *Managing for healthy labour relations: A practical guide for health services in southern Africa*. Pretoria: Van Schaik.

Bostrom, RN. 1983. *Persuasion*. Englewood Cliffs, NJ: Prentice-Hall.

Cloete, JNN. 1997. *Personnel administration and management*. Pretoria: Van Schaik.

Denhardt, RB, & Hammond, BR. 1992. *Public administration in action: Readings, profiles, and cases*. Pacific Grove, CA: Brooks/Cole.

De Witt, D. 1998. HR challenges for organisational transformation. *Management Today*, 14(1), 28–31.

Fenton, B. 1993. Honest workplace conversations at South African Breweries. *People Dynamics*, 11(7), 15–17.

Finnemore, M, & Van der Merwe, R. 1992. *Introduction to industrial relations in South Africa*. 3rd edn. Johannesburg: Lexicon.

Finnemore, M, & Van der Merwe, R. 1996. *Introduction to labour relations in South Africa*. 4th edn. Durban: Butterworth.

Finnemore, M, & Van Rensburg, R. 2000. *Contemporary labour relations*. Durban: Butterworth.

Fisher, R, & Brown, S. 1988. *Getting together: Building a relationship that gets to yes*. Boston, MA: Houghton Mifflin.

Fisher, R, & Ury, W. 1981. *Getting to yes*. London: Hutchinson.

Flanders, A. 1965. *Industrial relations: What is wrong with the system?* London: Institute of Personnel Management.

Grogan, J. 2008. *Workplace law*. Cape Town: Juta.

Grogan, J, Jordaan, B, Maserumule, P, & Stelzner, S. 2009. *Juta's annual labour law update 2009*. Cape Town: Juta.

Grosset, M. 1999. *Discipline and dismissal: A practical guide for South African managers*. Johannesburg: Thomson.

Hock, C. 1991/92. Interest bargaining: The way ahead? *IPM Journal*, 10(4), 15–18.

Horwitz, FM, & Townsend, M. 1993. Elements in participation, teamwork and flexibility in South Africa. *International Journal of Human Resource Management*, 4(4), 917–932.

Israelstam, I, Healy, T, Hayward, Randall, L, Jackson, D, Squire, D, Molefi, N, Meyerson, D. 2004. *Labour law for managers practical handbook*. Northriding: Fleet Street Publications [http://www.fsp.co.za].

Jaffee, G. 1990. Worker co-operatives: Their emergence, problems and potential. In M Anstey (ed.), *Worker participation*. Cape Town: Juta.

Kearney, RC. 2010. Public sector labor–management relations: Change or status quo? *Review of Public Personnel Administration*, 30(1) 89–111.

Kemp, N. 1992. *Labour relations strategies: An interactional approach*. Cape Town: Juta.

Kniveron, BH. 1974. Industrial negotiating: Some training implications. *Industrial Relations Journal*, 5(3), 27–37.

Labour law for managers. 2004. *When is it your business if your employee commits an offence out of the office*. Northriding: Fleet Street Publications.

Lee, YS. 1992. *Public personnel administration and constitutional values*. London: Quorum.

Macun, I. 1998. Democratising companies? Union representation on company boards. *South African Labour Bulletin*, 22(4), 61–66.

Moore, P. 1987. *Public personnel management: A contingency approach*. Lexington, MA: Lexington Books.

Nel, PS. 1997. *South African industrial relations: Theory and practice*. Pretoria: Van Schaik.

Nel, PS, Erasmus, BJ, & Swanepoel, BJ. 1993. *Successful labour relations: Guidelines for practice*. Pretoria: Van Schaik.

Nieuwmeijer, L. 1988. *Negotiation: Methodology and training*. Pretoria: Owen Burgess.

Pienaar, WD, & Spoelstra, HIJ. 1991. *Negotiation: Theories, strategies and skills*. Cape Town: Juta.

Pondy, LR. 1969. Organisation conflict, concepts and models. *Administrative Science Quarterly*, 12, 27–36.

Power, DF. 1991. Target specific bargaining. *IPM Journal*, 9(8), 15–20.

Reeves, TZ. 1998. *Cases in public human resource management*. New York: Thomson Wadsworth.

Riley, DD. 1993. *Public personnel administration*. New York: Harper Collins.

Salamon, M. 1992. *Industrial relations: Theory and practice*. 2nd edn. New York: Prentice-Hall.

Sylvia, RD. 1994. *Public personnel administration*. Belmont, CA: Wadsworth.

Thompson, FJ. 2003. *Classics of public personnel policy*. New York: Thomson Wadsworth.

Van der Walt, R. 1999. Workplace forums: Efficiency and democracy? *South African Labour Bulletin*, 23(1), 69–71.

Walton, RE, & McKersie, RB. 1965. *A behavioral theory of labour negotiation*. New York: McGraw Hill.

Webster, E, & Macun, I. 1998. A trend towards co-determination? Case studies of South African enterprises. *Law, Democracy and Development*, 63–84.

Acts of legislation

Republic of South Africa.1995. The Labour Relations Act (Act 66 of 1995). Government Printer. [http://www.polity.org.za/html/govdocs/legislation/1995]

Management guides

Republic of South Africa. 2003. Senior management service: Public service handbook. Department of Public Service and Administration. [http://www.dpsa.gov.za/documents/ sms/publications/ smshb2003]

17 Terminating the services of public sector employees

Purpose

The purpose of this chapter is to discuss the principles, requirements and procedures for terminating the services of public servants.

Learning outcomes

After you have read this chapter, you should be able to:
- Explain what counts as dismissal in terms of the Labour Relations Act 66 of 1995.
- List dismissals that will be characterised as automatically unfair dismissals.
- Briefly discuss the three grounds of justification for dismissal and explain the fairness standards for dismissal associated with each of these.
- Discuss the statutory remedies for unfair dismissal.

17.1 Introduction

Despite all human resource management efforts to ensure that employment relationships remain sound and that the match or fit between the parties adds value to the organisation's quest for success, the employment relationship between individual employees and the employing organisation will inevitably break down from time to time. Sometimes employees terminate the relationship by resigning in order to take up a position elsewhere. It may also happen that the initiative to terminate the relationship may come from the employer (or rather from management). This chapter focuses on the latter situation.

Both internationally and in terms of South African law, the services of an employee may be terminated for any one of the following reasons: as a result of misconduct on the part of the employee, for operational reasons, or because of the incapacity or incompetence (poor worker performance) of the employee. In order for a termination of employment to be fair, the employer must comply with the necessary standards of substantive and procedural fairness, and must be able to justify the termination of the employee's services in terms of any one of the three reasons mentioned above.

Through its jurisdiction in terms of 'unfair labour practice' as defined in the Labour Relations Act 66 of 1956, the Industrial Court has, over a period of little more than fifteen years, developed an impressive body of law dealing with issues relating, inter alia, to dismissal law (both collective and individual). In Chapter VIII of the Labour Relations Act of 1995 (henceforward called the Act or the LRA), the legislator has endeavoured to codify the dismissal law formulated in terms of the Industrial Court's jurisprudence.

17.2   Definition of dismissal

In the LRA, the chapter on unfair dismissals starts by stating clearly that '(e)very employee has the right not to be unfairly dismissed'. It then proceeds to spell out in some detail what is meant by 'dismissal'. It should be noted that, at this stage, the fairness or unfairness of a dismissal is not at issue; the Act simply tells us what conduct will, legally speaking, amount to dismissal. Logically, an enquiry into the fairness of a dismissal should be preceded by asking whether or not there has, in fact, been a dismissal in the first place. This is also the sequence followed by the Act. The definition of 'dismissal' in terms of the LRA is outlined below.

'Dismissal' is defined as any one of the following:
- An employer terminates a contract of employment with or without notice;   or
- An employee has reasonably expected an employer to renew a fixed-term contract of employment on the same or similar terms, but the employer offers to renew it on less favourable terms, or does not renew it;
- An employer refuses to allow an employee to resume work after she has taken maternity leave in terms of any law, collective agreement, or her contract of employment;
- An employer who has dismissed a number of employees for the same or similar reasons offers to re-employ one or more of them, but refuses to re-employ another; or
- An employee terminates a contract of employment with or without notice because the employer has made continued employment intolerable for the employee.

Regarding the above possible instances of dismissal enumerated in the Act, we must note the following:
- The Act does away with the nicety of distinguishing between 'termination of employment' and 'dismissal' – both count as 'dismissal'.
- Employers who think that fixed-term contracts can be used as a device to cause the termination of the employment relationship without having to adhere to the fairness standards required by the Act are mistaken.
- Women who go on maternity leave enjoy security of employment (although they are not entitled to paid maternity leave – see also the discussion of the Basic Conditions of Employment Act in chapter 15).
- An employer who has terminated a number of employees' services in a perfectly legal and fair manner may nevertheless incur liability should he or she afterwards decide to re-employee some (but not all) of the dismissed employees.
- The last instance of 'dismissal' is the so-called constructive dismissal, when an employee tenders notice, but then alleges that he or she had no option but to resign due to the employer's actions.

17.3   The fairness of a dismissal

Not all dismissals are fair. Unfair dismissals can be divided into two categories: automatically unfair dismissals and dismissals which are not automatically unfair.

17.3.1   Automatically unfair dismissals

Obviously not all dismissals are unfair; employers should be entitled, given appropriate justification and having followed a fair procedure, to dismiss employees. Nevertheless, having ascertained that a dismissal, as defined above, has indeed occurred, the next step is to determine whether the dismissal was fair or unfair. The LRA introduces an innovation into dismissal law by providing that certain types of dismissal constitute automatically unfair dismissals. We may consider that the legislator regards the listed instances of automatically unfair dismissals as the worst kinds of unfair dismissal. The reason why these instances of dismissal have been given special treatment is not difficult to ascertain: the listed reasons involve instances of undermining collective bargaining, undermining the authority of the Act, and dismissals that amount to unfair discrimination. Dismissing an employee for any of the reasons listed below will be regarded as automatically unfair.

Automatically unfair dismissals in terms of the LRA
- Victimisation or interference with the freedom of association;
- The employee participated in or supported, or indicated an intention to participate in or to support, a protected strike or protected protest action;
- The employee refused, or indicated an intention to refuse, to do any work normally done by an employee who at the time was taking part in a protected strike or was locked out (unless such work is necessary to prevent the actual endangering of the life, personal safety or health of other persons);
- The employer wanted to compel the employee to accept a demand in respect of any matter of mutual interest between the employer and employee;
- The employee took action, or indicated an intention to take action, against the employer by exercising any right conferred by this Act or by participating in any proceedings in terms of this Act;
- The employee's pregnancy, intended pregnancy, or any reason related to her pregnancy;
- The employer unfairly discriminated against an employee, directly or indirectly, on any arbitrary ground, including (but not limited to) race, gender, sex, ethnic or social origin, colour, sexual orientation, age, disability, religion, conscience, belief, political opinion, culture, language, marital status, or family responsibility (despite the preceding, a dismissal may be fair if the reason for dismissal is based on an inherent requirement of the particular job, or, in the case of a dismissal based on age, if the employee has reached the normal or agreed retirement age for persons employed in that capacity); and
- A contravention of the Protected Disclosures Act, 2000, by the employer, on account of an employee having made protected disclosure defined in that Act.

In the light of this information, the following observations are worth noting:

- Dismissing an employee for participating in a protected strike is unfair.
- An employer may not compel non-striking employees to do the work of protected strikers or of workers who have been locked out by the employer, except in crisis situations where life or health are endangered.
- The so-called lockout dismissal that enjoyed statutory recognition under the old Act is now as automatically unfair.
- Dismissing an employee for exercising his or her rights as a worker will not be tolerated.
- Women who are pregnant or intend to become pregnant enjoy job security for the first time. The ambit of the disconcertingly wide 'or any reason related to her pregnancy' will have to await clearer definition through arbitration awards and court decisions.
- A dismissal amounting to discrimination in terms of any one of the listed protected grounds will be automatically unfair unless it falls within the ambit of the savings clause.

Two examples will serve to illustrate how the discrimination clause will work. Assume that a woman has been dismissed for using foul language and she challenges her dismissal on the basis that men using similar language are not even disciplined, let alone dismissed. She, as applicant, will bear the onus of proving the fact of her dismissal, after which the onus will shift to the employer to prove that the dismissal did not amount to discrimination and was therefore not unfair (automatically or otherwise). The employer may discharge himself or herself of this onus either by showing that men who use foul language are similarly disciplined or by showing that the inherent requirements of the job are such that foul-mouthed women cannot be tolerated (it is difficult to think of a justification in this example that would not in itself amount to an impermissible expression of male chauvinism!).

Assume that the minister of a Protestant church is dismissed after he has undergone a change of faith and has converted to Catholicism. The dismissal would have been for religious reasons (one of the listed protected grounds), but the employer would be able to justify it on the basis that the inherent requirements of the particular job (that is, ministering to Protestant members of the congregation) justified his dismissal.

This anti-discrimination provision proscribes direct as well as indirect discrimination. Direct discrimination occurs where the discrimination is explicit; for example, when an employer unfairly refuses to employ women. On the other hand, indirect discrimination occurs when an employer follows standards which appear to be neutral on the surface, but which have the effect of unfairly disadvantaging a particular group. An example of indirect discrimination would be the use of selection criteria such as height and weight, which could, although neutral, exclude more women than men. In the case of indirect discrimination, the American term, disparate impact discrimination, is perhaps more appropriate: the criteria have a disparate impact on one group when compared with the impact on another group. It should be borne in mind that, after the complainant has proved that direct discrimination or indirect/disparate impact discrimination has taken place (usually by adducing statistical evidence) and the onus has shifted to the respondent (employer), the latter can still show that either the discrimination was not unfair or that the discriminatory dismissal was 'based on the inherent requirements of the particular job' (Section 187(2)(a)).

It is very important to understand how the provision of unfair discriminatory dismissals in terms of the Labour Relations Act relates to the provisions of Chapter II of the Employment Equity Act (discussed in Chapter 6). In terms of Section 10(1) of the latter Act, unfair discriminatory dismissals 'must be referred to the appropriate body for conciliation and arbitration or adjudication in terms of Chapter VIII of the Labour Relations Act'.

17.3.2 Other unfair dismissals

If a dismissal was not automatically unfair, it must still be determined whether the dismissal was fair or not. Employers will have less trouble in acting fairly when dismissing employees if they take note of the points summarised below.

Fairness standards and the three justifications for dismissals

Fair reason for dismissal

There are only THREE justifications (fair reasons) for dismissals:
- (Mis)conduct by the employee;
- (In)capacity on the part of the employee; or
- Because of the operational requirements of the employer.

The fairness standards differ, depending on which of the above reasons is relied upon to justify the dismissal.

Fair procedure

Regardless of the reason for the dismissal, a fair procedure must always be followed, which can be summed up by the following two principles:

Nemo judex in sua causa[1] – The person hearing the matter must be unbiased and not have an improper interest in the outcome of the case; and

Audi alteram partem[2] – The employee must be given a proper opportunity to state his or her side of the story

[1] No one may be a judge in his or her own case.
[2] I have heard the other party.

A dismissal must be both substantively as well as procedurally fair: the one element of fairness cannot substitute for the other. Thus, to dismiss an employee for some extremely gross form of misconduct (for example, a grievous and unprovoked assault on a co-worker) may very well be substantively fair, but it will be procedurally unfair if the dismissed employee is not given an opportunity to state his or her case; the dismissal as a whole will then be tainted with unfairness.

Requirements for a fair dismissal
Fair dismissal = Substantive fairness + Procedural fairness

The Act places the onus on the employer to show the following:
- That the reason for dismissal is a fair reason (related to the employee's conduct or capacity or based on the employer's operational requirements);
- That the dismissal has been effected in accordance with a fair procedure.

Shifting onus in dismissal disputes

Proof of dismissal	Proof of fair dismissal
On employee	On employer

In addition, the person considering whether or not the reason for dismissal is a fair reason or whether or not the dismissal has been effected in accordance with a fair procedure must take into account the Code of Good Practice contained in Schedule 8 of the Act. It should be noted that Schedule 8 deals only with dismissals based on misconduct or incapacity; dismissals based on the operational requirements of the employer are dealt with in Section 189 of the Act.

We shall now discuss in more detail each of the three grounds of justification for terminating the services of an employee: conduct, capacity and operational reasons.

17.4 Dismissal for misconduct

Schedule 8 to the Act contains a Code of Good Practice relating to dismissals based on conduct or capacity. Although it would be technically wrong to state that Schedule 8 represents a codification of our labour law on dismissals, it is in fact largely reflective of the positive law. As the Code itself makes clear, one should, when interpreting and applying the Code, always bear the following key principles in mind.

The Code is general in nature; therefore, departures from the norms established by this Code may be justified in appropriate circumstances. The Code is not intended to replace collective agreements; therefore disciplinary codes and procedures which have been agreed to between the parties (either during collective bargaining or as the outcome of joint decision making with a workplace forum), will take precedence over the guidelines provided in the Code of Good Practice. Mutual respect: The Code states the following:

[The] key principle in this Code is that employers and employees should treat one another with mutual respect [...] [a] premium is placed on both employment justice and the efficient operation of business [...] [w]hile employees should be protected from arbitrary action, employers are entitled to satisfactory conduct and work performance from their employees.

Therefore, formal compliance with the Act and the guidelines set out in the Code may be seen simply as putting into operation this basic norm: employers and employees should treat one another (as well as each other's divergent interests) with respect.

Mindful of the fact that the Code of Good Practice provides guidelines which may be departed from under appropriate circumstances, the Code suggests that the following principles should be adhered to with regard to dismissals based on conduct.

(Note: The following section has largely been taken from Schedule 8.)

17.4.1 Disciplinary procedures prior to dismissal

All employers should adopt disciplinary rules that establish the standard of conduct required of their employees. The form and content of disciplinary rules will obviously vary according to the size and nature of the employer's business. In general, a larger business will require a more formal approach to discipline. An employer's rules must create certainty and consistency in the application of discipline. This requires that the standards of conduct are clear and made available to employees in a manner that is easily understood. Some rules or standards may be so well established and known that it is not necessary to communicate them.

The courts have endorsed the concept of corrective or progressive discipline. This approach regards the purpose of discipline as a means for employees to know and understand what standards are required of them. Efforts should be made to correct employees' behaviour through a system of graduated disciplinary measures such as counselling and warnings. Formal procedures do not have to be invoked every time a rule is broken or a standard is not met; informal advice and correction is the best and most effective way for an employer to deal with minor violations of work discipline. Repeated misconduct will warrant warnings, which may themselves be graded according to degrees of severity. More serious infringements or repeated misconduct may call for a final warning, or other action short of dismissal. Dismissal should be reserved for cases of serious misconduct or repeated offences.

Generally, it is not appropriate to dismiss an employee for a first offence, except if the misconduct is serious and of such gravity that it makes a continued employment relationship intolerable. Examples of serious misconduct, subject to the rule that each case should be judged on its merits, are gross dishonesty or wilful damage to the property of the employer, wilful endangering of the safety of others, physical assault on the employer, a fellow employee, client, or customer, and gross insubordination. Whatever the merits of the case for dismissal may be, a dismissal will not be fair if it is not done in accordance with a fair procedure. When deciding whether or not to impose the penalty of dismissal, the employer should, in addition to the gravity of the misconduct, consider such factors as the employee's circumstances (including length of service, previous disciplinary record, and personal circumstances), the nature of the job, and the circumstances of the infringement itself. The employer should apply the penalty of dismissal consistently with the way in which it has been applied to the same and other employees in the past, and consistently as between two or more employees who participate in the misconduct under consideration.

17.4.1.1 Fair procedures

Normally the employer should conduct an investigation to determine whether there are sufficient grounds for dismissal. This does not need to be a formal enquiry. The employer should notify the employee of the allegations, using a form and language that the employee can reasonably understand. The employee should be allowed the opportunity to state a case in response to the allegations. The employee should be entitled to a reasonable time to prepare the response and be entitled to engage the assistance of a trade union representative or fellow employee. After the enquiry, the employer should communicate the decision taken, and should preferably furnish the employee with written notification of that decision. Discipline against a trade union representative or an employee who is an office-bearer or official of a trade union should not be instituted without first informing and consulting the trade union. If the employee is dismissed, the employee should be given the reason for dismissal and be reminded of any rights to refer the matter to a council with jurisdiction or to the Commission for Conciliation, Mediation and Arbitration (CCMA), or to any dispute resolution procedures established in terms of a collective agreement. In exceptional circumstances, if the employer cannot reasonably be expected to comply with these guidelines, the employer may dispense with pre-dismissal procedures.

SPOTLIGHT OF THE LAW 17.1
Substantive fairness of a dismissal for misconduct

The criteria for assessing the substantive fairness of a dismissal for misconduct are as follows (South Africa, 1995. Labour Relations Act, 66 of 1995, Schedule 8, Item 7):

7. Guidelines in cases of dismissal for misconduct
Any person who is determining whether a dismissal for misconduct is unfair should consider:
- (a) Whether or not the employee contravened a rule or standard regulating conduct in, or of relevance to, the workplace; and
- (b) If a rule or standard was contravened, whether or not:
  - (i) The rule was a valid or reasonable rule or standard;
  - (ii) The employee was aware, or could reasonably be expected to have been aware, of the rule or standard;
  - (iii) The rule or standard has been consistently applied by the employer; and
  - (iv) Dismissal was an appropriate sanction for the contravention of the rule or standard.

17.4.1.2 Disciplinary records

Employers should keep records for each employee specifying the nature of any disciplinary transgressions, the actions taken by the employer, and the reasons for the actions.

17.4.2   Dismissals and industrial action

Participation in an unprotected strike is misconduct. However, like any other act of misconduct, it does not always deserve dismissal. The substantive fairness of dismissal in these circumstances must be determined according to the facts of the case, including the seriousness of the contravention of the Act, whether attempts were made to comply with the Act, and whether or not the strike was in response to unjustified conduct by the employer. Prior to dismissal, the employer should, at the earliest opportunity, contact a trade union official to discuss the course of action it intends to adopt. The employer should issue an ultimatum in clear and unambiguous terms that should state what is required of the employees and what sanction will be imposed if they do not comply with the ultimatum. The employees should be allowed sufficient time to reflect on the ultimatum and respond to it, either by complying with it or rejecting it. If the employer cannot reasonably be expected to extend these steps to the employees in question, the employer may dispense with them.

17.5   Dismissals relating to the employee's capacity

17.5.1   Case 1 Incapacity: Poor work performance

A newly hired employee may be placed on probation for a reasonable period, given the circumstances of the job. The period should be determined by the nature of the job and the time it takes to determine the employee's suitability for continued employment. The Public Service Regulations of 2001 specify that this period should not exceed one year (Republic of South Africa 2001a: Chapter 1, Part VII.E).

The task of the supervisor in the public service with regard to officials serving a probationary period
- The supervisor of a probationer is expected to ensure the following:
- That the probationer, at the commencement of the probationary period, knows the performance and other requirements for obtaining confirmation of probation;
- That the probationer, on a quarterly basis, receives written feedback on her or his performance and compliance with other requirements;
- That, if necessary, the probationer receives training, counselling, or other assistance to meet the requirements for confirmation;
- That the probationer receives written confirmation of appointment at the end of the probationary period if she or he has been found suitable for the relevant post; and
- That, when dismissal as a result of poor performance is considered, the probationer is afforded the opportunity to state her or his case, during which process the probationer may be assisted by a personal representative, including a colleague or a trade union representative.

Source: Adapted from Republic of South Africa (2001a: Chapter 1, part VII.E.2)

When appropriate, an employer should give an employee whatever evaluation, instruction, training, guidance, or counselling the employee requires in order to render satisfactory service. Dismissal during the probationary period should be preceded by an opportunity for the employee to state a case in response and to be assisted by a trade union representative or fellow employee. After probation, an employee should not be dismissed for unsatisfactory performance unless the employer has (1) given the employee appropriate evaluation, instruction, training, guidance, or counselling; and (2) after a reasonable period of time for improvement, the employee continues to perform unsatisfactorily. The responsibilities of a supervisor in the South African public service with regard to employees on probation are summarised below.

Guidelines for dismissal for poor work performance
Any person determining whether a dismissal for poor work performance is unfair should consider the following:
- Whether or not the employee failed to meet a performance standard; and
- If the employee did not meet a required performance standard, whether or not:
  - The employee was aware, or could reasonably be expected to have been aware, of the required performance standards;
  - The employee was given a fair opportunity to meet the required performance standard; and
  - Dismissal was an appropriate sanction for not meeting the required performance standard.

Source: Republic of South Africa (1995: Schedule 8, item 11)

The procedure leading to dismissal should include an investigation to establish the reasons for the unsatisfactory performance, and the employer should consider other ways, short of dismissal, to remedy the matter. In the process, the employee should have the right to be heard and to be assisted by a trade union representative or a fellow employee.

17.5.2   Case 2 incapacity: Ill-health or injury

Incapacity on the grounds of ill-health or injury may be temporary or permanent. If an employee is temporarily unable to work in these circumstances, the employer should investigate the extent of the incapacity or the injury. If the employee is likely to be absent for a time that is unreasonably long in the circumstances, the employer should investigate all the possible alternatives short of dismissal. To this end, an executing authority may require an employee to undergo a medical examination by a registered physician (Republic of South Africa 2001a: Chapter 1, Part VII.G.3.1).

When alternatives are considered, relevant factors might include the nature of the job, the period of absence, the seriousness of the illness or injury, and the possibility of securing a temporary replacement for the ill or injured employee. In cases of permanent incapacity, the employer should ascertain the possibility of securing alternative employment, or of adapting the duties or work circumstances of the employee to accommodate the employee's disability.

In the process of this investigation, the employee should be allowed the opportunity to state a case in response and to be assisted by a trade union representative or fellow employee. The degree of incapacity is relevant to the fairness of any dismissal. The cause of the incapacity may also be relevant.

In the case of certain kinds of incapacity – for example, alcoholism or drug abuse – counselling and rehabilitation may be appropriate steps for an employer to consider (see Chapter 14).

Particular consideration should be given to employees who are injured at work or who are incapacitated by work-related illness. The courts have indicated that the duty placed on the employer to accommodate the incapacity of the employee is more onerous in these circumstances.

A discharge on account of ill health shall occur with due regard to item 10 of Schedule 8 to the Labour Relations Act (Republic of South Africa 2001a: Chapter 1, Part VII.G.3.2). The guidelines to be followed for dismissal arising from ill-health or injury are set out below.

SPOTLIGHT ON THE LAW 17.2
Dismissal arising from ill-health of injury

Guidelines for dismissal arising from ill-health of injury are as follows (South Africa. 1995. Labour Relations Act, 66 of 1995, Schedule 8, Item 11):

Any person determining whether a dismissal arising from ill-health or injury is unfair should consider the following:
- Whether or not the employee is capable of performing the work; and
- If the employee is not capable:
  - The extent to which the employee is able to perform the work;
  - The extent to which the employee's work circumstances might be adapted to accommodate disability, or, where this is not possible, the extent to which the employee's duties might be adapted; and
  - The availability of any suitable alternative work.

17.6 Dismissals based on operational requirements

It has been observed that the sequence in which the three grounds for justification of dismissal (misconduct, incapacity, or operational reasons) are normally listed represents a descending order of fault or guilt that can be attributed to the employee. Whereas an employee is clearly at fault in cases of misconduct, the employee who loses his or her job because of events not of his or her making and beyond his or her control, such as economic forces impacting on the employer's business (or because of other reasons such as technological innovation), is blameless. The so-called no-fault dismissals are deemed to be deserving of special treatment. It has been said that losing one's job is 'economic capital punishment'. Losing one's job when one has not even committed a 'capital crime' (committing serious misconduct) is doubly unfortunate and cries out for special compassion on the part of the employer. The Public Service Regulations (Republic of South Africa 2001a: Chapter 1, Part VII.G4.1) make provision for discharging public servants for operational reasons, if the discharge complies with Sections 17(2)(b) and (c) of the Public Service Act, 1994 and Sections 189 and 190 of the Labour Relations Act, as well as Section 189A of the Labour Relations Amendment Act of 2002. The requirements of a fair dismissal for operational reasons are summarised below.

Fair dismissals for operational reasons

Substantive fairness
* A valid and fair reason for the retrenchment.

Procedural fairness
* Prior consultation;
* Prior consensus over certain matters; Disclosure of certain information;
* Allowing employees to make representations;
* Genuine consideration of these representations;
* Selection of employees to be retrenched; and
* Payment of retrenchment package.

We shall now look at the above requirements in greater detail.

17.6.1   Substantive fairness

The Act does not tell us what will constitute a valid and fair reason, but this has been well-established by the Industrial Court. In brief, the employer's reason for the dismissal must be a genuine reason based on the operational requirements of the business. The factors that may cause employees' services no longer to be needed can be as diverse as a downswing in the economy, the implementation of new technology, restructuring of the business, or the shutting down of a plant or part of the business – or even the closing down of the business as a whole.

If an employer tries to rid himself or herself of employees for whatever reason (for example, because they had joined a trade union or because the employer is dissatisfied with their conduct or capacity) under the guise of operational reasons, such a scheme will indubitably be found to be grossly unfair. If an employee's conduct or ability to perform his or her duties is not to his or her employer's satisfaction, the fairness standards relating to dismissal for misconduct or incapacity must be complied with; to dismiss the 'undesirable' employee under the pretence of operational reasons (because the employer has insufficient proof, for example, or wants to save the costs of holding a hearing, or does not want to waste time on the employee, etc.), will always be unfair.

17.6.2   Procedural fairness

In this section, we shall discuss the seven requirements for a procedurally fair retrenchment. They are presented in terms of a seven-step process.

Step 1: Consulting the other party (LRA, Section 189(1))

> When an employer contemplates dismissing one or more employees for reasons based on the employer's operational requirements, the employer must consult [...] (Republic of South Africa 1995: Section 189(1))

First, 'consultation' means that the decision maker must seek advice or information from someone else. It does not mean that the decision maker must accept the advice or that he or she is constrained to reach consensus with the other party. A duty to consult is not a duty to reach agreement; it is simply a duty to give another party the opportunity to provide inputs into the decision-making process and to consider these inputs seriously before the decision maker makes a final decision (unilaterally).

Second, the duty to consult arises before the employer reaches the final conclusion that retrenchments will have to take place. In effect, this means that, as soon as the employer senses that there may be a possibility of retrenchments, the duty to consult arises. That this must be so is clear from the use of the word 'contemplates' in Section 189(1), as well as the meaning of 'consultation', as explained above. The decision maker cannot seriously consider representations made to him or her (for example, trade union suggestions on how to avoid retrenchments), if he or she has already reached a final decision on the course of action to be taken (that is, prior to hearing the representations). The primary purpose of consultation is to inform the employees (and their trade union) of the possibility of retrenchments and to invite their inputs on how the retrenchments may be avoided or on how the impact on the affected employees can be ameliorated as much as possible.

Who must be consulted? In Section 189(1), the legislator prescribes a preferential sequence of persons with whom the employer must consult:

- First, if the employer is bound by a collective agreement, and that agreement specifies with whom he or she must consult regarding retrenchments, the employer is obliged to consult with that person or party.
- Second, if there is no such collective agreement, the employer must consult with the workplace forum, if such a forum exists.
- Third, if there is no workplace forum, the employer must consult with any registered trade union whose members are likely to be affected by the proposed dismissals.
- Fourth, if there is no such trade union, the employer must consult directly with the employees likely to be affected by the proposed retrenchments, or other representatives nominated for that purpose.

Step 2: Attempting to reach consensus (LRA, Section 189(2))

The second procedural step is specified in Section 189(2) of the Act. This entails an effort on the part of the consulting parties to try to reach consensus on 'appropriate measures' on the following matters (Republic of South Africa 1995: Section 189(2)):

- To avoid the dismissals;
- To minimise the number of dismissals;
- To change the timing of the dismissals;
- To mitigate the adverse effects of the dismissals;
- The method for selecting the employees to be dismissed; and
- The severance pay for dismissed employees.

The matters specified in Section 189(2) over which consultations take place can be summarised in the following words: avoidance, minimising, timing, mitigation, selection, and compensation. The process is summarised in Figure 17.1.

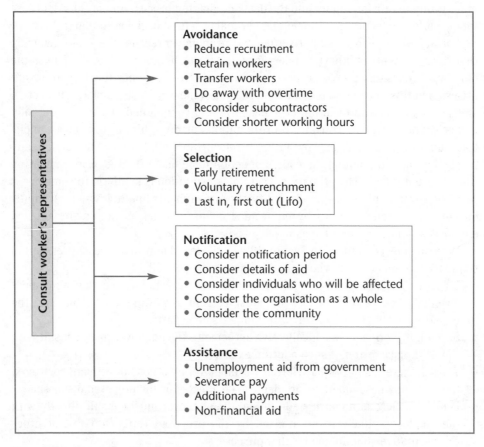

Figure 17.1   Procedural fairness in dismissals for operational reasons

Step 3: Providing relevant information to the other party (LRA, Section 189(3))
The Act, (Section 189(3) read together with Section 16), places an explicit duty on an employer to provide the other party, in writing, with any information relevant to the possible retrenchment. This information is summarised on page 515.

Retrenchments: Written disclosure of information

The employer must disclose all relevant information including, but not limited to:

- The reasons for the proposed dismissals;
- The alternatives that the employer has considered before proposing the dismissals, and the reasons for rejecting each of those alternatives;
- The number of employees likely to be affected and the job categories in which they are employed;
- The proposed method for selecting which employees to dismiss;
- The time when, or the period during which, the dismissals are likely to take effect;
- The severance pay proposed;
- Any assistance that the employer proposes to offer the employees to be dismissed; and
- The possibility of the future re-employment of the employees who are dismissed.

Furthermore, it should be noted that the provisions relating to the disclosure of information in Section 16 of the Act also apply to the disclosure of information during retrenchment consultations. This implies the following:

- 'All relevant information' would entail all information that would put the other party in a position to consult effectively;
- The employer would not be obliged to disclose information that:
  - Is legally privileged;
  - The employer cannot disclose without contravening a prohibition imposed on the employer by any law or order of any court;
  - Is confidential and, if disclosed, may cause substantial harm to an employee or to the employer; or
  - Is private personal information relating to an employee, unless that employee consents to the disclosure of that information.

Note that the relevance of the information that an employer is obliged to disclose is determined, in part, by the reasons advanced by the employer for having to embark on retrenchments. For example, if an employer cites financial difficulties as the reason for retrenchments, the union is entitled to the financial information of the organisation, whereas, if the employer advances a non-financial reason (for example, a strategic reason), the union has no automatic right to disclosure of financial information.

Step 4: Affording the other party an opportunity to make representations (LRA, Section 189(5))

The employer must allow the other consulting party an opportunity during consultation to make representations about any matter on which they are consulting. (Republic of South Africa 1955: Section 189(5))

The employer must, in good faith, consult with the trade union about the intended retrenchments. Should the employer not allow the trade union (or other party) to make representations during consultations, the retrenchments will be unfair. Issues on which the other party may make representations include 'any matter' and would presumably include at least those matters mentioned in Section 189(2).

Step 5: Considering and responding to the representations made by the other party (LRA, Section 189(6))

> The employer must consider and respond to the representations made by the other consulting party and, if the employer does not agree with them, the employer must state the reasons for disagreeing. (Republic of South Africa 1955: Section 189(6))

Having received the representations of the other party, the employer is under a statutory obligation to consider these proposals in good faith, and to give reasons should he or she not agree with them. Although not explicitly required, it would be best to give this response and reasons in writing to the other party. It is important to note that, although an employer is obliged to consider the representations carefully, he or she is under no obligation to reach agreement on these issues. On the other hand, true consideration of representations implies that, at the time these are under consideration, the employer must not have already firmly decided upon a course of action: considering representations against the background of a *fait accompli* cannot amount to good faith consultations. The employer is, of course, not bound either to accept or reject all the representations made as a package; for instance, the employer could reject (with supporting reasons) the proposals made relating to alternatives to retrenchments (for example to work short time), but still accept representations made in respect of certain deserving individuals who were earmarked for retrenchments and who, but for these representations, would have been dismissed.

Step 6: Selecting employees for retrenchment (LRA, Section 189(7))

> The employer must select the employees to be dismissed according to selection criteria:
> (a)   That have been agreed to by the consulting parties; or
> (b)   If no criteria have been agreed, criteria that are fair and objective. (Republic of South Africa 1955: Section 189(7))

It will be recalled that the employer must inform the trade union (or whoever is the other consulting party) in writing regarding 'the proposed method for selecting which employees to dismiss' (Section 189(3)(d)). If the employer and trade union have agreed on the selection criteria, these must be applied; if no agreement was reached, the employer must apply criteria that are fair and objective. 'Fairness' in this context would entail a balancing of the interests of the various stakeholders, including, for example: retrenchees, the employer, the workers not to be retrenched, the trade union, shareholders of the organisation, and the public at large. 'Objective' would mean criteria that are susceptible to external or third party verification.

Please note that criteria other than the popular last-in-first-out (LIFO) may be used, as long as these criteria are not left to the subjective opinion of any individual. For instance, productivity would be an acceptable criterion if it could be objectively verified by means of production figures, and/or absenteeism figures, and/or accident figures, and/or reject figures. But measuring productivity by asking the subjective opinion of supervisors regarding which of their subordinates they would consider as more or less productive will not do.

Step 7: Payment of retrenchment packages (LRA, Section 196)

Prior to the new Act, there was no obligation on an employer to pay a severance package to retrenchees, except under the following circumstances: if the employer had paid packages in the past, or if he or she had promised to pay a package, or if he or she was contractually bound (either in terms of a collective agreement or in accordance with an employment contract) to pay a package. The payment of retrenchment packages was held to be a substantive issue over which the courts had no jurisdiction (except in the case of any of the three circumstances listed above); it had to be regulated by agreement between the employer and his or her employees.

However, although the principle is sound that the courts should not involve themselves in substantive issues, there are some very cogent reasons (if not legal, then at least moral and as a matter of sound industrial relations) why retrenchment packages should be paid. First, remember that a retrenchment is an instance of no-fault dismissal (that is, the worker loses his or her livelihood through no fault of his or her own (as opposed to the case of dismissal for misconduct). Under these circumstances, it seems appropriate that the employer should pay the employee something in recognition of his or her loyal service and the hardship of losing his or her job. Second, the obligation to pay retrenchment packages may act as a deterrent or brake on employers who may otherwise too easily resort to retrenchments. Third, in terms of the organisation's wider social responsibility, it may be expected of an employer to tide the employee and his or her family over for the period that the employee will be unemployed. Fourth, bearing in mind the interest that the employer has in a motivated workforce, it may make good business sense to pay retrenchment packages, if only in order to reassure the remaining employees of their employer's good faith and loyalty towards his or her workforce. After a retrenchment exercise, the morale among the survivors is typically low, and some show of compassion on the part of their employer may go some way towards addressing the survivors' fears and feelings of job insecurity.

We can define a retrenchment package (or severance pay as it is also called) as monetary and other benefits which are given to an employee in addition to any other benefit to which he or she may be legally entitled.

From this definition, it is clear, first, that the payment of accrued leave, pro rata bonuses, contractual notice pay, and withdrawal benefits in terms of a pension/provident fund, etc., cannot be regarded as part of the retrenchment package. Second, should an employee be offered a reasonably similar position and he or she unreasonably refuses to accept the alternative employment, he or she loses the entitlement to a severance package. Finally, note that, for the purposes of calculating the monetary value of the package, it is only completed years of service (which service must have been continuous) that are used to calculate the severance package. For example, an employee who worked for an employer for two years, then resigned and was later re-employed by the same employer, for whom he or she then worked uninterrupted for ten and a half years prior to retrenchment, will be regarded as having had only ten years' service for the purpose of calculating the severance package (although in reality the person had had twelve and a half years of service with the employer).

Prescribed severance pay (LRA, Section 196)

- An employer must pay a retrenchment package equal to at least one week's remuneration for each year of continuous service with the employer.
- Remuneration includes payment in kind.
- Employers may apply for exemption from the duty to pay retrenchment packages.
- The payment of a package is in addition to any other amount the worker may be entitled to in terms of law.
- An employee who unreasonably refuses to accept the employer's offer of alternative employment with that employer or any other employer forfeits the right to a retrenchment package.

Some new details in the Act warrant special mention. The Labour Relations Amendment Act, Act 12 of 2002, Section 189A, provides for dismissals due to operational requirements by employers who employ 50 or more employees, according to the ratios listed below. The legislation applies if the employer contemplates dismissing at least:

- Ten employees, if the employer employs up to 200 employees;
- Twenty employees, if the employer employs more than 200, but not more than 300, employees;
- Thirty employees, if the employer employs more than 300, but not more than 400 employees;
- Forty employees, if the employer employs more than 400, but not more than 500 employees;

- Fifty employees, if the employer employs more than 500 employees; or the number of employees that the employer contemplates dismissing together with the number of employees that have been dismissed by reason of the employer's operational requirements in the 12 months prior to the employer issuing a notice, is equal to or exceeds the relevant number specified above. (Republic of South Africa 2002: Section 189A(1))

Under these circumstances, a facilitator may be appointed to assist the parties in resolving the dispute. If a facilitator is appointed and 60 days have elapsed from the date on which notice was given by the employer that he or she contemplates retrenching employees, the employer may give notice to terminate the contracts of employment in accordance with the Basic Conditions of Employment Act, and a registered trade union or the employees who have received notice of termination may either give notice of a strike or refer a dispute to the Labour Court over the question of fair reason for dismissal.

If a facilitator is not appointed, a party may not refer a dispute to a council or the Commission unless a period of 30 days has elapsed from the date on which notice of the impending retrenchments was given. Once this period has lapsed, the parties' rights are as explained in the previous paragraph.

If a dispute about a dismissal for operational requirements is referred to the Labour Court, the Court must find that the employee was dismissed for a fair reason if the following conditions apply:

- The dismissal was to give effect to a requirement based on the employer's economic, technological, structural, or similar needs;
- The dismissal was operationally justifiable on rational grounds;
- There was a proper consideration of alternatives; and
- Selection criteria were fair and objective.

Before we consider the next topic in this chapter, let us recap the grounds for dismissal: Remember that there are only three grounds of justification for dismissal – each dismissal must be capable of being classified as either a conduct, or a capacity, or an operational reasons dismissal, and must be justified in terms of the standards of fairness pertaining to those particular grounds of justification. A checklist is provided below to aid in determining fairness of dismissal.

Checklist for fair dismissal: Some questions to ask

- Was/is there an employment relationship?
- Was there a dismissal? (Onus on employee)
- Was the dismissal automatically unfair or just unfair? (Onus on employer to show that it was a fair dismissal)
- What are the grounds for justification? (Conduct, capacity, or operational reasons?)
- Legality? ▷

- Substantive fairness?
- Valid reason?
- Proportionality of sanction?
- Procedural fairness?
- *Nemo judex in sua causa* (chairperson must be unbiased and must not have any interest in the outcome of the hearing).
- *Audi alteram partem* (timeliness, reasonable notice, cross-examination, translator, call witnesses, appeal, etc.)

17.7   Remedies for unfair dismissal

The LRA provides for action that may be taken to remedy an unfair dismissal or to provide compensation or relief to the unfairly dismissed employee and his or her family.

17.7.1   Reinstatement, re-employment, and/or compensation (LRA, Section 193)

The natural remedy for an unfair dismissal is reinstatement or re-employment.

- Reinstatement occurs when an employee is placed back in the same position that he or she held before his or her putative dismissal.
- Re-employment occurs when an employer is required to accept the dismissed employee back into service, but not necessarily in the same position.

In both instances, the order may be from any date between the date of the order and the date of the unfair dismissal. In terms of the LRA, the person adjudicating an alleged unfair dismissal must, upon a finding in favour of the employee, order reinstatement or re-employment, unless the following conditions apply (Section 193(2)):

- The employee does not wish to be reinstated or re-employed;
- The circumstances surrounding the dismissal are such that a continued employment relationship would be intolerable;
- It is not reasonably practicable for the employer to reinstate or re-employ the employee;
- The dismissal is unfair only because the employer did not follow a fair procedure.

Of great importance to employers is a new provision in the Act which limits the amount of compensation that may be granted to an employee who has been unfairly dismissed. In the past employers suffered great prejudice when disputes, frequently due to no fault on the part of either party, were resolved after lengthy delays between the date the matter was brought to court and the date of the dismissals. Unfairly dismissed employees should not be disadvantaged by these limits, since the Act requires disputes regarding allegedly unfair dismissals to be resolved speedily (hence the absence of any status quo remedies, as provided for under the previous Act, in recognition of the fact that the final determination of dismissal disputes could often take very long, resulting in the need for some interim relief).[1] The limits on compensation are summarised below.

17.7.1.1 Limits on compensation awards for unfair dismissals (LRA, Section 194)

The compensation awarded to an employee whose dismissal is found to be unfair must be just and equitable in all the circumstances. However, it may not be more than the equivalent of 12 months' remuneration calculated at the employee's rate of remuneration on the date of dismissal. (As we have previously seen, dismissal is found to be unfair if the employer did not prove that the reason for dismissal was a fair reason relating to the employee's conduct or capacity or to the employer's operational requirements, or if the employer did not follow a fair procedure.)

The compensation awarded to an employee whose dismissal is automatically unfair must be just and equitable in all the circumstances, but not more than the equivalent of 24 months' remuneration calculated at the employee's rate of remuneration on the date of dismissal.

The compensation awarded to an employee in respect of an unfair labour practice must be just and equitable in all the circumstances, but not more than the equivalent of 12 months' remuneration. An order or award of compensation is in addition to, and not a substitute for, any other amount to which the employee is entitled in terms of any law, collective agreement, or contract of employment.

17.7.2 Urgent interim relief (LRA, Section 158(1))

In terms of Section 158(1)(a)(i) of the Act, the Labour Court may grant urgent interim relief. The purpose of granting relief is to come to the speedy assistance of an applicant pending the final resolution of a dispute by the ordinary (and more time-consuming) court procedures. In common law, the requirements for the granting of urgent interim relief are as follows:

- The matter must be urgent;
- A *prima facie* right in respect of which irreparable harm will be suffered if the relief sought is not granted;[2]
- No adequate alternative remedy;
- The damage and inconvenience that the applicant will suffer, should the application be refused, will be greater than the damage and inconvenience that the respondent will suffer, should the application for interim relief be granted.[3]

FOCUS ON RESEARCH 17.1
Employment laws and the public sector employer

RESEARCH

In an article 'Employment laws and the public sector employer: Lessons to be learned from a Review of lawsuits filed against local governments', (French, RE. 2009. *Public Administration Review*, 69(1): 92–103)) 'evaluates several areas of concern in the human ▷

resource administration of municipal governments with respect to the management of public employees within the protections set forth by the legislative and judicial branches of the federal government. Sample cases filed from 2000 to 2007 against local governments in Tennessee involving Title VII violations, retaliation, hostile work environment, Family and Medical Leave Act violations, and other employee grievances are detailed. The intent of this analysis is to highlight many of the laws and legal principles that relate to municipal human resources management and to provide scholars and practitioners with a brief overview of the liabilities that may arise from the employment relationship between local governments and their employees.'

It is about time for similar research within the South African context.

17.8 Agreement for pre-dismissal arbitration

The Labour Relations Amendment Act, Act 12 of 2002 provides for employers to dispense with disciplinary enquiries and replace these with arbitration under certain circumstances, provided that the employee consents to this. An employer may with the consent of the employee, request a council, an accredited agency, or the Commission for Conciliation, Mediation and Arbitration (CCMA) to conduct arbitration into allegations about the conduct or capacity of that employee. Once again, this amendment is aimed at speeding up the process and saving costs.

17.8.1 The conduct of proceedings before the Commission for Conciliation, Mediation and Arbitration (CCMA)

In 2002, the CCMA finally published its rules. As the CCMA plays such a crucial role in dispute resolution, it is advisable for any practitioner to obtain the most recent version of these rules from the CCMA. Rules and regulations, process guides, referral forms, and codes and procedures are available from the CCMA's website at http://www.ccma.org.za.

17.9 Review

In this final chapter, we have focused on the appropriate way to go about terminating employment relationships. Technically speaking, if the services of all an organisation's employees have been terminated, this will mean that the full cycle of the human resource management process has been completed. In practice this is, however, very rare – except in those instances where organisations actually close down or go out of business. In most cases, organisations continue to exist, work still needs to be done, and employees are still needed to perform that work. The termination of employment relationships in a procedurally correct and equitable manner under such circumstances therefore implies the start of the human resource management process all over again. In that case, generally speaking, one will already have to start planning and organising around the work to be done and the replacement employee(s) required to do the work.

If employment relationships are not terminated fairly and in the correct way, this could have major negative effects on the organisation, in the sense that its image in the labour market may be damaged to such an extent that it may become difficult to attract, employ, and keep the right numbers and quality of employees. Such an approach clearly does not fit in with a strategic approach to the management of human resources, as advocated throughout this book.

Remember too that, although dismissal of an employee is one way of improving the quality of the employer's human resource capital, it nevertheless reflects a failure on the employer's part, in that the appropriate time and place to enhance and protect the employer's interest in having the best possible workforce should be at the point of entry into the employment relationship; that is during the selection process.

17.10   Self-evaluation questions

1. Define 'dismissal' in the South African context.
2. When will a dismissal be regarded as automatically unfair? Explain your answer.
3. What are the two basic requirements for ensuring that a dismissal is regarded as fair? Explain your answer.
4. Differentiate between fair and unfair dismissal, and discuss fair dismissal in the context of:
    *   Misconduct,
    *   Incapacity, and
    *   Operational requirements.
5. Explain the potential remedies for unfair dismissal in South Africa.

17.11   End notes

1. Compensation may, however, not be awarded in respect of any unreasonable period of delay that was caused by the employee in initiating or prosecuting a claim.
2. 'Prima facie' means that, 'on the face of it' or from the documentation before the court, it appears as if the applicant's rights are infringed. No oral evidence is led, and the final determination of whether the applicant indeed has a right which has been violated is left for the proper court proceedings that are to follow in due course.
3. This could be called a 'balance of harm' test. Typically, an employee who has allegedly been unfairly dismissed and ejected from the organisation's accommodation would suffer greater prejudice should an order not be granted than his or her employer would, should it be granted.

Bibliography

Acts of legislation

Republic of South Africa. 1995. The Labour Relations Act (Act 66 of 1995). Government Printer. [http://www.polity.org.za/html/govdocs/legislation/1995]

Republic of South Africa. 2002. The Labour Relations Amendment Act (Act 12 of 2002). Government Printer. [http://www.labour.gov.za.docs/legislation/lra/LRA%20amend]

Government regulations

Republic of South Africa. 2001a. Public Service Regulations, 2001a. Government Gazette, 427(1): No. 21951, 5 January 2001.

Management guides

Republic of South Africa. 2001b. The Employment Equity Act: User guide. [http://www.labour.gov.za/docs/legislation/eea/guides01]

Index

Please note: Page numbers in italics refer to figures and tables.